2000–2001

53rd edition

Editors: GLENDA ROLLIN
and JACK ROLLIN

HEADLINE

First published in 2000
by HEADLINE BOOK PUBLISHING

10 9 8 7 6 5 4 3 2 1

Cover photographs Front: Kevin Phillips (Sunderland); back: Paolo di Canio (West Ham United) – both *ASP*.

ISBN 0 7472 6620 4

Typeset by Wearset, Boldon, Tyne and Wear

Printed and bound in Great Britain by
Clays Ltd, St Ives plc

HEADLINE BOOK PUBLISHING
A division of Hodder Headline
338 Euston Road
London NW1 3BH

www.headline.co.uk
www.hodderheadline.com

CONTENTS

EDITORIAL

It appears to count for nothing that the England team returned from its sterile Euro 2000 venture having shown no imagination, precious little creation, devoid of tactical awareness and lacking basic technique. The reason? The domestic game continues to flourish and even the failure to secure the World Cup in 2006 has not of course immediately affected the game at club level.

Money from new TV deals and other forms of modern communications should at least in the short term ensure further financial rewards. At the same time much of this increased revenue has already been earmarked for higher salaries and transfer fees which have shown no sign of diminishing in spite of the Bosman ruling now affecting players over 24 and out of contract. Clearly clubs are more concerned to buy and sell rather than be caught out in this fashion to see players go free.

High on the summer list of movements came the return to these shores of Jimmy Floyd Hasselbaink, the former Leeds United striker who spent last season with Atletico Madrid in Spain. He signed for Chelsea in a £15 million deal which equalled Alan Shearer's move to Newcastle United back in 1996. Tottenham Hotspur also paid the substantial sum of £11 million for the services of Sergei Rebrov the Ukranian from Dynamo Kiev.

It was ironic that of the 16 finalists in Euro 2000 no fewer than 12 of them had representatives from the FA Carling Premiership in their squads. Only Spain, Italy, Slovenia and Yugoslavia were not so blessed. And joint top scorer in the tournament with Patrick Kluivert of Holland with five goals was Savo Milosevic, once of Aston Villa who scored in every game!

Many will criticise the influx of foreigners into English football and point the finger at our sustained inability to perform well on the international stage as the cause of the problem. In this vein, it is interesting to note that the Italians who came so close to winning the final against France until tiredness overtook them, relied on home grown talent.

Analysing our defects at Euro 2000 the naive tactics could and should have been overcome. Less easy to put right is the absence of technique and anything approaching flair. It has been said that this is simply not our style. It will have to become so, if we are to improve on a record which still shows just one major trophy at international level, the World Cup in 1966 when it was held in this country and all our games were played at Wembley.

However, there is a movement at grass roots level to change the way youngsters are encouraged to play. This has come from Brazil of all places, where the aspiring lads of Rio, Sao Paulo and other states play a kind of football with a smaller and heavier ball, which has to be controlled and is ideal for short passing, simply because it is impossible for it to be used in the long ball game.

The thinking behind this innovation is that if it improves the ball control of our boys, the traditional assets of grit, determination and stamina, characteristic of countless England teams down the years, will at last give us the opportunity of competing at the highest level without the embarrassment which accompanies inevitable defeat.

This is the theory. Changing attitudes may not be as easy in practice. Lads are now taught at an early age to play in formation regardless of whether they have the basic skills to master the ball.

With the Scots, Welsh and Irish who have graced our game for a century or more, we are used to foreigners in our teams. That nowadays these are from France, Italy, Holland and Spain among others should surely make no difference to the concept.

It is also worth noting that not all the English born players in Manchester United's team – clearly our best – have looked world class when on international duty and this again is an aspect which is frequently overlooked.

Who was the last English-born manager of a League Championship winning team in this country? It has not happened during the lifetime of the Premier League, but was in the season prior to this competition's debut. In 1991-92 Leeds won the title with Howard Wilkinson at the helm. He is now coaching supremo at the Football Association and as such could be the man upon whom much of the future direction of the game will rest for better or worse.

STOP PRESS

World Cup 2006 fiasco: Germany pips South Africa, England lose out ... World cup 2002 North Korea to get two games with finals in Japan and South Korea ... Chelsea head summer spending spree paying £25m for three players ... Bradford sink Atlantas in the Inter-Toto Cup.

Top Transfers: Jimmy Floyd Hasselbaink, Atletico Madrid to Chelsea £15m; Sergei Rebrov, Dynamo Kiev to Tottenham H £11m; Fabien Barthez, Monaco to Manchester U £10m; Carl Cort, Wimbledon to Newcastle U £7m; Robert Pires, Marseille to Arsenal £7m; Oliver Dacourt, Lens to Leeds U £7.2m; Chris Sutton, Chelsea to Celtic £6m.

Other moves completed and pending: Mario Stanic, Parma to Chelsea; Eidur Gudjohnsen, Bolton W to Chelsea; Christian Karembeu, Real Madrid to Middlesbrough; Gary Rowett, Birmingham C to Leicester C; Steve Watson, Aston Villa to Everton; David Hopkin, Leeds U to Bradford C; Neil Sullivan, Wimbledon to Tottenham H; Ian Nolan, Sheffield W to Bradford C; Peter Atherton, Sheffield W to Bradford C; Ben Thatcher, Wimbledon to Tottenham H; Danny Higginbotham, Manchester U to Derby Co; Craig Hignett, Barnsley to Blackburn R; Geoff Horsfield, Fulham to Birmingham C; Bernard Diomede, Auxerre to Liverpool; Louis Saha, Metz to Fulham; John Curtis, Manchester U to Blackburn R; Stig Inge Bjornebye, Liverpool to Blackburn R; Mikkel Beck, Derby Co to Lille; Callum Davidson, Blackburn R to Leicester C; Paul Shaw, Millwall to Gillingham; Chris Hope, Scunthorpe U to Gillingham; Iain Anderson, Toulouse to Preston NE; Massimo Taibi, Manchester U to Reggina; Paul Okon, Fiorentina to Middlesbrough; Nigel Winterburn, Arsenal to West Ham U; Frederic Kanoute, Lyon to West Ham U; Marlon King, Barnet to Gillingham; Martin Hiden, Leeds U to Salzburg; Mark Robins, Walsall to Rotherham U; Adrian Williams, Wolverhampton W to Reading; Dean Delany, Everton to Port Vale; Alf Inge Haaland, Leeds U to Manchester C; Anthony Barness, Charlton Ath to Bolton W; Paul Wheatcroft, Manchester U to Bolton W; Keith Curle, Wolverhampton W to Sheffield U; Georges Santos, WBA to Sheffield U; Lee Jones, Tranmere R to Barnsley; Keith Jones, Charlton Ath to Reading; Neil Clement, Chelsea to WBA; Sinclair Le Geyt, Derby Co to Port Vale; Phil Babb, Liverpool to Sporting Lisbon; John Boardman, Liverpool to Burnley; Sam Aiston, Sunderland to Shrewsbury T; Alex Neil, Airdrie to Barnsley; Nicky Eaden, Barnsley to Birmingham C; Wayne Gill, Blackburn R to Tranmere R; Mark Lever, Grimsby T to Bristol C; Lee Glover, Rotherham U to Macclesfield T; Stuart Barlow, Wigan Ath to Tranmere R; Alan Mahon, Tranmere R to Sporting Lisbon; Damon Searle, Carlisle U to Southend U; Phil Whelan, Oxford U to Southend U; David Greene, Colchester U to Cardiff C; Matt Hewlett, Bristol C to Swindon T; Juan Cobian, Aberdeen to Swindon T; Martin Williams, Reading to Swindon T; Ian Brightwell, Walsall to Reading; Lee Steele, Shrewsbury T to Brighton & HA; Mark Walton, Brighton & HA to Cardiff C; Gary Hobson, Brighton & HA to York C; Jamie Campbell, Brighton & HA to Exeter C; Paul Beesley, Blackpool to Cardiff C; Michael Oliver, Darlington to Rochdale; Mark Burrows, Coventry C to Exeter C; Chris Freestone, Hartlepool U to Shrewsbury T; Scott Eustace, Cambridge U to Lincoln C; Jason Peake, Rochdale to Plymouth Arg; Iain Jenkins, Dundee U to Shrewsbury T; Jordi Cruyff, Manchester U to Alaves; Christian Bassedas, Velez Sarsfield to Newcastle U; Carlos Cordone, Racing to Newcastle U; Lee Collins, Swindon T to Blackpool; Karl Connolly, Wrexham to QPR; Alessandro Pistone, Newcastle U to Everton.

LEAGUE REVIEW AND CLUB SECTION

Manchester United won the FA Carling Premiership for the sixth time in eight years and while their achievement did not quite match that of 1998-99 when they completed an unbeaten run of 33 matches grabbing the European Cup and the FA Cup as a breathtaking threesome in the process, it was a just reward.

With a forced winter break while the team was playing in the inaugural FIFA Club World Championship in Brazil, United were able to resume without too much of a problem. No League matches were played from 28 December when United were a point behind Leeds with a game in hand, until the 24 January when they were held to a 1-1 draw at Old Trafford by Arsenal. This left United three points behind Leeds, but with two games in hand, Arsenal on the same number of points yet having played three more matches than United.

A lesser team might well have been badly affected by this result against one of its main rivals, but though the early part of the game had seen Arsenal well on top, United levelled the scores in the 73rd minute through Teddy Sheringham.

Freed from the task of defending their FA Cup success and out of the Worthington Cup which had never really interested them, United had just twin sights: the League and the Champions Cup. While others were concerned with the fifth round of the FA Cup, United continued League fare and edged out Middlesbrough with a late David Beckham goal to go top on goal difference from Leeds – moreover with a precious game to the good over the Yorkshiremen.

The gap between the two teams gradually widened despite a blip when United crashed 3-0 at Newcastle early in February. As in many other instances, United's opponents failed to capitalize on such a gift. And more importantly, Manchester United won 1-0 at Leeds on 20 February, courtesy of an Andy Cole goal.

On 22 April United clinched the title with a 3-1 win at Southampton. By then their nearest challengers were Liverpool, but 13 points adrift with four matches still to be played.

United called upon the services of 29 different players. The strength of the squad system at Old Trafford being such that not one player was ever-present. Dwight Yorke with 20 goals was their leading marksman, while Cole had 19 and Ole-Gunnar Solksjaer weighed in with a creditable 12 goals himself.

Liverpool just as Leeds had done before them had fallen away and it was Arsenal who finished runners-up some 18 points away.

Relegated were Wimbledon, Sheffield Wednesday and Watford with Bradford City escaping against popular conception to remain in the Premier League. Their places were taken by Charlton Athletic, Manchester City and Ipswich Town, who finished third but who came through via the play-offs.

Walsall, Port Vale and Swindon Town went down into the Second Division, replaced by Preston North End, Burnley and Gillingham, who themselves had been third but like Ipswich won through the play-off system. The quartet relegated were Cardiff City, Blackpool, Scunthorpe United and Chesterfield, with Swansea City, Rotherham United and Northampton Town gaining automatic promotion and Peterborough United making the fourth place via the play-offs having finished fifth in the table.

There was another nail-biting end at the foot of the Third Division, with Chester City being the unlucky ones to go into the Conference. On the last day of the season, Chester were beaten 1-0 at home by Peterborough, while Shrewsbury Town were winning 2-1 at Exeter. Carlisle United survived on goal difference even though they lost 1-0 themselves at Brighton. Shrewsbury escaped by just a point. Chester's place will be taken by newcomers Kidderminster Harriers.

Attendances in the Premier League showed a small increase and prospects for 2000–2001 appear good with Manchester City, hitherto the best supported team outside the Premiership, now back in the top flight after an absence of four years. Old Trafford's capacity has increased to 68,936 and other clubs will have the benefit of larger grounds including Newcastle United and Sunderland from the north-east.

Charlton bounced back after just one season in the First Division, while for Ipswich it has been five seasons away from the elite.

FA Carling Premiership

			Home			Goals		Away			Goals			
		P	W	D	L	F	A	W	D	L	F	A	GD	Pts
1	Manchester U	38	15	4	0	59	16	13	3	3	38	29	52	91
2	Arsenal	38	14	3	2	42	17	8	4	7	31	26	30	73
3	Leeds U	38	12	2	5	29	18	9	4	6	29	25	15	69
4	Liverpool	38	11	4	4	28	13	8	6	5	23	17	21	67
5	Chelsea	38	12	5	2	35	12	6	6	7	18	22	19	65
6	Aston Villa	38	8	8	3	23	12	7	5	7	23	23	11	58
7	Sunderland	38	10	6	3	28	17	6	4	9	29	39	1	58
8	Leicester C	38	10	3	6	31	24	6	4	9	24	31	0	55
9	West Ham U	38	11	5	3	32	23	4	5	10	20	30	–1	55
10	Tottenham H	38	10	3	6	40	26	5	5	9	17	23	8	53
11	Newcastle U	38	10	5	4	42	20	4	5	10	21	34	9	52
12	Middlesbrough	38	8	5	6	23	26	6	5	8	23	26	–6	52
13	Everton	38	7	9	3	36	21	5	5	9	23	28	10	50
14	Coventry C	38	12	1	6	38	22	0	7	12	9	32	–7	44
15	Southampton	38	8	4	7	26	22	4	4	11	19	40	–17	44
16	Derby Co	38	6	3	10	22	25	3	8	8	22	32	–13	38
17	Bradford C	38	6	8	5	26	29	3	1	15	12	39	–30	36
18	Wimbledon	38	6	7	6	30	28	1	5	13	16	46	–28	33
19	Sheffield W	38	6	3	10	21	23	2	4	13	17	47	–32	31
20	Watford	38	5	4	10	24	31	1	2	16	11	46	–42	24

LEADING GOALSCORERS 1999-2000

FA CARLING PREMIERSHIP

	League	*FA Cup*	*Worthington Cup*	*Other*	*Total*
Kevin Phillips *(Sunderland)*	30	0	0	0	30
Alan Shearer *(Newcastle U)*	23	5	0	2	30
Dwight Yorke *(Manchester U)*	20	0	0	4	24
Andy Cole *(Manchester U)*	19	0	0	3	22
Michael Bridges *(Leeds U)*	19	0	0	2	21
Thierry Henry *(Arsenal)*	17	0	1	8	26
Paolo Di Canio *(West Ham U)*	16	0	0	1	17
Steffan Iversen *(Tottenham H)*	14	1	1	1	17
Chris Armstrong *(Tottenham H)*	14	0	0	0	14
Niall Quinn *(Sunderland)*	14	0	0	0	14
Tony Cottee *(Leicester C)*	13	0	0	0	13
Marian Pahars *(Southampton)*	13	0	0	0	13
Dion Dublin *(Aston Villa)*	12	1	2	0	15
Nwankwo Kanu *(Arsenal)*	12	0	1	4	17
Ole Gunnar Solskjaer *(Manchester U)*	12	0	0	3	15
Hamilton Ricard *(Middlesbrough)*	12	0	2	0	14
Paolo Wanchope *(West Ham U)*	12	0	0	3	15
Kevin Campbell *(Everton)*	12	0	0	0	12
Robbie Keane *(Coventry C)*	12	0	0	0	12

Other matches consist of European games, Auto Windscreens Shield, Charity Shield and Football League play-offs.

Nationwide Football League Division 1

			Home			Goals		Away			Goals			
		P	W	D	L	F	A	W	D	L	F	A	GD	Pts
1	Charlton Ath	46	15	3	5	37	18	12	7	4	42	27	34	91
2	Manchester C	46	17	2	4	48	17	9	9	5	30	23	38	89
3	Ipswich T	46	16	3	4	39	17	9	9	5	32	25	29	87
4	Barnsley	46	15	4	4	48	24	9	6	8	40	43	21	82
5	Birmingham C	46	15	5	3	37	16	7	6	10	28	28	21	77
6	Bolton W	46	14	5	4	43	26	7	8	8	26	24	19	76
7	Wolverhampton W	46	15	5	3	45	20	6	6	11	19	28	16	74
8	Huddersfield T	46	14	5	4	43	21	7	6	10	19	28	13	74
9	Fulham	46	13	7	3	33	13	4	9	10	16	28	8	67
10	QPR	46	9	12	2	30	20	7	6	10	32	33	9	66
11	Blackburn R	46	10	9	4	33	20	5	8	10	22	31	4	62
12	Norwich C	46	11	6	6	26	22	3	9	11	19	28	–5	57
13	Tranmere R	46	10	8	5	35	27	5	4	14	22	41	–11	57
14	Nottingham F	46	9	10	4	29	18	5	4	14	24	37	–2	56
15	Crystal Palace	46	7	11	5	33	26	6	4	13	24	41	–10	54
16	Sheffield U	46	10	8	5	38	24	3	7	13	21	47	–12	54
17	Stockport Co	46	8	8	7	33	31	5	7	11	22	36	–12	54
18	Portsmouth	46	9	6	8	36	27	4	6	13	19	39	–11	51
19	Crewe Alex	46	9	5	9	27	31	5	4	14	19	36	–21	51
20	Grimsby T	46	10	8	5	27	25	3	4	16	14	42	–26	51
21	WBA	46	6	11	6	25	26	4	8	11	18	34	–17	49
22	Walsall	46	7	6	10	26	34	4	7	12	26	43	–25	46
23	Port Vale	46	6	6	11	27	30	1	9	13	21	39	–21	36
24	Swindon T	46	5	6	12	23	37	3	6	14	15	40	–39	36

NATIONWIDE DIVISION 1

	League	*FA Cup*	*Worthington Cup*	*Other Cups*	*Total*
Andy Hunt *(Charlton Ath)*	24	1	0	0	25
Shaun Goater *(Manchester C)*	23	3	3	0	29
David Johnson *(Ipswich T)*	22	0	1	0	23
Craig Hignett *(Barnsley)*	19	0	0	2	21
Iwan Roberts *(Norwich C)*	17	0	2	0	19
Wayne Allison *(Tranmere R)*	16	3	0	0	19
Marcus Stewart *(Ipswich T)*	16	0	1	3	20
(Including 14 League and 1 Worthington Cup goal for Huddersfield T)					
Ade Akinbiyi *(Wolverhampton W)*	16	0	0	0	16
Marcus Bent *(Sheffield U)*	15	1	0	0	16
Clyde Wijnhard *(Huddersfield T)*	15	0	1	0	16
Steve Claridge *(Portsmouth)*	14	0	0	0	14
Eidur Gudjohnsen *(Bolton W)*	13	4	3	1	21
Chris Kiwomya *(QPR)*	13	1	0	0	14
Darren Barnard *(Barnsley)*	13	0	2	0	15
Clinton Morrison *(Crystal Palace)*	13	0	2	0	15
James Scowcroft *(Ipswich T)*	13	0	2	0	15
Neil Shipperley *(Barnsley)*	13	0	1	1	15

Nationwide Football League Division 2

			Home			Goals		Away			Goals			
		P	W	D	L	F	A	W	D	L	F	A	GD	Pts
1	Preston NE	46	15	4	4	37	23	13	7	3	37	14	37	95
2	Burnley	46	16	3	4	42	23	9	10	4	27	24	22	88
3	Gillingham	46	16	3	4	46	21	9	7	7	33	27	31	85
4	Wigan Ath	46	15	3	5	37	14	7	14	2	35	24	34	83
5	Millwall	46	14	7	2	41	18	9	6	8	35	32	26	82
6	Stoke C	46	13	7	3	37	18	10	6	7	31	24	26	82
7	Bristol R	46	13	7	3	34	19	10	4	9	35	26	24	80
8	Notts Co	46	9	6	8	32	27	9	5	9	29	28	6	65
9	Bristol C	46	7	14	2	31	18	8	5	10	28	39	2	64
10	Reading	46	10	9	4	28	18	6	5	12	29	45	–6	62
11	Wrexham	46	9	6	8	23	24	8	5	10	29	37	–9	62
12	Wycombe W	46	11	4	8	32	24	5	9	9	24	29	3	61
13	Luton T	46	10	7	6	41	35	7	3	13	20	30	–4	61
14	Oldham Ath	46	8	5	10	27	28	8	7	8	23	27	–5	60
15	Bury	46	8	10	5	38	33	5	8	10	23	31	–3	57
16	AFC Bournemouth	46	11	6	6	37	19	5	3	15	22	43	–3	57
17	Brentford	46	8	6	9	27	31	5	7	11	20	30	–14	52
18	Colchester U	46	9	4	10	36	40	5	6	12	23	42	–23	52
19	Cambridge U	46	8	6	9	38	33	4	6	13	26	32	–1	48
20	Oxford U	46	6	5	12	24	38	6	4	13	19	35	–30	45
21	Cardiff C	46	5	10	8	23	34	4	7	12	22	33	–22	44
22	Blackpool	46	4	10	9	26	37	4	7	12	23	40	–28	41
23	Scunthorpe U	46	4	6	13	16	34	5	6	12	24	40	–34	39
24	Chesterfield	46	5	7	11	17	25	2	8	13	17	38	–29	36

NATIONWIDE DIVISION 2

	League	*FA Cup*	*Worthington Cup*	*Other Cups*	*Total*
Andy Payton *(Burnley)*	27	0	0	0	27
Neil Harris *(Millwall)*	25	0	0	0	25
Peter Thorne *(Stoke C)*	24	0	1	5	30
Sean Devine *(Wycombe W)*	23	1	1	0	25
Jonathan Macken *(Preston NE)*	22	1	2	0	25
Jason Roberts *(Bristol R)*	22	0	3	0	25
Jamie Cureton *(Bristol R)*	22	0	1	1	24
Trevor Benjamin *(Cambridge U)*	20	3	0	0	23
Martin Butler *(Reading)*	18	2	3	0	23
(Including 14 League, 2 FA Cup and 3 Worthington Cup goals for Cambridge U)					
Stuart Barlow *(Wigan Ath)*	18	2	2	1	23
Darren Caskey *(Reading)*	17	3	2	1	23
Steve McGavin *(Colchester U)*	16	0	0	0	16
Robert Taylor *(Gillingham)*	15	2	1	0	18
David Reeves *(Chesterfield)*	14	0	2	2	18
Mark Stallard *(Notts Co)*	14	0	0	0	14

Nationwide Football League Division 3

			Home			Goals		Away			Goals			
		P	W	D	L	F	A	W	D	L	F	A	GD	Pts
1	Swansea C	46	15	6	2	32	11	9	7	7	19	19	21	85
2	Rotherham U	46	13	5	5	43	17	11	7	5	29	19	36	84
3	Northampton T	46	16	2	5	36	18	9	5	9	27	27	18	82
4	Darlington	46	13	9	1	43	15	8	7	8	23	21	30	79
5	Peterborough U	46	14	4	5	39	30	8	8	7	24	24	9	78
6	Barnet	46	12	6	5	36	24	9	6	8	23	29	6	75
7	Hartlepool U	46	16	1	6	32	17	5	8	10	28	32	11	72
8	Cheltenham T	46	13	4	6	28	17	7	6	10	22	25	8	70
9	Torquay U	46	12	6	5	35	20	7	6	10	27	32	10	69
10	Rochdale	46	8	7	8	21	25	10	7	6	36	29	3	68
11	Brighton & HA	46	10	7	6	38	25	7	9	7	26	21	18	67
12	Plymouth Arg	46	12	10	1	38	18	4	8	11	17	33	4	66
13	Macclesfield T	46	9	7	7	36	30	9	4	10	30	31	5	65
14	Hull C	46	7	8	8	26	23	8	6	9	17	20	0	59
15	Lincoln C	46	11	6	6	38	23	4	8	11	29	46	–2	59
16	Southend U	46	11	5	7	37	31	4	6	13	16	30	–8	56
17	Mansfield T	46	9	6	8	33	26	7	2	14	17	39	–15	56
18	Halifax T	46	7	5	11	22	24	8	4	11	22	34	–14	54
19	Leyton Orient	46	7	7	9	22	22	6	6	11	25	30	–5	52
20	York C	46	7	10	6	21	21	5	6	12	18	32	–14	52
21	Exeter C	46	8	6	9	27	30	3	5	15	19	42	–26	44
22	Shrewsbury T	46	5	6	12	20	27	4	7	12	20	40	–27	40
23	Carlisle U	46	6	8	9	23	27	3	4	16	19	48	–33	39
24	Chester C	46	5	5	13	20	36	5	4	14	24	43	–35	39

NATIONWIDE DIVISION 3

	League	*FA Cup*	*Worthington Cup*	*Other Cups*	*Total*
Marco Gabbiadini *(Darlington)*	24	1	1	2	28
Martin Carruthers *(Southend U)*	19	0	0	0	19
Leo Fortune-West *(Rotherham U)*	17	0	0	0	17
Gary Alexander *(Exeter C)*	16	1	0	2	19
Anthony Bedeau *(Torquay U)*	16	1	0	0	17
Lee Thorpe *(Lincoln C)*	16	0	1	0	17
Richard Barker *(Macclesfield T)*	16	0	0	1	17
Andy Clarke *(Peterborough U)*	15	1	0	2	18
John Askey *(Macclesfield T)*	15	0	0	0	15
Luke Beckett *(Chester C)*	14	2	3	0	19
Tommy Miller *(Hartlepool U)*	14	0	1	1	16
Carlo Corazzin *(Northampton T)*	14	0	1	0	15
Paul McGregor *(Plymouth Arg)*	13	3	0	0	16
Ken Charlery *(Barnet)*	13	0	0	1	14

FA CARLING PREMIERSHIP

HOME TEAM	Arsenal	Aston Villa	Bradford C	Chelsea	Coventry C	Derby Co	Everton	Leeds U	Leicester C	Liverpool
Arsenal	—	3-1	2-0	2-1	3-0	2-1	4-1	2-0	2-1	0-1
Aston Villa	1-1	—	1-0	0-0	1-0	2-0	3-0	1-0	2-2	0-0
Bradford C	2-1	1-1	—	1-1	1-1	4-4	0-0	1-2	3-1	1-0
Chelsea	2-3	1-0	1-0	—	2-1	4-0	1-1	0-2	1-1	2-0
Coventry C	3-2	2-1	4-0	2-2	—	2-0	1-0	3-4	0-1	0-3
Derby Co	1-2	0-2	0-1	3-1	0-0	—	1-0	0-1	3-0	0-2
Everton	0-1	0-0	4-0	1-1	1-1	2-1	—	4-4	2-2	0-0
Leeds U	0-4	1-2	2-1	0-1	3-0	0-0	1-1	—	2-1	1-2
Leicester C	0-3	3-1	3-0	2-2	1-0	0-1	1-1	2-1	—	2-2
Liverpool	2-0	0-0	3-1	1-0	2-0	2-0	0-1	3-1	0-2	—
Manchester U	1-1	3-0	4-0	3-2	3-2	3-1	5-1	2-0	2-0	1-1
Middlesbrough	2-1	0-4	0-1	0-1	2-0	1-4	2-1	0-0	0-3	1-0
Newcastle U	4-2	0-1	2-0	0-1	2-0	2-0	1-1	2-2	0-2	2-2
Sheffield W	1-1	0-1	2-0	1-0	0-0	0-2	0-2	0-3	4-0	1-2
Southampton	0-1	2-0	1-0	1-2	0-0	3-3	2-0	0-3	1-2	1-1
Sunderland	0-0	2-1	0-1	4-1	1-1	1-1	2-1	1-2	2-0	0-2
Tottenham H	2-1	2-4	1-1	0-1	3-2	1-1	3-2	1-2	2-3	1-0
Watford	2-3	0-1	1-0	1-0	1-0	0-0	1-3	1-2	1-1	2-3
West Ham U	2-1	1-1	5-4	0-0	5-0	1-1	0-4	0-0	2-1	1-0
Wimbledon	1-3	2-2	3-2	0-1	1-1	2-2	0-3	2-0	2-1	1-2

1999–2000 RESULTS

Manchester U	Middlesbrough	Newcastle U	Sheffield W	Southampton	Sunderland	Tottenham H	Watford	West Ham U	Wimbledon
1-2	5-1	0-0	3-3	3-1	4-1	2-1	1-0	2-1	1-1
0-1	1-0	0-1	2-1	0-1	1-1	1-1	4-0	2-2	1-1
0-4	1-1	2-0	1-1	1-2	0-4	1-1	3-2	0-3	3-0
5-0	1-1	1-0	3-0	1-1	4-0	1-0	2-1	0-0	3-1
1-2	2-1	4-1	4-1	0-1	3-2	0-1	4-0	1-0	2-0
1-2	1-3	0-0	3-3	2-0	0-5	0-1	2-0	1-2	4-0
1-1	0-2	0-2	1-1	4-1	5-0	2-2	4-2	1-0	4-0
0-1	2-0	3-2	2-0	1-0	2-1	1-0	3-1	1-0	4-1
0-2	2-1	1-2	3-0	2-1	5-2	0-1	1-0	1-3	2-1
2-3	0-0	2-1	4-1	0-0	1-1	2-0	0-1	1-0	3-1
—	1-0	5-1	4-0	3-3	4-0	3-1	4-1	7-1	1-1
3-4	—	2-2	1-0	3-2	1-1	2-1	1-1	2-0	0-0
3-0	2-1	—	8-0	5-0	1-2	2-1	1-0	2-2	3-3
0-1	1-0	0-2	—	0-1	0-2	1-2	2-2	3-1	5-1
1-3	1-1	4-2	2-0	—	1-2	0-1	2-0	2-1	2-0
2-2	1-1	2-2	1-0	2-0	—	2-1	2-0	1-0	2-1
3-1	2-3	3-1	0-1	7-2	3-1	—	4-0	0-0	2-0
2-3	1-3	1-1	1-0	3-2	2-3	1-1	—	1-2	2-3
2-4	0-1	2-1	4-3	2-0	1-1	1-0	1-0	—	2-1
2-2	2-3	2-0	0-2	1-1	1-0	1-1	5-0	2-2	—

NATIONWIDE FOOTBALL LEAGUE

HOME TEAM	Barnsley	Blackburn R	Birmingham C	Bolton W	Charlton Ath	Crewe Alex	Crystal Palace	Fulham	Grimsby T	Huddersfield T
Barnsley	—	5-1	2-1	1-1	1-1	0-2	2-3	1-0	3-0	4-2
Blackburn R	1-2	—	1-0	3-1	1-1	0-1	1-1	2-0	1-1	2-0
Birmingham C	3-1	1-0	—	2-1	1-0	5-1	2-0	2-2	0-0	1-0
Bolton W	2-2	3-1	3-3	—	0-2	2-2	2-0	3-1	2-0	1-0
Charlton Ath	3-1	1-2	1-0	2-1	—	1-0	2-1	1-0	4-0	0-1
Crewe Alex	0-1	0-0	2-3	1-3	0-2	—	2-0	1-1	1-1	1-1
Crystal Palace	0-2	2-1	0-2	0-0	0-1	1-1	—	0-0	3-0	2-2
Fulham	1-3	2-2	0-0	1-1	2-1	3-0	1-0	—	0-1	3-0
Grimsby T	0-3	0-0	1-1	0-1	2-5	1-1	1-0	1-1	—	0-0
Huddersfield T	2-1	3-2	0-0	0-3	1-2	3-0	7-1	1-1	3-1	—
Ipswich T	6-1	0-0	0-1	1-0	4-2	2-1	1-0	1-0	2-0	2-1
Manchester C	3-1	2-0	1-0	2-0	1-1	4-0	2-1	4-0	2-1	0-1
Norwich C	2-2	0-2	0-1	2-1	0-3	2-1	0-1	1-2	3-0	1-1
Nottingham F	3-0	0-1	1-0	1-1	1-1	1-0	2-0	0-0	2-1	1-3
Port Vale	2-2	0-0	3-1	0-1	2-2	1-0	2-2	0-2	3-1	1-2
Portsmouth	3-0	1-2	2-2	0-0	0-2	0-2	3-1	0-1	1-2	0-0
QPR	2-2	0-0	2-2	0-1	0-0	1-0	0-1	0-0	1-0	3-1
Sheffield U	3-3	2-1	1-2	1-2	1-2	1-1	3-1	2-0	0-0	0-1
Stockport Co	1-3	0-1	2-0	0-0	1-3	2-1	1-2	2-1	2-1	1-1
Swindon T	1-2	2-1	1-4	0-4	1-2	0-1	2-4	1-0	0-1	2-0
Tranmere R	2-2	2-1	2-1	0-0	2-2	2-0	1-2	1-1	3-2	1-0
Walsall	1-4	1-1	1-0	2-0	2-4	1-4	2-2	1-3	1-0	2-0
WBA	0-2	2-2	0-3	4-4	2-0	1-0	0-0	0-0	2-1	0-1
Wolverhampton W	2-0	2-1	2-1	1-0	2-3	2-0	2-1	3-0	3-0	0-1

DIVISION 1 1999–2000 RESULTS

Ipswich T	Manchester C	Norwich C	Nottingham F	Port Vale	Portsmouth	QPR	Sheffield U	Stockport Co	Swindon T	Tranmere R	Walsall	WBA	Wolverhampton W
0-2	2-1	2-1	1-0	3-1	6-0	1-1	2-0	2-1	1-0	3-0	3-2	2-2	1-2
2-2	1-4	1-1	2-1	0-0	1-1	0-2	5-0	2-0	0-0	2-0	2-0	2-1	1-1
1-1	0-1	2-0	0-1	4-2	1-0	2-0	0-2	2-1	1-1	3-1	2-0	1-1	1-0
1-1	0-1	1-0	3-2	2-1	3-0	2-1	2-0	0-1	2-0	2-3	4-3	1-1	2-1
1-3	0-1	1-0	3-0	2-2	1-1	2-1	1-0	4-0	0-1	3-2	2-1	0-0	2-0
1-2	1-1	1-0	0-3	2-1	1-3	2-1	1-0	3-2	2-1	0-2	2-3	2-0	1-0
2-2	1-1	1-0	2-0	1-1	4-0	3-0	1-1	3-3	1-2	2-2	3-2	0-2	1-1
0-0	0-0	1-1	1-1	3-1	1-0	1-0	4-0	4-1	1-0	1-0	2-0	1-0	0-1
2-1	1-1	2-1	4-3	2-0	1-0	2-1	2-2	0-1	1-0	1-2	1-0	1-1	1-0
3-1	1-1	1-0	2-1	2-2	0-1	1-0	4-1	0-2	4-0	1-0	1-1	1-0	2-0
—	2-1	0-2	3-1	3-0	0-1	1-4	1-1	1-0	3-0	0-0	2-0	3-1	1-0
1-0	—	3-1	1-0	2-1	4-2	1-3	6-0	1-2	3-0	2-0	1-1	2-1	0-1
0-0	1-0	—	1-0	0-0	2-1	2-1	2-1	2-0	0-2	1-1	1-1	2-1	1-0
0-1	1-3	1-1	—	2-0	2-0	1-1	0-0	1-1	3-1	1-1	4-1	0-0	1-1
1-2	1-2	0-1	0-2	—	2-0	1-1	2-3	1-1	2-0	1-0	1-2	1-2	0-1
1-1	2-2	2-1	2-1	0-0	—	1-3	2-0	2-0	4-1	1-2	5-1	2-0	2-3
3-1	1-1	2-2	1-1	3-2	0-0	—	3-1	1-1	2-1	2-1	2-1	0-0	1-1
2-2	1-0	0-0	2-1	1-3	1-0	1-1	—	1-0	2-2	3-1	1-1	6-0	3-0
0-1	2-2	2-2	2-3	1-0	1-1	3-3	1-1	—	3-0	2-1	1-1	0-1	3-2
1-4	0-2	0-0	0-0	2-1	1-1	0-1	2-2	1-1	—	3-1	1-1	1-2	1-2
0-2	1-1	1-2	3-0	2-1	2-4	1-1	1-3	0-0	3-1	—	1-1	3-0	1-0
0-1	0-1	2-2	0-2	0-0	1-0	2-3	2-1	1-2	0-0	1-2	—	2-1	1-1
1-1	0-2	1-1	1-1	0-0	3-2	0-1	2-2	2-0	1-1	2-0	0-1	—	1-1
2-1	4-1	1-0	3-0	2-2	1-1	3-2	1-0	2-2	1-1	4-0	1-2	1-1	—

NATIONWIDE FOOTBALL LEAGUE

HOME TEAM	Blackpool	AFC Bournemouth	Brentford	Bristol C	Bristol R	Burnley	Bury	Cambridge U	Cardiff C	Chesterfield
Blackpool	—	0-0	0-1	1-2	2-1	1-1	0-5	2-1	2-2	2-2
AFC Bournemouth	2-0	—	4-1	2-3	0-1	0-1	1-1	2-1	1-0	1-1
Brentford	2-0	0-2	—	2-1	0-3	2-3	2-1	1-1	2-1	1-1
Bristol C	5-2	3-1	1-0	—	0-0	0-0	1-1	1-1	0-0	3-0
Bristol R	3-1	2-2	0-0	2-0	—	1-0	0-0	1-0	1-1	3-1
Burnley	1-0	2-1	2-2	2-0	1-0	—	2-2	2-0	2-1	2-1
Bury	3-2	2-2	2-2	0-0	0-0	4-2	—	0-2	3-2	1-1
Cambridge U	0-2	0-2	2-2	3-0	1-1	0-1	3-0	—	0-0	2-0
Cardiff C	1-1	1-2	1-1	0-0	1-0	1-2	0-2	0-4	—	2-1
Chesterfield	0-0	0-1	1-0	0-2	0-1	1-1	0-1	4-2	1-1	—
Colchester U	1-1	3-1	0-3	3-4	5-4	1-2	1-3	3-1	0-3	1-0
Gillingham	1-3	4-1	2-0	3-0	0-1	2-2	1-0	2-1	4-1	1-0
Luton T	3-2	1-2	1-2	1-2	1-4	2-1	1-1	2-2	1-0	1-1
Millwall	1-1	3-1	3-2	4-1	3-0	1-1	3-0	2-1	2-0	1-1
Notts Co	2-1	5-1	0-1	4-4	0-2	2-0	2-2	2-3	2-1	1-0
Oldham Ath	1-1	1-0	3-0	1-1	1-4	0-1	2-0	1-0	1-2	1-2
Oxford U	0-1	1-0	1-1	3-0	0-5	1-2	1-1	1-0	2-3	2-1
Preston NE	3-0	3-0	2-1	1-0	2-1	0-0	1-1	2-1	0-0	0-2
Reading	1-1	2-0	1-0	2-1	2-0	0-0	2-0	0-0	0-1	1-0
Scunthorpe U	1-0	3-1	0-0	1-2	0-2	1-2	0-2	0-3	0-0	0-0
Stoke C	3-0	1-0	1-0	1-1	1-2	2-2	3-0	1-0	2-1	5-1
Wigan Ath	5-1	3-1	1-0	2-1	3-1	1-1	1-0	1-1	2-0	3-0
Wrexham	1-1	1-0	0-1	0-1	2-1	0-1	1-0	1-1	2-1	1-1
Wycombe W	0-2	2-1	2-0	1-2	1-1	1-1	3-0	1-0	3-1	3-0

DIVISION 2 1999–2000 RESULTS

Colchester U	Gillingham	Luton T	Millwall	Notts Co	Oldham Ath	Oxford U	Preston NE	Reading	Scunthorpe U	Stoke C	Wigan Ath	Wrexham	Wycombe W
1-1	1-1	3-3	1-2	2-1	1-2	1-1	0-0	0-2	0-2	1-2	2-2	2-1	1-2
4-0	0-1	1-0	1-2	1-1	3-0	4-0	0-1	3-1	1-1	1-1	2-2	1-0	2-0
0-0	1-2	2-0	1-3	0-2	2-0	2-0	2-2	1-1	4-3	0-1	0-2	0-2	0-0
1-1	0-1	0-0	0-0	2-2	1-1	2-2	0-2	3-1	2-1	2-2	0-0	4-0	0-0
2-1	2-1	3-0	1-0	0-1	3-2	1-0	0-2	0-1	1-1	3-3	1-1	3-1	1-0
3-0	0-3	0-2	4-3	2-1	3-0	3-2	0-3	3-0	1-2	1-0	0-0	5-0	1-0
5-2	2-1	1-0	2-2	1-3	2-2	1-2	1-3	1-1	3-0	0-0	2-2	0-2	2-0
5-2	2-2	3-1	0-2	1-1	2-3	2-0	2-0	3-1	1-3	1-3	1-1	3-4	1-2
3-2	1-2	1-3	1-1	2-1	1-1	1-1	0-4	1-0	1-1	1-2	0-0	1-1	2-2
0-1	0-0	1-3	2-0	2-1	0-1	0-0	0-1	2-0	1-1	0-2	1-1	0-3	1-2
—	2-1	3-0	1-2	0-3	0-1	1-2	2-2	3-2	0-1	1-0	2-2	2-2	1-0
2-1	—	2-0	2-0	0-1	2-1	1-0	0-2	2-2	3-1	3-0	2-1	5-1	2-2
3-2	3-1	—	0-2	2-2	1-1	4-2	0-2	3-1	4-1	2-1	1-1	3-1	1-1
1-0	2-2	1-0	—	1-0	1-0	1-0	0-2	5-0	1-2	1-0	3-3	0-0	1-1
1-2	1-1	0-0	1-1	—	0-1	0-1	1-0	1-2	3-0	0-0	0-2	2-1	2-1
1-2	1-3	2-1	2-1	1-2	—	2-0	0-1	1-2	1-1	0-1	2-1	0-0	2-2
1-1	1-2	0-1	1-3	2-3	1-0	—	0-4	1-3	2-0	1-1	1-2	1-4	0-0
2-3	0-2	1-0	3-2	2-0	2-0	3-1	—	2-2	1-0	2-1	1-4	1-0	3-2
2-0	2-2	1-2	2-0	0-0	1-1	1-2	2-2	—	1-1	1-0	0-2	2-2	2-1
0-0	1-4	1-2	1-4	1-0	1-2	1-0	1-1	2-2	—	0-2	1-2	0-2	0-1
1-1	1-1	2-1	3-1	0-1	0-0	1-2	2-1	2-1	1-0	—	1-1	2-0	1-1
0-1	2-0	1-0	1-1	2-0	0-1	2-0	0-1	1-0	3-0	1-2	—	0-1	2-1
1-0	1-0	1-0	1-1	2-3	0-3	1-0	0-0	0-1	3-1	2-3	1-1	—	1-3
3-0	1-0	0-1	1-2	2-0	0-0	0-1	1-1	5-3	2-1	0-4	0-2	0-1	—

NATIONWIDE FOOTBALL LEAGUE

HOME TEAM	Barnet	Brighton & HA	Carlisle U	Cheltenham T	Chester C	Darlington	Exeter C	Halifax T	Hartlepool U	Hull C
Barnet	—	0-1	3-0	3-2	2-0	1-0	2-2	0-1	1-1	0-0
Brighton & HA	1-1	—	1-0	1-0	2-3	1-1	4-2	2-1	1-0	3-0
Carlisle U	3-1	0-1	—	1-1	4-1	1-1	0-0	1-1	0-3	0-4
Cheltenham T	1-2	0-0	3-1	—	1-0	0-0	3-1	3-0	2-1	1-0
Chester C	0-2	1-7	0-1	2-1	—	1-2	1-1	2-1	1-1	0-0
Darlington	4-0	1-1	3-1	1-0	3-1	—	1-0	4-0	1-1	0-0
Exeter C	0-0	0-0	1-1	1-2	0-2	1-4	—	1-0	1-2	1-0
Halifax T	1-2	2-1	5-2	1-1	0-1	0-1	1-0	—	1-1	0-1
Hartlepool U	3-0	0-0	1-0	0-1	1-0	2-0	2-1	0-2	—	2-0
Hull C	1-3	2-0	2-1	1-1	2-1	0-1	4-0	0-1	0-3	—
Leyton Orient	0-0	1-2	0-1	1-0	1-2	2-1	4-1	1-0	2-1	0-0
Lincoln C	0-0	1-3	5-0	1-2	4-1	1-0	1-0	1-1	1-2	2-1
Macclesfield T	2-0	1-1	2-1	1-2	1-1	2-1	1-0	0-2	3-3	0-2
Mansfield T	0-1	1-0	1-1	0-1	2-1	1-2	1-1	0-2	2-3	0-1
Northampton T	1-0	1-0	0-0	3-2	3-1	0-3	2-1	3-4	2-1	1-0
Peterborough U	1-2	0-0	0-2	1-0	2-1	4-2	3-1	2-1	2-1	2-1
Plymouth Arg	4-1	3-3	2-0	1-0	0-0	0-0	1-0	1-1	1-1	0-1
Rochdale	1-1	1-0	3-2	0-0	2-1	0-0	0-2	0-1	2-0	0-2
Rotherham U	2-0	1-3	4-2	2-0	4-0	2-1	5-0	0-1	3-0	3-1
Shrewsbury T	1-1	1-2	4-1	0-2	0-1	0-1	1-4	0-0	0-0	3-0
Southend U	1-3	2-1	2-0	2-1	3-1	1-2	1-2	4-1	2-1	1-2
Swansea C	1-2	2-0	1-0	0-0	2-1	0-0	3-0	3-1	2-1	0-0
Torquay U	0-1	0-0	4-1	1-1	2-2	1-0	1-0	4-0	0-0	0-1
York C	1-0	0-0	1-1	1-2	2-2	0-0	0-0	2-0	2-1	1-1

DIVISION 3 1999–2000 RESULTS

Leyton Orient	Lincoln C	Macclesfield T	Mansfield T	Northampton T	Peterborough U	Plymouth Arg	Rochdale	Rotherham U	Shrewsbury T	Southend U	Swansea C	Torquay U	York C
2-2	5-3	2-1	0-0	2-1	0-2	1-0	1-0	1-0	1-1	2-1	0-1	1-2	6-3
0-1	2-2	5-2	6-0	1-3	0-0	1-1	3-4	1-1	1-0	1-0	1-1	0-1	0-1
2-1	1-0	0-1	0-2	0-1	1-1	4-2	1-2	0-1	1-1	1-1	2-0	0-0	0-1
2-0	0-2	1-1	1-0	2-1	2-1	2-0	0-2	0-2	0-1	2-1	0-0	2-0	0-1
1-5	1-3	1-2	5-0	0-2	0-1	0-1	0-2	0-2	0-0	0-0	0-1	2-1	2-0
3-1	2-0	3-0	0-0	0-1	2-0	2-0	4-1	2-2	2-2	1-0	1-1	1-1	2-2
1-3	3-0	0-3	1-0	1-2	2-2	1-1	2-0	3-1	1-2	0-1	1-1	3-2	2-1
0-2	3-0	0-1	0-1	2-2	2-1	0-1	0-2	0-0	2-1	0-0	0-1	2-0	0-2
1-0	2-0	1-4	1-0	2-1	1-0	3-0	3-2	1-2	1-0	1-2	0-1	2-0	2-1
2-0	1-1	2-3	2-0	0-1	2-3	0-1	2-2	0-0	0-0	0-0	2-0	0-0	1-1
—	2-3	0-0	1-3	0-0	1-1	3-0	0-0	0-1	1-2	2-1	0-1	0-2	0-0
0-0	—	1-1	3-0	2-2	1-2	3-0	1-1	2-1	1-2	1-0	0-1	2-1	4-2
1-0	1-1	—	5-2	1-0	1-1	4-1	1-2	1-1	4-2	1-2	1-2	1-2	1-1
1-1	5-2	1-0	—	0-0	3-1	2-2	0-0	1-2	4-0	3-1	0-1	4-3	1-0
2-1	1-0	2-0	1-0	—	0-1	1-1	0-1	0-1	3-0	2-0	2-1	3-0	3-0
2-1	2-2	2-2	1-0	1-0	—	2-0	3-3	0-5	4-1	1-0	2-3	0-2	2-0
5-0	1-1	3-2	2-1	2-1	2-1	—	1-1	1-1	0-0	3-1	1-0	2-2	2-0
1-4	1-1	0-1	2-1	0-3	1-2	0-0	—	0-1	2-1	2-0	0-0	1-1	2-1
0-1	1-1	2-1	2-3	3-0	1-1	1-1	0-1	—	4-0	0-0	1-1	1-0	1-0
1-0	1-2	0-1	1-2	1-0	0-1	0-0	2-4	0-0	—	2-1	1-1	1-2	0-1
1-1	2-2	1-0	1-0	2-2	0-1	2-1	3-3	1-2	3-2	—	2-1	0-2	0-0
0-0	2-1	1-0	0-1	4-1	0-0	1-0	1-0	2-0	1-1	3-1	—	2-1	1-0
0-0	5-2	3-2	4-0	1-2	2-1	0-4	1-0	2-1	3-1	0-1	1-0	—	0-0
2-1	2-0	0-2	0-1	0-1	0-0	0-0	0-3	1-2	1-0	2-2	1-0	2-2	—

Player	*Ht*	*Wt*	*Birthplace*	*D.O.B.*	*Source*
Adams Tony (D)	6 3	13 02	Romford	10 10 66	Apprentice
Aliadiere Jeremie (F)			France	30 3 83	Scholar
Barrett Graham (F)	5 10	11 07	Dublin	6 10 81	Trainee
Bergkamp Dennis (F)	6 0	12 05	Amsterdam	18 5 69	Internazionale
Black Tommy (M)	5 7	11 04	Chigwell	26 11 79	Trainee
Bothroyd Jay (F)			London	5 5 82	Trainee
Canoville Lee (D)			Ealing	14 3 81	Trainee
Cole Ashley (D)	5 8	10 08	Stepney	20 12 80	Trainee
Dixon Lee (D)	5 9	10 12	Manchester	17 3 64	Stoke C
Gray Julian (M)			Lewisham	21 9 79	Trainee
Grimandi Gilles (M)	5 10	11 08	Gap	11 11 70	Monaco
Grondin David (D)	5 9	11 11	Paris	8 5 80	St Etienne
Harper James (M)			Chelmsford	9 11 80	Trainee
Henry Thierry (F)	6 2	13 01	Paris	17 8 77	Juventus
Kanu Nwankwo (F)	6 5	12 01	Owerri	1 8 76	Internazionale
Keown Martin (D)	6 1	12 04	Oxford	24 7 66	Everton
Lincoln Greg (M)			Cheshunt	23 3 80	Trainee
Ljungberg Frederik (M)	5 9	10 13	Halmstad	16 4 77	Halmstad
Lukic John (G)	6 4	13 07	Chesterfield	11 12 60	Leeds U
Luzhny Oleg (D)	5 10	12 01	Ukraine	5 8 68	Dynamo Kiev
MacDonald James (M)	6 0	12 05	Inverness	21 2 79	Trainee
Malz Stefan (M)	5 10	12 01	Ludwigshafen	15 6 72	Munich 1860
Manninger Alex (G)	6 2	13 03	Salzburg	4 6 77	Graz
McGovern Brian (D)	6 3	12 07	Dublin	28 4 80	Cherry Orchard
Mendez Alberto (M)	5 11	11 09	Nuremberg	24 10 74	FC Feucht
Overmars Marc (F)	5 8	11 05	Emst	29 3 73	Ajax
Parlour Ray (M)	5 10	11 12	Romford	7 3 73	Trainee
Pennant Jermaine (M)			Nottingham	15 1 83	
Petit Emmanuel (M)	6 1	12 04	Dieppe	22 9 70	Monaco
Seaman David (G)	6 3	13 00	Rotherham	19 9 63	QPR
Silvinho(D)	5 7	10 06	Sao Paulo	12 4 74	Corinthians
Taylor Stuart (G)	6 4	13 07	Romford	28 11 80	Trainee
Upson Matthew (D)	6 1	11 04	Hartismere	18 4 79	Luton T
Vernazza Paulo (M)	5 10	10 13	Islington	1 11 79	Trainee
Vieira Patrick (M)	6 4	13 00	Dakar	23 6 76	AC Milan
Vivas Nelson (D)	5 5	10 06	San Nicolas	18 10 69	Lugano
Volz Moritz (D)			Germany	21 1 83	
Weston Rhys (D)	6 0	12 03	Kingston	27 10 80	Trainee
Winterburn Nigel (D)	5 10	10 07	Nuneaton	11 12 63	Wimbledon
Wreh Christopher (F)	5 9	11 05	Monrovia	14 5 75	Guincamp

League Appearances: Adams, T. 21; Barrett, G. (2); Bergkamp, D. 23(5); Black, T. (1); Boa Morte, L. (2); Cole, A. 1; Dixon, L. 28; Gray, J. (1); Grimandi, G. 27(1); Henry, T. 26(5); Hughes, S. 1(1); Kanu, N. 24(7); Keown, M. 27; Ljungberg, F. 22(4); Luzhny, O. 16(5); Malz, S. 2(3); Manninger, A. 14(1); McGovern, B. (1); Overmars, M. 22(9); Parlour, R. 29(1); Petit, E. 24(2); Seaman, D. 24; Silvinho 23(8); Suker, D. 8(14); Upson, M. 5(3); Vernazza, P. 1(1); Vieira, P. 29(1); Vivas, N. 1(4); Weston, R. 1; Winterburn, N. 19(9).
Goals – League (73): Henry 17 (2 pens), Kanu 12 (1 pen), Suker 8, Overmars 7, Bergkamp 6, Ljungberg 6, Dixon 4, Petit 3, Grimandi 2, Vieira 2, Keown 1, Malz 1, Parlour 1, Silvinho 1, own goals 2.
Worthington Cup (4): Henry 1, Kanu 1, Malz 1, Suker 1.
FA Cup (3): Adams 1, Grimandi 1, Overmars 1.

Ground: Arsenal Stadium, Highbury, London N5 1BU. Telephone (020) 7704 4000.
Record attendance: 73,295 v Sunderland, Div 1, 9 March 1935. **Capacity:** 38,500.
Manager: Arsène Wenger.
Secretary: David Miles.
Most League Goals: 127, Division 1, 1930–31.
Highest League Scorer in Season: Ted Drake, 42, 1934–35.
Most League Goals in Total Aggregate: Cliff Bastin, 150, 1930–47.
Most Capped Player: Kenny Sansom, 77 (86), England, 1981–1988.
Most League Appearances: David O'Leary, 558, 1975–93.
Honours – FA Premier League: Champions – 1997–98. **Football League:** Division 1 Champions – 1930–31, 1932–33, 1933–34, 1934–35, 1937–38, 1947–48, 1952–53, 1970–71, 1988–89, 1990–91. **FA Cup winners** 1929–30, 1935–36, 1949–50, 1970–71, 1978–79, 1992–93, 1997–98. **Football League Cup winners** 1986–87, 1992–93. **European Competitions: European Cup-Winners' Cup winners:** 1993–94. **Fairs Cup winners:** 1969–70.
Colours: Red shirts with white sleeves, white shorts, red and white stockings.

ASTON VILLA — FA PREMIERSHIP

Barry Gareth (D)	5 11	12 06	Hastings	23 2 81	Trainee
Bewers Jonathan (D)	5 8	9 13	Kettering	10 9 82	Trainee
Boateng George (M)	5 9	10 12	Nkawkaw	5 9 75	Coventry C
Carbone Benito (F)	5 6	10 06	Begnara	14 8 71	Sheffield W
Cooke Stephen (M)			Walsall	15 2 83	
Curtolo David (M)	5 9	11 00	Stockholm	30 9 80	
Cutler Neil (G)	6 1	12 00	Birmingham	3 9 76	Chester C
De Bolla Mark (F)			London	1 1 83	Trainee
Delaney Mark (D)	6 1	11 07	Haverfordwest	13 5 76	Carmarthen T
Draper Mark (M)	5 10	12 04	Long Eaton	11 11 70	Leicester C
Dublin Dion (F)	6 2	12 04	Leicester	22 4 69	Coventry C
Edwards Rob (D)			Telford	25 12 82	Trainee
Ehiogu Ugo (D)	6 2	14 10	Hackney	3 11 72	Trainee
Enckelman Peter (G)	6 2	12 05	Turku	10 3 77	TPS Turku
Evans Stephen (F)	5 8	10 08	Coventry	12 11 80	Trainee
Fahey Keith (M)			Dublin	15 1 83	
Ghent Matthew (G)	6 3	14 01	Burton	5 10 80	Trainee
Ghrayib Najwan (D)	5 8	11 04	Nazareth	30 1 74	Hapoel Haifa
Hendrie Lee (F)	5 10	10 02	Birmingham	18 5 77	Trainee
Hylton Leon (D)			Birmingham	27 1 83	
James David (G)	6 5	14 02	Welwyn	1 8 70	Liverpool
Joachim Julian (F)	5 6	12 00	Boston	20 9 74	Leicester C
Lescott Aaron (M)	5 8	10 10	Birmingham	2 12 78	Trainee
McGrath John (M)	5 10	10 04	Limerick	27 3 80	Belvedere
Melaugh Gavin (M)	5 7	9 07	Derry	9 7 81	Trainee
Merson Paul (F)	6 0	13 02	Northolt	20 3 68	Middlesbrough
Nkubi Isaac (F)			Uganda	5 3 81	Vasteras
Samuel J Lloyd (D)	5 11	11 04	Trinidad	29 3 81	Charlton Ath
Southgate Gareth (D)	6 0	12 03	Watford	3 9 70	Crystal Palace
Standing Michael (M)	5 10	10 07	Brighton	20 3 81	Trainee
Stone Steve (M)	5 8	12 07	Gateshead	20 8 71	Nottingham F
Tarrant Neil (F)	6 1	11 05	Darlington	24 6 79	Ross Co
Taylor Ian (M)	6 1	12 00	Birmingham	4 6 68	Sheffield W
Thompson Alan (M)	6 0	12 08	Newcastle	22 12 73	Bolton W
Thornley Stuart (D)	5 8	11 04	Wrexham	28 10 80	Trainee
Vassell Darius (F)	5 7	12 00	Birmingham	13 6 80	Trainee
Walker Richard (F)	6 0	12 00	Sutton Coldfield	8 11 77	Trainee

Watson Steve (D)	6 1	12 07	North Shields	1 4 74	Newcastle U
Willetts Benjamin (D)			Sandwell	10 2 83	
Wright Alan (D)	5 4	9 09	Ashton-under-Lyme	28 9 71	Blackburn R

League Appearances: Barry, G. 30; Bewers, J. (1); Boateng, G. 30(3); Calderwood, C. 15(3); Carbone, B. 22(2); Cutler, N. (1); Delaney, M. 25(3); Draper, M. (1); Dublin, D. 23(3); Ehiogu, U. 31; Enckelman, P. 9(1); Ghrayib, N. 1(4); Hendrie, L. 18(11); James, D. 29; Joachim, J. 27(6); Merson, P. 24(8); Samuel, J. 5(4); Southgate, G. 31; Stone, S. 10(14); Taylor, I. 25(4); Thompson, A. 16(5); Vassell, D. 1(10); Walker, R. 2(3); Watson, S. 13(1); Wright, A. 31(1).
Goals – League (46): Dublin 12 (1 pen), Joachim 6, Merson 5, Taylor 5, Carbone 3, Boateng 2, Southgate 2, Thompson 2, Walker 2, Barry 1, Delaney 1, Ehiogu 1, Hendrie 1, Stone 1, Wright 1, own goal 1.
Worthington Cup (16): Taylor 4, Hendrie 3, Joachim 3, Dublin 2, Boateng 1, Stone 1, Thompson 1, Watson 1.
FA Cup (8): Carbone 5, Dublin 1, Southgate 1, Stone 1.
Ground: Villa Park, Trinity Rd, Birmingham B6 6HE. Telephone (0121) 327 2299.
Record attendance: 76,588 v Derby Co, FA Cup 6th rd, 2 March 1946.
Capacity: 39,217.
Manager: John Gregory.
Secretary: Steven Stride.
Most League Goals: 128, Division 1, 1930–31.
Highest League Scorer in Season: 'Pongo' Waring, 49, Division 1, 1930–31.
Most League Goals in Total Aggregate: Harry Hampton, 215, 1904–15.
Most Capped Player: Paul McGrath, 51 (83), Republic of Ireland.
Most League Appearances: Charlie Aitken, 561, 1961–76.
Honours – Football League: Division 1 Champions – 1893–94, 1895–96, 1896–97, 1898–99, 1899–1900, 1909–10, 1980–81. Division 2 Champions – 1937–38, 1959–60. Division 3 Champions – 1971–72. **FA Cup:** Winners 1887, 1895, 1897, 1905, 1913, 1920, 1957. **Football League Cup:** Winners 1961, 1975, 1977, 1994, 1996. **European Competitions: European Cup winners:** 1981–82, **European Super Cup winners:** 1982–83.
Colours: Claret and blue shirts, sky blue shorts, claret stockings.

BARNET DIV. 3

Arber Mark (D)	6 1	12 11	Johannesburg	8 10 77	Tottenham H
Basham Mike (D)	6 2	13 09	Barking	27 9 73	Peterborough U
Bell Leon (M)	5 7	9 07	Hitchin	19 12 80	Trainee
Bossu Bertrand (G)	6 7	14 00	Calais	14 10 80	
Brown Daniel (M)	6 0	12 06	Bethnal Green	12 9 80	Leyton Orient
Chapman Danny (M)			London	19 4 81	Trainee
Charlery Ken (F)	6 1	13 12	Stepney	28 11 64	Stockport Co
Currie Darren (M)	5 10	12 07	Hampstead	29 11 74	Plymouth Arg
Darcy Ross (D)	6 0	12 02	Balbriggan	21 3 78	Tottenham H
Doolan John (M)	6 1	13 00	Liverpool	7 5 74	Mansfield T
Gledhill Lee (D)	5 10	11 02	Bury	7 11 80	Trainee
Goodhind Warren (D)	5 11	11 02	Johannesburg	16 8 77	Trainee
Hackett Warren (D)	6 0	12 05	Plaistow	16 12 71	Mansfield T
Harrison Lee (G)	6 2	12 07	Billericay	12 9 71	Fulham
Heald Greg (D)	6 1	13 01	Enfield	26 9 71	Peterborough U
King Marlon (F)	6 1	12 03	Dulwich	26 4 80	Trainee
McCann Peter (D)			Paisley	27 6 82	Trainee
McGleish Scott (F)	5 10	11 07	Camden Town	10 2 74	Leyton Orient
Naisbitt Danny (G)	6 1	11 12	Bishop Auckland	25 11 78	Walsall
Sawyers Robert (D)	5 10	11 03	Dudley	20 11 78	Wolverhampton W
Searle Stevie (M)	5 10	11 08	Lambeth	7 3 77	Sittingbourne

Stockley Sam (D)	6 0	12 00	Tiverton	5 9 77	Trainee
Strevens Ben (F)	6 1	11 00	Islington	24 5 80	Wingate & Finchley
Toms Frazer (M)	6 1	11 00	Ealing	13 9 79	Trainee

League Appearances: Ansell, G. (3); Arber, M. 43(2); Barnes, S. 1(2); Basham, M. 15; Bell, L. (1); Brown, D. 20(4); Charlery, K. 42(1); Currie, D. 44; Darcy, R. 1(2); Davidson, R. 8(1); Doolan, J. 44; Gledhill, L. 8(2); Goodhind, W. 5(4); Hackett, W. 34; Harrison, L. 43; Heald, G. 40; King, M. 19(12); McGleish, S. 30(12); Naisbitt, D. 3(1); Omoyinmi, E. 1(5); Sawyers, R. 31(1); Searle, S. 8(11); Stockley, S. 31(3); Strevens, B. (6); Toms, F. 27(12); Wilson, P. 8(11).
Goals – League (59): Charlery 13, McGleish 10, King 8, Arber 6, Currie 5 (1 pen), Heald 5, Brown 3, Doolan 2, Sawyers 2, Hackett 1, Stockley 1, Toms 1, Wilson 1 (pen), own goal 1.
Worthington Cup (3): McGleish 2 (1 pen), Hackett 1.
FA Cup (0).
Ground: Underhill Stadium, Barnet Lane, Barnet, Herts EN5 2BE. Telephone (020) 8441 6932.
Record attendance: 11,026 v Wycombe Wanderers. FA Amateur Cup 4th Round 1951–52.
Capacity: 5560.
Manager: John Still.
Most League Goals: 81, Division 4, 1991–92.
Highest League Scorer in Season: Dougie Freedman, 24, Division 3, 1994–95.
Most League Goals in Total Aggregate: Sean Devine, 47, 1995–99.
Most Capped Player: Ken Charlery, St Lucia.
Most League Appearances: Paul Wilson, 263, 1991–2000.
Honours – FA Amateur Cup winners 1945–46. **GM Vauxhall Conference winners** 1990–91.
Colours: Amber and black shirts, amber shorts, amber stockings.

BARNSLEY DIV. 1

Appleby Matty (D)	5 10	11 08	Middlesbrough	16 4 72	Darlington
Austin Kevin (D)	6 1	15 00	Hackney	12 2 73	Lincoln C
Austin Neil (D)	5 10	11 00	Barnsley	26 4 83	Trainee
Barker Christopher (D)	6 0	11 08	Sheffield	2 3 80	Alfreton
Barnard Darren (D)	5 9	12 03	Rinteln	30 11 71	Bristol C
Bernard Curtis (F)	5 10	12 05	Leeds	3 7 80	Trainee
Brown Keith (D)	5 11	11 02	Edinburgh	24 12 79	Blackburn R
Bullock Martin (M)	5 6	9 04	Derby	5 3 75	Eastwood T
Chettle Steve (D)	6 1	13 07	Nottingham	27 9 68	Nottingham F
Crookes Dale (M)	5 9	12 03	Sheffield	10 3 80	Trainee
Dudgeon James (D)	6 2	12 04	Newcastle	19 3 81	Trainee
Dyer Bruce (F)	5 11	12 06	Ilford	13 4 75	Crystal Palace
Evans Andy (F)	6 2	12 02	Aberystwyth	25 11 75	Cardiff C
Fallon Rory (F)	6 2	11 09	Gisbourne	20 3 82	North Shore U
Goodyear Craig (M)	5 7	10 07	Barnsley	7 11 80	Trainee
Hignett Craig (M)	5 9	11 03	Whiston	12 1 70	Aberdeen
Hood Nathan (M)	5 5	10 05	Rotherham	24 2 82	
Hristov Georgi (F)	6 0	12 09	Bitola	30 1 76	Partizan Belgrade
Jackson Paul (F)	5 8	11 04	Rochdale	14 5 81	Trainee
Jones Scott (D)	5 10	12 01	Sheffield	1 5 75	Trainee
Kay Antony (M)	5 11	11 08	Barnsley	21 10 82	Trainee
McClare Sean (M)	5 11	11 08	Rotherham	12 1 78	Trainee
Miller Kevin (G)	6 1	16 00	Falmouth	15 3 69	Crystal Palace
Morgan Chris (D)	6 1	12 09	Barnsley	9 11 77	Trainee

Moses Adrian (D)	6 0	12 07	Doncaster	4 5 75	School
O'Callaghan Brian (D)	6 1	12 01	Limerick	24 2 81	Pike Rovers
Parkin Jonathan (F)	6 4	13 07	Barnsley	30 12 81	Scholar
Ravenhill Richard (M)	5 10	11 01	Doncaster	16 1 81	Trainee
Rose Karl (F)	5 10	11 00	Barnsley	12 10 78	
Sheron Mike (F)	5 10	12 07	Liverpool	11 1 72	QPR
Shipperley Neil (F)	6 0	14 01	Chatham	30 10 74	Nottingham F
Siddall Richard (G)	6 1	11 06	Sheffield	24 1 82	Scholar
Turner Mike (F)	6 2	13 03	Stoke	2 4 76	Bilston T
Walker Leigh (G)	5 10	12 06	Sheffield	12 2 81	Trainee
Watson David (G)	6 0	12 09	Barnsley	10 11 73	Trainee
Young Darren (M)	5 8	10 07	Whitehaven	20 2 81	

League Appearances: Appleby, M. 33(3); Austin, K. 3; Barker, C. 28(1); Barnard, D. 32(9); Brown, K. 7(3); Bullock, M. 1(3); Bullock, T. 5(1); Chettle, S. 25; Curtis, J. 28; Dyer, B. 13(19); Eaden, N. 38(4); Hignett, C. 38(4); Hristov, G. 5(13); Jackson, M. 1; Jones, S. 20; McClare, S. 1(9); Miller, K. 41; Morgan, C. 36(1); Moses, A. 12; Richardson, K. 4; Sheron, M. 28(8); Shipperley, N. 32(7); Thomas, G. 13(14); Tinkler, E. 28(5); Tuttle, D. 11(1); Van der Laan, R. 23(9).
Goals – League (88): Hignett 19 (3 pens), Barnard 13 (5 pens), Shipperley 13, Sheron 9, Dyer 6, Appleby 5, Hristov 4, Thomas 4, Tinkler 4, Van der Laan 3, Chettle 2, Curtis 2, McClare 2, Eaden 1, own goal 1.
Worthington Cup (13): Barnard 2 (1 pen), Eaden 2, Hristov 2, Sheron 2, Van der Laan 2, Jones 1, Morgan 1, Shipperley 1.
FA Cup (0).
Ground: Oakwell Ground, Grove St, Barnsley S71 1ET. Telephone (01226) 211211.
Record attendance: 40,255 v Stoke C, FA Cup 5th rd, 15 February 1936. **Capacity:** 23,186.
Manager: Dave Bassett.
Secretary: Michael Spinks.
Most League Goals: 118, Division 3 (N), 1933–34.
Highest League Scorer in Season: Cecil McCormack, 33, Division 2, 1950–51.
Most League Goals in Total Aggregate: Ernest Hine, 123, 1921–26 and 1934–38.
Most Capped Player: Gerry Taggart, 35 (45), Northern Ireland.
Most League Appearances: Barry Murphy, 514, 1962–78.
Honours – Football League: Division 3 (N) Champions – 1933–34, 1938–39, 1954–55. **FA Cup:** Winners 1912.
Colours: Red shirts, white shorts, red stockings.

BIRMINGHAM CITY — DIV. 1

Adebola Dele (F)	6 3	12 08	Lagos	23 6 75	Crewe Alex
Bass Jonathan (D)	6 0	12 02	Weston-Super-Mare	1 1 76	Birmingham C
Bennett Ian (G)	6 0	12 10	Worksop	10 10 71	Peterborough U
Capaldi Tony (D)	6 0	12 00	Porsgrunn	12 8 81	Trainee
Dyson James (D)	6 2	12 00	Wordsley	20 4 79	Trainee
Furlong Paul (F)	6 0	11 00	London	1 10 68	Chelsea
Gill Jeremy (D)	5 11	11 00	Clevedon	8 9 70	Yeovil T
Grainger Martin (D)	5 10	11 07	Enfield	23 8 72	Brentford
Haarhoff Jimmy (M)	5 5	10 02	Lusaka	27 5 81	Trainee
Holdsworth David (D)	6 1	12 10	Walthamstow	8 11 68	Sheffield U
Hughes Bryan (M)	5 9	10 00	Liverpool	19 6 76	Wrexham
Hyde Graham (M)	5 7	12 04	Doncaster	10 11 70	Sheffield W
Johnson Andrew (F)	5 7	10 00	Bedford	10 2 81	Trainee
Johnson Michael (D)	5 11	11 00	Nottingham	4 7 73	Notts Co
Lazaridis Stan (M)	5 9	12 00	Perth	16 8 72	West Ham U

Luntala Tresor (M)	5 9	11 00	Dreux	31 5 82	
Marcelo (F)	6 0	13 04	Niteroi	11 10 69	Sheffield U
Marsh Simon (D)	5 11	12 00	Ealing	29 1 77	Oxford U
McCarthy Jon (M)	5 9	11 05	Middlesbrough	18 8 70	Port Vale
Ndlovu Peter (F)	5 8	10 02	Zimbabwe	25 2 73	Coventry C
O'Connor Martin (M)	5 8	10 08	Walsall	10 12 67	Peterborough U
Parker Sonny (M)			Middlesbrough	28 2 83	Trainee
Pinkney Grant (M)			Evesham	31 1 83	
Poole Kevin (G)	5 10	11 11	Bromsgrove	21 7 63	Leicester C
Purse Darren (D)	6 2	13 08	Stepney	14 2 76	Oxford U
Robinson Steve (M)	5 9	11 00	Nottingham	17 10 75	Trainee
Rowett Gary (D)	6 0	12 10	Bromsgrove	6 3 74	Derby Co
Williams Jacques (M)	5 9	11 00	Wallasey	25 4 81	

League Appearances: Adebola, D. 21(21); Bass, J. 5(3); Bennett, I. 21; Beresford, J. 1; Campbell, S. (2); Carrick, M. 1(1); Charlton, S. 19(1); Dyson, J. (2); Forinton, H. (1); Furlong, P. 17(2); Gill, J. 2(9); Grainger, M. 34; Haarhoff, J. (1); Holdsworth, D. 43(1); Holland, C. 2(12); Hughes, B. 41(4); Hyde, G. 20(11); Johnson, A. 15(7); Johnson, M. 29(5); Johnston, A. 7(2); Lazaridis, S. 26(5); Marcelo 14(11); McCarthy, J. 21; Myhre, T. 7; Ndlovu, P. 2(11); Newton, E. 2(2); O'Connor, M. 38(1); Poole, K. 18; Purse, D. 33(5); Rankin, I. 11(2); Robinson, S. 5(1); Rowett, G. 45; Wreh, C. 6(1).
Goals – League (65): Furlong 11 (4 pens), Hughes 10, Adebola 5, Grainger 5 (1 pen), Holdsworth 5, Marcelo 5, McCarthy 4, Rankin 4, Johnson M 2, Lazaridis 2, O'Connor 2 (1 pen), Purse 2, Hyde 1, Johnson A 1, Ndlovu 1, Rowett 1, Wreh 1, own goals 3.
Worthington Cup (12): O'Connor 3 (2 pens), Adebola 1, Grainger 1, Holdsworth 1, Hyde 1, Johnson A 1, Purse 1, Rowett 1, own goals 2.
FA Cup (1): Rowett 1.
Ground: St Andrews, Birmingham B9 4NH. Telephone 0709 111 25837.
Record attendance: 66,844 v Everton, FA Cup 5th rd,11 February 1939. **Capacity:** 30,009.
Manager: Trevor Francis.
Secretary: Alan Jones BA, MBA
Most League Goals: 103, Division 2, 1893–94 (only 28 games).
Highest League Scorer in Season: Joe Bradford, 29, Division 1, 1927–28.
Most League Goals in Total Aggregate: Joe Bradford, 249, 1920–35.
Most Capped Player: Malcolm Page, 28, Wales.
Most League Appearances: Frank Womack, 491, 1908–28.
Honours – Football League: Division 2 Champions – 1892–93, 1920–21, 1947–48, 1954–55, 1994–95. **Football League Cup:** Winners 1963. **Leyland Daf Cup:** Winners 1991. **Auto Windscreens Shield:** Winners 1995.
Colours: Blue shirts, white shorts, blue/white stockings.

BLACKBURN ROVERS — DIV. 1

Baldacchino Ryan (F)	5 9	12 03	Leicester	13 1 81	Trainee
Bingham Michael (G)	6 0	12 05	Preston	21 5 81	Trainee
Blake Nathan (F)	5 11	13 12	Cardiff	27 1 72	Bolton W
Blakeman Liam (M)			Southport	6 9 82	Scholar
Broomes Marlon (D)	6 1	13 00	Meriden	28 11 77	Trainee
Burgess Ben (F)	6 3	14 04	Buxton	9 11 81	Trainee
Carsley Lee (M)	5 10	12 06	Birmingham	28 2 74	Derby Co
Chamberlain Robert (M)			Chester	5 6 82	Trainee
Corbett Jimmy (F)	5 10	12 00	Hackney	6 7 80	Trainee
Dailly Christian (D)	6 0	12 10	Dundee	23 10 73	Derby Co

Davidson Callum (D)	5 10	12 07	Stirling	25 6 76	St Johnstone
Douglas Jonathan (M)			Monaghan	22 11 81	Trainee
Doyle Robert (M)			Dublin	15 4 82	Trainee
Duff Damien (F)	5 9	11 07	Ballyboden	2 3 79	Lourdes Celtic
Dunn David (M)	5 10	12 06	Gt Harwood	27 12 79	Trainee
Dunning Darren (M)	5 6	11 12	Scarborough	8 1 81	Trainee
Filan John (G)	6 2	12 12	Sydney	8 2 70	Coventry C
Flitcroft Garry (M)	6 0	11 08	Bolton	6 11 72	Manchester C
Flitcroft Steven (M)	5 10	11 01	Bolton	17 10 81	Trainee
Forsyth Paul (F)	5 8	10 05	Dublin	11 4 81	Trainee
Foster Steve (F)	5 9	13 01	Manchester	30 12 81	Trainee
Frandsen Per (M)	5 11	12 10	Copenhagen	6 2 70	Bolton W
Gillespie Keith (F)	5 10	11 03	Bangor	18 2 75	Newcastle U
Grayson Simon (D)	6 0	13 07	Ripon	16 12 69	Aston Villa
Hamilton Gary (F)			Bambridge	6 10 80	Trainee
Harkness Steve (D)	5 9	11 09	Carlisle	27 8 71	Benfica
Hawe Steven (F)			Machbrafelt	23 12 80	Trainee
Howson Stuart (M)			Chorley	30 9 81	Trainee
Jansen Matt (F)	5 11	12 06	Carlisle	20 10 77	Crystal Palace
Johnson Damien (M)	5 9	11 07	Lisburn	18 11 78	Trainee
Kelly Alan (G)	6 3	14 02	Preston	11 8 68	Sheffield U
Kenna Jeff (D)	5 11	12 03	Dublin	28 8 70	Southampton
Lawless Michael (M)	5 6	10 13	Dublin	15 8 81	Trainee
McAteer Jason (M)	5 11	12 04	Birkenhead	18 6 71	Liverpool
McCann Peter (D)	5 6	10 13	Dublin	18 8 81	Trainee
McKinlay Billy (M)	5 8	11 06	Glasgow	22 4 69	Dundee U
McNamee David (D)	5 11	11 02	Glasgow	10 10 80	St Mirren BC
Miller Alan (G)	6 3	14 06	Epping	29 3 70	WBA
Murphy Peter (D)	5 11	12 10	Dublin	27 10 80	Trainee
Murray Frederick (M)			Clonmel	22 5 82	Trainee
O'Brien Burton (M)	5 10	10 12	South Africa	10 6 81	S Form
Ostenstad Egil (F)	5 11	13 00	Haugesund	2 1 72	Southampton
Peacock Darren (D)	6 2	12 12	Bristol	3 2 68	Newcastle U
Richards Marc (M)			Wolverhampton	8 7 82	Trainee
Richardson Leam (D)	5 8	11 04	Leeds	19 11 79	Trainee
Short Craig (D)	6 1	11 10	Bridlington	25 6 68	Everton
Taylor Martin (D)	6 4	14 00	Ashington	9 11 79	Trainee
Taylor Michael (M)			Liverpool	21 11 82	Scholar
Taylor Stuart (M)			Rochdale	14 9 81	Trainee
Thomas James (F)	6 1	13 04	Swansea	16 1 79	Trainee
Ward Ashley (F)	6 1	12 04	Manchester	24 11 70	Barnsley

League Appearances: Blake, N. 17(11); Broomes, M. 13; Burgess, B. 1(1); Carsley, L. 30; Dailly, C. 43; Davidson, C. 28(2); Davies, K. 2; Duff, D. 33(6); Dunn, D. 17(5); Fettis, A. (1); Filan, J. 16; Flitcroft, G. 18(1); Frandsen, P. 26(5); Gallacher, K. 3(2); Gillespie, K. 11(11); Grayson, S. 31(3); Harkness, S. 17; Jansen, M. 16(14); Johnson, D. 11(5); Kelly, A. 29(1); Kenna, J. 11; McAteer, J. 24(4); Miller, A. 1; Ostenstad, E. 21(7); Peacock, D. 15(2); Short, C. 17; Taylor, M. 4(2); Ward, A. 35(2); Wilcox, J. 16(4).
Goals – League (55): Carsley 10 (7 pens), Ostenstad 8, Ward 8, Duff 5, Frandsen 5, Dailly 4, Jansen 4, Blake 3, Dunn 2, Gillespie 2, McAteer 2, Broomes 1, Johnson 1.
Worthington Cup (6): Jansen 2, Duff 1, Dunn 1, Gallacher 1, own goal 1.
FA Cup (6): Blake 2, Carsley 1 (pen), Duff 1, Frandsen 1, Jansen 1.
Ground: Ewood Park, Blackburn BB2 4JF. Telephone (01254) 698888.
Record attendance: 61,783 v Bolton W, FA Cup 6th rd, 2 March, 1929. **Capacity:** 31,367.
Manager: Graeme Souness.

Secretary: Tom Finn.
Most League Goals: 114, Division 2, 1954–55.
Highest League Scorer in Season: Ted Harper, 43, Division 1, 1925–26.
Most League Goals in Total Aggregate: Simon Garner, 168, 1978–92.
Most Capped Player: Bob Crompton, 41, England.
Most League Appearances: Derek Fazackerley, 596, 1970–86.
Honours – FA Premier League: Champions – 1994–95. Football League: Division 1 Champions – 1911–12, 1913–14. Division 2 Champions – 1938–39. Division 3 Champions – 1974–75. **FA Cup:** Winners 1884, 1885, 1886, 1890, 1891, 1928. **Full Members' Cup:** Winners 1986–87.
Colours: Blue and white halved shirts, white shorts, white stockings, blue trim.

BLACKPOOL — DIV. 3

Barnes Phil (G)	6 1	11 01	Rotherham	2 3 79	Trainee
Beesley Paul (D)	6 1	12 06	Liverpool	21 7 65	Port Vale
Bent Junior (F)	5 5	10 06	Huddersfield	1 3 70	Bristol C
Bushell Steve (M)	5 9	11 06	Manchester	28 12 72	York C
Caig Tony (G)	6 1	12 00	Whitehaven	11 4 74	Carlisle U
Carlisle Clarke (D)	6 1	12 07	Preston	14 10 79	Trainee
Clarkson Phil (M)	5 10	12 05	Garstang	13 11 68	Scunthorpe U
Forsyth Richard (M)	5 11	13 00	Dudley	3 10 70	Stoke C
Garvey Steve (M)	5 9	11 01	Stalybridge	22 11 73	Crewe Alex
Gill Wayne (M)	5 9	11 00	Chorley	28 11 75	Blackburn R
Hills John (D)	5 8	10 08	St Annes-on-Sea	21 4 78	Everton
Hughes Ian (M)	5 10	12 08	Bangor	2 8 74	Bury
Jaszczun Tommy (D)	5 11	11 02	Kettering	16 9 77	Aston Villa
Jones Eifion (D)	6 3	13 00	Llanrug	28 9 80	Liverpool
Murphy John (F)	6 2	14 00	Whiston	18 10 76	Chester C
Newell Mike (F)	6 0	13 00	Liverpool	27 1 65	Crewe Alex
Nowland Adam (F)	5 11	11 06	Preston	6 7 81	Trainee
Ormerod Brett (F)	5 11	11 04	Blackburn	18 10 76	Accrington S
Rachel Adam (G)	5 11	12 08	Birmingham	10 12 76	Aston Villa
Thompson Phil (D)	5 11	12 00	Blackpool	1 4 81	Trainee
Wellens Richard (M)	5 9	11 05	Manchester	26 3 80	Manchester U

League Appearances: Ablett, G. 9(1); Aldridge-deceased, M. (5); Bardsley, D. 35; Barnes, P. 12; Beesley, P. 15(3); Bent, J. 18(10); Bryan, M. 14(4); Bushell, S. 17(7); Byfield, D. 3; Caig, T. 33; Carlisle, C. 43; Clarkson, P. 34(1); Coid, D. 13(8); Connell, D. 1(2); Couzens, A. 12(3); Durnin, J. 4(1); Forsyth, R. 10(3); Garvey, S. 1(1); Gill, W. 12; Hills, J. 32(1); Hughes, I. 31(3); Jaszczun, T. 19; Jones, E. 1; Lambert, R. (3); Lee, D. 9; Lumsdon, C. 6; Matthews, R. 5(1); Murphy, J. 34(5); Newell, M. 12(1); Nowland, A. 5(16); Ormerod, B. 13; Quailey, B. 1; Rachel, A. 1; Richardson, K. 20; Robinson, P. 4(2); Shuttleworth, B. 4(1); Thomas, J. 9; Thompson, P. 2(1); Wellens, R. 5(3); Whitley, J. 7(1).
Goals – League (49): Murphy 10, Gill 7, Ormerod 5, Carlisle 4, Clarkson 3, Nowland 3, Bushell 2, Hills 2 (2 pens), Matthews 2, Newell 2, Thomas 2, Ablett 1, Bent 1, Coid 1, Durnin 1, Lee 1, Lumsdon 1, Richardson 1.
Worthington Cup (3): Clarkson 2, Hughes 1.
FA Cup (5): Clarkson 2, Carlisle 1, Durnin 1, Nowland 1.
Ground: Bloomfield Rd Ground, Blackpool FY1 6JJ. Telephone (01253) 404331.
Record attendance: 38,098 v Wolverhampton W, Division 1, 17 September 1955.
Capacity: 11,295.
Manager: Steve McMahon.
Secretary: Carol Banks.
Most League Goals: 98, Division 2, 1929–30.

Highest League Scorer in Season: Jimmy Hampson, 45, Division 2, 1929–30.
Most League Goals in Total Aggregate: Jimmy Hampson, 246, 1927–38.
Most Capped Player: Jimmy Armfield, 43, England.
Most League Appearances: Jimmy Armfield, 568, 1952–71.
Honours – Football League: Division 2 Champions – 1929–30. **FA Cup:** Winners 1953. **Anglo-Italian Cup:** Winners 1971.
Colours: All tangerine.

BOLTON WANDERERS DIV. 1

Banks Steve (G)	6 0	13 12	Hillingdon	9 2 72	Blackpool
Crumblehulme Danny (M)	5 6	10 07	Blackpool	7 2 82	Trainee
Elliott Robbie (M)	5 10	12 03	Gosforth	25 12 73	Newcastle U
Evans James (M)			Glasgow	27 1 82	Scholar
Farrelly Gareth (M)	6 1	13 07	Dublin	28 8 75	Everton
Fish Mark (D)	6 4	13 06	Cape Town	14 3 74	Lazio
Gardner Ricardo (M)	5 9	11 01	St Andrews	25 9 78	Harbour View
Glennon Matthew (G)	6 2	14 09	Stockport	8 10 78	Trainee
Gudjohnsen Eidur (F)	6 0	13 09	Reykjavik	15 9 78	KR
Hansen Bo (F)	6 1	12 02	Jutland	16 6 72	Brondby
Haveron Gary (D)	6 1	14 00	Belfast	6 3 81	Wolverhampton W
Holden Dean (D)	6 0	12 03	Salford	15 9 79	
Holdsworth Dean (F)	5 11	13 06	Walthamstow	8 11 68	Wimbledon
Jaaskelainen Jussi (G)	6 3	13 05	Mikkeli	19 4 75	VPS
Jensen Claus (M)	5 11	12 13	Nykobing	29 4 77	Lyngby
Johnston Allan (F)	5 7	9 07	Glasgow	14 12 73	Rennes
Kaprielian Mickael (F)	5 10	11 00	Marseille	6 10 80	
Morrison Peter (M)	5 11	10 00	Manchester	29 6 80	Trainee
Nolan Kevin (D)	6 0	14 00	Liverpool	24 6 82	Scholar
Norris David (M)	5 7	11 06	Peterborough	22 2 81	Boston U
O'Kane John (D)	5 10	12 06	Nottingham	15 11 74	Everton
Snorrason Olaf (F)			Reykjavik	22 4 82	
Strong Greg (D)	6 2	14 04	Bolton	5 9 75	Wigan Ath
Warhurst Paul (D)	6 0	13 07	Stockport	26 9 69	Crystal Palace
Whitlow Mike (D)	6 1	13 03	Northwich	13 1 68	Leicester C

League Appearances: Aljofree, H. 3(5); Banks, S. 2; Bergsson, G. 37(1); Branagan, K. 11; Cox, N. 15; Elliott, R. 22(5); Farrelly, G. 8(3); Fish, M. 31; Frandsen, P. 7; Gardner, R. 26(3); Gudjohnsen, E. 40(1); Hansen, B. 15(15); Holden, D. 6(6); Holdsworth, D. 22(13); Holloway, D. 3(1); Jaaskelainen, J. 33(1); Jensen, C. 41(1); Johansen, M. 44(1); Johnston, A. 17(2); Kaprielian, M. (1); Nolan, K. (4); O'Kane, J. 7(4); Passi, F. 7(8); Phillips, J. 15(8); Ritchie, P. 13(1); Strong, G. 6; Taylor, B. 15(12); Todd, A. 10(2); Warhurst, P. 15(4); Whitlow, M. 35(2).
Goals – League (69): Gudjohnsen 13, Holdsworth 11 (6 pens), Hansen 9, Jensen 6, Gardner 5, Bergsson 4, Elliott 3, Johansen 3 (1 pen), Johnston 3, Taylor 3, Cox 2, Frandsen 2, Farrelly 1, O'Kane 1, Phillips 1, Whitlow 1, own goal 1.
Worthington Cup (17): Gudjohnsen 3, Johansen 3 (2 pens), Frandsen 2, Bergsson 1, Cox 1, Elliott 1, Fish 1, Gardner 1, Hansen 1, Holdsworth 1, Taylor 1, own goal 1.
FA Cup (7): Gudjohnsen 4, Taylor 2, Hansen 1.
Ground: Reebok Stadium, Burnden Way, Lostock, Bolton BL6 6JW. Telephone Bolton (01204) 673673.
Record attendance: 69,912 v Manchester C, FA Cup 5th rd, 18 February 1933.
Capacity: 27,879.

Manager: Sam Allardyce.
Secretary: Des McBain.
Most League Goals: 100, Division 1, 1996–97.
Highest League Scorer in Season: Joe Smith, 38, Division 1, 1920–21.
Most League Goals in Total Aggregate: Nat Lofthouse, 255, 1946–61.
Most Capped Player: Nat Lofthouse, 33, England.
Most League Appearances: Eddie Hopkinson, 519, 1956–70.
Honours – Football League: Division 1 Champions – 1996–97. Division 2 Champions – 1908–09, 1977–78. Division 3 Champions – 1972–73. **FA Cup winners** 1923, 1926, 1929, 1958. **Sherpa Van Trophy:** Winners 1989.
Colours: White shirts, navy blue shorts, blue stockings.

AFC BOURNEMOUTH DIV. 2

Bailey John (M)	5 8	10 02	London	6 5 69	Enfield
Broadhurst Karl (D)	6 1	11 07	Portsmouth	18 3 80	Trainee
Day Jamie (M)	5 10	11 04	Sidcup	13 9 79	Arsenal
Elliott Wade (F)	5 9	11 01	Southampton	14 12 78	
Fletcher Carl (M)	5 10	11 07	Camberley	7 4 80	Trainee
Fletcher Steve (F)	6 2	14 09	Hartlepool	26 6 72	Hartlepool U
Ford James (M)	5 8	11 00	Portsmouth	23 10 81	Trainee
Hayter James (F)	5 9	10 13	Newport (IW)	9 4 79	Trainee
Howe Eddie (D)	5 9	11 02	Amersham	29 11 77	Trainee
Huck Willie (M)	5 10	11 09	Paris	17 3 79	Monaco
Hughes Richard (M)	6 2	12 00	Glasgow	25 6 79	Atalanta
Jorgensen Claus (M)	5 10	10 06	Holstebro	27 4 76	AC Horsens
Keeler Justin (F)	5 11	11 06	Hillingdon	17 4 78	Christchurch
Ovendale Mark (G)	6 2	13 10	Leicester	22 11 73	Wisbech T
Robinson Steve (F)	5 9	11 02	Crumlin	10 12 74	Tottenham H
Sheerin Joe (F)	6 1	12 13	Hammersmith	1 2 79	Chelsea
Smith Daniel (D)	5 11	11 04	Southampton	17 8 82	Trainee
Stewart Gareth (G)	6 0	12 08	Preston	3 2 80	Blackburn R
Stock Brian (F)	5 11	11 02	Winchester	24 12 81	Trainee
Tindall Jason (M)	6 1	12 01	Stepney	15 11 77	Charlton Ath
Town David (F)	5 7	11 13	Bournemouth	9 12 76	Trainee
Young Neil (D)	5 9	12 00	Harlow	31 8 73	Tottenham H

League Appearances: Bailey, J. (1); Betsy, K. 1(4); Broadhurst, K. 16; Cox, I. 28; Day, J. 9(2); Elliott, S. 6(2); Elliott, W. 6(6); Fenton, N. 8; Fletcher, C. 20(5); Fletcher, S. 35(1); Forbes, T. 3; Ford, J. (2); Hayter, J. 21(10); Howe, E. 28; Huck, W. 4(13); Hughes, R. 20(1); Jorgensen, C. 34(10); Keeler, J. (3); Lovell, S. (1); Mean, S. 26(6); O'Neill, J. 18(12); O'Shea, J. 10; Ovendale, M. 43; Rawlinson, M. 2(1); Robinson, S. 40; Sheerin, J. 3(3); Smith, D. (1); Stein, M. 36; Stewart, G. 3; Stock, B. 4(1); Tindall, J. 4(4); Warren, C. 39(2); Watson, G. 2(4); Young, N. 37.
Goals – League (59): Stein 11, Robinson 9 (4 pens), Fletcher S 7, Jorgensen 6, Mean 4, Elliott 3, Fletcher C 3, O'Neill 3, Hayter 2, Hughes 2, Warren 2, Day 1, Howe 1, O'Shea 1, Sheerin 1, own goals 3.
Worthington Cup (4): Stein 2, Hayter 1, Huck 1.
FA Cup (5): Fletcher S 2, Robinson 1 (pen), Stein 1, Warren 1.
Ground: Dean Court Ground, Bournemouth BH7 7AF. Telephone (01202) 395381.
Record attendance: 28,799 v Manchester U, FA Cup 6th rd, 2 March 1957.
Capacity: 10,770.
Manager: Mel Machin.
Secretary: K. R. J. MacAlister.

Most League Goals: 88, Division 3 (S), 1956–57.
Highest League Scorer in Season: Ted MacDougall, 42, 1970–71.
Most League Goals in Total Aggregate: Ron Eyre, 202, 1924–33.
Most Capped Player: Gerry Peyton, 7 (33), Republic of Ireland.
Most League Appearances: Sean O'Driscoll, 423, 1984–95.
Honours – Football League: Division 3 Champions – 1986–87. **Associate Members' Cup:** Winners 1984.
Colours: Red shirts with black stripe, black shorts, black stockings.

BRADFORD CITY — FA PREMIERSHIP

Beagrie Peter (M)	5 8	12 00	Middlesbrough	28 11 65	Manchester C
Blake Robbie (F)	5 8	11 00	Middlesbrough	4 3 76	Darlington
Bower Mark (D)	5 10	10 11	Bradford	23 1 80	Trainee
Clarke Matthew (G)	6 3	12 02	Sheffield	3 11 73	Sheffield W
Davison Aidan (G)	6 1	13 12	Sedgefield	11 5 68	Sheffield U
Dreyer John (D)	6 1	13 02	Alnwick	11 6 63	Stoke C
Grant Gareth (F)	5 10	10 04	Leeds	6 9 80	Trainee
Halle Gunnar (D)	6 0	12 07	Lillestrom	11 8 65	Leeds U
Jacobs Wayne (D)	5 8	11 02	Sheffield	3 2 69	Rotherham U
Lawrence Jamie (M)	6 0	12 00	Balham	8 3 70	Leicester C
McCall Stuart (M)	5 9	11 04	Leeds	10 6 64	Rangers
Mills Lee (F)	6 2	12 09	Mexborough	10 7 70	Port Vale
Myers Andy (D)	5 10	13 11	Hounslow	3 11 73	Chelsea
O'Brien Andrew (D)	5 10	10 06	Harrogate	29 6 79	Trainee
Rankin Isiah (F)	5 10	11 00	London	22 5 78	Arsenal
Saunders Dean (F)	5 8	10 06	Swansea	21 6 64	Benfica
Sharpe Lee (M)	6 0	12 10	Halesowen	27 5 71	Sampdoria
Todd Lee (D)	5 7	11 01	Hartlepool	7 3 72	Southampton
Walsh Gary (G)	6 3	14 11	Wigan	21 3 68	Middlesbrough
Westwood Ashley (D)	5 11	11 02	Bridgnorth	31 8 76	Crewe Alex
Wetherall David (D)	6 4	13 05	Sheffield	14 3 71	Leeds U
Whalley Gareth (M)	5 10	11 06	Manchester	19 12 73	Crewe Alex
Windass Dean (F)	5 10	12 06	Hull	1 4 69	Oxford U

League Appearances: Beagrie, P. 30(5); Blake, R. 15(13); Cadete, J. 2(5); Clarke, M. 21; Davison, A. 5(1); Dreyer, J. 11(3); Grant, G. (1); Halle, G. 37(1); Jacobs, W. 22(2); Lawrence, J. 19(4); McCall, S. 33(1); Mills, L. 19(2); Myers, A. 10(3); O'Brien, A. 36; Rankin, I. (9); Redfearn, N. 14(3); Rodriguez, B. (2); Saunders, D. 28(6); Sharpe, L. 13(5); Southall, N. 1; Walsh, G. 11; Westwood, A. 1(4); Wetherall, D. 38; Whalley, G. 16; Windass, D. 36(2).
Goals – League (38): Windass 10, Beagrie 7 (5 pens), Mills 5, Lawrence 3, Saunders 3, Blake 2, Wetherall 2, Dreyer 1, McCall 1, O'Brien 1, Redfearn 1, Whalley 1, own goal 1.
Worthington Cup (5): Wetherall 2, Blake 1 (pen), Mills 1, Saunders 1.
FA Cup (3): Saunders 2, Blake 1.
Ground: Valley Parade, Bradford BD8 7DY. Telephone (01274) 773355.
Record attendance: 39,146 v Burnley, FA Cup 4th rd, 11 March 1911. **Capacity:** 25,000.
Manager: Chris Hutchings.
Secretary: Jon Pollard.
Most League Goals: 128, Division 3 (N), 1928–29.
Highest League Scorer in Season: David Layne, 34, Division 4, 1961–62.
Most League Goals in Total Aggregate: Bobby Campbell, 121, 1981–84, 1984–86.
Most Capped Player: Harry Hampton, 9, Northern Ireland.
Most League Appearances: Cec Podd, 502, 1970–84.

Honours – Football League: Division 2 Champions – 1907–08. Division 3 Champions – 1984–85. Division 3 (N) Champions – 1928–29. **FA Cup:** Winners 1911.
Colours: Claret and amber shirts, claret shorts, amber stockings.

BRENTFORD DIV. 2

Anderson Ijah (D)	5 8	10 06	Hackney	30 12 75	Tottenham H
Boxall Danny (D)	5 8	11 06	Croydon	24 8 77	Crystal Palace
Bryan Derek (F)	5 10	11 05	London	11 11 74	Hampton
Charles Julian (M)	5 9	11 00	Plaistow	5 2 77	Hampton & Richmond B
Dobson Michael (D)	5 11	12 04	Isleworth	9 4 81	Trainee
Evans Paul (M)	5 8	11 06	Oswestry	1 9 74	Shrewsbury T
Folan Tony (F)	5 11	11 08	Lewisham	18 9 78	Crystal Palace
Graham Gareth (M)	5 7	10 02	Belfast	6 12 78	Crystal Palace
Ingimarsson Ivar (M)	6 0	12 07	Reykjavik	20 8 77	Torquay U
Kennedy Richard (M)	5 8	10 05	Waterford	28 8 78	Wycombe W
Mahon Gavin (M)	6 0	13 02	Birmingham	2 1 77	Hereford U
Marshall Scott (D)	6 2	12 12	Edinburgh	1 5 73	Southampton
O'Connor Kevin (D)	5 11	12 00	Blackburn	24 2 82	Trainee
Owusu Lloyd (F)	6 0	14 00	Slough	12 12 76	Slough T
Partridge Scott (F)	5 9	11 02	Leicester	13 10 74	Torquay U
Pearcey Jason (G)	6 1	13 12	Leamington Spa	23 7 71	Grimsby T
Pinamonte Lorenzo (F)	6 3	13 04	Foggia	9 5 78	Bristol C
Powell Darren (D)	6 3	13 02	Hammersmith	10 3 76	Hampton
Quinn Robert (D)	5 11	11 02	Sidcup	8 11 76	Crystal Palace
Rowlands Martin (M)	5 9	10 10	Hammersmith	8 2 79	Farnborough T
Saroya Nevin (M)	6 3	14 00	Hillingdon	15 9 80	Trainee
Scott Andy (F)	6 1	11 05	Epsom	2 8 72	Sheffield U
Theobald David (D)	6 2	11 00	Cambridge	15 12 78	Ipswich T
Woodman Andy (G)	6 3	13 07	Camberwell	11 8 71	Northampton T

League Appearances: Agyemang, P. 3(9); Anderson, I. 30(1); Boxall, D. 25; Bryan, D. 5(13); Charles, J. (2); Clement, N. 7(1); Einarsson, G. 1(2); Evans, P. 33; Folan, T. 1(8); Glass, J. 1(1); Graham, G. 5(8); Hreidarsson, H. 8; Hutchings, C. 7(1); Ingimarsson, I. 21(4); James, C. (1); Jenkins, S. 2(3); Jones, S. 6(2); Kennedy, R. 4(5); Mahon, G. 37; Marshall, S. 22; O'Connor, K. 6; Owusu, L. 39(2); Partridge, S. 38(3); Pearcey, J. 6; Pinamonte, L. 5(10); Powell, D. 36; Quinn, R. 42(2); Rowlands, M. 38(2); Saroya, N. (1); Scott, A. 32(4); Theobald, D. 6(4); Warner, P. 1(13); Woodman, A. 39.
Goals – League (47): Owusu 12, Evans 7 (1 pen), Partridge 6, Rowlands 6, Mahon 3, Scott 3, Hreidarsson 2, Marshall 2, Powell 2, Bryan 1, Folan 1, Ingimarsson 1, Pinamonte 1.
Worthington Cup (0).
FA Cup (3): Marshall 1, Owusu 1, Quinn 1.
Ground: Griffin Park, Braemar Rd, Brentford, Middlesex TW8 0NT. Telephone (020) 8847 2511.
Record attendance: 39,626 v Preston NE, FA Cup 6th rd, 5 March 1938. **Capacity:** 12,763.
Manager: Ron Noades.
Secretary: Polly Kates.
Most League Goals: 98, Division 4, 1962–63.
Highest League Scorer in Season: Jack Holliday, 38, Division 3 (S), 1932–33.
Most League Goals in Total Aggregate: Jim Towers, 153, 1954–61.
Most Capped Player: John Buttigieg, (63), Malta.

Most League Appearances: Ken Coote, 514, 1949–64.
Honours – Football League: Division 2 Champions – 1934–35. Division 3 Champions – 1991–92, 1998–99. Division 3 (S) Champions – 1932–33. Division 4 Champions – 1962–63.
Colours: Red and white vertical striped shirts, black shorts, black stockings.

BRIGHTON & HOVE ALBION — DIV. 3

Andrews Ben (D)	6 1	12 13	Burton-on-Trent	18 11 80	Trainee
Campbell Jamie (D)	6 1	12 07	Birmingham	21 10 72	Cambridge U
Carr Darren (D)	6 2	13 07	Bristol	4 9 68	Gillingham
Crosby Andy (D)	6 2	13 07	Rotherham	3 3 73	Chester C
Cullip Danny (D)	6 1	12 07	Bracknell	17 9 76	Brentford
Davis Danny (M)	5 10	11 04	Brighton	3 10 80	Trainee
Freeman Darren (F)	5 11	13 00	Brighton	22 8 73	Brentford
Hart Gary (F)	5 9	12 08	Harlow	6 11 75	Stansted
Mayo Kerry (D)	5 8	11 07	Cuckfield	21 9 77	Trainee
McArthur Duncan (M)	5 9	12 06	Brighton	6 5 81	Trainee
Oatway Charlie (M)	5 7	10 10	Hammersmith	28 11 73	Brentford
Packham Will (G)	6 2	13 00	Brighton	13 1 81	Trainee
Ramsay Scott (F)	6 0	13 00	Hastings	16 10 80	Trainee
Rogers Paul (M)	6 0	13 02	Portsmouth	21 3 65	Wigan Ath
Thomas Rod (F)	5 6	11 11	London	10 10 70	Chester C
Watson Paul (D)	5 8	10 10	Hastings	4 1 75	Brentford

League Appearances: Armstrong, P. (5); Arnott, A. (1); Aspinall, W. 19(12); Brooker, P. 15; Cameron, D. 6(11); Campbell, J. 22(1); Carr, D. 16(3); Crosby, A. 36; Cullip, D. 32(1); Culverhouse, I. 1; Freeman, D. 36(2); Hart, G. 42(1); Hobson, G. 6; Johnson, R. 4(5); Ling, M. 2(6); Mayo, K. 25(6); McPhee, C. (4); McPherson, K. 23(2); Newhouse, A. 1(11); Oatway, C. 42; Ormerod, M. 7; Palmer, R. 1; Pinamonte, L. 8(1); Ramsay, S. 8(16); Rogers, P. 44(1); Thomas, R. 14(20); Walton, M. 39; Watson, P. 40(2); Wilder, C. 11; Wilkinson, S. (2); Zamora, B. 6.
Goals – League (64): Freeman 12 (3 pens), Hart 9, Rogers 8, Zamora 6 (1 pen), Oatway 4, Watson 4, Aspinall 3, Crosby 3, Brooker 2, Cullip 2, Newhouse 2, Pinamonte 2, Ramsay 2, Campbell 1, Ling 1, Mayo 1, McPherson 1, Thomas 1.
Worthington Cup (0).
FA Cup (5): Cullip 1, Freeman 1, Mayo 1, Rogers 1, Watson 1.
Offices: Hanover House, 118 Queens Road, Brighton BN1 3XG. Telephone: (01273) 778855. **Ground:** Withdean Stadium, Tongdean Lane, Brighton.
Record attendance: 36,747 v Fulham, Division 2, 27 December 1958.
Capacity: 6960.
Manager: Micky Adams.
Secretary: Derek Allan.
Most League Goals: 112, Division 3 (S), 1955–56.
Highest League Scorer in Season: Peter Ward, 32, Division 3, 1976–77.
Most League Goals in Total Aggregate: Tommy Cook, 114, 1922–29.
Most Capped Player: Steve Penney, 17, Northern Ireland.
Most League Appearances: 'Tug' Wilson, 509, 1922–36.
Honours – Football League: Division 3 (S) Champions – 1957–58. Division 4 Champions – 1964–65.
Colours: Blue and white striped shirts, white shorts, blue stockings.

BRISTOL CITY DIV. 2

Ashley Neil (M)	5 9	11 04	Chesterfield	16 9 80	Leicester C
Ball Alex (D)	5 9	10 06	Bristol	4 8 81	Trainee
Beadle Peter (F)	6 2	14 07	Lambeth	13 5 72	Notts Co
Bell Mickey (D)	5 8	11 13	Newcastle	15 11 71	Wycombe W
Brown Aaron (M)	5 10	11 12	Bristol	14 3 80	Trainee
Burnell Joe (D)	5 9	11 11	Bristol	10 10 80	Trainee
Burns John (M)	5 8	11 04	Dublin	4 12 77	Nottingham F
Carey Louis (D)	5 10	12 05	Bristol	22 1 77	Trainee
Clist Simon (M)	5 9	11 00	Bournemouth	13 6 81	Tottenham H
Doherty Tom (M)	5 8	11 07	Bristol	17 3 79	Trainee
Edwards Jamie (M)			Hereford	18 2 83	Scholar
Hill Matt (D)	5 8	11 09	Bristol	26 3 81	Trainee
Holland Paul (M)	5 9	13 05	Lincoln	8 7 73	Chesterfield
Hulbert Robin (M)	5 9	10 05	Plymouth	14 3 80	Swindon T
Hutchings Carl (M)	6 1	12 00	Hammersmith	24 9 74	Brentford
Jones Steve (F)	6 1	12 07	Cambridge	17 3 70	Charlton Ath
Jordan Andrew (D)	6 2	13 04	Manchester	14 12 79	Trainee
Lavin Gerard (D)	5 10	11 10	Corby	5 2 74	Millwall
Malessa Antony (G)	5 11	11 12	Ascot	13 11 80	
Meechan Alex (F)	5 8	10 06	Plymouth	29 1 80	Trainee
Mercer Billy (G)	6 1	11 00	Liverpool	22 5 69	Chesterfield
Millen Keith (D)	6 1	13 02	Croydon	26 9 66	Watford
Mortimer Paul (M)	5 9	12 13	Kensington	8 5 68	Charlton Ath
Murray Scott (M)	5 8	11 00	Aberdeen	26 5 74	Aston Villa
Phillips Steve (G)	6 1	12 07	Bath	6 5 78	Paulton R
Pike James (M)			Bristol	15 11 82	Scholar
Scope Tynan (G)	6 3	13 08	Sydney	30 7 79	Coventry C
Testimitanu Ivan (M)	5 10	11 02	Moldova	27 4 74	Zimbru Chisinau
Thorpe Tony (F)	5 8	12 06	Leicester	10 4 74	Fulham
Tinnion Brian (M)	5 11	12 13	Stanley	23 2 68	Bradford C
Turner Danny (M)	6 3	13 02	Maidstone	8 1 81	
Woodman Craig (M)			Tiverton	22 12 82	Trainee
Wright Ben (F)	6 1	13 07	Munster	1 7 80	Kettering T

League Appearances: Akinbiyi, A. 3; Amankwaah, K. 4(1); Beadle, P. 22(3); Bell, M. 34(2); Black, T. 4; Brennan, J. 11(1); Brown, A. 10(3); Brown, M. (2); Burnell, J. 15(2); Burns, J. 6(5); Carey, L. 20(2); Clist, S. 8(1); Coles, D. (1); Doherty, T. (1); Goodridge, G. 13(8); Hewlett, M. 5(2); Hill, M. 8(6); Holland, P. 22(5); Hulbert, R. 1(1); Hutchings, C. 17(4); Jones, S. 12(2); Jordan, A. 8; Lavin, G. 18(1); Meechan, A. 5(7); Mercer, B. 25; Millen, K. 28; Mortimer, P. 22(1); Murray, S. 31(10); Odejayi, K. (3); Phillips, S. 21; Pinamonte, L. 2(4); Sebok, V. 8(3); Shail, M. (1); Spencer, D. 6(3); Taylor, S. 25; Testimitanu, I. 11(5); Thorpe, T. 24(7); Tinnion, B. 42(1); Torpey, S. 15(5); Wright, B. (2).
Goals – League (59): Thorpe 13 (2 pens), Beadle 6, Murray 6, Bell 5, Meechan 4, Taylor 4, Tinnion 3, Akinbiyi 2, Brennan 2, Brown A 2, Jones 2, Millen 2, Testimitanu 2, Hutchings 1, Spencer 1, Torpey 1, own goals 3.
Worthington Cup (5): Hutchings 1, Jordan 1, Mortimer 1, Thorpe 1, Torpey 1.
FA Cup (5): Murray 3, Tinnion 2.
Ground: Ashton Gate, Bristol BS3 2EJ. Telephone (0117) 9630630.
Record attendance: 43,335 v Preston NE, FA Cup 5th rd, 16 February 1935.
Capacity: 21,479.
Manager: Danny Wilson.
Secretary: Michelle McDonald.

Most League Goals: 104, Division 3 (S), 1926–27.
Highest League Scorer in Season: Don Clark, 36, Division 3 (S), 1946–47.
Most League Goals in Total Aggregate: John Atyeo, 314, 1951–66.
Most Capped Player: Billy Wedlock, 26, England.
Most League Appearances: John Atyeo, 597, 1951–66.
Honours – Football League: Division 2 Champions – 1905–06. Division 3 (S) Champions – 1922–23, 1926–27, 1954–55. **Welsh Cup winners** 1934. **Anglo-Scottish Cup:** Winners 1977–78. **Freight Rover Trophy winners** 1985–86.
Colours: Red shirts, red shorts, white stockings.

BRISTOL ROVERS — DIV. 2

Andreasson Marcus (D)	6 4	13 02	Liberia	13 7 78	Osters
Astafjevs Vitalijs (M)	5 11	12 05	Riga	3 4 71	Skonto Riga
Bryant Simon (M)	5 11	12 11	Bristol	22 11 82	Scholar
Challis Trevor (D)	5 8	11 06	Paddington	23 10 75	QPR
Cureton Jamie (F)	5 7	11 00	Bristol	28 8 75	Norwich C
Ellington Nathan (F)	5 10	12 10	Bradford	2 7 81	Walton & Hersham
Ellis Clinton (M)			Ealing	7 7 77	
Foster Stephen (D)	6 1	13 00	Mansfield	3 12 74	Trainee
Hillier David (M)	5 10	12 07	Blackheath	19 12 69	Portsmouth
Hogg Lewis (M)	5 8	10 07	Bristol	13 9 82	Trainee
Jones Lee (G)	6 3	14 10	Pontypridd	9 8 70	Swansea C
Mauge Ronnie (M)	5 10	10 06	Islington	10 3 69	Plymouth Arg
Meaker Michael (M)	5 11	12 12	Greenford	18 8 71	Reading
Pethick Robbie (D)	5 10	12 07	Tavistock	8 9 70	Portsmouth
Pierre Nigel (F)	5 11	11 11	Port of Spain	2 6 79	Joe Public
Pritchard David (D)	5 7	12 00	Wolverhampton	27 5 72	WBA
Roberts Jason (F)	6 1	13 06	Park Royal	25 1 78	Hayes
Shore Jamie (M)	5 9	12 05	Bristol	1 9 77	Norwich C
Smith Mark (D)	6 0	13 07	Bristol	13 9 79	Trainee
Thomson Andy (D)	6 3	14 03	Swindon	28 3 74	Portsmouth
Tillson Andy (D)	6 2	13 05	Huntingdon	30 6 66	QPR
Trees Robert (M)	5 10	12 07	Manchester	18 12 77	Trainee
Trought Michael (D)	6 2	14 03	Bristol	19 10 80	Trainee
Walters Mark (M)	5 9	11 05	Birmingham	2 6 64	Swindon T
Zabek Lee (M)	6 0	13 08	Bristol	13 10 78	Trainee
Zamora Bobby (F)	6 1	11 08	Barking	16 1 81	Trainee

League Appearances: Andreasson, M. 6; Astafjevs, V. 13(3); Bennett, F. (10); Bryant, S. 9(6); Byrne, S. 1(1); Challis, T. 36(4); Cureton, J. 46; Ellington, N. 12(25); Evans, R. 4; Foster, S. 43; Hillier, D. 39; Jones, L. 36; Leoni, S. 2(6); Mauge, R. 22; Meaker, M. (2); Parkin, B. 2(1); Penrice, G. (3); Pethick, R. 40(1); Pierre, N. 1(2); Pritchard, D. 21; Roberts, J. 41; Stewart, J. 1(3); Taylor, S. 4; Thomson, A. 43; Tillson, A. 43; Trees, R. 5(5); Trought, M. 2(2); Walters, M. 28(2); White, T. 3; Wolleaston, R. (4); Zabek, L. 3(1); Zamora, B. (4).
Goals – League (69): Cureton 22 (6 pens), Roberts 22, Walters 9, Ellington 4, Thomson 3, Astafjevs 2, Pethick 2, Challis 1, Foster 1, Pritchard 1, Tillson 1, Trees 1.
Worthington Cup (4): Roberts 3, Cureton 1.
FA Cup (0).
Ground: The Memorial Ground, Filton Avenue, Horfield, Bristol BS7 0AQ.
Record attendance: 9464 v Liverpool, FA Cup 4th rd, 8 February 1992 (Twerton Park). 38,472 v Preston NE, FA Cup 4th rd, 30 January 1960 (Eastville). 9274 v Leyton Orient, FA Cup 4th rd, 23 January 1999 (Memorial Ground).
Capacity: 10,861.

Manager: Ian Holloway.
Secretary: Roger Brinsford.
Most League Goals: 92, Division 3 (S), 1952–53.
Highest League Scorer in Season: Geoff Bradford, 33, Division 3 (S), 1952–53.
Most League Goals in Total Aggregate: Geoff Bradford, 242, 1949–64.
Most Capped Player: Neil Slatter, 10 (22), Wales.
Most League Appearances: Stuart Taylor, 546, 1966–80.
Honours – Football League: Division 3 (S) Champions – 1952–53. Division 3 Champions – 1989–90.
Colours: Blue and white quartered shirts, white shorts, blue stockings.

BURNLEY DIV. 1

Armstrong Gordon (D)	6 0	13 04	Newcastle	15 7 67	Bury
Brass Chris (D)	5 9	12 06	Easington	24 7 75	Trainee
Cooke Andy (F)	5 11	12 08	Stoke	20 1 74	Newtown
Cox Ian (D)	6 0	12 00	Croydon	25 3 71	Bournemouth
Crichton Paul (G)	6 1	13 08	Pontefract	3 10 68	WBA
Davis Steve (D)	6 2	14 07	Hexham	30 10 68	Luton T
Devenney Michael (D)	5 8	10 05	Bolton	8 2 80	Trainee
Heywood Matthew (D)	6 3	14 00	Chatham	26 8 79	Trainee
Johnrose Lenny (M)	5 11	12 06	Preston	27 11 69	Bury
Kevan Alex (M)	5 10	11 00	Liverpool	23 2 81	Trainee
Lee Alan (F)	6 2	13 09	Galway	21 8 78	Aston Villa
Little Glen (M)	6 3	13 00	Wimbledon	15 10 75	Glentoran
Mawson Craig (G)	6 2	13 04	Keighley	16 5 79	Trainee
Maylett Bradley (M)	5 8	10 07	Manchester	24 12 80	Trainee
Mellon Micky (D)	5 10	12 11	Paisley	18 3 72	Tranmere R
Mullin John (F)	6 0	11 05	Bury	11 8 75	Sunderland
Payton Andy (F)	5 9	11 13	Burnley	23 10 67	Huddersfield T
Robertson Mark (M)	5 9	11 09	Sydney	6 4 77	Marconi
Scott Christopher (D)	5 11	12 05	Burnley	12 2 80	Trainee
Smith Paul (M)	6 0	13 03	Leeds	22 7 76	Trainee
Weller Paul (M)	5 8	11 02	Brighton	6 3 75	Trainee
West Dean (D)	5 10	11 07	Leeds	5 12 72	Bury
Williamson John (D)	6 1	11 06	Derby	3 3 81	Trainee

League Appearances: Armstrong, G. 22; Branch, G. 31(13); Brass, C. 4(3); Cook, P. 44; Cooke, A. 33(3); Cowan, T. 5(3); Cox, I. 17; Crichton, P. 46; Davis, S. 42; Jepson, R. 1(30); Johnrose, L. 28(7); Lee, A. 2(13); Little, G. 36(5); Mellon, M. 33(9); Mullin, J. 27(10); Payton, A. 39(2); Robertson, M. (1); Smith, P. 17(7); Swan, P. (2); Thomas, M. 44; Weller, P. 1(6); West, D. 30(4); Wright, I. 4(11).
Goals – League (69): Payton 27 (4 pens), Cooke 7, Davis 7, Mullin 5, Wright 4, Branch 3, Cook 3, Little 3, Mellon 3, Jepson 2, Johnrose 2, Armstrong 1, Cox 1, Weller 1.
Worthington Cup (0).
FA Cup (4): Cook 2, Cooke 1, Mullin 1.
Ground: Turf Moor, Burnley BB10 4BX. Telephone (01282) 700000.
Record attendance: 54,775 v Huddersfield T, FA Cup 3rd rd, 23 February 1924.
Capacity: 22,546.
Manager: Stan Ternent.
Secretary: Cathy Pickup.
Most League Goals: 102, Division 1, 1960–61.
Highest League Scorer in Season: George Beel, 35, Division 1, 1927–28.
Most League Goals in Total Aggregate: George Beel, 178, 1923–32.
Most Capped Player: Jimmy McIlroy, 51 (55), Northern Ireland.

Most League Appearances: Jerry Dawson, 522, 1907–28.
Honours – Football League: Division 1 Champions – 1920–21, 1959–60. Division 2 Champions – 1897–98, 1972–73. Division 3 Champions – 1981–82. Division 4 Champions – 1991–92. **FA Cup winners** 1913–14. **Anglo-Scottish Cup:** Winners 1978–79.
Colours: Claret and blue shirts, white shorts, white stockings.

BURY DIV. 2

Barnes Paul (F)	5 11	13 00	Leeds	16 11 67	Huddersfield T
Barrass Matt (D)	5 11	12 00	Bury	28 2 81	Trainee
Barrick Dean (D)	5 8	12 00	Hemsworth	30 9 69	Preston NE
Bhutia Baichung (F)	5 8	10 02	Sikkim	15 6 76	East Bengal
Billy Chris (D)	5 11	12 06	Huddersfield	2 1 71	Notts Co
Buggie Lee (F)	5 9	11 00	Bury	11 2 81	Trainee
Bullock Darren (M)	5 9	12 10	Worcester	12 2 69	Swindon T
Collins Sam (D)	6 2	14 04	Pontefract	5 6 77	Huddersfield T
Connell Lee (D)	6 0	12 00	Bury	24 6 81	Trainee
Daws Nick (M)	5 11	12 13	Salford	15 3 70	Altrincham
Forrest Martyn (M)	5 10	12 02	Bury	2 1 79	Trainee
Halford Stephen (M)	5 10	12 10	Bury	21 9 80	Trainee
Hill Nicky (D)	6 0	12 03	Accrington	26 2 81	Trainee
James Lutel (F)	5 8	11 00	Manchester	2 6 72	
Kenny Paddy (G)	6 1	14 06	Halifax	17 5 78	Bradford PA
Littlejohn Adrian (M)	5 10	11 00	Wolverhampton	26 9 71	Oldham Ath
Preece Andy (F)	6 1	12 00	Evesham	27 3 67	Blackpool
Reid Paul (M)	5 10	10 12	Oldbury	19 1 68	Oldham Ath
Souter Ryan (M)	5 10	12 00	Bedford	5 2 78	Weston-Super-Mare
Swailes Chris (D)	6 2	13 07	Gateshead	19 10 70	Ipswich T
Swailes Danny (D)	6 3	12 06	Bolton	1 4 79	Trainee

League Appearances: Avdiu, K. 8(13); Barnes, P. 13(17); Barrass, M. 24(1); Barrick, D. 12(5); Bhutia, B. 6(8); Billy, C. 32(4); Bryan, M. 6(3); Buggie, L. (1); Bullock, D. 22(5); Challinor, P. (1); Collins, S. 19; Connell, L. 1(1); Crowe, D. 4; Daws, N. 43; Forrest, M. 9(6); Halford, S. 1(1); Hill, N. 4(1); James, L. 17(6); Kenny, P. 46; Lawson, I. 20(5); Linighan, B. 2(1); Littlejohn, A. 34(8); Preece, A. 30(13); Redmond, S. 28(5); Reid, P. 37(2); Richardson, L. 5; Rocha, C. (3); Souter, R. 2(2); Swailes, C. 27; Swailes, D. 18(6); Williams, P. 22(4); Woodward, A. 14.
Goals – League (61): Preece 12 (5 pens), Lawson 11, Littlejohn 9, Barnes 4, Billy 4, Swailes D 3, Bhutia 2, Bullock 2, Daws 2, James 2, Reid 2 (1 pen), Swailes C 2, Barrass 1, Crowe 1, Redmond 1, Richardson 1, own goals 2.
Worthington Cup (1): Lawson 1.
FA Cup (4): Billy 1, Bullock 1, James 1, Littlejohn 1.
Ground: Gigg Lane, Bury BL9 9HR. Telephone (0161) 764 4881.
Record attendance: 35,000 v Bolton W, FA Cup 3rd rd, 9 January 1960. **Capacity:** 11,841.
Manager: Andy Preece.
Secretary: Jill Neville.
Most League Goals: 108, Division 3, 1960–61.
Highest League Scorer in Season: Craig Madden, 35, Division 4, 1981–82.
Most League Goals in Total Aggregate: Craig Madden, 129, 1978–86.
Most Capped Player: Bill Gorman, 11 (13), Republic of Ireland and (4), Northern Ireland.
Most League Appearances: Norman Bullock, 506, 1920–35.

Honours – Football League: Division 2 Champions – 1894–95, 1996–97. Division 3 Champions – 1960–61. **FA Cup winners** 1900, 1903. **Auto Windscreens Shield winners** 1997.
Colours: White shirts, royal blue shorts, royal blue stockings.

CAMBRIDGE UNITED DIV. 2

Abbey Zema (F)	6 1	12 11	Luton	17 4 77	Hitchin T
Ashbee Ian (M)	6 1	14 04	Birmingham	6 9 76	Derby Co
Benjamin Trevor (F)	6 2	14 02	Kettering	8 2 79	Trainee
Cassidy Jamie (M)	5 9	11 05	Liverpool	21 11 77	Liverpool
Chillingworth Daniel (F)	6 0	12 06	Cambridge	13 9 81	Scholar
Duncan Andy (D)	5 11	14 03	Hexham	20 10 77	Manchester U
Hansen John (M)	5 11	13 01	Mannheim	17 9 73	
Joseph Marc (D)	6 1	13 00	Leicester	10 11 76	Trainee
Kavanagh Jason (D)	5 9	12 13	Meriden	23 11 71	Stoke C
Lamey Nathan (F)	5 10	13 04	Sandwell	14 10 80	Wolverhampton W
MacKenzie Neil (M)	6 2	13 06	Birmingham	15 4 76	Stoke C
Marshall Shaun (G)	6 1	13 03	Fakenham	3 10 78	Trainee
McNeil Martin (D)	6 0	13 02	Rutherglen	28 9 80	Trainee
Mustoe Neil (M)	5 9	12 02	Gloucester	5 11 76	Manchester U
Preece David (M)	5 6	11 05	Bridgnorth	28 5 63	Derby Co
Russell Alex (M)	5 8	11 12	Crosby	17 3 73	Rochdale
Tann Adam (D)	6 0	11 05	Fakenham	12 5 82	Scholar
Taylor John (F)	6 2	15 00	Norwich	24 10 64	Luton T
Wanless Paul (M)	6 1	14 08	Banbury	14 12 73	Lincoln C
Youngs Tom (F)	5 9	11 01	Bury St Edmunds	31 8 79	Trainee

League Appearances: Abbey, Z. 2(6); Ashbee, I. 43(2); Benjamin, T. 42(2); Butler, M. 26; Byfield, D. 3(1); Cassidy, J. 4(4); Chenery, B. 17(1); Chillingworth, D. (3); Cowan, T. 4; Duncan, A. 13; Eustace, S. 34(2); Graham, M. (1); Guinan, S. 4(2); Hansen, J. 12(4); Hunt, J. 3(4); Joseph, M. 27(6); Kavanagh, J. 19; Kyd, M. 12(6); Lamey, N. 2(1); MacKenzie, N. 19(3); Marshall, S. 23(1); McNeil, M. 29; Miller, R. (1); Mustoe, N. 28(5); Paterson, S. 6; Perez, L. 9; Preece, D. 1(11); Russell, A. 14(1); Taylor, J. 18(22); Van Heusden, A. 14(1); Wanless, P. 39(3); Wilson, C. 27; Youngs, T. 12(9).
Goals – League (64): Benjamin 20, Butler 14 (3 pens), Youngs 8, Taylor 6 (1 pen), Hansen 3, Kyd 3, Wanless 3, Ashbee 1, Duncan 1, Eustace 1, Hunt 1, own goals 3.
Worthington Cup (3): Butler 3.
FA Cup (7): Benjamin 3, Butler 2 (1 pen), Taylor 1, Wanless 1.
Ground: Abbey Stadium, Newmarket Rd, Cambridge CB5 8LN. Telephone (01223) 566500. **Capacity:** 9247.
Record attendance; 14,000 v Chelsea, Friendly, 1 May 1970.
Manager: Roy McFarland.
Secretary: Andrew Pincher.
Most League Goals: 87, Division 4, 1976–77.
Highest League Scorer in Season: David Crown, 24, Division 4, 1985–86.
Most League Goals in Total Aggregate: John Taylor, 77, 1988–92; 1996–99.
Most Capped Player: Tom Finney, 7 (15), Northern Ireland.
Most League Appearances: Steve Spriggs, 416, 1975–87.
Honours – Football League: Division 3 Champions – 1990–91. Division 4 Champions – 1976–77.
Colours: Amber shirts with black trim, black shorts, amber stockings.

CARDIFF CITY DIV. 3

Boland Willie (M)	5 9	11 02	Ennis	6 8 75	Coventry C
Bonner Mark (M)	5 8	11 00	Ormskirk	7 6 74	Blackpool
Bowen Jason (F)	5 8	11 02	Merthyr	24 8 72	Reading
Brazier Matt (M)	5 8	11 08	Whipps Cross	2 7 76	Fulham
Earnshaw Robert (F)	5 6	9 09	Zambia	6 4 81	Trainee
Faerber Winston (D)	5 11	12 06	Surinam	27 3 71	
Hughes Jamie (F)	6 0	13 05	Liverpool	5 4 77	Trainee
Kelly Seamus (G)	6 1	13 13	Tullamore	6 5 74	UCD
Legg Andy (D)	5 8	11 01	Swansea	28 7 66	Reading
Low Josh (F)	6 0	14 00	Bristol	15 2 79	Leyton Orient
Nogan Kurt (F)	5 10	11 01	Cardiff	9 9 70	Preston NE
Nugent Kevin (F)	6 2	13 00	Edmonton	10 4 69	Bristol C
Perrett Russell (D)	6 2	13 00	Barton-on-Sea	18 6 73	Portsmouth
Roberts Chris (F)	5 10	12 03	Cardiff	22 10 79	Trainee
Schwinkendorf Jorn (D)	6 7	13 00	Hamburg	27 1 71	Waldhof Mannheim
Thomas Dai (F)	5 11	13 07	Caerphilly	26 9 75	Watford
Young Scott (D)	6 2	13 04	Llywnypia	14 1 76	Trainee

League Appearances: Boland, W. 20(8); Bonner, M. 29(2); Bowen, J. 32(7); Brayson, P. 7(2); Brazier, M. 20(10); Carpenter, R. 28(5); Cornforth, J. 6(4); Earnshaw, R. 4(2); Eckhardt, J. 39(2); Faerber, W. 31(2); Ford, M. 23(3); Fowler, J. 28; Hallworth, J. 39; Hill, D. 12(11); Hughes, J. (2); Humphreys, R. 8(1); Jarman, L. (1); Kelly, S. 7(1); Legg, A. 42; Low, J. 12(5); Middleton, C. 7(3); Nogan, K. 4(2); Nugent, K. 37(2); Perrett, R. 26(1); Phillips, L. (3); Roberts, C. 1(7); Schwinkendorf, J. 5; Thomas, D. 5(2); Vaughan, T. 14; Young, S. 20(2).
Goals – League (45): Bowen 12, Nugent 10 (1 pen), Humphreys 2, Legg 2, Low 2, Young 2, Boland 1 (pen), Brayson 1, Brazier 1, Carpenter 1, Cornforth 1, Earnshaw 1, Eckhardt 1, Faerber 1, Fowler 1, Hill 1, Hughes 1, Perrett 1, Thomas 1, own goals 2.
Worthington Cup (5): Bowen 2, Brazier 1, Hughes 1, Nugent 1 (pen).
FA Cup (5): Nugent 2 (1 pen), Brazier 1, Ford 1, Perrett 1.
Ground: Ninian Park, Cardiff CF1 8SX. Telephone (029) 2022 1001.
Record attendance: 61,566, Wales v England, 14 October 1961. **Capacity:** 15,585.
Manager: Billy Ayre.
Secretary: Jim Finney.
Most League Goals: 93, Division 3 (S), 1946–47.
Highest League Scorer in Season: Stan Richards, 30, Division 3 (S), 1946–47.
Most League Goals in Total Aggregate: Len Davies, 128, 1920–31.
Most Capped Player: Alf Sherwood, 39 (41), Wales.
Most League Appearances: Phil Dwyer, 471, 1972–85.
Honours – Football League: Division 3 (S) Champions – 1946–47. **FA Cup winners** 1926–27 (only occasion the Cup has been won by a club outside England). **Welsh Cup winners** 21 times.
Colours: Blue shirts, white shorts, blue stockings.

CARLISLE UNITED DIV. 3

Clark Peter (D)	6 1	12 04	Romford	10 12 79	Arsenal
Dobie Scott (F)	6 2	12 09	Workington	10 10 78	Trainee
Harries Paul (F)	6 1	13 00	Sydney	19 11 77	Crystal Palace
Hopper Tony (M)	5 11	12 08	Carlisle	31 5 76	Trainee
Keen Peter (G)	6 0	11 10	Middlesbrough	16 11 76	Newcastle U

McKinnon Rob (D)	5 11	11 01	Glasgow	31 7 66	Hearts
Pitts Matthew (D)	5 11	12 06	Middlesbrough	25 12 79	Trainee
Prokas Richard (M)	5 9	11 05	Penrith	22 1 76	Trainee
Reid Paul (D)	6 2	11 08	Carlisle	18 2 82	Trainee
Skelton Gavin (M)	5 7	10 00	Carlisle	27 3 81	Trainee
Soley Steve (M)	5 11	12 08	Widnes	22 4 71	Portsmouth
Thurston Mark (M)	6 2	11 08	Carlisle	10 2 80	Trainee
Weaver Luke (G)	6 2	13 02	Woolwich	26 6 79	Sunderland
Whitehead Stuart (D)	6 0	12 02	Bromsgrove	17 7 76	Bolton W

League Appearances: Anthony, G. 12(6); Baker, P. 12(5); Barr, B. 28(1); Black, T. 5; Bowman, R. 12(3); Brightwell, D. 37; Clark, P. 42(1); Clarke, A. 7; Dalton, P. 3; Dibble, A. 2; Dobie, S. 25(9); Durnin, J. 20(2); Gregory, A. 6(1); Halliday, S. 16; Harries, P. 6(14); Hopper, T. 25(2); Hore, J. 1; Ingham, M. 7; Keen, P. 6; McKinnon, R. 8; Pitts, M. 20(9); Prokas, R. 28(7); Reid, P. 17(2); Roddie, A. 1(1); Searle, D. 14(7); Skelton, G. 1(6); Skinner, S. (2); Soley, S. 35(2); Teale, S. 18; Thorpe, J. 4(9); Tracey, R. 25(11); Van der Kwaak, P. 2; Walker, A. 3; Weaver, L. 29; Whitehead, S. 29.
Goals – League (42): Soley 8 (2 pens), Dobie 7, Halliday 7, Tracey 7, Baker 2, Durnin 2, Harries 2, Black 1, Clark 1, Dalton 1, Gregory 1, Pitts 1, Prokas 1, Searle 1.
Worthington Cup (0).
FA Cup (1): Harries 1.
Ground: Brunton Park, Carlisle CA1 1LL. Telephone (01228) 526237.
Record attendance: 27,500 v Birmingham C, FA Cup 3rd rd, 5 January 1957 and v Middlesbrough, FA Cup 5th rd, 7 February 1970. **Capacity:** 16,651.
Manager: Ian Atkins.
Secretary: Sarah McKnight.
Most League Goals: 113, Division 4, 1963–64.
Highest League Scorer in Season: Jimmy McConnell, 42, Division 3 (N), 1928–29.
Most League Goals in Total Aggregate: Jimmy McConnell, 126, 1928–32.
Most Capped Player: Eric Welsh, 4, Northern Ireland.
Most League Appearances: Allan Ross, 466, 1963–79.
Honours – Football League: Division 3 Champions – 1964–65, 1994–95. **Auto Windscreens Shield winners:** 1997
Colours: Blue shirts, white shorts, white stockings.

CHARLTON ATHLETIC — FA PREMIERSHIP

Allman Anthony (D)	5 9	10 07	Sidcup	14 12 80	Trainee
Berti Nicola (M)	6 1	12 02	Salsomaggiore Terme	14 4 67	Alaves
Brown Steve (D)	6 1	14 04	Brighton	13 5 72	Trainee
Collis David (M)			London	8 11 81	Trainee
Brown Steve (D)	6 1	14 04	Brighton	13 5 72	Trainee
Fortune Jonathan (D)	6 2	11 00	Islington	23 8 80	Trainee
Hales Lee (F)	5 10	11 00	Gillingham	1 5 81	Trainee
Hockley David (M)	5 11	11 05	Gillingham	23 2 81	Trainee
Hunt Andy (F)	6 0	12 02	Thurrock	9 6 70	WBA
Ilic Sasa (G)	6 4	14 00	Melbourne	18 7 72	St Leonards Stamcroft
Izzet Kemal (M)	5 8	10 05	Whitechapel	29 9 80	Trainee
Jones Keith (M)	5 9	11 07	Dulwich	14 10 65	Southend U
Kiely Dean (G)	6 0	12 13	Salford	10 10 70	Bury
Kinsella Mark (M)	5 9	11 07	Dublin	12 8 72	Colchester U
Konchesky Paul (D)	5 10	11 07	Barking	15 5 81	Trainee
Lisbie Kevin (F)	5 9	11 00	Hackney	17 10 78	Trainee

MacDonald Charlie (F)	5 9	11 00	Southwark	13 2 81	Trainee
McCammon Mark (F)	6 2	14 06	Barnet	7 8 78	Cambridge U
Mendonca Clive (F)	5 10	12 07	Islington	9 9 68	Grimsby T
Newton Shaun (F)	5 8	11 04	Camberwell	20 8 75	Trainee
Parker Scott (M)	5 9	10 12	Lambeth	13 10 80	Trainee
Powell Chris (D)	5 10	11 10	Lambeth	8 9 69	Derby Co
Pringle Martin (F)	6 2	12 02	Gothenburg	18 11 70	Benfica
Robinson John (F)	5 10	11 08	Bulawayo	29 8 71	Brighton & HA
Royal Mark (M)			London	20 12 81	Chelsea
Rufus Richard (D)	6 1	12 10	Lewisham	12 1 75	Trainee
Salako John (F)	5 9	12 03	Nigeria	11 2 69	Fulham
Shields Greg (D)	5 10	11 06	Falkirk	21 8 76	Dunfermline Ath
Shittu Daniel (M)			Lagos	2 9 80	
Stuart Graham (M)	5 8	11 12	Tooting	24 10 70	Sheffield U
Svensson Mathias (F)	6 0	12 06	Boras	24 9 74	Crystal Palace
Tiler Carl (D)	6 2	13 10	Sheffield	11 2 70	Everton
Todd Andy (D)	5 10	10 11	Derby	21 9 74	Bolton W
Youds Eddie (D)	6 1	14 09	Liverpool	3 5 70	Bradford C

League Appearances: Barness, A. 17(2); Brown, S. 29(11); Hunt, A. 43(1); Ilic, S. 1; Jones, K. 16(1); Jones, S. 1(1); Kiely, D. 45; Kinsella, M. 38; Kitson, P. 2(4); Konchesky, P. 6(2); MacDonald, C. (3); McCammon, M. 1(3); Mendonca, C. 19; Newton, S. 41(1); Parker, S. 5(10); Powell, C. 40; Pringle, M. 12(20); Robinson, J. 43(2); Rufus, R. 44; Salako, J. 4(23); Shields, G. 21; Stuart, G. 33(4); Svensson, M. 13(5); Tiler, C. 4(7); Todd, A. 5(7); Youds, E. 23.
Goals – League (79): Hunt 24, Mendonca 9 (4 pens), Robinson 7, Stuart 7, Rufus 6, Newton 5, Pringle 4, Kinsella 3, Brown 2, Salako 2, Shields 2, Svensson 2, Jones K 1, Kitson 1, Parker 1, Tiler 1, own goals 2.
Worthington Cup (0).
FA Cup (6): Kinsella 2, Hunt 1, MacDonald 1, Newton 1, Robinson 1.
Ground: The Valley, Floyd Road, Charlton, London SE7 8BL. Telephone (020) 8333 4000.
Record attendance: 75,031 v Aston Villa, FA Cup 5th rd, 12 February 1938 (at The Valley). **Capacity:** 20,043.
Manager: Alan Curbishley.
Secretary: Chris Parkes.
Most League Goals: 107, Division 2, 1957–58.
Highest League Scorer in Season: Ralph Allen, 32, Division 3 (S), 1934–35.
Most League Goals in Total Aggregate: Stuart Leary, 153, 1953–62.
Most Capped Player: John Robinson, 22, Wales.
Most League Appearances: Sam Bartram, 583, 1934–56.
Honours – Football League: Division 1 Champions – 1999–2000. Division 3 (S) Champions – 1928–29, 1934–35. **FA Cup winners** 1947.
Colours: Red shirts, white shorts, red stockings.

CHELSEA — FA PREMIERSHIP

Aleksidze Rati (M)	6 0	12 02	Georgia	6 8 78	Dynamo Tbilisi
Ambrosetti Gabriele (M)	5 11	11 05	Varese	7 8 73	Vicenza
Babayaro Celestine (D)	5 9	11 09	Kaduna	29 8 78	Anderlecht
Broad Stephen (D)	6 0	11 05	Epsom	10 6 80	Trainee
Casiraghi Pierluigi (F)	6 1	13 05	Monza	4 3 69	Lazio
Clement Neil (D)	6 0	14 07	Reading	3 10 78	Trainee
Cudicini Carlo (G)	6 1	12 02	Milan	6 9 73	
Cummings Warren (D)	5 9	11 05	Aberdeen	15 10 80	Trainee
Dalla Bona Samuele (F)	6 0	13 04	San Dona di Piave	6 2 81	

De Goey Ed (G)	6 6	14 05	Gouda	20 12 66	Feyenoord
Demetrious Shayne (M)	5 9	10 01	Perivale	6 12 80	Trainee
Desailly Marcel (D)	6 0	13 05	Accra	7 9 68	AC Milan
Deschamps Didier (M)	5 8	12 11	Bayonne	15 10 68	Juventus
Di Matteo Roberto (M)	5 10	12 04	Schaffhausen	29 5 70	Lazio
Emerson (D)	6 1	13 12	Porto Alegre	30 3 72	Sheffield W
Evans Rhys (G)	6 1	12 02	Swindon	27 1 82	Trainee
Ferrer Albert (D)	5 9	12 02	Barcelona	6 6 70	Barcelona
Flo Tore Andre (F)	6 4	13 08	Strin	15 6 73	Brann
Forssell Mikael (F)	6 0	12 08	Steinfurt	15 3 81	HJK Helsinki
Harley Jon (D)	5 9	11 05	Maidstone	26 9 79	Trainee
Hitchcock Kevin (G)	6 1	13 00	Custom House	5 10 62	Mansfield T
Hogh Jes (D)	6 0	11 11	Aalborg	7 5 66	Fenerbahce
Keenan Joseph (M)	5 8	10 00	Southampton	14 10 82	Trainee
Knight Leon (F)	5 4	9 06	Hackney	16 9 82	Trainee
Lambourde Bernard (D)	6 0	13 05	Pointe-A-Pitre	11 5 71	Bordeaux
Le Saux Graeme (D)	5 10	11 09	Jersey	17 10 68	Blackburn R
Leboeuf Franck (D)	6 1	11 11	Marseille	22 1 68	Strasbourg
Melchiot Mario (D)	6 2	11 11	Amsterdam	4 11 76	Ajax
Morris Jody (M)	5 5	10 03	Hammersmith	22 12 78	Trainee
Nicholls Mark (M)	5 10	10 12	Hillingdon	30 5 77	Trainee
Parkin Sam (F)	6 2	13 00	Roehampton	14 3 81	School
Percassi Luca (M)	5 9	11 09	Milan	25 8 80	
Petrescu Dan (M)	5 10	11 02	Bucharest	22 12 67	Sheffield W
Poyet Gustavo (M)	6 1	13 00	Montevideo	15 11 67	Zaragoza
Reddington Stuart (D)			Lincoln	21 2 78	Lincoln U
Richardson Jay (M)	5 9	11 09	Keston	14 11 79	Trainee
Slatter Danny (D)	5 8	10 02	Cardiff	15 11 80	Trainee
Sutton Chris (F)	6 3	13 08	Nottingham	10 3 73	Blackburn R
Terry John (D)	6 1	12 13	Barking	7 12 80	Trainee
Thornton Paul (D)	5 7	11 00	Surrey	7 1 83	Trainee
Vialli Gianluca (F)	5 10	13 06	Cremona	9 7 64	Juventus
Weah George (F)	6 1	12 10	Liberia	1 10 66	AC Milan
Wise Dennis (M)	5 6	10 11	Kensington	16 12 66	Wimbledon
Wolleaston Robert (M)	5 11	11 07	Perivale	21 12 79	Trainee
Zola Gianfranco (F)	5 6	10 08	Oliena	5 7 66	Parma

League Appearances: Ambrosetti, G. 9(7); Babayaro, C. 23(2); Cudicini, C. 1; Dalla Bona, S. (2); De Goey, E. 37; Desailly, M. 23; Deschamps, D. 24(3); Di Matteo, R. 14(4); Emerson 18(2); Ferrer, A. 24(1); Flo, T. 20(14); Goldbaek, B. 2(4); Harley, J. 13(4); Hogh, J. 6(3); Lambourde, B. 12(3); Le Saux, G. 6(2); Leboeuf, F. 28; Melchiot, M. 4(1); Morris, J. 19(11); Petrescu, D. 24(5); Poyet, G. 25(8); Sutton, C. 21(7); Terry, J. 2(2); Weah, G. 9(2); Wise, D. 29(1); Wolleaston, R. (1); Zola, G. 25(8).
Goals – League (53): Flo 10, Poyet 10, Petrescu 4, Wise 4, Zola 4, Morris 3, Weah 3, Di Matteo 2, Harley 2, Lambourde 2, Leboeuf 2 (1 pen), Desailly 1, Sutton 1, own goals 5.
Worthington Cup (0).
FA Cup (18): Poyet 6, Di Matteo 2, Weah 2, Flo 1, Leboeuf 1, Morris 1, Sutton 1, Terry 1, Wise 1, Zola 1 (pen), own goal 1.
Ground: Stamford Bridge, London SW6 1HS. Telephone (020) 7385 5545.
Record attendance: 82,905 v Arsenal, Division 1, 12 October 1935.
Capacity: 35,421 (up to 41,000).
Player-Manager: Gianluca Vialli.
Secretary: Alan Shaw.
Most League Goals: 98, Division 1, 1960–61.
Highest League Scorer in Season: Jimmy Greaves, 41, 1960–61.

Most League Goals in Total Aggregate: Bobby Tambling, 164, 1958–70.
Most Capped Player: Dan Petrescu, 43 (92), Romania.
Most League Appearances: Ron Harris, 655, 1962–80.
Honours – Football League: Division 1 Champions – 1954–55. **FA Cup winners** 1970, 1997, 2000. **Football League Cup winners** 1964–65, 1997–98. **Full Members' Cup winners** 1985–86. **Zenith Data Systems Cup winners** 1989–90. **European Cup-Winners' Cup winners** 1970–71, 1997–98. **Super Cup Winners:** 1999.
Colours: Royal blue with white and amber shirts and shorts, white stockings with royal blue and amber trim.

CHELTENHAM TOWN — DIV. 3

Banks Chris (D)	5 11	12 04	Stone	22 11 65	Exeter C
Benbow Steve (G)	5 10	10 07	Cheltenham	5 4 82	
Bloomer Bob (M)	5 10	12 07	Sheffield	21 6 66	Bristol R
Book Steve (G)	5 11	11 02	Bournemouth	7 7 69	Lincoln C
Brough John (D)	6 0	12 11	Ilkeston	8 1 73	Hereford U
Devaney Martin (F)	5 11	12 06	Cheltenham	1 6 80	Coventry C
Duff Michael (D)	6 1	11 08	Belfast	11 1 78	Trainee
Freeman Mark (D)	6 2	13 08	Walsall	27 1 70	Bilston T
Grayson Neil (F)	5 10	12 09	York	1 11 64	Northampton T
Griffin Anthony (M)	5 11	11 03	Bournemouth	22 3 79	Bournemouth
Higgs Shane (G)	6 3	14 02	Oxford	13 5 77	Bristol R
Hopkins Gareth (F)	6 2	13 08	Cheltenham	14 6 80	Trainee
Howarth Neil (D)	6 2	13 06	Bolton	15 11 71	Macclesfield T
Howells Lee (M)	5 11	11 02	Fremantle	14 10 68	Apprentice
Jackson Michael D (M)	5 7	10 10	Cheltenham	26 6 80	Trainee
McAuley Hugh (F)	5 10	11 06	Plymouth	13 5 77	Leek T
Milton Russell (M)	5 8	12 01	Folkestone	12 1 69	Arsenal
Mitchinson Stuart (F)	5 6	10 08	Cheltenham	15 10 80	Trainee
Victory Jamie (D)	5 11	12 02	London	14 11 75	Bournemouth
Walker Richard (D)	5 10	11 09	Derby	9 11 71	Notts Co
Yates Mark (M)	5 11	13 02	Birmingham	24 1 70	Doncaster R

League Appearances: Banks, C. 41(1); Bloomer, B. 1(10); Book, S. 46; Brissett, J. 5(3); Brough, J. 15(22); Devaney, M. 19(7); Duff, M. 31; Freeman, M. 36(2); Freestone, C. 5; Grayson, N. 39(4); Griffin, A. 14(10); Hopkins, G. (1); Howarth, N. 43(1); Howells, L. 45; Jackson, M. (2); Jones, M. 3; McAuley, H. 22(17); Milton, R. 38; Stevens, I. 1; Victory, J. 46; Walker, R. 6(1); Watkins, D. 4(5); Yates, M. 46.
Goals – League (50): Grayson 10, Milton 9 (4 pens), Devaney 6, McAuley 4 (1 pen), Victory 4, Howells 3, Brough 2, Duff 2, Freeman 2, Freestone 2, Howarth 2, Yates 2, own goals 2.
Worthington Cup (2): Grayson 1 (pen), Victory 1.
FA Cup (3): Brough 1, Howarth 1, Milton 1.
Ground: Whaddon Road, Cheltenham, Gloucester GL52 5NA. Telephone (01242) 573558.
Record attendance: at Whaddon Road: 8326 v Reading, FA Cup 1st rd, 17 November 1956; at Cheltenham Athletic Ground: 10,389 v Blackpool, FA Cup 3rd rd, 13 January 1934.
Capacity: 6114.
Manager: Steve Cotterill.
Secretary: Reg Woodward.
Most League Goals: 115, Southern League, 1957–58.
Highest League Scorer in Season: Dave Lewis, 33 (53 in all competitions), Southern League Division 1, 1974–75.

Most League Goals in Total Aggregate: Dave Lewis, 205 (290 in all competitions), 1970–83.
Most League Appearances: Roger Thorndale, 523 (702 in all competitions), 1958–76.
Honours – Football Conference: Champions – 1998–99. **FA Trophy winners** 1997–98.
Colours: Red and white striped shirts, white shorts, red stockings.

CHESTER CITY — NATIONWIDE CONFERENCE

Ajetunmobi Adewale (M)			Glasgow	27 10 77	
Beckett Luke (F)	5 11	11 06	Sheffield	25 11 76	Barnsley
Berry Paul (M)	5 9	10 08	Warrington	6 12 78	Warrington T
Brown Wayne (G)	6 1	11 06	Southampton	14 1 77	Bristol C
Carden Paul (M)	5 9	11 10	Liverpool	29 3 79	Rochdale
Eve Angus (M)	5 7	11 02	Trinidad	23 2 72	Joe Public
Finney Steve (F)	5 11	12 08	Hexham	31 10 73	Leyton Orient
Fisher Neil (M)	5 10	10 09	St Helens	7 11 70	Bolton W
Hemmings Tony (F)	5 10	12 09	Burton	21 9 67	Wycombe W
Hicks Stuart (D)	6 1	13 03	Peterborough	30 5 67	Leyton Orient
Lancaster Martin (D)	6 0	12 07	Wigan	10 11 80	Trainee
Moss Darren (M)	5 10	11 00	Wrexham	24 5 81	Trainee
Richardson Nick (M)	6 0	12 06	Halifax	11 4 67	Bury
Robinson Jamie (D)	6 1	12 08	Liverpool	26 2 72	Exeter C
Shelton Andy (M)	5 10	12 00	Sutton Coldfield	19 6 80	Trainee
Woods Matt (D)	6 1	12 03	Gosport	9 9 76	Trainee
Wright Darren (F)	5 6	10 00	Warrington	7 9 79	Trainee

League Appearances: Agogo, M. 10; Beckett, L. 46; Berry, P. (9); Blackburn, C. (1); Blackwood, M. 9; Brown, W. 46; Carden, P. 9(2); Carver, J. 1(1); Cross, J. 13(4); Davidson, R. 9; Doughty, M. 19(14); Eve, A. 9(5); Eyjolfsson, S. 9; Finney, S. 4(9); Fisher, N. 34(7); Heggs, C. 11; Hemmings, T. 19; Hicks, S. 13; Hobson, G. 20; Jones, J. 4(2); Keister, J. 8(2); Laird, K. 2(1); Lancaster, M. 14(3); Milosavljevic, G. 11(1); Moss, D. 28(7); Nash, M. 12(4); Pickering, A. 7; Porter, A. 16; Reid, S. 10(3); Richardson, N. 31(5); Robinson, J. 9; Shelton, A. 9(2); Spooner, N. 9; Woods, M. 40(2); Wright, D. 15(10).
Goals – League (44): Beckett 14 (1 pen), Agogo 6, Eve 4, Eyjolfsson 3, Blackwood 2, Heggs 2, Hemmings 2, Richardson 2, Berry 1, Doughty 1, Fisher 1, Laird 1, Pickering 1, Wright 1, own goals 3.
Worthington Cup (6): Beckett 3 (2 pens), Jones 1, Richardson 1, Shelton 1.
FA Cup (6): Cross 3, Beckett 2, Richardson 1.
Ground: The Deva Stadium, Bumpers Lane, Chester CH1 4LT. Telephone (01244) 371376, 371809.
Record attendance: 20,500 v Chelsea, FA Cup 3rd rd (replay), 16 January, 1952 (at Sealand Road). **Capacity:** 6000.
Secretary: Gill Dugan.
Most League Goals: 119, Division 4, 1964–65.
Highest League Scorer in Season: Dick Yates, 36, Division 3 (N), 1946–47.
Most League Goals in Total Aggregate: Stuart Rimmer, 135, 1985–88, 1991–98.
Most Capped Player: Bill Lewis, 13 (27), Wales.
Most League Appearances: Ray Gill, 406, 1951–62.
Honours – Welsh Cup winners 1908, 1933, 1947. **Debenhams Cup:** Winners 1977.
Colours: Blue and white striped shirts, white shorts, blue and white stockings.

CHESTERFIELD DIV. 3

Barratt Danny (D)	6 0	11 12	Bradford	25 9 80	Trainee
Blatherwick Steve (D)	6 1	15 00	Nottingham	20 9 73	Burnley
Breckin Ian (D)	5 11	11 07	Rotherham	24 2 75	Rotherham U
Curtis Tom (M)	5 8	10 08	Exeter	1 3 73	Derby Co
D'Auria David (M)	5 9	11 11	Swansea	26 3 70	Hull C
Ebdon Marcus (M)	5 10	11 02	Pontypool	17 10 70	Peterborough U
Galloway Mick (M)	5 11	11 05	Nottingham	13 10 74	Gillingham
Howard Jonathan (F)	5 11	11 07	Sheffield	7 10 71	Rotherham U
Payne Steve (D)	5 11	12 05	Castleford	1 8 75	Macclesfield T
Pearce Greg (M)	6 0	11 00	Bolton	26 5 80	Trainee
Perkins Chris (D)	5 11	10 09	Nottingham	9 1 74	Hartlepool U
Simpkins Mike (D)	6 0	11 11	Sheffield	28 11 78	Trainee
Williams Danny (D)	5 9	9 13	Sheffield	2 3 81	Trainee
Williams Ryan (F)	5 4	11 02	Chesterfield	31 8 78	Tranmere R
Woods Steve (D)	5 11	11 13	Davenham	15 12 76	Stoke C

League Appearances: Agogo, M. 3(1); Armstrong, J. 3; Barratt, D. (2); Beaumont, C. 32(1); Bettney, C. 7(6); Blatherwick, S. 36; Breckin, I. 37(1); Carss, T. 24(7); Curtis, T. 17(1); D'Auria, D. 4(1); Dudley, C. (2); Ebdon, M. 10(1); Galloway, M. 14(1); Gayle, M. 29(1); Hewitt, J. 38(2); Holland, P. 4; Howard, J. 19(8); Leaning, A. 6; Lee, J. 3(3); Lomas, J. 10(7); Muggleton, C. 5; Payne, S. 15(3); Pearce, G. 8(2); Perkins, C. 29(2); Pointon, N. 9(1); Reeves, D. 43; Simpkins, M. 8(1); Vaughan, J. 3; Wilkinson, S. 15(7); Williams, D. 3(2); Williams, R. 30; Willis, R. 20(8); Woods, S. 22(3).
Goals – League (34): Reeves 14 (4 pens), Williams R 5, Willis 4, Payne 3, Beaumont 2, Howard 2, Breckin 1, Carss 1, Galloway 1, Wilkinson 1.
Worthington Cup (5): Reeves 2, Ebdon 1, own goals 2.
FA Cup (1): Lomas 1.
Ground: Recreation Ground, Chesterfield S40 4SX. Telephone (01246) 209765.
Record attendance: 30,968 v Newcastle U, Division 2, 7 April 1939. **Capacity:** 8880.
Manager: Nicky Law.
Secretary: Stephanie Otter.
Most League Goals: 102, Division 3 (N), 1930–31.
Highest League Scorer in Season: Jimmy Cookson, 44, Division 3 (N), 1925–26.
Most League Goals in Total Aggregate: Ernie Moss, 161, 1969–76, 1979–81 and 1984–86.
Most Capped Player: Walter McMillen, 4 (7), Northern Ireland; Mark Williams, 4 (11), Northern Ireland.
Most League Appearances: Dave Blakey, 613, 1948–67.
Honours – Football League: Division 3 (N) Champions – 1930–31, 1935–36. Division 4 Champions – 1969–70, 1984–85. **Anglo-Scottish Cup winners** 1980–81.
Colours: Blue shirts, white shorts, blue stockings.

COLCHESTER UNITED DIV. 2

Arnott Andy (M)	6 0	13 07	Chatham	18 10 73	Brighton & HA
Brown Simon (G)	6 2	15 01	Chelmsford	3 12 76	Tottenham H
Duguid Karl (F)	5 11	11 00	Letchworth	21 3 78	Trainee
Dunne Joe (D)	5 9	11 08	Dublin	25 5 73	Gillingham
Farley Craig (D)	6 0	11 00	Oxford	17 3 81	
Johnson Gavin (D)	5 11	11 07	Eye	10 10 70	Dunfermline Ath
Johnson Ross (D)	6 0	13 00	Brighton	2 1 76	Brighton & HA

Keeble Chris (M)	5 9	11 00	Colchester	17 9 78	Ipswich T
Keith Joey (D)	5 7	10 06	London	1 10 78	West Ham U
Lua-Lua Lomano (F)	5 8	10 00	Zaire	28 12 80	
McGavin Steve (F)	5 9	12 08	North Walsham	24 1 69	Northampton T
Pinault Thomas (M)	5 10	11 01	Grasse	4 12 81	Cannes

League Appearances: Arnott, A. 4(8); Aspinall, W. 7; Bramble, T. 2; Brown, S. 38; Burton, S. 9; Dozzell, J. 38(1); Duguid, K. 40(1); Dunne, J. 19(1); Farley, C. 8(6); Ferguson, B. 5(1); Forbes, S. (2); Germain, S. 1(2); Greene, D. 29; Gregory, D. 45; Johnson, G. 24(3); Johnson, R. 17(1); Keeble, C. 2(3); Keith, J. 45; Launders, B. 6; Lock, T. 12(12); Lua-Lua, L. 24(17); McGavin, S. 30(4); Moralee, J. 20(7); Opara, C. 2(14); Pinault, T. 1(3); Richard, F. 13(1); Skelton, A. 27(6); Sodje, E. 3; Vaughan, J. 6; Walker, A. 2; White, A. 4; Wignall, J. (1); Wilkins, R. 23(1).
Goals – League (59): McGavin 16, Duguid 12, Lua-Lua 12, Dozzell 5, Skelton 4 (1 pen), Aspinall 2 (1 pen), Lock 2, Wilkins 2, Greene 1 (pen), Keeble 1, Keith 1, Moralee 1.
Worthington Cup (3): Dozzell 1, Keith 1, Lua-Lua 1.
FA Cup (1): Lua-Lua 1.
Ground: Layer Rd Ground, Colchester CO2 7JJ. Telephone (01206) 508800.
Record attendance: 19,072 v Reading, FA Cup 1st rd, 27 Nov, 1948. **Capacity:** 7556.
Manager: Steve Whitton.
Secretary: Mrs Marie Partner.
Most League Goals: 104, Division 4, 1961–62.
Highest League Scorer in Season: Bobby Hunt, 38, Division 4, 1961–62.
Most League Goals in Total Aggregate: Martyn King, 130, 1956–64.
Most Capped Player: None.
Most League Appearances: Micky Cook, 613, 1969–84.
Honours – GM Vauxhall Conference winners 1991–92. **FA Trophy winners** 1991–92.
Colours: Blue and white striped shirts, navy shorts, white stockings.

COVENTRY CITY — FA PREMIERSHIP

Aloisi John (F)	6 1	12 06	Adelaide	5 2 76	Portsmouth
Betts Robert (D)	5 10	11 00	Doncaster	21 12 81	School
Breen Gary (D)	6 1	11 12	London	12 12 73	Birmingham C
Chippo Youssef (M)	5 11	12 00	Morocco	10 6 73	Porto
Cudworth Thomas (D)	5 10	11 00	Coventry	3 8 82	Trainee
Davenport Calum (D)	6 4	14 00	Bedford	1 1 83	Trainee
Delorge Laurent (M)	5 10	11 12	Leuven	21 7 79	
Doyle Daire (M)	5 10	11 06	Dublin	18 10 80	Cherry Orchard
Edworthy Marc (D)	5 11	10 03	Barnstaple	24 12 72	Crystal Palace
Eustace John (M)	5 11	11 12	Solihull	3 11 79	Dundee U
Ferguson Barry (D)	6 3	13 00	Dublin	7 9 79	Home Farm
Ford Brian (D)	5 11	12 00	Edinburgh	23 9 82	Trainee
Froggatt Steve (F)	5 11	11 00	Lincoln	9 3 73	Wolverhampton W
Grant Martin (F)	5 7	10 10	Kirkcaldy	16 1 82	Trainee
Gustafsson Tomas (D)	5 10	11 00	Stockholm	7 5 73	AIK Stockholm
Hadji Mustapha (M)	6 0	12 00	Ifrane	16 11 71	La Coruna
Hall Daniel (D)	5 8	10 06	Rugby	29 12 81	Trainee
Hall Marcus (D)	6 1	12 02	Coventry	24 3 76	Trainee
Hedman Magnus (G)	6 3	14 00	Stockholm	19 3 73	AIK Stockholm
Hendry Colin (D)	6 1	12 07	Keith	7 12 65	Rangers
Hyldgaard Morten (G)	6 6	14 00	Herning	26 1 78	Ikast
Keane Robbie (F)	5 9	11 07	Dublin	8 7 80	Wolverhampton W

Kirkland Christopher (G)	6 3	11 07	Leicester	2 5 81	Trainee
Konjic Muhamed (D)	6 3	13 00	Bosnia	14 5 70	Monaco
Mathie Graeme (D)	6 1	12 00	Lanark	17 10 82	Trainee
McAllister Gary (M)	6 1	11 11	Motherwell	25 12 64	Leeds U
McConnell Peter (M)	5 10	11 12	Rutherglen	16 9 82	Trainee
McPhee Gary (F)	6 0	12 00	Glasgow	18 4 80	
McPhee Stephen (M)	5 7	10 08	Glasgow	5 6 81	
McSheffrey Gary (F)	5 8	10 06	Coventry	13 8 82	Trainee
Normann Runar (M)	5 11	12 00	Harstad	1 3 78	Lillestrom
Palmer Carlton (M)	6 3	13 00	Oldbury	5 12 65	Nottingham F
Pead Craig (M)	5 9	11 06	Bromsgrove	15 9 81	Trainee
Quinn Barry (M)	6 0	12 02	Dublin	9 5 79	Trainee
Roussel Cedric (F)	6 3	13 00	Mons	6 1 78	La Louviere
Shaw Richard (D)	5 9	12 08	Brentford	11 9 68	Crystal Palace
Strachan Craig (M)	5 8	10 06	Aberdeen	19 5 82	Trainee
Strachan Gavin (M)	5 10	11 07	Aberdeen	23 12 78	Trainee
Telfer Paul (M)	5 9	11 06	Edinburgh	21 10 71	Luton T
Whelan Noel (F)	6 2	12 03	Leeds	30 12 74	Leeds U
Williams Paul (D)	5 11	12 10	Burton	26 3 71	Derby Co
Zuniga Ysrael (F)	5 9	11 00	Lima	27 8 76	

League Appearances: Aloisi, J. 3(4); Betts, R. (2); Breen, G. 20(1); Burrows, D. 11(4); Chippo, Y. 33; Edworthy, M. 10; Eustace, J. 12(4); Froggatt, S. 21(5); Gustafsson, T. 7(3); Hadji, M. 33; Hall, M. 7(2); Hall, P. (1); Hedman, M. 35; Hendry, C. 9; Huckerby, D. 1; Keane, R. 30(1); Konjic, M. 3(1); McAllister, G. 38; McSheffrey, G. (3); Normann, R. 1(7); Ogrizovic, S. 3; Palmer, C. 15; Quinn, B. 5(6); Roussel, C. 18(4); Shaw, R. 27(2); Strachan, G. 1(2); Telfer, P. 26(4); Whelan, N. 20(6); Williams, P. 26(2); Zuniga, Y. 3(3).
Goals – League (47): Keane 12, McAllister 11 (4 pens), Hadji 6, Roussel 6, Aloisi 2, Chippo 2, Zuniga 2, Eustace 1, Froggatt 1, Palmer 1, Whelan 1, Williams 1, own goal 1.
Worthington Cup (4): Chippo 2, McAllister 2.
FA Cup (8): Roussel 3, Chippo 2, Whelan 2, Eustace 1.
Ground: Highfield Road Stadium, King Richard Street, Coventry CV2 4FW. Telephone (024) 7623 4000.
Record attendance: 51,455 v Wolverhampton W, Division 2, 29 April 1967.
Capacity: 23,611.
Manager: Gordon Strachan.
Secretary: Graham Hover.
Most League Goals: 108, Division 3 (S), 1931–32.
Highest League Scorer in Season: Clarrie Bourton, 49, Division 3 (S), 1931–32.
Most League Goals in Total Aggregate: Clarrie Bourton, 171, 1931–37.
Most Capped Player: Peter Ndlovu, 26 (37), Zimbabwe.
Most League Appearances: Steve Ogrizovic, 507, 1984–2000.
Honours – Football League: Division 2 Champions – 1966–67. Division 3 Champions – 1963–64. Division 3 (S) Champions 1935–36. **FA Cup winners** 1986–87.
Colours: Sky blue and navy striped shirts with white trim, sky blue shorts and stockings with navy trim.

CREWE ALEXANDRA — DIV. 1

Charles Anthony (D)			Isleworth	11 3 81	Brook House
Charnock Phil (M)	5 10	11 03	Southport	14 2 75	Liverpool
Collins James (M)	5 8	10 00	Liverpool	28 5 78	Trainee
Cramb Colin (F)	6 0	12 09	Lanark	23 6 74	Bristol C

Foster Stephen (D)	5 11	11 00	Warrington	10 9 80	Trainee
Grant John (F)	5 11	10 08	Manchester	9 8 81	Trainee
Hulse Robert (F)	6 1	12 00	Crewe	25 10 79	Trainee
Ince Clayton (G)	6 3	13 00	Trinidad	13 7 72	Defence Force
Jack Rodney (F)	5 7	10 07	Kingston, Jamaica	28 9 72	Torquay U
Kearton Jason (G)	6 1	12 03	Ipswich (Aus)	9 7 69	Everton
Lightfoot Chris (D)	6 1	12 00	Penketh	1 4 70	Wigan Ath
Little Colin (F)	5 10	11 00	Wythenshaw	4 11 72	Hyde U
Lunt Kenny (M)	5 10	10 00	Runcorn	20 11 79	Trainee
Macauley Steve (D)	6 1	12 03	Lytham	4 3 69	Fleetwood T
Rivers Mark (F)	5 10	11 00	Crewe	26 11 75	Trainee
Smith Peter (F)	5 10	10 00	Rhuddlan	15 9 78	Trainee
Smith Shaun (D)	5 10	11 00	Leeds	9 4 71	Halifax T
Sorvel Neil (M)	6 0	12 09	Widnes	2 3 73	Macclesfield T
Street Kevin (M)	5 10	11 00	Crewe	25 11 77	Trainee
Trainer Phil (M)			Wolverhampton	3 7 81	
Walker Richard (D)	6 2	13 00	Stafford	17 9 80	Trainee
Walton David (D)	6 2	14 07	Bellingham	10 4 73	Shrewsbury T
Welsby Kevin (G)	6 0	10 06	Crewe	27 8 80	Trainee
Wright David (D)	5 11	10 09	Warrington	1 5 80	Trainee

League Appearances: Bignot, M. 25(2); Boertien, P. 2; Charnock, P. 14(2); Collins, J. 8(5); Cramb, C. 33(4); Critchley, N. (1); Foran, M. 11(2); Grant, J. 1(3); Hulse, R. (4); Ince, C. (1); Jack, R. 21(2); Kearton, J. 46; Lightfoot, C. 16(5); Little, C. 34(3); Lunt, K. 39(4); Macauley, S. 35(2); Newby, J. 5(1); Rivers, M. 29(3); Smith, P. (6); Smith, S. 30(1); Sorvel, N. 46; Street, K. 20(8); Tait, P. 19(14); Unsworth, L. 3(5); Walton, D. 8(3); Wright, D. 44(1); Wright, S. 17(6).
Goals – League (46): Rivers 7, Cramb 6, Sorvel 6, Tait 6, Jack 4, Little 4, Macauley 4 (1 pen), Lunt 3, Smith S 2 (2 pens), Charnock 1, Hulse 1, Lightfoot 1, Street 1.
Worthington Cup (8): Little 4, Rivers 2, Cramb 1, Smith S 1 (pen).
FA Cup (1): Little 1.
Ground: Football Ground, Gresty Rd, Crewe CW2 6EB. Telephone (01270) 213014.
Record attendance: 20,000 v Tottenham H, FA Cup 4th rd, 30 January 1960.
Capacity: 10,046.
Manager: Dario Gradi MBE.
Secretary: Mrs Gill Palin.
Most League Goals: 95, Division 3 (N), 1931–32.
Highest League Scorer in Season: Terry Harkin, 35, Division 4, 1964–65.
Most League Goals in Total Aggregate: Bert Swindells, 126, 1928–37.
Most Capped Player: Bill Lewis, 9 (27), Wales.
Most League Appearances: Tommy Lowry, 436, 1966–78.
Honours – Welsh Cup: Winners 1936, 1937.
Colours: Red shirts, white shorts, red stockings.

CRYSTAL PALACE DIV. 1

Amsalem David (D)	6 1	12 01	Israel	4 9 71	Beitar Jerusalem
Austin Dean (D)	5 11	11 11	Hemel Hempstead	26 4 70	Tottenham H
Carlisle Wayne (M)	6 0	11 06	Lisburn	9 9 79	Trainee
Curcic Sasa (M)	5 9	11 00	Belgrade	14 2 72	Aston Villa
Del Rio Walter (D)	6 0	12 06	Buenos Aires	16 6 76	Boca Juniors
Digby Fraser (G)	6 1	12 12	Sheffield	23 4 67	Swindon T
Dimond Kristian (M)			Cardiff	1 2 83	Trainee
Evans Stephen (M)	5 11	11 02	Caerphilly	25 9 80	Trainee
Foster Craig (M)	5 11	12 00	Melbourne	15 4 69	Portsmouth
Fowler Michael (M)			Cardiff	22 8 81	Trainee

Frampton Andrew (D)	5 11	10 10	Wimbledon	3 9 79	Trainee
Fullarton Jamie (M)	5 9	10 09	Bellshill	20 7 74	Bastia
Gregg Matt (G)	5 11	12 00	Cheltenham	30 11 78	Torquay U
Hankin Sean (M)	5 11	12 04	Camberley	28 2 81	Trainee
Harris Richard (D)	5 11	10 09	Croydon	23 10 80	Trainee
Hibburt James (D)	6 0	12 08	Ashford	30 10 79	Trainee
Howell Richard (M)			Hitchin	29 8 82	
Hunt Steve (M)	5 9	12 06	Laois	1 8 81	Trainee
Jihai Sun (D)	5 10	10 07	Dalian	30 9 77	Dalian Wanda
Kabba Steven (D)	5 10	11 12	Lambeth	7 3 81	Trainee
Kendall Lee (G)	5 10	10 05	Newport	8 1 81	Trainee
Linighan Andy (D)	6 4	13 10	Hartlepool	18 6 62	Arsenal
Martin Andrew (F)	6 0	10 12	Cardiff	28 2 80	Trainee
McKenzie Leon (F)	5 10	10 03	Croydon	17 5 78	Trainee
Morrison Clinton (F)	6 1	11 02	Tooting	14 5 79	Trainee
Mullins Hayden (M)	6 0	11 12	Reading	27 3 79	Trainee
Ormshaw Gareth (G)	6 0	12 10	Durban	8 7 79	Ramblers
Petric Gordan (D)	6 1	12 03	Belgrade	30 7 69	Rangers
Rizzo Nicky (M)	5 10	12 00	Sydney	9 6 79	Liverpool
Rodger Simon (M)	5 9	11 09	Shoreham	3 10 71	Trainee
Sharpling Christopher (F)	5 11	11 10	Bromley	21 4 81	Trainee
Smith Jamie (D)	5 8	11 02	Birmingham	17 9 74	Wolverhampton W
Thomson Steve (M)	5 8	10 04	Glasgow	23 1 78	Trainee
Walsh Ronald (M)			Glasnevin	15 9 82	Scholar
Woozley David (D)	6 0	12 10	Berkshire	6 12 79	Trainee
Zhiyi Fan (M)	6 0	12 01	Shanghai	22 1 70	Shanghai Shenhua

League Appearances: Austin, D. 45; Bradbury, L. 9(1); Carlisle, W. 23(3); Cole, A. 14; De Ornelas, F. 5(4); Digby, F. 38; Evans, S. (1); Forssell, M. 13; Foster, C. 17(3); Frampton, A. 6(3); Fullarton, J. 13; Fumaca, J. 2(1); Gregg, M. 6; Hankin, S. (1); Harris, R. 1(5); Hibburt, J. 1(3); Hunt, S. (3); Kabba, S. 1; Launders, B. 1(1); Linighan, A. 44(1); Martin, A. 10(9); Mautone, S. 2; McKenzie, L. 24(1); Morrison, C. 28(1); Mullins, H. 45; Phelan, T. 14; Rizzo, N. 2(15); Rodger, S. 34; Sharpling, C. 1(5); Smith, J. 27; Svensson, M. 20(4); Thomson, S. 17(4); Tuttle, D. (1); Woozley, D. 14(9); Zhiyi, F. 29.
Goals – League (57): Morrison 13, Mullins 10 (2 pens), Svensson 9 (1 pen), McKenzie 4, Carlisle 3, Forssell 3, Austin 2, Bradbury 2, Linighan 2, Martin 2, Rodger 2, Cole 1, Foster 1, Zhiyi 1, own goals 2.
Worthington Cup (10): Morrison 2, Smith 2, Bradbury 1, Mullins 1, Rizzo 1, Rodger 1, Thomson 1, Zhiyi 1.
FA Cup (0).
Ground: Selhurst Park, London SE25 6PU. Telephone (0181) 768 6000.
Record attendance: 51,482 v Burnley, Division 2, 11 May 1979. **Capacity:** 26,400.
Manager: Steve Coppell.
Club Secretary: Mike Hurst.
Most League Goals: 110, Division 4, 1960–61.
Highest League Scorer in Season: Peter Simpson, 46, Division 3 (S), 1930–31.
Most League Goals in Total Aggregate: Peter Simpson, 153, 1930–36.
Most Capped Player: Eric Young, 19 (21), Wales.
Most League Appearances: Jim Cannon, 571, 1973–88.
Honours – Football League: Division 1 – Champions 1993–94. Division 2 Champions – 1978–79. Division 3 (S) 1920–21. **Zenith Data Systems Cup winners** 1991.
Colours: Red shirts with blue trim, red shorts with blue and white trim, red stockings.

DARLINGTON — DIV. 3

Aspin Neil (D)	6 0	13 00	Gateshead	12 4 65	Port Vale
Atkinson Brian (M)	5 10	12 10	Darlington	19 1 71	Sunderland
Campbell Paul (M)	6 1	11 00	Middlesbrough	29 1 80	Trainee
Duffield Peter (F)	5 6	10 04	Middlesbrough	4 2 69	Raith R
Gabbiadini Marco (F)	5 10	13 04	Nottingham	21 1 68	York C
Gray Martin (M)	5 9	11 05	Stockton	17 8 71	Oxford U
Heaney Neil (M)	5 11	12 00	Middlesbrough	3 11 71	Manchester C
Heckingbottom Paul (D)	6 0	12 03	Barnsley	17 7 77	Sunderland
Himsworth Gary (M)	5 8	11 00	York	19 12 69	York C
Hjorth Jesper (F)	6 0	12 04	Denmark	3 4 75	Odense
Kilty Mark (D)	6 0	12 00	Sunderland	24 6 81	Trainee
Liddle Craig (D)	5 11	12 07	Chester-le-Street	21 10 71	Middlesbrough
Nogan Lee (F)	5 10	11 00	Cardiff	21 5 69	Grimsby T
Pepper Carl (D)	5 11	11 00	Darlington	26 7 80	Trainee
Reed Adam (D)	6 1	11 00	Bishop Auckland	18 2 75	Blackburn R
Tutill Steve (D)	5 10	12 06	Derwent	1 10 69	York C
Wells David (D)	5 9	12 00	Stockton	19 2 81	Trainee

League Appearances: Aspin, N. 29; Atkinson, B. 26(4); Baker, S. 4(1); Bennett, G. 4(1); Brumwell, P. 9(9); Campbell, P. 3(6); Carruthers, M. (6); Collett, A. 13; Duffield, P. 21(12); Gabbiadini, M. 41(1); Gray, M. 40(1); Heaney, N. 33(3); Heckingbottom, P. 44(1); Himsworth, G. 13(6); Holsgrove, P. 1(2); Hyorth, J. 8(14); Kilty, M. 1(1); Liddle, C. 45; Naylor, G. 8(17); Nogan, L. 19(12); Oliver, M. 35(2); Reed, A. 20(3); Russell, C. 11(1); Samways, M. 33(1); Taylor, M. 4; Tutill, S. 25(2); Wainwright, N. 16(1).
Goals – League (66): Gabbiadini 24 (3 pens), Duffield 12, Hyorth 6, Heaney 5, Wainwright 4, Naylor 3, Campbell 2, Nogan 2, Oliver 2, Russell 2, Heckingbottom 1, Liddle 1, own goals 2.
Worthington Cup (4): Nogan 2, Gabbiadini 1, Oliver 1.
FA Cup (4): Duffield 1, Gabbiadini 1 (pen), Heckingbottom 1, Tutill 1.
Ground: Feethams Ground, Darlington DL1 5JB. Telephone (01325) 240240.
Record attendance: 21,023 v Bolton W, League Cup 3rd rd, 14 November 1960.
Capacity: 8500.
Manager: David Hodgson.
Secretary: Lisa Charlton.
Most League Goals: 108, Division 3 (N), 1929–30.
Highest League Scorer in Season: David Brown, 39, Division 3 (N), 1924–25.
Most League Goals in Total Aggregate: Alan Walsh, 90, 1978–84.
Most Capped Player: Jason Devos, 3, Canada.
Most League Appearances: Ron Greener, 442, 1955–68.
Honours – Football League: Division 3 (N) Champions – 1924–25. Division 4 Champions – 1990–91.
Colours: Black and white.

DERBY COUNTY — FA PREMIERSHIP

Beck Mikkel (F)	6 2	12 13	Aarhus	4 5 73	Middlesbrough
Boertien Paul (D)	5 10	11 07	Carlisle	21 1 79	Carlisle U
Bohinen Lars (M)	6 1	12 03	Vadso	8 9 69	Blackburn R
Bolder Adam (M)	5 8	11 05	Hull	25 10 80	Hull C
Burley Craig (M)	6 2	13 03	Ayr	24 9 71	Celtic
Burton Deon (F)	5 9	12 02	Reading	25 10 76	Portsmouth

Carbonari Horace Angel (D)	6 3	14 03	Rosario	2 5 73	Rosario Central
Christie Malcolm (F)	6 0	11 11	Peterborough	11 4 79	Nuneaton B
Delap Rory (D)	6 2	13 00	Sutton Coldfield	6 7 76	Carlisle U
Doherty Gerard (M)			Derry	24 8 81	Derry C
Elliott Steve (D)	6 2	14 03	Derby	29 10 78	Trainee
Eranio Stefano (M)	5 10	12 04	Genoa	29 12 68	AC Milan
Evatt Ian (D)			Coventry	19 11 81	Trainee
Fuertes Esteban (F)	6 1	13 12	Coronel Dorredo	26 12 72	Coronel de Santa Fe
Jackson Richard (D)	5 8	10 00	Whitby	18 4 80	Scarborough
Johnson Seth (M)	5 10	11 11	Birmingham	12 3 79	Crewe Alex
Kinkladze Georgiou (M)	5 8	11 05	Tbilisi	6 7 73	Ajax
Laursen Jacob (D)	6 0	12 13	Vejle	6 10 71	Silkeborg
Morris Lee (F)	5 9	10 12	Driffield	30 4 80	Sheffield U
Murray Adam (M)	5 8	10 12	Birmingham	30 9 81	Trainee
Oakes Andy (G)	6 3	10 12	Crewe	11 1 77	Hull C
Poom Mart (G)	6 4	13 04	Tallinn	3 2 72	Flora Tallinn
Powell Darryl (M)	6 0	13 01	Lambeth	15 11 71	Portsmouth
Riggott Chris (D)	6 2	12 05	Derby	1 9 80	Trainee
Robinson Marvin (F)	6 0	12 13	Crewe	11 4 80	Trainee
Schnoor Stefan (D)	6 2	12 11	Neumunster	24 4 71	Hamburg
Strupar Branko (F)	6 3	14 00	Zagreb	9 2 70	Genk
Sturridge Dean (F)	5 8	12 02	Birmingham	27 7 73	Trainee

League Appearances: Baiano, F. 5(4); Beck, M. 5(6); Boertien, P. (2); Bohinen, L. 8(5); Borbokis, V. 6(6); Burley, C. 18; Burton, D. 15(4); Carbonari, H. 29; Christie, M. 10(11); Delap, R. 34; Dorigo, T. 20(3); Elliott, S. 18(2); Eranio, S. 17(2); Fuertes, E. 8; Harper, K. (5); Hoult, R. 10; Jackson, R. (2); Johnson, S. 36; Kinkladze, G. 12(5); Laursen, J. 36; Morris, L. 2(1); Murray, A. 1(7); Nimni, A. 2(2); Poom, M. 28; Powell, D. 31; Prior, S. 15(5); Riggott, C. (1); Robinson, M. 3(5); Schnoor, S. 22(7); Strupar, B. 13(2); Sturridge, D. 14(11).

Goals – League (44): Delap 8, Sturridge 6, Burley 5 (2 pens), Christie 5, Strupar 5, Burton 4, Carbonari 2, Powell 2, Beck 1, Fuertes 1, Johnson 1, Kinkladze 1, Laursen 1, Nimni 1, own goal 1.

Worthington Cup (4): Beck 1, Borbokis 1, Fuertes 1, Sturridge 1.

FA Cup (0).

Ground: Pride Park Stadium, Derby DE24 8XL. Telephone: (01332) 202202.

Record attendance: 41,826 v Tottenham H, Division 1, 20 September 1969. **Capacity:** 33,597.

Manager: Jim Smith.

Secretary: Keith Pearson ACIS.

Most League Goals: 111, Division 3 (N), 1956–57.

Highest League Scorer in Season: Jack Bowers, 37, Division 1, 1930–31; Ray Straw, 37 Division 3 (N), 1956–57.

Most League Goals in Total Aggregate: Steve Bloomer, 292, 1892–1906 and 1910–14.

Most Capped Player: Peter Shilton, 34 (125), England.

Most League Appearances: Kevin Hector, 486, 1966–78 and 1980–82.

Honours – Football League: Division 1 Champions – 1971–72, 1974–75. Division 2 Champions – 1911–12, 1914–15, 1968–69, 1986–87. Division 3 (N) 1956–57. **FA Cup winners** 1945–46.

Colours: White shirts with black trim, black shorts with white stripes, white stockings.

Ball Michael (D)	5 10	12 02	Liverpool	2 10 79	Trainee
Barmby Nick (F)	5 8	11 04	Hull	11 2 74	Middlesbrough
Cadamarteri Danny (F)	5 9	12 10	Bradford	12 10 79	Trainee
Campbell Kevin (F)	6 1	13 08	Lambeth	4 2 70	Trabzonspor
Chadwick Nick (F)	6 0	12 04	Stoke	26 10 82	
Clarke Peter (D)	6 0	12 00	Southport	3 1 82	Trainee
Cleland Alex (D)	5 9	11 07	Glasgow	10 12 70	Rangers
Collins John (M)	5 7	10 13	Galashiels	30 1 68	Monaco
Curran Damien (M)	5 9	12 01	Antrim	17 10 81	Trainee
Degn Peter (M)	5 10	12 06	Denmark	6 4 77	Aarhus
Dunne Richard (D)	6 2	14 06	Dublin	21 9 79	Trainee
Gemmill Scot (M)	5 9	11 11	Paisley	2 1 71	Nottingham F
Gerrard Paul (G)	6 2	14 00	Heywood	22 1 73	Oldham Ath
Gough Richard (D)	6 0	12 00	Stockholm	5 4 62	Nottingham F
Hibbert Anthony (M)	5 8	11 01	Liverpool	20 2 81	Trainee
Hogg Craig (D)	6 1	11 12	Liverpool	8 10 81	Trainee
Hughes Mark (F)	5 11	13 00	Wrexham	1 11 63	Southampton
Hughes Stephen (M)	6 0	12 12	Wokingham	18 9 76	Arsenal
Hutchison Don (M)	6 1	12 05	Gateshead	9 5 71	Sheffield U
Jeffers Francis (F)	5 10	10 05	Liverpool	25 1 81	Trainee
Jevons Phil (F)	5 10	11 12	Liverpool	1 8 79	Trainee
Kearney Thomas (M)	5 9	10 12	Liverpool	7 10 81	Trainee
Lester John (M)	5 11	12 09	Dublin	5 8 82	Trainee
McKay Matt (M)	6 0	11 05	Warrington	21 1 81	Trainee
McLeod Kevin (M)	5 11	11 00	Liverpool	12 9 80	Trainee
Milligan Jamie (M)	5 7	9 12	Blackpool	3 1 80	Trainee
Moore Joe-Max (F)	5 8	11 06	USA	23 2 71	New England Rev
Myhre Thomas (G)	6 4	13 12	Sarpsborg	16 10 73	Viking
O'Hanlon Sean (D)	6 1	12 02	Liverpool	2 1 83	
Osman Leon (M)	5 8	9 11	Billinge	17 5 81	Trainee
Pembridge Mark (M)	5 7	11 09	Merthyr	29 11 70	Benfica
Penman Craig (D)	5 11	11 06	Falkirk	9 9 82	Trainee
Pilkington George (D)	5 11	11 00	Rugeley	7 11 81	Trainee
Price Michael (D)	5 8	11 01	Wrexham	29 4 82	Trainee
Regan Carl (D)	6 0	11 05	Liverpool	9 9 80	Trainee
Simonsen Steve (G)	6 3	13 11	South Shields	3 4 79	Tranmere R
Southern Keith (M)			Gateshead	24 4 81	Trainee
Unsworth Dave (D)	6 1	14 09	Chorley	16 10 73	Aston Villa
Valentine Ryan (M)	5 10	11 07	Wrexham	19 8 82	Trainee
Ward Mitch (D)	5 8	11 13	Sheffield	19 6 71	Sheffield U
Watson Dave (D)	6 1	13 10	Liverpool	20 11 61	Norwich C
Weir David (D)	6 3	13 13	Falkirk	10 5 70	Hearts
Williamson Danny (M)	6 0	13 13	West Ham	5 12 73	West Ham U
Xavier Abel (M)	6 2	13 06	Mozambique	30 11 72	PSV Eindhoven

League Appearances: Ball, M. 14(11); Barmby, N. 37; Cadamarteri, D. 3(14); Campbell, K. 26; Cleland, A. 3(6); Collins, J. 33(2); Dunne, R. 27(4); Gemmill, S. 6(8); Gerrard, P. 34; Gough, R. 29; Grant, T. (2); Hughes, M. 9; Hughes, S. 11; Hutchison, D. 28(3); Jeffers, F. 16(5); Jevons, P. 2(1); Johnson, T. (3); Milligan, J. (1); Moore, J. 11(4); Myhre, T. 4; Pembridge, M. 29(2); Phelan, T. (1); Simonsen, S. (1); Unsworth, D. 32(1); Ward, M. 6(4); Watson, D. 5(1); Weir, D. 35; Xavier, A. 18(2).
Goals – League (59): Campbell 12, Barmby 9, Hutchison 6, Jeffers 6, Moore 6,

Unsworth 6 (5 pens), Collins 2, Pembridge 2, Weir 2, Ball 1 (pen), Cadamarteri 1, Gemmill 1, Gough 1, Hughes M 1, Hughes S 1, own goals 2.
Worthington Cup (1): Cadamarteri 1.
FA Cup (6): Unsworth 3 (2 pens), Moore 2, Barmby 1.
Ground: Goodison Park, Liverpool L4 4EL. Telephone (0151) 330 2200.
Record attendance: 78,299 v Liverpool, Division 1, 18 September 1948. **Capacity:** 40,200.
Manager: Walter Smith OBE.
Secretary: Michael J. Dunford.
Most League Goals: 121, Division 2, 1930–31.
Highest League Scorer in Season: William Ralph 'Dixie' Dean, 60, Division 1, 1927–28 (All-time League record).
Most League Goals in Total Aggregate: William Ralph 'Dixie' Dean, 349, 1925–37.
Most Capped Player: Neville Southall, 92, Wales.
Most League Appearances: Neville Southall, 578, 1981–98.
Honours – Football League: Division 1 Champions – 1890–91, 1914–15, 1927–28, 1931–32, 1938–39, 1962–63, 1969–70, 1984–85, 1986–87. Division 2 Champions – 1930–31. **FA Cup:** Winners 1906, 1933, 1966, 1984, 1995. **European Competitions: European Cup-Winners' Cup winners:** 1984–85.
Colours: Royal blue shirts with white trim, white shorts, royal blue stockings.

EXETER CITY — DIV. 3

Breslan Geoff (M)	5 9	10 05	Torbay	4 6 80	Trainee
Buckle Paul (M)	5 8	11 08	Welwyn	16 12 70	Colchester U
Cornforth John (M)	5 11	14 06	Whitley Bay	7 10 67	Scunthorpe U
Curran Chris (D)	5 11	12 12	Birmingham	17 9 71	Plymouth Arg
Flack Steve (F)	6 1	14 07	Cambridge	29 5 71	Cardiff C
Holloway Chris (M)	5 10	11 10	Swansea	5 2 80	Trainee
Power Graeme (D)	5 11	11 07	Northwick Park	7 3 77	Bristol R
Richardson Jon (D)	6 1	12 02	Nottingham	29 8 75	Trainee
Smith Peter (M)	5 10	11 00	Skelmersdale	31 10 80	Trainee
Speakman Robert (F)	5 10	11 07	Swansea	5 12 80	Trainee
Vanninen Jukka (M)	5 7	12 01	Riihimaki	31 1 77	Rops
Waugh Warren (F)	6 0	13 07	Harlesden	9 10 80	Trainee
Wilkinson John (M)	5 9	10 06	Exeter	24 8 79	Trainee

League Appearances: Alexander, G. 37; Bennett, F. 8(1); Blake, N. 2(5); Boylan, L. 3(3); Bradley, S. 6(2); Breslan, G. 16(13); Brown, A. 4(1); Buckle, P. 27; Cornforth, J. 12; Curran, C. 36(2); Dewhurst, R. 21(2); Ellington, L. (1); Flack, S. 19(21); Gale, S. 18(5); Gittens, J. 38; Holloway, C. 20(4); Inglethorpe, A. (1); Jarman, L. 7; Lee, D. 3(1); Lovell, S. 4(1); Matthews, J. 11(1); McConnell, B. 16(9); Naylor, S. 31; Nyamah, K. 23(12); Potter, D. 4; Power, G. 28(1); Rees, J. 42(1); Richardson, J. 35; Robinson, J. 11(1); Rowbotham, D. 13(5); Smith, P. 3(4); Speakman, R. 4(13); Vanninen, J. 3(2); Waugh, W. (3); Worrall, B. 1(3).
Goals – League (46): Alexander 16 (1 pen), Rees 4 (1 pen), Speakman 3, Cornforth 2 (2 pens), Dewhurst 2, Flack 2, Gittens 2, Rowbotham 2, Bennett 1, Blake 1, Boylan 1, Bradley 1, Brown 1, Buckle 1, Curran 1, Gale 1, Holloway 1, Lovell 1, McConnell 1 (pen), Nyamah 1, Richardson 1.
Worthington Cup (1): McConnell 1 (pen).
FA Cup (4): Flack 2, Alexander 1, Gale 1.
Ground: St James Park, Exeter EX4 6PX. Telephone (01392) 254073.
Record attendance: 20,984 v Sunderland, FA Cup 6th rd (replay), 4 March 1931.
Capacity: 10,570.
Manager: Noel Blake.
Secretary: Stuart Brailey.

Most League Goals: 88, Division 3 (S), 1932–33.
Highest League Scorer in Season: Fred Whitlow, 33, Division 3 (S), 1932–33.
Most League Goals in Total Aggregate: Tony Kellow, 129, 1976–78, 1980–83, 1985–88.
Most Capped Player: Dermot Curtis, 1 (17), Eire.
Most League Appearances: Arnold Mitchell, 495, 1952–66.
Honours – Football League: Division 4 Champions – 1989–90. **Division 3 (S) Cup:** Winners 1934.
Colours: Red and white striped shirts, red shorts, red stockings.

FULHAM — DIV. 1

Ball Kevin (M)	5 10	12 04	Hastings	12 11 64	Sunderland
Betsy Kevin (F)	6 0	12 02	Seychelles	20 3 78	Woking
Bracewell Paul (M)	5 9	12 03	Heswall	19 7 62	Sunderland
Brevett Rufus (D)	5 8	11 09	Derby	24 9 69	QPR
Brooker Paul (F)	5 8	10 01	Hammersmith	25 11 76	Trainee
Clark Lee (M)	5 8	11 08	Wallsend	27 10 72	Sunderland
Coleman Chris (D)	6 2	15 00	Swansea	10 6 70	Blackburn R
Collins Wayne (M)	5 10	12 01	Manchester	4 3 69	Sheffield W
Cornwall Luke (F)	5 10	11 00	Lambeth	23 7 80	Trainee
Davis Sean (M)	5 11	12 07	Clapham	20 9 79	Trainee
Finnan Steve (D)	6 0	12 04	Limerick	20 4 76	Notts Co
Goldbaek Bjarne (M)	5 9	12 08	Denmark	6 10 68	Chelsea
Hahnemann Marcus (G)	6 3	16 02	Seattle	15 6 72	Colorado Rapids
Hammond Elvis (F)	5 10	10 09	Accra	6 10 80	Trainee
Hayles Barry (F)	5 9	13 02	London	17 4 72	Bristol R
Hayward Steve (M)	5 11	13 00	Walsall	8 9 71	Carlisle U
Horsfield Geoff (F)	6 1	13 07	Barnsley	1 11 73	Halifax T
Hudson Mark (D)	6 1	12 01	Guildford	30 3 82	Trainee
Hutchinson Tom (D)	6 0	11 03	Hammersmith	23 2 82	
Keevill Sam (M)	5 8	10 01	Lewisham	8 5 81	Trainee
Knight Zatyiah (D)	6 6	13 08	Solihull	2 5 80	
Lewis Eddie (M)	5 9	11 12	California	17 5 74	San Jose Clash
Melville Andy (D)	6 0	13 02	Swansea	29 11 68	Sunderland
Morgan Simon (D)	5 11	12 05	Birmingham	5 9 66	Leicester C
Neilson Alan (D)	5 11	12 06	Wegburg	26 9 72	Southampton
Peschisolido Paul (F)	5 7	10 09	Canada	25 5 71	WBA
Phelan Terry (D)	5 6	10 06	Manchester	16 3 67	Everton
Riedle Karlheinz (F)	5 11	11 07	Weiler	16 9 65	Liverpool
Symons Kit (D)	6 3	13 00	Basingstoke	8 3 71	Manchester C
Taylor Maik (G)	6 3	14 02	Hildeshein	4 9 71	Southampton
Thompson Glyn (G)	6 3	11 03	Shrewsbury	24 2 81	Shrewsbury T
Trollope Paul (M)	5 11	11 04	Swindon	3 6 72	Derby Co
Tucker Anthony (G)	5 11	11 04	Barking	12 10 81	Trainee

League Appearances: Ball, K. 15(3); Betsy, K. (2); Brevett, R. 22(1); Cadamarteri, D. 3(2); Clark, L. 42; Coleman, C. 40; Collins, W. 6(13); Collymore, S. 3(3); Davis, S. 15(11); Finnan, S. 35; Goldbaek, B. 16(2); Hayles, B. 21(14); Hayward, S. 34(3); Horsfield, G. 28(3); Hughes, S. 3; Lewis, E. 6(2); Melville, A. 40; Morgan, S. 26(2); Neilson, A. 4(1); Peschisolido, P. 18(12); Phelan, T. 17; Riedle, K. 15(6); Symons, K. 27(2); Taylor, M. 46; Trollope, P. 13(9); Uhlenbeek, G. 11(5).
Goals – League (49): Clark 8 (1 pen), Horsfield 7, Hayles 5, Riedle 5 (1 pen), Peschisolido 4 (1 pen), Coleman 3, Goldbaek 3, Melville 3, Finnan 2, Phelan 2, Symons 2, Cadamarteri 1, Collins 1, Neilson 1, own goals 2.

Worthington Cup (19): Horsfield 6, Peschisolido 3, Collins 2, Davis 2, Hayles 2, Clark 1, Coleman 1, Collymore 1, own goal 1.
FA Cup (9): Collins 2, Hayles 2, Coleman 1, Davis 1, Finnan 1, Hayward 1, Horsfield 1.
Ground: Craven Cottage, Stevenage Rd, Fulham, London SW6 6HH. Telephone (020) 7893 8383.
Record attendance: 49,335 v Millwall, Division 2, 8 October 1938. **Capacity:** 19,250.
Manager: Jean Tigana.
Secretary: Etain Wist.
Most League Goals: 111, Division 3 (S), 1931–32.
Highest League Scorer in Season: Frank Newton, 43, Division 3 (S), 1931–32.
Most League Goals in Total Aggregate: Gordon Davies, 159, 1978–84, 1986–91.
Most Capped Player: Johnny Haynes, 56, England.
Most League Appearances: Johnny Haynes, 594, 1952–70.
Honours – Football League: Division 2 Champions – 1948–49, 1998–99. Division 3 (S) Champions – 1931–32.
Colours: White shirts, red and black trim, black shorts, white stockings red and black trim.

GILLINGHAM DIV. 1

Asaba Carl (F)	6 2	13 00	London	28 1 73	Reading
Ashby Barry (D)	6 2	13 08	London	2 11 70	Brentford
Bartram Vince (G)	6 2	13 04	Birmingham	8 8 68	Arsenal
Browning Marcus (M)	6 0	12 10	Bristol	22 4 71	Huddersfield T
Bryant Matthew (D)	6 1	13 01	Bristol	21 9 70	Bristol C
Butler Steve (F)	6 1	12 02	Birmingham	21 1 62	Peterborough U
Butters Guy (D)	6 3	13 12	Hillingdon	30 10 69	Portsmouth
Edge Roland (D)	5 10	11 10	Gillingham	25 11 78	Trainee
Gooden Ty (M)	5 8	12 06	Canvey Island	23 10 72	Swindon T
Hessenthaler Andy (M)	5 7	11 05	Gravesend	17 6 65	Watford
Lee Christian (F)	6 2	11 07	Aylesbury	8 10 76	Northampton T
Lewis Junior (F)	6 2	11 08	Wembley	9 10 73	Trainee
McGlinchey Brian (D)	5 8	10 05	Derry	26 10 77	Port Vale
Miller Barry (D)	6 0	11 07	Greenford Ealing	29 3 76	
Mitten Charlie (G)	6 2	12 07	Woolwich	9 10 74	Dover Ath
Nosworthy Nayron (M)	6 1	12 07	London	11 10 80	Trainee
Onuora Iffy (F)	6 1	13 10	Glasgow	28 7 67	Swindon T
Patterson Mark (D)	5 9	12 04	Leeds	13 9 68	Plymouth Arg
Pennock Adrian (M)	6 1	13 05	Ipswich	27 3 71	Bournemouth
Pinnock James (F)	5 9	11 05	Dartford	1 8 78	Trainee
Rowe Rodney (F)	5 8	12 08	Plymouth	30 7 75	York C
Saunders Mark (M)	5 11	11 12	Reading	23 7 71	Plymouth Arg
Smith Paul (M)	5 11	12 08	East Ham	18 9 71	Brentford
Southall Nicky (M)	5 10	12 12	Middlesbrough	28 1 72	Grimsby T
Thomson Andy (F)	5 10	11 05	Motherwell	1 4 71	Oxford U

League Appearances: Asaba, C. 7(4); Ashby, B. 41; Bartram, V. 43; Bass, J. 4(3); Browning, M. (1); Bryant, M. 3(3); Butler, S. 2(8); Butters, G. 38(2); Edge, R. 25(1); Galloway, M. 1(1); Gooden, T. 15(1); Hessenthaler, A. 41(1); Hodge, J. 1(14); Lee, C. 1(2); Lewis, J. 37(5); Matthews, L. 2(3); Mautone, S. 1; McGlinchey, B. 6(7); Miller, B. 1(3); Nosworthy, N. 15(14); Omoyinmi, E. 7(2); Onuora, I. 21(1); Patterson, M. 9; Pennock, A. 34; Pinnock, J. (2); Rowe, R. 8(14); Saunders, M. 20(6); Smith, P. 43(1); Southall, N. 45; Taylor, R. 13(2); Thomson, A. 20(8); Williams, A. 2.

Goals – League (79): Taylor 15 (1 pen), Southall 9 (2 pens), Thomson 9, Asaba 6, Lewis 6, Onuora 6, Hessenthaler 5, Gooden 4, Rowe 4, Ashby 3, Omoyinmi 3, Butler 2, Butters 2, Edge 1, McGlinchey 1, Nosworthy 1, Saunders 1, Smith 1.
Worthington Cup (5): Hessenthaler 2, Southall 1, Taylor 1, own goal 1.
FA Cup (16): Thomson 4, Southall 3, Taylor 2, Ashby 1, Butters 1, Hodge 1, McGlinchey 1, Pennock 1, Saunders 1, own goal 1.
Ground: Priestfield Stadium, Gillingham ME7 4DD. Telephone (01634) 851854, 576828.
Record attendance: 23,002 v QPR, FA Cup 3rd rd 10 January 1948. **Capacity:** 10,600.
Player-Manager: Andy Hessenthaler.
Secretary: Mrs G. E. Poynter.
Most League Goals: 90, Division 4, 1973–74.
Highest League Scorer in Season: Ernie Morgan, 31, Division 3 (S), 1954–55; Brian Yeo, 31, Division 4, 1973–74.
Most League Goals in Total Aggregate: Brian Yeo, 135, 1963–75.
Most Capped Player: Tony Cascarino, 3 (88), Republic of Ireland.
Most League Appearances: John Simpson, 571, 1957–72.
Honours – Football League: Division 4 Champions – 1963–64.
Colours: Blue and black.

GRIMSBY TOWN — DIV. 1

Allen Bradley (F)	5 8	11 00	Harold Wood	13 9 71	Charlton Ath
Ashcroft Lee (F)	5 9	12 07	Preston	7 9 72	Preston NE
Bloomer Matthew (D)	6 0	11 08	Cleethorpes	3 11 78	Trainee
Buckley Adam (M)	5 9	11 07	Nottingham	2 8 79	WBA
Butterfield Danny (D)	5 10	11 06	Boston	21 11 79	Trainee
Chapman Ben (D)	5 6	11 00	Scunthorpe	2 3 79	Trainee
Clare Daryl (F)	5 9	12 05	Jersey	1 8 78	Trainee
Coldicott Stacy (M)	5 8	12 08	Worcester	29 4 74	WBA
Coyne Danny (G)	6 0	13 04	Prestatyn	27 8 73	Tranmere R
Croudson Steve (G)	6 0	11 12	Grimsby	14 9 79	Trainee
Donovan Kevin (F)	5 8	11 13	Halifax	17 12 71	WBA
Gallimore Tony (D)	5 11	13 04	Crewe	21 2 72	Carlisle U
Groves Paul (M)	5 11	13 04	Derby	28 2 66	WBA
Handyside Peter (D)	6 1	13 07	Dumfries	31 7 74	Trainee
Livingstone Steve (F)	6 1	15 03	Middlesbrough	8 9 68	Chelsea
McDermott John (D)	5 7	10 13	Middlesbrough	3 2 69	Trainee
Rowan Jonathan (M)	5 10	11 00	Grimsby	5 10 11	Trainee
Pouton Alan (M)	6 0	12 10	Newcastle	1 2 77	York C
Smith David (M)	5 7	11 11	Gloucester	29 5 68	WBA
Smith Richard (D)	6 0	13 11	Leicester	3 10 70	Leicester C

League Appearances: Allen, B. 12(19); Ashcroft, L. 31(3); Black, K. 15(16); Bloomer, M. (2); Buckley, A. 8(5); Burnett, W. 7(3); Butterfield, D. 21(8); Chapman, B. 1; Clare, D. 13(4); Coldicott, S. 42(2); Coyne, D. 44; Croudson, S. 2(1); Donovan, K. 41; Gallimore, T. 38(1); Groves, P. 43; Hamilton, I. 6; Lester, J. 23(3); Lever, M. 35; Livingstone, S. 23(6); McDermott, J. 23(3); Nicholls, M. 6; Pouton, A. 19(16); Smith, D. 34(2); Smith, R. 19.
Goals – League (41): Ashcroft 12 (6 pens), Allen 8, Lester 4, Clare 3, Donovan 3, Groves 3 (2 pens), Black 2, Coldicott 2, Hamilton 1, Pouton 1, Smith D 1 (pen), own goal 1.
Worthington Cup (10): Lester 3, Groves 2, Ashcroft 1 (pen), Coldicott 1, Donovan 1, Gallimore 1, Smith D 1.

FA Cup (3): Livingstone 2, Allen 1.
Ground: Blundell Park, Cleethorpes, North-East Lincolnshire DN35 7PY. Telephone (01472) 605050.
Record attendance: 31,651 v Wolverhampton W, FA Cup 5th rd, 20 February 1937.
Capacity: 10,033.
Manager: Alan Buckley.
Secretary: Ian Fleming.
Most League Goals: 103, Division 2, 1933–34.
Highest League Scorer in Season: Pat Glover, 42, Division 2, 1933–34.
Most League Goals in Total Aggregate: Pat Glover, 180, 1930–39.
Most Capped Player: Pat Glover, 7, Wales.
Most League Appearances: Keith Jobling, 448, 1953–69.
Honours – Football League: Division 2 Champions – 1900–01, 1933–34. Division 3 (N) Champions – 1925–26, 1955–56. Division 3 Champions – 1979–80. Division 4 Champions – 1971-72. **League Group Cup:** Winners 1981–82. **Auto Windscreens Shield:** Winners 1997–98.
Colours: Black and white striped shirts, black shorts, black stockings.

HALIFAX TOWN DIV. 3

Butler Lee (G)	6 1	13 08	Sheffield	30 5 66	Dunfermline Ath
Butler Peter (M)	5 9	11 01	Halifax	27 8 66	WBA
Clarke Chris (D)	6 3	12 02	Leeds	18 12 80	Wolverhampton W
Clarke Matthew (F)	6 3	13 00	Leeds	18 12 80	Wolverhampton W
Fitzpatrick Ian (F)	5 9	10 00	Manchester	22 9 80	Manchester U
Gaughan Steve (M)	5 11	11 08	Doncaster	14 4 70	Darlington
Holt Grant (M)	6 0	12 06	Carlisle	12 4 81	Workington
Jules Mark (D)	5 7	10 09	Bradford	5 9 71	Chesterfield
Kerrigan Steve (F)	6 1	12 04	Bailleston	9 10 72	Shrewsbury T
Middleton Craig (M)	5 11	12 00	Nuneaton	10 9 70	Cardiff C
Mitchell Graham (D)	6 1	13 01	Shipley	16 2 68	Cardiff C
Ord Michael (M)	6 1	11 06	Huddersfield	22 5 81	Ripon C
Painter Robbie (F)	5 10	12 02	Ince	26 1 71	Rochdale
Potter Lee (F)	5 11	12 10	Salford	3 9 78	Bolton W
Reilly Alan (M)	5 11	12 01	Dublin	22 8 80	Manchester C
Richards Ian (M)	5 8	11 04	Barnsley	5 10 79	Blackburn R
Stansfield James (D)	6 1	13 04	Dewsbury	18 9 78	Trainee
Stoneman Paul (D)	6 0	13 06	Whitley Bay	26 2 73	Blackpool

League Appearances: Adamson, C. 7; Bradshaw, M. 17(8); Butler, L. 38; Butler, P. 30; Clarke, C. (1); Clarke, M. 8(11); Cullen, J. 11; Fitzpatrick, I. 2(6); Gaughan, S. 29(9); Herbert, R. 1(3); Holt, G. (4); Hulme, K. 2(1); Jackson, J. (1); Jones, G. 8; Jules, M. 38(4); Kerrigan, S. 7; Lucas, R. 10(2); Middleton, C. 10; Mitchell, G. 45; Murphy, S. 10(5); Newton, C. 4(4); Painter, R. 38(4); Parks, T. 1; Paterson, J. 37(3); Potter, L. 13(6); Power, L. 3(4); Reilly, A. 15(5); Richards, I. 5(1); Rowe, R. 7(2); Russell, M. 3(4); Sertori, M. 5; Stamp, D. 5; Stansfield, J. 10(2); Stoneman, P. 36(1); Tate, C. 18; Wilder, C. 31; Williams, M. 2(1).
Goals – League (44): Painter 8, Paterson 7 (4 pens), Cullen 5 (1 pen), Stoneman 4, Tate 4, Kerrigan 3, Mitchell 2, Potter 2, Rowe 2, Bradshaw 1, Jones 1, Middleton 1, Murphy S 1, Power 1, Wilder 1, own goal 1.
Worthington Cup (1): Gaughan 1.
FA Cup (3): Mitchell 1, Paterson 1, Tate 1.
Ground: The Shay Stadium, Shaw Hill, Halifax HX1 2YS. Telephone Halifax (01422) 345543.
Record attendance: 36,885 v Tottenham H, FA Cup 5th rd, 15 February 1953.
Capacity: 9,900.

Manager: Mark Lillis.
Secretary: Mike Riley.
Most League Goals: 83, Division 3 (N), 1957–58.
Highest League Scorer in Season: Albert Valentine, 34, Division 3 (N), 1934–35.
Most League Goals in Total Aggregate: Ernest Dixon, 129, 1922–30.
Most Capped Player: None.
Most League Appearances: John Pickering, 367, 1965–74.
Honours – Football League: Division 3 (N)—Runners-up 1934–35; Division 4: Runners-up 1968–69. **Vauxhall Conference:** Champions 1997–98.
Colours: Blue shirts, white trim, blue shorts, white trim, white stockings.

HARTLEPOOL UNITED — DIV. 3

Arnison Paul (D)	5 10	11 08	Hartlepool	18 9 77	Newcastle U
Barron Micky (D)	5 11	11 11	Lumley	22 12 74	Middlesbrough
Boyd Adam (F)	5 9	10 12	Hartlepool	25 5 82	Scholar
Fitzpatrick Lee (M)	5 10	11 02	Manchester	31 10 78	Blackburn R
Freestone Chris (F)	5 11	12 05	Nottingham	4 9 71	Northampton T
Henderson Kevin (F)	5 11	13 04	Ashington	8 6 74	Burnley
Hollund Martin (G)	6 2	12 09	Stord	11 8 74	Brann
Jones Gary (F)	6 1	12 08	Huddersfield	6 4 69	Notts Co
Knowles Darren (D)	5 6	11 02	Sheffield	8 10 70	Scarborough
Lee Graeme (D)	6 2	13 07	Middlesbrough	31 5 78	Trainee
McAvoy Andy (M)	6 0	13 06	Middlesbrough	28 8 79	Blackburn R
Midgley Craig (F)	5 7	11 03	Bradford	24 5 76	Bradford C
Miller Tommy (M)	6 1	12 01	Easington	8 1 79	Trainee
Robinson Mark (D)	5 9	11 00	Guisborough	24 7 81	Trainee
Shilton Sam (M)	5 11	11 06	Nottingham	21 7 78	Coventry C
Strodder Gary (D)	6 1	13 07	Cleckheaton	1 4 65	Notts Co
Tennebo Thomas (M)	6 2	12 00	Bergen	19 3 75	Fana
Westwood Chris (D)	5 11	12 03	Dudley	13 2 77	Wolverhampton W

League Appearances: Arnison, P. 5(3); Barron, M. 40; Beavers, P. 2(5); Boyd, A. (4); Clark, I. 34(10); Coppinger, J. 6(4); Di Lella, G. 3; Dibble, A. 6; Fitzpatrick, L. 16(8); Freestone, C. 15(12); Henderson, K. 23(12); Hollund, M. 40; Ingram, D. 6(1); Jones, G. 30(3); Knowles, D. 43(1); Lee, G. 38; Mason, G. 5(1); McAvoy, A. 5(11); Midgley, C. 2(15); Miller, T. 44; Perkins, C. 7(1); Shilton, S. 16(5); Stephenson, P. 46; Strodder, G. 28(1); Tennebo, T. 6(5); Vindheim, R. 7; West, C. (1); Westwood, C. 33(4).
Goals – League (60): Miller 14 (2 pens), Henderson 8, Lee 7, Clark 6 (1 pen), Jones 6, Stephenson 5, Freestone 4, Coppinger 3, Shilton 3, Fitzpatrick 2, Arnison 1, Boyd 1.
Worthington Cup (3): Di Lella 1, Miller 1, Stephenson 1.
FA Cup (1): Jones 1.
Ground: Victoria Park, Clarence Road, Hartlepool TS24 8BZ. Telephone (01429) 272584.
Record attendance: 17,426 v Manchester U, FA Cup 3rd rd, 5 January 1957. **Capacity:** 7229.
Manager: Chris Turner.
Secretary: Maureen Smith.
Most League Goals: 90, Division 3 (N), 1956–57.
Highest League Scorer in Season: William Robinson, 28, Division 3 (N), 1927–28; Joe Allon, 28, Division 4, 1990–91.
Most League Goals in Total Aggregate: Ken Johnson, 98, 1949–64.

Most Capped Player: Ambrose Fogarty, 1 (11), Republic of Ireland.
Most League Appearances: Wattie Moore, 447, 1948–64.
Honours – Nil.
Colours: Royal blue and white stripes.

HUDDERSFIELD TOWN — DIV. 1

Armstrong Craig (D)	5 11	12 10	South Shields	23 5 75	Nottingham F
Baldry Simon (M)	5 10	11 06	Huddersfield	12 2 76	Trainee
Beech Chris (M)	5 10	11 12	Blackpool	16 9 74	Hartlepool U
Beresford David (M)	5 7	10 06	Middleton	11 11 76	Oldham Ath
Brown Nathaniel (F)	6 2	12 05	Sheffield	15 6 81	Trainee
Donis George (F)	6 0	13 00	Greece	29 10 69	Sheffield U
Dyson Jon (D)	6 1	12 09	Mirfield	18 12 71	School
Edwards Rob (M)	5 9	12 04	Manchester	23 2 70	Crewe Alex
Facey Delroy (F)	6 0	13 00	Huddersfield	22 4 80	Trainee
Gorre Dean (M)	5 8	11 07	Surinam	10 9 70	Ajax
Gray Kevin (D)	6 0	14 00	Sheffield	7 1 72	Mansfield T
Hay Chris (F)	5 11	11 07	Glasgow	28 8 74	Swindon T
Holland Chris (M)	5 9	11 05	Whalley	11 9 75	Birmingham C
Irons Kenny (M)	5 10	11 02	Liverpool	4 11 70	Tranmere R
Jenkins Steve (D)	5 11	12 03	Merthyr	16 7 72	Swansea C
Lucketti Chris (D)	6 1	13 04	Littleborough	21 9 71	Bury
Margetson Martyn (G)	6 0	14 00	West Neath	8 9 71	Southend U
Mattis Dwayne (M)	5 10	11 00	Huddersfield	31 7 81	Trainee
Monkou Ken (D)	6 3	14 06	Surinam	29 11 64	Southampton
Muangsem Kiatisuk (M)			Thailand	11 8 76	
Richardson Lee J (M)	5 11	10 06	Halifax	12 3 69	Oldham Ath
Schofield Danny (F)	5 10	11 06	Doncaster	10 4 80	Brodsworth
Scott Paul (M)	5 11	12 00	Wakefield	5 11 79	Trainee
Sellars Scott (M)	5 7	9 10	Sheffield	27 11 65	Bolton W
Senior Michael (M)	5 9	11 06	Huddersfield	3 3 81	Trainee
Senior Philip (M)			Huddersfield	30 10 82	Trainee
Smith Martin (F)	5 11	12 00	Sunderland	13 11 74	Sheffield U
Thornley Ben (F)	5 9	11 08	Bury	21 4 75	Manchester U
Vaesen Nico (G)	6 1	13 08	Hasselt	28 9 69	Aalst
Vincent Jamie (D)	5 10	11 09	London	18 6 75	Bournemouth
Wijnhard Clyde (F)	5 10	13 04	Paramaribo	1 11 73	Leeds U

League Appearances: Allison, W. (3); Armstrong, A. 4(2); Armstrong, C. 37(2); Baker, S. 3; Baldry, S. 5(14); Beech, C. 34(1); Donis, G. 10(10); Dyson, J. 22(6); Edmondson, D. 2(3); Edwards, R. 1(8); Facey, D. (2); Gorre, D. 26(2); Gray, K. 16(2); Hay, C. 2(5); Heary, T. 1; Hodouto, K. 1(1); Holland, C. 16(1); Horne, B. 6(8); Irons, K. 39(1); Jenkins, S. 33; Lucketti, C. 26; May, D. 1; Monkou, K. 19; Ngonge, M. (4); Schofield, D. (2); Sellars, S. 23(11); Smith, M. 10(2); Stewart, M. 29; Thornley, B. 16(12); Vaesen, N. 46; Vincent, J. 33(3); Wijnhard, C. 45.
Goals – League (62): Wijnhard 15, Stewart 14 (2 pens), Beech 9, Gorre 4, Smith 4, Irons 3 (1 pen), Dyson 2, Gray 2, Vincent 2, Baldry 1, Edwards 1, Holland 1, Monkou 1, Sellars 1, Thornley 1, own goal 1.
Worthington Cup (8): Irons 2, Beech 1, Gorre 1, Lucketti 1, Sellars 1, Stewart 1, Wijnhard 1.
FA Cup (0).
Ground: The Alfred McAlpine Stadium, Leeds Road, Huddersfield HD1 6PX. Telephone (01484) 484100.

Record attendance: 67,037 v Arsenal, FA Cup 6th rd, 27 February 1932. **Capacity:** 25,000.
Manager: Steve Bruce.
Secretary: Ann Hough.
Most League Goals: 101, Division 4, 1979–80.
Highest League Scorer in Season: Sam Taylor, 35, Division 2, 1919–20; George Brown, 35, Division 1, 1925–26.
Most League Goals in Total Aggregate: George Brown, 142, 1921–29; Jimmy Glazzard, 142, 1946–56.
Most Capped Player: Jimmy Nicholson, 31 (41), Northern Ireland.
Most League Appearances: Billy Smith, 520, 1914–34.
Honours – Football League: Division 1 Champions – 1923–24, 1924–25, 1925–26. Division 2 Champions – 1969–70. Division 4 Champions – 1969–70. **FA Cup winners** 1922.
Colours: Blue and white striped shirts, white shorts, white stockings with blue trim.

HULL CITY — DIV. 3

Brabin Gary (M)	5 11	14 08	Liverpool	9 12 70	Blackpool
Bracey Lee (G)	6 2	13 02	Barking	11 9 68	Ipswich T
Brown David (F)	5 10	12 07	Bolton	2 10 78	Manchester U
Edwards Michael (D)	6 1	12 00	Hessle	25 4 80	Trainee
Eyre John (F)	6 0	12 06	Hull	9 10 74	Scunthorpe U
Goodison Ian (D)	6 1	12 06	St James, Jamaica	5 8 72	Olympic Gardens
Greaves Mark (D)	6 1	13 00	Hull	22 1 75	Brigg Town
Harper Steve (M)	5 10	11 12	Newcastle-under-Lyme	3 2 69	Mansfield T
Harris Jason (F)	6 1	11 07	Sutton	24 11 76	Preston NE
Joyce Warren (M)	5 9	12 00	Oldham	20 1 65	Burnley
Mann Neil (M)	5 10	12 01	Nottingham	19 11 72	Grantham T
Morley Ben (M)	5 9	10 01	Hull	22 12 80	Trainee
Perry Jason (D)	5 11	11 12	Newport	2 4 70	Lincoln C
Swales Steve (D)	5 8	10 06	Whitby	26 12 73	Reading
Whitmore Theodore (M)	6 2	12 10	Jamaica	21 11 72	Seba U
Whitney Jon (D)	5 10	13 08	Nantwich	23 12 70	Lincoln C
Whittle Justin (D)	6 1	12 12	Derby	18 3 71	Stoke C
Wilson Steve (G)	5 10	10 12	Hull	24 4 74	Trainee
Wood Jamie (F)	5 10	13 04	Salford	21 9 78	Manchester U

League Appearances: Alcide, C. 10(2); Baker, M. (2); Betsy, K. 1(1); Bolder, A. 18(1); Brabin, G. 37; Bracey, L. 10; Bradshaw, G. 5(7); Brown, D. 39(6); Bywater, S. 4; Culkin, N. 4; D'Auria, D. 10(2); Edwards, M. 36(4); Eyre, J. 24; Goodison, I. 17(1); Greaves, M. 38; Harper, S. 36(2); Harris, J. 18(11); Harrison, G. 3; Joyce, W. 19; Knight, R. 1; Mann, N. 2; Morgan, S. 17(2); Morley, B. (1); Perry, J. 1; Quigley, M. (3); Schofield, J. 13(12); Swales, S. 17(3); Whitmore, T. 17; Whitney, J. 19(2); Whittle, J. 38; Whitworth, N. (1); Williams, G. 12(1); Wilson, S. 27; Wood, J. 13(19).
Goals – League (43): Eyre 8 (2 pens), Brown 6, Wood 6, Harper 4, Harris 4, Brabin 3, Greaves 3, Whitmore 2, Alcide 1, Edwards 1, Joyce 1, Morgan 1, Whitney 1, Williams 1, own goal 1.
Worthington Cup (6): Alcide 2, Brown 2, Eyre 2 (1 pen).
FA Cup (10): Brown 3, Edwards 2, Eyre 2, Greaves 1, Wood 1, own goal 1.
Ground: Boothferry Park, Hull HU4 6EU. Telephone (01482) 575263.
Record attendance: 55,019 v Manchester U, FA Cup 6th rd, 26 February 1949. **Capacity:** 15,159.
Manager: Brian Little.

Assistant Secretary: Jackie Bell.
Most League Goals: 109, Division 3, 1965–66.
Highest League Scorer in Season: Bill McNaughton, 39, Division 3 (N), 1932–33.
Most League Goals in Total Aggregate: Chris Chilton, 195, 1960–71.
Most Capped Player: Terry Neill, 15 (59), Northern Ireland.
Most League Appearances: Andy Davidson, 520, 1952–67.
Honours – Football League: Division 3 (N) Champions – 1932–33, 1948–49. Division 3 Champions – 1965–66.
Colours: Amber shirts, black and white trim, black shorts, black stockings with amber turnovers.

IPSWICH TOWN — FA PREMIERSHIP

Artun Erdem (D)			London	11 11 82	Trainee
Bramble Titus (D)	6 1	13 10	Ipswich	21 7 81	Trainee
Brown Wayne (D)	6 0	12 00	Barking	20 8 77	Trainee
Clapham Jamie (D)	5 9	11 08	Lincoln	7 12 75	Tottenham H
Croft Gary (D)	5 8	10 08	Stafford	17 2 74	Blackburn R
Daly Colm (M)			Dublin	4 1 82	
Friars Sean (M)	5 8	10 07	Derry	15 5 79	Liverpool
Holland Matt (M)	5 10	11 10	Bury	11 4 74	Bournemouth
Johnson David (F)	5 6	12 00	Kingston, Jam	15 8 76	Bury
Logan Richard (F)	6 0	12 00	Bury St Edmunds	4 1 82	Trainee
Magilton Jim (M)	6 0	14 13	Belfast	6 5 69	Sheffield W
McGreal John (D)	5 11	11 00	Birkenhead	2 6 72	Tranmere R
Midgley Neil (F)	5 11	11 08	Cambridge	21 10 78	Trainee
Miller Justin (D)	6 0	11 07	Johannesburg	16 12 80	Academy
Naylor Richard (F)	6 0	13 07	Leeds	28 2 77	Trainee
Niven Stuart (M)	5 11	12 08	Glasgow	24 12 78	Trainee
Pullen James (G)	6 2	14 00	Chelmsford	18 3 82	Heybridge S
Salmon Mike (G)	6 2	14 00	Leyland	14 7 64	Charlton Ath
Scowcroft James (F)	6 2	14 02	Bury St Edmunds	15 11 75	Trainee
Stewart Marcus (F)	5 10	10 06	Bristol	7 11 72	Huddersfield T
Thetis Manuel (D)	6 3	14 13	France	5 11 71	Sevilla
Venus Mark (D)	6 1	12 12	Hartlepool	6 4 67	Wolverhampton W
Wilnis Fabian (D)	5 8	12 06	Paramaribo	23 8 70	De Graafschap
Wright Jermaine (M)	5 10	11 09	Greenwich	21 10 75	Crewe Alex
Wright Richard (G)	6 2	13 02	Ipswich	5 11 77	Trainee

League Appearances: Axeldal, J. 1(15); Brown, W. 20(5); Clapham, J. 44(2); Clegg, M. 3; Croft, G. 14(7); Friars, S. (1); Holland, M. 46; Johnson, D. 44; Logan, R. (1); Magilton, J. 33(5); McGreal, J. 34; Midgley, N. 1(3); Mowbray, T. 35(1); Naylor, R. 19(17); Reuser, M. 2(6); Scowcroft, J. 40(1); Stewart, M. 9(1); Stockwell, M. 21(14); Thetis, M. 15(1); Venus, M. 28; Wilnis, F. 30(5); Wright, J. 21(13); Wright, R. 46.
Goals – League (71): Johnson 22 (1 pen), Scowcroft 13, Holland 10, Naylor 8, Magilton 4 (1 pen), Clapham 2, Reuser 2, Stewart 2, Stockwell 2, Venus 2, Croft 1, Midgley 1, Mowbray 1, Wright J 1.
Worthington Cup (6): Clapham 2, Scowcroft 2, Johnson 1, Venus 1.
FA Cup (0).
Ground: Portman Road, Ipswich, Suffolk IP1 2DA. Telephone (01473) 400500.
Record attendance: 38,010 v Leeds U, FA Cup 6th rd, 8 March 1975.
Capacity: 22,700.
Manager: George Burley.
Secretary: David C. Rose.

Most League Goals: 106, Division 3 (S), 1955–56.
Highest League Scorer in Season: Ted Phillips, 41, Division 3 (S), 1956–57.
Most League Goals in Total Aggregate: Ray Crawford, 203, 1958–63 and 1966–69.
Most Capped Player: Allan Hunter, 47 (53), Northern Ireland.
Most League Appearances: Mick Mills, 591, 1966–82.
Honours – Football League: Division 1 Champions – 1961–62. Division 2 Champions – 1960–61, 1967–68, 1991–92. Division 3 (S) Champions – 1953–54, 1956–57. **FA Cup:** Winners 1977–78. **European Competitions: UEFA Cup winners:** 1980–81.
Colours: Blue shirts, white shorts, blue stockings.

KIDDERMINSTER HARRIERS — DIV. 3

Conference Appearances: Barnett, G. 4(5); Bennett, D. 35(4); Brock, S. 11(1); Brownrigg, A. 16(5); Burgess, R. (3); Clarke, T. 29(1); Clarkson, I. 27(1); Collins, J. 5; Cunnington, S. 5(3); Davies, B. (1); Druce, M. 15(7); Foster, I. 34(3); Hadley, S. 26(12); Hines, L. 6(5); Hinton, C. 38(3); King, P. 7(7); Marsh, M. 23(1); Midgley, N. 4(1); Petersen, R. 16(2); Pope, S. 15(6); Skovbjerg, T. 30(1); Smith, A. 42; Stamps, S. 34(1); Taylor, S. 4(7); Webb, P. 33(2); Weir, M. 1; Williams, L. 2.
Goals – League (75): Foster 17 (5 pens), Hadley 12, Bennett 10, Druce 7, Marsh 4, Skovbjerg 4, Brownrigg 3, Hinton 3, Petersen 3 (1 pen), Barnett 2, King 2, Midgley 2, Stamps 2, Smith 1, Taylor 1, Webb 1, own goal 1.
FA Cup (0).
Trophy (2): Clarkson 1, Pope 1.
NM Trophy (0).
Ground: Aggborough Stadium, Hoo Road, Kidderminster DY10 1NB. Telephone (01562) 823 931.
Record attendance: 9,155 v Hereford U, 27 November 1948.
Capacity: 6,293 (1,100 seated).
Manager: Jan Molby.
Football Secretary: Roger Barlow.
Most League Goals: 98, Division 2, 1927–28.
Honours – Conference: Champions 1993–94, 1999–2000; Runners-up 1996–97. **FA Trophy:** 1986–87 (winners); 1990–91 (runners-up), 1994–95 (runners-up). **League Cup:** 1996–97 (winners). **Welsh FA Cup:** 1985–86 (runners-up), 1988–89 (runners-up). **Southern League Cup:** 1979–80 (winners). **Worcester Senior Cup:** (21). **Birmingham Senior Cup:** (7). **Staffordshire Senior Cup:** (4). **West Midland League Champions:** (6), Runners-up (3). **Southern Premier:** Runners-up (1). **West Midland League Cup:** Winners (7). **Keys Cup:** Winners (7). **Border Counties Floodlit League Champions:** (3). **Camkin Floodlit Cup:** Winners (3). **Bass County Vase:** Winners (1). **Conference Fair Play Trophy:** (5)
Colours: Red shirts with white flash, red shorts and stockings with white trim.

LEEDS UNITED — FA PREMIERSHIP

Allaway Shaun (M)			Reading	16 2 83	Trainee
Bakke Eirik (M)	6 1	13 11	Sogndal	13 9 77	Sogndal
Batty David (M)	5 8	11 10	Leeds	2 12 68	Newcastle U
Bowyer Lee (M)	5 9	10 09	London	3 1 77	Charlton Ath
Boyle Wes (F)	5 10	11 01	Portadown	30 3 79	Trainee
Bridges Michael (F)	6 1	11 00	North Shields	5 8 78	Sunderland

Cansdell-Sheriff Shane (M)	6 0	12 00	Sydney	10 11 82	NSW Academy
Cawley Alan (M)	6 2	10 01	Sligo	3 1 82	Belvedere
Cramer Martin (M)	5 4	10 01	Dublin	15 11 82	Maryland Boys
Dixon Kevin (M)	5 9	12 03	Easington	27 6 80	Trainee
Duberry Michael (D)	6 1	14 00	Enfield	14 10 75	Chelsea
Evans Gareth (D)	6 0	11 11	Leeds	15 2 81	Trainee
Evans Kevin (D)	6 2	12 10	Carmarthen	16 12 80	Trainee
Farrell Craig (F)	5 11	12 00	Middlesbrough	5 12 82	Trainee
Feeney Warren (F)	5 10	11 00	Belfast	17 1 81	Trainee
Ferguson Steven (M)	5 6	9 03	Newry	25 2 83	St Andrew's
Folan Caleb (F)	6 1	12 00	Leeds	26 10 82	Trainee
Haaland Alf-Inge (M)	6 1	12 06	Stavanger	23 11 72	Nottingham F
Hackworth Tony (F)	6 1	13 07	Durham	19 5 80	Trainee
Harte Ian (D)	6 0	12 04	Drogheda	31 8 77	Trainee
Hay Danny (D)	6 4	14 11	Auckland	15 5 75	Perth Glory
Hiden Martin (D)	6 1	12 00	Stainz	11 3 73	Rapid Vienna
Hopkin David (M)	6 1	13 13	Greenock	21 8 70	Crystal Palace
Huckerby Darren (F)	5 11	11 04	Nottingham	23 4 76	Coventry C
Jones Matthew (M)	5 11	11 09	Llanelli	1 9 80	Trainee
Kelly Gary (D)	5 8	11 00	Drogheda	9 7 74	Home Farm
Kewell Harry (F)	6 0	12 10	Sydney	22 9 78	NSW Academy
Lanns Jason (D)	5 8	10 07	Birmingham	2 11 81	Birmingham C
Lennon Anthony (F)	5 9	10 08	Leeds	16 5 82	Trainee
Lynch Damien (D)	5 10	11 00	Dublin	31 7 79	
Martin Alan (D)	5 10	11 05	Dublin	21 11 81	Trainee
Martyn Nigel (G)	6 2	14 10	St Austell	11 8 66	Crystal Palace
Matthews Lee (F)	6 2	13 05	Middlesbrough	6 1 79	Trainee
Maybury Alan (D)	5 9	10 04	Dublin	8 8 78	Trainee
McCargo Gerard (F)	5 4	9 02	Belfast	3 11 82	Celtic (Belfast) Boy
McMaster Jamie (M)	5 10	11 12	Sydney	29 11 82	NSW Academy
McPhail Stephen (M)	5 10	11 06	London	9 12 79	Trainee
Mills Danny (D)	5 11	11 09	Norwich	18 5 77	Charlton Ath
Milosevic Dejan (G)	6 3	14 12	Carlton	26 6 78	Perth Glory
Molenaar Robert (D)	6 2	14 09	Zaandam	27 2 69	Volendam
Radebe Lucas (D)	6 1	12 04	Johannesburg	12 4 69	Kaiser Chiefs
Richardson Frazer (D)	5 11	11 08	Rotherham	29 10 82	Trainee
Robinson Paul (G)	6 4	14 04	Beverley	15 10 79	Trainee
Singh Harpal (F)	5 7	10 02	Bradford	15 9 81	Trainee
Smith Alan (F)	5 9	10 13	Leeds	28 10 80	Trainee
Watson Simon (M)	5 9	10 00	Strabane	22 9 80	Trainee
Wilcox Jason (F)	6 0	11 00	Bolton	15 7 71	Blackburn R
Woodgate Jonathan (D)	6 2	12 09	Middlesbrough	22 1 80	Trainee

League Appearances: Bakke, E. 24(5); Batty, D. 16; Bowyer, L. 31(2); Bridges, M. 32(2); Duberry, M. 12(1); Haaland, A. 7(6); Harte, I. 33; Hiden, M. (1); Hopkin, D. 10(4); Huckerby, D. 9(24); Jones, M. 5(6); Kelly, G. 28(3); Kewell, H. 36; Martyn, N. 38; McPhail, S. 23(1); Mills, D. 16(1); Radebe, L. 31; Smith, A. 20(6); Wilcox, J. 15(5); Woodgate, J. 32(2).
Goals – League (58): Bridges 19, Kewell 10, Harte 6 (4 pens), Bowyer 5, Smith 4, Wilcox 3, Bakke 2, Huckerby 2, McPhail 2, Duberry 1, Hopkin 1, Mills 1, Woodgate 1, own goal 1.
Worthington Cup (1): Mills 1.
FA Cup (9): Bakke 4, Kewell 2, Bowyer 1, Harte 1, Smith 1.
Ground: Elland Road, Leeds LS11 0ES. Telephone (0113) 2266000.
Record attendance: 57,892 v Sunderland, FA Cup 5th rd (replay), 15 March 1967.
Capacity: 40,204.
Manager: David O'Leary.

Secretary: Ian Silvester.
Most League Goals: 98, Division 2, 1927–28.
Highest League Scorer in Season: John Charles, 42, Division 2, 1953–54.
Most League Goals in Total Aggregate: Peter Lorimer, 168, 1965–79 and 1983–86.
Most Capped Player: Billy Bremner, 54, Scotland.
Most League Appearances: Jack Charlton, 629, 1953–73.
Honours – Football League: Division 1 Champions – 1968–69, 1973–74, 1991–92. Division 2 Champions – 1923–24, 1963–64, 1989–90. **FA Cup:** Winners 1972. **Football League Cup:** Winners 1967–68. **European Competitions: European Fairs Cup winners:** 1967–68, 1970–71.
Colours: All white, yellow and blue trim.

LEICESTER CITY — FA PREMIERSHIP

Arphexad Pegguy (G)	6 2	13 13	Abymes	18 5 73	Lens
Boateng Danny (F)	5 10	12 07	London	14 11 80	Arsenal
Campbell Stuart (M)	5 10	10 13	Corby	9 12 77	Trainee
Collymore Stan (F)	6 3	13 10	Cannock	22 1 71	Aston Villa
Cottee Tony (F)	5 10	12 06	West Ham	11 7 65	West Ham U
Dudfield Lawrie (F)	6 0	12 04	London	7 5 80	Kettering T
Eadie Darren (F)	5 7	10 09	Chippenham	10 6 75	Norwich C
Elliott Matt (D)	6 3	15 00	Roehampton	1 11 68	Oxford U
Flowers Tim (G)	6 2	14 00	Kenilworth	3 2 67	Blackburn R
Gilchrist Phil (D)	6 0	13 03	Stockton	25 8 73	Oxford U
Goodwin Tommy (D)	6 0	12 07	Leicester	8 11 79	Trainee
Gunnlaugsson Arnar (F)	5 10	11 06	Akranes	6 3 73	Bolton W
Guppy Steve (M)	5 11	11 11	Winchester	29 3 69	Port Vale
Impey Andrew (M)	5 8	11 06	Hammersmith	13 9 71	West Ham U
Izzet Muzzy (M)	5 10	11 02	Hackney	31 10 74	Chelsea
Lennon Neil (M)	5 9	13 02	Belfast	25 6 71	Crewe Alex
McCann Tim (M)	5 9	12 00	Belfast	22 3 80	Trainee
Mortimer Alex (D)	5 10	10 06	Manchester	28 11 82	Trainee
Oakes Stefan (M)	5 11	12 08	Leicester	6 9 78	Trainee
Piper Matthew (M)	6 1	13 02	Leicester	29 9 81	Trainee
Savage Robbie (M)	5 11	11 01	Wrexham	18 10 74	Crewe Alex
Sinclair Frank (D)	5 10	12 03	Lambeth	3 12 71	Chelsea
Stewart Jordan (M)	6 0	12 04	Birmingham	3 3 82	Trainee
Taggart Gerry (D)	6 2	14 01	Belfast	18 10 70	Bolton W
Thomas Danny (D)	5 7	10 10	Leamington Spa	1 5 81	Trainee
Walsh Steve (D)	6 3	15 02	Fulwood	3 11 64	Wigan Ath
Wilson Stuart (F)	5 8	10 03	Leicester	16 9 77	Trainee

League Appearances: Arphexad, P. 9(2); Campbell, S. 1(3); Collymore, S. 6; Cottee, T. 30(3); Dudfield, L. (2); Eadie, D. 15(1); Elliott, M. 37; Fenton, G. 1(1); Flowers, T. 29; Gilchrist, P. 17(10); Goodwin, T. 1; Gunnlaugsson, A. 2; Guppy, S. 29(1); Heskey, E. 23; Impey, A. 28(1); Izzet, M. 32; Lennon, N. 31; Marshall, I. 2(19); Oakes, S. 15(7); Savage, R. 35; Sinclair, F. 34; Stewart, J. (1); Taggart, G. 30(1); Thomas, D. (3); Walsh, S. 5(6); Zagorakis, T. 6(11).
Goals – League (55): Cottee 13, Izzet 8 (3 pens), Heskey 7, Elliott 6, Taggart 6, Collymore 4, Guppy 2, Gilchrist 1, Impey 1, Lennon 1, Oakes 1, Savage 1, Zagorakis 1, own goals 3.
Worthington Cup (15): Elliott 3, Marshall 3, Oakes 2 (1 pen), Fenton 1, Heskey 1, Izzet 1, Lennon 1, Taggart 1, Walsh 1, own goal 1.
FA Cup (3): Elliott 2, Izzet 1.
Ground: City Stadium, Filbert St, Leicester LE2 7FL. Telephone (0116) 2915000.

Record attendance: 47,298 v Tottenham H, FA Cup 5th rd, 18 February 1928.
Capacity: 22,215.
Manager: Peter Taylor.
Football Secretary: Andrew Neville.
Most League Goals: 109, Division 2, 1956–57.
Highest League Scorer in Season: Arthur Rowley, 44, Division 2, 1956–57.
Most League Goals in Total Aggregate: Arthur Chandler, 259, 1923–35.
Most Capped Player: John O'Neill, 39, Northern Ireland.
Most League Appearances: Adam Black, 528, 1920–35.
Honours – Football League: Division 2 Champions – 1924–25, 1936–37, 1953–54, 1956–57, 1970–71, 1979–80. **Football League Cup:** Winners 1964, 1997, 2000.
Colours: Royal blue shirts, white shorts, blue stockings.

LEYTON ORIENT — DIV. 3

Barrett Scott (G)	5 11	13 00	Ilkeston	2 4 63	Cambridge U
Bayes Ashley (G)	6 1	13 05	Lincoln	19 4 72	Exeter C
Beall Billy (M)	5 6	12 00	Enfield	4 12 77	Cambridge U
Christie Iyseden (F)	5 10	12 02	Coventry	14 11 76	Mansfield T
Downer Simon (D)	5 11	12 08	Romford	19 10 81	Trainee
Griffiths Carl (F)	5 9	11 04	Welshpool	15 7 71	Port Vale
Harris Andy (D)	5 10	12 02	Springs	26 2 77	Southend U
Inglethorpe Alex (F)	5 11	11 04	Epsom	14 11 71	Watford
Lockwood Matt (D)	5 9	10 12	Rochford	17 10 76	Bristol R
Martin John (M)	5 5	10 00	Bethnal Green	15 7 81	Trainee
McGhee Dave (D)	6 0	12 01	Worthing	19 6 76	Brentford
Richards Tony (F)	6 0	13 06	Newham	17 9 73	Cambridge U
Shorey Nicky (D)	5 9	10 08	Romford	19 2 81	Trainee
Smith Dean (D)	6 0	13 00	West Bromwich	19 3 71	Hereford U
Uka Niam (M)	5 7	10 01	Kosovo	26 10 81	Partizani
Walschaerts Wim (M)	5 11	12 00	Antwerp	5 11 72	FC Tielen
Watts Steve (F)	6 1	13 00	Peckham	11 7 76	Fisher Ath

League Appearances: Ampadu, K. 43; Barrett, S. 29; Bayes, A. 17; Beall, B. 22(11); Brkovic, A. 25(4); Canham, S. 1; Carter, R. (2); Christie, I. 22(14); Clark, S. 19; Downer, S. 24; Gough, N. 1(3); Gould, R. (2); Griffiths, C. 11; Harris, A. 11(4); Hicks, S. 13(1); Hockton, D. 1(4); Holligan, G. 1; Ibehre, J. (3); Inglethorpe, A. 12(4); Joseph, M. 38(3); Joseph, R. (1); Ling, M. 14; Lockwood, M. 41; Low, J. 2(3); Martin, J. 8; McElholm, B. 3; McGhee, D. 17(6); McLean, A. (3); Morrison, D. 5(8); Murray, J. (2); Parsons, D. 1; Richards, T. 9(8); Rowbotham, D. 4(2); Shorey, N. 4(3); Simba, A. 8(5); Smith, D. 44; Walschaerts, W. 32(4); Watts, S. 21(11); Webb, S. 3(1).
Goals – League (47): Christie 7, Lockwood 6 (2 pens), Watts 6, Brkovic 5, Griffiths 4 (2 pens), Smith 4, Simba 3, Walschaerts 3, Inglethorpe 2, Richards 2, Beall 1, Clark 1, Ling 1, Low 1, McGhee 1.
Worthington Cup (4): Lockwood 2 (1 pen), Inglethorpe 1, Watts 1.
FA Cup (2): Ampadu 1, Smith 1.
Ground: Leyton Stadium, Brisbane Road, Leyton, London E10 5NE. Telephone (020) 8926 1111.
Record attendance: 34,345 v West Ham U, FA Cup 4th rd, 25 January 1964.
Capacity: 13,842.
Manager: Tommy Taylor.
Secretary: Frank Woolf.
Most League Goals: 106, Division 3 (S), 1955–56.
Highest League Scorer in Season: Tom Johnston, 35, Division 2, 1957–58.

Most League Goals in Total Aggregate: Tom Johnston, 121, 1956–58, 1959–61.
Most Capped Players: Tunji Banjo, 7 (7), Nigeria; John Chiedozie, 7 (9), Nigeria; Tony Grealish, 7 (45), Eire.
Most League Appearances: Peter Allen, 432, 1965–78.
Honours – Football League: Division 3 Champions – 1969–70. Division 3 (S) Champions – 1955–56.
Colours: White shirts with red V, black shorts, red stockings.

LINCOLN CITY — DIV. 3

Barnett Dave (D)	6 0	12 08	Birmingham	16 4 67	Port Vale
Barnett Jason (D)	5 9	10 10	Shrewsbury	21 4 76	Wolverhampton W
Battersby Tony (F)	6 0	12 09	Doncaster	30 8 75	Bury
Bimson Stuart (D)	5 11	11 08	Liverpool	29 9 69	Bury
Brown Grant (D)	6 0	11 12	Sunderland	19 11 69	Leicester C
Finnigan John (M)	5 8	10 11	Wakefield	29 3 76	Nottingham F
Gain Peter (M)	5 9	11 00	Hammersmith	2 11 76	Tottenham H
Gordon Gavin (F)	6 2	12 00	Manchester	24 6 79	Hull C
Henry Anthony (D)	6 0	13 00	London	13 9 79	West Ham U
Holmes Steve (D)	6 2	13 00	Middlesbrough	13 1 71	Preston NE
Marriott Alan (G)	5 11	12 05	Bedford	3 9 78	Tottenham H
Mayo Paul (D)	5 11	11 09	Lincoln	13 10 81	Scholar
Miller Paul (M)	6 0	11 07	Bisley	31 1 68	Bristol R
Peacock Richard (M)	6 1	11 05	Sheffield	29 10 72	Hull C
Smith Paul (M)	5 11	11 07	Hastings	25 1 76	Nottingham F
Thorpe Lee (F)	6 0	11 06	Wolverhampton	14 12 75	Blackpool
Welsh Steve (D)	6 0	12 03	Glasgow	19 4 68	Ayr U

League Appearances: Agogo, M. 3; Barnett, D. 20(2); Barnett, J. 17(1); Battersby, T. 7(9); Bimson, S. 15(5); Branston, G. 4; Brown, G. 25(1); Finnigan, J. 36(1); Fleming, T. 41; Gain, P. 20(12); Galloway, M. 5; Gordon, G. 39(2); Henry, A. 14(3); Holmes, S. 9; Lescott, A. 3(2); Lewis, G. 3(2); Marriott, A. 18; Mayo, P. 19; Miller, P. 37(3); Peacock, R. 16(8); Phillips, D. 6(2); Philpott, L. 18(5); Poppleton, D. 4(1); Richardson, B. 22; Smith, P. 23(4); Stant, P. 3(15); Stones, C. (3); Thorpe, L. 38(4); Vaughan, J. 6; Welsh, S. 32; Wilkins, I. 3(1).
Goals – League (67): Thorpe 16, Gordon 11, Miller 7, Fleming 5 (4 pens), Smith 5, Barnett D 3, Battersby 3 (1 pen), Peacock 3, Philpott 3, Stant 3, Finnigan 2, Gain 2, Holmes 2, Agogo 1, Henry 1.
Worthington Cup (4): Fleming 1, Gordon 1, Peacock 1, Thorpe 1.
FA Cup (3): Barnett D 1, Gordon 1, Smith 1.
Ground: Sincil Bank, Lincoln LN5 8LD. Telephone (01522) 880011.
Record attendance: 23,196 v Derby Co, League Cup 4th rd, 15 November 1967.
Capacity: 11,729.
Manager: Phil Stant.
Secretary: F. J. Martin.
Most League Goals: 121, Division 3 (N), 1951–52.
Highest League Scorer in Season: Allan Hall, 42, Division 3 (N), 1931–32.
Most League Goals in Total Aggregate: Andy Graver, 144, 1950–55 and 1958–61.
Most Capped Player: David Pugh, 3 (7), Wales; George Moulson, 3, Republic of Ireland.
Most League Appearances: Tony Emery, 402, 1946–59.
Honours – Football League: Division 3 (N) Champions – 1931–32, 1947–48, 1951–52. Division 4 Champions – 1975–76.
Colours: Red and white striped shirts, black shorts, black stockings.

Armstrong Ian (F)			Fazackerley	16 11 81	Trainee
Berger Patrik (M)	6 1	12 06	Prague	10 11 73	Borussia Dortmund
Camara Titi (F)	6 0	13 00	Donka	17 11 72	Marseille
Carragher Jamie (M)	6 1	13 00	Liverpool	28 1 78	Trainee
Doherty Kevin (M)			Dublin	18 4 80	
Foley-Sheridan Michael (M)			Dublin	9 3 83	
Fowler Robbie (F)	5 11	11 10	Liverpool	9 4 75	Trainee
Friedel Brad (G)	6 3	14 00	Lakewood	18 5 71	Columbus Crew
Gerrard Steven (M)	6 1	13 00	Whiston	30 5 80	Trainee
Gudnason Haukar (F)	5 10	12 00	Keflavik	8 9 78	Keflavik
Hamann Dietmar (M)	6 2	12 06	Waldasson	27 8 73	Newcastle U
Heggem Vegard (D)	5 11	12 00	Trondheim	13 7 75	Rosenborg
Henchoz Stephane (D)	6 1	12 08	Billens	7 9 74	Blackburn R
Heskey Emile (F)	6 2	14 03	Leicester	11 1 78	Leicester C
Hyypia Sami (D)	6 4	14 00	Porvoo	7 10 73	Willem II
Kippe Frode (D)	6 4	14 10	Oslo	17 1 78	Lillestrom
Matteo Dominic (D)	6 1	11 10	Dumfries	24 4 74	Trainee
Maxwell Leyton (M)	5 8	11 00	St Asaph	3 10 79	Trainee
Meijer Erik (F)	6 2	13 05	Meersen	2 8 69	Leverkusen
Miles John (F)			Fazackerley	28 9 81	Trainee
Murphy Danny (M)	5 9	10 08	Chester	18 3 77	Crewe Alex
Navarro Alan (D)			Liverpool	31 5 81	Trainee
Newby Jon (F)	6 0	12 00	Warrington	28 11 78	Trainee
O'Brien Chris (M)			Liverpool	13 1 82	Trainee
Otsemobor John (D)			Liverpool	23 3 83	Trainee
Owen Michael (F)	5 8	11 00	Chester	14 12 79	Trainee
Partridge Richie (M)	5 8	10 10	Dublin	12 9 80	Trainee
Redknapp Jamie (M)	6 0	12 10	Barton-on-Sea	25 6 73	Bournemouth
Smicer Vladimir (M)	5 10	11 10	Degin	24 5 73	Lens
Song Rigobert (D)	6 0	13 00	Nkenlicock	1 7 76	Salernitana
Staunton Steve (D)	6 1	12 11	Drogheda	19 1 69	Aston Villa
Thompson David (M)	5 7	10 00	Birkenhead	12 9 77	Trainee
Torpey Steve (M)			Fazackerley	16 9 81	Trainee
Traore Djimi (D)	6 3	13 10	Saint Ouen	1 3 80	Laval
Warnock Stephen (M)			Ormskirk	12 12 81	Trainee
Westerveld Sander (G)	6 4	14 00	Enschede	23 10 74	Vitesse
Wright Stephen (D)	6 0	12 00	Liverpool	8 2 80	Trainee

League Appearances: Berger, P. 34; Camara, T. 22(11); Carragher, J. 33(3); Fowler, R. 8(6); Friedel, B. 2; Gerrard, S. 26(3); Hamann, D. 27(1); Heggem, V. 10(12); Henchoz, S. 29; Heskey, E. 12; Hyypia, S. 38; Matteo, D. 32; Meijer, E. 7(14); Murphy, D. 9(14); Newby, J. (1); Owen, M. 22(5); Redknapp, J. 18(4); Riedle, K. (1); Smicer, V. 13(8); Song, R. 14(4); Staunton, S. 7(5); Thompson, D. 19(8); Westerveld, S. 36.
Goals – League (51): Owen 11 (1 pen), Berger 9 (1 pen), Camara 9, Fowler 3, Heskey 3, Murphy 3, Redknapp 3 (1 pen), Thompson 3, Hyypia 2, Gerrard 1, Hamann 1, Heggem 1, Smicer 1, own goal 1.
Worthington Cup (10): Murphy 3, Meijer 2, Riedle 2, Maxwell 1, Owen 1, Staunton 1.
FA Cup (2): Camara 1, Matteo 1.
Ground: Anfield Road, Liverpool L4 0TH. Telephone (0151) 263 2361.
Record attendance: 61,905 v Wolverhampton W, FA Cup 4th rd, 2 February 1952.
Capacity: 45,362.
Manager: Gerard Houllier.

Secretary: Bryce Morrison.
Most League Goals: 106, Division 2, 1895–96.
Highest League Scorer in Season: Roger Hunt, 41, Division 2, 1961–62.
Most League Goals in Total Aggregate: Roger Hunt, 245, 1959–69.
Most Capped Player: Ian Rush, 67 (73), Wales.
Most League Appearances: Ian Callaghan, 640, 1960–78.
Honours – Football League: Division 1 – Champions 1900–01, 1905–06, 1921–22, 1922–23, 1946–47, 1963–64, 1965–66, 1972–73, 1975–76, 1976–77, 1978–79, 1979–80, 1981–82, 1982–83, 1983–84, 1985–86, 1987–88, 1989–90 (Liverpool have a record number of 18 **League** Championship wins). Division 2 Champions – 1893–94, 1895–96, 1904–05, 1961–62. **FA Cup**: Winners 1965, 1974, 1986, 1989, 1992. League **Cup:** Winners 1981, 1982, 1983, 1984, 1995. Super Cup: Winners 1985–86. **European Competitions: European Cup winners:** 1976–77, 1977–78, 1980–81, 1983–84. **UEFA Cup winners:** 1972–73, 1975–76. **Super Cup winners:** 1977.
Colours: All red.

LUTON TOWN — DIV. 2

Ayres James (D)	6 3	13 00	Luton	18 9 80	Trainee
Boyce Emmerson (D)	5 11	11 02	Aylesbury	24 9 79	Trainee
Douglas Stuart (F)	5 8	11 05	London	9 4 78	Trainee
Fotiadis Andrew (F)	5 11	11 07	Hitchin	6 9 77	School
Fraser Stuart (D)	5 9	10 06	Edinburgh	9 1 80	Trainee
George Liam (F)	5 9	11 04	Luton	2 2 79	Trainee
Locke Adam (M)	5 11	12 07	Croydon	20 8 70	Bristol C
McGowan Gavin (D)	5 10	12 06	Blackheath	16 1 76	Arsenal
McLaren Paul (M)	6 1	13 00	High Wycombe	17 11 76	Trainee
Scarlett Andre (M)	5 4	9 12	Brent	11 1 80	Trainee
Spring Matthew (M)	5 11	11 07	Harlow	17 11 79	Trainee
Standen Dean (M)			Lewisham	23 3 82	Welling U
Stirling Jude (D)	6 2	11 12	Enfield	29 6 82	Trainee
Taylor Matthew (D)	5 10	11 08	Oxford	27 11 81	Trainee
Ward Scott (G)	6 2	13 00	Brent	5 10 81	Trainee
Watts Julian (D)	6 2	13 06	Sheffield	17 3 71	Bristol C

League Appearances: Abbey, N. 32(1); Boyce, E. 23(7); Doherty, G. 40; Douglas, S. 35(5); Fotiadis, A. 8(15); Fraser, S. 20; George, L. 35(7); Gray, P. 28(1); Johnson, M. 44; Kandol, T. 1(3); Locke, A. 27(7); McGowan, G. 10(3); McIndoe, M. 2(15); McKinnon, R. (3); McLaren, P. 25(4); Midgley, N. 8(2); Roberts, B. 14; Scarlett, A. 2(1); Sodje, E. 5(4); Spring, M. 44(1); Taylor, M. 39(2); Thorpe, T. 3(1); Watts, J. 45; White, A. 16(3); Zahana-Oni, L. (1).
Goals – League (61): George 13 (1 pen), Gray 11, Doherty 6, Spring 6 (1 pen), Taylor 4, Watts 4, Douglas 3, Locke 3, Midgley 3, Fotiadis 2, Boyce 1, Fraser 1, McLaren 1, Thorpe 1, White 1, own goal 1.
Worthington Cup (2): Doherty 1, Kandol 1.
FA Cup (9): Doherty 2, George 2, Spring 2, Douglas 1, Gray 1, Taylor 1.
Ground: Kenilworth Road Stadium, 1 Maple Rd, Luton, Beds. LU4 8AW. Telephone (01582) 411622.
Record attendance: 30,069 v Blackpool, FA Cup 6th rd replay, 4 March 1959.
Capacity: 9975.
Manager: Ricky Hill.
Secretary: Cherry Newbery.
Most League Goals: 103, Division 3 (S), 1936–37.
Highest League Scorer in Season: Joe Payne, 55, Division 3 (S), 1936–37.
Most League Goals in Total Aggregate: Gordon Turner, 243, 1949–64.
Most Capped Player: Mal Donaghy, 58 (91), Northern Ireland.

Most League Appearances: Bob Morton, 494, 1948–64.
Honours – Football League: Division 2 Champions – 1981–82. Division 4 Champions – 1967–68. Division 3 (S) Champions – 1936–37. **Football League Cup winners** 1987–88.
Colours: Orange shirts with blue side panels and blue and white knitted colar, blue shorts with orange and white stripe, blue stockings with orange stripes.

MACCLESFIELD TOWN — DIV. 3

Abbey George (D)	5 8	10 08	Port Harcourt	20 10 78	Sharks
Askey John (F)	6 0	12 02	Stoke	4 11 64	Port Vale
Bamber Michael (M)	5 7	10 02	Preston	1 10 80	Blackpool
Barker Richard (F)	6 1	13 12	Sheffield	30 5 75	Brighton & HA
Collins Simon (D)	6 0	13 00	Pontefract	16 12 73	Plymouth Arg
Durkan Kieron (M)	5 10	12 09	Chester	1 12 73	Stockport Co
Hitchen Steve (D)	5 8	11 07	Salford	28 11 76	Blackburn R
Ingram Rae (D)	5 11	12 09	Manchester	6 12 74	Manchester C
Martin Lee (G)	6 0	13 07	Huddersfield	9 9 68	Halifax T
Priest Chris (M)	5 10	12 00	Leigh	18 10 73	Chester C
Rioch Greg (D)	5 10	12 08	Sutton Coldfield	24 6 75	Hull C
Sedgemore Ben (M)	6 0	12 07	Wolverhampton	5 8 75	Mansfield T
Tinson Darren (D)	6 0	13 07	Birmingham	15 11 69	Northwich V
Tomlinson Graeme (F)	5 10	12 00	Watford	10 12 75	Manchester U
Ware Paul (M)	5 9	11 05	Congleton	7 11 70	Stockport Co
Whitehead Damien (F)	5 10	12 00	Whiston	24 4 79	Warrington T

League Appearances: Abbey, G. 12(6); Askey, J. 37(3); Bamber, M. (1); Barker, R. 35; Brown, G. 2(3); Byrne, C. 5; Collins, S. 37(2); Davies, S. 30(6); Durkan, K. 41(1); Hitchen, S. 2(3); Ingram, R. 35(1); Knight, R. 3; Martin, L. 21; Moore, N. 12(3); Munroe, K. 1(4); O'Neill, P. (1); Price, R. 11(1); Priest, C. 34(2); Rioch, G. 42; Sedgemore, B. 31(4); Tinson, D. 46; Tomlinson, G. 7(11); Ware, P. 9(9); Whitehead, D. 10(13); Whittaker, S. 2(7); Williams, A. 11; Wood, S. 30(6).
Goals – League (66): Barker 16, Askey 15, Durkan 6, Whitehead 6, Rioch 5 (3 pens), Priest 4, Collins 3, Moore 2, Tomlinson 2, Ware 2, Davies 1, Sedgemore 1, Tinson 1, Wood 1, own goal 1.
Worthington Cup (1): Priest 1.
FA Cup (0).
Ground: The Moss Rose Ground, London Road, Macclesfield, Cheshire SK11 7SP. Telephone: (01625) 264686.
Record attendance: 9008 v Winsford U, Cheshire Senior Cup 2nd rd, 4 February 1948. **Capacity:** 6028 (seated 1053, standing 4975).
Assistant Manager: Peter Davenport.
Secretary: Colin Garlick.
Most League Goals: 66, Division 3, 1999–2000.
Highest League Scorer in Season: Richard Barker, 16, Division 3, 1999–2000.
Most League Goals in Total Aggregate: John Askey, 25, 1997–2000.
Most League Appearances: Darren Tinson, 127, 1997–2000.
Honours – Nil.
Colours: Royal blue shirts, white shorts, blue stockings.

MANCHESTER CITY — FA PREMIERSHIP

Allsopp Danny (F)	6 0	12 08	Melbourne	10 8 78	Port Melbourne
Cooke Terry (F)	5 8	10 03	Marston Green	5 8 76	Manchester U
Crooks Lee (D)	6 1	12 09	Wakefield	14 1 78	Trainee

Day Rhys (M)	6 1	12 08	Bridgend	31 8 82	Scholar
Dickov Paul (F)	5 5	11 09	Glasgow	1 11 72	Arsenal
Dunfield Terry (M)	5 7	10 03	Canada	20 2 82	Trainee
Edghill Richard (D)	5 9	11 00	Oldham	23 9 74	Trainee
Etuhu Dixon (M)			Kano	8 6 82	Scholar
Fenton Nick (D)	6 1	11 08	Preston	23 11 79	Trainee
Goater Shaun (F)	6 0	12 10	Bermuda	25 2 70	Bristol C
Grant Tony (M)	5 10	10 08	Liverpool	14 11 74	Everton
Granville Danny (D)	6 1	12 11	Islington	19 1 75	Leeds U
Hodgson Steven (G)	5 11	11 00	Macclesfield	23 12 81	Scholar
Holmes Shaun (D)	5 9	10 07	Derry	27 12 80	Trainee
Horlock Kevin (M)	6 0	12 00	Erith	1 11 72	Swindon T
Jobson Richard (D)	6 2	12 12	Holderness	9 5 63	Leeds U
Jordan Stephen (M)	6 0	11 00	Warrington	6 3 82	Scholar
Joyce Damien (M)			Dublin	8 3 83	Scholar
Kennedy Mark (F)	5 11	11 00	Dublin	15 5 76	Wimbledon
Killen Chris (F)	5 11	11 03	Wellington	8 10 81	Miramar R
Laycock David (M)	5 10	10 07	Hull	1 10 80	Trainee
Mason Gary (M)	5 8	10 01	Edinburgh	15 10 79	Trainee
McKinney Richard (G)			Ballymoney	18 5 79	Ballymena U
Mike Leon (F)	6 0	12 02	Manchester	4 9 81	Scholar
Morrison Andy (D)	5 11	12 12	Inverness	30 7 70	Huddersfield T
Murphy Brian (M)				7 5 83	Waterford
Peacock Lee (F)	6 1	13 12	Paisley	9 10 76	Mansfield T
Pollock Jamie (M)	6 0	13 03	Stockton	16 2 74	Bolton W
Prior Spencer (D)	6 1	13 00	Rochford	22 4 71	Derby Co
Russell Craig (F)	5 10	12 07	Jarrow	4 2 74	Sunderland
Shuker Chris (M)	5 5	9 03	Liverpool	9 5 82	Scholar
Taylor Gareth (F)	6 1	12 02	Weston-Super-Mare	25 2 73	Sheffield U
Taylor Robert (F)	6 1	13 08	Norwich	30 4 71	Gillingham
Tiatto Danny (D)	5 8	11 01	Melbourne	22 5 73	Baden
Weaver Nick (G)	6 3	13 01	Sheffield	2 3 79	Mansfield T
Whitley Jeff (M)	5 9	10 10	Zambia	28 1 79	Trainee
Whitley Jim (M)	5 9	10 12	Zambia	14 4 75	Trainee
Wiekens Gerard (D)	6 0	12 06	Tolhuiswyk	25 2 73	
Wright-Phillips Shaun (F)	5 6	10 01	London	25 10 81	

League Appearances: Allsopp, D. (4); Bishop, I. 25(12); Cooke, T. 6(7); Crooks, L. 9(11); Dickov, P. 22(12); Edghill, R. 40(1); Goater, S. 40; Grant, T. 4(4); Granville, D. 28(7); Horlock, K. 36(2); Jobson, R. 43(1); Kennedy, M. 41; Mills, L. 1(2); Morrison, A. 12; Peacock, L. 4(4); Pollock, J. 17(7); Prior, S. 9; Taylor, G. 8(9); Taylor, R. 14(2); Tiatto, D. 26(9); Vaughan, T. (1); Weaver, N. 45; Whitley, Jeff 41(1); Whitley, Jim (1); Wiekens, G. 32(2); Wright, T. 1; Wright-Phillips, S. 2(2).
Goals – League (78): Goater 23, Horlock 10 (4 pens), Kennedy 8, Dickov 5, Taylor G 5, Taylor R 5, Jeff Whitley 4, Jobson 3, Pollock 3, Prior 3, Bishop 2, Granville 2, Crooks 1, Edghill 1, Wiekens 1, own goals 2.
Worthington Cup (9): Goater 3, Kennedy 2, Cooke 1, Dickov 1, Horlock 1 (pen), Taylor G 1.
FA Cup (6): Goater 3, Bishop 2, own goal 1.
Ground: Maine Road, Moss Side, Manchester M14 7WN. Telephone (0161) 232 3000.
Record attendance: 84,569 v Stoke C, FA Cup 6th rd, 3 March 1934 (British record for any game outside London or Glasgow). **Capacity:** 31,458.
Manager: Joe Royle.
General Secretary: J. B. Halford.
Most League Goals: 108, Division 2, 1926–27.

Highest League Scorer in Season: Tommy Johnson, 38, Division 1, 1928–29.
Most League Goals in Total Aggregate: Tommy Johnson, 158, 1919–30.
Most Capped Player: Colin Bell, 48, England.
Most League Appearances: Alan Oakes, 565, 1959–76.
Honours – Football League: Division 1 Champions – 1936–37, 1967–68. Division 2 Champions – 1898–99, 1902–03, 1909–10, 1927–28, 1946–47, 1965–66. **FA Cup winners** 1904, 1934, 1956, 1969. **Football League Cup winners** 1970, 1976.
European Competitions: European Cup-Winners' Cup winners: 1969–70.
Colours: Lazer blue shirts, white shorts, navy stockings.

MANCHESTER UNITED FA PREMIERSHIP

Beckham David (M)	6 0	11 13	Leytonstone	2 5 75	Trainee
Berg Henning (D)	6 0	12 04	Eidsvoll	1 9 69	Blackburn R
Blomqvist Jesper (F)	5 9	11 03	Tavelsjo	5 2 74	Parma
Bosnich Mark (G)	6 2	15 07	Fairfield	13 1 72	Aston Villa
Brown Wes (D)	6 1	13 11	Manchester	13 10 79	Trainee
Butt Nicky (M)	5 10	11 11	Manchester	21 1 75	Trainee
Chadwick Luke (F)	5 11	11 08	Cambridge	18 11 80	Trainee
Clegg George (F)	5 10	11 11	Manchester	16 11 80	Trainee
Clegg Michael (D)	5 8	11 10	Ashton-under-Lyne	3 7 77	Trainee
Coates Craig (F)	5 7	10 11	Dryburn	26 10 82	Trainee
Cole Andy (F)	5 11	12 02	Nottingham	15 10 71	Newcastle U
Cosgrove Stephen (M)	5 9	10 06	Glasgow	29 12 80	Trainee
Culkin Nick (G)	6 2	13 09	York	6 7 78	York C
Curtis John (D)	5 10	11 13	Nuneaton	3 9 78	Trainee
Davis James (F)	5 8	11 05	Bromsgrove	6 2 82	Trainee
Djordjic Bojan (M)	5 10	11 01	Belgrade	6 2 82	
Dodd Ashley (M)	5 10	10 02	Stafford	7 1 82	Trainee
Evans Wayne (M)	5 9	9 08	Carmarthen	23 10 80	Trainee
Fortune Quinton (M)	5 9	11 09	Cape Town	21 5 77	Atletico Madrid
Giggs Ryan (F)	5 11	11 00	Cardiff	29 11 73	School
Greening Jonathan (F)	6 0	11 13	Scarborough	2 1 79	York C
Healy David (F)	5 8	11 01	Downpatrick	5 8 79	Trainee
Higginbotham Danny (D)	6 1	12 07	Manchester	29 12 78	Trainee
Hilton Kirk (D)	5 7	10 01	Flixton	2 4 81	Trainee
Irwin Denis (D)	5 8	10 11	Cork	31 10 65	Oldham Ath
Johnsen Ronny (D)	6 3	13 06	Sandefjord	10 6 69	Besiktas
Jones Rhodri (D)	6 0	12 04	Cardiff	19 1 82	Trainee
Keane Roy (M)	5 11	11 10	Cork	10 8 71	Nottingham F
Lynch Mark (D)	5 11	11 03	Manchester	2 9 81	Trainee
May David (D)	6 0	13 05	Oldham	24 6 70	Blackburn R
McDermott Alan (D)	6 1	11 07	Dublin	22 1 82	Trainee
Muirhead Ben (F)	5 9	10 05	Doncaster	5 1 83	Trainee
Nardiello Daniel (F)	5 11	11 04	Coventry	22 10 82	Trainee
Neville Gary (D)	5 11	12 04	Bury	18 2 75	Trainee
Neville Phil (D)	5 11	12 00	Bury	21 1 77	Trainee
Notman Alex (F)	5 7	10 11	Edinburgh	10 12 79	Trainee
O'Shea John (D)	6 3	12 10	Waterford	30 4 81	Waterford
Rachubka Paul (G)	6 1	13 01	San Luis Obispo	21 5 81	Trainee
Roche Lee (D)	5 10	10 10	Bolton	28 10 80	Trainee
Rose Michael (D)	5 11	11 01	Salford	28 7 82	Trainee
Scholes Paul (M)	5 7	11 00	Salford	16 11 74	Trainee
Sheringham Teddy (F)	6 0	12 09	Highams Park	2 4 66	Tottenham H
Silvestre Mikael (D)	6 0	13 01	Chambray les Tours	9 8 77	Internazionale

Solskjaer Ole Gunnar (F)	5 10	11 11	Kristiansund	26 2 73	Molde
Stam Jaap (D)	6 3	15 00	Kampen	17 7 72	PSV Eindhoven
Stewart Michael (M)	5 11	11 11	Edinburgh	26 2 81	Trainee
Strange Gareth (M)	5 9	10 05	Bolton	3 10 81	Trainee
Studley Mark (D)	5 6	10 00	Manchester	21 12 81	Trainee
Szmid Marek (D)	5 8	11 06	Nuneaton	2 3 82	Trainee
Taibi Massimo (G)	6 3	14 09	Palermo	18 2 70	Venezia
Teather Paul (D)	6 0	11 13	Rotherham	28 12 77	Trainee
Van der Gouw Raimond (G)	6 3	13 09	Oldenzaal	24 3 63	Vitesse
Walker Joshua (M)	6 1	11 01	Birmingham	20 12 81	Trainee
Wallwork Ronnie (D)	5 10	13 01	Manchester	10 9 77	Trainee
Webber Danny (F)	5 9	10 08	Manchester	28 12 81	Trainee
Williams Matthew (F)	5 8	9 11	St Asaph	5 11 82	
Wilson Mark (M)	6 0	12 07	Scunthorpe	9 2 79	Trainee
Wood Neil (F)	5 10	13 02	Manchester	4 1 83	Trainee
Yorke Dwight (F)	5 10	12 03	Canaan	3 11 71	Aston Villa

League Appearances: Beckham, D. 30(1); Berg, H. 16(6); Bosnich, M. 23; Butt, N. 21(11); Clegg, M. (2); Cole, A. 23(5); Cruyff, J. 1(7); Culkin, N. (1); Curtis, J. (1); Fortune, Q. 4(2); Giggs, R. 30; Greening, J. 1(3); Higginbotham, D. 2(1); Irwin, D. 25; Johnsen, R. 2(1); Keane, R. 28(1); May, D. (1); Neville, G. 22; Neville, P. 25(4); Scholes, P. 27(4); Sheringham, T. 15(12); Silvestre, M. 30(1); Solskjaer, O. 15(13); Stam, J. 33; Taibi, M. 4; Van der Gouw, R. 11(3); Wallwork, R. (5); Wilson, M. 1(2); Yorke, D. 29(3).
Goals – League (97): Yorke 20, Cole 19, Solskjaer 12, Scholes 9 (1 pen), Beckham 6, Giggs 6, Keane 5, Sheringham 5, Butt 3, Cruyff 3, Irwin 3 (3 pens), Fortune 2, Berg 1, own goals 3.
Worthington Cup (0).
Ground: Old Trafford, Sir Matt Busby Way, Manchester M16 0RA. Telephone (0161) 868 8000.
Record attendance: 76,962 Wolverhampton W v Grimsby T, FA Cup semi-final. 25 March 1939. **Capacity:** 68,936.
Manager: Sir Alex Ferguson CBE.
Secretary: Kenneth Merrett.
Most League Goals: 103, Division 1, 1956–57 and 1958–59.
Highest League Scorer in Season: Dennis Viollet, 32, 1959–60.
Most League Goals in Total Aggregate: Bobby Charlton, 199, 1956–73.
Most Capped Player: Bobby Charlton, 106, England.
Most League Appearances: Bobby Charlton, 606, 1956–73.
Honours – FA Premier League: Champions – 1992–93, 1993–94, 1995–96, 1996–97, 1998–99, 1999–2000. **Football League:** Division 1 Champions – 1907–8, 1910–11, 1951–52, 1955–56, 1956–57, 1964–65, 1966–67. Division 2 Champions – 1935–36, 1974–75. **FA Cup winners** 1909, 1948, 1963, 1977, 1983, 1985, 1990, 1994, 1996, 1999. **Football League Cup winners** 1991–92. **European Competitions: European Cup winners:** 1967–68, 1998–99. **European Cup-Winners' Cup winners:** 1990–91. **Super Cup winners:** 1991. **Inter-Continental Cup winners:** 1999.
Colours: Red shirts, white shorts, black stockings.

MANSFIELD TOWN — DIV. 3

Andrews John (D)	6 1	12 08	Cork	27 9 78	Coventry C
Asher Alistair (D)	5 11	11 07	Leicester	14 10 80	Trainee
Bacon Danny (D)	5 10	10 12	Mansfield	20 9 80	Trainee
Boulding Mick (F)	5 10	11 03	Sheffield	8 2 76	Hallam
Clarke Darrell (M)	5 10	11 06	Mansfield	16 12 77	Trainee
Disley Craig (M)	5 10	10 12	Worksop	24 8 81	Trainee

Greenacre Chris (F)	5 11	10 06	Halifax	23 12 77	Manchester C
Hassell Bobby (D)	5 9	12 04	Derby	4 6 80	Trainee
Kerr David (M)	6 0	12 11	Dumfries	6 9 74	Manchester C
Lormor Tony (F)	6 1	14 02	Ashington	29 10 70	Preston NE
Sisson Michael (M)	5 10	11 05	Sutton-in-Ashfield	24 11 78	Trainee
Tallon Gary (M)	5 10	11 10	Drogheda	5 9 73	Kilmarnock
Willis Scott (M)			Liverpool	20 2 82	Wigan Ath

League Appearances: Allardyce, C. 1(3); Andrews, J. 29(1); Asher, A. 29(6); Bacon, D. 6(2); Bassinder, G. 1(3); Blake, M. 40(3); Boulding, M. 16(17); Bowling, I. 10; Bromby, L. 10; Camilleri, C. (2); Clarke, D. 39; Cowling, L. 3(5); Disley, C. 2(3); Evans, A. 4(2); Fortune, J. 4; Garratt, M. 4(2); Greenacre, C. 31; Hassell, B. 8(3); Kerr, D. 10(8); Lawrence, L. (2); Linighan, D. 28; Lormor, T. 33; Mimms, B. 5; Muggleton, C. 9; Peacock, L. 12; Porter, A. 5; Richardson, B. 6; Richardson, N. 31; Roscoe, A. 29(10); Sisson, M. 24(1); Tallon, G. 11(2); Thomas, W. 4(1); Thompson, G. 16; Williams, L. 46; Williamson, L. (4).
Goals – League (50): Greenacre 9, Lormor 9 (2 pens), Clarke 7, Peacock 7, Boulding 6, Bacon 2, Roscoe 2, Sisson 2, Andrews 1, Blake 1, Bromby 1, Hassell 1, own goals 2.
Worthington Cup (1): Peacock 1.
FA Cup (2): Blake 1, Lormor 1 (pen).
Ground: Field Mill Ground, Quarry Lane, Mansfield NG18 5DA. Telephone (01623) 623567.
Record attendance: 24,467 v Nottingham F, FA Cup 3rd rd, 10 January 1953.
Capacity: 5289.
Manager: Bill Dearden.
Secretary: Christine Reynolds.
Most League Goals: 108, Division 4, 1962–63.
Highest League Scorer in Season: Ted Harston, 55, Division 3 (N), 1936–37.
Most League Goals in Total Aggregate: Harry Johnson, 104, 1931–36.
Most Capped Player: John McClelland, 6 (53), Northern Ireland.
Most League Appearances: Rod Arnold, 440, 1970–83.
Honours – Football League: Division 3 Champions – 1976–77. Division 4 Champions – 1974–75. **Freight Rover Trophy winners** 1986–87.
Colours: Amber & royal blue shirts, royal blue shorts, royal blue stockings with amber trim.

MIDDLESBROUGH — FA PREMIERSHIP

Armstrong Alun (F)	6 0	13 08	Gateshead	22 2 75	Stockport Co
Baker Steve (D)	6 0	12 06	Pontefract	8 9 78	Trainee
Bennion Chris (G)	6 2	12 00	Edinburgh	30 8 80	Trainee
Beresford Marlon (G)	6 1	13 08	Lincoln	2 6 69	Burnley
Bernhardt Arturo (M)	6 1	12 00	Santa Catarino	27 8 82	Nova Hamburgo
Campbell Andy (F)	6 0	11 13	Middlesbrough	18 4 79	Trainee
Close Brian (M)			Belfast	27 1 82	
Cooper Colin (D)	5 11	11 11	Sedgefield	28 2 67	Nottingham F
Deane Brian (F)	6 3	14 00	Leeds	7 2 68	Sheffield U
Festa Gianluca (D)	5 11	13 00	Cagliari	15 3 69	Internazionale
Fleming Curtis (D)	5 10	12 05	Manchester	8 10 68	St Patrick's Ath
Gascoigne Paul (M)	5 10	12 09	Gateshead	27 5 67	Rangers
Gavin Jason (D)	6 0	11 12	Dublin	14 3 80	Trainee
Gordon Dean (D)	6 0	13 08	Thornton Heath	10 2 73	Crystal Palace
Hanson Christian (D)	6 1	11 05	Middlesbrough	3 8 81	Trainee
Harrison Craig (D)	6 0	11 08	Gateshead	10 11 77	Trainee
Hudson Mark (M)	5 10	11 03	Bishop Auckland	24 10 80	Trainee

Ince Paul (M)	5 10	12 04	Ilford	21 10 67	Liverpool
Jones Bradley (G)	6 3	12 01	Armadale	19 3 82	Trainee
Jones Thomas (F)	5 10	11 02	Middlesbrough	26 3 80	Trainee
Kell Richard (M)	6 1	10 13	Bishop Auckland	15 9 79	Trainee
Kilgannon Sean (M)	5 11	11 08	Stirling	8 3 81	Trainee
Maddison Neil (M)	5 10	11 10	Darlington	2 10 69	Southampton
Marinelli Carlos (M)	5 8	11 06	Buenos Aires	14 3 82	Boca Juniors
McStea Anthony (D)	5 10	11 07	Gateshead	16 5 81	Trainee
Moat David (D)	5 8	11 02	Gateshead	1 10 81	Trainee
Moore Alan (M)	5 10	11 02	Dublin	25 11 74	Rivermount
Mustoe Robbie (M)	6 0	12 03	Oxford	28 8 68	Oxford U
O'Neill Keith (F)	6 1	12 13	Dublin	16 2 76	Norwich C
Ormerod Anthony (M)	5 11	12 00	Middlesbrough	31 3 79	Trainee
Pallister Gary (D)	6 5	15 02	Ramsgate	30 6 65	Manchester U
Parnaby Stuart (M)	5 11	11 00	Durham City	19 7 82	Trainee
Ricard Hamilton (F)	6 1	13 12	Choco	12 1 74	Deportivo Cali
Roberts Ben (G)	6 2	13 05	Bishop Auckland	22 6 75	Trainee
Robinson Gerard (M)			Dublin	9 6 82	Trainee
Schwarzer Mark (G)	6 5	15 01	Sydney	6 10 72	Bradford C
Stamp Phil (M)	5 11	14 09	Middlesbrough	12 12 75	Trainee
Stockdale Robbie (D)	6 0	12 03	Redcar	30 11 79	Trainee
Summerbell Mark (M)	5 9	11 01	Durham	30 10 76	Trainee
Taylor Andrew (D)	5 11	11 01	Middlesbrough	6 9 81	Trainee
Vickers Steve (D)	6 2	13 01	Bishop Auckland	13 10 67	Tranmere R
Wilford Aaron (D)	6 3	14 01	Scarborough	14 1 82	Harrogate College
Wiltshire Luke (M)			Australia	2 10 81	
Ziege Christian (D)	6 2	12 13	Berlin	1 2 72	AC Milan

League Appearances: Armstrong, A. 3(9); Beresford, M. 1; Campbell, A. 16(9); Cooper, C. 26; Cummins, M. (1); Deane, B. 29; Festa, G. 27(2); Fleming, C. 27; Gascoigne, P. 7(1); Gavin, J. 2(4); Gordon, D. 3(1); Ince, P. 32; Juninho 24(4); Kilgannon, S. (1); Maddison, N. 6(7); Marinelli, C. (2); Mustoe, R. 18(10); O'Neill, K. 14(2); Ormerod, A. (1); Pallister, G. 21; Ricard, H. 28(6); Schwarzer, M. 37; Stamp, P. 13(3); Stockdale, R. 6(5); Summerbell, M. 16(3); Townsend, A. 3(2); Vickers, S. 30(2); Ziege, C. 29.
Goals – League (46): Ricard 12 (3 pens), Deane 9 (1 pen), Ziege 6 (1 pen), Campbell 4, Juninho 4, Ince 3, Festa 2, Armstrong 1, Gascoigne 1 (pen), Pallister 1, Stockdale 1, own goals 2.
Worthington Cup (6): Ricard 2 (1 pen), Ince 1, Juninho 1, Vickers 1, Ziege 1.
FA Cup (1): Deane 1.
Ground: Cellnet Riverside Stadium, Middlesbrough, Cleveland TS3 6RS. Telephone (01642) 877700
Record attendance: 53,596 v Newcastle U, Division 1, 27 December 1949. **Capacity:** 35,049.
Manager: Bryan Robson.
Secretary: Karen Nelson.
Most League Goals: 122, Division 2, 1926–27.
Highest League Scorer in Season: George Camsell, 59, Division 2, 1926–27 (Second Division record).
Most League Goals in Total Aggregate: George Camsell, 325, 1925–39.
Most Capped Player: Wilf Mannion, 26, England.
Most League Appearances: Tim Williamson, 563, 1902–23.
Honours – Football League: Division 1 Champions 1994–95. Division 2 Champions 1926–27, 1928–29, 1973–74. **Amateur Cup winners** 1895, 1898, **Anglo-Scottish Cup:** Winners 1975–76.
Colours: Red shirts, white shorts, red stockings.

MILLWALL DIV. 2

Bircham Marc (D)	5 11	12 02	Brent	11 5 78	Trainee
Bowry Bobby (M)	5 9	10 08	Croydon	19 5 71	Crystal Palace
Braniff Kevin (M)			Belfast	4 3 83	Scholar
Bubb Byron (M)	5 7	10 05	Harrow	17 12 81	Scholar
Bull Ronnie (D)	5 7	10 11	Hackney	27 12 80	Trainee
Cahill Tim (M)	5 10	10 10	Sydney	6 12 79	Sydney U
Cort Leon (D)	6 2	12 13	Southwark	11 9 79	Dulwich H
Dolan Joe (D)	6 3	13 05	Harrow	27 5 80	Chelsea
Dunne Alan (M)			Dublin	23 8 82	
Dyche Sean (D)	6 0	13 07	Kettering	28 6 71	Bristol C
Harris Neil (F)	5 11	12 04	Orsett	12 7 77	Cambridge C
Hicks Mark (F)	5 8	10 04	Belfast	24 7 81	
Ifill Paul (M)	6 0	12 09	Brighton	20 10 79	Trainee
Kinet Christophe (M)	5 8	10 12	Huy	31 12 74	Strasbourg
Lawrence Matthew (D)	6 1	12 12	Northampton	19 6 74	Wycombe W
Livermore David (M)	5 11	12 04	Edmonton	20 5 80	Trainee
Meade Darren (M)			Dublin	3 2 82	Belvedere
Moody Paul (F)	6 3	14 08	Portsmouth	13 6 67	Fulham
Neill Lucas (M)	6 0	12 03	Sydney	9 3 78	NSW Academy
Nethercott Stuart (D)	6 0	13 00	Chadwell Heath	21 3 73	Tottenham H
Newman Ricky (M)	5 10	12 06	Guildford	5 8 70	Crystal Palace
Odunsi Leke (M)	5 9	11 07	Walworth	5 12 80	Trainee
Phillips Mark (M)			London	27 1 82	Scholar
Rees Matthew (M)			Swansea	2 9 82	Trainee
Reid Steven (F)	6 0	12 03	Kingston	10 3 81	Trainee
Ryan Robbie (D)	5 10	12 03	Dublin	6 5 77	Huddersfield T
Sadlier Richard (F)	6 2	13 01	Dublin	14 1 79	Belvedere
Shaw Paul (F)	5 10	12 10	Burnham	4 9 73	Arsenal
Smith Phil (G)	6 1	13 11	Harrow	14 12 79	Trainee
Stuart Jamie (D)	5 9	11 10	Southwark	15 10 76	Charlton Ath
Tuttle David (D)	6 2	14 02	Reading	6 2 72	Barnsley
Tyne Tommy (F)	6 1	12 05	Lambeth	2 3 81	
Warner Tony (G)	6 4	15 01	Liverpool	11 5 74	Liverpool

League Appearances: Bircham, M. 22; Bowry, B. 3(2); Bubb, B. (2); Bull, R. 5(4); Cahill, T. 45; Dolan, J. 16(1); Dyche, S. 1; Fitzgerald, S. 31; Gilkes, M. 26(3); Harris, N. 34(4); Ifill, P. 38(6); Kinet, C. (3); Lawrence, M. 9; Livermore, D. 29(3); Moody, P. 24(8); Neill, L. 27(4); Nethercott, S. 37; Newman, R. 14; Odunsi, L. 1(3); Reid, S. 11(10); Ryan, R. 33(1); Sadlier, R. 21(6); Shaw, P. 17(18); Spink, N. 1; Stuart, J. 9; Tuttle, D. 7(1); Warner, T. 45.
Goals – League (76): Harris 25 (3 pens), Cahill 12, Ifill 11, Moody 11, Sadlier 5, Shaw 5 (1 pen), Gilkes 2, Livermore 2, Bircham 1, Dolan 1, Neill 1.
Worthington Cup (1): Sadlier 1.
FA Cup (0).
Ground: The Den, Zampa Road, Bermondsey SE16 3LN. Telephone (020) 7232 1222.
Record attendance: 20,093 v Arsenal, FA Cup 3rd rd, 10 January 1994. **Capacity:** 20,146.
Joint managers: Keith Stevens and Alan McLeary.
Secretary: Yvonne Haines.
Most League Goals: 127, Division 3 (S), 1927–28.
Highest League Scorer in Season: Richard Parker, 37, Division 3 (S), 1926–27.
Most League Goals in Total Aggregate: Teddy Sheringham, 93, 1984–91.

Most Capped Player: Eamonn Dunphy, 22 (23), Republic of Ireland.
Most League Appearances: Barry Kitchener, 523, 1967–82.
Honours – Football League: Division 2 Champions – 1987–88. Division 3 (S) Champions – 1927–28, 1937–38. Division 4 Champions – 1961–62. **Football League Trophy winners** 1982–83.
Colours: White with black trim.

NEWCASTLE UNITED — FA PREMIERSHIP

Ameobi Foluwashola (F)	6 2	12 00	Zaria	12 10 81	Trainee
Barton Warren (D)	6 0	12 00	Islington	19 3 69	Wimbledon
Beharall David (D)	6 2	11 07	Newcastle	8 3 79	Trainee
Boyd Mark (M)	5 9	11 02	Carlisle	22 10 81	Trainee
Brady Garry (M)	5 10	11 02	Glasgow	7 9 76	Tottenham H
Brennan Stephen (M)	5 8	10 03	Dublin	26 3 83	
Caldwell Gary (D)	5 11	11 10	Stirling	12 4 82	Trainee
Caldwell Stephen (D)	6 0	11 05	Stirling	12 9 80	Trainee
Charvet Laurent (D)	5 11	12 03	Beziers	8 5 73	Chelsea
Coppinger James (F)	5 7	10 03	Middlesbrough	18 1 81	Darlington
Cowan David (D)	5 11	11 10	Carlisle	5 3 82	Trainee
Dabizas Nikos (D)	6 1	12 07	Amindeo	3 8 73	Olympiakos
Domi Didier (D)	5 10	11 03	Sarcelles	2 5 78	Paris St Germain
Dyer Kieron (M)	5 7	9 07	Ipswich	29 12 78	Ipswich T
Elliott Stuart (D)	5 8	11 05	London	27 8 77	Trainee
Ferguson Duncan (F)	6 4	14 06	Stirling	27 12 71	Everton
Fumaca Jose Antunes (M)	6 0	11 08	Belem	15 7 76	Crystal Palace
Gall Kevin (F)	5 9	11 01	Merthyr	4 2 82	Trainee
Gallacher Kevin (F)	5 8	11 03	Clydebank	23 11 66	Blackburn R
Gavilan Diego	5 8	10 07	Asuncion	1 3 80	Cerro Porteno
Given Shay (G)	6 1	13 04	Lifford	20 4 76	Blackburn R
Glass Stephen (M)	5 9	10 11	Dundee	23 5 76	Aberdeen
Goma Alain (D)	6 0	13 00	Sault	5 10 72	Paris St Germain
Griffin Andy (D)	5 9	10 10	Billinge	7 3 79	Stoke C
Hamilton Des (M)	5 11	13 02	Bradford	15 8 76	Bradford C
Harper Steve (G)	6 2	13 00	Easington	14 3 75	Seaham Red Star
Helder Rodrigues (D)	5 11	13 00	Luanda	21 3 71	La Coruna
Howey Steve (D)	6 2	11 12	Sunderland	26 10 71	Trainee
Hughes Aaron (D)	6 1	11 02	Cookstown	8 11 79	Trainee
Karelse John (G)	6 3	13 07	Kapelle	17 5 70	NAC Breda
Kerr Brian (M)	5 8	11 00	Motherwell	12 10 81	Trainee
Ketsbaia Temuri (M)	5 8	10 12	Gale	18 3 68	AEK Athens
Lee Robert (M)	5 10	11 13	Plaistow	1 2 66	Charlton Ath
Marcelino Elena (D)	6 2	13 00	Gijon	26 9 71	Mallorca
Maric Silvio (M)	5 9	11 02	Zagreb	20 3 75	Croatia Zagreb
McClen Jamie (M)	5 8	10 07	Newcastle	13 5 79	Trainee
McMahon David (F)	6 1	11 05	Dublin	17 1 81	Trainee
Perez Lionel (G)	5 11	13 04	Bagnols Coze	24 4 67	Sunderland
Pistone Alessandro (D)	5 11	11 05	Milan	27 7 75	Internazionale
Robinson Paul (F)	5 11	12 11	Sunderland	20 11 78	Darlington
Serrant Carl (D)	5 11	11 02	Bradford	12 9 75	Oldham Ath
Shearer Alan (F)	6 0	12 06	Newcastle	13 8 70	Blackburn R
Solano Nolberto (M)	5 9	11 06	Callao	12 12 74	Boca Juniors
Speed Gary (M)	5 10	10 12	Mancot	8 9 69	Everton

League Appearances: Barton, W. 33(1); Beharall, D. (2); Charvet, L. 1(1); Dabizas, N. 29; Domi, D. 19(8); Dumas, F. 6; Dyer, K. 27(3); Ferguson, D. 17(6); Fumaca, J. 1(4); Gallacher, K. 15(5); Gavilan, D. 2(4); Given, S. 14; Glass, S. 1(6); Goma, A. 14; Griffin, A. 1(2); Harper, S. 18; Helder, R. 8; Howey, S. 7(2); Hughes, A. 22(5); Karelse, J. 3; Ketsbaia, T. 11(10); Lee, R. 30; Marcelino, E. 10(1); Maric, S. 3(10); McClen, J. 3(6); Pistone, A. 15; Robinson, P. 2(9); Serrant, C. 2; Shearer, A. 36(1); Solano, N. 29(1); Speed, G. 36; Wright, T. 3.
Goals – League (63): Shearer 23 (5 pens), Speed 9, Ferguson 6, Dabizas 3, Domi 3, Dyer 3, Solano 3 (1 pen), Gallacher 2, Hughes 2, Gavilan 1, Glass 1, Griffin 1, Helder 1, Pistone 1, own goals 4.
Worthington Cup (0).
FA Cup (17): Shearer 5 (1 pen), Ferguson 3, Speed 3, Dabizas 2, Domi 1, Dyer 1, Gallacher 1, Lee 1.
Ground: St James' Park, Newcastle-upon-Tyne NE1 4ST. Telephone (0191) 201 8400.
Record attendance: 68,386 v Chelsea, Division 1, 3 Sept 1930. **Capacity:** 52,167.
Manager: Bobby Robson CBE.
Secretary: Russell Cushing.
Most League Goals: 98, Division 1, 1951–52.
Highest League Scorer in Season: Hughie Gallacher, 36, Division 1, 1926–27.
Most League Goals in Total Aggregate: Jackie Milburn, 177, 1946–57.
Most Capped Player: Alf McMichael, 40, Northern Ireland.
Most League Appearances: Jim Lawrence, 432, 1904–22.
Honours – Football League: Division 1 – Champions 1904–05, 1906–07, 1908–09, 1926–27, 1992–93. Division 2 Champions – 1964–65. **FA Cup winners** 1910, 1924, 1932, 1951, 1952, 1955. **Texaco Cup winners** 1973–74, 1974–75. **European Competitions: European Fairs Cup winners:** 1968–69. **Anglo-Italian Cup winners:** 1973.
Colours: Black and white striped shirts, white and blue shorts and stockings.

NORTHAMPTON TOWN — DIV. 2

Frain John (D)	5 10	12 04	Birmingham	8 10 68	Birmingham C
Hendon Ian (D)	6 1	13 08	Ilford	5 12 71	Notts Co
Hodge John (F)	5 7	11 06	Skelmersdale	1 4 69	Gillingham
Hope Richard (D)	6 3	13 05	Stockton	22 6 78	Darlington
Howard Steve (F)	6 3	14 06	Durham	10 5 76	Hartlepool U
Howey Lee (D)	6 3	14 06	Sunderland	1 4 69	Burnley
Hughes Garry (D)	6 0	12 00	Birmingham	19 11 79	Trainee
Hunt James (M)	5 11	12 07	Derby	17 12 76	Notts Co
Hunter Roy (M)	5 10	12 08	Saltburn	29 10 73	WBA
Morrow Andrew (F)	5 8	9 07	Bangor	5 10 80	Trainee
Sampson Ian (D)	6 2	13 05	Wakefield	14 11 68	Sunderland
Savage Dave (M)	6 2	13 00	Dublin	30 7 73	Millwall
Spedding Duncan (M)	6 2	12 01	Frimley	7 9 77	Southampton
Welch Keith (G)	6 2	13 07	Bolton	3 10 68	Bristol C

League Appearances: Battersby, T. (3); Byfield, D. 6; Clare, D. 9(1); Clarkson, I. 1(1); Corazzin, C. 27(12); Crowe, D. 3(2); Dobson, T. 1; Forrester, J. 9(1); Frain, J. 40; Gibb, A. 6(8); Green, R. 21; Hendon, I. 44; Hodge, J. 5(3); Hope, R. 14(3); Howard, S. 32(9); Howey, L. 20; Hughes, G. 1(1); Hunt, J. 33(4); Hunter, R. 15(2); Matthew, D. (1); Morrow, A. (4); O'Reilly, A. 7; Parrish, S. 21(4); Peer, D. 6(3); Sampson, I. 45; Savage, D. 43; Spedding, D. 44; Sturridge, S. 10(8); Welch, K. 39; Wilson, K. 4(4).

Goals – League (63): Corazzin 14 (1 pen), Howard 10, Forrester 6, Sampson 6, Savage 5, Clare 3, Hunter 3, Parrish 3, Frain 2, Green 2, Hendon 2 (1 pen), Battersby 1, Byfield 1, Hunt 1, Peer 1, Spedding 1, Sturridge 1, Wilson 1.
Worthington Cup (2): Byfield 1, Corazzin 1 (pen).
FA Cup (1): Hendon 1.
Ground: Sixfields Stadium, Upton Way, Northampton NN5 5QA. Telephone (01604) 757773.
Record attendance: 24,523 v Fulham, Division 1, 23 April 1966. **Capacity:** 7653.
Manager: Kevin WIlson.
Secretary: Norman Howells.
Most League Goals: 109, Division 3, 1962–63 and Division 3 (S), 1952–53.
Highest League Scorer in Season: Cliff Holton, 36, Division 3, 1961–62.
Most League Goals in Total Aggregate: Jack English, 135, 1947–60.
Most Capped Player: E. Lloyd Davies, 12 (16), Wales.
Most League Appearances: Tommy Fowler, 521, 1946–61.
Honours – Football League: Division 3 Champions – 1962–63. Division 4 Champions – 1986–87.
Colours: Claret with white shirts, white shorts, white stockings.

NORWICH CITY — DIV. 1

Anselin Cedric (M)	5 7	11 02	Lens	24 7 77	Bordeaux
Bellamy Craig (F)	5 8	11 00	Cardiff	13 7 79	Trainee
Coote Adrian (F)	6 1	11 11	Gt Yarmouth	30 9 78	Trainee
Dalglish Paul (F)	5 10	11 00	Glasgow	18 2 77	Newcastle U
De Waard Raymond (F)	6 1	12 03	Rotterdam	27 3 73	Cambuur
Derveld Fernando (D)	6 2	13 00	Vlissingen	22 10 76	Haarlem
Fleming Craig (D)	5 11	12 10	Halifax	6 10 71	Oldham Ath
Forbes Adrian (F)	5 7	11 04	Greenford	23 1 79	Trainee
Green Robert (G)	6 3	13 00	Chertsey	18 1 80	Trainee
Jackson Matt (D)	6 0	12 09	Leeds	19 10 71	Everton
Kenton Darren (D)	5 11	11 10	Wandsworth	13 9 78	Trainee
Llewellyn Chris (F)	6 0	11 11	Merthyr	29 8 79	Trainee
MacKay Malky (D)	6 3	13 03	Bellshill	19 2 72	Celtic
Marshall Andy (G)	6 2	13 08	Bury	14 4 75	Trainee
Marshall Lee (M)	6 2	12 00	Islington	21 1 79	Enfield
McVeigh Paul (F)	5 6	10 06	Belfast	6 12 77	Tottenham H
Mulryne Phil (M)	5 9	11 05	Belfast	1 1 78	Manchester U
Roberts Iwan (F)	6 3	13 01	Bangor	26 6 68	Wolverhampton W
Russell Darel (M)	6 0	12 02	Mile End	22 10 80	Trainee
Sutch Daryl (D)	5 11	12 06	Lowestoft	11 9 71	Trainee
de Blasiis Yves (M)	5 9	11 05	Bordeaux	25 9 73	Red Star 93

League Appearances: Anselin, C. 15(4); Bellamy, C. 2(2); Brady, G. 6; Carey, S. 18(3); Coote, A. 4(7); Dalglish, P. 22(9); De Waard, R. 4; Derveld, F. 5; Diop, P. 2(5); Eadie, D. 12(1); Fleming, C. 38(1); Forbes, A. 15(10); Fuglestad, E. 26; Giallanza, G. 2(1); Green, R. 2(1); Hamilton, D. 7; Jackson, M. 38; Kenton, D. 23(3); Llewellyn, C. 24(12); MacKay, M. 16(5); Marshall, A. 44; Marshall, L. 21(12); McVeigh, P. (1); Milligan, M. 9(2); Mulryne, P. 7(2); Roberts, I. 44; Russell, D. 28(5); Sutch, D. 44(1); Wilson, C. 2(3); de Blasiis, Y. 26(2).
Goals – League (45): Roberts 17 (1 pen), Marshall L 5, Russell 4, Fleming 3, Llewellyn 3, Bellamy 2, Dalglish 2, Sutch 2, Coote 1, Eadie 1, Forbes 1, Kenton 1, own goals 3.
Worthington Cup (3): Roberts 2, Marshall L 1.
FA Cup (1): Llewellyn 1.

Ground: Carrow Road, Norwich NR1 1JE. Telephone (01603) 760760.
Record attendance: 43,984 v Leicester C, FA Cup 6th rd, 30 March 1963. **Capacity:** 21,414.
Manager: Bryan Hamilton.
Secretary: Kevin Platt.
Most League Goals: 99, Division 3 (S), 1952–53.
Highest League Scorer in Season: Ralph Hunt, 31, Division 3 (S), 1955–56.
Most League Goals in Total Aggregate: Johnny Gavin, 122, 1945–54, 1955–58.
Most Capped Player: Mark Bowen, 35 (41), Wales.
Most League Appearances: Ron Ashman, 592, 1947–64.
Honours – Football League: Division 2 Champions – 1971–72, 1985–86. Division 3 (S) Champions – 1933–34. **Football League Cup:** Winners 1962, 1985.
Colours: All yellow.

NOTTINGHAM FOREST — DIV. 1

Allou Bernard (M)	5 8	11 00	Cocody	19 6 75	Paris St Germain
Bart-Williams Chris (M)	5 11	12 07	Freetown	16 6 74	Sheffield W
Beasant Dave (G)	6 4	14 02	Willesden	20 3 59	Southampton
Brennan Jim (D)	5 9	11 06	Toronto	8 5 77	Bristol C
Calderwood Colin (D)	6 0	13 00	Stranraer	20 1 65	Aston Villa
Cash Brian (M)			Dublin	24 11 82	Trainee
Cooper Richard (D)	5 9	10 07	Nottingham	27 9 79	Trainee
Dawson Kevin (D)	6 0	10 07	Northallerton	18 6 81	Trainee
Doig Chris (D)	6 2	12 06	Dumfries	13 2 81	Trainee
Doyle Kevin (D)	5 11	12 02	Wexford	13 10 80	Leeds U
Edds Gareth (M)	5 11	10 12	Sydney	3 2 81	Trainee
Edwards Christian (D)	6 2	12 03	Caerphilly	23 11 75	Swansea C
Fenton Paul (M)			Cork	8 3 83	Scholar
Foy Keith (M)	5 11	12 03	Crumlin	30 12 81	Trainee
Freedman Dougie (F)	5 9	12 05	Glasgow	21 1 74	Wolverhampton W
Freeman David (F)	5 10	11 07	Dublin	25 11 79	Cherry Orchard
Gray Andy (M)	6 0	13 00	Harrogate	15 11 77	Leeds U
Harewood Marlon (F)	6 1	13 03	Hampstead	25 8 79	Trainee
Hjelde Jon Olav (D)	6 2	13 05	Levanger	30 7 72	Rosenborg
Hudson Niall (M)	5 10	10 02	Ilkeston	7 1 82	Trainee
Jenas Jermaine (M)			Nottingham	18 2 83	Scholar
John Stern (F)	6 1	13 07	Trinidad	30 10 76	Columbus Crew
Johnson Andy (M)	6 1	13 03	Bristol	2 5 74	Norwich C
Kearney Liam (M)			Dublin	10 1 83	Scholar
Lester Jack (F)	5 10	11 10	Sheffield	8 10 75	Grimsby T
Louis-Jean Mathieu (D)	5 9	10 08	Mont-St-Aignan	22 2 76	Le Havre
Love Gordon (M)			Bellshill	17 3 83	Scholar
Matrecano Salvatore (D)	6 2	14 00	Naples	5 10 70	Perugia
Mattsson Jesper (D)	6 1	13 01	Visby	18 4 68	Halmstad
McNamara Niall (F)	5 11	11 09	Eire	26 1 82	Trainee
Merino Carlos (M)	5 8	10 04	Bilbao	15 3 80	Urdaneta
Petrachi Gianluca (M)	5 9	11 05	Lecce	14 1 69	Perugia
Prutton David (D)	6 1	11 06	Hull	12 9 81	Trainee
Quashie Nigel (M)	5 9	12 08	Nunhead	20 7 78	QPR
Reid Andrew (M)			Dublin	29 7 82	Trainee
Roche Barry (G)	6 4	12 06	Dublin	6 4 82	Trainee
Rogers Alan (D)	5 10	12 08	Liverpool	3 1 77	Tranmere R
Scimeca Riccardo (D)	6 0	13 11	Leamington Spa	13 6 75	Aston Villa
Shevlin Anthony (M)			Dublin	9 12 82	Trainee
Thompson John (M)			Dublin	12 10 81	

Turner Matthew (F)	5 9	10 00	Nottingham	29 12 81	Trainee
Vaughan Tony (D)	6 1	12 10	Manchester	11 10 75	Manchester C
Williams Gareth (M)	5 11	11 08	Glasgow	16 12 81	Trainee

League Appearances: Allou, B. 1(3); Bart-Williams, C. 38; Beasant, D. 27; Beck, M. 5; Bonalair, T. 10(2); Brennan, J. 22(3); Burns, J. 3; Calderwood, C. 6; Chettle, S. 10(1); Cooper, R. (1); Crossley, M. 19(1); Dawson, K. 4(3); Doig, C. 8(3); Edds, G. 2; Freedman, D. 28(6); Freeman, D. (3); Gray, A. 12(10); Guinan, S. (1); Harewood, M. 18(16); Hjelde, J. 26(7); John, S. 13(4); Johnson, A. 24(1); Lester, J. 12(3); Louis-Jean, M. 26(1); Mannini, M. 7(1); Matrecano, S. 11; Melton, S. 1(1); Merino, C. 3(6); Palmer, C. 1(2); Petrachi, G. 10(3); Platt, D. 1(2); Prutton, D. 33(1); Quashie, N. 25(3); Rogers, A. 36(1); Scimeca, R. 38; Terry, J. 5(1); Vaughan, T. 10; Williams, G. (2); Woan, I. 1(10); Wright, I. 10.
Goals – League (53): Freedman 9, Rogers 9, Bart-Williams 5 (3 pens), Wright 5 (1 pen), Harewood 4, John 3, Bonalair 2, Johnson 2, Lester 2, Prutton 2, Quashie 2, Allou 1, Beck 1, Chettle 1 (pen), Palmer 1, own goals 4.
Worthington Cup (6): Allou 1, Bart-Williams 1, Freedman 1, Harewood 1, Quashie 1, Rogers 1.
FA Cup (4): Bart-Williams 2 (1 pen), Freedman 1, Rogers 1.
Ground: City Ground, Nottingham NG2 5FJ. Telephone (0115) 9824444.
Record attendance: 49,945 v Manchester U, Division 1, 28 October 1967. **Capacity:** 30,602.
Manager: David Platt.
Secretary: Paul White.
Most League Goals: 110, Division 3 (S), 1950–51.
Highest League Scorer in Season: Wally Ardron, 36, Division 3 (S), 1950–51.
Most League Goals in Total Aggregate: Grenville Morris, 199, 1898–1913.
Most Capped Player: Stuart Pearce, 76 (78), England.
Most League Appearances: Bob McKinlay, 614, 1951–70.
Honours – Football League: Division 1 – Champions 1977–78, 1997–98. Division 2 Champions – 1906–07, 1921–22. Division 3 (S) Champions – 1950–51. **FA Cup:** Winners 1898, 1959. **Football League Cup:** Winners 1977–78, 1978–79, 1988–89, 1989–90. **Anglo-Scottish Cup:** Winners 1976–77. **Simod Cup:** Winners 1989. **Zenith Data Systems Cup:** Winners 1991–92. **European Competitions: European Cup winners:** 1978–79, 1979–80. **Super Cup winners:** 1979–80.
Colours: Red shirts, white shorts, red stockings.

NOTTS COUNTY — DIV. 2

Bolland Paul (M)	6 0	12 01	Bradford	23 12 79	Bradford C
Brough Michael (M)	6 0	11 07	Nottingham	1 8 81	Trainee
Darby Duane (F)	6 0	13 02	Birmingham	17 10 73	Hull C
Dyer Alex (M)	6 1	13 01	Forest Gate	14 11 65	Huddersfield T
Farrell Sean (F)	6 2	13 01	Watford	28 1 69	Peterborough U
Ford Ryan (M)	5 10	10 05	Worksop	3 9 78	Manchester U
Gibson Paul (G)	6 3	13 00	Sheffield	1 11 76	Manchester U
Heffernan Paul (F)	5 10	11 00	Dublin	29 12 81	Newton
Holmes Richard (D)	5 11	10 12	Grantham	7 11 80	Trainee
Hughes Andy (M)	6 0	12 07	Manchester	2 1 78	Oldham Ath
Liburd Richard (D)	5 9	11 06	Nottingham	26 9 73	Carlisle U
Lindley James (G)	6 1	13 00	Sutton-in-Ashfield	23 7 81	Trainee
Murray Shaun (M)	5 8	10 12	Newcastle	7 10 70	Bradford C
Owers Gary (M)	6 0	12 09	Newcastle	3 10 68	Bristol C
Pearce Dennis (D)	5 9	11 07	Wolverhampton	10 9 74	Wolverhampton W
Ramage Craig (M)	5 11	12 10	Derby	30 3 70	Bradford C
Rapley Kevin (F)	5 10	11 07	Reading	21 9 77	Brentford

Redmile Matt (D)	6 3	15 03	Nottingham	12 11 76	Trainee
Richardson Ian (D)	5 10	12 00	Barking	22 1 70	Dagenham & Redbridge
Stallard Mark (F)	6 0	12 13	Derby	24 10 74	Wycombe W
Ward Darren (G)	5 11	12 09	Worksop	11 5 74	Mansfield T
Warren Mark (D)	6 0	12 08	Clapton	12 11 74	Leyton Orient

League Appearances: Allsopp, D. 3; Angell, B. 6; Beadle, P. 1(7); Blackmore, C. 21; Bolland, P. 18(7); Brough, M. 11; Cross, D. (1); Darby, D. 22(6); Dyer, A. 21(9); Farrell, S. (9); Fenton, N. 13; Ford, R. (1); Gibson, P. 1; Heffernan, P. (2); Holmes, R. 38(3); Howell, D. (1); Hughes, A. 32(3); Liburd, R. 24(7); Lindley, J. (1); Murray, S. 4(5); Owers, G. 45; Pearce, D. 14(6); Ramage, C. 36(4); Rapley, K. 11(18); Redmile, M. 39(2); Richardson, I. 33; Robson, M. (2); Stallard, M. 31(5); Tierney, F. 6(7); Ward, D. 45; Warren, M. 31(2); Webster, A. (1).
Goals – League (61): Stallard 14, Hughes 7 (4 pens), Dyer 6, Angell 5, Darby 5, Owers 4, Ramage 4, Richardson 4, Blackmore 2, Rapley 2, Allsopp 1, Bolland 1, Fenton 1, Liburd 1, Redmile 1, Tierney 1, Warren 1, own goal 1.
Worthington Cup (5): Blackmore 2, Ramage 2 (1 pen), Darby 1.
FA Cup (3): Rapley 1, Redmile 1, Tierney 1.
Ground: County Ground, Meadow Lane, Nottingham NG2 3HJ. Telephone (0115) 952 9000.
Record attendance: 47,310 v York C, FA Cup 6th rd, 12 March 1955. **Capacity:** 20,300.
Manager: Jocky Scott.
Secretary: Tony Cuthbert.
Most League Goals: 107, Division 4, 1959–60.
Highest League Scorer in Season: Tom Keetley, 39, Division 3 (S), 1930–31.
Most League Goals in Total Aggregate: Les Bradd, 124, 1967–78.
Most Capped Player: Kevin Wilson, 15 (42), Northern Ireland.
Most League Appearances: Albert Iremonger, 564, 1904–26.
Honours – Football League: Division 2 Champions – 1896–97, 1913–14, 1922–23. Division 3 Champions – 1997–98. Division 3 (S) Champions – 1930–31, 1949–50. Division 4 Champions – 1970–71. **FA Cup:** Winners 1893–94. **Anglo-Italian Cup:** Winners 1995.
Colours: Black and white striped shirts, black shorts, black stockings.

OLDHAM ATHLETIC DIV. 2

Adams Neil (M)	5 9	11 04	Stoke	23 11 65	Norwich C
Allott Mark (F)	5 11	10 12	Middleton	16 3 78	Trainee
Beavers Paul (F)	6 3	14 07	Blackpool	2 10 78	Sunderland
Boshell Daniel (M)	5 11	11 10	Bradford	30 5 81	Trainee
Campbell Jamie (G)			Glasgow	2 12 80	Trainee
Dudley Craig (F)	5 11	11 02	Ollerton	12 9 79	Notts Co
Duxbury Lee (M)	5 10	10 07	Keighley	7 10 69	Bradford C
Futcher Ben (D)	6 6	12 02	Bradford	4 6 81	Trainee
Garnett Shaun (D)	6 2	13 01	Wallasey	22 11 69	Swansea C
Holt Andy (D)	6 1	11 02	Manchester	21 5 78	Trainee
Hotte Mark (M)	5 11	11 00	Bradford	27 9 78	Trainee
Innes Mark (D)	5 10	12 04	Bellshill	27 9 78	Trainee
Jones Paul (D)	6 1	11 09	Liverpool	3 6 78	Tranmere R
Kelly Gary (G)	5 11	12 08	Fulwood	3 8 66	Bury
McLaughlin Gerard (M)			Rutherglen	26 9 81	Trainee
McLean Ian (D)	5 10	11 04	Leeds	13 9 78	Trainee
McNiven Scott (D)	5 10	10 08	Leeds	27 5 78	Trainee
Miskelly David (G)	6 0	12 02	Ards	3 9 79	Trainee

Philliskirk Tony (F)	6 2	12 12	Sunderland	10 2 65	Cardiff C
Rickers Paul (M)	5 10	11 04	Dewsbury	9 5 75	Trainee
Ritchie Andy (F)	5 11	12 04	Manchester	28 11 60	Scarborough
Salt Philip (M)	5 10	11 02	Huddersfield	2 3 79	Trainee
Sheridan John (M)	5 10	11 12	Stretford	1 10 64	Bolton W
Sugden Ryan (F)	6 0	12 07	Bradford	26 12 80	Trainee
Tait Jordan (D)	5 10	11 05	Berwick	27 9 79	Trainee
Thom Stuart (D)	6 3	13 01	Dewsbury	27 12 76	Nottingham F
Tipton Matthew (F)	5 10	11 02	Bridgend	29 6 80	Trainee
Walsh Danny (M)	5 11	12 03	Manchester	16 9 78	Trainee
Whitehall Steve (F)	5 11	11 09	Bromborough	8 12 66	Mansfield T

League Appearances: Adams, N. 29; Agogo, M. 2; Allott, M. 28(4); Beavers, P. 3(1); Boshell, D. 4(4); Dudley, C. 18(7); Duxbury, L. 43; Futcher, B. 1(4); Garnett, S. 32; Graham, R. 14(3); Holt, A. 46; Hotte, M. 34(1); Innes, M. 15(6); Jones, P. 16; Kelly, G. 44; McLean, I. 1; McNiven, D. 3(1); McNiven, S. 45; Miskelly, D. 2; Rickers, P. 40(1); Salt, P. 4(1); Sheridan, J. 34(2); Sugden, R. 3(14); Tait, J. (1); Thom, S. 9; Tipton, M. 9(20); Walsh, D. (1); Whitehall, S. 27(11).
Goals – League (50): Allott 10 (1 pen), Whitehall 9, Dudley 5, Duxbury 4, Holt 3, Rickers 3, Tipton 3 (1 pen), Adams 2, Garnett 2, Graham 2, Thom 2, Jones 1, McNiven D 1, McNiven S 1, Sheridan 1, Sugden 1.
Worthington Cup (1): Allott 1.
FA Cup (6): Whitehall 2, Adams 1, Dudley 1, Duxbury 1, Sheridan 1.
Ground: Boundary Park, Oldham OL1 2PA. Telephone (0161) 624 4972.
Record attendance: 47,671 v Sheffield W, FA Cup 4th rd. 25 January 1930.
Capacity: 13,559.
Manager: Andy Ritchie.
Secretary: Alan Hardy.
Most League Goals: 95, Division 4, 1962–63.
Highest League Scorer in Season: Tom Davis, 33, Division 3 (N), 1936–37.
Most League Goals in Total Aggregate: Roger Palmer, 141, 1980–94.
Most Capped Player: Gunnar Halle, 24 (62), Norway.
Most League Appearances: Ian Wood, 525, 1966–80.
Honours – Football League: Division 2 Champions – 1990–91, Division 3 (N) Champions – 1952–53. Division 3 Champions – 1973–74.
Colours: All blue.

OXFORD UNITED — DIV. 2

Abbey Ben (F)	5 7	11 00	London	13 5 78	Crawley T
Anthrobus Steve (F)	6 2	14 07	Lewisham	10 11 68	Crewe Alex
Arendse Andre (G)	6 1	11 08	Cape Town	27 6 67	Fulham
Beauchamp Joey (M)	5 10	12 07	Oxford	13 3 71	Swindon T
Cook Jamie (F)	5 10	10 10	Oxford	2 8 79	Trainee
Davis Steve (D)	6 1	13 05	Birmingham	26 7 65	Barnsley
Fear Peter (M)	5 10	11 10	Sutton	10 9 73	Wimbledon
Folland Robbie (F)	5 9	10 07	Swansea	16 9 79	Trainee
Hackett Christopher (D)	6 0	11 06	Oxford	1 3 83	Scholar
Lilley Derek (F)	5 9	11 10	Paisley	9 2 74	Leeds U
McGowan Neil (D)	5 8	11 07	Glasgow	15 4 77	Albion R
Murphy Matt (M)	6 0	12 02	Northampton	20 8 71	Corby T
Powell Paul (M)	5 8	11 01	Wallingford	30 6 78	Trainee
Ricketts Sam (M)			Aylesbury	11 10 81	Trainee
Shepheard Jon (D)	6 2	12 04	Oxford	31 3 81	Trainee
Tait Paul (M)	5 11	11 10	Sutton Coldfield	31 7 71	Birmingham C

Weatherstone Ross (D)	5 11	11 10	Reading	16 5 81	Trainee
Weatherstone Simon (F)	5 10	12 04	Reading	26 1 80	Trainee
Whitehead Dean (M)	5 11	12 01	Oxford	12 1 82	Trainee

League Appearances: Abbey, B. (10); Anthrobus, S. 25(11); Arendse, A. 13; Banger, N. 1(2); Beauchamp, J. 33(1); Cook, J. 11(18); Davis, S. 20(4); Edwards, C. 5; Fear, P. 13(6); Folland, R. 17(6); Francis, K. (3); Gilchrist, P. 1; Hackett, C. (2); Jemson, N. 13(5); Knight, R. 12(1); Lambert, J. 8(5); Lewis, M. 3(2); Lilley, D. 36(8); Lundin, P. 21(1); McGowan, N. 15(5); Murphy, M. 46; Newton, E. 7; Powell, P. 39(1); Robinson, L. 46; Russell, C. 5(1); Shepheard, J. 1(1); Tait, P. 34; Watson, M. 34(1); Weatherstone, R. 3; Weatherstone, S. 13(8); Whelan, P. 31.
Goals – League (43): Murphy 11 (3 pens), Lilley 7, Powell 6 (1 pen), Beauchamp 4, Cook 3, Anthrobus 2, Lambert 2, Whelan 2, Davis 1, Edwards 1, Fear 1, Folland 1, Weatherstone S 1, own goal 1.
Worthington Cup (5): Murphy 3, Beauchamp 2.
FA Cup (9): Murphy 3, Powell 3, Abbey 1, Folland 1, Lilley 1.
Ground: Manor Ground, Headington, Oxford OX3 7RS. Telephone (01865) 761503.
Record attendance: 22,750 v Preston NE, FA Cup 6th rd, 29 February 1964.
Capacity: 9650.
Manager: Denis Smith.
Secretary: Mick Brown.
Most League Goals: 91, Division 3, 1983–84.
Highest League Scorer in Season: John Aldridge, 30, Division 2, 1984–85.
Most League Goals in Total Aggregate: Graham Atkinson, 77, 1962–73.
Most Capped Player: Jim Magilton, 18 (40), Northern Ireland.
Most League Appearances: John Shuker, 478, 1962–77.
Honours – Football League: Division 2 Champions – 1984–85. Division 3 Champions – 1967–68, 1983–84. **Football League Cup:** Winners 1985–86.
Colours: Yellow shirts with navy trim, navy shorts and stockings.

PETERBOROUGH UNITED DIV. 2

Broughton Drewe (F)	6 3	12 04	Hitchin	25 10 78	Brentford
Campbell James (D)	6 2	11 12	Kent	16 11 79	Trainee
Chapple Phil (D)	6 2	13 01	Norwich	21 11 66	Charlton Ath
Clarke Andy (F)	5 10	11 07	Islington	22 7 67	Wimbledon
Connor Dan (G)	6 2	13 04	Dublin	31 1 81	Trainee
Cullen Jon (M)	6 0	13 00	Durham	10 1 73	Sheffield U
Danielsson Helgi (M)	6 0	12 00	Reykjavik	13 7 81	Fylkir
Drury Adam (D)	5 10	11 04	Cottenham	29 8 78	Trainee
Edwards Andy (D)	6 2	12 13	Epping	17 9 71	Birmingham C
Farrell Dave (M)	5 11	11 08	Birmingham	11 11 71	Wycombe W
Forinton Howard (F)	5 11	12 04	Boston	18 9 75	Birmingham C
French Daniel (M)	5 11	11 00	Peterborough	25 11 79	Trainee
Gill Matthew (M)	5 11	11 07	Cambridge	8 11 80	Trainee
Green Francis (F)	5 9	11 04	Derby	23 4 80	Ilkeston T
Haley Grant (D)	5 8	10 02	Bristol	20 9 79	Trainee
Hanlon Ritchie (M)	6 1	12 13	Kenton	25 5 78	Southend U
Hann Matthew (F)	5 9	10 04	Saffron Walden	6 9 80	Trainee
Hooper Dean (D)	5 11	12 06	Harefield	13 4 71	Swindon T
Inman Niall (M)	5 9	11 06	Wakefield	6 2 78	Trainee
Jelleyman Gareth (D)	5 10	10 03	Holywell	14 11 80	Trainee
Lee Jason (F)	6 3	13 03	Newham	9 5 71	Chesterfield
Lewis Neil (D)	5 8	10 05	Wolverhampton	28 6 74	Leicester C
Lyttle Gerard (D)	5 9	11 04	Belfast	27 11 77	Star of the Stea

Murray Dan (D)	6 2	12 12	Cambridge	16 5 82	Scholar
Oldfield David (M)	6 1	13 04	Perth (Aus)	30 5 68	Stoke C
Rea Simon (D)	6 1	13 00	Coventry	20 9 76	Birmingham C
Scott Richard (M)	5 11	12 08	Dudley	29 9 74	Shrewsbury T
Shields Tony (M)	5 8	10 01	Derry	4 6 80	Trainee
Showler Paul (M)	5 10	11 00	Doncaster	10 10 66	Luton T
Tyler Mark (G)	5 11	12 00	Norwich	2 4 77	Trainee
Wicks Matthew (D)	6 2	13 05	Reading	8 9 78	Crewe Alex

League Appearances: Broughton, D. 5(5); Castle, S. 36(3); Chapple, P. 15(1); Clarke, A. 33(4); Connor, D. (1); Cullen, J. 12(1); Davies, S. 16; Drury, A. 41(1); Edwards, A. 44; Etherington, M. 19; Farrell, D. 33(2); Forinton, H. 19(6); French, D. (6); Gill, M. 7(13); Green, F. 8(12); Griemink, B. 14; Haley, G. 1; Hanlon, R. 9(7); Hooper, D. 28(1); Inman, N. (1); Jelleyman, G. 14(6); Knight, Z. 8; Koogi, A. (1); Lee, J. 23; Martin, J. 7(8); Murray, D. 2; Oldfield, D. 9; Rea, S. 11(3); Scott, R. 28(6); Shields, T. 15(9); Tyler, M. 32; Wicks, M. 17(3).
Goals – League (63): Clarke 15, Castle 10 (4 pens), Forinton 7, Lee 6, Cullen 3, Etherington 3, Farrell 3, Scott 3, Davies 2, Edwards 2, Broughton 1, Chapple 1, Drury 1, Gill 1, Green 1, Hanlon 1, Martin 1, Rea 1, Shields 1.
Worthington Cup (1): Shields 1.
FA Cup (1): Clarke 1.
Ground: London Road Ground, Peterborough PE2 8AL. Telephone (01733) 563947.
Record attendance: 30,096 v Swansea T, FA Cup 5th rd, 20 February 1965.
Capacity: 15,314.
Manager: Barry Fry.
Secretary: Julie Etherington.
Most League Goals: 134, Division 4, 1960–61.
Highest League Scorer in Season: Terry Bly, 52, Division 4, 1960–61.
Most League Goals in Total Aggregate: Jim Hall, 122, 1967–75.
Most Capped Player: Tony Millington, 8 (21), Wales.
Most League Appearances: Tommy Robson, 482, 1968–81.
Honours – Football League: Division 4 Champions – 1960–61, 1973–74.
Colours: Royal blue shirts, white shorts, blue stockings with white tops.

PLYMOUTH ARGYLE — DIV. 3

Adams Steve (D)	6 0	12 00	Plymouth	25 9 80	Trainee
Barrett Adam (M)	5 10	12 00	Dagenham	29 11 79	
Bastow Darren (M)	5 11	12 00	Torquay	22 12 81	Trainee
Beswetherick John (D)	5 11	11 04	Liverpool	15 1 78	Trainee
Gritton Martin (F)	6 1	12 02	Glasgow	1 6 78	Porthleven
Guinan Stephen (F)	6 1	13 06	Birmingham	24 12 75	Cambridge U
Leadbitter Chris (M)	5 9	10 06	Middlesbrough	17 10 67	Apprentice
McCarthy Sean (F)	6 1	12 05	Bridgend	12 9 67	Oldham Ath
McGregor Paul (F)	5 10	11 06	Liverpool	17 12 74	Preston NE
Morrison-Hill Jamie (M)	5 8	10 04	Plymouth	8 6 81	Trainee
O'Sullivan Wayne (M)	5 7	10 11	Akrotiri	25 2 74	Cardiff C
Phillips Lee (F)	5 10	12 00	Penzance	16 9 80	School
Stonebridge Ian (F)	6 0	11 04	Lewisham	30 8 81	Tottenham H
Taylor Craig (D)	6 1	12 03	Plymouth	24 1 74	Swindon T
Wills Kevin (F)	5 7	10 04	Torbay	15 10 80	Trainee
Wotton Paul (M)	5 11	11 08	Plymouth	17 8 77	Trainee

League Appearances: Adams, S. 1; Ashton, J. 5(3); Barlow, M. 1(1); Barrett, A. 38(4); Bastow, D. 7(6); Belgrave, B. 2(13); Beswetherick, J. 44(1); Etherington, C.

4(1); Gibbs, P. 3(4); Gritton, M. 14(16); Guinan, S. 8; Hargreaves, C. 44; Heathcote, M. 27(2); Leadbitter, C. 28(3); McCall, S. 14(2); McCarthy, S. 21(8); McGregor, P. 44; Middleton, C. 6; Morrison-Hill, J. (1); O'Sullivan, W. 45; Paterson, S. 5; Phillips, L. 3(14); Rowbotham, J. 7(4); Sheffield, J. 41; Stonebridge, I. 27(4); Taylor, C. 41; Veysey, K. 5(1); Wills, K. (2); Wotton, P. 21(2).
Goals – League (55): McGregor 13, Stonebridge 9, Gritton 6, McCarthy 6, Barrett 3, Hargreaves 3, Taylor 3, Guinan 2, Leadbitter 2, Middleton 2, O'Sullivan 2, Bastow 1, Heathcote 1, McCall 1, Rowbotham 1.
Worthington Cup (2): Gritton 1, Stonebridge 1.
FA Cup (8): McGregor 3, Hargreaves 2, Bastow 1, Heathcote 1, Stonebridge 1.
Ground: Home Park, Plymouth, Devon PL2 3DQ. Telephone (01752) 562561.
Record attendance: 43,596 v Aston Villa, Division 2, 10 October 1936.
Capacity: 19,630.
Manager: Kevin Hodges.
Secretary: Roger Matthews.
Most League Goals: 107, Division 3 (S), 1925–26 and 1951–52.
Highest League Scorer in Season: Jack Cock, 32, Division 3 (S), 1925–26.
Most League Goals in Total Aggregate: Sammy Black, 180, 1924–38.
Most Capped Player: Moses Russell, 20 (23), Wales.
Most League Appearances: Kevin Hodges, 530, 1978–92.
Honours – Football League: Division 3 (S) Champions – 1929–30, 1951–52. Division 3 Champions – 1958–59.
Colours: Green and white shirts, white shorts, green, black and white stockings.

PORTSMOUTH — DIV. 1

Allen Rory (F)	5 11	11 10	Beckenham	17 10 77	Tottenham H
Awford Andy (D)	5 9	11 09	Worcester	14 7 72	Worcester C
Birmingham David (D)	5 8	11 01	Portsmouth	16 4 81	Bournemouth
Bradbury Lee (F)	6 2	13 10	Isle of Wight	3 7 75	Crystal Palace
Claridge Steve (F)	5 9	12 09	Portsmouth	10 4 66	Wolverhampton W
Crowe Jason (D)	5 9	11 02	Sidcup	30 9 78	Arsenal
Cundy Jason (D)	6 0	13 11	Wimbledon	12 11 69	Ipswich T
Derry Shaun (M)	5 10	13 02	Nottingham	6 12 77	Sheffield U
Edinburgh Justin (D)	5 10	12 01	Basildon	18 12 69	Tottenham H
Flahavan Aaron (G)	6 1	11 12	Southampton	15 12 75	Trainee
Griffiths Ben (M)			Bournemouth	27 11 81	Trainee
Harper Kevin (F)	5 7	12 00	Oldham	15 1 76	Derby Co
Hiley Scott (D)	5 8	11 08	Plymouth	27 9 68	Southampton
Holbrook Adam (D)	5 9	11 06	Newport (IW)	17 10 80	Trainee
Hoult Russell (G)	6 4	14 07	Ashby	22 11 72	Derby Co
Hughes Ceri (M)	5 10	12 07	Pontypridd	26 2 71	Wimbledon
Lovell Stephen (F)	5 11	11 08	Amersham	6 12 80	Bournemouth
McNab Joe (M)	5 4	9 00	Brighton	29 10 80	Manchester C
McNab Neil (M)	5 6	10 03	Brighton	29 10 80	Manchester C
Miglioranzi Stefani (M)	6 1	12 12	Pacos de Caldas	20 9 77	St Johns Univ
Moore Darren (D)	6 3	15 08	Birmingham	22 4 74	Bradford C
Nightingale Luke (F)	5 11	11 07	Portsmouth	22 12 80	Trainee
Panopoulos Mike (M)	6 1	12 10	Melbourne	9 10 76	Heidelberg U
Pettefer Carl (M)	5 7	10 02	Taplow	22 3 81	Trainee
Petterson Andy (G)	6 2	15 02	Fremantle	29 9 69	Charlton Ath
Phillips Martin (M)	5 8	10 03	Exeter	13 3 76	Manchester C
Stoner Craig (M)			Chichester	5 11 81	Trainee
Tardif Chris (G)	5 11	12 07	Guernsey	19 9 79	Trainee
Thogersen Thomas (M)	6 2	13 01	Copenhagen	2 4 68	Brondby

Waterman David (D)	5 10	12 02	Guernsey	16 5 77	Trainee
Whitbread Adrian (D)	6 0	12 12	Epping	22 10 71	West Ham U
Whittingham Guy (F)	6 1	12 04	Evesham	10 11 64	Sheffield W
Wilson Michael (M)			Guernsey	5 10 81	Trainee

League Appearances: Allen, R. 10(5); Awford, A. 28(6); Berntsen, T. 1(1); Birmingham, D. 1(1); Bradbury, L. 35; Brown, M. 4; Claridge, S. 31(3); Crowe, J. 21(4); Cundy, J. 9; Derry, S. 9; Durnin, J. 2; Edinburgh, J. 11; Fenton, A. (1); Flahavan, A. 10; Harper, K. 12; Hiley, S. 4(4); Hoult, R. 18; Hughes, C. 15; Igoe, S. 14(12); Knight, A. 1; Lovell, S. (3); McLoughlin, A. 18(1); Miglioranzi, S. 12(1); Moore, D. 25; Myers, A. 4(4); Newton, A. 1(2); Nightingale, L. 1(6); O'Neil, G. (1); Pamarot, N. 1(1); Panopoulos, M. 18(4); Peron, J. 9(1); Petterson, A. 17; Phillips, M. 2(5); Robinson, M. 23(2); Simpson, F. 17; Thogersen, T. 32(3); Vernazza, P. 7; Vlachos, M. 11(1); Waterman, D. 19(1); Whitbread, A. 38(1); Whittingham, G. 15(10).
Goals – League (55): Claridge 14 (2 pens), Bradbury 10 (1 pen), McLoughlin 5 (5 pens), Thogersen 5, Whittingham 4, Allen 3, Harper 2, Hughes 2, Miglioranzi 2, Peron 2, Awford 1, Derry 1, Igoe 1, Moore 1, Panopoulos 1, Whitbread 1.
Worthington Cup (4): Nightingale 2, Lovell 1, McLoughlin 1.
FA Cup (0).
Ground: Fratton Park, Frogmore Rd, Portsmouth PO4 8RA. Telephone (01705) 731204.
Record attendance: 51,385 v Derby Co, FA Cup 6th rd, 26 February 1949.
Capacity: 19,179.
Manager: Tony Pulis.
Secretary: Paul Weld.
Most League Goals: 91, Division 4, 1979–80.
Highest League Scorer in Season: Guy Whittingham, 42, Division 1, 1992–93.
Most League Goals in Total Aggregate: Peter Harris, 194, 1946–60.
Most Capped Player: Jimmy Dickinson, 48, England.
Most League Appearances: Jimmy Dickinson, 764, 1946–65.
Honours – Football League: Division 1 Champions – 1948–49, 1949–50. Division 3 (S) Champions – 1923–24. Division 3 Champions – 1961–62, 1982–83. **FA Cup:** Winners 1939.
Colours: Blue shirts, white shorts, red stockings.

PORT VALE — DIV. 2

Brammer Dave (M)	5 11	12 00	Bromborough	28 2 75	Wrexham
Brisco Neil (M)	5 11	13 01	Billinge	26 1 78	Manchester C
Burton Sagi (D)	6 2	13 06	Birmingham	25 11 77	Colchester U
Burns Liam (D)	6 0	13 03	Belfast	30 10 78	Trainee
Carragher Matthew (D)	5 9	11 06	Liverpool	14 1 76	Wigan Ath
Cummins Michael (M)	6 0	12 08	Dublin	1 6 78	Middlesbrough
Donnelly Paul (D)	5 7	11 00	Newcastle under Lyme	16 2 81	Trainee
Eyre Richard (M)	5 8	11 08	Poynton	15 9 76	Trainee
Goodlad Mark (G)	6 0	13 02	Barnsley	9 9 80	Nottingham F
Minton Jeffrey (F)	5 10	12 04	Hackney	28 12 73	Brighton & HA
Naylor Tony (F)	5 4	10 07	Manchester	29 3 68	Crewe Alex
O'Callaghan George (M)	6 1	10 05	Cork	5 9 79	Trainee
Rougier Tony (F)	5 10	14 07	Trinidad	17 7 71	Hibernian
Smith Alex (M)	5 8	10 06	Liverpool	15 2 76	Chester C
Tankard Allen (D)	5 10	13 04	Fleet	21 5 69	Wigan Ath
Taylor Paul (M)	5 11	12 06	Stoke	16 9 80	Trainee
Walsh Michael (D)	6 0	12 08	Rotherham	5 8 77	Scunthorpe U
Widdrington Tommy (M)	5 9	11 12	Newcastle	1 10 71	Grimsby T

League Appearances: Aldridge-deceased, M. (3); Barker, S. 3(2); Bent, M. 7(1); Bogie, I. 8(1); Brammer, D. 29; Brisco, N. 11(1); Bullock, M. 6; Burns, L. 24; Burton, S. 19(1); Butler, T. 15; Carragher, M. 36(1); Corden, W. (2); Cummins, M. 12; Donnelly, P. 4; Eyre, R. 17(13); Foyle, M. 13(9); Gardner, A. 26; Goodlad, M. 1; Griffiths, C. (5); Healy, D. 15(1); Minton, J. 23; Musselwhite, P. 30; Naylor, T. 25(11); O'Callaghan, G. 8(3); Pilkington, K. 15; Rimmer, S. (2); Rougier, T. 33(5); Smith, A. 9(4); Snijders, M. 18(3); Talbot, S. 6; Tankard, A. 31(4); Taylor, G. 4; Viljanen, V. 11(4); Walsh, M. 10(2); Widdrington, T. 37(1).
Goals – League (48): Rougier 8, Foyle 6, Naylor 6, Widdrington 5 (4 pens), Viljanen 4, Gardner 3, Healy 3, Minton 3 (2 pens), Burton 2, Bent 1, Bullock 1, Carragher 1, Cummins 1, Eyre 1, Tankard 1, Walsh 1, own goal 1.
Worthington Cup (5): Naylor 2, Griffiths 1, Minton 1 (pen), Rougier 1.
FA Cup (0).
Ground: Vale Park, Burslem, Stoke-on-Trent ST6 1AW. Telephone (01782) 814134.
Record attendance: 50,000 v Aston Villa, FA Cup 5th rd, 20 February 1960.
Capacity: 22,356
Manager: Brian Horton.
Secretary: F. W. Lodey.
Most League Goals: 110, Division 4, 1958–59.
Highest League Scorer in Season: Wilf Kirkham 38, Division 2, 1926–27.
Most League Goals in Total Aggregate: Wilf Kirkham, 154, 1923–29, 1931–33.
Most Capped Player: Sammy Morgan, 7 (18), Northern Ireland.
Most League Appearances: Roy Sproson, 761, 1950–72.
Honours – Football League: Division 3 (N) Champions – 1929–30, 1953–54. Division 4 Champions – 1958–59.
Colours: White shirts, black shorts, black and white stockings.

PRESTON NORTH END DIV. 1

Alexander Graham (D)	5 10	12 00	Coventry	10 10 71	Luton T
Anderson Iain (F)	5 8	9 07	Glasgow	23 7 77	Dundee
Appleton Michael (M)	5 8	11 00	Salford	4 12 75	Manchester U
Barry-Murphy Brian (M)	6 0	12 04	Cork	27 7 78	Cork City
Basham Steve (F)	5 11	12 05	Southampton	2 12 77	Southampton
Cartwright Lee (F)	5 8	10 07	Rossendale	19 9 72	Trainee
Eaton Adam (D)	5 10	11 08	Wigan	2 5 80	Everton
Edwards Robert (D)	6 0	12 07	Kendal	1 7 73	Bristol C
Gregan Sean (M)	6 2	12 03	Stockton	29 3 74	Darlington
Gunnlaugsson Bjarki (F)	5 9	11 05	Iceland	6 3 73	KR
Jackson Michael (D)	5 11	11 10	Chester	4 12 73	Bury
Kidd Ryan (D)	5 11	10 10	Radcliffe	16 10 71	Port Vale
King Stuart (M)	5 11	10 00	Derry	20 3 81	Trainee
Lucas David (G)	6 1	11 06	Preston	23 11 77	Trainee
Macken Jonathan (F)	5 10	12 00	Manchester	7 9 77	Trainee
Mathie Alex (F)	5 10	11 13	Bathgate	20 12 68	Dundee U
McKenna Paul (M)	5 8	11 11	Chorley	20 10 77	Trainee
Moilanen Teuvo (G)	6 5	12 09	Oulu	12 12 73	Jaro
Morgan Paul (D)	6 0	11 05	Belfast	23 10 78	Trainee
Murdock Colin (D)	6 1	12 00	Ballymena	2 7 75	Manchester U
Rankine Mark (M)	5 9	11 05	Doncaster	30 9 69	Wolverhampton W
Wright Mark (F)	5 10	11 05	Chorley	4 9 81	Schoolboy

League Appearances: Alexander, G. 46; Anderson, I. 11(1); Angell, B. 9(6); Appleton, M. 21(5); Barry-Murphy, B. (1); Basham, S. 11(13); Beesley, M. (1);

Beresford, D. 1(3); Cartwright, L. 22(8); Darby, J. 2(1); Diaf, F. 1(2); Edwards, R. 37(4); Eyres, D. 26(15); Gregan, S. 33; Gunnlaugsson, B. 12(14); Jackson, M. 46; Kidd, R. 28(1); Lucas, D. 6; Ludden, D. 3; Macken, J. 40(4); Mathie, A. 5(7); McKenna, P. 17(7); Moilanen, T. 40(1); Morgan, P. ; Murdock, C. 29(4); Nogan, K. 16(6); Parkinson, G. (1); Rankine, M. 44; Wright, M. (2).
Goals – League (74): Macken 22, Angell 8, Eyres 7, Alexander 6 (5 pens), Jackson 5, Nogan 4, Appleton 3, Gregan 3, Anderson 2, Basham 2, Edwards 2, Mathie 2, McKenna 2, Murdock 2, Cartwright 1, Gunnlaugsson 1, own goals 2.
Worthington Cup (7): Macken 2, Mathie 2, Alexander 1, Appleton 1, Basham 1.
FA Cup (9): Alexander 3 (3 pens), Eyres 1, Gunnlaugsson 1, McKenna 1, Macken 1, own goals 2.
Ground: Deepdale, Preston PR1 6RU. Telephone (01772) 902020.
Record attendance: 42,684 v Arsenal, Division 1, 23 April 1938. **Capacity:** 21,412.
Manager: David Moyes.
Secretary: M. Wearmouth.
Most League Goals: 100, Division 2, 1927–28 and Division 1, 1957–58.
Highest League Scorer in Season: Ted Harper, 37, Division 2, 1932–33.
Most League Goals in Total Aggregate: Tom Finney, 187, 1946–60.
Most Capped Player: Tom Finney, 76, England.
Most League Appearances: Alan Kelly, 447, 1961–75.
Honours – Football League: Division 1 Champions – 1888–89 (first champions), 1889–90. Division 2 Champions – 1903–04, 1912–13, 1950–51, 1999–2000. Division 3 Champions – 1970–71, 1995–96. **FA Cup winners** 1889, 1938.
Colours: White shirts, navy shorts, white stockings.

QUEENS PARK RANGERS — DIV. 1

Bankole Ademola (G)	6 3	14 11	Lagos	9 9 69	Crewe Alex
Baraclough Ian (D)	6 1	12 10	Leicester	4 12 70	Notts Co
Brady Richard (F)	5 8	10 04	Dartford	17 9 82	Trainee
Breacker Tim (D)	6 0	13 00	Bicester	2 7 65	West Ham U
Brown Carlos (D)	6 0	11 07	Edmonton	22 4 81	Trainee
Browne Rickey (D)	6 1	12 05	Edmonton	19 10 81	Scholar
Bruce Paul (F)	5 10	12 06	London	18 2 78	Trainee
Bubb Alvin (F)	5 4	10 03	Paddington	11 10 80	Trainee
Bull Nikki (G)	6 1	11 13	Hastings	2 10 81	Scholar
Cochrane Justin (M)	5 11	11 07	Hackney	26 1 82	Scholar
Currie Michael (F)	5 10	11 00	Westminster	19 10 79	Trainee
D'Austin Ryan (M)	5 9	10 13	Edgware	29 11 82	Trainee
Darlington Jermaine (D)	5 9	13 00	Hackney	11 4 74	Aylesbury U
Duncan Lyndon (D)	5 8	11 02	Ealing	12 1 83	Trainee
Gallen Kevin (F)	5 11	13 05	Hammersmith	21 9 75	Trainee
Graham Richard (M)	5 8	10 06	Newry	5 8 79	Trainee
Harper Lee (G)	6 1	14 07	Chelsea	30 10 71	Arsenal
Heinola Antti (D)	5 10	12 03	Helsinki	20 3 73	Heracles
Jeanne Leon (F)	5 8	10 10	Cardiff	17 11 80	Trainee
Koejoe Sammy (F)	6 2	14 07	Surinam	17 8 74	Salzburg
Kulcsar George (M)	6 1	12 08	Budapest	12 8 67	Bradford C
Langley Richard (M)	5 10	11 04	London	27 12 79	Trainee
Lusardi Mario (F)	5 9	12 00	Islington	27 9 79	Trainee
Maddix Danny (D)	5 11	12 00	Ashford	11 10 66	Tottenham H
McFlynn Terry (M)	5 9	11 11	Magherafelt	27 3 81	Trainee
Mills Danny (G)	6 0	12 07	Sidcup	8 9 82	Trainee
Morrow Steve (D)	6 0	12 06	Bangor	2 7 70	Arsenal
Murphy Danny (D)	5 6	10 04	London	4 12 82	Trainee

Murray Paul (M)	5 8	10 05	Carlisle	31 8 76	Carlisle U
Pacquette Richard (F)	6 0	12 07	Paddington	28 1 83	Trainee
Peacock Gavin (M)	5 9	11 08	Eltham	18 11 67	Chelsea
Perry Mark (M)	5 11	13 06	Perivale	19 10 78	Trainee
Piercewright Brad (D)	6 0	12 00	Northampton	21 9 80	Northampton T
Plummer Chris (D)	6 2	12 12	Isleworth	12 10 76	Trainee
Ready Karl (D)	6 3	13 08	Neath	14 8 72	Trainee
Rose Matthew (D)	5 11	11 09	Dartford	24 9 75	Arsenal
Rowland Keith (M)	5 10	10 07	Portadown	1 9 71	West Ham U
Rustem Adam (F)	6 0	11 07	Whipps Cross	18 9 81	Scholar
Scully Tony (M)	5 7	11 06	Dublin	12 6 76	Manchester C
Steiner Rob (F)	6 2	13 05	Finsprong	20 6 73	Bradford C
Wardley Stuart (M)	5 11	12 03	Cambridge	10 9 75	Saffron Walden T
Weare Ross (F)	6 2	13 09	Perivale	19 3 77	East Ham U
Wright Danny (M)	5 7	10 13	London	24 9 81	Trainee

League Appearances: Bankole, A. (1); Baraclough, I. 45; Beck, M. 10(1); Breacker, T. 15(1); Bruce, P. 11(1); Darlington, J. 34; Gallen, K. 7(24); Harper, L. 37(1); Jeanne, L. 1(1); Kiwomya, C. 42(2); Koejoe, S. 5(6); Kulcsar, G. 5(8); Langley, R. 36(5); Maddix, D. 17; McGovern, B. 3(2); Miklosko, L. 9; Morrow, S. 6(1); Murray, P. 21(9); Peacock, G. 26(4); Perry, M. 9(1); Plummer, C. 17(1); Ready, K. 32(1); Rose, M. 27(2); Rowland, K. 5(10); Scully, T. 2(6); Slade, S. 3(6); Steiner, R. 24; Taylor, G. 2(4); Ward, D. 14; Wardley, S. 41(2); Weare, R. (4).
Goals – League (62): Kiwomya 13, Wardley 11, Peacock 8 (2 pens), Steiner 6, Beck 4 (3 pens), Gallen 4, Langley 3, Darlington 2, Ready 2, Breacker 1, Koejoe 1, Maddix 1, Rose 1, Slade 1, Taylor 1, own goals 3.
Worthington Cup (3): Langley 1, Peacock 1 (pen), own goal 1.
FA Cup (4): Wardley 3, Kiwomya 1.
Ground: South Africa Road, W12 7PA. Telephone (020) 8743 0262.
Record attendance: 35,353 v Leeds U, Division 1, 27 April 1974. **Capacity:** 19,148.
Manager: Gerry Francis.
Secretary: Sheila Marson.
Most League Goals: 111, Division 3, 1961–62.
Highest League Scorer in Season: George Goddard, 37, Division 3 (S), 1929–30.
Most League Goals in Total Aggregate: George Goddard, 172, 1926–34.
Most Capped Player: Alan McDonald, 52, Northern Ireland.
Most League Appearances: Tony Ingham, 519, 1950–63.
Honours – Football League: Division 2 Champions – 1982–83. Division 3 (S) Champions – 1947–48. Division 3 Champions – 1966–67. **Football League Cup winners** 1966–67.
Colours: Blue and white hooped shirts, blue shorts, blue stockings.

READING — DIV. 2

Allaway Ricky (D)	6 2	11 08	Reading	16 2 83	Trainee
Ashdown Jamie (G)	6 3	14 07	Wokingham	30 11 80	
Brayson Paul (F)	5 4	10 10	Newcastle	16 9 77	Newcastle U
Butler Martin (F)	6 0	11 07	Wordsley	15 9 74	Cambridge U
Caskey Darren (M)	5 8	11 09	Basildon	21 8 74	Tottenham H
Casper Chris (D)	6 0	11 02	Burnley	28 4 75	Manchester U
Crawford Jimmy (M)	5 10	11 00	Chicago	1 5 73	Newcastle U
Evers Sean (M)	5 9	9 07	Hitchin	10 10 77	Luton T
Forster Nicky (F)	5 9	10 11	Caterham	8 9 73	Birmingham C
Gray Stuart (D)	5 11	12 00	Harrogate	18 12 73	Celtic
Gurney Andy (D)	5 8	10 08	Bristol	25 1 74	Torquay U

Haddow Alex (M)	5 8	11 02	Fleet	8 1 82	Trainee
Henderson Darius (F)	6 1	13 09	Doncaster	7 9 81	Trainee
Howie Scott (G)	6 4	13 07	Motherwell	4 1 72	Motherwell
Igoe Sammy (M)	5 6	10 08	Spelthorne	30 9 75	Portsmouth
Lockwood Adam (D)	6 0	12 00	Wakefield	26 10 81	Trainee
Mackie John (D)	6 0	12 06	London	5 7 76	Sutton U
McIntyre Jim (F)	5 11	11 05	Alexandria	24 5 72	Kilmarnock
Murty Graeme (M)	5 10	11 10	Saltburn	13 11 74	York C
Parkinson Phil (M)	6 0	11 06	Chorley	1 12 67	Bury
Polston John (D)	5 11	11 12	Walthamstow	10 6 68	Norwich C
Robinson Matt (D)	5 10	11 02	Exeter	23 12 74	Portsmouth
Scott Keith (F)	6 3	14 03	Westminster	9 6 67	Wycombe W
Smith Christopher (D)	5 11	11 01	Derby	30 6 81	Trainee
Smith Neil (M)	5 9	12 00	Lambeth	30 9 71	Fulham
Stamp Neville (D)	5 11	12 07	Reading	7 7 81	Trainee
Tyson Nathan (F)	6 0	10 01	Reading	4 5 82	Trainee
Whitehead Phil (G)	6 3	13 07	Halifax	17 12 69	WBA

League Appearances: Bernal, A. 19(4); Brayson, P. (7); Brebner, G. 2; Butler, M. 17; Caskey, D. 43(1); Casper, C. 14(1); Crawford, J. 3(1); Evers, S. 8(9); Forster, N. 31(5); Grant, P. 27(2); Gray, S. 12(3); Gurney, A. 35(3); Haddow, A. 1(1); Henderson, D. 2(4); Hodges, L. 15(10); Howie, S. 35(1); Hunter, B. 27(4); Igoe, S. 3(3); Lisbie, K. 1(1); McIntyre, J. 15(11); McLaren, A. 2; Murty, G. 14(3); Newman, R. 4(3); Nicholls, M. 4(1); Parkinson, P. 22; Polston, J. 12(2); Potter, G. 4; Primus, L. 27(1); Robinson, M. 19; Sarr, M. (3); Scott, K. 14(11); Smith, N. 26(10); Tyson, N. (1); Van der Kwaak, P. (1); Whitehead, P. 11; Williams, A. 15; Williams, M. 22(7).
Goals – League (57): Caskey 17 (5 pens), Forster 10, Williams M 5 (1 pen), Butler 4, McIntyre 4, Scott 3, Gurney 2, Hodges 2, Brebner 1, Crawford 1, Grant 1, Hunter 1, Newman 1, Nicholls 1, Parkinson 1, Polston 1, Smith 1, Williams A 1.
Worthington Cup (5): Caskey 2 (1 pen), Scott 2, Hunter 1.
FA Cup (7): Caskey 3 (3 pens), Bernal 1, Hunter 1, McIntyre 1, Williams M 1.
Ground: Madejski Stadium, Junction 11, M4, Reading, Berks RG2 0FL. Telephone (0118) 968 1100.
Record attendance: 33,042 v Brentford, FA Cup 5th rd, 19 February 1927. **Capacity:** 15,000.
Manager: Alan Pardew.
Secretary: Ms Andrea Barker.
Most League Goals: 112, Division 3 (S), 1951–52.
Highest League Scorer in Season: Ronnie Blackman, 39, Division 3 (S), 1951–52.
Most League Goals in Total Aggregate: Ronnie Blackman, 158, 1947–54.
Most Capped Player: Jimmy Quinn, 17 (46), Northern Ireland.
Most League Appearances: Martin Hicks, 500, 1978–91.
Honours – Football League: Division 2 Champions – 1993–94. Division 3 Champions – 1985–86. Division 3 (S) Champions – 1925–26. Division 4 Champions – 1978–79. **Simod Cup winners** 1987–88.
Colours: Royal blue and white hooped shirts, blue shorts, white and blue stockings.

ROCHDALE DIV. 3

Atkinson Graeme (D)	5 7	11 04	Hull	11 11 71	Scarborough
Bayliss Dave (D)	5 11	12 00	Liverpool	8 6 76	Trainee
Edwards Neil (G)	5 9	11 11	Aberdare	5 12 70	Stockport Co
Evans Wayne (D)	5 10	12 03	Welshpool	25 8 71	Walsall
Flitcroft David (M)	5 11	13 05	Bolton	14 1 74	Chester C

Ford Tony (M)	5 9	13 00	Grimsby	14 5 59	Mansfield T
Hicks Graham (D)	5 10	13 05	Oldham	17 2 81	Trainee
Hill Keith (D)	6 1	12 07	Bolton	17 5 69	Plymouth Arg
Jones Gary (M)	5 11	11 07	Birkenhead	3 6 77	Caernarfon Town
McAuley Sean (D)	5 9	11 13	Sheffield	23 6 72	Scunthorpe U
Platt Clive (F)	6 3	12 13	Wolverhampton	27 10 77	Trainee
Priestley Phil (G)	6 0	12 09	Wigan	30 3 76	Atherton LR

League Appearances: Atkinson, G. 32(8); Bayliss, D. 26(3); Bettney, C. 12(12); Carden, P. 3(10); Dowe, J. 1(6); Edwards, N. 40; Ellis, T. 30(1); Evans, W. 46; Flitcroft, D. 40(3); Ford, T. 28(6); Gibson, P. 5; Green, R. 6; Hill, K. 37(1); Holt, M. 8(6); Jones, G. 31(8); Lancashire, G. 21(8); McAuley, S. 10(3); McClare, S. 5(4); Monington, M. 22(2); Morris, A. 1(6); Peake, J. 38(5); Peyton, W. 1; Platt, C. 31(10); Priestley, P. 1(1); Searle, D. 13(1); Stokes, D. 18(1); Taylor, D. (1); Wilson, S. (1).
Goals – League (57): Ellis 11, Platt 9, Lancashire 8, Jones 7 (3 pens), Peake 6, Atkinson 5, Bayliss 3, Flitcroft 2, Ford 2, Monington 2, Evans 1, own goal 1.
Worthington Cup (2): Evans 1, Lancashire 1.
FA Cup (4): Atkinson 1, Dowe 1, Peake 1, Platt 1.
Ground: Spotland, Sandy Lane, Rochdale OL11 5DS. Telephone (01706) 644648.
Record attendance: 24,231 v Notts Co, FA Cup 2nd rd, 10 December 1949.
Capacity: 10,249.
Manager: Steve Parkin.
Secretary: Hilary Molyneux Horrocks.
Most League Goals: 105, Division 3 (N), 1926–27.
Highest League Scorer in Season: Albert Whitehurst, 44, Division 3 (N), 1926–27.
Most League Goals in Total Aggregate: Reg Jenkins, 119, 1964–73.
Most Capped Player: None.
Most League Appearances: Graham Smith, 317, 1966–74.
Honours – Nil.
Colours: Blue shirts with white trim, blue shorts, blue stockings with white hoop.

ROTHERHAM UNITED — DIV. 2

Artell David (D)	6 2	13 00	Rotherham	22 11 80	Trainee
Beech Chris (D)	5 9	12 09	Congleton	5 11 75	Cardiff C
Branston Guy (D)	6 1	13 11	Leicester	9 1 79	Leicester C
Dillon Paul (D)	5 9	10 11	Limerick	22 10 78	Trainee
Fortune-West Leo (F)	6 4	13 01	Stratford	9 4 71	Brentford
Hudson Danny (M)	5 8	10 03	Mexborough	25 6 79	Trainee
Monkhouse Andy (F)	6 0	13 09	Leeds	23 10 80	Trainee
Pettinger Paul (G)	6 0	13 00	Sheffield	1 10 75	Carlisle U
Scott Rob (F)	6 1	12 04	Epsom	15 8 73	Fulham
Sedgwick Chris (F)	5 11	10 10	Sheffield	28 4 80	Trainee
Turner Andy (M)	5 10	11 10	Woolwich	23 3 75	Wolverhampton W
Varty Will (D)	6 0	12 00	Workington	1 10 76	Carlisle U
Warne Paul (F)	5 8	11 01	Norwich	8 5 73	Wigan Ath
Watson Kevin (M)	5 10	12 08	Hackney	3 1 74	Swindon T
Wilsterman Brian (D)	6 1	14 02	Surinam	19 11 66	Oxford U

League Appearances: Artell, D. (1); Beech, C. 5(1); Berry, T. 18(18); Branston, G. 30; Dillon, P. 15; Fortune-West, L. 39; Garner, D. 33(2); Glover, L. (7); Hudson, D. 3(4); Hurst, P. 25(5); Ingledow, J. 2(2); Martindale, G. 4(5); Pollitt, M. 46; Scott, R. 33(1); Sedgwick, C. 29(9); Thompson, S. 27(4); Turner, A. 26(6); Varty, W. 26(1); Warne, P. 39(4); Warner, V. 16(2); Watson, K. 44; White, J. 8(12); Wilsterman, B. 38(4).

Goals – League (72): Fortune-West 17, Warne 10, Garner 9, Thompson 6 (3 pens), Sedgwick 5 (1 pen), Berry 4, Branston 4, White 4, Wilsterman 3, Hurst 2, Martindale 2 (2 pens), Glover 1 (pen), Hudson 1, Scott 1, Turner 1, Watson 1, own goal 1.
Worthington Cup (0).
FA Cup (3): Garner 1, Martindale 1 (pen), Thompson 1.
Ground: Millmoor Ground, Rotherham S60 1HR. Telephone (01709) 512434.
Record attendance: 25,000 v Sheffield U, Division 2, 13 December 1952 and v Sheffield W, Division 2, 26 January 1952. **Capacity:** 11,514
Manager: Ronnie Moore.
Most League Goals: 114, Division 3 (N), 1946–47.
Highest League Scorer in Season: Wally Ardron, 38, Division 3 (N), 1946–47.
Most League Goals in Total Aggregate: Gladstone Guest, 130, 1946–56.
Most Capped Player: Shaun Goater, 18, Bermuda.
Most League Appearances: Danny Williams, 459, 1946–62.
Honours – Football League: Division 3 Champions – 1980–81. Division 3 (N) Champions – 1950–51. Division 4 Champions – 1988–89. **Auto Windscreens Shield:** Winners 1996
Colours: Red shirts, white shorts, red stockings.

SCUNTHORPE UNITED — DIV. 3

Calvo-Garcia Alexander (M)	5 11	11 10	Ordizia	1 1 72	Eibar
Dawson Andrew (D)	5 9	11 05	Northallerton	20 10 78	Nottingham F
Evans Tom (G)	6 1	13 02	Doncaster	31 12 76	Crystal Palace
Graves Wayne (M)	5 8	10 09	Scunthorpe	18 9 80	Trainee
Harsley Paul (M)	5 10	11 03	Scunthorpe	29 5 78	Trainee
Hodges Lee (M)	5 5	11 00	Newham	2 3 78	West Ham U
Hope Chris (D)	6 1	12 08	Sheffield	14 11 73	Nottingham F
Housham Steven (M)	5 10	12 03	Gainsborough	24 2 76	Trainee
Ipoua Guy (F)	6 1	13 02	Douala	14 1 76	Novelda
Quailey Brian (F)	6 0	13 04	Leicester	21 3 78	Nuneaton B
Jackson Mark (D)	5 11	12 04	Barnsley	30 9 77	Leeds U
Sheldon Gareth (F)	5 11	12 06	Birmingham	31 1 80	Trainee
Stamp Darryn (F)	6 1	11 10	Beverley	21 9 78	
Stanton Nathan (D)	5 9	12 06	Nottingham	6 5 81	Trainee
Torpey Steve (F)	6 3	13 06	Islington	8 12 70	Bristol C

League Appearances: Barwick, T. (1); Bull, G. 3(3); Calvo-Garcia, A. 18; Clarke, R. 1; Cornforth, J. 2(2); Dawson, A. 40(3); Evans, T. 27(1); Fickling, A. 24(6); Gayle, J. 2(10); Graves, W. 9(10); Guinan, S. 2(1); Harsley, P. 45(1); Hodges, L. 39(1); Hodgson, R. 1; Hope, C. 43(1); Housham, S. 6(3); Humphreys, R. 6; Hyldgaard, M. 5; Ipoua, G. 28(12); Jackson, M. 6; Logan, R. 39; Marcelle, C. 8(2); Marshall, L. 1(4); McAuley, S. 8; Omoyinmi, E. 6; Perez, L. 13; Quailey, B. 13(1); Sheldon, G. 8(14); Sparrow, M. 2(9); Stamp, D. 5(5); Stanton, N. 27(7); Torpey, S. 15; Turner, R. 1; Walker, J. 40(2); Wilcox, R. 13(1).
Goals – League (40): Ipoua 9 (2 pens), Hodges 6, Quailey 5, Harsley 3, Hope 3, Dawson 2, Humphreys 2 (1 pen), Sheldon 2, Bull 1, Calvo-Garcia 1, Cornforth 1, Fickling 1, Guinan 1, Logan 1, Omoyinmi 1, Torpey 1.
Worthington Cup (0).
FA Cup (0).
Ground: Glanford Park, Scunthorpe, South Humberside DN15 8TD. Telephone (01724) 848077.
Record attendance: Old Showground: 23,935 v Portsmouth, FA Cup 4th rd, 30 January 1954. Glanford Park: 8775 v Rotherham U, Division 4, 1 May 1989.

Capacity: 9183.
Manager: Brian Laws.
Secretary: A. D. Rowing.
Most League Goals: 88, Division 3 (N), 1957–58.
Highest League Scorer in Season: Barrie Thomas, 31, Division 2, 1961–62.
Most League Goals in Total Aggregate: Steve Cammack, 110, 1979–81, 1981–86.
Most Capped Player: None.
Most League Appearances: Jack Brownsword, 595, 1950–65.
Honours – Division 3 (N) Champions – 1957–58.
Colours: White shirt with claret and blue trim, white shorts and stockings with claret and blue trim.

SHEFFIELD UNITED — DIV. 1

Bent Marcus (F)	6 2	12 04	Hammersmith	19 5 78	Port Vale
Brown Michael R (M)	5 9	10 07	Hartlepool	25 1 77	Manchester C
Burley Adam (M)	5 10	12 06	Sheffield	27 11 80	Trainee
Cryan Colin (M)			Dublin	23 3 81	Scholar
D'Jaffo Laurent (F)	6 0	13 05	Aquitane	5 11 70	Stockport Co
Devlin Paul (F)	5 8	11 08	Birmingham	14 4 72	Birmingham C
Doane Ben (D)	5 10	10 05	Sheffield	22 12 79	Trainee
El Banna Wassim (F)	5 11	12 04	Zambia	10 5 79	Oldham Ath
Ford Bobby (M)	5 8	10 07	Bristol	22 9 74	Oxford U
Gijsbrechts Davy (D)	6 1	13 08	Heusden	20 9 72	Lokeren
Hamilton Ian (M)	5 10	12 07	Stevenage	14 12 67	WBA
Hunt Jonathan (M)	5 10	11 13	London	2 11 71	Derby Co
Jagielka Philip (M)	5 11	12 08	Manchester	17 8 82	Scholar
Kozluk Robert (D)	5 8	10 07	Sutton-in-Ashfield	5 8 77	Derby Co
Mbome Kingsley (M)			Yaounde	21 11 81	
Murphy Shaun (D)	6 1	13 10	Sydney	5 11 70	WBA
Quinn Wayne (D)	5 10	12 10	Truro	19 11 76	Trainee
Ribeiro Bruno (M)	5 8	12 07	Setubal	22 10 75	Leeds U
Sandford Lee (D)	6 0	13 06	Basingstoke	22 4 68	Stoke C
Smith Andy (F)	5 11	11 10	Lisburn	25 9 80	
Tracey Simon (G)	6 0	14 00	Woolwich	9 12 67	Wimbledon
Woodhouse Curtis (M)	5 8	11 06	Driffield	17 4 80	Trainee
Woodward Andy (D)	6 0	13 04	Stockport	13 9 73	Bury
Yohanna Buba (M)			Yaounde	16 6 82	

League Appearances: Bent, M. 32; Brown, M. 21(3); Burley, A. (2); Craddock, J. 10; D'Jaffo, L. 6(9); Davison, A. 1(1); Derry, S. 31(3); Devlin, P. 40(4); Doane, B. (1); Ford, B. 38(3); Gijsbrechts, D. 9(8); Hall, P. 1(3); Hamilton, I. 3(4); Hunt, J. 8(6); Jagielka, P. (1); Katchuro, P. 8(15); Kozluk, R. 36(3); Launders, B. (1); Marcelo 9(1); Morris, L. (1); Murphy, S. 42; Notman, A. 7(3); Quinn, W. 41(2); Ribeiro, B. 9(11); Sandford, L. 43; Smeets, A. 2(3); Smith, M. 24(2); Tracey, S. 45; Wilson, S. 4(2); Woodhouse, C. 34(3); Woodward, A. 2(1).
Goals – League (59): Bent 15, Devlin 11 (1 pen), Smith 10, Brown 3, Murphy 3, Notman 3, Woodhouse 3, Ford 2, Marcelo 2, Burley 1, D'Jaffo 1, Hall 1, Katchuro 1, Quinn 1, Ribeiro 1, Sandford 1.
Worthington Cup (8): Smith 4, Katchuro 2, Marcelo 2.
FA Cup (3): Bent 1, Derry 1, Smith 1.
Ground: Bramall Lane Ground, Sheffield S2 4SU. Telephone (0114) 2215757
Record attendance: 68,287 v Leeds U, FA Cup 5th rd, 15 February 1936.
Capacity: 30,370.
Manager: Neil Warnock.
Secretary: D. Capper AFA.

Most League Goals: 102, Division 1, 1925–26.
Highest League Scorer in Season: Jimmy Dunne, 41, Division 1, 1930–31.
Most League Goals in Total Aggregate: Harry Johnson, 205, 1919–30.
Most Capped Player: Billy Gillespie, 25, Northern Ireland.
Most League Appearances: Joe Shaw, 629, 1948–66.
Honours – Football League: Division 1 Champions – 1897–98. Division 2 Champions – 1952–53. Division 4 Champions – 1981–82. **FA Cup:** Winners 1899, 1902, 1915, 1925.
Colours: Red and white striped shirts with black trim, black shorts and black stockings with red trim.

SHEFFIELD WEDNESDAY DIV. 1

Alexandersson Niclas (M)	6 2	11 08	Halmstad	29 12 71	IFK Gothenburg
Atherton Peter (D)	5 11	13 12	Orrell	6 4 70	Coventry C
Bettney Scott (D)	5 9	13 00	Hull	12 3 80	Trainee
Billington David (D)	5 9	10 06	Oxford	15 10 80	Trainee
Booth Andy (F)	6 0	13 00	Huddersfield	6 12 73	Huddersfield T
Briscoe Lee (D)	5 11	11 12	Pontefract	30 9 75	Trainee
Bromby Leigh (D)	5 11	11 06	Dewsbury	2 6 80	
Crane Anthony (M)	6 1	12 06	Liverpool	8 9 82	Trainee
Cresswell Richard (F)	6 0	11 08	Bridlington	20 9 77	York C
De Bilde Gilles (F)	5 11	11 04	Brussels	9 6 71	PSV Eindhoven
Donnelly Simon (M)	5 9	10 06	Glasgow	1 12 74	Celtic
Geary Derek (D)	5 6	10 08	Dublin	19 6 80	
Hamshaw Matthew (M)	5 9	11 09	Rotherham	1 1 82	Trainee
Haslam Steven (D)	5 11	10 10	Sheffield	6 9 79	Trainee
Higgins Alex (M)	5 9	11 04	Sheffield	22 7 81	Trainee
Hinchcliffe Andy (D)	5 10	13 07	Manchester	5 2 69	Everton
Holmes Peter (M)	5 10	10 00	Bishop Auckland	18 11 80	Trainee
Houlahan Martin (M)	6 0	12 13	Bishop Auckland	17 9 81	Trainee
Humphreys Richie (F)	5 11	14 07	Sheffield	30 11 77	Trainee
Hutton John (F)	5 10	11 07	Easington	23 9 80	Trainee
Jonk Wim (M)	6 0	12 02	Volendam	12 10 66	PSV Eindhoven
McKeever Mark (M)	5 9	11 08	Derry	16 11 78	Trainee
Morrison Owen (F)	5 8	11 12	Derry	8 12 81	Trainee
Muller Adam (M)			Leeds	17 4 82	
Nicholson Kevin (D)	5 9	11 07	Derby	2 10 80	Trainee
Nolan Ian (D)	6 0	12 01	Liverpool	9 7 70	Tranmere R
O'Donnell Phil (M)	5 10	11 07	Bellshill	25 3 72	Celtic
Pressman Kevin (G)	6 1	15 05	Fareham	6 11 67	Apprentice
Quinn Alan (F)	5 9	10 02	Dublin	13 6 79	Cherry Orchard
Rand Craig (M)	6 1	11 00	Bishop Auckland	24 6 82	Trainee
Rudi Petter (M)	6 2	12 00	Kristiansund	17 9 73	Molde
Scott Philip (M)	5 9	11 01	Perth	14 11 74	St Johnstone
Sibon Gerald (F)	6 3	13 04	Emmen	19 4 74	Ajax
Sonner Danny (M)	5 11	12 08	Wigan	9 1 72	Ipswich T
Srnicek Pavel (G)	6 2	14 09	Bohumin	10 3 68	Newcastle U
Staniforth Thomas (D)	5 10	13 00	Carlisle	15 12 80	Trainee
Walker Des (D)	5 11	11 13	Enfield	26 11 65	Sampdoria

League Appearances: Alexandersson, N. 37; Atherton, P. 35; Booth, A. 20(3); Briscoe, L. 7(9); Carbone, B. 3(4); Cresswell, R. 2(18); De Bilde, G. 37(1); Donnelly, S. 3(9); Emerson 16(1); Haslam, S. 16(7); Hinchcliffe, A. 29; Horne, B. 7; Jonk, W. 29(1); McKeever, M. 1(1); Newsome, J. 5(1); Nolan, I. 28(1);

O'Donnell, P. (1); Pressman, K. 18(1); Quinn, A. 18(1); Rudi, P. 18(2); Scott, P. 2(3); Sibon, G. 12(16); Sonner, D. 18(9); Srnicek, P. 20; Walker, D. 37.
Goals – League (38): De Bilde 10 (2 pens), Alexandersson 5, Sibon 5, Jonk 3 (1 pen), Quinn 3, Booth 2, Carbone 2 (1 pen), Rudi 2, Atherton 1, Cresswell 1, Donnelly 1, Hinchcliffe 1, own goals 2.
Worthington Cup (7): Alexandersson 2, Booth 1, Cresswell 1, De Bilde 1, Rudi 1, Sonner 1.
FA Cup (3): Alexandersson 1, Booth 1, Sibon 1.
Ground: Hillsborough, Sheffield, S6 1SW. Telephone (0114) 2212121
Record attendance: 72,841 v Manchester C, FA Cup 5th rd, 17 February 1934.
Capacity: 39,859
Manager: Paul Jewell.
Secretary: Alan D. Sykes.
Most League Goals: 106, Division 2, 1958–59.
Highest League Scorer in Season: Derek Dooley, 46, Division 2, 1951–52.
Most League Goals in Total Aggregate: Andy Wilson, 199, 1900–20.
Most Capped Player: Nigel Worthington, 50 (66), Northern Ireland.
Most League Appearances: Andy Wilson, 502, 1900–20.
Honours – Football League: Division 1 Champions – 1902–03, 1903–04, 1928–29, 1929–30. Division 2 Champions – 1899–1900, 1925–26, 1951–52, 1955–56, 1958–59.
FA Cup winners 1896, 1907, 1935. **Football League Cup winners** 1990–91.
Colours: Blue and white striped shirts, black shorts, black stockings.

SHREWSBURY TOWN — DIV. 3

Davidson Ross (D)	5 9	12 04	Chertsey	13 11 73	Barnet
Drysdale Leon (D)	5 9	10 12	Walsall	3 2 81	Trainee
Dunbavin Ian (G)	6 1	10 10	Knowsley	27 5 80	Liverpool
Edwards Paul (G)	6 1	12 05	Liverpool	22 2 65	Crewe Alex
Gayle John (F)	6 3	15 04	Bromsgrove	30 7 64	Scunthorpe U
Hanmer Gary (D)	5 6	10 02	Shrewsbury	12 10 73	Newtown
Hughes David (D)	6 4	13 06	Wrexham	1 2 78	Aston Villa
Jagielka Steve (F)	5 8	11 03	Manchester	10 3 78	Trainee
Jones Matthew (M)	6 1	11 03	Shrewsbury	11 10 80	Trainee
Murray Karl (M)	5 10	12 00	Islington	24 6 82	Trainee
Peer Dean (M)	6 2	12 04	Stourbridge	8 8 69	Northampton T
Seabury Kevin (D)	5 10	11 06	Shrewsbury	24 11 73	Trainee
Thomas Wayne (M)	5 11	11 10	Walsall	28 8 78	Walsall
Tretton Andrew (D)	6 0	12 08	Derby	9 10 76	Chesterfield
Whelan Spencer (D)	6 2	13 00	Liverpool	17 9 71	Chester C
Wilding Peter (D)	6 1	12 09	Shrewsbury	28 11 68	Telford U

League Appearances: Aiston, S. 10; Berkley, A. 27(6); Brown, M. 35(9); Cullen, J. 10; Davidson, R. 9(1); Dunbavin, I. 6(1); Edwards, P. 40; Gayle, J. 17(1); Hanmer, G. 31(2); Herbert, C. 1(1); Hughes, D. 18(4); Jagielka, S. 14(19); Jobling, K. 25(3); Kerrigan, S. 20(5); Murray, K. 6(6); Peer, D. 19; Preece, R. 5; Rigby, T. 4(4); Rodgers, L. (6); Seabury, K. 31(1); Spink, D. 1(3); Steele, L. 34(3); Sturridge, S. 10(1); Thomas, W. 11(2); Tolley, J. (2); Tretton, A. 33; Whelan, S. 16; Wilding, P. 41; Winstanley, M. 32(1).
Goals – League (40): Steele 11 (3 pens), Brown 7, Kerrigan 3, Tretton 3, Gayle 2, Jobling 2, Wilding 2, Cullen 1, Hughes 1, Jagielka 1, Murray 1, Rigby 1, Rodgers 1, Sturridge 1, Thomas 1 (pen), Winstanley 1, own goal 1.
Worthington Cup (0).
FA Cup (5): Kerrigan 3, Jagielka 1, Wilding 1.
Ground: Gay Meadow, Shrewsbury SY2 6AB. Telephone (01743) 360111.

Record attendance: 18,917 v Walsall, Division 3, 26 April 1961. **Capacity:** 8000.
Manager: Kevin Ratcliffe.
Secretary: M. J. Starkey.
Most League Goals: 101, Division 4, 1958–59.
Highest League Scorer in Season: Arthur Rowley, 38, Division 4, 1958–59.
Most League Goals in Total Aggregate: Arthur Rowley, 152, 1958–65 (completing his League record of 434 goals).
Most Capped Player: Jimmy McLaughlin, 5 (12), Northern Ireland; Bernard McNally, 5, Northern Ireland.
Most League Appearances: Colin Griffin, 406, 1975–89.
Honours – Football League: Division 3 Champions – 1978–79, 1993–94. **Welsh Cup winners** 1891, 1938, 1977, 1979, 1984, 1985.
Colours: Amber and blue striped shirts, blue shorts, blue stockings, amber trim.

SOUTHAMPTON — FA PREMIERSHIP

Player	Ht	Wt	Birthplace	Birthdate	Source
Beattie James (F)	6 1	13 03	Lancaster	27 2 78	Blackburn R
Benali Francis (M)	5 9	11 01	Southampton	30 12 68	Apprentice
Beresford John (M)	5 7	12 00	Sheffield	4 9 66	Newcastle U
Bevan Scott (G)	6 6	15 07	Southampton	16 9 79	Trainee
Bleidelis Imants (M)	5 9	12 00	Latvia	16 8 75	Skonto Riga
Boa Morte Luis (F)	5 9	11 10	Lisbon	4 8 77	Arsenal
Bradley Shayne (F)	6 0	13 12	Gloucester	8 12 79	Trainee
Bridge Wayne (F)	5 10	12 07	Southampton	5 8 80	Trainee
Colleter Patrick (D)	5 10	11 04	Brest	6 11 65	Marseille
Davies Kevin (F)	6 0	14 10	Sheffield	26 3 77	Blackburn R
Dodd Jason (D)	5 8	12 07	Bath	2 11 70	Bath C
Dryden Richard (D)	6 0	13 04	Stroud	14 6 69	Bristol C
El Khalej Tahar (D)	6 2	13 08	Morocco	16 6 68	Benfica
Gibbens Kevin (M)	5 10	14 02	Southampton	4 11 79	Trainee
Gray Steven (M)			Dublin	17 10 81	
Howard Brian (M)			Winchester	23 1 83	Trainee
Hughes David (M)	5 11	11 01	St Albans	30 12 72	Trainee
Hughes Paul (M)	6 0	12 05	Hammersmith	19 4 76	Chelsea
Jones Paul (G)	6 3	15 00	Chirk	18 4 67	Stockport Co
Kachloul Hassan (M)	6 2	13 02	Agadir	19 2 73	St Etienne
Le Tissier Matthew (F)	6 1	14 01	Guernsey	14 10 68	Trainee
Lundekvam Claus (D)	6 4	12 12	Austevoll	22 2 73	Brann
Marsden Chris (M)	6 0	12 08	Sheffield	3 1 69	Birmingham C
Monk Gary (D)	6 0	13 12	Bedford	6 3 79	Trainee
Moss Neil (G)	6 3	14 00	New Milton	10 5 75	Bournemouth
Oakley Matthew (M)	5 10	12 00	Peterborough	17 8 77	Trainee
Pakhar (Pahars) Marian (F)	5 8	10 08	Latvia	5 8 76	Skonto Riga
Richards Dean (D)	6 2	14 01	Bradford	9 6 74	Wolverhampton W
Ripley Stuart (F)	6 0	13 09	Middlesbrough	20 11 67	Blackburn R
Rodrigues Danny (F)	5 11	11 05	Madeira	3 3 80	Farense
Soltvedt Trond Egil (M)	6 0	12 09	Vaksdal	15 2 67	Coventry C
Tealdi Daniele (M)			Italy	15 11 82	Atletico 2000
Tessem Jo (M)	6 2	13 05	Norway	28 2 72	Molde
Warner Phil (D)	5 10	11 09	Southampton	2 2 79	Trainee

League Appearances: Almeida, M. (1); Beattie, J. 8(10); Benali, F. 25(1); Beresford, J. (3); Boa Morte, L. 6(8); Bradley, S. (1); Bridge, W. 15(4); Colleter, P. 8; Davies, K. 19(4); Dodd, J. 30(1); Dryden, R. 1; El Khalej, T. 11; Hiley, S. 3; Hughes, M. 18(2); Jones, P. 31; Kachloul, H. 29(3); Le Tissier, M. 9(9); Lundekvam, C. 25(2); Marsden, C. 19(2); Monk, G. 1(1); Moss, N. 7(2); Oakley, M. 26(5); Ostenstad, E. 3; Pakhar (Pahars), M. 31(2); Richards, D. 35; Ripley, S. 18(5); Rodrigues, D. (2); Soltvedt, T. 17(7); Tessem, J. 23(2).
Goals – League (45): Pakhar (Pahars) 13, Davies 6, Kachloul 5, Tessem 4, Le Tissier 3 (1 pen), Oakley 3, Richards 2, Boa Morte 1, Bridge 1, El Khalej 1, Hughes 1, Ostenstad 1, Ripley 1, Soltvedt 1, own goals 2.
Worthington Cup (6): Oakley 2, Richards 2, Dodd 1 (pen), Soltvedt 1.
FA Cup (1): Richards 1.
Ground: The Dell, Milton Road, Southampton SO15 2XH. Telephone (023) 8022 0505.
Record attendance: 31,044 v Manchester U, Division 1, 8 October 1969. **Capacity:** 15,000.
Manager: Glenn Hoddle.
Secretary: Brian Truscott.
Most League Goals: 112, Division 3 (S), 1957–58.
Highest League Scorer in Season: Derek Reeves, 39, Division 3, 1959–60.
Most League Goals in Total Aggregate: Mike Channon, 185, 1966–77, 1979–82.
Most Capped Player: Peter Shilton, 49 (125), England.
Most League Appearances: Terry Paine, 713, 1956–74.
Honours – Football League: Division 3 (S) Champions – 1921–22. Division 3 Champions – 1959–60. **FA Cup:** Winners 1975–76.
Colours: Red and white striped shirts, black shorts, black stockings with red trim.

SOUTHEND UNITED DIV. 3

Abiodun Yemi (F)	5 10	10 07	Clapton	29 12 80	Norwich C
Booty Martyn (D)	5 8	12 03	Kirby Muxloe	30 5 71	Reading
Byrne Paul (M)	5 11	13 00	Dublin	30 6 72	Celtic
Capleton Mel (G)	6 0	13 00	London	24 10 73	Trainee
Carruthers Martin (F)	5 10	12 02	Nottingham	7 8 72	Darlington
Connelly Gordon (F)	6 0	12 04	Glasgow	1 11 76	York C
Cross Garry (D)	5 9	12 00	Chelmsford	7 10 80	Trainee
Fitzpatrick Trevor (F)	6 1	13 00	Surrey	19 2 80	Trainee
Houghton Scott (M)	5 5	12 02	Hitchin	22 10 71	Peterborough U
Johnson Leon (M)	6 0	12 00	London	10 5 81	Scholar
Maher Kevin (M)	5 11	13 04	Ilford	17 10 76	Tottenham H
McDonald Thomas (D)	6 2	12 00	London	15 9 80	Trainee
Morley David (D)	6 2	13 05	St Helens	25 9 77	Manchester C
Perkins Chris (D)	5 11	13 08	Stepney	1 3 80	Trainee
Prudhoe Mark (G)	6 0	14 00	Washington	8 11 63	Bradford C
Roget Leo (D)	6 1	12 02	Ilford	1 8 77	Trainee
Tinkler Mark (M)	6 2	13 00	Bishop Auckland	24 10 74	York C
Tolson Neil (F)	6 2	12 11	Wordsley	25 10 73	York C

League Appearances: Abiodun, Y. 1(2); Beard, M. 38(3); Booty, M. 28; Campbell, N. 6(6); Capleton, M. 40(2); Carruthers, M. 38; Clarke, A. (4); Coleman, S. 43; Connelly, G. 29(4); Cross, G. 7(1); Fitzpatrick, T. 1(15); Gooding, M. (2); Hails, J. (1); Houghton, S. 42(1); Jones, N. 43; Jones, S. 9; Kerrigan, D. (4); Maher, K. 18(6); McDonald, T. 1(2); Morley, D. 29(3); Newman, R. 14(5); Pepper, N. 9(3); Prudhoe, M. 6; Roach, N. 6(2); Roget, L. 28(8); Tinkler, M. 41; Tolson, N. 29(2).

Goals – League (53): Carruthers 19 (3 pens), Tolson 10 (3 pens), Coleman 5, Houghton 4, Connelly 2, Jones N 2, Jones S 2, Pepper 2, Roget 2, Beard 1, Campbell 1, Roach 1, own goals 2.
Worthington Cup (0).
FA Cup (0).
Ground: Roots Hall Football Ground, Victoria Avenue, Southend-on-Sea SS2 6NQ. Telephone (01702) 304050
Record attendance: 31,090 v Liverpool FA Cup 3rd rd, 10 January 1979. **Capacity:** 12,306
Manager: Alan Little.
Secretary: Miss H. Giles.
Most League Goals: 92, Division 3 (S), 1950–51.
Highest League Scorer in Season: Jim Shankly, 31, 1928–29; Sammy McCrory, 1957–58, both in Division 3 (S).
Most League Goals in Total Aggregate: Roy Hollis, 122, 1953–60.
Most Capped Player: George Mackenzie, 9, Eire.
Most League Appearances: Sandy Anderson, 452, 1950–63.
Honours – Football League: Division 4 Champions – 1980–81.
Colours: Royal blue and white.

STOCKPORT COUNTY DIV. 1

Angell Brett (F)	6 2	13 10	Marlborough	20 8 68	Sunderland
Bailey Alan (F)	5 11	12 03	Macclesfield	1 11 78	Manchester C
Bennett Tom (M)	5 11	11 08	Falkirk	12 12 69	Stockport Co
Bergersen Kent (M)	5 10	11 07	Oslo	8 2 67	Stromsgodset
Briggs Keith (D)	6 0	11 00	Glossop	11 12 81	Trainee
Byrne Chris (M)	5 9	10 02	Hulme	9 2 75	Macclesfield T
Clare Robert (M)			Belper	28 2 83	Trainee
Connelly Sean (D)	5 10	11 10	Sheffield	26 6 70	Hallam
Cooper Kevin (F)	5 8	10 07	Derby	8 2 75	Derby Co
Daly Jon (F)	6 3	12 00	Dublin	8 1 83	Trainee
Dinning Tony (M)	6 0	12 04	Wallsend	12 4 75	Trainee
Evans Lee (M)			Cardiff	30 11 81	Trainee
Flynn Mike (D)	6 0	11 02	Oldham	23 2 69	Preston NE
Fradin Karim (M)	5 11	12 00	Ste Martin d'Hyeres	2 2 72	Niort
Gibb Ali (F)	5 9	11 07	Salisbury	17 2 76	Northampton T
Hancock Glynn (D)	6 0	12 02	Biddulph	24 5 82	Trainee
Johnson Ben (D)	6 0	12 00	Manchester	27 8 80	Trainee
Larsson Jonas (M)			Vanersborg	1 4 82	Trainee
Lawson Ian (F)	5 11	11 00	Huddersfield	4 11 77	Bury
Matthews Rob (F)	6 0	12 05	Slough	14 10 70	Bury
Moore Ian (F)	5 11	12 02	Birkenhead	26 8 76	Nottingham F
Nash Carlo (G)	6 5	14 01	Bolton	13 9 73	Crystal Palace
Nicholson Shane (D)	5 10	11 10	Newark	3 6 70	Chesterfield
Ross Neil (F)	6 1	12 02	West Bromwich	10 8 82	Trainee
Smith David (M)	5 10	12 11	Liverpool	26 12 70	Oxford U
Wilbraham Aaron (F)	6 3	12 04	Knutsford	21 10 79	Trainee
Woodthorpe Colin (D)	6 0	11 08	Ellesmere Pt	13 1 69	Aberdeen

League Appearances: Allen, C. 10(6); Angell, B. 5; Bailey, A. 5(9); Bennett, T. 8(1); Bergersen, K. 10(7); Briggs, K. 4(3); Byrne, C. 11(7); Connelly, S. 42(1); Cooper, K. 44(2); D'Jaffo, L. 20(1); Daly, J. (4); Dinning, T. 43(1); Elliott, S. 4(1); Ellis, T. 1(3); Flynn, M. 46; Fradin, K. 19(2); Francis, K. 4; Gannon, J. 20(9); Gibb, A. 13(1); Gibbens, K. 1(1); Gray, I. 8(2); Lawson, I. 13(2); Matthews, R. 3(1); McIntosh, M. 17(3); Monk, G. 2; Moore, I. 34(4); Nash, C. 38; Nicholson, S. 42; Ross, N. (2); Smith, D. 7(2); Taylor, M. 7; Wilbraham, A. 13(13); Woodthorpe, C. 12(14).
Goals – League (55): Dinning 12 (6 pens), Moore 10, D'Jaffo 7, Cooper 4, Lawson 4, Wilbraham 4, Connelly 3, Byrne C 2, Bailey 1, Briggs 1, Flynn 1, Fradin 1, Matthews 1, Nicholson 1, Smith 1, own goals 2.
Worthington Cup (7): Angell 1, Briggs 1, Cooper 1, Dinning 1 (pen), D'Jaffo 1, Wilbraham 1, Woodthorpe 1.
FA Cup (2): Bailey 1, Moore 1.
Ground: Edgeley Park, Hardcastle Road, Stockport, Cheshire SK3 9DD. Telephone (0161) 286 8888.
Record attendance: 27,833 v Liverpool, FA Cup 5th rd, 11 February 1950.
Capacity: 11,541.
Manager: Andy Kilner.
Secretary: Gary Glendenning BA (HONS) FCCA.
Most League Goals: 115, Division 3 (N), 1933–34.
Highest League Scorer in Season: Alf Lythgoe, 46, Division 3 (N), 1933–34.
Most League Goals in Total Aggregate: Jack Connor, 132, 1951–56.
Most Capped Player: Martin Nash, 8, Canada.
Most League Appearances: Andy Thorpe, 489, 1978–86, 1988–92.
Honours – Football League: Division 3 (N) Champions – 1921–22, 1936–37. Division 4 Champions – 1966–67.
Colours: Blue shirts with white chest band, blue shorts, white stockings.

STOKE CITY DIV. 2

Bullock Matthew (M)	5 8	11 00	Stoke	1 11 80	Trainee
Clarke Clive (D)	6 1	12 03	Dublin	14 1 80	Trainee
Collins Lee (D)	6 1	12 06	Birmingham	10 9 77	Aston Villa
Connor Paul (F)	6 2	11 08	Bishop Auckland	12 1 79	Middlesbrough
Crowe Dean (F)	5 5	11 02	Stockport	6 6 79	Trainee
Goodfellow Marc (M)			Burton	20 9 81	
Gudjonsson Bjarni (F)	5 8	11 02	Reykjavik	26 2 79	Genk
Gunnarsson Brynjar (M)	6 1	11 00	Reykjavik	16 10 75	Moss
Hansson Mikael (D)	5 8	11 08	Norrkoping	15 3 68	Norrkoping
Heath Robert (M)	5 9	10 00	Newcastle-Under-Lyme	31 8 78	
Henry Karl (M)			Wolverhampton	26 11 82	Trainee
Iwelumo Chris (F)	6 4	13 00	Coatbridge	1 8 78	Aarhus Fremad
Kavanagh Graham (M)	5 10	12 06	Dublin	2 12 73	Middlesbrough
Lightbourne Kyle (F)	6 2	12 00	Bermuda	29 9 68	Coventry C
Mohan Nicky (D)	6 1	14 00	Middlesbrough	6 10 70	Wycombe W
Neal Lewis (M)			Leicester	14 7 81	
O'Connor James (M)	5 8	11 00	Dublin	1 9 79	Trainee
Petty Ben (D)	6 0	12 05	Solihull	22 3 77	Aston Villa
Short Chris (D)	5 10	12 04	Munster	9 5 70	Sheffield U
Sigurdsson Kris (D)	5 11	11 11	Akureyri	7 10 80	
Taaffe Steven (F)	5 7	9 00	Stoke	10 9 79	Trainee
Thorne Peter (F)	6 0	13 07	Manchester	21 6 73	Swindon T
Ward Gavin (G)	6 2	12 02	Sutton Coldfield	30 6 70	Bolton W
Wooliscroft Ashley (D)	5 10	11 02	Stoke	28 12 79	Trainee

League Appearances: Aiston, S. 2(4); Bullock, M. 4(3); Clarke, C. 39(3); Connor, P. 15(11); Crowe, D. (6); Danielsson, E. 3(5); Dryden, R. 11(2); Gislason, S. 4(4); Gudjonsson, B. 7(1); Gunnarsson, B. 21(1); Gunnlaugsson, A. 10(3); Hansson, M. 24(3); Heath, R. (3); Iwelumo, C. (3); Jacobsen, A. 29(4); Kavanagh, G. 44(1); Keen, K. 20(3); Kippe, F. 15; Lightbourne, K. 35(5); MacKenzie, N. (2); Melton, S. (5); Mohan, N. 40; O'Connor, J. 42; Oldfield, D. 7(12); Petty, B. 7(6); Robinson, P. 14(8); Short, C. 14; Sigurdsson, L. 5; Small, B. 5(3); Taaffe, S. 2; Thorne, P. 41(4); Ward, G. 46.
Goals – League (68): Thorne 24, Kavanagh 7 (1 pen), Lightbourne 7, O'Connor 6, Connor 5, Mohan 5, Gunnlaugsson 2 (1 pen), Jacobsen 2, Clarke 1, Danielsson 1, Gudjonsson 1, Gunnarsson 1, Keen 1, Kippe 1, Oldfield 1, Robinson 1, Sigurdsson 1, own goal 1.
Worthington Cup (5): Connor 1, Kavanagh 1, Keen 1, O'Connor 1, Thorne 1.
FA Cup (0).
Ground: Britannia Stadium, Stoke-on-Trent ST4 4EG. Telephone: (01782) 592222.
Record attendance: 51,380 v Arsenal, Division 1, 29 March 1937. **Capacity:** 24,054.
Manager: Gudjon Thordarson.
Most League Goals: 92, Division 3 (N), 1926–27.
Highest League Scorer in Season: Freddie Steele, 33, Division 1, 1936–37.
Most League Goals in Total Aggregate: Freddie Steele, 142, 1934–49.
Most Capped Player: Gordon Banks, 36 (73), England.
Most League Appearances: Eric Skeels, 506, 1958–76.
Honours – Football League: Division 2 Champions – 1932–33, 1962–63, 1992–93. Division 3 (N) Champions – 1926–27. **Football League Cup:** Winners 1971–72. **Autoglass Trophy winners** 1992. **Auto Windscreens Shield winners** 2000.
Colours: Red and white striped shirts, white shorts, red and white stockings.

SUNDERLAND — FA PREMIERSHIP

Aiston Sam (M)	6 0	13 09	Newcastle	21 11 76	Newcastle U
Bould Steve (D)	6 4	14 02	Stoke	16 11 62	Arsenal
Butler Paul (D)	6 3	14 09	Manchester	2 11 72	Bury
Butler Thomas (M)	5 7	10 06	Ballymun	25 4 81	Trainee
Byrne Clifford (M)			Dublin	27 4 82	
Convery Mark (F)	5 6	10 05	Newcastle	29 5 81	Trainee
Craddock Jody (D)	6 2	12 05	Bromsgrove	25 7 75	Cambridge U
Dichio Danny (F)	6 4	13 09	Hammersmith	19 10 74	Lecce
Dickman Jonjo (D)	5 8	10 05	Hexham	22 9 81	
Duke David (M)	5 10	11 01	Inverness	7 11 78	Redby CA
Fredgaard Carsten (M)	6 1	12 01	Hillesod	20 5 76	
Gray Michael (D)	5 9	11 01	Sunderland	3 8 74	Trainee
Graydon Keith (M)			Dublin	10 2 83	
Helmer Thomas (D)	6 1	12 04	Herford	21 4 65	Bayern Munich
Holloway Darren (D)	6 0	12 09	Crook	3 10 77	Trainee
Ingham Michael (G)	6 4	13 10	Preston	9 7 80	Malachians
Kennedy Jon (G)			Rotherham	30 11 80	Worksop T
Kilbane Kevin (M)	6 2	13 07	Preston	1 2 77	WBA
Kyle Kevin (F)	5 8	12 00	Stranraer	7 6 81	
Lumsdon Chris (M)	5 10	10 09	Newcastle	15 12 79	Trainee
Lynch Finbar (F)	5 8	10 01	Dublin	24 1 82	
Makin Chris (D)	5 11	12 11	Manchester	8 5 73	Marseille
Maley Mark (D)	6 0	13 00	Newcastle	26 1 81	Trainee
Marriott Andy (G)	6 2	13 04	Sutton-in-Ashfield	11 10 70	Wrexham
McCann Gavin (M)	6 1	12 08	Blackpool	10 1 78	Everton
McCartney George (D)	6 0	12 06	Belfast	29 4 81	Trainee

McGill Brendan (M)	5 8	9 02	Dublin	22 3 81	
Nunez Milton (F)	5 5	10 08	Honduras	30 10 72	
Oster John (M)	5 9	10 09	Boston	8 12 78	Everton
Phillips Kevin (F)	5 8	11 05	Hitchin	25 7 73	Watford
Proctor Michael (F)	6 0	11 08	Sunderland	3 10 80	Trainee
Quinn Niall (F)	6 5	14 08	Dublin	6 10 66	Manchester C
Rae Alex (M)	5 10	11 09	Glasgow	30 9 69	Millwall
Reddy Michael (F)	6 1	11 07	Graignamanagh	24 3 80	Kilkenny C
Roy Eric (M)	6 2	13 00	Nice	26 9 67	Marseille
Schwarz Stefan (M)	6 0	12 00	Malmo	18 4 69	Valencia
Sorensen Thomas (G)	6 4	14 08	Odense	12 6 76	Odense
Summerbee Nicky (M)	5 11	12 03	Altrincham	26 8 71	Manchester C
Thirlwell Paul (M)	5 11	12 00	Springwell Village	13 2 79	Trainee
Wainwright Neil (M)	6 1	11 07	Warrington	4 11 77	Wrexham
Williams Darren (D)	5 11	12 00	Middlesbrough	28 4 77	York C

League Appearances: Ball, K. 6(5); Bould, S. 19(1); Butler, P. 31(1); Butler, T. (1); Craddock, J. 18(1); Dichio, D. (12); Fredgaard, C. (1); Gray, M. 32(1); Helmer, T. 1(1); Holloway, D. 8(7); Kilbane, K. 17(3); Lumsdon, C. 1; Makin, C. 34; Marriott, A. 1; McCann, G. 21(3); Nunez, M. (1); Oster, J. 4(6); Phillips, K. 36; Quinn, N. 35(2); Rae, A. 22(4); Reddy, M. (8); Roy, E. 19(5); Schwarz, S. 27; Sorensen, T. 37; Summerbee, N. 29(3); Thirlwell, P. 7(1); Williams, D. 13(12).
Goals – League (57): Phillips 30 (6 pens), Quinn 14, McCann 4, Rae 3, Butler P 1, Kilbane 1, Makin 1, Reddy 1, Schwarz 1, Summerbee 1.
Worthington Cup (10): Dichio 4, Fredgaard 2, Ball 1, Roy 1, Williams 1, own goal 1.
FA Cup (1): McCann 1.
Ground: Sunderland Stadium of Light, Sunderland, Tyne and Wear SR5 1SU. Telephone: (0191) 551 5000.
Record attendance: 75,118 v Derby Co, FA Cup 6th rd replay, 8 March 1933 (at Roker Park). **Capacity:** 48,500.
Manager: Peter Reid.
Secretary: Mark Blackbourne.
Most League Goals: 109, Division 1, 1935–36.
Highest League Scorer in Season: Dave Halliday, 43, Division 1, 1928–29.
Most League Goals in Total Aggregate: Charlie Buchan, 209, 1911–25.
Most Capped Player: Charlie Hurley, 38 (40), Republic of Ireland.
Most League Appearances: Jim Montgomery, 537, 1962–77.
Honours – Football League: Division 1 Champions – 1891–92, 1892–93, 1894–95, 1901–02, 1912–13, 1935–36, 1995–96, 1998–99. Division 2 Champions – 1975–76. Division 3 Champions – 1987–88. **FA Cup:** Winners 1937, 1973.
Colours: Red and white striped shirts with black trim, black shorts, black stockings, red turnover.

SWANSEA CITY — DIV. 2

Appleby Ritchie (M)	5 9	11 04	Stockton	18 9 75	Ipswich T
Barwood Danny (F)	5 9	11 00	Caerphilly	7 7 80	Trainee
Casey Ryan (M)	6 2	12 05	Coventry	3 1 79	Trainee
Coates Jonathan (M)	5 8	11 04	Swansea	27 6 75	Trainee
Cusack Nick (M)	6 0	12 05	Rotherham	24 12 65	Fulham
De-Vulgt Leigh (M)	5 10	10 07	Swansea	17 3 81	Trainee
Freestone Roger (G)	6 2	14 04	Newport	19 8 68	Chelsea
Howard Mike (D)	5 7	10 07	Birkenhead	2 12 78	Tranmere R
Jenkins Lee (M)	5 8	11 02	Pontypool	28 6 79	Trainee
Jones Jason (G)	6 2	12 10	Wrexham	10 5 79	Liverpool

Jones Steve (D)	5 10	12 09	Bristol	25 12 70	Cheltenham T
Keegan Michael (M)	5 10	11 00	Liskeard	12 5 81	Trainee
Lacey Damien (D)	5 8	11 10	Bridgend	3 8 77	Trainee
Morgan Bari (M)	5 6	10 08	Carmarthen	13 8 80	Trainee
Mutton Tommy (F)	5 8	10 02	Huddersfield	17 1 78	Bangor C
O'Leary Kristian (D)	6 0	13 07	Port Talbot	30 8 77	Trainee
Phillips Gareth (M)	5 7	11 02	Pontypridd	19 8 79	Trainee
Price Jason (D)	6 2	11 05	Aberdare	12 4 77	Aberaman Ath
Roberts Stuart (M)	5 6	9 08	Carmarthen	22 7 80	Trainee
Smith Jason (D)	6 3	14 00	Bromsgrove	6 9 74	Coventry C
Thomas Martin (G)	6 1	12 01	Swansea	12 9 73	Trainee
Watkin Steve (F)	5 10	11 12	Wrexham	16 6 71	Wrexham

League Appearances: Alsop, J. 29(8); Appleby, R. 10(10); Bird, T. 8(8); Bound, M. 43; Boyd, W. 21(6); Casey, R. (11); Coates, J. 41(1); Cusack, N. 43; De-Vulgt, L. (2); Evans, K. 1(1); Freestone, R. 46; Howard, M. 39(1); Jenkins, L. 7(9); Jones, S. 34(4); Keegan, M. 3(1); Lacey, D. 14(2); Mutton, T. 1(1); O'Leary, K. 9(11); Phillips, G. 2(1); Price, J. 35(4); Roberts, S. 9(2); Smith, J. 43; Thomas, M. 32(8); Watkin, S. 36(3).
Goals – League (51): Boyd 7, Cusack 7 (1 pen), Watkin 7 (1 pen), Coates 6, Price 6, Appleby 4, Thomas 4, Alsop 3, Bound 2 (2 pens), Bird 1, Roberts 1, Smith 1, own goals 2.
Worthington Cup (4): Bird 1 (pen), Bound 1 (pen), Price 1, Watkin 1.
FA Cup (2): Cusack 1, Watkin 1.
Ground: Vetch Field, Swansea SA1 3SU. Telephone (01792) 474114.
Record attendance: 32,796 v Arsenal, FA Cup 4th rd, 17 February 1968. **Capacity:** 10,402.
Team Manager: John Hollins MBE.
Secretary: Vicki Townsend.
Most League Goals: 90, Division 2, 1956–57.
Highest League Scorer in Season: Cyril Pearce, 35, Division 2, 1931–32.
Most League Goals in Total Aggregate: Ivor Allchurch, 166, 1949–58, 1965–68.
Most Capped Player: Ivor Allchurch, 42 (68), Wales.
Most League Appearances: Wilfred Milne, 585, 1919–37.
Honours – Football League: Division 3 Champions – 1999–2000. Division 3 (S) Champions – 1924–25, 1948–49. **Autoglass Trophy:** Winners 1994. **Welsh Cup:** Winners 9 times.
Colours: White shirts with maroon and black trim, white shorts, white stockings.

SWINDON TOWN — DIV. 2

Campagna Sam (D)	6 1	11 07	Worcester	19 11 80	Trainee
Davies Gareth (D)	6 1	11 12	Hereford	11 12 73	Reading
Davis Sol (D)	5 8	11 00	Cheltenham	4 9 79	Trainee
Grazioli Guiliano (F)	5 11	12 11	London	23 3 75	Peterborough U
Griffin Charlie (F)	6 0	12 07	Bath	25 6 79	Bristol R
Hall Gareth (D)	5 8	12 00	Croydon	20 3 69	Sunderland
Howe Bobby (M)	5 7	10 04	Annisford	6 11 73	Nottingham F
McAreavey Paul (M)	5 10	11 00	Belfast	3 12 80	Trainee
McHugh Frazer (M)	5 9	12 05	Nottingham	14 7 81	Trainee
Mildenhall Steve (G)	6 5	13 05	Swindon	13 5 78	Trainee
Mills Jamie (M)	5 10	11 00	Swindon	31 8 81	Trainee
Reeves Alan (D)	6 0	12 00	Birkenhead	19 11 67	Wimbledon
Williams Andy (M)	5 10	10 10	Bristol	8 10 77	Southampton
Williams James (M)	5 7	10 08	Liverpool	15 7 82	Trainee
Willis Adam (D)	6 1	12 02	Nuneaton	21 9 76	Coventry C

League Appearances: Campagna, S. 1(2); Carrick, M. 6; Collins, L. 23(1); Cowe, S. 12(5); Cuervo, P. (6); Davies, G. 17; Davis, S. 24(5); Flanagan, A. (1); Glass, J. 8; Gooden, T. 8(2); Gray, W. 8(4); Grazioli, G. 11(8); Griemink, B. 4; Griffin, C. 6(15); Hall, G. 38(1); Hay, C. 27(4); Howe, B. 24(7); Hulbert, R. 5(7); Leitch, S. 28(1); McCammon, M. 4; McHugh, F. 9(5); Meaker, M. 6; Mildenhall, S. 3(2); Ndah, G. 12; Onuora, I. 18(6); Quinn, J. 1(6); Reeves, A. 43; Robinson, M. 40(2); Smith, B. (1); Talia, F. 31; Taylor, C. 1(1); Thirlwell, P. 12; Walters, M. 11(2); Williams, A. 35(1); Williams, J. 14(12); Willis, A. 16(7).
Goals – League (38): Hay 10 (3 pens), Grazioli 8, Onuora 4 (1 pen), Carrick 2, Gray 2, Hall 2, Walters 2, Collins 1, Cowe 1, Griffin 1, Howe 1, Ndah 1, Reeves 1, Williams A 1, Williams J 1.
Worthington Cup (1): Walters 1 (pen).
FA Cup (1): Gordon 1.
Ground: County Ground, Swindon, Wiltshire SN1 2ED. Telephone (01793) 333 700.
Record attendance: 32,000 v Arsenal, FA Cup 3rd rd, 15 January 1972. **Capacity:** 15,728.
Manager: Colin Todd.
Secretary: Steve Jones.
Most League Goals: 100, Division 3 (S), 1926–27.
Highest League Scorer in Season: Harry Morris, 47, Division 3 (S), 1926–27.
Most League Goals in Total Aggregate: Harry Morris, 216, 1926–33.
Most Capped Player: Rod Thomas, 30 (50), Wales.
Most League Appearances: John Trollope, 770, 1960–80.
Honours – Football League: Division 2 Champions – 1995–96. Division 4 Champions – 1985–86. **Football League Cup:** Winners 1968–69. **Anglo-Italian Cup:** Winners 1970.
Colours: Red shirts, white shorts, red stockings.

TORQUAY UNITED — DIV. 3

Aggrey Jimmy (D)	6 3	13 06	London	26 10 78	Chelsea
Bedeau Anthony (F)	5 10	11 00	Hammersmith	24 3 79	Trainee
Brandon Chris (M)	5 7	10 00	Bradford	7 4 76	Bradford PA
Healy Brian (M)	6 1	13 02	Glasgow	27 12 68	Morecambe
Herrera Robbie (D)	5 7	10 06	Torbay	12 6 70	Fulham
Hill Kevin (M)	5 8	10 03	Exeter	6 3 76	Torrington
Holmes Paul (D)	5 10	11 00	Stocksbridge	18 2 68	WBA
Jones Stuart (G)	6 0	13 07	Bristol	24 10 77	Sheffield W
Neil Gary (F)	6 0	12 10	Glasgow	16 8 78	Leicester C
Northmore Ryan (G)	6 1	13 00	Plymouth	5 9 80	Trainee
O'Brien Mick (M)	5 5	10 06	Liverpool	25 9 79	Everton
Platts Mark (F)	5 8	11 12	Sheffield	23 5 79	Sheffield W
Russell Lee (D)	5 10	11 09	Southampton	3 9 69	Portsmouth
Thomas Wayne (D)	5 11	11 02	Gloucester	17 5 79	Trainee
Tully Stephen (M)	5 7	10 04	Paignton	10 2 80	Trainee
Watson Alex (D)	6 1	12 00	Liverpool	5 4 68	Bournemouth
Williams Eifion (F)	5 11	11 00	Bangor	15 11 75	Barry T

League Appearances: Aggrey, J. 22(5); Bedeau, A. 37(1); Brandon, C. 41(1); Donaldson, O. 4(11); Forrester, M. (1); Griffiths, M. 8(14); Gutteridge, L. (1); Healy, B. 37(1); Herrera, R. 34(1); Hill, K. 39(4); Holmes, P. 30; Ingimarsson, I. 4; Jones, S. 16; Neil, G. 4(3); Nichols, J. 1; Northmore, R. 2(1); O'Brien, M. 25(5); Platts, M. 7(15); Russell, L. 35; Simb, J. 1(10); Southall, N. 28; Stocco, T. 2(6); Thomas, W. 38(2); Tully, S. 10(3); Watson, A. 43; Williams, E. 38(4).

Goals – League (62): Bedeau 16, Healy 9 (5 pens), Williams 9, Brandon 5, O'Brien 4 (1 pen), Watson 4, Griffiths 3, Thomas 3, Hill 2, Stocco 2, Ingimarsson 1, Platts 1, own goals 3.
Worthington Cup (0).
FA Cup (7): O'Brien 2, Bedeau 1, Brandon 1, Donaldson 1, Hill 1, Thomas 1.
Ground: Plainmoor Ground, Torquay, Devon TQ1 3PS. Telephone (01803) 328666.
Record attendance: 21,908 v Huddersfield T, FA Cup 4th rd, 29 January 1955.
Capacity: 6003.
Manager: Wes Saunders.
Secretary: Miss H. Kindeleit.
Most League Goals: 89, Division 3 (S), 1956–57.
Highest League Scorer in Season: Sammy Collins, 40, Division 3 (S), 1955–56.
Most League Goals in Total Aggregate: Sammy Collins, 204, 1948–58.
Most Capped Player: Rodney Jack, St Vincent.
Most League Appearances: Dennis Lewis, 443, 1947–59.
Honours – Nil
Colours: Yellow and white striped shirts, navy shorts, navy stockings.

TOTTENHAM HOTSPUR — FA PREMIERSHIP

Player	Ht	Wt	Birthplace	Birthdate	Source
Anderton Darren (F)	6 1	12 05	Southampton	3 3 72	Portsmouth
Armstrong Chris (F)	6 0	12 10	Newcastle	19 6 71	Crystal Palace
Baardsen Espen (G)	6 5	13 03	San Rafael	7 12 77	San Francisco AB
Campbell Sol (D)	6 21	14 04	Newham	18 9 74	Trainee
Carr Stephen (D)	5 9	12 04	Dublin	29 8 76	Trainee
Clemence Stephen (M)	5 11	11 07	Liverpool	31 3 78	Trainee
Consorti Maurizio (M)			Rome	6 3 82	Trainee
Crouch Peter (F)	6 2	11 12	Macclesfield	30 1 81	Trainee
Davies Simon (M)	5 10	11 04	Haverfordwest	23 10 79	Peterborough U
Doherty Gary (D)	6 2	13 01	Carndonagh	31 1 80	Luton T
Dominguez Jose (F)	5 3	10 00	Lisbon	16 2 74	Sporting Lisbon
Etherington Matthew (F)	5 10	11 02	Truro	14 8 81	Peterborough U
Fenn Neale (F)	5 10	12 08	Edmonton	18 1 77	Trainee
Ferdinand Les (F)	5 11	13 05	Paddington	8 12 66	Newcastle U
Fox Ruel (F)	5 6	10 05	Ipswich	14 1 68	Newcastle U
Freund Steffen (M)	5 11	12 06	Brandenburg	19 1 70	Borussia Dortmund
Gardner Anthony (D)	6 5	13 11	Tittensor	19 9 80	Port Vale
Ginola David (F)	5 11	11 10	Gassin	25 1 67	Newcastle U
Gower Mark (M)	5 11	11 12	Edmonton	5 10 78	Trainee
Hillier Ian (D)	5 11	11 05	Neath	26 12 79	Trainee
Iversen Steffen (F)	6 1	11 08	Oslo	10 11 76	
Jackson Johnnie (M)			Camden	15 8 82	Trainee
Kamanan Yannick (F)			St Pol-sur-Mer	5 10 82	Le Mans
Kelly Gavin (G)	6 0	13 05	Hammersmith	3 6 81	Trainee
King Ledley (D)	6 2	13 08	London	12 10 80	Trainee
Korsten Willem (F)	6 4	13 04	Boxtel	21 1 75	Leeds U
Leonhardsen Oyvind (M)	5 10	11 02	Kristiansund	17 8 70	Liverpool
McEwen Dave (F)	6 0	11 00	Westminster	2 11 77	Dulwich H
Nielsen Allan (M)	5 8	11 02	Esbjerg	13 3 71	Brondby
Partin Jonatan (M)			Kungsbacka	24 2 83	Edsbyns
Perry Chris (D)	5 8	10 08	Carshalton	26 4 73	Wimbledon
Piercy John (M)	5 11	11 12	Forest Gate	18 9 79	Trainee
Sherwood Tim (M)	6 1	12 09	St Albans	2 2 69	Blackburn R
Taricco Mauricio (D)	5 8	11 05	Buenos Aires	10 3 73	Ipswich T

Thelwell Alton (D)	6 0	12 07	London	5 9 80	Trainee
Toner Ciaran (M)	6 1	12 02	Craigavon	30 6 81	Trainee
Vega Ramon (D)	6 3	13 00	Olten	14 6 71	Cagliari
Walker Ian (G)	6 2	13 01	Watford	31 10 71	Trainee
Young Luke (M)	6 0	12 04	Harlow	19 7 79	Trainee

League Appearances: Anderton, D. 22; Armstrong, C. 29(2); Campbell, S. 29; Carr, S. 34; Clemence, S. 16(4); Davies, S. 1(2); Doherty, G. (2); Dominguez, J. 2(10); Edinburgh, J. 7(1); Etherington, M. 1(4); Ferdinand, L. 5(4); Fox, R. 1(2); Freund, S. 24(3); Ginola, D. 36; Iversen, S. 36; King, L. 2(1); Korsten, W. 4(5); Leonhardsen, O. 21(1); McEwen, D. (1); Nielsen, A. 5(9); Perry, C. 36(1); Piercy, J. 1(2); Scales, J. 3(1); Sherwood, T. 23(4); Taricco, M. 29; Vega, R. 2(3); Walker, I. 38; Young, L. 11(9).
Goals – League (57): Armstrong 14, Iversen 14, Sherwood 8, Leonhardsen 4, Anderton 3 (1 pen), Carr 3, Ginola 3, Ferdinand 2, Clemence 1, Perry 1, Vega 1, own goals 3.
Worthington Cup (4): Ginola 1, Iversen 1, Leonhardsen 1, Sherwood 1.
FA Cup (2): Ginola 1, Iversen 1.
Ground: 748 High Rd, Tottenham, London N17 0AP. Telephone (020) 8365 5000.
Record attendance: 75,038 v Sunderland, FA Cup 6th rd, 5 March 1938.
Capacity: 36,236.
Manager: George Graham.
Secretary: John Alexander.
Most League Goals: 115, Division 1, 1960–61.
Highest League Scorer in Season: Jimmy Greaves, 37, Division 1, 1962–63.
Most League Goals in Total Aggregate: Jimmy Greaves, 220, 1961–70.
Most Capped Player: Pat Jennings, 74 (119), Northern Ireland.
Most League Appearances: Steve Perryman, 655, 1969–86.
Honours – Football League: Division 1 Champions – 1950–51, 1960–61. Division 2 Champions – 1919–20, 1949–50. **FA Cup:** Winners 1901 (as non-**League** club), 1921, 1961, 1962, 1967, 1981, 1982, 1991. **Football League Cup:** Winners 1970–71, 1972–73, 1998–99. **European Competitions: European Cup-Winners' Cup winners:** 1962–63. **UEFA Cup winners:** 1971–72, 1983–84.
Colours: White shirts, navy blue shorts, navy blue stockings.

TRANMERE ROVERS DIV. 1

Achterberg John (G)	6 1	13 00	Utrecht	8 7 71	Eindhoven
Aldridge Paul (F)	5 11	11 07	Liverpool	2 12 81	Scholar
Allen Graham (D)	6 0	12 00	Bolton	8 4 77	Everton
Allison Wayne (F)	6 0	14 07	Huddersfield	16 10 68	Huddersfield T
Black Michael (M)	5 8	11 08	Chigwell	6 10 76	Arsenal
Challinor Dave (D)	6 1	12 00	Chester	2 10 75	Brombrough Pool
Hay Alexander (M)			Wirral	14 10 81	Scholar
Hazell Reuben (D)	5 11	11 11	Birmingham	24 4 79	Aston Villa
Henry Nick (M)	5 6	10 12	Liverpool	21 2 69	Walsall
Hill Clint (D)	6 0	11 06	Liverpool	19 10 78	Trainee
Hinds Richard (D)	6 2	12 00	Sheffield	22 8 80	Schoolboy
Koumas Jason (M)	5 10	11 06	Wrexham	25 9 79	Trainee
Mahon Alan (M)	5 9	11 05	Dublin	4 4 78	Crumplin U
Moran Andy (F)	5 11	11 02	Wigan	7 10 79	Trainee
Murphy Joe (G)	6 2	13 06	Dublin	21 8 81	Trainee
Parkinson Andy (F)	5 8	10 12	Liverpool	27 5 79	Liverpool
Roberts Gareth (D)	5 8	11 00	Wrexham	6 2 78	Liverpool
Sharps Ian (M)	6 3	13 05	Warrington	23 10 80	Trainee

Taylor Perry (M)	5 11	12 02	Birkenhead	29 1 81	Trainee
Taylor Scott (F)	5 10	11 06	Chertsey	5 5 76	Bolton W
Yates Steve (D)	5 10	12 02	Bristol	29 1 70	QPR

League Appearances: Achterberg, J. 24(2); Aldridge, P. (4); Allen, G. 21(3); Allison, W. 40; Babb, P. 4; Black, M. 7(15); Challinor, D. 39(2); Frail, S. 1(2); Grant, T. 8(1); Hazell, R. 21(2); Henry, N. 28(2); Hill, C. 28(1); Hinds, R. 5(1); Hume, I. (3); Jones, G. 27(4); Jones, L. 3(11); Kelly, D. 25(7); Koumas, J. 9(14); Mahon, A. 33(3); Matias, P. 1(3); Morgan, A. 20(6); Murphy, J. 21; Nixon, E. 1(1); Parkinson, A. 30(7); Roberts, G. 36(1); Santos, G. 9(1); Taylor, S. 23(12); Thompson, A. 10(5); Yates, S. 32(1).
Goals – League (57): Allison 16, Parkinson 7, Kelly 6, Hill 5, Mahon 4 (3 pens), Challinor 3, Jones G 3, Taylor 3, Koumas 2, Yates 2, Hazell 1, Henry 1, Roberts 1, Santos 1, own goals 2.
Worthington Cup (23): Kelly 8, Taylor 4, Hill 2, Parkinson 2, Black 1, Grant 1, Henry 1, Mahon 1 (pen), Morgan 1, Yates 1, own goal 1.
FA Cup (6): Allison 3, Henry 1, Jones 1, Kelly 1.
Ground: Prenton Park, Prenton Road West, Prenton, Wirral L42 9PN. Telephone (0151) 608 4194.
Record attendance: 24,424 v Stoke C, FA Cup 4th rd, 5 February 1972. **Capacity:** 16,789.
Manager: John Aldridge.
Secretary: Mick Horton.
Most League Goals: 111, Division 3 (N), 1930–31.
Highest League Scorer in Season: Bunny Bell, 35, Division 3 (N), 1933–34.
Most League Goals in Total Aggregate: Ian Muir, 142, 1985–95.
Most Capped Player: John Aldridge, 30 (69), Republic of Ireland.
Most League Appearances: Harold Bell, 595, 1946–64 (incl. League record 401 consecutive appearances).
Honours – Football League Division 3 (N) Champions – 1937–38. **Welsh Cup:** Winners 1935. **Leyland Daf Cup:** Winners 1990.
Colours: White shirts, blue shorts.

WALSALL — DIV. 2

Barras Tony (D)	6 0	13 00	Billingham	29 3 71	Reading
Birch Gary (M)			Birmingham	8 10 81	Trainee
Bukran Gabby (M)	5 11	12 01	Eger	16 11 75	Xerxes
Carter Alfie (F)	5 10	10 05	Birmingham	13 8 80	Trainee
Emberson Carl (G)	6 2	14 07	Epsom	13 7 73	Colchester U
Eyjolfsson Siggi (F)	6 2	12 07	Reykjavik	1 12 73	
Gadsby Matthew (D)	6 1	11 12	Sutton Coldfield	6 9 79	Trainee
Keates Dean (M)	5 5	10 06	Walsall	30 6 78	Trainee
Marsh Chris (D)	5 11	13 02	Dudley	14 1 70	Trainee
Matias Pedro (M)	6 0	12 00	Madrid	11 10 73	Tranmere R
Padula Gino (D)	5 9	12 01	Buenos Aires	11 7 76	Xerex
Rammell Andy (F)	6 1	13 12	Nuneaton	10 2 67	Southend U
Ricketts Michael (F)	6 2	11 12	Birmingham	4 12 78	Trainee
Roper Ian (D)	6 3	14 00	Nuneaton	20 6 77	Trainee
Scott Dion (D)	5 11	11 00	Bearwood	24 12 80	Trainee
Walker James (G)	5 11	12 13	Sutton-in-Ashfield	9 7 73	Notts Co
Wrack Darren (F)	5 9	12 02	Cleethorpes	5 5 76	Grimsby T

League Appearances: Abou, S. 7(1); Barras, T. 19(5); Bennett, T. 11; Bica (1); Brightwell, I. 9(1); Brissett, J. 5(2); Bukran, G. 33(4); Carter, A. 1; Daley, T. 3(4); Emberson, C. 3(2); Eyjolfsson, S. 1(12); Fenton, G. 8(1); Forrester, J. 2(3); Gadsby, M. 1(2); Hall, P. 10; Harper, K. 8(1); Keates, D. 27(8); Keister, J. (1); Larusson, B. 12(11); Marsh, C. 40; Matias, P. 30(3); Mavrak, D. 1(3); Padula, G. 23(2); Pointon, N. 18; Rammell, A. 21(9); Ricketts, M. 21(11); Robins, M. 30(10); Roper, I. 32(2); Thomas, W. (1); Todd, L. 1; Viveash, A. 41(2); Vlachos, M. 11; Walker, J. 43; Wrack, D. 34(10).
Goals – League (52): Ricketts 11 (1 pen), Matias 6, Robins 6 (1 pen), Rammell 5, Barras 4, Hall 4, Wrack 4, Bennett 3, Bukran 2, Eyjolfsson 1, Fenton 1, Harper 1, Keates 1, Roper 1, Viveash 1, Vlachos 1.
Worthington Cup (10): Bukran 3, Eyjolfsson 3, Barras 1, Keates 1, Robins 1, own goal 1.
FA Cup (2): Larusson 1, Robins 1 (pen).
Ground: Bescot Stadium, Bescot Cresent, Walsall WS1 4SA. Telephone (01922) 622791.
Record attendance: 10,628 B International, England v Switzerland, 20 May 1991.
Capacity: 9000.
Manager: Ray Graydon.
Secretary/Commercial Manager: Roy Whalley.
Most League Goals: 102, Division 4, 1959–60.
Highest League Scorer in Season: Gilbert Alsop, 40, Division 3 (N), 1933–34 and 1934–35.
Most League Goals in Total Aggregate: Tony Richards, 184, 1954–63; Colin Taylor, 184, 1958–63, 1964–68, 1969–73.
Most Capped Player: Mick Kearns, 15 (18), Republic of Ireland.
Most League Appearances: Colin Harrison, 467, 1964–82.
Honours – Football League: Division 4 Champions – 1959–60.
Colours: Red shirts with black trim, black shorts with white trim, red stockings with white band.

WATFORD — DIV. 1

Bakalli Adrian (M)	6 3	13 00	Brussels	22 11 76	Molenbeek
Bonnot Alex (M)	5 8	11 05	Poissy	31 7 73	Angers
Brooker Stephen (F)	5 10	12 04	Newport Pagnell	21 5 81	Trainee
Chamberlain Alec (G)	6 2	13 10	March	20 6 64	Sunderland
Cook Lee (F)			Hammersmith	3 8 82	Aylesbury U
Cox Neil (D)	6 0	12 01	Scunthorpe	8 10 71	Bolton W
Easton Clint (M)	5 11	10 04	Barking	1 11 77	Trainee
Fisken Gary (M)			Watford	27 10 81	Scholar
Foley Dominic (F)	6 1	12 08	Cork	7 7 76	Wolverhampton W
Gibbs Nigel (D)	5 7	11 06	St Albans	20 11 65	Apprentice
Gudmundsson Johann (M)	6 0	11 07	Reykjavik	5 12 77	Keflavik
Helguson Heidar (F)	5 10	11 00	Akureyri	22 8 77	Lillestrom
Hyde Micah (M)	5 10	11 07	Newham	10 11 74	Cambridge U
Ifil Jerel (D)			London	27 6 82	Academy
Johnson Lee (M)	5 6	10 07	Newmarket	7 6 81	Trainee
Johnson Richard (M)	5 10	11 13	Kurri Kurri	27 4 74	Trainee
Kennedy Peter (M)	5 10	11 11	Lisburn	10 9 73	Portadown
Kodra Elis (M)			Pristina	20 5 82	Academy
Langston Matthew (D)	6 2	12 04	Brighton	2 4 81	Trainee
Lyttle Des (D)	5 9	12 00	Wolverhampton	24 9 71	Nottingham F
Miller Charlie (M)	5 7	12 02	Glasgow	18 3 76	Rangers
Mooney Tommy (F)	5 11	12 10	Teeside North	11 8 71	Southend U
Ngonge Michel (F)	6 0	12 00	Huy	10 1 67	Samsunspor

Noel-Williams Gifton (F)	6 1	12 04	Islington	21 1 80	Trainee
Page Robert (D)	6 0	12 05	Llwynipia	9 9 74	Trainee
Palmer Steve (M)	6 1	12 03	Brighton	31 3 68	Ipswich T
Panayi James (D)	6 1	12 06	Hammersmith	24 1 80	Trainee
Perpetuini David (D)	5 9	10 00	Hitchin	26 9 79	Trainee
Robinson Paul (D)	5 9	11 11	Watford	14 12 78	Trainee
Smart Allan (F)	6 2	12 04	Perth	8 7 74	Carlisle U
Smith Tommy (F)	5 9	10 00	Hemel Hempstead	22 5 80	Trainee
Walker Herwig (G)	6 1	13 00	Linz	4 5 72	Linz ASK
Ward Darren (D)	6 3	12 11	Kenton	13 9 78	Trainee
Warner David (F)			Hillingdon	27 4 81	Brook House
Williams Mark (D)	6 0	12 04	Stalybridge	28 9 70	Chesterfield
Wooter Nordin (F)	5 6	10 08	Breda	24 8 76	Zaragoza
Wright Nick (F)	5 10	11 08	Derby	15 10 75	Carlisle U
Yates Dean (D)	6 2	12 08	Leicester	26 10 67	Derby Co

League Appearances: Bakalli, A. (2); Bonnot, A. 7(5); Brooker, S. (1); Chamberlain, A. 27; Cox, N. 20(1); Day, C. 11; Easton, C. 13(4); Foley, D. 5(7); Gibbs, N. 11(6); Gravelaine, X. 7; Gudmundsson, J. 1(8); Helguson, H. 14(2); Hyde, M. 33(1); Johnson, R. 20(3); Kennedy, P. 17(1); Lyttle, D. 11; Miller, C. 9(5); Mooney, T. 8(4); Ngonge, M. 16(7); Noel-Williams, G. 1(2); Page, R. 36; Palmer, S. 38; Panayi, J. 2; Perpetuini, D. 12(1); Robinson, P. 29(3); Smart, A. 13(1); Smith, T. 13(9); Ward, D. 7(2); Williams, M. 20(2); Wooter, N. 16(4); Wright, N. 1(3).
Goals – League (35): Helguson 6, Ngonge 5, Smart 5, Hyde 3, Johnson 3 (1 pen), Gravelaine 2, Mooney 2, Smith 2, Foley 1, Kennedy 1 (pen), Page 1, Perpetuini 1, Ward 1, Williams 1, Wooter 1.
Worthington Cup (3): Easton 1, Hyde 1, Kennedy 1.
FA Cup (0).
Ground: Vicarage Road Stadium, Watford WD1 8ER. Telephone (01923) 496000.
Record attendance: 34,099 v Manchester U, FA Cup 4th rd (replay), 3 February 1969. **Capacity:** 20,800.
General Manager: Graham Taylor.
Secretary: Catherine Alexander.
Most League Goals: 92, Division 4, 1959–60.
Highest League Scorer in Season: Cliff Holton, 42, Division 4, 1959–60.
Most League Goals in Total Aggregate: Luther Blissett, 148, 1976–83, 1984–88, 1991–92.
Most Capped Player: John Barnes, 31 (79), England and Kenny Jackett, 31, Wales.
Most League Appearances: Luther Blissett, 415, 1976–83, 1984–88, 1991–92.
Honours – Football League: Division 3 Champions – 1968–69. Division 2 Champions – 1997–98. Division 4 Champions – 1977–78.
Colours: Yellow shirts with red and black trim, red shorts, red stockings with yellow trim.

WEST BROMWICH ALBION — DIV. 1

Adamson Chris (G)	6 3	12 00	Ashington	4 11 78	Trainee
Burgess Daryl (D)	5 11	11 04	Birmingham	24 1 71	Trainee
Butler Tony (D)	6 2	12 00	Stockport	28 9 72	Port Vale
Carbon Matt (D)	6 2	12 05	Nottingham	8 6 75	Derby Co
Chambers Adam (D)	5 10	11 08	Sandwell	20 11 80	Trainee
Chambers James (D)	5 10	11 08	Sandwell	20 11 80	Trainee
De Freitas Fabian (F)	6 0	12 00	Paramaribo	28 7 72	Osasuna
Evans Micky (F)	6 0	12 03	Plymouth	1 1 73	Southampton
Gabbidon Daniel (D)	5 10	11 02	Cwmbran	8 8 79	Trainee
Hughes Lee (F)	5 10	11 06	Birmingham	22 5 76	Kidderminster H

Jensen Brian (G)	6 1	12 04	Copenhagen	8 6 75	AZ
Lezzi Massamiliano (M)			Rome	1 2 81	
Mardon Paul (D)	6 0	11 10	Bristol	14 9 69	Birmingham C
Morris Elliott (M)			Belfast	4 5 81	Trainee
Oliver Adam (M)	5 9	11 02	Sandwell	25 10 80	Trainee
Quinn James (F)	6 1	12 10	Coventry	15 12 74	Blackpool
Raven Paul (D)	6 1	12 11	Salisbury	28 7 70	Doncaster R
Richards Justin (F)	6 0	11 10	Sandwell	16 10 80	Trainee
Sigurdsson Larus (D)	6 0	13 11	Akureyri	4 6 73	Stoke C
Sneekes Richard (M)	5 11	12 03	Amsterdam	30 10 68	Bolton W
Taylor Bob (F)	5 11	13 05	Easington	3 2 67	Bolton W
Townsend Andy (M)	6 0	13 05	Maidstone	27 7 63	Middlesbrough
Van Blerk Jason (D)	6 1	13 00	Sydney	16 3 68	Manchester C

League Appearances: Adamson, C. 9; Angel, M. (3); Burgess, D. 23(3); Butler, T. 7; Carbon, M. 33(1); Chambers, J. 10(2); Clement, N. 7(1); De Freitas, F. 12(12); Evans, M. 16(17); Flynn, S. 36; Fredgaard, C. 5; Gabbidon, D. 18; Hall, P. 4; Hughes, L. 36; Jensen, B. 12; Kilbane, K. 19; Lyttle, D. 8(1); Maresca, E. 19(6); McDermott, A. 10(3); Miller, A. 25; Oliver, A. 1(14); Potter, G. 6(4); Quinn, J. 30(7); Raven, P. 27(5); Santos, G. 8; Sigurdsson, L. 27; Sneekes, R. 42; Taylor, B. 8; Townsend, A. 15(3); Van Blerk, J. 33(2).
Goals – League (43): Hughes 12 (1 pen), Kilbane 5, Taylor 5, Flynn 4, Evans 3, Maresca 3, Sneekes 3 (2 pens), Carbon 2, Burgess 1, De Freitas 1, McDermott 1, Oliver 1, Raven 1, Van Blerk 1.
Worthington Cup (11): Hughes 3, De Freitas 2, Kilbane 2, Evans 1, Flynn 1, Quinn 1, Raven 1.
FA Cup (2): Evans 1, Hughes 1.
Ground: The Hawthorns, West Bromwich B71 4LF. Telephone (0121) 525 8888.
Record attendance: 64,815 v Arsenal, FA Cup 6th rd, 6 March 1937. **Capacity:** 25,396.
Manager: Gary Megson.
Secretary: Dr. John J. Evans BA, PHD. (Wales).
Most League Goals: 105, Division 2, 1929–30.
Highest League Scorer in Season: William 'Ginger' Richardson, 39, Division 1, 1935–36.
Most League Goals in Total Aggregate: Tony Brown, 218, 1963–79.
Most Capped Player: Stuart Williams, 33 (43), Wales.
Most League Appearances: Tony Brown, 574, 1963–80.
Honours – Football League: Division 1 Champions – 1919–20. Division 2 Champions – 1901–02, 1910–11. **FA Cup:** Winners 1888, 1892, 1931, 1954, 1968. **Football League Cup:** Winners 1965–66.
Colours: Navy blue and white striped shirts, white shorts, blue and white stockings.

WEST HAM UNITED — FA PREMIERSHIP

Alexander Gary (F)	6 0	12 00	South London	15 8 79	Trainee
Angus Stevland (D)	6 0	12 00	Essex	16 9 80	Trainee
Britton Leon (M)			London	16 9 82	Trainee
Bullard Jimmy (M)	5 10	11 07	Newham	23 10 78	Gravesend & N
Byrne Shaun (D)	5 9	11 08	Taplow	21 1 81	Trainee
Bywater Steve (G)	6 2	12 00	Manchester	7 6 81	Trainee
Carrick Michael (M)	6 0	11 10	Wallsend	28 7 81	Trainee
Charles Gary (D)	5 9	11 03	East London	13 4 70	Benfica
Cole Joe (M)	5 7	9 08	Islington	8 11 81	Trainee
Defoe Jermaine (F)	5 7	10 04	Beckton	7 10 82	Charlton Ath
Di Canio Paolo (F)	5 9	11 09	Rome	9 7 68	Sheffield W

Etherington Craig (M)	6 0	11 10	Basildon	16 9 79	Trainee
Ferdinand Rio (D)	6 2	12 00	Peckham	8 11 78	Trainee
Ferrante Michael (M)			Melbourne	28 4 81	Australia IOS
Feuer Ian (G)	6 6	15 06	Las Vegas	20 5 71	Cardiff C
Forbes Terrell (D)	6 0	12 05	Southwark	17 8 81	
Forrest Craig (G)	6 4	14 04	Vancouver	20 9 67	Ipswich T
Garcia Richard (F)			Perth	4 9 81	Trainee
Hislop Shaka (G)	6 4	14 04	Hackney	22 2 69	Newcastle U
Holligan Gavin (F)	5 10	13 00	Lambeth	13 6 80	Kingstonian
Iriekpen Ezomo (D)	6 1	12 02	East London	14 5 82	Trainee
Kanoute Frederic (F)	6 3	12 04	Ste. Foy-Les-Lyon	2 9 77	Lyon
Keller Marc (M)	5 10	11 05	Colmar	14 1 68	Karlsruhe
Kitson Paul (F)	5 11	10 12	Murton	9 1 71	Newcastle U
Lampard Frank (M)	6 0	11 12	Romford	20 6 78	Trainee
Laurie Steve (D)			Melbourne	30 10 82	
Lomas Steve (M)	6 0	12 08	Hanover	14 3 72	Manchester C
Margas Javier (D)	6 1	13 00	Santiago	10 5 69	Univ Catolica
McCann Grant (M)			Belfast	14 4 80	Trainee
Minto Scott (D)	5 10	10 00	Wirral	6 8 71	Benfica
Moncur John (M)	5 8	9 10	Mile End	22 9 66	Swindon T
Newton Adam (D)	5 10	11 00	Ascot	4 12 80	Trainee
O'Reilly Alex (G)			Epping	15 9 79	Trainee
Pearce Ian (D)	6 3	14 04	Bury St Edmunds	7 5 74	Blackburn R
Pearce Stuart (D)	5 10	12 13	Shepherds Bush	24 4 62	Newcastle U
Potts Steve (D)	5 7	10 11	Hartford (USA)	7 5 67	Apprentice
Riza Omer (F)			Edmonton	8 11 79	Arsenal
Ruddock Neil (D)	6 2	12 12	Wandsworth	9 5 68	Liverpool
Sinclair Trevor (F)	5 10	12 05	Dulwich	2 3 73	QPR
Sjolund Danny (M)			Sweden	22 4 83	
Stimac Igor (D)	6 2	13 00	Metkovic	6 9 67	Derby Co
Wanchope Paulo (F)	6 4	12 00	Heredia	31 7 76	Derby Co
Williams Thomas (M)			Carshalton	8 7 80	Walton & Hersham

League Appearances: Byrne, S. (1); Bywater, S. 3(1); Carrick, M. 4(4); Charles, G. 2(2); Cole, J. 17(5); Di Canio, P. 29(1); Ferdinand, R. 33; Feuer, I. 3; Foe, M. 25; Forrest, C. 9(2); Hislop, S. 22; Ilic, S. 1; Kanoute, F. 8; Keller, M. 19(4); Kitson, P. 4(6); Lampard, F. 34; Lomas, S. 25; Margas, J. 15(3); Minto, S. 15(3); Moncur, J. 20(2); Newton, A. (2); Pearce, I. 1; Pearce, S. 8; Potts, S. 16(1); Ruddock, N. 12(3); Sinclair, T. 36; Stimac, I. 24; Wanchope, P. 33(2).
Goals – League (52): Di Canio 16 (2 pens), Wanchope 12, Lampard 7, Sinclair 7, Kanoute 2, Carrick 1, Cole 1, Foe 1, Lomas 1, Margas 1, Moncur 1, Stimac 1, own goal 1.
Worthington Cup (6): Lampard 2, Cole 1, Keller 1, Kitson 1, Lomas 1.
FA Cup (0).
Ground: Boleyn Ground, Green Street, Upton Park, London E13 9AZ. Telephone (020) 8548 2748.
Record attendance: 42,322 v Tottenham H, Division 1, 17 October 1970. **Capacity:** 26,012.
Manager: Harry Redknapp.
Secretary: Peter Barnes.
Most League Goals: 101, Division 2, 1957–58.
Highest League Scorer in Season: Vic Watson, 42, Division 1, 1929–30.
Most League Goals in Total Aggregate: Vic Watson, 298, 1920–35.
Most Capped Player: Bobby Moore, 108, England.
Most League Appearances: Billy Bonds, 663, 1967–88.

Honours – Football League: Division 2 Champions – 1957–58, 1980–81. **FA Cup:** Winners 1964, 1975, 1980. **European Competitions: European Cup-Winners' Cup winners:** 1964–65. **Intertoto Cup winners** 1999.
Colours: Claret shirts with blue sleeves, white shorts, light blue with claret hooped stockings.

WIGAN ATHLETIC DIV. 2

Balmer Stuart (D)	6 0	13 02	Falkirk	20 9 69	Charlton Ath
Carroll Roy (G)	6 2	13 12	Enniskillen	30 9 77	Hull C
De Zeeuw Arjan (D)	6 3	13 07	Castricum	16 4 70	Barnsley
Griffiths Gareth (D)	6 4	14 01	Winsford	10 4 70	Port Vale
Haworth Simon (F)	6 1	14 02	Cardiff	30 3 77	Coventry C
Jones Graeme (F)	6 0	13 11	Gateshead	13 3 70	Doncaster R
Liddell Andy (F)	5 8	11 05	Leeds	28 6 73	Barnsley
Martinez Roberto (M)	5 11	12 03	Balaguer	13 7 73	Balaguer
McLaughlin Brian (M)	5 5	9 02	Bellshill	14 5 74	Dundee U
McLoughlin Alan (M)	5 8	10 10	Manchester	20 4 67	Portsmouth
Nicholls Kevin (M)	5 11	12 04	Newham	2 1 79	Charlton Ath
Porter Andy (M)	5 9	12 03	Holmes Chapel	17 9 68	Port Vale
Redfearn Neil (M)	5 8	12 00	Dewsbury	20 6 65	Bradford C
Roberts Neil (F)	5 10	11 02	Wrexham	7 4 78	Wrexham
Sharp Kevin (D)	5 9	11 04	Ontario	19 9 74	Leeds U
Sheridan Darren (M)	5 6	11 04	Manchester	8 12 67	Barnsley
Stillie Derek (G)	6 0	12 05	Cumnock	3 12 73	Aberdeen

League Appearances: Balmer, S. 41; Barlow, S. 24(9); Bowen, M. 7; Bradshaw, C. 21(5); Carroll, R. 34; Clegg, G. 6; Cooke, T. 10; De Zeeuw, A. 39; Green, S. 32(1); Griffiths, G. 10(6); Haworth, S. 36(4); Jones, G. 1(2); Kilford, I. 18(3); Lee, D. (4); Liddell, A. 41; Martinez, R. 14(11); McGibbon, P. 30(4); McLoughlin, A. 11(4); Nicholls, K. 6(2); O'Neill, M. 30; Peron, J. 19(4); Porter, A. 2(3); Redfearn, N. 12; Roberts, N. 8(1); Sharp, K. 17(4); Sheridan, D. 25(6); Stillie, D. 12(1).
Goals – League (72): Barlow 18 (3 pens), Haworth 13, Liddell 8, Redfearn 6 (5 pens), De Zeeuw 3, Martinez 3, Sheridan 3, Balmer 2, Green 2, McGibbon 2, O'Neill 2, Bradshaw 1 (pen), Cooke 1, Griffiths 1, Jones 1, Kilford 1, McLoughlin 1, Roberts 1, own goals 3.
Worthington Cup (6): Haworth 3, Barlow 2 (1 pen), Bradshaw 1 (pen).
FA Cup (6): Haworth 3, Barlow 2, Liddell 1.
Ground: J. J. B. Stadium, Robin Park, Newtown, Wigan WN6 7BA. Telephone (01942) 774 000.
Record attendance: 27,500 v Hereford U, FA Cup 2nd rd, 12 December 1953.
Capacity: 25,000
Manager: Bruce Rioch.
Secretary: Mrs Brenda Spencer.
Most League Goals: 84, Division 3, 1996–97.
Highest League Scorer in Season: Graeme Jones, 31, Division 3, 1996–97.
Most League Goals in Total Aggregate: David Lowe, 66, 1982–87 and 1995–99.
Most Capped Player: Roy Carroll, 4, Northern Ireland.
Most League Appearances: Kevin Langley, 317, 1981–86, 1990–94.
Honours – Football League: Division 3 Champions – 1996–97. **Freight Rover Trophy:** Winners 1984–85. **Auto Windscreens Shield:** Winners 1998–99.
Colours: Blue shirts with white side panel, blue shorts and stockings.

WIMBLEDON DIV. 1

Agyemang Patrick (F)	6 1	12 00	Walthamstow	29 9 80	Trainee
Ainsworth Gareth (M)	5 9	11 00	Blackburn	10 5 73	Port Vale
Andersen Trond (M)	6 0	11 06	Kristiansund	6 1 75	Molde
Andresen Martin (M)	5 11	11 04	Norway	2 2 77	Stabaek
Ardley Neal (M)	5 11	11 09	Epsom	1 9 72	Trainee
Badir Walid (M)	5 10	12 07	Kafr Kasm	12 3 74	Hapoel P-T
Blackwell Dean (D)	6 1	12 10	Camden	5 12 69	Trainee
Cort Carl (F)	6 4	12 07	Southwark	1 11 77	Trainee
Cunningham Kenny (D)	5 11	11 04	Dublin	28 6 71	Millwall
Davis Kelvin (G)	6 1	11 02	Bedford	29 9 76	Luton T
Euell Jason (F)	5 11	11 02	Lambeth	6 2 77	Trainee
Francis Damien (M)	6 0	10 10	Wandsworth	27 2 79	Trainee
Gayle Marcus (F)	6 1	12 09	Hammersmith	27 9 70	Brentford
Gier Robert (M)	5 9	11 07	Ascot	6 1 80	Trainee
Gray Wayne (F)	5 10	11 10	South London	7 11 80	Trainee
Hartson John (F)	6 0	13 07	Swansea	5 4 75	West Ham U
Hawkins Peter (D)	6 0	11 04	Maidstone	19 9 78	Trainee
Heald Paul (G)	6 2	12 05	Wath-on-Dearne	20 9 68	Leyton Orient
Hinds Leigh (F)	5 9	10 10	Beckenham	17 8 78	Trainee
Hreidarsson Hermann (D)	6 3	11 12	Iceland	11 7 74	Brentford
Hughes Michael (M)	5 6	10 08	Larne	2 8 71	West Ham U
Jupp Duncan (D)	6 0	12 11	Guildford	25 1 75	Fulham
Kimble Alan (D)	5 10	12 04	Poole	6 8 66	Cambridge U
Leaburn Carl (F)	6 3	13 00	Lewisham	30 3 69	Charlton Ath
Lund Andreas (F)	6 1	11 04	Kristiansand	7 5 75	Molde
Mensing Simon (M)	5 10	11 06	Woifenbuttel	27 6 82	
Owusu Ansah (M)	5 11	11 02	Hackney	22 11 79	Trainee
Pedersen Tore (D)	6 0	11 00	Fredrikstad	29 9 69	Eintracht Frankfurt
Roberts Andy (M)	5 10	13 00	Dartford	20 3 74	Crystal Palace
Tapp Alex (M)	5 8	11 10	Redhill	7 6 82	Trainee
Thatcher Ben (D)	5 11	12 00	Swindon	30 11 75	Millwall
Vella Simon (D)	6 2	11 11	Westminster	19 9 79	Trainee
Waehler Kjetil (M)	5 10	11 00	Oslo	16 3 76	Lyn
Willmott Chris (D)	5 11	10 12	Bedford	30 9 77	Luton T

League Appearances: Ainsworth, G. (2); Andersen, T. 35(1); Andresen, M. 4(10); Ardley, N. 10(7); Badir, W. 12(9); Blackwell, D. 16(1); Cort, C. 32(2); Cunningham, K. 37; Earle, R. 23(2); Euell, J. 32(5); Francis, D. 1(8); Gayle, M. 35(1); Gray, W. (1); Hartson, J. 15(1); Heald, P. 1; Hreidarsson, H. 24; Hughes, M. 13(7); Jupp, D. 6(3); Kimble, A. 24(4); Leaburn, C. 5(13); Lund, A. 10(2); Pedersen, T. 6; Roberts, A. 14(2); Sullivan, N. 37; Thatcher, B. 19(1); Willmott, C. 7.
Goals – League (46): Cort 9, Hartson 9, Gayle 7, Euell 4, Earle 3, Ainsworth 2, Ardley 2 (1 pen), Hughes 2, Lund 2, Andresen 1, Badir 1, Hreidarsson 1, own goals 3.
Worthington Cup (10): Cort 5, Earle 2, Euell 1, Hughes 1, Kimble 1.
FA Cup (1): Cort 1.
Ground: Selhurst Park, South Norwood, London SE25 6PY. Telephone (020) 8771 2233.
Record attendance: 30,115 v Manchester U, FA Premier **League**, 9 May 1993. **Capacity:** 26,297.
Manager: Terry Burton.
Secretary: Steve Rooke.
Most League Goals: 97, Division 3, 1983–84.

Highest League Scorer in Season: Alan Cork, 29, 1983–84.
Most League Goals in Total Aggregate: Alan Cork, 145, 1977–92.
Most Capped Player: Kenny Cunningham, 31, Republic of Ireland.
Most League Appearances: Alan Cork, 430, 1977–92.
Honours – Football League: Division 4 Champions – 1982–83. **FA Cup:** Winners 1987–88.
Colours: All navy blue with yellow trim.

WOLVERHAMPTON WANDERERS DIV. 1

Akinbiyi Ade (F)	6 1	13 09	Hackney	10 10 74	Bristol C
Andrews Keith (M)	5 10	12 04	Dublin	13 9 80	Trainee
Barrett Shane (M)			Luton	23 11 81	Trainee
Bazeley Darren (D)	5 11	10 09	Northampton	5 10 72	Watford
Branch Michael (F)	5 10	11 09	Liverpool	18 10 78	Everton
Bull Steve (F)	5 11	11 04	Tipton	28 3 65	WBA
Corica Steve (M)	5 8	10 10	Cairns	24 3 73	Marconi
Crowe Seamie (M)	5 7	11 07	Galway	18 11 80	Trainee
Curle Keith (D)	6 0	12 07	Bristol	14 11 63	Manchester C
Downes Lee (M)			Wolverhampton	27 2 83	Trainee
Emblen Neil (M)	6 1	13 03	Bromley	19 6 71	Crystal Palace
Flo Havard (F)	6 2	13 08	Volda	4 4 70	Werder Bremen
Green Ryan (D)	5 8	10 10	Cardiff	20 10 80	Danes Court
Hagan Conor (M)			Belfast	31 3 82	Trainee
Larkin Colin (F)	5 9	11 07	Dundalk	27 4 82	Trainee
Leonard Gerard (M)			Drogheda	7 7 82	Trainee
Lescott Jolean (M)			Birmingham	16 8 82	Trainee
Loughlin Paul (M)			Dublin	5 10 81	Stella Maris
Murray Matt (G)	6 3	13 07	Solihull	2 5 81	Trainee
Muscat Kevin (D)	5 11	11 07	Crawley	7 8 73	Crystal Palace
Naylor Lee (D)	5 8	12 00	Bloxwich	19 3 80	Trainee
Ndah George (F)	6 1	11 04	Dulwich	23 12 74	Swindon T
Niestroj Robert (M)	5 10	11 03	Oppeln	2 12 74	Fortuna Dusseldorf
Oakes Michael (G)	6 2	14 07	Northwich	30 10 73	Aston Villa
Osborn Simon (M)	5 10	11 04	New Addington	9 1 72	QPR
Pollet Ludovic (D)	6 0	12 06	Vieux-conde	18 6 70	Le Havre
Proudlock Adam (M)			Wellington	9 5 81	Trainee
Robinson Carl (M)	5 10	12 10	Llandrindod Wells	13 10 76	Trainee
Sedgley Steve (D)	6 1	13 13	Enfield	26 5 68	Ipswich T
Simms Gordon (D)	6 2	12 06	Larne	23 3 81	Trainee
Simpson Paul (M)	5 8	11 11	Carlisle	26 7 66	Derby Co
Sinton Andy (M)	5 7	10 07	Newcastle	19 3 66	Tottenham H
Stowell Mike (G)	6 2	13 10	Portsmouth	19 4 65	Everton
Tudor Shane (M)			Wolverhampton	10 2 82	Trainee

League Appearances: Akinbiyi, A. 36(1); Andrews, K. (2); Bazeley, D. 46; Branch, M. 25(2); Corica, S. 10(5); Curle, K. 44(1); Emblen, N. 45(1); Flo, H. 9(10); Jones, M. (1); Keane, R. 2; Larkin, C. 1; Muscat, K. 45; Naylor, L. 24(6); Ndah, G. 3(1); Nielsen, A. 7; Niestroj, R. (1); Oakes, M. 28; Osborn, S. 22(3); Pollet, L. 38(1); Robinson, C. 21(12); Sedgley, S. 32(6); Simpson, P. 1(12); Sinton, A. 31(4); Stowell, M. 18; Taylor, S. 18(10); Williams, A. (1).
Goals – League (64): Akinbiyi 16, Branch 6, Emblen 5, Pollet 5, Sedgley 5, Flo 4, Muscat 4 (2 pens), Bazeley 3, Robinson 3, Taylor 3, Curle 2 (2 pens), Keane 2, Naylor 2, Nielsen 2, Corica 1, own goal 1.
Worthington Cup (3): Curle 1 (pen), Emblen 1, Larkin 1.
FA Cup (2): Robinson 1, Sedgley 1.

Ground: Molineux Grounds, Wolverhampton WV1 4QR. Telephone (01902) 655000.
Record attendance: 61,315 v Liverpool, FA Cup 5th rd, 11 February 1939.
Capacity: 28,525.
Manager: Colin Lee.
Secretary: Richard Skirrow.
Most League Goals: 115, Division 2, 1931–32.
Highest League Scorer in Season: Dennis Westcott, 38, Division 1, 1946–47.
Most League Goals in Total Aggregate: Steve Bull, 250, 1986–99.
Most Capped Player: Billy Wright, 105, England (70 consecutive).
Most League Appearances: Derek Parkin, 501, 1967–82.
Honours – Football League: Division 1 Champions – 1953–54, 1957–58, 1958–59. Division 2 Champions – 1931–32, 1976–77. Division 3 (N) Champions – 1923–24. Division 3 Champions – 1988–89. Division 4 Champions – 1987–88. **FA Cup:** Winners 1893, 1908, 1949, 1960. **Football League Cup:** Winners 1973–74, 1979–80. **Sherpa Van Trophy winners** 1988.
Colours: Gold shirts, black shorts, gold stockings.

WREXHAM DIV. 2

Barrett Paul (M)	5 9	11 04	Newcastle	13 4 78	Newcastle U
Carey Brian (D)	6 3	13 02	Cork	31 5 68	Leicester C
Cartwright Mark (G)	6 2	13 06	Chester	13 1 73	York C
Chalk Martyn (F)	5 6	11 03	Swindon	30 8 69	Stockport Co
Dearden Kevin (G)	5 11	12 06	Luton	8 3 70	Brentford
Edwards Jake (F)	6 1	12 08	Manchester	11 5 76	USA College
Faulconbridge Craig (F)	6 1	13 00	Nuneaton	20 4 78	Dunfermline Ath
Ferguson Darren (M)	5 10	11 10	Glasgow	9 2 72	Wolverhampton W
Gibson Robin (F)	5 7	10 07	Crewe	15 11 79	Trainee
Hardy Phil (D)	5 7	11 08	Chester	9 4 73	Trainee
Lowe David (F)	5 10	11 04	Liverpool	30 8 65	Wigan Ath
McGregor Mark (D)	5 10	11 05	Chester	16 2 77	Trainee
Owen Gareth (M)	5 8	12 00	Chester	21 10 71	Trainee
Phillips Wayne (M)	5 11	11 00	Bangor	15 12 70	Stockport Co
Ridler Dave (D)	6 0	12 02	Liverpool	12 3 76	Prescot T
Roberts Steve (D)	6 2	11 06	Wrexham	24 2 80	Trainee
Rogers Kristian (G)	6 0	11 07	Chester	2 10 80	
Russell Kevin (M)	5 9	10 12	Portsmouth	6 12 66	Notts Co
Thomas Steve (M)	5 10	11 07	Hartlepool	23 6 79	Trainee
Walsh Dave (G)	6 1	12 05	Wrexham	29 4 79	Trainee
Williams Danny (M)	6 2	13 01	Wrexham	12 7 79	Liverpool

League Appearances: Allsopp, D. 3; Barrett, P. 17(1); Brace, D. 3(3); Carey, B. 43; Chalk, M. 10(10); Connolly, K. 35(6); Dearden, K. 45; Edwards, J. (2); Faulconbridge, C. 23(12); Ferguson, D. 37; Gibson, R. 18(6); Hannon, K. (1); Hardy, P. 38; Jarrett, J. 1; Lowe, D. 4(6); McGregor, M. 45; Morrell, A. 4(9); Owen, G. 35(4); Phillips, W. 3; Ridler, D. 22(3); Roberts, N. 18(1); Roberts, S. 16(3); Rogers, K. 1; Russell, K. 29(4); Ryan, M. 4(3); Spink, D. 13(2); Stevens, I. 14(2); Thomas, S. (2); Warren, D. 1; Williams, D. 24.
Goals – League (52): Connolly 9 (1 pen), Faulconbridge 8, Roberts N 6 (1 pen), Allsopp 4, Ferguson 4 (1 pen), Russell 4, Stevens 4, Owen 3, Barrett 2, Carey 1, Edwards 1, Gibson 1, Hardy 1 (pen), Lowe 1, McGregor 1, Morrell 1, Williams 1.
Worthington Cup (0).
FA Cup (8): Roberts N 2 (1 pen), Connolly 1, Faulconbridge 1, Ferguson 1, Gibson 1, Roberts S 1, Williams 1.
Ground: Racecourse Ground, Mold Road, Wrexham LL11 2AH. Telephone (01978) 262129.
Record attendance: 34,445 v Manchester U, FA Cup 4th rd, 26 January 1957.

Capacity: 15,500.
Manager: Brian Flynn.
Secretary: D. L. Rhodes.
Most League Goals: 106, Division 3 (N), 1932–33.
Highest League Scorer in Season: Tom Bamford, 44, Division 3 (N), 1933–34.
Most League Goals in Total Aggregate: Tom Bamford, 175, 1928–34.
Most Capped Player: Joey Jones, 29 (72), Wales.
Most League Appearances: Arfon Griffiths, 592, 1959–61, 1962–79.
Honours – Football League: Division 3 Champions – 1977–78. **Welsh Cup:** Winners 22 times.
Colours: Red shirts, white shorts, red stockings.

WYCOMBE WANDERERS DIV. 2

Baird Andy (F)	5 10	11 13	East Kilbride	18 1 79	Trainee
Bates Jamie (D)	6 2	14 06	Croydon	24 2 68	Brentford
Beeton Alan (D)	5 11	11 13	Watford	4 10 78	Trainee
Brady Matt (M)	5 10	10 04	Barnet	27 10 77	Barnet
Brown Steve (M)	5 10	11 12	Northampton	6 7 66	Northampton T
Bulman Dannie (M)	5 9	11 12	Ashford	24 1 79	Ashford T
Carroll Dave (M)	5 10	11 12	Paisley	20 9 66	Ruislip Manor
Cousins Jason (D)	5 10	12 07	Hayes	4 10 70	Brentford
Devine Sean (F)	5 11	13 00	Lewisham	6 9 72	Barnet
Emblen Paul (M)	5 9	12 12	Bromley	3 4 76	Charlton Ath
Harkin Maurice (M)	5 8	11 05	Derry	16 8 79	Trainee
Holsgrove Peter (M)			Wendover	16 4 82	Scholar
Lee Martyn (M)	5 6	9 00	Guilford	10 8 80	Trainee
McCarthy Paul (D)	5 10	13 10	Cork	4 8 71	Brighton & HA
McSporran Jermaine (F)	5 10	10 12	Manchester	1 1 77	Oxford C
Osborn Mark (G)	6 0	14 01	Bletchley	19 6 81	Trainee
Robson Mark (M)	5 10	10 00	Newham	22 5 69	Charlton Ath
Rogers Mark (D)	5 11	12 12	Geulph	3 11 75	
Ryan Keith (M)	5 10	12 06	Northampton	25 6 70	Berkhamsted T
Senda Danny (F)	5 10	10 02	Harrow	17 4 81	Southampton
Simpson Michael (M)	5 8	11 07	Nottingham	28 2 74	Notts Co
Vinnicombe Chris (D)	5 9	10 12	Exeter	20 10 70	Burnley
Westhead Mark (G)	6 1	14 05	Blackpool	19 7 75	Bolton W

League Appearances: Ablett, G. 4; Baird, A. 20(10); Bates, J. 30(2); Beeton, A. 10(6); Brady, M. 4(3); Brown, S. 34(5); Bulman, D. 10(19); Bywater, S. 2; Carroll, D. 36; Cousins, J. 30(7); Devine, S. 39; Emblen, P. 12(4); Harkin, M. 2(15); Holsgrove, L. 5(4); Johnson, L. (1); Lawrence, M. 29; Lee, M. 3(1); McCarthy, P. 21(1); McSporran, J. 32(6); Osborn, M. 1; Rogers, M. 19(6); Ryan, K. 38; Senda, D. 5(22); Simpson, M. 42(1); Taylor, M. 42; Thompson, R. 1(5); Townsend, B. 1; Vinnicombe, C. 33(2); Westhead, M. 1(1).
Goals – League (56): Devine 23 (4 pens), McSporran 9, Ryan 6, Baird 4, Brown 3 (1 pen), Brady 2, Carroll 2, Lawrence 2, Bates 1, Bulman 1, Cousins 1, McCarthy 1, Senda 1.
Worthington Cup (8): McSporran 2, Brown 1 (pen), Carroll 1, Devine 1, McCarthy 1, Ryan 1, own goal 1.
FA Cup (5): Baird 1, Brown 1, Devine 1, Ryan 1, Simpson 1.
Ground: Adams Park, Hillbottom Road, Sands, High Wycombe HP12 4HJ. Telephone (01494) 472100.
Record attendance: 9002 v West Ham U, FA Cup 3rd rd, 7 January 1995. **Capacity:** 10,000.
Manager: Lawrie Sanchez.

Secretary: Keith J. Allen.
Most League Goals: 67, Division 3, 1993–94.
Highest League Goalscorer in Season: Sean Devine, 23, 1999–2000.
Most League Goals in Total Aggregate: Dave Carroll, 38, 1993–2000.
Most Capped Player: None.
Most League Appearances: Dave Carroll, 278, 1993–2000.
Honours – GM Vauxhall Conference winners: 1993. **FA Trophy winners:** 1991, 1993.
Colours: Light & dark blue quartered shirts, light blue shorts, light blue stockings.

YORK CITY — DIV. 3

Agnew Steve (M)	5 10	10 06	Shipley	9 11 65	Sunderland
Alcide Colin (F)	6 2	13 11	Huddersfield	14 4 72	Hull C
Bullock Lee (M)	6 1	12 07	Stockton	22 5 81	Trainee
Conlon Barry (F)	6 2	13 07	Drogheda	1 10 78	Southend U
Dawson Andrew (D)	6 0	12 00	York	8 12 79	Trainee
Fairclough Chris (D)	5 11	11 07	Nottingham	12 4 64	Notts Co
Fox Christian (M)	5 11	11 00	Auchenbrae	11 4 81	Trainee
Hall Wayne (D)	5 9	10 06	Rotherham	25 10 68	Darlington
Hocking Matt (D)	5 11	12 00	Boston	30 1 78	Hull C
Howarth Russell (G)	6 1	12 00	York	27 3 82	Scholar
Hulme Kevin (M)	5 10	13 07	Farnworth	7 12 67	Halifax T
Jordan Scott (M)	5 9	11 02	Newcastle	19 7 75	Trainee
Reed Martin (D)	5 11	11 07	Scarborough	10 1 78	Trainee
Sertori Mark (D)	6 2	14 02	Manchester	1 9 67	Halifax T
Skinner Craig (M)	5 8	11 00	Bury	21 10 70	Wrexham
Swan Peter (D)	6 2	14 02	Leeds	28 9 66	Burnley
Turley James (F)	5 8	10 07	Manchester	24 6 81	Trainee
Williams John (F)	6 2	13 08	Birmingham	11 5 68	Cardiff C
Williams Marc (F)	5 9	11 07	Bangor	8 2 73	Halifax T

League Appearances: Agnew, S. 20(2); Alcide, C. 9(6); Atkins, M. 10; Bower, M. 15; Bullock, L. 16(8); Conlon, B. 31(9); Darlow, K. (2); Dawson, A. 11(6); Dixon, K. 3; Edmondson, D. 7; Fairclough, C. 25(1); Fettis, A. 13; Fox, C. 28(6); Garratt, M. 2(5); Hall, W. 23; Hawkins, P. 14; Hocking, M. 26(6); Howarth, R. 5(1); Hulme, K. 23; Jones, B. 35(2); Jordan, S. 26(2); Keegan, J. 2(1); Mimms, B. 28; Ormerod, A. 9(3); Reed, M. 7(1); Rowe, R. 3(4); Sertori, M. 37(3); Skinner, C. 1(4); Swan, P. 9; Talbot, P. 5(1); Thompson, M. 9(1); Thompson, N. 6; Turley, J. 9(2); Williams, J. 28(8); Williams, M. 11(11).
Goals – League (39): Conlon 11, Williams M 5 (1 pen), Hulme 4, Williams J 3, Alcide 2, Atkins 2, Hocking 2, Jordan 2, Turley 2, Bower 1, Fox 1, Jones 1, Sertori 1, own goals 2.
Worthington Cup (1): Rowe 1.
FA Cup (0).
Ground: Bootham Crescent, York YO3 7AQ. Telephone (01904) 624447.
Record attendance: 28,123 v Huddersfield T, FA Cup 6th rd, 5 March 1938.
Capacity: 9534.
Manager: Terry Dolan.
Secretary: Keith Usher.
Most League Goals: 96, Division 4, 1983–84.
Highest League Scorer in Season: Bill Fenton, 31, Division 3 (N), 1951–52; Arthur Bottom, 31, Division 3 (N), 1954–55 and 1955–56.
Most League Goals in Total Aggregate: Norman Wilkinson, 125, 1954–66.
Most Capped Player: Peter Scott, 7 (10), Northern Ireland.
Most League Appearances: Barry Jackson, 481, 1958–70.
Honours – Football League: Division 4 Champions – 1983–84.
Colours: Red shirts, navy shorts, red stockings.

LEAGUE POSITIONS: FA PREMIER from 1992–93 and DIVISION 1 1974–75 to 1991–92

	1998–99	1997–98	1996–97	1995–96	1994–95	1993–94	1992–93	1991–92	1990–91	1989–90	1988–89	1987–88	1986–87
Arsenal	2	1	3	5	12	4	10	4	1	4	1	6	4
Aston Villa	6	7	5	4	18	10	2	7	17	2	17	–	22
Barnsley	–	19	–	–	–	–	–	–	–	–	–	–	–
Birmingham C	–	–	–	–	–	–	–	–	–	–	–	–	–
Blackburn R	19	6	13	7	1	2	4	–	–	–	–	–	–
Bolton W	–	18	–	20	–	–	–	–	–	–	–	–	–
Brighton & HA	–	–	–	–	–	–	–	–	–	–	–	–	–
Bristol C	–	–	–	–	–	–	–	–	–	–	–	–	–
Burnley	–	–	–	–	–	–	–	–	–	–	–	–	–
Carlisle U	–	–	–	–	–	–	–	–	–	–	–	–	–
Charlton Ath	18	–	–	–	–	–	–	–	–	19	14	17	19
Chelsea	3	4	6	11	11	14	11	14	11	5	–	18	14
Coventry C	15	11	17	16	16	11	15	19	16	12	7	10	10
Crystal Palace	–	20	–	–	19	–	20	10	3	15	–	–	–
Derby Co	8	9	12	–	–	–	–	–	20	16	5	15	–
Everton	14	17	15	6	15	17	13	12	9	6	8	4	1
Ipswich T	–	–	–	–	22	19	16	–	–	–	–	–	–
Leeds U	4	5	11	13	5	5	17	1	4	–	–	–	–
Leicester C	10	10	9	–	21	–	–	–	–	–	–	–	20
Liverpool	7	3	4	3	4	8	6	6	2	1	2	1	2
Luton T	–	–	–	–	–	–	–	20	18	17	16	9	7
Manchester C	–	–	–	18	17	16	9	5	5	14	–	–	21
Manchester U	1	2	1	1	2	1	1	2	6	13	11	2	11
Middlesbrough	9	–	19	12	–	–	21	–	–	–	18	–	–
Millwall	–	–	–	–	–	–	–	–	–	20	10	–	–
Newcastle U	13	13	2	2	6	3	–	–	–	–	20	8	17
Norwich C	–	–	–	–	20	12	3	18	15	10	4	14	5
Nottingham F	20	–	20	9	3	–	22	8	8	9	3	3	8
Notts Co	–	–	–	–	–	–	–	21	–	–	–	–	–
Oldham Ath	–	–	–	–	–	21	19	17	–	–	–	–	–
Oxford U	–	–	–	–	–	–	–	–	–	–	–	21	18
Portsmouth	–	–	–	–	–	–	–	–	–	–	–	19	–
QPR	–	–	–	19	8	9	5	11	12	11	9	5	16
Sheffield U	–	–	–	–	–	20	14	9	13	–	–	–	–
Sheffield W	12	16	7	15	13	7	7	3	–	18	15	11	13
Southampton	17	12	16	17	10	18	18	16	14	7	13	12	12
Stoke C	–	–	–	–	–	–	–	–	–	–	–	–	–
Sunderland	–	–	18	–	–	–	–	–	19	–	–	–	–
Swansea C	–	–	–	–	–	–	–	–	–	–	–	–	–
Swindon T	–	–	–	–	–	22	–	–	–	–	–	–	–
Tottenham H	11	14	10	8	7	15	8	15	10	3	6	13	3
Watford	–	–	–	–	–	–	–	–	–	–	–	20	9
WBA	–	–	–	–	–	–	–	–	–	–	–	–	–
West Ham U	5	8	14	10	14	13	–	22	–	–	19	16	15
Wimbledon	16	15	8	14	9	6	12	13	7	8	12	7	6
Wolv'hampton W	–	–	–	–	–	–	–	–	–	–	–	–	–

1985–86	1984–85	1983–84	1982–83	1981–82	1980–81	1979–80	1978–79	1977–78	1976–77	1975–76	1974–75	
7	7	6	10	5	3	4	7	5	8	17	16	Arsenal
16	10	10	6	11	1	7	8	8	4	16	–	Aston Villa
–	–	–	–	–	–	–	–	–	–	–	–	Barnsley
21	–	20	17	16	13	–	21	11	13	19	17	Birmingham C
–	–	–	–	–	–	–	–	–	–	–	–	Blackburn R
–	–	–	–	–	22	17	–	–	–	–	–	Bolton W
–	–	–	22	13	19	16	–	–	–	–	–	Brighton & HA
–	–	–	–	–	–	20	13	17	18	–	–	Bristol C
–	–	–	–	–	–	–	–	–	–	21	10	Burnley
–	–	–	–	–	–	–	–	–	–	–	22	Carlisle U
–	–	–	–	–	–	–	–	–	–	–	–	Charlton Ath
6	6	–	–	–	–	–	22	16	–	–	21	Chelsea
17	18	19	19	14	16	15	10	7	19	14	14	Coventry C
–	–	–	–	–	22	13	–	–	–	–	–	Crystal Palace
–	–	–	–	–	–	21	19	12	15	4	1	Derby Co
2	1	7	7	8	15	19	4	3	9	11	4	Everton
20	17	12	9	2	2	3	6	18	3	6	3	Ipswich T
–	–	–	–	20	9	11	5	9	10	5	9	Leeds U
19	15	15	–	–	21	–	–	22	11	7	18	Leicester C
1	2	1	1	1	5	1	1	2	1	1	2	Liverpool
9	13	16	18	–	–	–	–	–	–	–	20	Luton T
15	–	–	20	10	12	17	15	4	2	8	8	Manchester C
4	4	4	3	3	8	2	9	10	6	3	–	Manchester U
–	–	–	–	22	14	9	12	14	12	13	7	Middlesbrough
–	–	–	–	–	–	–	–	–	–	–	–	Millwall
11	14	–	–	–	–	–	–	21	5	15	15	Newcastle U
–	20	14	14	–	20	12	16	13	16	10	–	Norwich C
8	9	3	5	12	7	5	2	1	–	–	–	Nottingham F
–	–	21	15	15	–	–	–	–	–	–	–	Notts Co
–	–	–	–	–	–	–	–	–	–	–	–	Oldham Ath
18	–	–	–	–	–	–	–	–	–	–	–	Oxford U
–	–	–	–	–	–	–	–	–	–	–	–	Portsmouth
13	19	5	–	–	–	–	20	19	14	2	11	QPR
–	–	–	–	–	–	–	–	–	–	22	6	Sheffield U
5	8	–	–	–	–	–	–	–	–	–	–	Sheffield W
14	5	2	12	7	6	8	14	–	–	–	–	Southampton
–	22	18	13	18	11	18	–	–	21	12	5	Stoke C
–	21	13	16	19	17	–	–	–	20	–	–	Sunderland
–	–	–	21	6	–	–	–	–	–	–	–	Swansea C
–	–	–	–	–	–	–	–	–	–	–	–	Swindon T
10	3	8	4	4	10	14	11	–	22	9	19	Tottenham H
12	11	11	2	–	–	–	–	–	–	–	–	Watford
22	12	17	11	17	4	10	3	6	7	–	–	WBA
3	16	9	8	9	–	–	–	20	17	18	13	West Ham U
–	–	–	–	–	–	–	–	–	–	–	–	Wimbledon
–	–	22	–	21	18	6	18	15	–	20	12	Wolv'hampton W

LEAGUE POSITIONS: DIVISION 1 from 1992–93 and DIVISION 2 1974–75 to 1991–92

	1998–99	1997–98	1996–97	1995–96	1994–95	1993–94	1992–93	1991–92	1990–91	1989–90	1988–89	1987–88	1986–87
Aston Villa	–	–	–	–	–	–	–	–	–	–	–	2	–
Barnsley	13	–	2	10	6	18	13	16	8	19	7	14	11
Birmingham C	4	7	10	15	–	22	19	–	–	–	23	19	19
Blackburn R	–	–	–	–	–	–	–	6	19	5	5	5	12
Blackpool	–	–	–	–	–	–	–	–	–	–	–	–	–
Bolton W	6	–	1	–	3	14	–	–	–	–	–	–	–
Bournemouth	–	–	–	–	–	–	–	–	–	22	12	17	–
Bradford C	2	13	21	–	–	–	–	–	–	23	14	4	10
Brentford	–	–	–	–	–	–	22	–	–	–	–	–	–
Brighton & HA	–	–	–	–	–	–	–	23	6	18	19	–	22
Bristol C	24	–	–	–	23	13	15	17	9	–	–	–	–
Bristol R	–	–	–	–	–	–	24	13	13	–	–	–	–
Burnley	–	–	–	–	22	–	–	–	–	–	–	–	–
Bury	22	17	–	–	–	–	–	–	–	–	–	–	–
Cambridge U	–	–	–	–	–	–	23	5	–	–	–	–	–
Cardiff C	–	–	–	–	–	–	–	–	–	–	–	–	–
Carlisle U	–	–	–	–	–	–	–	–	–	–	–	–	–
Charlton Ath	–	4	15	6	15	11	12	7	16	–	–	–	–
Chelsea	–	–	–	–	–	–	–	–	–	–	1	–	–
Crewe Alex	18	11	–	–	–	–	–	–	–	–	–	–	–
Crystal Palace	14	–	6	3	–	1	–	–	–	–	3	6	6
Derby Co	–	–	–	2	9	6	8	3	–	–	–	–	1
Fulham	–	–	–	–	–	–	–	–	–	–	–	–	–
Grimsby T	11	–	22	17	10	16	9	19	–	–	–	–	21
Hereford U	–	–	–	–	–	–	–	–	–	–	–	–	–
Huddersfield T	10	16	20	8	–	–	–	–	–	–	–	23	17
Hull C	–	–	–	–	–	–	–	–	24	14	21	15	14
Ipswich T	3	5	4	7	–	–	–	1	14	9	8	8	5
Leeds U	–	–	–	–	–	–	–	–	–	1	10	7	4
Leicester C	–	–	–	5	–	4	6	4	22	13	15	13	–
Leyton Orient	–	–	–	–	–	–	–	–	–	–	–	–	–
Luton T	–	–	–	24	16	20	20	–	–	–	–	–	–
Manchester C	–	22	14	–	–	–	–	–	–	–	2	9	–
Manchester U	–	–	–	–	–	–	–	–	–	–	–	–	–
Mansfield T	–	–	–	–	–	–	–	–	–	–	–	–	–
Middlesbrough	–	2	–	–	1	9	–	2	7	21	–	3	–
Millwall	–	–	–	22	12	3	7	15	5	–	–	1	16
Newcastle U	–	–	–	–	–	–	1	20	11	3	–	–	–
Norwich C	9	15	13	16	–	–	–	–	–	–	–	–	–
Nottingham F	–	1	–	–	–	2	–	–	–	–	–	–	–
Notts Co	–	–	–	–	24	7	17	–	4	–	–	–	–
Oldham Ath	–	–	23	18	14	–	–	–	1	8	16	10	3
Oxford U	23	12	17	–	–	23	14	21	10	17	17	–	–
Peterborough U	–	–	–	–	–	24	10	–	–	–	–	–	–
Plymouth Arg	–	–	–	–	–	–	–	22	18	16	18	16	7
Port Vale	21	19	8	12	17	–	–	24	15	11	–	–	–
Portsmouth	19	20	7	21	18	17	3	9	17	12	20	–	2
Preston NE	–	–	–	–	–	–	–	–	–	–	–	–	–
QPR	20	21	9	–	–	–	–	–	–	–	–	–	–

1985–86	1984–85	1983–84	1982–83	1981–82	1980–81	1979–80	1978–79	1977–78	1976–77	1975–76	1974–75	
–	–	–	–	–	–	–	–	–	–	–	2	Aston Villa
12	11	14	10	6	–	–	–	–	–	–	–	Barnsley
–	2	–	–	–	–	3	–	–	–	–	–	Birmingham C
19	5	6	11	10	4	–	22	5	12	15	–	Blackburn R
–	–	–	–	–	–	–	–	20	5	10	7	Blackpool
–	–	–	22	19	18	–	–	1	4	4	10	Bolton W
–	–	–	–	–	–	–	–	–	–	–	–	Bournemouth
13	–	–	–	–	–	–	–	–	–	–	–	Bradford C
–	–	–	–	–	–	–	–	–	–	–	–	Brentford
11	6	9	–	–	–	–	2	4	–	–	–	Brighton & HA
–	–	–	–	–	21	–	–	–	–	2	5	Bristol C
–	–	–	–	–	22	19	16	18	15	18	19	Bristol R
–	–	–	21	–	–	21	13	11	16	–	–	Burnley
–	–	–	–	–	–	–	–	–	–	–	–	Bury
–	–	22	12	14	13	8	12	–	–	–	–	Cambridge U
–	21	15	–	20	19	15	9	19	18	–	21	Cardiff C
20	16	7	14	–	–	–	–	–	20	19	–	Carlisle U
2	17	13	17	13	–	22	19	17	7	9	–	Charlton Ath
–	–	1	18	12	12	4	–	–	2	11	–	Chelsea
–	–	–	–	–	–	–	–	–	–	–	–	Crewe Alex
5	15	18	15	15	–	–	1	9	–	–	–	Crystal Palace
–	–	20	13	16	6	–	–	–	–	–	–	Derby Co
22	9	11	4	–	–	20	10	10	17	12	9	Fulham
15	10	5	19	17	7	–	–	–	–	–	–	Grimsby T
–	–	–	–	–	–	–	–	–	22	–	–	Hereford U
16	13	12	–	–	–	–	–	–	–	–	–	Huddersfield T
6	–	–	–	–	–	–	–	22	14	14	8	Hull C
–	–	–	–	–	–	–	–	–	–	–	–	Ipswich T
14	7	10	8	–	–	–	–	–	–	–	–	Leeds U
–	–	–	3	8	–	1	17	–	–	–	–	Leicester C
–	–	–	–	22	17	14	11	14	19	13	12	Leyton Orient
–	–	–	–	1	5	6	18	13	6	7	–	Luton T
–	3	4	–	–	–	–	–	–	–	–	–	Manchester C
–	–	–	–	–	–	–	–	–	–	–	1	Manchester U
–	–	–	–	–	–	–	–	21	–	–	–	Mansfield T
21	19	17	16	–	–	–	–	–	–	–	–	Middlesbrough
9	–	–	–	–	–	–	21	16	10	–	20	Millwall
–	–	3	5	9	11	9	8	–	–	–	–	Newcastle U
1	–	–	–	3	–	–	–	–	–	–	3	Norwich C
–	–	–	–	–	–	–	–	–	3	8	16	Nottingham F
–	20	–	–	–	2	17	6	15	8	5	14	Notts Co
8	14	19	7	11	15	11	14	8	13	17	18	Oldham Ath
–	1	–	–	–	–	–	–	–	–	20	11	Oxford U
–	–	–	–	–	–	–	–	–	–	–	–	Peterborough U
–	–	–	–	–	–	–	–	–	21	16	–	Plymouth Arg
–	–	–	–	–	–	–	–	–	–	–	–	Port Vale
4	4	16	–	–	–	–	–	–	–	22	17	Portsmouth
–	–	–	–	–	20	10	7	–	–	–	–	Preston NE
–	–	–	1	5	8	5	–	–	–	–	–	QPR

LEAGUE POSITIONS: DIVISION 1 from 1992–93 and DIVISION 2 1974–75 to 1991–92 (cont.)

	1998–99	1997–98	1996–97	1995–96	1994–95	1993–94	1992–93	1991–92	1990–91	1989–90	1988–89	1987–88	1986–87
Reading	–	24	18	19	2	–	–	–	–	–	–	22	13
Rotherham U	–	–	–	–	–	–	–	–	–	–	–	–	–
Sheffield U	8	6	5	9	8	–	–	–	–	2	–	21	9
Sheffield W	–	–	–	–	–	–	–	–	3	–	–	–	–
Shrewsbury T	–	–	–	–	–	–	–	–	–	–	22	18	18
Southampton	–	–	–	–	–	–	–	–	–	–	–	–	–
Southend U	–	–	24	14	13	15	18	12	–	–	–	–	–
Stockport Co	16	8	–	–	–	–	–	–	–	–	–	–	–
Stoke C	–	23	12	4	11	10	–	–	–	24	13	11	8
Sunderland	1	3	–	1	20	12	21	18	–	6	11	–	20
Swansea C	–	–	–	–	–	–	–	–	–	–	–	–	–
Swindon T	17	18	19	–	21	–	5	8	21	4	6	12	–
Tottenham H	–	–	–	–	–	–	–	–	–	–	–	–	–
Tranmere R	15	14	11	13	5	5	4	14	–	–	–	–	–
Walsall	–	–	–	–	–	–	–	–	–	–	24	–	–
Watford	5	–	–	23	7	19	16	10	20	15	4	–	–
WBA	12	10	16	11	19	21	–	–	23	20	9	20	15
West Ham U	–	–	–	–	–	–	2	–	2	7	–	–	–
Wimbledon	–	–	–	–	–	–	–	–	–	–	–	–	–
Wolv'hampton W	7	9	3	20	4	8	11	11	12	10	–	–	–
Wrexham	–	–	–	–	–	–	–	–	–	–	–	–	–
York C	–	–	–	–	–	–	–	–	–	–	–	–	–

LEAGUE POSITIONS: DIVISION 2 from 1992–93 and DIVISION 3 1974–75 to 1991–92

	1998–99	1997–98	1996–97	1995–96	1994–95	1993–94	1992–93	1991–92	1990–91	1989–90	1988–89	1987–88	1986–87
Aldershot	–	–	–	–	–	–	–	–	–	–	24	20	–
Barnet	–	–	–	–	–	24	–	–	–	–	–	–	–
Barnsley	–	–	–	–	–	–	–	–	–	–	–	–	–
Birmingham C	–	–	–	–	1	–	–	2	12	7	–	–	–
Blackburn R	–	–	–	–	–	–	–	–	–	–	–	–	–
Blackpool	14	12	7	3	12	20	18	–	–	23	19	10	9
Bolton W	–	–	–	–	–	–	2	13	4	6	10	–	21
Bournemouth	7	9	16	14	19	17	17	8	9	–	–	–	1
Bradford C	–	–	–	6	14	7	10	16	8	–	–	–	–
Brentford	–	21	4	15	2	16	–	1	6	13	7	12	11
Brighton & HA	–	–	–	23	16	14	9	–	–	–	–	2	–
Bristol C	–	2	5	13	–	–	–	–	–	2	11	5	6
Bristol R	13	5	17	10	4	8	–	–	–	1	5	8	19

1985–86	1984–85	1983–84	1982–83	1981–82	1980–81	1979–80	1978–79	1977–78	1976–77	1975–76	1974–75	
–	–	–	20	7	–	–	–	–	–	–	–	Reading
–	–	–	20	7	–	–	–	–	–	–	–	Rotherham U
7	18	–	–	–	–	–	20	12	11	–	–	Sheffield U
–	–	2	6	4	10	–	–	–	–	–	22	Sheffield W
17	8	8	9	18	14	13	–	–	–	–	–	Shrewsbury T
–	–	–	–	–	–	–	–	2	9	6	13	Southampton
–	–	–	–	–	–	–	–	–	–	–	–	Southend U
–	–	–	–	–	–	–	–	–	–	–	–	Stockport Co
10	–	–	–	–	–	–	3	7	–	–	–	Stoke C
18	–	–	–	–	–	2	4	6	–	1	4	Sunderland
–	–	21	–	–	3	12	–	–	–	–	–	Swansea C
–	–	–	–	–	–	–	–	–	–	–	–	Swindon T
–	–	–	–	–	–	–	–	3	–	–	–	Tottenham H
–	–	–	–	–	–	–	–	–	–	–	–	Tranmere R
–	–	–	–	–	–	–	–	–	–	–	–	Walsall
–	–	–	–	2	9	18	–	–	–	–	–	Watford
–	–	–	–	–	–	–	–	–	–	3	6	WBA
–	–	–	–	–	1	7	5	–	–	–	–	West Ham U
3	12	–	–	–	–	–	–	–	–	–	–	Wimbledon
–	22	–	2	–	–	–	–	–	1	–	–	Wolv'hampton W
–	–	–	–	21	16	16	15	–	–	–	–	Wrexham
–	–	–	–	–	–	–	–	–	–	21	15	York C

1985–86	1984–85	1983–84	1982–83	1981–82	1980–81	1979–80	1978–79	1977–78	1976–77	1975–76	1974–75	
–	–	–	–	–	–	–	–	–	–	21	20	Aldershot
–	–	–	–	–	–	–	–	–	–	–	–	Barnet
–	–	–	–	–	2	11	–	–	–	–	–	Barnsley
–	–	–	–	–	–	–	–	–	–	–	–	Birmingham C
–	–	–	–	–	–	2	–	–	–	–	1	Blackburn R
12	–	–	–	–	23	18	12	–	–	–	–	Blackpool
18	17	10	–	–	–	–	–	–	–	–	–	Bolton W
15	10	17	14	–	–	–	–	–	–	–	21	Bournemouth
–	1	7	12	–	–	–	–	22	–	–	–	Bradford C
10	13	20	9	8	9	19	10	–	–	–	–	Brentford
–	–	–	–	–	–	–	–	–	2	4	19	Brighton & HA
9	5	–	–	23	–	–	–	–	–	–	–	Bristol C
16	6	5	7	15	–	–	–	–	–	–	–	Bristol R

LEAGUE POSITIONS: DIVISION 2 from 1992–93 and DIVISION 3 1974–75 to 1991–92 (cont.)

	1998–99	1997–98	1996–97	1995–96	1994–95	1993–94	1992–93	1991–92	1990–91	1989–90	1988–89	1987–88	1986–87
Burnley	15	20	9	17	–	6	13	–	–	–	–	–	–
Bury	–	–	1	–	–	–	–	21	7	5	13	14	16
Cambridge U	–	–	–	–	20	10	–	–	1	–	–	–	–
Cardiff C	–	–	–	–	22	19	–	–	–	21	16	–	–
Carlisle U	–	23	–	21	–	–	–	–	–	–	–	–	22
Charlton Ath	–	–	–	–	–	–	–	–	–	–	–	–	–
Chester C	–	–	–	–	23	–	24	18	19	16	8	15	15
Chesterfield	9	10	10	7	–	–	–	–	–	–	22	18	17
Colchester U	18	–	–	–	–	–	–	–	–	–	–	–	–
Crewe Alex	–	–	6	5	3	–	–	–	22	12	–	–	–
Crystal Palace	–	–	–	–	–	–	–	–	–	–	–	–	–
Darlington	–	–	–	–	–	–	–	24	–	–	–	–	22
Derby Co	–	–	–	–	–	–	–	–	–	–	–	–	–
Doncaster R	–	–	–	–	–	–	–	–	–	–	–	24	13
Exeter C	–	–	–	–	–	22	19	20	16	–	–	–	–
Fulham	1	6	–	–	–	21	12	9	21	20	4	9	18
Gillingham	4	8	11	–	–	–	–	–	–	–	23	13	5
Grimsby T	–	3	–	–	–	–	–	3	–	–	22	–	–
Halifax T	–	–	–	–	–	–	–	–	–	–	–	–	–
Hartlepool U	–	–	–	–	–	23	16	11	–	–	–	–	–
Hereford U	–	–	–	–	–	–	–	–	–	–	–	–	–
Huddersfield T	–	–	–	–	5	11	15	3	11	8	14	–	–
Hull C	–	–	–	24	8	9	20	14	–	–	–	–	–
Leyton Orient	–	–	–	–	24	18	7	10	13	14	–	–	–
Lincoln C	23	–	–	–	–	–	–	–	–	–	–	–	21
Luton T	12	17	3	–	–	–	–	–	–	–	–	–	–
Macclesfield T	24	–	–	–	–	–	–	–	–	–	–	–	–
Manchester C	3	–	–	–	–	–	–	–	–	–	–	–	–
Mansfield T	–	–	–	–	–	–	22	–	24	15	15	19	10
Middlesbrough	–	–	–	–	–	–	–	–	–	–	–	–	2
Millwall	10	18	14	–	–	–	–	–	–	–	–	–	–
Newport Co	–	–	–	–	–	–	–	–	–	–	–	–	23
Northampton T	22	4	–	–	–	–	–	–	–	22	20	6	–
Notts Co	16	–	24	4	–	–	–	–	–	3	9	4	7
Oldham Ath	20	13	–	–	–	–	–	–	–	–	–	–	–
Oxford U	–	–	–	2	7	–	–	–	–	–	–	–	–
Peterborough U	–	–	21	19	15	–	–	6	–	–	–	–	–
Plymouth Arg	–	22	19	–	21	3	14	–	–	–	–	–	–
Portsmouth	–	–	–	–	–	–	–	–	–	–	–	–	–
Port Vale	–	–	–	–	–	2	3	–	–	–	3	11	12
Preston NE	5	15	15	–	–	–	21	17	17	19	6	16	–
Reading	11	–	–	–	–	1	8	12	15	10	18	–	–
Rochdale	–	–	–	–	–	–	–	–	–	–	–	–	–
Rotherham U	–	–	23	16	17	15	11	–	23	9	–	21	14
Scunthorpe U	–	–	–	–	–	–	–	–	–	–	–	–	–
Sheffield U	–	–	–	–	–	–	–	–	–	–	2	–	–
Sheffield W	–	–	–	–	–	–	–	–	–	–	–	–	–
Shrewsbury T	–	–	22	18	18	–	–	22	18	11	–	–	–
Southend U	–	24	–	–	–	–	–	–	2	–	21	17	–

1985–86	1984–85	1983–84	1982–83	1981–82	1980–81	1979–80	1978–79	1977–78	1976–77	1975–76	1974–75	
–	21	12	–	1	8	–	–	–	–	–	–	Burnley
20	–	–	–	–	–	21	19	15	7	13	14	Bury
–	24	–	–	–	–	–	–	2	–	–	–	Cambridge U
22	–	–	2	–	–	–	–	–	–	2	–	Cardiff C
–	–	–	–	2	19	6	6	13	–	–	–	Carlisle U
–	–	–	–	–	3	–	–	–	–	–	3	Charlton Ath
–	–	–	–	24	18	9	16	5	13	17	–	Chester C
17	–	–	24	11	5	4	20	9	18	15	15	Chesterfield
–	–	–	–	–	22	5	7	8	–	22	11	Colchester U
–	–	–	–	–	–	–	–	–	–	–	–	Crewe Alex
–	–	–	–	–	–	–	–	–	3	5	5	Crystal Palace
13	–	–	–	–	–	–	–	–	–	–	–	Darlington
3	7	–	–	–	–	–	–	–	–	–	–	Derby C
11	14	–	23	19	–	–	–	–	–	–	–	Doncaster R
–	–	24	19	18	11	8	9	17	–	–	–	Exeter C
–	–	–	–	3	13	–	–	–	–	–	–	Fulham
5	4	8	13	6	15	16	4	7	12	14	10	Gillingham
–	–	–	–	–	–	1	–	–	23	18	16	Grimsby T
–	–	–	–	–	–	–	–	–	–	24	17	Halifax T
–	–	–	–	–	–	–	–	–	–	–	–	Hartlepool U
–	–	–	–	–	–	–	–	23	–	1	12	Hereford U
–	–	–	3	17	4	–	–	–	–	–	24	Huddersfield T
–	3	4	–	–	24	20	8	–	–	–	–	Hull C
–	22	11	20	–	–	–	–	–	–	–	–	Leyton Orient
19	14	6	4	–	–	–	24	16	9	–	–	Lincoln C
–	–	–	–	–	–	–	–	–	–	–	–	Luton T
–	–	–	–	–	–	–	–	–	–	–	–	Macclesfield T
–	–	–	–	–	–	–	–	–	–	–	–	Manchester C
–	–	–	–	–	–	23	18	–	1	11	–	Mansfield T
–	–	–	–	–	–	–	–	–	–	–	–	Middlesbrough
–	2	9	17	9	16	14	–	–	–	3	–	Millwall
19	18	13	4	16	12	–	–	–	–	–	–	Newport Co
–	–	–	–	–	–	–	–	–	22	–	–	Northampton T
8	–	–	–	–	–	–	–	–	–	–	–	Notts Co
–	–	–	–	–	–	–	–	–	–	–	–	Oldham Ath
–	–	1	5	5	14	17	11	18	17	–	–	Oxford U
–	–	–	–	–	–	–	21	4	16	10	7	Peterborough U
2	15	19	8	10	7	15	15	19	–	–	2	Plymouth Arg
–	–	–	1	13	6	–	–	24	20	–	–	Portsmouth
–	–	23	–	–	–	–	–	21	19	12	6	Port Vale
–	23	16	16	14	–	–	–	3	6	8	9	Preston NE
1	9	–	21	12	10	7	–	–	21	–	–	Reading
–	–	–	–	–	–	–	–	–	–	–	–	Rochdale
14	12	18	–	–	1	13	17	20	4	16	–	Rotherham U
–	–	21	–	–	–	–	–	–	–	–	–	Scunthorpe U
–	–	3	11	–	21	12	–	–	–	–	–	Sheffield U
–	–	–	–	–	–	3	14	14	8	20	–	Sheffield W
–	–	–	–	–	–	–	1	11	10	9	–	Shrewsbury T
–	–	22	15	7	–	22	13	–	–	23	18	Southend U

LEAGUE POSITIONS: DIVISION 2 from 1992–93 and DIVISION 3 1974–75 to 1991–92 (cont.)

	1998–99	1997–98	1996–97	1995–96	1994–95	1993–94	1992–93	1991–92	1990–91	1989–90	1988–89	1987–88	1986–87
Stockport Co	–	–	2	9	11	4	6	5	–	–	–	–	–
Stoke C	8	–	–	–	–	–	1	4	14	–	–	–	–
Sunderland	–	–	–	–	–	–	–	–	–	–	–	1	–
Swansea C	–	–	–	22	10	13	5	19	20	17	12	–	–
Swindon T	–	–	–	1	–	–	–	–	–	–	–	–	3
Torquay U	–	–	–	–	–	–	–	23	–	–	–	–	–
Tranmere R	–	–	–	–	–	–	–	–	5	4	–	–	–
Walsall	2	19	12	11	–	–	5	–	–	24	–	3	8
Watford	–	1	13	–	–	–	–	–	–	–	–	–	–
WBA	–	–	–	–	–	–	4	7	–	–	–	–	–
Wigan Ath	6	11	–	–	–	–	23	15	10	18	17	7	4
Wimbledon	–	–	–	–	–	–	–	–	–	–	–	–	–
Wolv'hampton W	–	–	–	–	–	–	–	–	–	–	1	–	–
Wrexham	17	7	8	8	13	12	–	–	–	–	–	–	–
Wycombe W	19	14	18	12	6	–	–	–	–	–	–	–	–
York C	21	16	20	20	9	5	–	–	–	–	–	23	20

LEAGUE POSITIONS: DIVISION 3 from 1992–93 and DIVISION 4 1974–75 to 1991–92

	1998–99	1997–98	1996–97	1995–96	1994–95	1993–94	1992–93	1991–92	1990–91	1989–90	1988–89	1987–88	1986–87
Aldershot	–	–	–	–	–	–	–	*	23	22	–	–	6
Barnet	16	7	15	9	11	–	3	7	–	–	–	–	–
Barnsley	–	–	–	–	–	–	–	–	–	–	–	–	–
Blackpool	–	–	–	–	–	–	–	4	5	–	–	–	–
Bolton W	–	–	–	–	–	–	–	–	–	–	–	3	–
Bournemouth	–	–	–	–	–	–	–	–	–	–	–	–	–
Bradford C	–	–	–	–	–	–	–	–	–	–	–	–	–
Brentford	–	–	–	–	–	–	–	–	–	–	–	–	–
Brighton & HA	17	23	23	–	–	–	–	–	–	–	–	–	–
Bristol C	–	–	–	–	–	–	–	–	–	–	–	–	–
Burnley	15	–	–	–	–	–	–	1	6	16	16	10	22
Bury	–	–	–	3	4	13	7	–	–	–	–	–	–
Cambridge U	2	16	10	16	–	–	–	–	–	6	8	15	11
Cardiff C	3	21	7	22	–	–	1	9	13	–	–	2	13
Carlisle U	23	–	3	–	1	7	18	22	20	8	12	23	–
Chester C	14	14	6	8	–	2	–	–	–	–	–	–	–
Chesterfield	–	–	–	–	3	8	12	13	18	7	–	–	–

*Record expunged

1985–86	1984–85	1983–84	1982–83	1981–82	1980–81	1979–80	1978–79	1977–78	1976–77	1975–76	1974–75	
–	–	–	–	–	–	–	–	–	–	–	–	Stockport Co
–	–	–	–	–	–	–	–	–	–	–	–	Stoke C
–	–	–	–	–	–	–	–	–	–	–	–	Sunderland
24	20	–	–	–	–	–	3	–	–	–	–	Swansea C
–	–	–	–	22	17	10	5	10	11	19	4	Swindon T
–	–	–	–	–	–	–	–	–	–	–	–	Torquay U
–	–	–	–	–	–	–	23	12	14	–	22	Tranmere R
6	11	6	10	20	20	–	22	6	15	7	8	Walsall
–	–	–	–	–	–	–	2	–	–	–	23	Watford
–	–	–	–	–	–	–	–	–	–	–	–	WBA
4	16	15	18	–	–	–	–	–	–	–	–	Wigan Ath
–	–	2	–	21	–	24	–	–	–	–	–	Wimbledon
23	–	–	–	–	–	–	–	–	–	–	–	Wolv'hampton W
–	–	–	22	–	–	–	–	1	5	6	13	Wrexham
–	–	–	–	–	–	–	–	–	–	–	–	Wycombe W
7	8	–	–	–	–	–	–	–	24	–	–	York C

1985–86	1984–85	1983–84	1982–83	1981–82	1980–81	1979–80	1978–79	1977–78	1976–77	1975–76	1974–75	
16	13	5	18	16	6	10	5	5	17	–	–	Aldershot
–	–	–	–	–	–	–	–	–	–	–	–	Barnet
–	–	–	–	–	–	–	4	7	6	12	15	Barnsley
–	2	6	21	12	–	–	–	–	–	–	–	Blackpool
–	–	–	–	–	–	–	–	–	–	–	–	Bolton W
–	–	–	–	4	13	11	18	17	13	6	–	Bournemouth
–	–	–	–	2	14	5	15	–	4	17	10	Bradford C
–	–	–	–	–	–	–	–	4	15	18	8	Brentford
–	–	–	–	–	–	–	–	–	–	–	–	Brighton & HA
–	–	4	14	–	–	–	–	–	–	–	–	Bristol C
14	–	–	–	–	–	–	–	–	–	–	–	Burnley
–	4	15	5	9	12	–	–	–	–	–	–	Bury
22	–	–	–	–	–	–	–	–	1	13	6	Cambridge U
–	–	–	–	–	–	–	–	–	–	–	–	Cardiff C
–	–	–	–	–	–	–	–	–	–	–	–	Carlisle U
2	16	24	13	9	–	–	–	–	–	–	4	Chester C
–	1	13	–	–	–	–	–	–	–	–	–	Chesterfield

LEAGUE POSITIONS: DIVISION 3 from 1992–93 and DIVISION 4 1974–75 to 1991–92 (cont.)

	1998–99	1997–98	1996–97	1995–96	1994–95	1993–94	1992–93	1991–92	1990–91	1989–90	1988–89	1987–88	1986–87
Colchester U	–	4	8	7	10	17	10	–	–	24	22	9	5
Crewe Alex	–	–	–	–	–	3	6	6	–	–	3	17	17
Darlington	11	19	18	5	20	21	15	–	1	–	24	13	–
Doncaster R	–	24	19	13	9	15	16	21	11	20	23	–	–
Exeter C	12	15	22	14	22	–	–	–	–	1	13	22	14
Fulham	–	–	2	17	8	–	–	–	–	–	–	–	–
Gillingham	–	–	–	2	19	16	21	11	15	14	–	–	–
Grimsby T	–	–	–	–	–	–	–	–	–	2	9	–	–
Halifax T	10	–	–	–	–	–	22	20	22	23	21	18	15
Hartlepool U	22	17	20	20	18	–	–	–	3	19	19	16	18
Hereford U	–	–	24	6	16	20	17	17	17	17	15	19	16
Huddersfield T	–	–	–	–	–	–	–	–	–	–	–	–	–
Hull C	21	22	17	–	–	–	–	–	–	–	–	–	–
Leyton Orient	6	11	16	21	–	–	–	–	–	–	6	8	7
Lincoln C	–	3	9	18	12	18	8	10	14	10	10	–	24
Macclesfield T	–	2	–	–	–	–	–	–	–	–	–	–	–
Maidstone U	–	–	–	–	–	–	–	18	19	5	–	–	–
Mansfield T	8	12	11	19	6	12	–	3	–	–	–	–	–
Newport Co	–	–	–	–	–	–	–	–	–	–	–	24	–
Northampton T	–	–	4	11	17	22	20	16	10	–	–	–	1
Notts Co	–	1	–	–	–	–	–	–	–	–	–	–	–
Peterborough U	9	10	–	–	–	–	–	–	4	9	17	7	10
Plymouth Arg	13	–	–	4	–	–	–	–	–	–	–	–	–
Portsmouth	–	–	–	–	–	–	–	–	–	–	–	–	–
Port Vale	–	–	–	–	–	–	–	–	–	–	–	–	–
Preston NE	–	–	–	1	5	5	–	–	–	–	–	–	2
Reading	–	–	–	–	–	–	–	–	–	–	–	–	–
Rochdale	19	18	14	15	15	9	11	8	12	12	18	21	21
Rotherham U	5	9	–	–	–	–	–	2	–	–	1	–	–
Scarborough	24	6	12	23	21	14	13	12	9	18	5	12	–
Scunthorpe U	4	8	13	12	7	11	14	5	8	11	4	4	8
Sheffield U	–	–	–	–	–	–	–	–	–	–	–	–	–
Shrewsbury T	15	13	–	–	–	1	9	–	–	–	–	–	–
Southend U	18	–	–	–	–	–	–	–	–	3	–	–	3
Southport	–	–	–	–	–	–	–	–	–	–	–	–	–
Stockport Co	–	–	–	–	–	–	–	–	2	4	20	20	19
Swansea C	7	20	5	–	–	–	–	–	–	–	–	6	12
Swindon T	–	–	–	–	–	–	–	–	–	–	–	–	–
Torquay U	20	5	21	24	13	6	19	–	7	15	14	5	23
Tranmere R	–	–	–	–	–	–	–	–	–	–	2	14	20
Walsall	–	–	–	–	2	10	5	15	16	–	–	–	–
Watford	–	–	–	–	–	–	–	–	–	–	–	–	–
Wigan Ath	–	–	1	10	14	19	–	–	–	–	–	–	–
Wimbledon	–	–	–	–	–	–	–	–	–	–	–	–	–
Wolv'hampton W	–	–	–	–	–	–	–	–	–	–	–	1	4
Workington	–	–	–	–	–	–	–	–	–	–	–	–	–
Wrexham	–	–	–	–	–	–	2	14	24	21	7	11	9
Wycombe W	–	–	–	–	–	4	–	–	–	–	–	–	–
York C	–	–	–	–	–	–	4	19	21	13	11	–	–

1985–86	1984–85	1983–84	1982–83	1981–82	1980–81	1979–80	1978–79	1977–78	1976–77	1975–76	1974–75	
6	7	8	6	6	–	–	–	–	3	–	–	Colchester U
12	10	16	23	24	18	23	24	15	12	16	18	Crewe Alex
–	3	14	17	3	8	22	21	19	11	20	21	Darlington
–	–	2	–	–	3	12	22	12	8	10	17	Doncaster R
21	18	–	–	–				–	2	7	9	Exeter C
–	–	–	–	–	–	–	–	–	–	–	–	Fulham
–	–	–	–	–	–	–	–	–	–	–	–	Gillingham
–	–	–	–	–	–	–	2	6	–	–	–	Grimsby T
20	21	21	11	19	23	18	23	20	21	–	–	Halifax T
7	19	23	22	14	9	19	13	21	22	14	13	Hartlepool U
10	5	11	24	10	22	21	14	–	–	–	–	Hereford U
–	–	–	–	–	–	1	9	11	9	5	–	Huddersfield T
–	–	–	2	8	–	–	–	–	–	–	–	Hull C
5	–	–	–	–	–	–	–	–	–	–	–	Leyton Orient
–	–	–	–	–	2	7	–	–	–	1	5	Lincoln C
–	–	–	–	–	–	–	–	–	–	–	–	Macclesfield T
–	–	–	–	–	–	–	–	–	–	–	–	Maidstone U
3	14	19	10	20	7	–	–	–	–	–	1	Mansfield T
–	–	–	–	–	–	3	8	16	19	22	12	Newport C
8	23	18	15	22	10	13	19	10	–	2	16	Northampton T
–	–	–	–	–	–	–	–	–	–	–	–	Notts Co
17	11	7	9	5	5	8	–	–	–	–	–	Peterborough U
–	–	–	–	–	–	–	–	–	–	–	–	Plymouth Arg
–	–	–	–	–	–	4	7	–	–	–	–	Portsmouth
4	12	–	3	7	19	20	16	–	–	–	–	Port Vale
23	–	–	–	–	–	–	–	–	–	–	–	Preston NE
–	–	3	–	–	–	–	1	8	–	3	7	Reading
18	17	22	20	21	15	24	20	24	18	15	19	Rochdale
–	–	–	–	–	–	–	–	–	–	–	3	Rotherham U
–	–	–	–	–	–	–	–	–	–	–	–	Scarborough
15	9	–	4	23	16	14	12	14	20	19	24	Scunthorpe U
–	–	–	–	1	–	–	–	–	–	–	–	Sheffield U
–	–	–	–	–	–	–	–	–	–	–	2	Shrewsbury T
9	20	–	–	–	1	–	–	2	10	–	–	Southend U
–	–	–	–	–	–	–	–	23	23	23	11	Southport
11	22	12	16	18	20	16	17	18	14	21	20	Stockport Co
–	–	–	–	–	–	–	–	3	5	11	22	Swansea C
1	8	17	8	–	–	–	–	–	–	–	–	Swindon T
24	24	9	12	15	17	9	11	9	16	9	14	Torquay U
19	6	10	19	11	21	15	–	–	–	4	–	Tranmere R
–	–	–	–	–	–	2	–	–	–	–	–	Walsall
–	–	–	–	–	–	–	–	1	7	8	–	Watford
–	–	–	–	3	11	6	6	–	–	–	–	Wigan Ath
–	–	–	1	–	4	–	3	13	–	–	–	Wimbledon
–	–	–	–	–	–	–	–	–	–	–	–	Wolv'hampton W
–	–	–	–	–	–	–	–	–	24	24	23	Workington
13	15	20	–	–	–	–	–	–	–	–	–	Wrexham
–	–	–	–	–	–	–	–	–	–	–	–	Wycombe W
–	–	1	7	17	24	17	10	22	–	–	–	York C

LEAGUE CHAMPIONSHIP HONOURS

FA PREMIER LEAGUE

Maximum points: 126

	First	*Pts*	*Second*	*Pts*	*Third*	*Pts*
1992–93	Manchester U	84	Aston Villa	74	Norwich C	72
1993–94	Manchester U	92	Blackburn R	84	Newcastle U	77
1994–95	Blackburn R	89	Manchester U	88	Nottingham F	77

Maximum points: 114

1995–96	Manchester U	82	Newcastle U	78	Liverpool	71
1996–97	Manchester U	75	Newcastle U*	68	Arsenal*	68
1997–98	Arsenal	78	Manchester U	77	Liverpool	65
1998–99	Manchester U	79	Arsenal	78	Chelsea	75
1999–00	Manchester U	91	Arsenal	73	Leeds U	69

DIVISION 1

Maximum points: 138

1992–93	Newcastle U	96	West Ham U*	88	Portsmouth††	88
1993–94	Crystal Palace	90	Nottingham F	83	Millwall††	74
1994–95	Middlesbrough	82	Reading††	79	Bolton W	77
1995–96	Sunderland	83	Derby Co	79	Crystal Palace††	75
1996–97	Bolton W	98	Barnsley	80	Wolverhampton W††	76
1997–98	Nottingham F	94	Middlesbrough	91	Sunderland††	90
1998–99	Sunderland	105	Bradford C	87	Ipswich T††	86
1999–00	Charlton Ath	91	Manchester C	89	Ipswich T	87

DIVISION 2

Maximum points: 138

1992–93	Stoke C	93	Bolton W	90	Port Vale††	89
1993–94	Reading	89	Port Vale	88	Plymouth Arg††	85
1994–95	Birmingham C	89	Brentford††	85	Crewe Alex††	83
1995–96	Swindon T	92	Oxford U	83	Blackpool††	82
1996–97	Bury	84	Stockport Co	82	Luton T††	78
1997–98	Watford	88	Bristol C	85	Grimsby T	72
1998–99	Fulham	101	Walsall	87	Manchester C	82
1999–00	Preston NE	95	Burnley	88	Gillingham	85

DIVISION 3

Maximum points: 126

1992–93	Cardiff C	83	Wrexham	80	Barnet	79
1993–94	Shrewsbury T	79	Chester C	74	Crewe Alex	73
1994–95	Carlisle U	91	Walsall	83	Chesterfield	81

Maximum points: 138

1995–96	Preston NE	86	Gillingham	83	Bury	79
1996–97	Wigan Ath*	87	Fulham	87	Carlisle U	84
1997–98	Notts Co	99	Macclesfield T	82	Lincoln C	75
1998–99	Brentford	85	Cambridge U	81	Cardiff C	80
1999–00	Swansea C	85	Rotherham U	84	Northampton T	82

†† *Not promoted after play-offs.*

FOOTBALL LEAGUE

Maximum points: a 44; *b* 60

1888–89*a*	Preston NE	40	Aston Villa	29	Wolverhampton W	28
1889–90*a*	Preston NE	33	Everton	31	Blackburn R	27
1890–91*a*	Everton	29	Preston NE	27	Notts Co	26
1891–92*b*	Sunderland	42	Preston NE	37	Bolton W	36

DIVISION 1 to 1991–92

Maximum points: a 44; *b* 52; *c* 60; *d* 68; *e* 76; *f* 84; *g* 126; *h* 120; *k* 114.

1892–93*c*	Sunderland	48	Preston NE	37	Everton	36
1893–94*c*	Aston Villa	44	Sunderland	38	Derby Co	36

	First	Pts	Second	Pts	Third	Pts
1894–95*c*	Sunderland	47	Everton	42	Aston Villa	39
1895–96*c*	Aston Villa	45	Derby Co	41	Everton	39
1896–97*c*	Aston Villa	47	Sheffield U*	36	Derby Co	36
1897–98*c*	Sheffield U	42	Sunderland	37	Wolverhampton W*	35
1898–99*d*	Aston Villa	45	Liverpool	43	Burnley	39
1899–1900*d*	Aston Villa	50	Sheffield U	48	Sunderland	41
1900–01*d*	Liverpool	45	Sunderland	43	Notts Co	40
1901–02*d*	Sunderland	44	Everton	41	Newcastle U	37
1902–03*d*	The Wednesday	42	Aston Villa*	41	Sunderland	41
1903–04*d*	The Wednesday	47	Manchester C	44	Everton	43
1904–05*d*	Newcastle U	48	Everton	47	Manchester C	46
1905–06*e*	Liverpool	51	Preston NE	47	The Wednesday	44
1906–07*e*	Newcastle U	51	Bristol C	48	Everton*	45
1907–08*e*	Manchester U	52	Aston Villa*	43	Manchester C	43
1908–09*e*	Newcastle U	53	Everton	46	Sunderland	44
1909–10*e*	Aston Villa	53	Liverpool	48	Blackburn R*	45
1910–11*e*	Manchester U	52	Aston Villa	51	Sunderland*	45
1911–12*e*	Blackburn R	49	Everton	46	Newcastle U	44
1912–13*e*	Sunderland	54	Aston Villa	50	Sheffield W	49
1913–14*e*	Blackburn R	51	Aston Villa	44	Middlesbrough*	43
1914–15*e*	Everton	46	Oldham Ath	45	Blackburn R*	43
1919–20*f*	WBA	60	Burnley	51	Chelsea	49
1920–21*f*	Burnley	59	Manchester C	54	Bolton W	52
1921–22*f*	Liverpool	57	Tottenham H	51	Burnley	49
1922–23*f*	Liverpool	60	Sunderland	54	Huddersfield T	53
1923–24*f*	Huddersfield T*	57	Cardiff C	57	Sunderland	53
1924–25*f*	Huddersfield T	58	WBA	56	Bolton W	55
1925–26*f*	Huddersfield T	57	Arsenal	52	Sunderland	48
1926–27*f*	Newcastle U	56	Huddersfield T	51	Sunderland	49
1927–28*f*	Everton	53	Huddersfield T	51	Leicester C	48
1928–29*f*	Sheffield W	52	Leicester C	51	Aston Villa	50
1929–30*f*	Sheffield W	60	Derby Co	50	Manchester C*	47
1930–31*f*	Arsenal	66	Aston Villa	59	Sheffield W	52
1931–32*f*	Everton	56	Arsenal	54	Sheffield W	50
1932–33*f*	Arsenal	58	Aston Villa	54	Sheffield W	51
1933–34*f*	Arsenal	59	Huddersfield T	56	Tottenham H	49
1934–35*f*	Arsenal	58	Sunderland	54	Sheffield W	49
1935–36*f*	Sunderland	56	Derby Co*	48	Huddersfield T	48
1936–37*f*	Manchester C	57	Charlton Ath	54	Arsenal	52
1937–38*f*	Arsenal	52	Wolverhampton W	51	Preston NE	49
1938–39*f*	Everton	59	Wolverhampton W	55	Charlton Ath	50
1946–47*f*	Liverpool	57	Manchester U*	56	Wolverhampton W	56
1947–48*f*	Arsenal	59	Manchester U*	52	Burnley	52
1948–49*f*	Portsmouth	58	Manchester U*	53	Derby Co	53
1949–50*f*	Portsmouth*	53	Wolverhampton W	53	Sunderland	52
1950–51*f*	Tottenham H	60	Manchester U	56	Blackpool	50
1951–52*f*	Manchester U	57	Tottenham H*	53	Arsenal	53
1952–53*f*	Arsenal*	54	Preston NE	54	Wolverhampton W	51
1953–54*f*	Wolverhampton W	57	WBA	53	Huddersfield T	51
1954–55*f*	Chelsea	52	Wolverhampton W*	48	Portsmouth*	48
1955–56*f*	Manchester U	60	Blackpool*	49	Wolverhampton W	49
1956–57*f*	Manchester U	64	Tottenham H*	56	Preston NE	56
1957–58*f*	Wolverhampton W	64	Preston NE	59	Tottenham H	51
1958–59*f*	Wolverhampton W	61	Manchester U	55	Arsenal*	50
1959–60*f*	Burnley	55	Wolverhampton W	54	Tottenham H	53
1960–61*f*	Tottenham H	66	Sheffield W	58	Wolverhampton W	57

	First	Pts	Second	Pts	Third	Pts
1961–62*f*	Ipswich T	56	Burnley	53	Tottenham H	52
1962–63*f*	Everton	61	Tottenham H	55	Burnley	54
1963–64*f*	Liverpool	57	Manchester U	53	Everton	52
1964–65*f*	Manchester U*	61	Leeds U	61	Chelsea	56
1965–66*f*	Liverpool	61	Leeds U*	55	Burnley	55
1966–67*f*	Manchester U	60	Nottingham F*	56	Tottenham H	56
1967–68*f*	Manchester C	58	Manchester U	56	Liverpool	55
1968–69*f*	Leeds U	67	Liverpool	61	Everton	57
1969–70*f*	Everton	66	Leeds U	57	Chelsea	55
1970–71*f*	Arsenal	65	Leeds U	64	Tottenham H*	52
1971–72*f*	Derby Co	58	Leeds U*	57	Liverpool*	57
1972–73*f*	Liverpool	60	Arsenal	57	Leeds U	53
1973–74*f*	Leeds U	62	Liverpool	57	Derby Co	48
1974–75*f*	Derby Co	53	Liverpool*	51	Ipswich T	51
1975–76*f*	Liverpool	60	QPR	59	Manchester U	56
1976–77*f*	Liverpool	57	Manchester C	56	Ipswich T	52
1977–78*f*	Nottingham F	64	Liverpool	57	Everton	55
1978–79*f*	Liverpool	68	Nottingham F	60	WBA	59
1979–80*f*	Liverpool	60	Manchester U	58	Ipswich T	53
1980–81*f*	Aston Villa	60	Ipswich T	56	Arsenal	53
1981–82*g*	Liverpool	87	Ipswich T	83	Manchester U	78
1982–83*g*	Liverpool	82	Watford	71	Manchester U	70
1983–84*g*	Liverpool	80	Southampton	77	Nottingham F*	74
1984–85*g*	Everton	90	Liverpool*	77	Tottenham H	77
1985–86g	Liverpool	88	Everton	86	West Ham U	84
1986–87*g*	Everton	86	Liverpool	77	Tottenham H	71
1987–88*h*	Liverpool	90	Manchester U	81	Nottingham F	73
1988–89*k*	Arsenal*	76	Liverpool	76	Nottingham F	64
1989–90*k*	Liverpool	79	Aston Villa	70	Tottenham H	63
1990–91*k*	Arsenal†	83	Liverpool	76	Crystal Palace	69
1991–92*g*	Leeds U	82	Manchester U	78	Sheffield W	75

No official competition during 1915–19 and 1939–46; Regional Leagues operating.
** Won or placed on goal average (ratio)/goal difference.*
† 2 pts deducted

DIVISION 2 to 1991–92

Maximum points: a 44; *b* 56; *c* 60; *d* 68; *e* 76; *f* 84; *g* 126; *h* 132; *k* 138.

1892–93*a*	Small Heath	36	Sheffield U	35	Darwen	30
1893–94*b*	Liverpool	50	Small Heath	42	Notts Co	39
1894–95*c*	Bury	48	Notts Co	39	Newton Heath*	38
1895–96*c*	Liverpool*	46	Manchester C	46	Grimsby T*	42
1896–97*c*	Notts Co	42	Newton Heath	39	Grimsby T	38
1897–98*c*	Burnley	48	Newcastle U	45	Manchester C	39
1898–99*d*	Manchester C	52	Glossop NE	46	Leicester Fosse	45
1899–1900*d*	The Wednesday	54	Bolton W	52	Small Heath	46
1900–01*d*	Grimsby T	49	Small Heath	48	Burnley	44
1901–02*d*	WBA	55	Middlesbrough	51	Preston NE*	42
1902–03*d*	Manchester C	54	Small Heath	51	Woolwich A	48
1903–04*d*	Preston NE	50	Woolwich A	49	Manchester U	48
1904–05*d*	Liverpool	58	Bolton W	56	Manchester U	53
1905–06*e*	Bristol C	66	Manchester U	62	Chelsea	53
1906–07*e*	Nottingham F	60	Chelsea	57	Leicester Fosse	48
1907–08*e*	Bradford C	54	Leicester Fosse	52	Oldham Ath	50
1908–09*e*	Bolton W	52	Tottenham H*	51	WBA	51
1909–10*e*	Manchester C	54	Oldham Ath*	53	Hull C*	53
1910–11*e*	WBA	53	Bolton W	51	Chelsea	49

	First	Pts	Second	Pts	Third	Pts
1911–12*e*	Derby Co*	54	Chelsea	54	Burnley	52
1912–13*e*	Preston NE	53	Burnley	50	Birmingham	46
1913–14*e*	Notts Co	53	Bradford PA*	49	Woolwich A	49
1914–15*e*	Derby Co	53	Preston NE	50	Barnsley	47
1919–20*f*	Tottenham H	70	Huddersfield T	64	Birmingham	56
1920–21*f*	Birmingham*	58	Cardiff C	58	Bristol C	51
1921–22*f*	Nottingham F	56	Stoke C*	52	Barnsley	52
1922–23*f*	Notts Co	53	West Ham U*	51	Leicester C	51
1923–24*f*	Leeds U	54	Bury*	51	Derby Co	51
1924–25*f*	Leicester C	59	Manchester U	57	Derby Co	55
1925–26*f*	Sheffield W	60	Derby Co	57	Chelsea	52
1926–27*f*	Middlesbrough	62	Portsmouth*	54	Manchester C	54
1927–28*f*	Manchester C	59	Leeds U	57	Chelsea	54
1928–29*f*	Middlesbrough	55	Grimsby T	53	Bradford PA*	48
1929–30*f*	Blackpool	58	Chelsea	55	Oldham Ath	53
1930–31*f*	Everton	61	WBA	54	Tottenham H	51
1931–32*f*	Wolverhampton W	56	Leeds U	54	Stoke C	52
1932–33*f*	Stoke C	56	Tottenham H	55	Fulham	50
1933–34*f*	Grimsby T	59	Preston NE	52	Bolton W*	51
1934–35*f*	Brentford	61	Bolton W*	56	West Ham U	56
1935–36*f*	Manchester U	56	Charlton Ath	55	Sheffield U*	52
1936–37*f*	Leicester C	56	Blackpool	55	Bury	52
1937–38*f*	Aston Villa	57	Manchester U*	53	Sheffield U	53
1938–39*f*	Blackburn R	55	Sheffield U	54	Sheffield W	53
1946–47*f*	Manchester C	62	Burnley	58	Birmingham C	55
1947–48*f*	Birmingham C	59	Newcastle U	56	Southampton	52
1948–49*f*	Fulham	57	WBA	56	Southampton	55
1949–50*f*	Tottenham H	61	Sheffield W*	52	Sheffield U*	52
1950–51*f*	Preston NE	57	Manchester C	52	Cardiff C	50
1951–52*f*	Sheffield W	53	Cardiff C*	51	Birmingham C	51
1952–53*f*	Sheffield U	60	Huddersfield T	58	Luton T	52
1953–54*f*	Leicester C*	56	Everton	56	Blackburn R	55
1954–55*f*	Birmingham C*	54	Luton T*	54	Rotherham U	54
1955–56*f*	Sheffield W	55	Leeds U	52	Liverpool*	48
1956–57*f*	Leicester C	61	Nottingham F	54	Liverpool	53
1957–58*f*	West Ham U	57	Blackburn R	56	Charlton Ath	55
1958–59*f*	Sheffield W	62	Fulham	60	Sheffield U*	53
1959–60*f*	Aston Villa	59	Cardiff C	58	Liverpool*	50
1960–61*f*	Ipswich T	59	Sheffield U	58	Liverpool	52
1961–62*f*	Liverpool	62	Leyton Orient	54	Sunderland	53
1962–63*f*	Stoke C	53	Chelsea*	52	Sunderland	52
1963–64*f*	Leeds U	63	Sunderland	61	Preston NE	56
1964–65*f*	Newcastle U	57	Northampton T	56	Bolton W	50
1965–66*f*	Manchester C	59	Southampton	54	Coventry C	53
1966–67*f*	Coventry C	59	Wolverhampton W	58	Carlisle U	52
1967–68*f*	Ipswich T	59	QPR*	58	Blackpool	58
1968–69*f*	Derby Co	63	Crystal Palace	56	Charlton Ath	50
1969–70*f*	Huddersfield T	60	Blackpool	53	Leicester C	51
1970–71*f*	Leicester C	59	Sheffield U	56	Cardiff C*	53
1971–72*f*	Norwich C	57	Birmingham C	56	Millwall	55
1972–73*f*	Burnley	62	QPR	61	Aston Villa	50
1973–74*f*	Middlesbrough	65	Luton T	50	Carlisle U	49
1974–75*f*	Manchester U	61	Aston Villa	58	Norwich C	53
1975–76*f*	Sunderland	56	Bristol C*	53	WBA	53
1976–77*f*	Wolverhampton W	57	Chelsea	55	Nottingham F	52
1977–78*f*	Bolton W	58	Southampton	57	Tottenham H*	56
1978–79*f*	Crystal Palace	57	Brighton & HA*	56	Stoke C	56

	First	Pts	Second	Pts	Third	Pts
1979–80*f*	Leicester C	55	Sunderland	54	Birmingham C*	53
1980–81*f*	West Ham U	66	Notts Co	53	Swansea C*	50
1981–82*g*	Luton T	88	Watford	80	Norwich C	71
1982–83*g*	QPR	85	Wolverhampton W	75	Leicester C	70
1983–84*g*	Chelsea*	88	Sheffield W	88	Newcastle U	80
1984–85*g*	Oxford U	84	Birmingham C	82	Manchester C	74
1985–86*g*	Norwich C	84	Charlton Ath	77	Wimbledon	76
1986–87*g*	Derby Co	84	Portsmouth	78	Oldham Ath††	75
1987–88*h*	Millwall	82	Aston Villa*	78	Middlesbrough	78
1988–89*k*	Chelsea	99	Manchester C	82	Crystal Palace	81
1989–90*k*	Leeds U*	85	Sheffield U	85	Newcastle U††	80
1990–91*k*	Oldham Ath	88	West Ham U	87	Sheffield W	82
1991–92*k*	Ipswich T	84	Middlesbrough	80	Derby Co	78

No official competition during 1915–19 and 1939–46; Regional Leagues operating.
* *Won or placed on goal average (ratio)/goal difference.*
†† *Not promoted after play-offs.*

DIVISION 3 to 1991–92

Maximum points: 92; 138 from 1981–82.

1958–59	Plymouth Arg	62	Hull C	61	Brentford*	57
1959–60	Southampton	61	Norwich C	59	Shrewsbury T*	52
1960–61	Bury	68	Walsall	62	QPR	60
1961–62	Portsmouth	65	Grimsby T	62	Bournemouth*	59
1962–63	Northampton T	62	Swindon T	58	Port Vale	54
1963–64	Coventry C*	60	Crystal Palace	60	Watford	58
1964–65	Carlisle U	60	Bristol C*	59	Mansfield T	59
1965–66	Hull C	69	Millwall	65	QPR	57
1966–67	QPR	67	Middlesbrough	55	Watford	54
1967–68	Oxford U	57	Bury	56	Shrewsbury T	55
1968–69	Watford*	64	Swindon T	64	Luton T	61
1969–70	Orient	62	Luton T	60	Bristol R	56
1970–71	Preston NE	61	Fulham	60	Halifax T	56
1971–72	Aston Villa	70	Brighton & HA	65	Bournemouth*	62
1972–73	Bolton W	61	Notts Co	57	Blackburn R	55
1973–74	Oldham Ath	62	Bristol R*	61	York C	61
1974–75	Blackburn R	60	Plymouth Arg	59	Charlton Ath	55
1975–76	Hereford U	63	Cardiff C	57	Millwall	56
1976–77	Mansfield T	64	Brighton & HA	61	Crystal Palace*	59
1977–78	Wrexham	61	Cambridge U	58	Preston NE*	56
1978–79	Shrewsbury T	61	Watford*	60	Swansea C	60
1979–80	Grimsby T	62	Blackburn R	59	Sheffield W	58
1980–81	Rotherham U	61	Barnsley*	59	Charlton Ath	59
1981–82	Burnley*	80	Carlisle U	80	Fulham	78
1982–83	Portsmouth	91	Cardiff C	86	Huddersfield T	82
1983–84	Oxford U	95	Wimbledon	87	Sheffield U*	83
1984–85	Bradford C	94	Millwall	90	Hull C	87
1985–86	Reading	94	Plymouth Arg	87	Derby Co	84
1986–87	Bournemouth	97	Middlesbrough	94	Swindon T	87
1987–88	Sunderland	93	Brighton & HA	84	Walsall	82
1988–89	Wolverhampton W	92	Sheffield U*	84	Port Vale	84
1989–90	Bristol R	93	Bristol C	91	Notts Co	87
1990–91	Cambridge U	86	Southend U	85	Grimsby T*	83
1991–92	Brentford	82	Birmingham C	81	Huddersfield T	78

* *Won or placed on goal average (ratio)/goal difference.*

DIVISION 4 (1958–1992)

Maximum points: 92; 138 from 1981–82.

	First	*Pts*	*Second*	*Pts*	*Third*	*Pts*
1958–59	Port Vale	64	Coventry C*	60	York C	60
1959–60	Walsall	65	Notts Co*	60	Torquay U	60
1960–61	Peterborough U	66	Crystal Palace	64	Northampton T*	60
1961–62†	Millwall	56	Colchester U	55	Wrexham	53
1962–63	Brentford	62	Oldham Ath*	59	Crewe Alex	59
1963–64	Gillingham*	60	Carlisle U	60	Workington	59
1964–65	Brighton & HA	63	Millwall*	62	York C	62
1965–66	Doncaster R*	59	Darlington	59	Torquay U	58
1966–67	Stockport Co	64	Southport*	59	Barrow	59
1967–68	Luton T	66	Barnsley	61	Hartlepools U	60
1968–69	Doncaster R	59	Halifax T	57	Rochdale*	56
1969–70	Chesterfield	64	Wrexham	61	Swansea C	60
1970–71	Notts Co	69	Bournemouth	60	Oldham Ath	59
1971–72	Grimsby T	63	Southend U	60	Brentford	59
1972–73	Southport	62	Hereford U	58	Cambridge U	57
1973–74	Peterborough U	65	Gillingham	62	Colchester U	60
1974–75	Mansfield T	68	Shrewsbury T	62	Rotherham U	59
1975–76	Lincoln C	74	Northampton T	68	Reading	60
1976–77	Cambridge U	65	Exeter C	62	Colchester U*	59
1977–78	Watford	71	Southend U	60	Swansea C*	56
1978–79	Reading	65	Grimsby T*	61	Wimbledon*	61
1979–80	Huddersfield T	66	Walsall	64	Newport Co	61
1980–81	Southend U	67	Lincoln C	65	Doncaster R	56
1981–82	Sheffield U	96	Bradford C*	91	Wigan Ath	91
1982–83	Wimbledon	98	Hull C	90	Port Vale	88
1983–84	York C	101	Doncaster R	85	Reading*	82
1984–85	Chesterfield	91	Blackpool	86	Darlington	85
1985–86	Swindon T	102	Chester C	84	Mansfield T	81
1986–87	Northampton T	99	Preston NE	90	Southend U	80
1987–88	Wolverhampton W	90	Cardiff C	85	Bolton W	78
1988–89	Rotherham U	82	Tranmere R	80	Crewe Alex	78
1989–90	Exeter C	89	Grimsby T	79	Southend U	75
1990–91	Darlington	83	Stockport Co*	82	Hartlepool U	82
1991–92†*	Burnley	83	Rotherham U*	77	Mansfield T	77

†*Maximum points:* 88 owing to Accrington Stanley's resignation. ††*Not promoted after play-offs*.
†**Maximum points:* 126 owing to Aldershot being expelled.

DIVISION 3—SOUTH (1920–1958)

1920–21 Season as Division 3.
Maximum points: a 84; *b* 92.

1920–21*a*	Crystal Palace	59	Southampton	54	QPR	53
1921–22*a*	Southampton*	61	Plymouth Arg	61	Portsmouth	53
1922–23*a*	Bristol C	59	Plymouth Arg*	53	Swansea T	53
1923–24*a*	Portsmouth	59	Plymouth Arg	55	Millwall	54
1924–25*a*	Swansea T	57	Plymouth Arg	56	Bristol C	53
1925–26*a*	Reading	57	Plymouth Arg	56	Millwall	53
1926–27*a*	Bristol C	62	Plymouth Arg	60	Millwall	56
1927–28*a*	Millwall	65	Northampton T	55	Plymouth Arg	53
1928–29*a*	Charlton Ath*	54	Crystal Palace	54	Northampton T*	52
1929–30*a*	Plymouth Arg	68	Brentford	61	QPR	51
1930–31*a*	Notts Co	59	Crystal Palace	51	Brentford	50
1931–32*a*	Fulham	57	Reading	55	Southend U	53
1932–33*a*	Brentford	62	Exeter C	58	Norwich C	57

	First	Pts	Second	Pts	Third	Pts
1933–34*a*	Norwich C	61	Coventry C*	54	Reading*	54
1934–35*a*	Charlton Ath	61	Reading	53	Coventry C	51
1935–36*a*	Coventry C	57	Luton T	56	Reading	54
1936–37*a*	Luton T	58	Notts Co	56	Brighton & HA	53
1937–38*a*	Millwall	56	Bristol C	55	QPR*	53
1938–39*a*	Newport Co	55	Crystal Palace	52	Brighton & HA	49
1939–46	Competition cancelled owing to war.					
1946–47*a*	Cardiff C	66	QPR	57	Bristol C	51
1947–48*a*	QPR	61	Bournemouth	57	Walsall	51
1948–49*a*	Swansea T	62	Reading	55	Bournemouth	52
1949–50*a*	Notts Co	58	Northampton T*	51	Southend U	51
1950–51*b*	Nottingham F	70	Norwich C	64	Reading*	57
1951–52*b*	Plymouth Arg	66	Reading*	61	Norwich C	61
1952–53*b*	Bristol R	64	Millwall*	62	Northampton T	62
1953–54*b*	Ipswich T	64	Brighton & HA	61	Bristol C	56
1954–55*b*	Bristol C	70	Leyton Orient	61	Southampton	59
1955–56*b*	Leyton Orient	66	Brighton & HA	65	Ipswich T	64
1956–57*b*	Ipswich T*	59	Torquay U	59	Colchester U	58
1957–58*b*	Brighton & HA	60	Brentford*	58	Plymouth Arg	58

* *Won or placed on goal average (ratio).*

DIVISION 3—NORTH (1921–1958)

Maximum points: a 76; *b* 84; *c* 80; *d* 92.

	First	Pts	Second	Pts	Third	Pts
1921–22*a*	Stockport Co	56	Darlington*	50	Grimsby T	50
1922–23*a*	Nelson	51	Bradford PA	47	Walsall	46
1923–24*b*	Wolverhampton W	63	Rochdale	62	Chesterfield	54
1924–25*b*	Darlington	58	Nelson*	53	New Brighton	53
1925–26*b*	Grimsby T	61	Bradford PA	60	Rochdale	59
1926–27*b*	Stoke C	63	Rochdale	58	Bradford PA	55
1927–28*b*	Bradford PA	63	Lincoln C	55	Stockport Co	54
1928–29*g*	Bradford C	63	Stockport Co	62	Wrexham	52
1929–30*b*	Port Vale	67	Stockport Co	63	Darlington*	50
1930–31*b*	Chesterfield	58	Lincoln C	57	Wrexham*	54
1931–32*c*	Lincoln C*	57	Gateshead	57	Chester	50
1932–33*b*	Hull C	59	Wrexham	57	Stockport Co	54
1933–34*b*	Barnsley	62	Chesterfield	61	Stockport Co	59
1934–35*b*	Doncaster R	57	Halifax T	55	Chester	54
1935–36*b*	Chesterfield	60	Chester*	55	Tranmere R	55
1936–37*b*	Stockport Co	60	Lincoln C	57	Chester	53
1937–38*b*	Tranmere R	56	Doncaster R	54	Hull C	53
1938–39*b*	Barnsley	67	Doncaster R	56	Bradford C	52
1939–46	Competition cancelled owing to war.					
1946–47*b*	Doncaster R	72	Rotherham U	60	Chester	56
1947–48*b*	Lincoln C	60	Rotherham U	59	Wrexham	50
1948–49*b*	Hull C	65	Rotherham U	62	Doncaster R	50
1949–50*b*	Doncaster R	55	Gateshead	53	Rochdale*	51
1950–51*d*	Rotherham U	71	Mansfield T	64	Carlisle U	62
1951–52*d*	Lincoln C	69	Grimsby T	66	Stockport Co	59
1952–53*d*	Oldham Ath	59	Port Vale	58	Wrexham	56
1953–54*d*	Port Vale	69	Barnsley	58	Scunthorpe U	57
1954–55*d*	Barnsley	65	Accrington S	61	Scunthorpe U*	58
1955–56*d*	Grimsby T	68	Derby Co	63	Accrington S	59
1956–57*d*	Derby Co	63	Hartlepools U	59	Accrington S*	58
1957–58*d*	Scunthorpe U	66	Accrington S	59	Bradford C	57

* *Won or placed on goal average (ratio).*

PROMOTED AFTER PLAY-OFFS
(Not accounted for in previous section)
1986–87 Aldershot to Division 3.
1987–88 Swansea C to Divison 3.
1988–89 Leyton Orient to Division 3.
1989–90 Cambridge U to Division 3; Notts Co to Division 2; Sunderland to Division 1.
1990–91 Notts Co to Division 1; Tranmere R to Division 2; Torquay U to Division 3.
1991–92 Blackburn R to Premier League; Peterborough U to Division 1.
1992–93 Swindon T to Premier League; WBA to Division 1; York C to Division 2.
1993–94 Leicester C to Premier League; Burnley to Division 1; Wycombe W to Division 2.
1994–95 Huddersfield T to Division 1.
1995–96 Leicester C to Premier League; Bradford C to Division 1; Plymouth Arg to Division 2.
1996–97 Crystal Palace to Premier League; Crewe Alex to Division 1; Northampton T to Division 2.
1997–98 Charlton Ath to Premier League; Colchester U to Division 2.
1998–99 Watford to Premier League; Scunthorpe to Division 2.
1999–00 Peterborough U to Division 2.

RELEGATED CLUBS

FA PREMIER LEAGUE TO DIVISION 1

1992–93 Crystal Palace, Middlesbrough, Nottingham F
1993–94 Sheffield U, Oldham Ath, Swindon T
1994–95 Crystal Palace, Norwich C, Leicester C, Ipswich T
1995–96 Manchester C, QPR, Bolton W
1996–97 Sunderland, Middlesbrough, Nottingham F
1997–98 Bolton W, Barnsley, Crystal Palace
1998–99 Charlton Ath, Blackburn R, Nottingham F
1999–90 Wimbledon, Sheffield W, Watford

DIVISION 1 TO DIVISION 2

1898–99 Bolton W and Sheffield W
1899–1900 Burnley and Glossop
1900–01 Preston NE and WBA
1901–02 Small Heath and Manchester C
1902–03 Grimsby T and Bolton W
1903–04 Liverpool and WBA
1904–05 League extended. Bury and Notts Co, two bottom clubs in First Division, re-elected.
1905–06 Nottingham F and Wolverhampton W
1906–07 Derby Co and Stoke C
1907–08 Bolton W and Birmingham C
1908–09 Manchester C and Leicester Fosse
1909–10 Bolton W and Chelsea
1910–11 Bristol C and Nottingham F
1911–12 Preston NE and Bury
1912–13 Notts Co and Woolwich Arsenal
1913–14 Preston NE and Derby Co
1914–15 Tottenham H and Chelsea*
1919–20 Notts Co and Sheffield W
1920–21 Derby Co and Bradford PA
1921–22 Bradford C and Manchester U
1922–23 Stoke C and Oldham Ath
1923–24 Chelsea and Middlesbrough
1924–25 Preston NE and Nottingham F
1925–26 Manchester C and Notts Co
1926–27 Leeds U and WBA
1927–28 Tottenham H and Middlesbrough
1928–29 Bury and Cardiff C
1929–30 Burnley and Everton
1930–31 Leeds U and Manchester U
1931–32 Grimsby T and West Ham U
1932–33 Bolton W and Blackpool
1933–34 Newcastle U and Sheffield U
1934–35 Leicester C and Tottenham H
1935–36 Aston Villa and Blackburn R
1936–37 Manchester U and Sheffield W
1937–38 Manchester C and WBA
1938–39 Birmingham C and Leicester C
1946–47 Brentford and Leeds U
1947–48 Blackburn R and Grimsby T
1948–49 Preston NE and Sheffield U
1949–50 Manchester C and Birmingham C
1950–51 Sheffield W and Everton
1951–52 Huddersfield T and Fulham
1952–53 Stoke C and Derby Co
1953–54 Middlesbrough and Liverpool
1954–55 Leicester C and Sheffield W
1955–56 Huddersfield T and Sheffield U
1956–57 Charlton Ath and Cardiff C
1957–58 Sheffield W and Sunderland
1958–59 Portsmouth and Aston Villa

1959–60 Luton T and Leeds U
1960–61 Preston NE and Newcastle U
1961–62 Chelsea and Cardiff C
1962–63 Manchester C and Leyton Orient
1963–64 Bolton W and Ipswich T
1964–65 Wolverhampton W and Birmingham C
1965–66 Northampton T and Blackburn R
1966–67 Aston Villa and Blackpool
1967–68 Fulham and Sheffield U
1968–69 Leicester C and QPR
1969–70 Sunderland and Sheffield W
1970–71 Burnley and Blackpool
1971–72 Huddersfield T and Nottingham F
1972–73 Crystal Palace and WBA
1973–74 Southampton, Manchester U, Norwich C
1974–75 Luton T, Chelsea, Carlisle U
1975–76 Wolverhampton W, Burnley, Sheffield U
1976–77 Sunderland, Stoke C, Tottenham H
1977–78 West Ham U, Newcastle U, Leicester C
1978–79 QPR, Birmingham C, Chelsea
1979–80 Bristol C, Derby Co, Bolton W
1980–81 Norwich C, Leicester C, Crystal Palace
1981–82 Leeds U, Wolverhampton W, Middlesbrough
1982–83 Manchester C, Swansea C, Brighton & HA
1983–84 Birmingham C, Notts Co, Wolverhampton W
1984–85 Norwich C, Sunderland, Stoke C
1985–86 Ipswich T, Birmingham C, WBA
1986–87 Leicester C, Manchester C, Aston Villa
1987–88 Chelsea**, Portsmouth, Watford, Oxford U
1988–89 Middlesbrough, West Ham U, Newcastle U
1989–90 Sheffield W, Charlton Ath, Millwall
1990–91 Sunderland and Derby Co
1991–92 Luton T, Notts Co, West Ham U
1992–93 Brentford, Cambridge U, Bristol R
1993–94 Birmingham C, Oxford U, Peterborough U
1994–95 Swindon T, Burnley, Bristol C, Notts Co
1995–96 Millwall, Watford, Luton T
1996–97 Grimsby T, Oldham Ath, Southend U
1997–98 Manchester C, Stoke C, Reading
1998–99 Bury, Oxford U, Bristol C
1999–00 Walsall, Port Vale, Swindon T

***Relegated after play-offs.*
**Subsequently re-elected to Division 1 when League was extended after the War.*

DIVISION 2 TO DIVISION 3

1920–21 Stockport Co
1921–22 Bradford PA and Bristol C
1922–23 Rotherham Co and Wolverhampton W
1923–24 Nelson and Bristol C
1924–25 Crystal Palace and Coventry C
1925–26 Stoke C and Stockport Co
1926–27 Darlington and Bradford C
1927–28 Fulham and South Shields
1928–29 Port Vale and Clapton Orient
1929–30 Hull C and Notts Co
1930–31 Reading and Cardiff C
1931–32 Barnsley and Bristol C
1932–33 Chesterfield and Charlton Ath
1933–34 Millwall and Lincoln C
1934–35 Oldham Ath and Notts Co
1935–36 Port Vale and Hull C
1936–37 Doncaster R and Bradford C
1937–38 Barnsley and Stockport Co
1938–39 Norwich C and Tranmere R
1946–47 Swansea T and Newport Co
1947–48 Doncaster R and Millwall
1948–49 Nottingham F and Lincoln C
1949–50 Plymouth Arg and Bradford PA
1950–51 Grimsby T and Chesterfield
1951–52 Coventry C and QPR
1952–53 Southampton and Barnsley
1953–54 Brentford and Oldham Ath
1954–55 Ipswich T and Derby Co
1955–56 Plymouth Arg and Hull C
1956–57 Port Vale and Bury
1957–58 Doncaster R and Notts Co
1958–59 Barnsley and Grimsby T
1959–60 Bristol C and Hull C
1960–61 Lincoln C and Portsmouth
1961–62 Brighton & HA and Bristol R
1962–63 Walsall and Luton T
1963–64 Grimsby T and Scunthorpe U
1964–65 Swindon T and Swansea T
1965–66 Middlesbrough and Leyton Orient
1966–67 Northampton T and Bury
1967–68 Plymouth Arg and Rotherham U
1968–69 Fulham and Bury
1969–70 Preston NE and Aston Villa
1970–71 Blackburn R and Bolton W
1971–72 Charlton Ath and Watford
1972–73 Huddersfield T and Brighton & HA
1973–74 Crystal Palace, Preston NE, Swindon T
1974–75 Millwall, Cardiff C, Sheffield W

1975–76 Oxford U, York C, Portsmouth
1976–77 Carlisle U, Plymouth Arg, Hereford U
1977–78 Blackpool, Mansfield T, Hull C
1978–79 Sheffield U, Millwall, Blackburn R
1979–80 Fulham, Burnley, Charlton Ath
1980–81 Preston NE, Bristol C, Bristol R
1981–82 Cardiff C, Wrexham, Orient
1982–83 Rotherham U, Burnley, Bolton W
1983–84 Derby Co, Swansea C, Cambridge U
1984–85 Notts Co, Cardiff C, Wolverhampton W
1985–86 Carlisle U, Middlesbrough, Fulham
1986–87 Sunderland**, Grimsby T, Brighton & HA
1987–88 Huddersfield T, Reading, Sheffield U**
1988–89 Shrewsbury T, Birmingham C, Walsall
1989–90 Bournemouth, Bradford C, Stoke C
1990–91 WBA and Hull C
1991–92 Plymouth Arg, Brighton & HA, Port Vale
1992–93 Preston NE, Mansfield T, Wigan Ath, Chester C
1993–94 Fulham, Exeter C, Hartlepool U, Barnet
1994–95 Cambridge U, Plymouth Arg, Cardiff C, Chester C, Leyton Orient
1995–96 Carlisle U, Swansea C, Brighton & HA, Hull C
1996–97 Peterborough U, Shrewsbury T, Rotherham U, Notts Co
1997–98 Brentford, Plymouth Arg, Carlisle U, Southend U
1998–99 York C, Northampton T, Lincoln C, Macclesfield T
1999–00 Cardiff C, Blackpool, Scunthorpe U, Chesterfield

DIVISION 3 TO DIVISION 4

1958–59 Rochdale, Notts Co, Doncaster R, Stockport Co
1959–60 Accrington S, Wrexham, Mansfield T, York C
1960–61 Chesterfield, Colchester U, Bradford C, Tranmere R
1961–62 Newport Co, Brentford, Lincoln C, Torquay U
1962–63 Bradford PA, Brighton & HA, Carlisle U, Halifax T
1963–64 Millwall, Crewe Alex, Wrexham, Notts Co
1964–65 Luton T, Port Vale, Colchester U, Barnsley
1965–66 Southend U, Exeter C, Brentford, York C
1966–67 Doncaster R, Workington, Darlington, Swansea T
1967–68 Scunthorpe U, Colchester U, Grimsby T, Peterborough U (demoted)
1968–69 Oldham Ath, Crewe Alex, Hartlepool, Northampton T
1969–70 Bournemouth, Southport, Barrow, Stockport Co
1970–71 Reading, Bury, Doncaster R, Gillingham
1971–72 Mansfield T, Barnsley, Torquay U, Bradford C
1972–73 Rotherham U, Brentford, Swansea C, Scunthorpe U
1973–74 Cambridge U, Shrewsbury T, Southport, Rochdale
1974–75 Bournemouth, Tranmere R, Watford, Huddersfield T
1975–76 Aldershot, Colchester U, Southend U, Halifax T
1976–77 Reading, Northampton T, Grimsby T, York C
1977–78 Port Vale, Bradford C, Hereford U, Portsmouth
1978–79 Peterborough U, Walsall, Tranmere R, Lincoln C
1979–80 Bury, Southend U, Mansfield T, Wimbledon
1980–81 Sheffield U, Colchester U, Blackpool, Hull C
1981–82 Wimbledon, Swindon T, Bristol C, Chester
1982–83 Reading, Wrexham, Doncaster R, Chesterfield
1983–84 Scunthorpe U, Southend U, Port Vale, Exeter C
1984–85 Burnley, Orient, Preston NE, Cambridge U
1985–86 Lincoln C, Cardiff C, Wolverhampton W, Swansea C
1986–87 Bolton W**, Carlisle U, Darlington, Newport Co
1987–88 Doncaster R, York C, Grimsby T, Rotherham U**
1988–89 Southend U, Chesterfield, Gillingham, Aldershot
1989–90 Cardiff C, Northampton T, Blackpool, Walsall
1990–91 Crewe Alex, Rotherham U, Mansfield T
1991–92 Bury, Shrewsbury T, Torquay U, Darlington

***Relegated after play-offs.*

LEAGUE TITLE WINS

FA PREMIER LEAGUE – Manchester U 6, Arsenal 1, Blackburn R 1.

LEAGUE DIVISION 1 – Liverpool 18, Arsenal 10, Everton 9, Sunderland 8, Manchester U 7, Aston Villa 7, Newcastle U 5, Sheffield W 4, Huddersfield T 3, Leeds U 3, Wolverhampton W 3, Blackburn R 2, Nottingham F 2, Portsmouth 2, Preston NE 2, Burnley 2, Manchester C 2, Tottenham H 2, Derby Co 2, Bolton W 1, Chelsea 1, Sheffield U 1, WBA 1, Ipswich T 1, Crystal Palace 1, Middlesbrough 1, Charlton Ath 1.

LEAGUE DIVISION 2 – Leicester C 6, Manchester C 6, Sheffield W 5, Birmingham C (one as Small Heath) 5, Derby Co 4, Liverpool 4, Preston NE 4, Ipswich T 3, Leeds U 3, Notts Co 3, Middlesbrough 3, Stoke C 3, Bury 2, Grimsby T 2, Norwich C 2, Nottingham F 2, Tottenham H 2, WBA 2, Aston Villa 2, Burnley 2, Chelsea 2, Manchester U 2, West Ham U 2, Wolverhampton W 2, Bolton W 2, Fulham 2, Swindon T, Huddersfield T, Bristol C, Brentford, Bradford C, Everton, Sheffield U, Newcastle U, Coventry C, Blackpool, Blackburn R, Sunderland, Crystal Palace, Luton T, QPR, Oxford U, Millwall, Oldham Ath, Reading, Watford 1 each.

LEAGUE DIVISION 3 – Portsmouth 2, Oxford U 2, Carlisle U 2, Preston NE 2, Shrewsbury T 2, Brentford 2, Plymouth Arg, Southampton, Bury, Northampton T, Coventry C, Hull C, QPR, Watford, Leyton Orient, Aston Villa, Bolton W, Oldham Ath, Blackburn R, Hereford U, Mansfield T, Wrexham, Grimsby T, Rotherham U, Burnley, Bradford C, Bournemouth, Reading, Sunderland, Wolverhampton W, Bristol R, Cambridge U, Cardiff C, Wigan Ath, Notts Co, Swansea C 1 each.

LEAGUE DIVISION 4 – Chesterfield 2, Doncaster R 2, Peterborough U 2, Port Vale, Walsall, Millwall, Brentford, Gillingham, Brighton, Stockport Co, Luton T, Notts Co, Grimsby T, Southport, Mansfield T, Lincoln C, Cambridge U, Watford, Reading, Huddersfield T, Southend U, Sheffield U, Wimbledon, York C, Swindon T, Northampton T, Wolverhampton W, Rotherham U, Exeter C, Darlington, Burnley 1 each.

To 1957–58

DIVISION 3 (South) – Bristol C 3; Charlton Ath, Ipswich T, Millwall, Notts Co, Plymouth Arg, Swansea T 2 each; Brentford, Bristol R, Cardiff C, Crystal Palace, Coventry C, Fulham, Leyton Orient, Luton T, Newport Co, Nottingham F, Norwich C, Portsmouth, QPR, Reading, Southampton, Brighton & HA 1 each.

DIVISION 3 (North) – Barnsley, Doncaster R, Lincoln C 3 each; Chesterfield, Grimsby T, Hull C, Port Vale, Stockport Co 2 each; Bradford PA, Bradford C, Darlington, Derby Co, Nelson, Oldham Ath, Rotherham U, Stoke C, Tranmere R, Wolverhampton W, Scunthorpe U 1 each.

LEAGUE ATTENDANCES 1999–2000

FA CARLING PREMIERSHIP ATTENDANCES

	Average Gate			*Season 1999/2000*	
	1998/99	1999/2000	+/−%	Highest	Lowest
Arsenal	38,042	38,033	−0.02	38,147	37,271
Aston Villa	36,937	31,697	−14.19	39,217	23,885
Bradford City	14,289	18,030	+26.18	18,276	16,864
Chelsea	34,754	34,531	−0.64	35,113	31,591
Coventry City	20,773	20,786	+0.06	23,084	17,658
Derby County	29,193	29,351	+0.54	33,378	24,045
Everton	36,202	34,880	−3.65	40,052	30,490
Leeds United	35,773	39,155	+9.45	40,192	34,122
Leicester City	20,469	19,825	−3.15	22,170	17,550
Liverpool	43,231	44,074	+1.95	44,929	40,483
Manchester United	55,188	58,017	+5.13	61,629	54,941
Middlesbrough	34,386	33,263	−3.27	34,800	31,400
Newcastle United	36,690	36,311	−1.03	36,619	35,614
Sheffield Wednesday	26,745	24,855	−7.07	39,640	18,077
Southampton	15,140	15,132	−0.05	15,257	14,208
Sunderland	38,745	40,495	+4.52	42,079	37,879
Tottenham Hotspur	34,149	34,902	+2.21	36,233	28,701
Watford	11,822	18,544	+56.86	21,590	15,511
West Ham United	25,639	25,093	−2.13	26,044	22,438
Wimbledon	18,207	17,156	−5.77	26,129	8,248

NATIONWIDE FOOTBALL LEAGUE: DIVISION ONE ATTENDANCES

	Average Gate			*Season 1999/2000*	
	1998/99	1999/2000	+/−%	Highest	Lowest
Barnsley	16,269	15,412	−5.3	22,650	12,026
Birmingham City	20,794	21,895	+5.3	29,050	17,150
Blackburn Rovers	25,773	19,253	−25.3	29,913	15,671
Bolton Wanderers	18,240	14,244	−21.9	21,671	11,668
Charlton Athletic	19,816	19,558	−1.3	20,043	18,663
Crewe Alexandra	5,269	6,222	+18.1	10,066	4,741
Crystal Palace	17,123	15,662	−8.5	22,577	12,110
Fulham	11,387	13,092	+15.0	19,623	8,688
Grimsby Town	6,681	6,157	−7.8	8,742	4,036
Huddersfield Town	12,976	14,029	+8.1	18,173	10,656
Ipswich Town	16,920	18,524	+9.5	21,908	14,514
Manchester City	28,261	32,088	+13.5	33,027	30,057
Norwich City	15,761	15,539	−1.4	19,948	12,468
Nottingham Forest	24,415	17,196	−29.6	25,846	13,841
Port Vale	6,991	5,997	−14.2	10,250	3,737
Portsmouth	11,973	13,906	+16.1	19,015	9,042
Queens Park Rangers	11,793	12,589	+6.7	19,002	9,357
Sheffield United	16,243	13,718	−15.5	23,862	8,965
Stockport County	7,900	7,411	−6.2	11,212	4,868
Swindon Town	8,651	6,977	−19.4	12,397	4,701
Tranmere Rovers	6,930	7,273	+4.9	13,208	5,004
Walsall	5,457	6,779	+24.2	9,422	5,384
West Bromwich Albion	14,585	14,584	−0.0	22,101	9,201
Wolverhampton Wanderers	22,620	21,470	−5.1	25,500	18,186

NATIONWIDE FOOTBALL LEAGUE: DIVISION TWO ATTENDANCES

	Average Gate			*Season 1999/2000*	
	1998/99	1999/2000	+/−%	Highest	Lowest
AFC Bournemouth	7,117	4,917	−30.9	6,512	3,481
Blackpool	5,116	4,841	−5.4	9,042	2,819
Brentford	5,444	5,742	+5.5	7,100	4,055
Bristol City	12,860	9,803	−23.8	16,011	7,777
Bristol Rovers	6,263	8,402	+34.2	11,109	5,397
Burnley	10,605	12,937	+22.0	22,310	8,944
Bury	5,476	4,025	−26.5	9,115	2,606
Cambridge United	4,583	4,403	−3.9	6,211	3,016
Cardiff City	7,131	6,895	−3.3	11,168	4,389
Chesterfield	4,564	2,935	−35.7	4,726	1,903
Colchester United	4,479	3,782	−15.6	6,194	2,557
Gillingham	6,339	7,088	+11.8	9,178	5,884
Luton Town	5,527	5,658	+2.4	7,205	4,633
Millwall	6,958	9,260	+33.1	17,929	5,202
Notts County	5,617	5,667	+0.9	9,677	3,728
Oldham Athletic	5,628	5,391	−4.2	9,432	3,807
Oxford United	7,040	5,790	−17.8	7,638	4,318
Preston North End	11,926	12,819	+7.5	19,407	8,506
Reading	11,265	8,985	−20.2	13,348	5,393
Scunthorpe United	3,741	4,064	+8.6	5,862	2,686
Stoke City	12,732	11,426	−10.3	15,354	7,054
Wigan Athletic	4,250	7,007	+64.9	15,993	4,338
Wrexham	3,948	3,952	+0.1	8,811	2,139
Wycombe Wanderers	5,121	5,101	−0.4	7,042	3,821

NATIONWIDE FOOTBALL LEAGUE: DIVISION THREE ATTENDANCES

	Average Gate			*Season 1999/2000*	
	1998/99	1999/2000	+/−%	Highest	Lowest
Barnet	2,107	2,743	+30.2	4,030	1,769
Brighton & Hove Albion	3,253	5,733	+76.2	5,998	5,049
Carlisle United	3,319	3,192	−3.8	6,525	2,028
Cheltenham Town	3,112	4,125	+32.6	5,391	3,107
Chester City	2,526	2,686	+6.3	5,507	1,705
Darlington	3,181	5,523	+73.6	7,401	3,553
Exeter City	3,154	3,014	−4.4	5,263	1,652
Halifax Town	2,541	2,536	−0.2	3,721	1,657
Hartlepool United	2,690	2,982	+10.9	4,673	1,980
Hull City	6,051	5,736	−5.2	8,293	4,150
Leyton Orient	4,672	4,357	−6.7	7,200	2,990
Lincoln City	4,654	3,405	−26.8	5,032	2,556
Macclesfield Town	3,311	2,304	−30.4	3,456	1,541
Mansfield Town	2,963	2,594	−12.5	3,338	1,960
Northampton Town	6,073	5,459	−10.1	6,901	4,495
Peterborough United	5,306	6,568	+23.8	10,793	4,965
Plymouth Argyle	5,323	5,372	+0.9	14,893	3,782
Rochdale	2,125	2,774	+30.5	4,198	1,529
Rotherham United	3,988	4,426	+11.0	10,863	2,708
Shrewsbury Town	2,575	2,832	+10.0	7,654	1,785
Southend United	4,317	4,138	−4.1	6,187	2,563
Swansea City	5,225	5,895	+12.8	10,743	3,357
Torquay United	2,600	2,555	−1.7	5,010	1,756
York City	3,646	3,048	−16.4	5,308	1,857

TRANSFERS 1999–2000

May 1999	*From*	*To*
25 Brown, Daniel	Leyton Orient	Barnet
28 Burton, Sagi	Crystal Palace	Colchester United
13 Eaton, Jason	Cheltenham Town	Yeovil Town
26 Hocking, Matthew J.	Hull City	York City
21 Johnson, Seth A.M.	Crewe Alexandra	Derby County
27 Kiely, Dean L.	Bury	Charlton Athletic
27 Low, Joshua D.	Bristol Rovers	Leyton Orient
27 Read, David	Telford United	Stafford Rangers
27 Spiller, Lee M.	Margate	Gravesend & Northfleet
29 Walling, Dean A.	Lincoln City	Doncaster Rovers
Temporary transfers		
8 Varty, John W.	Carlisle United	Rotherham United
8 Whelan, Philip J.	Oxford United	Rotherham United
June 1999		
11 Dalglish, Paul	Newcastle United	Norwich City
29 Eaton, Adam P.	Everton	Preston North End
25 Forster, Nicholas	Birmingham City	Reading
4 Gray, Martin	Oxford United	Darlington
11 Halle, Gunnar	Leeds United	Bradford City
21 Higgs, Shane P.	Worcester City	Cheltenham Town
17 Irons, Kenneth	Tranmere Rovers	Huddersfield Town
23 James, David B.	Liverpool	Aston Villa
14 Lucketti, Christopher	Bury	Huddersfield Town
21 Nicholls, Kevin J.	Charlton Athletic	Wigan Athletic
7 Oakes, Andrew M.	Hull City	Derby County
5 Town, David	AFC Bournemouth	Rushden & Diamonds
15 Turley, William L.	Northampton Town	Rushden & Diamonds
19 Varty, John W.	Carlisle United	Rotherham United
July 1999		
16 Allen, Rory W.	Tottenham Hotspur	Portsmouth
28 Barras, Anthony	Reading	Walsall
7 Basham, Steven	Southampton	Preston North End
22 Boateng, George	Coventry City	Aston Villa
9 Bould, Stephen A.	Arsenal	Sunderland
9 Brazier, Matthew R.	Fulham	Cardiff City
2 Burns, Alexander	Southend United	Raith Rovers
14 Carr, Darren J.	Gillingham	Brighton & Hove Albion
13 Catlin, Neil	Hayes	Chesham United
2 Christie, Iyseden	Mansfield Town	Leyton Orient
13 Clark, Lee R.	Sunderland	Fulham
2 Collins, Sam J.	Huddersfield Town	Bury
20 Conlon, Barry J.	Southend United	York City
1 Connelly, Gordon J.	York City	Southend United
28 Crosby, Andrew K.	Chester City	Brighton & Hove Albion
7 Crowe, Jason W.R.	Arsenal	Portsmouth
15 Davis, Kelvin G.	Luton Town	Wimbledon
8 Dyche, Sean M.	Bristol City	Millwall
16 Dyer, Kieron C.	Ipswich Town	Newcastle United
23 Endersby, Lee A.	Slough Town	Farnborough Town
30 Flowers, Timothy D.	Blackburn Rovers	Leicester City
31 Francis, Delton M.	Kingstonian	Nuneaton Borough
14 Gaughan, Steven E.	Darlington	Halifax Town
29 Grayson, Simon N.	Aston Villa	Blackburn Rovers
27 Griffin, Antony R.	AFC Bournemouth	Cheltenham Town

23 Hamann, Dietmar	Newcastle United	Liverpool
12 Harris, Jason A.S.	Preston North End	Hull City
20 Henchoz, Stephane	Blackburn Rovers	Liverpool
8 Hodges, Lee L.	West Ham United	Scunthorpe United
30 Kelly, Alan T.	Sheffield United	Blackburn Rovers
19 Kennedy, Mark J.	Wimbledon	Manchester City
16 Lawson, Ian J.	Huddersfield Town	Bury
29 Lazaridis, Stan	West Ham United	Birmingham City
8 Lee, Alan D.	Aston Villa	Burnley
1 Mills, Daniel J.	Charlton Athletic	Leeds United
20 Mitchell, Graham L.	Cardiff City	Halifax Town
21 Moody, Paul	Fulham	Millwall
16 Myers, Andrew	Chelsea	Bradford City
9 Oatway, Anthony P.	Brentford	Brighton & Hove Albion
8 Payne, Stephen J.	Macclesfield Town	Chesterfield
21 Perrett, Russell	Portsmouth	Cardiff City
7 Perry, Christopher J.	Wimbledon	Tottenham Hotspur
23 Phillips, Wayne	Stockport County	Wrexham
30 Preece, David	Darlington	Aberdeen
5 Russell, Matthew L.	Scarborough	Halifax Town
24 Sale, Mark D.	Colchester United	Rushden & Diamonds
23 Scimeca, Riccardo	Aston Villa	Nottingham Forest
7 Shipperley, Neil J.	Nottingham Forest	Barnsley
29 Steiner, Robert H.	Bradford City	Queens Park Rangers
16 Sutton, Christopher R.	Blackburn Rovers	Chelsea
5 Tate, Christopher D.	Scarborough	Halifax Town
8 Tebily, Olivier	Sheffield United	Celtic
28 Wanchope, Watson P.	Derby County	West Ham United
21 Wardley, Stuart	Saffron Walden Town	Queens Park Rangers
9 Watson, Paul D.	Brentford	Brighton & Hove Albion
7 Weatherall, David	Leeds United	Bradford City
22 Wijnhard, Clyde	Leeds United	Huddersfield Town
15 Willmott, Christopher A.	Luton Town	Wimbledon
12 Winston, Samuel A.	Chesham United	Sutton United
23 Wright, Jermaine M.	Crewe Alexandra	Ipswich Town

Temporary transfers

1 Adamson, Christopher	West Bromwich Albion	Halifax Town
18 Agogo, Manuel	Sheffield Wednesday	Oldham Athletic
19 Collymore, Stanley V.	Aston Villa	Fulham
26 Hughes, Stephen J.	Arsenal	Fulham
30 Livermore, David	Arsenal	Millwall
2 Newton, Adam L.	West Ham United	Portsmouth
9 Warner, Philip	Southampton	Brentford

August 1999

12 Ashe, Ryan	Ruislip Manor	Chertsey Town
4 Bailey, Alan	Manchester City	Stockport County
9 Bailey, Dennis L.	Cheltenham Town	Forest Green Rovers
9 Beavers, Paul M.	Sunderland	Oldham Athletic
27 Boa Morte, Pereira L.	Arsenal	Southampton
19 Brebner, Grant I.	Reading	Hibernian
13 Carty, Paul	Hednesford Town	Worcester City
6 Cramb, Colin	Bristol City	Crewe Alexandra
18 Davies, Kevin C.	Blackburn Rovers	Southampton
13 D'Jaffo, Laurent	Bury	Stockport County
27 Edwards, Matthew	Hucknall Town	Yeading
10 Gilchrist, Philip A.	Oxford United	Leicester City
12 Hanlon, Ritchie K.	Peterborough United	Welling United
23 Hannigan, Al J.	Yeovil Town	Slough Town
6 Heaney, Neil A.	Manchester City	Darlington

12 Huckerby, Darren C.	Coventry City	Leeds United
6 Illingworth, Jeremy M.	Wisbech Town	Ashton United
3 Ince, Paul E.C.	Liverpool	Middlesbrough
20 Keane, Robert D.	Wolverhampton Wanderers	Coventry City
21 Kirkby, Martin J.	Workington	Bedlington Terriers
3 Lee, Christian	Northampton Town	Gillingham
6 Leonhardsen, Oyvind	Liverpool	Tottenham Hotspur
6 Lilley, Derek	Leeds United	Oxford United
13 Lovell, Stephen W.H.	AFC Bournemouth	Portsmouth
12 Margetson, Martyn W.	Southend United	Huddersfield Town
19 McGowan, Neil	Albion Rovers	Oxford United
4 McGreal, John	Tranmere Rovers	Ipswich Town
24 McKimm, Steven	Farnborough Town	Hayes
26 McKinney, Richard	Ballymena United	Manchester City
27 Miller, Kevin	Crystal Palace	Barnsley
27 Morton, Neil	Morecambe	Lancaster City
6 Murphy, John J.	Chester City	Blackpool
18 Ostenstad, Egil	Southampton	Blackburn Rovers
6 Oster, John	Everton	Sunderland
24 Reddington, Stuart	Lincoln United	Chelsea
3 Redfearn, Neil D.	Charlton Athletic	Bradford City
11 Robinson, Ian B.	Ilkeston Town	Hednesford Town
31 Samuels, Anthony	Boreham Wood	Stevenage Borough
26 Shields, Greg	Dunfermline Athletic	Charlton Athletic
4 Short, Craig J.	Everton	Blackburn Rovers
20 Smith, Neil J.	Fulham	Reading
13 Soley, Steven	Portsmouth	Carlisle United
13 Soltvedt, Trond E.	Coventry City	Southampton
20 Taylor, Craig	Swindon Town	Plymouth Argyle
5 Thomson, Andrew	Oxford United	Gillingham
13 Tinkler, Mark R.	York City	Southend United
18 Tuttle, David P.	Crystal Palace	Barnsley
6 Whitehead, Damien S.	Warrington Town	Macclesfield Town
12 Williams, John	Cardiff City	York City
3 Witney, Scott	St Albans City	Bishop's Stortford

Temporary transfers

2 Adamson, Christopher	West Bromwich Albion	Halifax Town
6 Aiston, Sam J.	Sunderland	Stoke City
19 Alexander, Gary G.	West Ham United	Exeter City
13 Baker, Joseph P.J.	Leyton Orient	Welling United
6 Baker, Steven R.	Middlesbrough	Huddersfield Town
25 Black, Thomas R.	Arsenal	Carlisle United
10 Branston, Guy P.B.	Leicester City	Lincoln City
24 Brunskill, Iain R.	Hednesford Town	Runcorn
13 Byfield, Darren	Aston Villa	Northampton Town
27 Byrne, Christopher T.	Stockport County	Macclesfield Town
13 Chapman, Danny P.	Barnet	Crawley Town
20 Clark, Dean W.	Brentford	Crawley Town
14 Collins, James I.	Crewe Alexandra	Kidderminster Harriers
17 Cook, Aaron	Havant & Waterlooville	Bognor Regis Town
13 Cooksey, Scott A.	Shrewsbury Town	Weymouth
13 Coward, Ronell	Woking	Whyteleafe
27 Craddock, Jody D.	Sunderland	Sheffield United
13 Cullen, David J.	Sheffield United	Shrewsbury Town
5 Dixon, Kevin R.	Leeds United	York City
20 Dudley, Craig B.	Oldham Athletic	Chesterfield
28 Fenton, Darren T.	Hitchen Town	Baldock Town
7 Granville, Daniel P.	Leeds United	Manchester City
13 Hendry, Iain	Woking	St Leonards

13 Humphreys, Richie J.	Sheffield Wednesday	Scunthorpe United
4 Knight, Richard	Derby County	Birmingham City
19 Love, Andrew M.	Grimsby Town	Ilkeston Town
6 Margetson, Martyn W.	Southend United	Huddersfield Town
26 Martin, John	Leyton Orient	Cambridge City
27 McCann, Grant S.	West Ham United	Livingston
21 Mildenhall, Stephen J.	Swindon Town	Salisbury City
14 Newell, Paul C.	St Albans City	Dagenham & Redbridge
1 Newton, Adam L.	West Ham United	Portsmouth
20 Oakes, Andrew M.	Derby County	Port Vale
6 O'Reilly, Alexander	West Ham United	Northampton Town
13 Ovens, Steven	Witney Town	Tiverton Town
16 Payne, Stuart	Kidderminster Harriers	Bromsgrove Rovers
5 Platt, Clive L.	Walsall	Rochdale
5 Pouton, Alan	York City	Grimsby Town
24 Rea, Simon	Birmingham City	Peterborough United
5 Richardson, Barry	Lincoln City	Mansfield Town
27 Richardson, Lee J.	Huddersfield Town	Bury
27 Ritchie, Stuart A.	Havant & Waterlooville	Wokingham Town
20 Salako, John A.	Fulham	Charlton Athletic
13 Samuels, Anthony	Boreham Wood	Stevenage Borough
13 Slinn, Kevin P.	Boston United	Stamford
6 Soley, Steven	Portsmouth	Carlisle United
13 Tardif, Christopher L.	Portsmouth	Havant & Waterlooville
6 Thomas, Wayne	Walsall	Mansfield Town
20 Townley, Leon	Brentford	Slough Town
12 Turkington, Edmund B.	Altrincham	Leigh RMI
6 Watts, Julian	Bristol City	Luton Town
6 Weaver, Luke D.S.	Sunderland	Carlisle United
20 Whitley, James	Manchester City	Blackpool
26 Whittle, David L.J.	Queens Park Rangers	Waterford United
5 Williams, Anthony S.	Blackburn Rovers	Gillingham
27 Wright, Ian E.	West Ham United	Nottingham Forest
6 Wright, Stephen J.	Liverpool	Crewe Alexandra
25 Wright, Thomas J.	Manchester City	Newcastle United

September 1999

29 Abbey, Benjamin	Crawley Town	Oxford United
7 Akinbiyi, Adeola P.	Bristol City	Wolverhampton Wanderers
24 Albrighton, Mark	Atherstone United	Telford United
6 Allison, Wayne A.	Huddersfield Town	Tranmere Rovers
24 Butler, Lee S.	Dunfermline Athletic	Halifax Town
22 Charles, Anthony D.	Brook House	Crewe Alexandra
10 Coupe, Matthew W.E.	Gloucester City	Clevedon Town
21 Croft, Gary	Blackburn Rovers	Ipswich Town
23 Forinton, Howard L.	Birmingham City	Peterborough United
16 Francis, Ruben M.	Burton Albion	Rocester
22 Frandsen, Per	Bolton Wanderers	Blackburn Rovers
30 Graham, Gareth L.	Crystal Palace	Brentford
23 Holland, Paul	Chesterfield	Bristol City
15 Holt, Grant	Workington	Halifax Town
22 Hughes, Robert D.	Aston Villa	Shrewsbury Town
14 Hulme, Kevin	Halifax Town	York City
10 Jones, Stephen G.	Charlton Athletic	Bristol City
6 Livermore, David	Arsenal	Millwall
28 McGrath, Stephen M.	Aldershot Town	Yeading
10 Platt, Clive L.	Walsall	Rochdale
7 Pouton, Alan	York City	Grimsby Town
28 Rachel, Adam	Aston Villa	Blackpool
28 Riedle, Karlheinz	Liverpool	Fulham

3 Sertori, Mark A.	Halifax Town	York City
17 Sigurdsson, Larus O.	Stoke City	West Bromwich Albion
3 Sparks, Christopher	Hayes	Yeovil Town
23 Telemaque, Errol	Stevenage Borough	Hayes
17 Townsend, Andrew D.	Middlesbrough	West Bromwich Albion
9 Watts, Julian	Bristol City	Luton Town
9 Weaver, Luke D.S.	Sunderland	Carlisle United
30 West, Mark	Farnborough Town	Thame United

Temporary transfers

13 Adams, Darren S.	Welling United	Hampton & Richmond Borough
3 Adamson, Christopher	West Bromwich Albion	Halifax Town
3 Agogo, Manuel	Sheffield Wednesday	Chester City
6 Aiston, Sam J.	Sunderland	Stoke City
29 Aldridge, Martin J.	Blackpool	Port Vale
19 Alexander, Gary G.	West Ham United	Exeter City
3 Allison, Wayne A.	Huddersfield Town	Tranmere Rovers
10 Ansell, Gary S.	Barnet	Hayes
24 Arnott, Andrew J.	Brighton & Hove Albion	Colchester United
24 Aspinall, Warren	Colchester United	Brighton & Hove Albion
21 Baillie, Lewis	Bishop's Stortford	Witham Town
24 Battersby, Anthony	Lincoln City	Northampton Town
3 Betsy, Kevin E.L.	Fulham	AFC Bournemouth
3 Blackwood, Michael	Aston Villa	Chester City
17 Bradley, Shayne	Southampton	Exeter City
10 Brown, John K.	Blackburn Rovers	Barnsley
21 Brunskill, Iain R.	Hednesford Town	Runcorn
17 Byfield, Darren	Aston Villa	Cambridge United
24 Bywater, Stephen M.	West Ham United	Wycombe Wanderers
9 Cadette, Nathan D.	Cardiff City	Aberystwyth Town
17 Carruthers, Martin G.	Darlington	Southend United
10 Claridge, Robert R.	Clevedon Town	Yate Town
21 Clark, Dean W.	Brentford	Crawley Town
10 Clarke, Adrian J.	Southend United	Carlisle United
3 Clarke, Tim	Scunthorpe United	Kidderminster Harriers
13 Connell, Lee A.	Bury	Workington
13 Cooksey, Scott A.	Shrewsbury Town	Weymouth
30 Craddock, Jody	Sunderland	Sheffield United
3 Culbertson, Richard D.J.	Swindon Town	Ballymena United
10 Cullen, David J.	Sheffield United	Shrewsbury Town
17 Cullip, Daniel	Brentford	Brighton & Hove Albion
17 Davies, Jamie	Swansea City	Bangor
28 Downey, Glen	Hartlepool United	Bishop Auckland
16 Dunwell, Michael	Hartlepool United	Whitby Town
17 Fettis, Alan	Blackburn Rovers	Leicester City
17 Fitzpatrick, Lee G.	Blackburn Rovers	Hartlepool United
29 Galloway, Michael A.	Gillingham	Lincoln City
6 Gant, Adam S.	Enfield	Bishop's Stortford
9 Gibbens, Kevin	Southampton	Stockport County
10 Glennon, Matthew W.	Bolton Wanderers	Port Vale
28 Graham, Gareth L.	Crystal Palace	Brentford
2 Grant, Anthony J.	Everton	Tranmere Rovers
24 Green, Richard E.	Walsall	Rochdale
17 Gregory, Andrew	Barnsley	Carlisle United
10 Guinan, Stephen	Nottingham Forest	Scunthorpe United
3 Hammatt, Bryan	Slough Town	Billericay Town
24 Hill, Graham E.	Chorley	Winsford United
13 Hockton, Danny J.	Millwall	Leyton Orient
17 Holligan, Gavin V.	West Ham United	Leyton Orient
17 Janney, Mark	Dagenham & Redbridge	Braintree Town

24 Johnson, Thomas	Celtic	Everton
16 Johnston, Ray	Bristol Rovers	Southampton
3 Knight, Richard	Derby County	Birmingham City
18 Love, Andrew	Grimsby Town	Ilkeston Town
24 McGrath, Stephen M.	Aldershot Town	Yeading
17 Mathie, Alexander	Dundee United	Preston North End
24 Midgley, Neil A.	Ipswich Town	Luton Town
9 Monk, Garry A.	Southampton	Stockport County
21 Morris, Andrew D.	Rochdale	Scarborough
9 Muggleton, Carl D.	Stoke City	Mansfield Town
8 Ndekine, Malcolm S.	Rushden & Diamonds	Spalding United
1 Newton, Adam L.	West Ham United	Portsmouth
3 Omoyimni, Emmanuel	West Ham United	Gillingham
24 Ormerod, Anthony	Middlesbrough	York City
17 Palmer, Carlton L.	Nottingham Forest	Coventry City
24 Payne, Stuart	Kidderminster Harriers	Halesowen Town
17 Prudhoe, Mark	Bradford City	Darlington
27 Ritchie, Stuart A.	Havant & Waterlooville	Wokingham Town
24 Rowe, Rodney C.	York City	Halifax Town
3 Russell, Craig S.	Manchester City	Darlington
20 Salako, John A.	Fulham	Charlton Athletic
17 Searle, Damon P.	Carlisle United	Rochdale
3 Simpson, Philip M.	Yeovil Town	Enfield
13 Slinn, Kevin P.	Boston United	Stamford AFC
11 Smith, Christopher G.	Blakenall	Solihull Borough
10 Smith, Philip A.	Millwall	Ashford Town
18 Stoker, Gareth	Rochdale	Scarborough
17 Stowell, Matthew D.	Bristol City	Yeovil Town
23 Sucharwycz, Gary	Hucknall Town	Spalding United
24 Taylor, Stuart J.	Arsenal	Bristol Rovers
8 Thirlwell, Paul	Sunderland	Swindon Town
17 Todd, Lee	Bradford City	Walsall
24 Trees, Robert V.	Bristol Rovers	Altrincham
22 Turner, Michael C.	Barnsley	Lincoln City
15 Vaughan, Anthony J.	Manchester City	Cardiff City
10 Walker, Keith C.	Swansea City	Merthyr Tydfil
24 Webster, Adam	Notts County	Grantham Town
10 Westcott, John P.J.	Brighton & Hove Albion	Newport (IW)
20 Whitley, James	Manchester City	Blackpool
8 Williams, Andrew P.	Southampton	Swindon Town
6 Williams, Anthony S.	Blackburn Rovers	Gillingham
27 Wright, Ian E.	West Ham United	Nottingham Forest
8 Wright, Stephen J.	Liverpool	Crewe Alexandra

October 1999

25 Arnott, Andrew J.	Brighton & Hove Albion	Colchester United
25 Aspinall, Warren	Colchester United	Brighton & Hove Albion
21 Beadle, Peter C.	Notts County	Bristol City
28 Bent, Marcus N.	Port Vale	Sheffield United
14 Bradbury, Lee M.	Crystal Palace	Portsmouth
21 Carbone, Benito	Sheffield Wednesday	Aston Villa
18 Carruthers, Martin G.	Darlington	Southend United
18 Cullip, Daniel	Brentford	Brighton & Hove Albion
1 Gallacher, Kevin W.	Blackburn Rovers	Newcastle United
14 Hreidarsson, Hermann	Brentford	Wimbledon
14 MacKenzie, Neil D.	Stoke City	Cambridge United
25 Marcelo	Sheffield United	Birmingham City
29 Marshall, Scott R.	Southampton	Brentford
28 Mercer, William	Chesterfield	Bristol City
1 Miller, Charles D.	Rangers	Watford

8 Mitten, Charles H.	Dover Athletic	Gillingham
15 Morris, Lee	Sheffield United	Derby County
21 Ndah, George E.	Swindon Town	Wolverhampton Wanderers
22 Nwadike, Chukweumeka B.	Grantham Town	Kings Lynn
29 Oakes, Michael C.	Aston Villa	Wolverhampton Wanderers
1 Pullen, James	Heybridge Swifts	Ipswich Town
25 Ribeiro, Bruno M.F.	Leeds United	Sheffield United
22 Russell, Matthew L.	Halifax Town	Scarborough
20 Salako, John A.	Fulham	Charlton Athletic
21 Thompson, Glyn W.	Shrewsbury Town	Fulham
7 Whitehead, Philip M.	West Bromwich Albion	Reading
22 Wilder, Christopher J.	Brighton & Hove Albion	Halifax Town
8 Williams, Andrew P.	Southampton	Swindon Town

Temporary transfers

1 Abou, Samassi	West Ham United	Walsall
4 Agogo, Manuel	Sheffield Wednesday	Chester City
18 Agyemang, Patrick	Wimbledon	Brentford
21 Alexander, Gary G.	West Ham United	Exeter City
29 Ansell, Gary S.	Barnet	Carshalton Athletic
29 Barry, Peter L.	Nuneaton Borough	Racing Club Warwick
1 Bartley, Daniel R.	Cambridge City	Bishop Stortford
19 Beadle, Peter C.	Notts County	Bristol City
7 Beresford, John	Southampton	Birmingham City
15 Bignall, Michael G.	Aylesbury United	Boreham Wood
4 Blackwood, Michael	Aston Villa	Chester City
21 Bradley, Shayne	Southampton	Exeter City
15 Branston, Guy P.B.	Leicester City	Rotherham United
29 Brennan, James G.	Bristol City	Nottingham Forest
30 Brockett, Luke	Chesham United	Chalfont St Peter
22 Brown, Greg J.	Macclesfield Town	Morecambe
21 Canham, Scott W.	Leyton Orient	Chesham United
22 Cartwright, Mark N.	Wrexham	Newry Town
10 Clarke, Adrian J.	Southend United	Carlisle United
29 Cleaver, Christopher W.	Peterborough United	Kings Lynn
14 Conner, Stephen J.	Dagenham & Redbridge	Billericay Town
29 Cooper, Mark N.	Rushden & Diamonds	Telford United
30 Corns, Stuart R.	Telford United	Droylsden
1 Dean, Michael J.	AFC Bournemouth	Basingstoke Town
8 Dibble, Andrew G.	Hartlepool United	Carlisle United
11 Di Lella, Gustavo M.	Hartlepool United	Blyth Spartans
9 Douglas, Andrew S.	Carlisle United	Gretna
1 Everitt, Leigh A.	Nuneaton Borough	Stafford Rangers
7 Fenton, Nicholas L.	Manchester City	Notts County
30 Fiore, Mark J.	Chesham United	Chalfont St Peter
18 Fitzpatrick, Lee G.	Blackburn Rovers	Hartlepool United
18 Forbes, Terrell	West Ham United	AFC Bournemouth
11 Glennon, Matthew	Bolton Wanderers	Port Vale
4 Grant, Anthony J.	Everton	Tranmere Rovers
4 Green, Richard E.	Walsall	Rochdale
8 Griffin, Charles J.	Swindon Town	Yeovil Town
1 Harrison, Gerald R.	Sunderland	Hull City
14 Hockton, Danny J.	Millwall	Leyton Orient
15 Housham, Steven J.	Scunthorpe United	Gainsborough Trinity
15 Hulse, Robert W.	Crewe Alexandra	Hyde United
15 Hume, Mark A.	Doncaster Rovers	Gainsborough Trinity
1 Ingham, Michael G.	Sunderland	Carlisle United
16 Janney, Mark	Dagenham & Redbridge	Braintree Town
15 Johnston, Allan	Sunderland	Birmingham City
10 Johnston, Ray	Bristol Rovers	Southampton

4 Jones, Mark A.	Wolverhampton Wanderers	Cheltenham Town
15 Kelly, Paul L.M.	Chesham United	Boreham Wood
30 Killick, Thomas M.	Basingstoke Town	Walton & Hersham
7 Knight, Richard	Derby County	Hull City
18 Lee, David M.	Wigan Athletic	Blackpool
10 Marcelle, Clinton S.	Barnsley	Scunthorpe United
15 Marshall, Scott R.	Southampton	Brentford
13 McLaren, Andrew	Reading	Livingston
25 Midgley, Neil	Ipswich Town	Luton Town
11 Miller, Matthew	Hampton & Richmond Borough	Fleet Town
14 Morris, Andrew D.	Rochdale	Scarborough
18 Morrish, Adam	Southend United	Dartford
11 Muggleton, Carl D.	Stoke City	Mansfield Town
30 Naylor, Dominic J.	Stevenage Borough	Dagenham & Redbridge
7 Omoyimni, Emmanuel	West Ham United	Gillingham
4 Pates, Bradley J.	Macclesfield Town	Winsford Town
8 Perez, Lionel	Newcastle United	Scunthorpe United
7 Perkins, Christopher P.	Hartlepool United	Chesterfield
23 Phelan, Terrence M.	Everton	Crystal Palace
23 Pinnock, James E.	Gillingham	Margate
22 Porter, Andrew M.	Wigan Athletic	Mansfield Town
22 Reece, Dominic M.A.	Hednesford Town	Atherstone United
22 Ribeiro, Bruno M.F.	Leeds United	Sheffield United
24 Rowe, Rodney C.	York City	Halifax Town
3 Russell, Craig S.	Manchester City	Darlington
18 Searle, Damon	Carlisle United	Rochdale
8 Simpson, Philip M.	Yeovil Town	Enfield
11 Smith, Philip A.	Millwall	Ashford Town
16 Smyth, Peter W.	Leigh RMI	Radcliffe Borough
11 Stoker, Gareth	Rochdale	Scarborough
20 Stowell, Matthew D.	Bristol City	Yeovil Town
19 Strong, Grant	Chelmsford City	Whitham Town
14 Thirlwell, Paul	Sunderland	Swindon Town
12 Thompson, Richard O.	Wycombe Wanderers	Kingstonian
14 Thurstan, Mark R.	Carlisle United	Gretna
26 Turkington, Edmond B.	Altrincham	Leigh RMI
30 Turpin, Simon J.	Leigh RMI	Winsford United
22 Westcott, John P.J.	Brighton & Hove Albion	Bognor Regis Town
29 Williams, Richard J.	Nuneaton Borough	Stafford Rangers
22 Wilmot, Ellis J.	Bristol City	Weymouth
30 Winter, Steven D.	Forest Green Rovers	Basingstoke Town
22 Wreh, Christopher	Arsenal	Birmingham City

November 1999

24 Alcide, Colin J.	Hull City	York City
19 Branston, Guy P.B.	Leicester City	Rotherham United
3 Brennan, James G.	Bristol City	Nottingham Forest
5 Burns, John C.	Nottingham Forest	Bristol City
19 Carr, Graeme	Scarborough	Workington
5 Cox, Neil J.	Bolton Wanderers	Watford
30 Cutler, Neil A.	Chester City	Aston Villa
25 D'Auria, David A.	Hull City	Chesterfield
19 Ejiofor, Emeke	Moor Green	Rocester
5 Galloway, Michael A.	Gillingham	Chesterfield
25 Gayle, John	Scunthorpe United	Shrewsbury Town
30 Gibbons, Daniel	Weston-Super-Mare	Newport (IW)
1 Granville, Daniel P.	Leeds United	Manchester City
11 Gutzmore, Leon	Aldershot Town	Bedford Town
19 Jones, Graeme A.	Wigan Athletic	St Johnstone
24 McAvoy, Andrew D.	Blackburn Rovers	Hartlepool United

12 Millen, Keith D.	Watford	Bristol City
15 Moore, Darren M.	Bradford City	Portsmouth
12 Payne, Grant	Woking	Aldershot Town
5 Peacock, Lee A.	Mansfield Town	Manchester City
4 Perkins, Christopher P.	Hartlepool United	Chesterfield
30 Peron, Jean F.	Portsmouth	Wigan Athletic
2 Rea, Simon	Birmingham City	Peterborough United
25 Rowe, Rodney C.	York City	Gillingham
4 Rowland, Lynden J.	Halesowen Town	Kings Lynn
19 Smith, Danny	Kingstonian	Hampton & Richmond Borough
30 Taylor, Robert A.	Gillingham	Manchester City
18 Todd, Andrew J.J.	Bolton Wanderers	Charlton Athletic
17 Walters, Mark E.	Swindon Town	Bristol Rovers

Temporary transfers

11 Agogo, Manuel	Sheffield Wednesday	Chesterfield
18 Agyemang, Patrick	Wimbledon	Brentford
23 Alcide, Colin J.	Hull City	York City
5 Allsop, Daniel	Manchester City	Notts County
30 Barry, Peter L.	Nuneaton Borough	Racing Club Warwick
12 Beck, Mikkel	Derby County	Nottingham Forest
19 Bernard, Curtis J.	Barnsley	Emley
26 Betsy, Kevin E.L.	Fulham	Hull City
9 Blaney, Steven D.	Billericay Town	Heybridge Swifts
27 Bonfield, Darren	Hitchen Town	Hemel Hempstead Town
11 Brady, Matthew J.	Boreham Wood	Wycombe Wanderers
25 Branch, Paul M.	Everton	Wolverhampton Wanderers
11 Brissett, Jason C.	Walsall	Cheltenham Town
19 Brown, Michael R.	Manchester City	Portsmouth
23 Bywater, Stephen M.	West Ham United	Hull City
4 Cadamarteri, Daniel L.	Everton	Fulham
22 Canham, Scott W.	Leyton Orient	Chesham United
12 Carmody, Michael	Altrincham	Ashton United
12 Carrick, Michael	West Ham United	Swindon Town
26 Chettle, Stephen	Nottingham Forest	Barnsley
12 Clare, Daryl A.	Grimsby Town	Northampton Town
12 Clarke, Daniel N.	Enfield	Leyton Pennant
13 Cleeve, Anthony G.	Basingstoke Town	Hampton & Richmond Borough
23 Clement, Neil	Chelsea	Brentford
27 Corns, Stuart R.	Telford United	Droylsden
18 Critchley, Neil	Crewe Alexandra	Hyde United
19 Curtis, John C.K.	Manchester United	Barnsley
24 Davies, Jamie	Swansea City	Llanelli
9 Di Lella, Gustavo M.	Hartlepool United	Blyth Spartans
18 Donnelly, Mark P.	Bury	Whitby Town
12 Douglas, Andrew S.	Carlisle United	Gretna
3 Dryden, Richard A.	Southampton	Stoke City
1 Durnin, John P.	Portsmouth	Blackpool
12 Farrelly, Gareth	Everton	Bolton Wanderers
7 Fenton, Nicholas L.	Manchester City	Notts County
12 Gibbons, Daniel	Weston-Super-Mare	Newport (IW)
18 Graham, Gareth L.	Brentford	Crawley Town
5 Greenacre, Christopher M.	Manchester City	Mansfield Town
9 Grime, Dominic	Boreham Wood	Chertsey Town
4 Hamilton, Ian R.	Sheffield United	Grimsby Town
15 Hulse, Robert W.	Crewe Alexandra	Hyde United
19 Hume, Mark A.	Doncaster Rovers	Barrow
22 Humphreys, Ritchie J.	Sheffield Wednesday	Cardiff City
7 Johnston, Ray	Bristol Rovers	Southampton
4 Keeble, Shaun R.	Kings Lynn	Raunds Town

28 Lee, David M.	Wigan Athletic	Blackpool
1 Linger, Paul H.	Billericay Town	Braintree Town
26 Lisbie, Kevin A.	Charlton Athletic	Reading
5 Lynch, Paul E.	Accrington Stanley	Netherfield Kendal
20 Marcelle, Clinton S.	Barnsley	Scunthorpe United
19 Marshall, Dwight W.	Kingstonian	Slough Town
12 Mason, Gary	Manchester City	Hartlepool United
18 Messer, Gary M.	Bury	Whitby Town
12 Miller, Matthew	Hampton & Richmond Borough	Fleet Town
15 Morris, Andrew D.	Rochdale	Scarborough
19 Morrish, Adam	Southend United	Dartford
9 Niemi, Antti	Rangers	Charlton Athletic
19 O'Kane, John A.	Everton	Bolton Wanderers
1 Ormerod, Anthony	Middlesbrough	York City
1 Perez, Lionel	Newcastle United	Scunthorpe United
1 Perkins, Christopher P.	Southend United	Kettering Town
25 Phelan, Terrence M.	Everton	Crystal Palace
30 Planck, Thomas	Margate	Sittingbourne
5 Potter, Daniel R.J.	Exter City	Weymouth
22 Price, Ryan	Macclesfield Town	Telford United
4 Ritchie, Stuart A.	Havant & Waterlooville	Wokingham Town
11 Rowbotham, Darren	Exeter City	Leyton Orient
3 Russell, Craig S.	Manchester City	Darlington
11 Sailesman, Neil A.	Burton Albion	Rocester
17 Searle, Damon	Carlisle United	Rochdale
15 Smith, Philip A.	Millwall	Ashford Town
5 Soares, Clifton J.	Newport (IW)	Wokingham Town
1 Spink, Dean P.	Wrexham	Shrewsbury Town
11 Stoker, Gareth	Rochdale	Scarborough
25 Stowell, Matthew D.	Bristol City	Rushden & Diamonds
26 Thorpe, Anthony	Bristol City	Luton Town
12 Thurstan, Mark R.	Carlisle United	Gretna
23 Vaughan, John	Lincoln City	Colchester United
19 Watkins, Dale A.	Cheltenham Town	Kettering Town
19 Watts, Stephen	Leyton Orient	Welling United
23 Westcott, John P.J.	Brighton & Hove Albion	Bognor Regis Town
26 White, Alan	Luton Town	Colchester United
5 Wilkinson, Lee A.	Spalding United	Hucknall Town
30 Williams, Richard J.	Nuneaton Borough	Stafford Rangers
10 Williams, Ryan N.	Tranmere Rovers	Chesterfield
12 Wright, Stephen J.	Liverpool	Crewe Alexandra

December 1999

23 Appleton, Arthur	Yeovil Town	Mangotsfield United
9 Ball, Kevin A.	Sunderland	Fulham
21 Brady, Matthew	Boreham Wood	Wycombe Wanderers
20 Brown, John K.	Blackburn Rovers	Barnsley
2 Burley, Craig W.	Celtic	Derby County
23 Campbell, Stephen J.	Chippenham Town	Devizes Town
15 Chettle, Stephen	Nottingham Forest	Barnsley
15 Dunne, Joseph J.	Dover Athletic	Colchester United
10 Eadie, Darren M.	Norwich City	Leicester City
1 Ellender, Paul	Altrincham	Scarborough
23 Emerson, Augusto T.	Sheffield Wednesday	Chelsea
6 Everitt, Leigh A.	Nuneaton Borough	Stafford Rangers
17 Farrelly, Gareth	Everton	Bolton Wanderers
10 Goodwin, Shaun	Doncaster Rovers	Altrincham
24 Grant, Anthony J.	Everton	Manchester City
16 Griffiths, Carl B.	Port Vale	Leyton Orient
17 Hanlon, Ritchie K.	Welling United	Peterborough United

3 Hiley, Scott P.	Southampton	Portsmouth
16 Kilbane, Kevin D.	West Bromwich Albion	Sunderland
10 McLoughlin, Alan F.	Portsmouth	Wigan Athletic
24 Nartey, Joseph H.	Aldershot Town	Chesham United
17 O'Connor, Joseph N.	Nuneaton Borough	Kingstonian
22 O'Kane, John A.	Everton	Bolton Wanderers
8 Ovens, Steven	Witney Town	Tiverton Town
17 Palmer, Carlton L.	Nottingham Forest	Coventry City
3 Reilly, Alan	Manchester City	Halifax Town
7 Riza, Omer K.	Arsenal	West Ham United
8 Simpson, Fitzroy	Portsmouth	Hearts
24 Stevens, David P.	Dulwich Hamlet	Hayes
21 Stowell, Matthew D.	Bristol City	Rushden & Diamonds
16 Tate, Christopher D.	Halifax Town	Scarborough
3 Tate, Steven K.	Havant & Waterlooville	Weymouth
17 Walker, Leigh D.	Sheffield United	Barnsley
22 Watkins, Dale A.	Cheltenham Town	Kettering Town
17 Wilcox, Jason M.	Blackburn Rovers	Leeds United
10 Williams, Gareth J.	Hull City	Scarborough

Temporary transfers

3 Ablett, Gary I.	Birmingham City	Wycombe Wanderers
17 Agogo, Manuel	Sheffield Wednesday	Lincoln City
21 Agyemang, Patrick	Wimbledon	Brentford
24 Aiston, Sam J.	Sunderland	Shrewsbury Town
21 Aldridge, Martin J.	Blackpool	Rushden & Diamonds
30 Allsop, Michael P.	Burton Albion	Belper Town
9 Angell, Brett A.M.	Stockport County	Notts County
27 Barry, Peter L.	Nuneaton Borough	Redditch United
30 Bennett, Thomas M.	Stockport County	Walsall
17 Beresford, David	Huddersfield Town	Preston North End
3 Bird, Anthony	Swansea City	Merthyr Tydfil
17 Black, Thomas R.	Arsenal	Bristol City
3 Blake, Marvin	Nuneaton Borough	Atherstone United
10 Bolt, Daniel A.	Woking	Dover Athletic
29 Bramble, Titus M.	Ipswich Town	Colchester United
13 Brissett, Jason C.	Walsall	Cheltenham Town
23 Broad, Stephen	Chelsea	Hayes
2 Brockett, Luke	Chesham United	Chalfont St Peter
10 Bromby, Leigh	Sheffield Wednesday	Mansfield Town
7 Brough, Michael	Notts County	Spalding United
17 Brown, Michael R.	Manchester City	Sheffield United
3 Cadette, Nathan D.	Cardiff City	Inter-Cardiff
22 Canham, Scott W.	Leyton Orient	Chesham United
17 Carrick, Michael	West Ham United	Swindon Town
20 Cartwright, Mark N.	Wrexham	Bury
10 Carty, Paul	Worcester City	Nuneaton Borough
24 Chambers, Leroy D.	Altrincham	Kettering Town
3 Cheal, Mark	Lancaster City	Netherfield Kendal
12 Clare, Daryl A.	Grimsby Town	Northampton Town
10 Clark, Dean W.	Brentford	Uxbridge
21 Clement, Neil	Chelsea	Brentford
20 Critchley, Neil	Crewe Alexandra	Hyde United
17 Culbertson, Richard D.J.	Swindon Town	Larne
24 Culkin, Nicholas J.	Manchester United	Hull City
17 Cullen, David J.	Sheffield United	Halifax Town
20 Curtis, John C.K.	Manchester United	Barnsley
16 Dalton, Paul	Huddersfield Town	Carlisle United
2 Davidson, Daniel	Burton Albion	Belper Town
3 Davison, Aidan J.	Sheffield United	Bradford City

13 Donnelly, Mark P.	Bury	Whitby Town
2 Dowe, Julian L.	Rochdale	Burton Albion
6 Dryden, Richard A.	Southampton	Stoke City
3 Durnin, John P.	Portsmouth	Carlisle United
9 Ellington, Lee S.	Hull City	Altrincham
3 Elliott, Stuart T.	Newcastle United	AFC Bournemouth
7 Fenton, Nicholas L.	Manchester City	Notts County
4 Flitter, Matthew A.H.	Chesham United	Hampton & Richmond Borough
6 Greenacre, Christopher M.	Manchester City	Mansfield Town
7 Gregory, Neil R.	Colchester United	Canvey Island
22 Grime, Dominic	Boreham Wood	Gravesend & Northfleet
16 Hadland, Philip J.	Reading	Aldershot Town
17 Hall, Paul A.	Coventry City	Sheffield United
17 Harper, Kevin P.	Derby County	Walsall
10 Hendry, Iain	Woking	Molesey
14 Holloway, Darren	Sunderland	Bolton Wanderers
7 Howell, Dean G.	Notts County	Spalding United
24 Hughes, John P.	Chelsea	Crewe Alexandra
17 Hulse, Robert W.	Crewe Alexandra	Hyde United
19 Hume, Mark A.	Doncaster Rovers	Barrow
21 Hurdle, Augustus A.J.	Basingstoke Town	Ashford Town
3 Kelly, Gavin R.	Tottenham Hotspur	Chelmsford City
3 Kenna, Warren J.	Peterborough United	Cambridge City
26 Killick, Thomas M.	Basingstoke Town	Fleet Town
24 Kippe, Frode	Liverpool	Stoke City
3 Knight, Richard	Derby County	Macclesfield Town
10 Lindley, James E.	Notts County	Ilkeston Town
2 Lynch, Paul E.	Accrington Stanley	Netherfield Kendal
2 Lyttle, Gerard F.	Peterborough United	Kingstonian
24 McGovern, Brian	Arsenal	Queens Park Rangers
3 Makel, Lee R.	Heart of Midlothian	Portsmouth
19 Marshall, Dwight W.	Kingstonian	Slough Town
15 Mason, Gary	Manchester City	Hartlepool United
28 Matthews, Robert D.	Stockport County	Blackpool
24 May, David	Manchester United	Huddersfield Town
3 Meredith, Thomas J.A.	St Albans City	Boreham Wood
15 Messer, Gary	Bury	Whitby Town
10 Metcalfe, Christian W.	Hayes	Boreham Wood
25 Mings, Adrian	Forest Green Rovers	Yate Town
17 Morrison, David E.	Leyton Orient	Stevenage Borough
11 Mputu, Fiston	Hampton & Richmond Borough	Chertsey Town
9 Muggleton, Carl D.	Stoke City	Chesterfield
3 Newton, Christopher J.	Halifax Town	Barrow
30 Nicholls, Mark	Chelsea	Reading
21 Omoyimni, Emmanuel	West Ham United	Scunthorpe United
1 Ormerod, Anthony	Middlesbrough	York City
24 Pepper, Colin N.	Aberdeen	Southend United
2 Perez, Lionel	Newcastle United	Scunthorpe United
1 Perkins, Christopher P.	Southend United	Kettering Town
30 Phelan, Terrence M.	Everton	Crystal Palace
17 Pinamonte, Lorenzo	Bristol City	Brighton & Hove Albion
2 Potter, Graham S.	West Bromwich Albion	Reading
17 Potter, Lee	Bolton Wanderers	Halifax Town
3 Quailey, Brian S.	West Bromwich Albion	Blackpool
1 Quinton, Bradley L.J.	Bishop's Stortford	Leyton Pennant
17 Randall, Adrian J.	Forest Green Rovers	Weymouth
10 Rew, Ian K.	Newport (IW)	Wokingham Town
17 Rigby, Malcolm	Stafford Rangers	Northwich Victoria
22 Ritchie, Paul M.	Heart of Midlothian	Bolton Wanderers
24 Scope, Tynan G.A.	Bristol City	Chesham United

3 Shuttlewood, Justin	Forest Green Rovers	Salisbury City
16 Smith, Christopher A.	Reading	Hayes
3 Thompson, Christopher N.	Ilkeston Town	Stamford
1 Thorpe, Anthony L.	Bristol City	Luton Town
3 Walker, Richard S.	Crewe Alexandra	Northwich Victoria
17 Ward, Darren P.	Watford	Queens Park Rangers
16 Ware, Paul D.	Macclesfield Town	Nuneaton Borough
3 Webster, Adam	Notts County	Bedworth United
17 White, Daniel A.J.	Hampton & Richmond Borough	Leatherhead
28 Williams, Richard J.	Nuneaton Borough	Stafford Rangers
14 Williams, Ryan N.	Tranmere Rovers	Chesterfield
13 Woolsey, Jeffrey A.	Dagenham & Redbridge	Enfield
21 Xavier, Mark J.	Basingstoke Town	Ashford Town
30 Zamora, Robert L.	Bristol Rovers	Bath City

January 2000

26 Barry, Peter L.	Nuneaton Borough	Redditch United
20 Branch, Paul M.	Everton	Wolverhampton Wanderers
14 Brown, Michael R.	Manchester City	Sheffield United
10 Davies, Simon	Peterborough United	Tottenham Hotspur
17 Dunbavin, Ian S.	Liverpool	Shrewsbury Town
10 Etherington, Matthew	Peterborough United	Tottenham Hotspur
27 Fitzpatrick, Lee G.	Blackburn Rovers	Hartlepool United
28 Gardner, Anthony	Port Vale	Tottenham Hotspur
18 Goldbaek, Bjarne	Chelsea	Fulham
1 Gooden, Ty M.	Swindon Town	Gillingham
24 Greenacre, Christopher M.	Manchester City	Mansfield Town
21 Hemmings, Anthony G.	Ilkeston Town	Chester City
21 Hughes, Ceri M.	Wimbledon	Portsmouth
20 Jaszczun, Anthony J.	Aston Villa	Blackpool
28 Lester, Jack W.	Grimsby Town	Nottingham Forest
5 Onuora, Ifem	Swindon Town	Gillingham
21 Potter, Lee	Bolton Wanderers	Halifax Town
12 Rigby, Malcolm R.	Stafford Rangers	Northwich Victoria
28 Svensson, Matthias	Crystal Palace	Charlton Athletic
21 Williams, Gary L.	Accrington Stanley	Doncaster Rovers
27 Williams, Richard J.	Nuneaton Borough	Stafford Rangers

Temporary transfers

24 Aiston, Sam J.	Sunderland	Shrewsbury Town
5 Aldridge, Martin J.	Blackpool	Rushden & Diamonds
14 Armstrong, Paul	Stevenage Borough	Aylesbury United
21 Babb, Philip A.	Liverpool	Tranmere Rovers
28 Baker, Matthew C.	Hull City	Bradford Park Avenue
29 Barker, Daniel T.	Basingstoke Town	Fleet Town
24 Behzadi, Bobby	Stevenage Borough	Wealdstone
17 Beresford, David	Huddersfield Town	Preston North End
21 Bettney, Scott	Sheffield Wednesday	Hednesford Town
3 Bonfield, Darren	Hitchin Town	Hemel Hempstead Town
4 Branch, Paul M.	Everton	Wolverhampton Wanderers
4 Brockett, Luke	Chesham United	Chalfont St Peter
12 Bromby, Leigh	Sheffield Wednesday	Mansfield Town
6 Brough, Michael	Notts County	Spalding United
6 Brown, Aaron W.	Bristol City	Exeter City
14 Bullock, Martin J.	Barnsley	Port Vale
7 Byrne, Shaun R.	West Ham United	Bristol Rovers
3 Cheal, Mark	Lancaster City	Netherfield Kendal
12 Clare, Daryl A.	Grimsby Town	Northampton Town
10 Clark, Dean W.	Brentford	Uxbridge
28 Cooksey, Scott A.	Shrewsbury Town	Hereford United
28 Critchley, Neil	Crewe Alexandra	Hyde United

21 Cullen, David J.	Sheffield United	Halifax Town
7 Curran, Danny	Leyton Orient	Purfleet
4 Davison, Aidan J.	Sheffield United	Bradford City
18 Doane, Ben N.D.C.	Sheffield United	Kettering Town
21 Drake, Kieron A.	Maidenhead United	Burnham
19 Dunwell, Richard K.	Enfield	Gravesend & Northfleet
20 Earnshaw, Robert	Cardiff City	Greenock Morton
21 Edwards, Ross P.	Gravesend & Northfleet	Croydon
5 Elliott, Stuart T.	Newcastle United	AFC Bournemouth
17 Evans, Kevin	Leeds United	Swansea City
7 Eyjolfsson, Sigurdur	Walsall	Chester City
14 Gledhill, Lee	Barnet	Slough Town
18 Glennon, Matthew W.	Bolton Wanderers	Stockport County
14 Gordon, Daniel	Aylesbury United	Tring Town
7 Green, Richard E.	Walsall	Northampton Town
7 Greenacre, Christopher M.	Manchester City	Mansfield Town
4 Gregory, Neil R.	Colchester United	Canvey Island
19 Harper, Kevin P.	Derby County	Walsall
14 Hendry, Iain	Woking	Molesey
21 Hibbins, John J.	Sheffield Wednesday	Hednesford Town
7 Hobson, Gary	Brighton & Hove Albion	Chester City
6 Hodson, Benjamin M.	Hayes	Wealdstone
21 Holmshaw, James	Worksop Town	Matlock Town
20 Holt, Michael A.	Rochdale	Northwich Victoria
21 Hoult, Russell	Derby County	Portsmouth
18 Housham, Steven J.	Scunthorpe United	Barrow
6 Howell, Dean G.	Notts County	Spalding United
21 Hughes, James J.	Cardiff City	Cwmbran Town
22 Hurdle, Augustus A.J.	Basingstoke Town	Crawley Town
7 Hylgaard, Morten L.	Coventry City	Scunthorpe United
14 Jackson, Mark G.	Leeds United	Barnsley
27 Johnston, Allan	Sunderland	Bolton Wanderers
28 Jones, Jonathan B.	Chester City	Caernafon Town
21 Jones, Stephen G.	Bristol City	Brentford
14 Kadi, Junior	Kingstonian	Hampton & Richmond Borough
6 Kelly, Gavin R.	Tottenham Hotspur	Chelmsford City
28 Kelly, Seamus	Cardiff City	Merthyr Tydfil
23 Kippe, Frode	Liverpool	Stoke City
19 Knight, Richard	Derby County	Oxford United
3 Lee, Jason	Chesterfield	Peterborough United
7 Lindley, James E.	Notts County	Ilkeston Town
3 McCammon, Mark J.	Charlton Athletic	Swindon Town
28 McCormack, Francis	St Albans City	Sutton United
20 McCoy, Barry J.	Aldershot Town	Fleet Town
23 McGovern, Brian	Arsenal	Queens Park Rangers
1 Meredith, Thomas J.A.	St Albans City	Boreham Wood
13 Metcalfe, Christian W.	Hayes	Boreham Wood
20 Morrison, David E.	Leyton Orient	Dover Athletic
10 Muggleton, Carl D.	Stoke City	Chesterfield
20 Notman, Alexander M.	Manchester United	Sheffield United
23 Omoyimni, Emmanuel	West Ham United	Scunthorpe United
3 Onuora, Ifem	Swindon Town	Gillingham
18 O'Shea, John F.	Manchester United	AFC Bournemouth
18 Pinamonte, Lorenzo	Bristol City	Brighton & Hove Albion
28 Potter, Daniel R.J.	Exeter City	Salisbury City
22 Randall, Adrian J.	Forest Green Rovers	Weymouth
19 Rankin, Isiah	Bradford City	Birmingham City
13 Rew, Ian K.	Newport (IW)	Wokingham Town
10 Richardson, Kevin	Barnsley	Blackpool
14 Roberts, Christian J.	Cardiff City	Drogheda

20 Saunders, Lee	Ilkeston Town	Shepshed Dynamo
29 Shaw, Darren R.	Stafford Rangers	Sutton Coldfield Town
14 Shuttlewood, Justin	Forest Green Rovers	Salisbury City
20 Strevens, Benjamin J.	Barnet	Slough Town
21 Sucharwycz, Gary	Hucknall Town	Matlock Town
21 Taylor, Gareth K.	Manchester City	Port Vale
18 Taylor, Martin	Blackburn Rovers	Darlington
28 Taylor, Stephen C.	Kidderminster Harriers	Halesowen Town
27 Thomas, David J.	Cardiff City	Drogheda
20 Thomas, Wayne	Walsall	Shrewsbury Town
21 Thompson, Glyn W.	Fulham	Mansfield Town
21 Turner, Michael C.	Barnsley	Finn Harps
22 Vaughan, John	Lincoln City	Chesterfield
14 Vernazza, Paulo A.P.	Arsenal	Portsmouth
4 Walker, Richard S.	Crewe Alexandra	Northwich Victoria
14 Ward, Darren P.	Watford	Queens Park Rangers
13 Ware, Paul D.	Macclesfield Town	Nuneaton Borough
1 Webster, Adam	Notts County	Bedworth United
28 Westcott, John P.J.	Brighton & Hove Albion	Sutton United
28 White, Thomas M.	Bristol Rovers	Hereford United
28 Williams, Anthony S.	Blackburn Rovers	Macclesfield Town
21 Wilson, Scott A.	Rochdale	Altrincham
12 Yorke-Johnson, Ross	Brighton & Hove Albion	Colchester United
February 2000		
11 Abbey, Zema	Hitchin Town	Cambridge United
11 Baptiste, Rocky	Wealdstone	Staines Town
24 Bennett, Gary	Sudbury AFC	Chelmsford City
1 Butler, Martin N.	Cambridge United	Reading
11 Collymore, Stanley V.	Aston Villa	Leicester City
4 Cox, Ian G.	AFC Bournemouth	Burnley
4 D'Jaffo, Laurent	Stockport County	Sheffield United
1 Ford, Ryan	Manchester United	Notts County
4 Frail, Stephen	Tranmere Rovers	St Johnstone
18 Gibb, Alistair S.	Northampton Town	Stockport County
4 Gregory, Neil R.	Colchester United	Canvey Island
11 Hayes, Adrian M.	Diss Town	Boston United
3 Holland, Christopher J.	Birmingham City	Huddersfield Town
17 Lawson, Ian J.	Bury	Stockport County
10 McIntosh, Martin	Stockport County	Hibernian
4 Marshall, Dwight W.	Kingstonian	Slough Town
28 Melton, Stephen	Nottingham Forest	Stoke City
15 Miller, Alan J.	West Bromwich Albion	Blackburn Rovers
7 Moore, Christian	Ilkeston Town	Burton Albion
11 Newell, Michael C.	Doncaster Rovers	Blackpool
2 Norris, David M.	Boston United	Bolton Wanderers
4 Pinamonte, Lorenzo	Bristol City	Brentford
3 Quailey, Brian S.	West Bromwich Albion	Scunthorpe United
18 Roberts, Neil W.	Wrexham	Wigan Athletic
28 Sheerin, Joseph E.	Chelsea	AFC Bournemouth
3 Smith, Martin	Sheffield United	Huddersfield Town
1 Stewart, Marcus P.	Huddersfield Town	Ipswich Town
22 Thomas, Wayne	Walsall	Shrewsbury Town
4 Torpey, Stephen D.J.	Bristol City	Scunthorpe United
18 Watson, Liam	Runcorn	Accrington Stanley
14 Williams, Ryan N.	Tranmere Rovers	Chesterfield
14 Yorke-Johnson, Ross	Brighton & Hove Albion	Colchester United
Temporary transfers		
25 Allsop, Daniel	Manchester City	Wrexham
24 Angell, Brett A.M.	Stockport County	Preston North End

11 Armstrong, Paul	Stevenage Borough	Aylesbury United
26 Ayres, James M.	Luton Town	Stevenage Borough
18 Barnett, David K.	Lincoln City	Forest Green Rovers
11 Beck, Mikkel	Derby County	Queens Park Rangers
21 Behzadi, Bobby	Stevenage Borough	Wealdstone
3 Bennett, Frank	Bristol Rovers	Exeter City
11 Boertien, Paul	Derby County	Crewe Alexandra
17 Bower, Mark J.	Bradford City	York City
18 Brooker, Paul	Fulham	Brighton & Hove Albion
4 Broughton, Drewe O.	Peterborough United	Nuneaton Borough
29 Burgess, Richard D.	Stoke City	Kidderminster Harriers
25 Campbell, James R.	Peterborough United	Spalding United
15 Canoville, Trevor	Hampton & Richmond Borough	Chertsey Town
11 Carmody, Michael	Altrincham	Ashton United
23 Carrick, Michael	West Ham United	Birmingham City
1 Cheal, Mark	Lancaster City	Netherfield Kendal
9 Clarke, Daniel N.	Enfield	Hertford Town
11 Cleaver, Christopher W.	Peterborough United	Cambridge United
16 Clegg, Michael J.	Manchester United	Ipswich Town
25 Cole, Ashley	Arsenal	Crystal Palace
26 Conner, Stephen J.	Dagenham & Redbridge	Billericay Town
28 Cooksey, Scott A.	Shrewsbury Town	Hereford United
18 Cort, Wayne	Harlow Town	Thame United
22 Cowan, Thomas	Burnley	Cambridge United
11 Crowe, Dean A.	Stoke City	Northampton Town
6 Curran, Danny	Leyton Orient	Purfleet
4 Davison, Aidan J.	Sheffield United	Bradford City
4 Dean, Michael J.	AFC Bournemouth	Dorchester Town
15 Doane, Ben N.D.C.	Sheffield United	Kettering Town
18 Donnelly, Mark P.	Bury	Workington
11 Durnin, John P.	Portsmouth	Carlisle United
24 Edwards, Christian N.H.	Nottingham Forest	Oxford United
29 Edwards, Ross P.	Gravesend & Northfleet	Croydon
25 Elliott, Stuart T.	Newcastle United	Stockport County
25 Evans, Rhys K.	Chelsea	Bristol Rovers
10 Eyjolfsson, Sigurdur	Walsall	Chester City
23 Forssell, Mikael K.	Chelsea	Crystal Palace
18 Fortune, Jonathan J.	Charlton Athletic	Mansfield Town
9 Fredgaard, Carsten	Sunderland	West Bromwich Albion
11 Freestone, Christopher M.	Hartlepool United	Cheltenham Town
4 Gibson, Paul R.	Notts County	Rochdale
14 Gledhill, Lee	Barnet	Slough Town
5 Griemink, Bart	Peterborough United	Swindon Town
2 Grime, Dominic	Boreham Wood	Gravesend & Northfleet
10 Hall, Paul A.	Coventry City	West Bromwich Albion
4 Hanson, David	Nuneaton Borough	Ashton United
21 Harper, Kevin P.	Derby County	Walsall
22 Hawkins, Peter S.	Wimbledon	York City
10 Healy, Brett W.	Nuneaton Borough	Solihull Borough
25 Healy, David J.	Manchester United	Port Vale
15 Hoult, Russell	Derby County	Portsmouth
11 Hutchings, Carl E.	Bristol City	Brentford
11 Hyldgaard, Morten	Coventry City	Scunthorpe United
24 Ilic, Sasa	Charlton Athletic	West Ham United
24 Inglethorpe, Alex M.	Leyton Orient	Exeter City
27 Johnston, Allan	Sunderland	Bolton Wanderers
27 Jones, Stephen G.	Bristol City	Brentford
3 Jones, Stuart C.	Sheffield Wednesday	Torquay United
18 Key, Lance W.	Northwich Victoria	Altrincham
27 Kippe, Frode	Liverpool	Stoke City

25 Knight, Zatyiah	Fulham	Peterborough United
25 Koogi, Anders B.	Peterborough United	Cambridge City
7 Lee, Jason	Chesterfield	Peterborough United
25 Lockwood, Adam B.	Reading	Maidenhead United
18 Love, Andrew M.	Grimsby Town	Ilkeston Town
3 Lumsdon, Christopher	Sunderland	Blackpool
22 Martin, Jae A.	Peterborough United	Welling United
25 McAlindon, Gareth E.	Scarborough	Gateshead
22 McCoy, Barry J.	Aldershot Town	Fleet Town
14 McKinnon, Robert	Heart of Midlothian	Carlisle United
11 McNiven, David J.	Oldham Athletic	Scarborough
10 Metcalfe, Christian W.	Hayes	Boreham Wood
21 Morrison, David E.	Leyton Orient	Dover Athletic
25 Muir, Ian J.	Nuneaton Borough	Moor Green
24 Nicholls, Mark	Chelsea	Grimsby Town
22 Notman, Alexander M.	Manchester United	Sheffield United
25 Omoyimni, Emmanuel	West Ham United	Barnet
8 Osborn, Mark	Wycombe Wanderers	Marlow
18 O'Shea, John F.	Manchester United	AFC Bournemouth
15 Petterson, Andrew K.	Portsmouth	Wolverhampton Wanderers
5 Porter, Andrew M.	Wigan Athletic	Chester City
25 Randall, Adrian J.	Forest Green Rovers	Weymouth
20 Rankin, Isaiah	Bradford City	Birmingham City
11 Richardson, Kevin	Barnsley	Blackpool
24 Roberts, Ben J.	Middlesbrough	Luton Town
18 Rose, Stephen D.	Manchester United	AFC Bournemouth
11 Russell, Craig S.	Manchester City	Oxford United
5 Ryder, Stuart H.	Nuneaton Borough	Stafford Rangers
2 Samuels, Anthony	Stevenage Borough	Boreham Wood
16 Saunders, Lee	Ilkeston Town	Shepshed Dynamo
24 Searle, Stuart A.	Aldershot Town	Molesey
11 Skelton, Craig E.	Darlington	Altrincham
12 Smyth, Peter W.	Leigh RMI	Chorley
18 Stamp, Darryn M.	Scunthorpe United	Halifax Town
16 Swan, Iain	Oldham Athletic	Leigh RMI
18 Telemaque, Errol	Hayes	Molesey
3 Thomas, Anton	Burton Albion	Hinckley United
21 Thompson, Glyn	Fulham	Mansfield Town
25 Tremble, David G.	Scarborough	Gateshead
22 Van der Kwaak, Peter	Reading	Carlisle United
8 Vaughan, Anthony J.	Manchester City	Nottingham Forest
23 Vaughan, John	Lincoln City	Chesterfield
4 Wainwright, Neil	Sunderland	Darlington
5 Walker, Richard S.	Crewe Alexandra	Northwich Victoria
25 Wall, James	Hereford United	Burton Albion
14 Ward, Darren P.	Watford	Queens Park Rangers
19 White, Devon W.	Ilkeston Town	Stafford Rangers
27 White, Thomas M.	Bristol Rovers	Hereford United
15 Williams, Adrian	Wolverhampton Wanderers	Reading
29 Williams, Anthony S.	Blackburn Rovers	Macclesfield Town
26 Woolsey, Jeffrey A.	Dagenham & Redbridge	Billericay Town
1 Zamora, Robert L.	Bristol Rovers	Brighton & Hove Albion

March 2000

7 Allaway, Shaun	Reading	Leeds United
24 Arnison, Paul S.	Newcastle United	Hartlepool United
23 Butler, Philip A.	Port Vale	West Bromwich Albion
15 Calderwood, Colin	Aston Villa	Nottingham Forest
20 Campbell, Neil A.	Southend United	Doncaster Rovers
17 Conner, Stephen J.	Dagenham & Redbridge	Billericay Town

17 Cort, Wayne	Harlow Town	Thame United
3 Cullen, David J.	Sheffield United	Peterborough United
17 Cummins, Michael T.	Middlesbrough	Port Vale
16 Davison, Aidan J.	Sheffield United	Bradford City
16 Derry, Shaun P.	Sheffield United	Portsmouth
9 Edinburgh, Justin C.	Tottenham Hotspur	Portsmouth
1 Fettis, Alan	Blackburn Rovers	York City
2 Fitzpatrick Ian M.	Manchester United	Halifax Town
10 Francis, Kevin M.D.	Oxford United	Stockport County
6 Gill, Wayne J.	Blackburn Rovers	Blackpool
23 Goodlad, Mark	Nottingham Forest	Port Vale
21 Hall, Paul A.	Coventry City	Walsall
6 Harper, Kevin P.	Derby County	Portsmouth
23 Hay, Christopher D.	Swindon Town	Huddersfield Town
3 Hendry, Edward C.J.	Rangers	Coventry City
10 Heskey, Emile W.	Leicester City	Liverpool
8 Hodge, John	Gillingham	Northampton Town
23 Horne, Barry	Huddersfield Town	Sheffield Wednesday
30 Hoult, Russell	Derby County	Portsmouth
10 Hughes, Stephen J.	Arsenal	Everton
23 Hulbert, Robin J.	Swindon Town	Bristol City
23 Igoe, Samuel G.	Portsmouth	Reading
23 Jones, Eifion P.	Liverpool	Blackpool
10 Jones, Stuart C.	Sheffield Wednesday	Torquay United
23 Kerrigan, Steven J.	Shrewsbury Town	Halifax Town
31 Kiely, Paul	Leek Town	Stafford Rangers
22 Lawrence, Matthew J.	Wycombe Wanderers	Millwall
15 Lee, Jason B.	Chesterfield	Peterborough United
23 Lewis, Ben	Heybridge Swifts	Chelmsford City
23 McVeigh, Paul F.	Tottenham Hotspur	Norwich City
21 Messer, Gary	Bury	Workington
16 Middleton, Craig D.	Cardiff City	Halifax Town
22 Nogan, Kurt	Preston North End	Cardiff City
23 Prior, Spencer J.	Derby County	Manchester City
17 Redfearn, Neil D.	Bradford City	Wigan Athletic
22 Ritchie, Paul M.	Heart of Midlothian	Bolton Wanderers
23 Santos, Georges	Tranmere Rovers	West Bromwich Albion
16 Standen, Dean	Welling United	Luton Town
23 Taylor, Robert	Bolton Wanderers	West Bromwich Albion
2 Tuttle, David P.	Barnsley	Millwall
23 Vaughan, Anthony J.	Manchester City	Nottingham Forest
23 Wellens, Richard P.	Manchester United	Blackpool
23 Woodward, Andrew S.	Bury	Sheffield United
17 Wormull, Simon J.	Dover Athletic	Rushden & Diamonds
10 Young, Ryan	Chasetown	Nuneaton Borough

Temporary transfers

30 Arkins, Steven	Reading	Basingstoke Town
23 Armstrong, Alun	Middlesbrough	Huddersfield Town
10 Armstrong, Paul	Stevenage Borough	Aylesbury United
10 Arnison, Paul S.	Newcastle United	Hartlepool United
31 Bailey, Jermaine A.	Ilkeston Town	VS Rugby
23 Baker, Steven R.	Middlesbrough	Darlington
23 Bankole, Ademola	Queens Park Rangers	Bradford City
21 Banya, Sahr M.	Kettering Town	Bedford Town
1 Barker, Daniel T.	Basingstoke Town	Fleet Town
30 Barnes, Steven L.	Barnet	Welling United
23 Bass, Jonathan D.M.	Birmingham City	Gillingham
10 Batty, Laurence W.	Woking	Chesham United
23 Beavers, Paul M.	Oldham Athletic	Hartlepool United

13 Beck, Mikkel	Derby County	Queens Park Rangers
30 Belgrave, Barrington	Plymouth Argyle	Yeovil Town
23 Bennett, Thomas M.	Stockport County	Walsall
3 Blake, Marvin	Nuneaton Borough	Halesowen Town
10 Bonfield, Darren	Hitchin Town	Gravesend & Northfleet
10 Bradshaw, Mark	Halifax Town	Nuneaton Borough
22 Brady, Gary	Newcastle United	Norwich City
6 Branagan, Keith G.	Bolton Wanderers	Ipswich Town
16 Brayson, Paul	Reading	Cardiff City
19 Brooker, Paul	Fulham	Brighton & Hove Albion
5 Broughton, Drewe O.	Peterborough United	Nuneaton Borough
27 Bullock, Darren J.	Bury	Rushden & Diamonds
2 Burke, Paul	Sheffield United	Whitby Town
27 Butterfield, John P.	Barnet	Boreham Wood
6 Byfield, Darren	Aston Villa	Blackpool
17 Campagna, Samuel P.P.	Swindon Town	Bath City
27 Campbell, James R.	Peterborough United	Spalding United
23 Campbell, Stuart P.	Leicester City	Birmingham City
18 Canoville, Trevor	Hampton & Richmond Borough	Chertsey Town
3 Charles, Julian	Brentford	Woking
3 Clark, Dean W.	Brentford	Uxbridge
14 Cleaver, Christopher W.	Peterborough United	Cambridge City
23 Clegg, Michael J.	Manchester United	Wigan Athletic
23 Clement, Neil	Chelsea	West Bromwich Albion
31 Connolly, Gary M.	Portsmouth	Havant & Waterlooville
7 Cooke, Terence J.	Manchester City	Wigan Athletic
23 Cook, Robert P.	Forest Green Rovers	Gloucester City
16 Cooksey, Scott A.	Shrewsbury Town	Hereford United
10 Coppinger, James	Newcastle United	Hartlepool United
3 Crouch, Peter J.	Tottenham Hotspur	Dulwich Hamlet
23 Crowe, Dean A.	Stoke City	Bury
5 Dean, Michael J.	AFC Bournemouth	Dorchester Town
23 Dryden, Richard A.	Southampton	Stoke City
21 Dunning, Richard	Blackburn Rovers	Oldham Athletic
6 Edinburgh, Justin C.	Tottenham Hotspur	Portsmouth
29 Elliott, Stuart T.	Newcastle United	Stockport County
23 Etherington, Craig	West Ham United	Plymouth Argyle
22 Evans, David A.	Barnsley	Mansfield Town
23 Fenton, Nicholas L.	Manchester City	AFC Bournemouth
23 Ferguson, Barry	Coventry City	Colchester United
21 Forrester, Jamie M.	Walsall	Northampton Town
17 Friars, Sean M.	Ipswich Town	Portadown
30 Girdler, Stuart K.	Woking	Basingstoke Town
17 Gordon, Daniel	Aylesbury United	Tring Town
23 Grant, Gareth M.	Bradford City	Bolton Wanderers
3 Gray, Wayne W.	Wimbledon	Swindon Town
30 Gummer, Sean M.	Derby County	Southport
3 Gunnlaugsson, Arnar B.	Leicester City	Stoke City
17 Hall, Paul A.	Coventry City	Walsall
22 Hamilton, Derrick V.	Newcastle United	Norwich City
23 Harrison, Gerald R.	Sunderland	Burnley
10 Harrison, Ross	Stevenage Borough	Basingstoke Town
30 Harvey, Lee	St Albans City	Boreham Wood
27 Hawkins, Peter S.	Wimbledon	York City
26 Healy, David J.	Manchester United	Port Vale
10 Heggs, Carl S.	Rushden & Diamonds	Chester City
17 Hendry, Iain	Woking	Kingstonian
31 Hibbins, John J.	Sheffield Wednesday	Worksop Town
7 Hodge, John	Gillingham	Northampton Town
24 Holbrook, Adam P.	Portsmouth	Havant & Waterlooville

3	Holmshaw, James	Worksop Town	Matlock Town
3	Holt, Grant	Halifax Town	Barrow
31	Hooker, Jonathan W.	Harlow Town	Braintree Town
23	Hoult, Russell	Derby County	Portsmouth
31	Hughes, James J.	Cardiff City	Cwmbran Town
23	Hunt, Jonathan R.	Sheffield United	Cambridge United
19	Hurdle, Augustus A.J.	Basingstoke Town	Crawley Town
13	Hutchings, Carl E.	Bristol City	Brentford
21	Ingram, Stuart D.	Hartlepool United	Scarborough
31	James, Kevin E.	Charlton Athletic	Farnborough Town
27	Johnston, Allan	Sunderland	Bolton Wanderers
23	Jones, Gary	Hartlepool United	Halifax Town
17	Jones, Stephen G.	Bristol City	Southend United
24	Kielty, Gerrard T.	Altrincham	Leigh RMI
21	Kitson, Paul	West Ham United	Charlton Athletic
13	Knight, Richard	Derby County	Oxford United
27	Knight, Zatyiah	Fulham	Peterborough United
16	Kotylo, Krystof J.	Nuneaton Borough	Redditch United
21	Lawrence, Matthew J.	Wycombe Wanderers	Millwall
14	Lescott, Aaron A.	Aston Villa	Lincoln City
31	Lindley, James E.	Notts County	Moor Green
20	Lovell, Stephen W.H.	Portsmouth	Exeter City
21	Lyttle, Desmond	Watford	West Bromwich Albion
24	Martindale, Gary	Rotherham United	Telford United
18	Martin, Jae A.	Peterborough United	Welling United
17	Matassa, Vincent	Basingstoke Town	Salisbury City
23	Matthews, Lee J.	Leeds United	Gillingham
31	McAlindon, Gareth E.	Scarborough	Gateshead
22	McClare, Sean P.	Barnsley	Rochdale
18	McCormack, Francis	St Albans City	Harrow Borough
17	McDonnell, Nicholas	Croydon	Tonbridge Angels
24	McNiven, David J.	Oldham Athletic	Southport
23	Meaker, Michael J.	Bristol Rovers	Swindon Town
30	Midgley, Neil	Ipswich Town	Kidderminster Harriers
3	Miller, Barry S.	Gillingham	Woking
10	Mills, Rowan L.	Bradford City	Manchester City
26	Morrison, David E.	Leyton Orient	Dover Athletic
23	Myers, Andrew	Bradford City	Portsmouth
31	Myhre, Thomas	Everton	Birmingham City
24	Naylor, Stuart W.	Exeter City	Rushden & Diamonds
3	Newby, Jon P.R.	Liverpool	Crewe Alexandra
17	Newman, Richard A.	Millwall	Reading
17	Ngonge, Felix M.	Watford	Huddersfield Town
28	Nicholls, Mark	Chelsea	Grimsby Town
23	Nielsen, Allan	Tottenham Hotspur	Wolverhampton Wanderers
6	Pepper, Colin N.	Aberdeen	Southend United
23	Perez, Lionel	Newcastle United	Cambridge United
24	Perkins, Christopher P.	Southend United	Kettering Town
7	Porter, Andrew M.	Wigan Athletic	Chester City
4	Randall, Adrian J.	Forest Green Rovers	Newport (IW)
21	Rankin, Isaiah	Bradford City	Birmingham City
17	Reece, Dominic M.A.	Hednesford Town	Redditch United
30	Reed, Ian P.	Nuneaton Borough	Halesowen Town
23	Richardson, Barry	Lincoln City	Sheffield Wednesday
24	Roberts, Ben J.	Middlesbrough	Luton Town
13	Roden, Craig L.	Rotherham United	Gainsborough Trinity
29	Russell, Craig S.	Manchester City	St Johnstone
5	Ryder, Stuart H.	Nuneaton Borough	Stafford Rangers
16	Samuels, Anthony	Stevenage Borough	Dagenham & Redbridge
17	Saunders, Edward	Woking	Kingstonian

23 Searle, Stuart A.	Aldershot Town	Molesey
10 Shaw, Darren R.	Stafford Rangers	Solihull Borough
24 Simba, Amara S.	Leyton Orient	Kingstonian
20 Stevens, Ian D.	Wrexham	Cheltenham Town
23 Stewart, Jordan B.	Leicester City	Bristol Rovers
31 Stones, Craig	Lincoln City	Grantham Town
17 Strong, Greg	Bolton Wanderers	Motherwell
2 Sturridge, Simon A.	Stoke City	Shrewsbury Town
17 Swan, Iain	Oldham Athletic	Partick Thistle
25 Tallentire, Dean	Corby Town	Aylesbury United
1 Tardif, Christopher L.	Portsmouth	Newport (IW)
15 Taylor, Gareth K.	Manchester City	Queens Park Rangers
23 Taylor, Martin	Blackburn Rovers	Stockport County
22 Terry, John G.	Chelsea	Nottingham Forest
30 Thomas, Anthony	Burton Albion	Worcester City
21 Thomas, James A.	Blackburn Rovers	Blackpool
20 Thompson, Glyn	Fulham	Mansfield Town
31 Tremble, David G.	Scarborough	Gateshead
31 Trundle, Lee C.	Southport	Bamber Bridge
4 Wainwright, Neil	Sunderland	Darlington
24 Wardle, Darren C.	Oldham Athletic	Stalybridge Celtic
24 Wall, James	Hereford United	Burton Albion
24 Wardle, Darren	Oldham Athletic	Stalybridge Celtic
24 Waugh, Warren A.	Exeter City	Dorchester Town
31 Webb, Simon J.	Leyton Orient	Purfleet
6 Whetton, Lee D.	Hucknall Town	Spennymoor United
24 White, Devon W.	Ilkeston Town	Stafford Rangers
27 White, Thomas M.	Bristol Rovers	Hereford United
17 Wilkins, Ian J.	Lincoln City	Ballymena United
22 Williams, Adrian	Wolverhampton Wanderers	Reading
23 Wilson, Stuart K.	Leicester City	Sheffield United
23 Wolleaston, Robert A.	Chelsea	Bristol Rovers
23 Woodman, Andrew J.	Brentford	Peterborough United
26 Woolsey, Jeffrey A.	Dagenham & Redbridge	Billericay Town

April 2000

4 Bolder, Adam P.	Hull City	Derby County
27 Doherty, Gary M.T.	Luton Town	Tottenham Hotspur

Temporary transfers

24 Armstrong, Alun	Middlesbrough	Huddersfield Town
30 Barnes, Steven L.	Barnet	Welling United
25 Bass, Jonathan	Birmingham City	Gillingham
17 Bower, Mark	Bradford City	York City
2 Burke, Paul	Sheffield United	Whitby Town
24 Campbell, Stuart P.	Leicester City	Birmingham City
3 Charles, Julian	Brentford	Woking
7 Cooke, Terence J.	Manchester City	Wigan Athletic
10 Coppinger, James	Newcastle United	Hartlepool United
25 Dryden, Richard A.	Southampton	Stoke City
27 Elliott, Stuart T.	Newcastle United	Stockport County
23 Fenton, Nicholas L.	Manchester City	AFC Bournemouth
28 Forssell, Mikael K.	Chelsea	Crystal Palace
3 Gray, Wayne W.	Wimbledon	Swindon Town
3 Gunnlaugsson, Arnar B.	Leicester City	Stoke City
26 Holbrook, Adam P.	Portsmouth	Havant & Waterlooville
18 Ingram, Stuart D.	Hartlepool United	Scarborough
7 James, Kevin E.	Charlton Athletic	Farnborough Town
27 Jones, Gary	Hartlepool United	Halifax Town
10 Knight, Richard	Derby County	Oxford United
20 Matassa, Vincent	Basingstoke Town	Salisbury City

23 McClare, Sean P.	Barnsley	Rochdale
18 McCormack, Francis	St Albans City	Harrow Borough
3 Miller, Barry S.	Gillingham	Woking
29 Myhre, Thomas	Everton	Birmingham City
4 Naylor, Stuart W.	Exeter City	Rushden & Diamonds
25 Nielsen, Allan	Tottenham Hotspur	Wolverhampton Wanderers
24 Perkins, Christopher P.	Southend United	Kettering Town
10 Porter, Andrew M.	Wigan Athletic	Chester City
22 Reece, Dominic M.A.	Hednesford Town	Redditch United
23 Searle, Stuart A.	Aldershot Town	Molesey
3 Sturridge, Simon A.	Northampton Town	Shrewsbury Town
27 Taylor, Martin	Blackburn Rovers	Stockport County
4 Wainwright, Neil	Sunderland	Darlington
20 White, Devon W.	Ilkeston Town	Stafford Rangers
25 Wilson, Stuart K.	Leicester City	Sheffield United

May 2000

17 Alford, Carl P.	Stevenage Borough	Doncaster Rovers
24 Carlisle, Clarke J.	Blackpool	Queens Park Rangers
24 Kelly, James	Hednesford Town	Doncaster Rovers
22 Marsh, Michael A.	Kidderminster Harriers	Southport
25 Matthews, Colin E.	Bognor Regis Town	Newport (IW)
9 Morrison, Peter A.	Bolton Wanderers	Scunthorpe United
25 Robinson, Stephen	AFC Bournemouth	Preston North End

Temporary transfers

8 Coppinger, James	Newcastle United	Hartlepool United
5 Gunnlaugsson, Arnar B.	Leicester City	Stoke City
8 Hendry, Iain	Woking	Kingstonian
9 Myhre, Thomas	Everton	Birmingham City
6 Saunders, Edward	Woking	Kingstonian
7 Simba, Amara S.	Leyton Orient	Kingstonian
6 Stewart, Jordan B.	Leicester City	Bristol Rovers
1 Trundle, Lee C.	Southport	Bamber Bridge
7 Webb, Simon J.	Leyton Orient	Purfleet

FA CUP REVIEW 1999–2000

Judged by its own previously high standards, the FA Cup had by far its worst season of all time in 1999–2000. Top of the list of factors which led to this state of affairs, there was the furore when Manchester United were allowed to opt out of defending their title in order to play in the inaugural FIFA Club World Championship. One of the reasons why this was agreed was said to be the need for an English team to compete in FIFA's new tournament for fear of not being considered as hosts for the 2006 World Cup!

This Manchester United absence, led to the farcical situation of one team being given a wild card reprieve after being knocked out in the second round.

The lucky team turned out to be Darlington, eliminated 3-1 at Gillingham but brought back to face Villa the eventual runners-up to whom they went down 2-1 at Villa Park. Even that final defeat for Villa at Wembley against Chelsea was watched by arguably the lowest TV audience at terrestial level in recent times, said to be only seven million on ITV. The BBC were, of course, unable to cover the match because of TV rights.

Live attendances at matches were also hit by the ridiculous decision to bring the rounds forward, giving the money-spinning third round a December slot against its traditional January fixture. Two weeks before Christmas was clearly not the best idea and normal service has been resumed for 2000–2001.

Even the minnows failed to enjoy their usual tally of giant-killing acts. However, the first round proper was kicked-off by Conference table-toppers Rushden & Diamonds accounting for Scunthorpe United 2-0. The following day, Ryman Premier League Enfield won 2-1 at Chesterfield and Ilkeston Town from the Doc Martens League had a similar success against Carlisle United. Other resolute performances included Tamworth holding Bury 2-2 and Whyteleafe from the Ryman First Division drawing 0-0 with Chester City. Kettering Town drew 1-1 at Wrexham. None of these aspirants survived the replays.

In addition, Forest Green Rovers did manage a few goals to beat Guiseley 6-0 in the first round only to be beaten 3-0 at home by Torquay United in the second round. Still the non-league fraternity was represented in the third round. Hereford United, not so long ago giant-killers themselves before entering and then subsequently losing their Football League status, returned to haunt Leicester City. They drew 0-0 at Edgar Street and took their opponents to extra time before losing the replay.

Rushden & Diamonds held Sheffield United 1-1 at Bramall Lane, repeated the feat on their own patch and only bowed out on penalties. Meanwhile Chelsea began what was to prove their successful campaign by trouncing Hull City 6-1 at Boothferry Park. It also brought Tottenham Hotspur's low point of the season when they crashed by exactly the same scoreline at Newcastle United in another replay.

Round Four saw further Premiership casualties, as Fulham put the skids under Wimbledon 3-0 while Tranmere Rovers beat Sunderland 1-0 in a controversial finish which produced a mix-up when it appeared that a substitute had replaced a player dismissed!

Blackburn also did well to win 1-0 at Liverpool and Gillingham helped themselves to a Premier League scalp of their own beating Bradford City 3-1.

In the fifth round results were not much kinder to the Premier clubs. Charlton Athletic won 3-2 at Coventry City, Gillingham overturned Sheffield Wednesday 3-1 before shipping five goals at rampant Chelsea. The other successful quarter-finalists were Bolton Wanderers 1-0 winners over Charlton, Villa 2-1 at Everton and Newcastle who ended Tranmere's best FA Cup run 3-2 at Prenton Park.

Both semi-finals were held at Wembley. Villa came through via penalties after a goalless draw with Bolton Wanderers, while a week later Chelseas edged out Newcastle 2-1. Chelsea won a rather disappointing final 1-0 at the expense of Villa with a goal from Roberto Di Matteo, who contributed to another slice of FA Cup history as being the last goalscorer in the competition at the ground before rebuilding, having in 1997 scored the fastest Wembley final goal in only an electronically-timed 43 seconds.

A match of few chances at either end saw the Villa goalkeeper David James fail to grasp the ball, which allowed an alert Di Matteo to take full advantage. The crowd of 78,217 was well up to recent attendances of course but the unconfirmed aggregate for the entire competition of 1,699,330 was over 400,000 down on the figures for 1998–99.

AXA FA CUP 1999–2000

FIRST ROUND

Rushden & D	(0) 2	Scunthorpe U	(0) 0
Aldershot T	(0) 1	Hednesford T	(0) 1
Bath C	(0) 0	Hendon	(0) 2
Blackpool	(1) 2	Stoke C	(0) 0
Brentford	(0) 2	Plymouth Arg	(1) 2
Bristol C	(1) 3	Mansfield T	(1) 2
Burton A	(0) 0	Rochdale	(0) 0
Cambridge C	(0) 0	Wigan Ath	(2) 2
Cambridge U	(0) 1	Gateshead	(0) 0
Cheltenham T	(0) 1	Gillingham	(1) 1
Chesterfield	(0) 1	Enfield	(1) 2
Darlington	(1) 2	Southport	(0) 1
Doncaster R	(0) 0	Halifax T	(0) 2
Exeter C	(1) 2	Eastwood T	(0) 1
Forest Green R	(4) 6	Guiseley	(0) 0
Hayes	(1) 2	Runcorn	(1) 1
Hereford U	(0) 1	York C	(0) 0
Ilkeston T	(1) 2	Carlisle U	(1) 1
Leyton Orient	(0) 1	Cardiff C	(1) 1
Lincoln C	(1) 1	Welling U	(0) 0
Luton T	(1) 4	Kingstonian	(1) 2
Macclesfield T	(0) 0	Hull C	(0) 0
Notts Co	(1) 1	Bournemouth	(0) 1
Oldham Ath	(2) 4	Chelmsford C	(0) 0
Oxford U	(1) 3	Morecambe	(1) 2
Peterborough U	(1) 1	Brighton & HA	(1) 1
Reading	(1) 4	Yeovil T	(1) 2
Rotherham U	(1) 3	Worthing	(0) 0
Shrewsbury T	(1) 2	Northampton T	(1) 1
St Albans C	(0) 0	Bamber Bridge	(1) 2
Swansea C	(0) 2	Colchester U	(0) 1
Tamworth	(1) 2	Bury	(1) 2
Torquay U	(0) 1	Southend U	(0) 0
Whyteleafe	(0) 0	Chester C	(0) 0
Wrexham	(0) 1	Kettering T	(0) 1
Wycombe W	(0) 1	Oxford C	(0) 1
Barnet	(0) 0	Burnley	(0) 1
Bristol R	(0) 0	Preston NE	(0) 1
Hartlepool U	(0) 1	Millwall	(0) 0
Merthyr T	(0) 2	Stalybridge C	(2) 2

FIRST ROUND REPLAYS

Hednesford T	(1) 1	Aldershot T	(0) 2
Bournemouth	(1) 4	Notts Co	(0) 2
Brighton & HA	(1) 3	Peterborough U	(0) 0
Bury	(0) 2	Tamworth	(1) 1
(aet)			
Cardiff C	(1) 3	Leyton Orient	(1) 1
Chester C	(1) 3	Whyteleafe	(1) 1
Gillingham	(2) 3	Cheltenham T	(0) 2
Hull C	(3) 4	Macclesfield T	(0) 0
Oxford C	(1) 1	Wycombe W	(0) 1

(Abandoned after extra time; fire.)

Plymouth Arg	(0) 2	Brentford	(0) 1
(aet)			
Rochdale	(1) 3	Burton A	(0) 0
Stalybridge C	(2) 3	Merthyr T	(1) 1
Kettering T	(0) 0	Wrexham	(2) 2
Oxford C	(0) 0	Wycombe W	(0) 1

SECOND ROUND

Luton T	(0) 2	Lincoln C	(1) 2
Blackpool	(0) 2	Hendon	(0) 0
(aet)			
Bournemouth	(0) 0	Bristol C	(1) 2
Burnley	(0) 2	Rotherham U	(0) 0
Bury	(0) 0	Cardiff C	(0) 0
Cambridge U	(0) 1	Bamber Bridge	(0) 0
Exeter C	(2) 2	Aldershot T	(0) 0
Gillingham	(2) 3	Darlington	(0) 1
Hayes	(1) 2	Hull C	(1) 2
Ilkeston T	(1) 1	Rushden & D	(0) 1
Oldham Ath	(1) 1	Swansea C	(0) 0
Plymouth Arg	(0) 0	Brighton & HA	(0) 0
Preston NE	(0) 0	Enfield	(0) 0
Reading	(0) 1	Halifax T	(0) 1
Shrewsbury T	(1) 2	Oxford U	(0) 2
Stalybridge C	(1) 1	Chester C	(1) 2
Wrexham	(1) 2	Rochdale	(1) 1
Wycombe W	(1) 2	Wigan Ath	(1) 2
Forest Green R	(0) 0	Torquay U	(0) 3
Hereford U	(0) 1	Hartlepool U	(0) 0

SECOND ROUND REPLAYS

Brighton & HA	(0) 1	Plymouth Arg	(1) 2
Cardiff C	(0) 1	Bury	(0) 0
(aet)			
Enfield	(0) 0	Preston NE	(0) 3
Halifax T	(0) 0	Reading	(0) 1
Hull C	(0) 3	Hayes	(0) 2
(aet)			
Lincoln C	(0) 0	Luton T	(0) 1
Oxford U	(0) 2	Shrewsbury T	(1) 1
(aet)			
Rushden & D	(2) 3	Ilkeston T	(0) 0
Wigan Ath	(1) 2	Wycombe W	(1) 1

THIRD ROUND

Cambridge U	(0) 2	Crystal Palace	(0) 0
Nottingham F	(1) 1	Oxford U	(0) 1
Aston Villa	(1) 2	Darlington	(0) 1
Darlington progressed to Third Round as 'Lucky Losers'.			
Charlton Ath	(0) 2	Swindon T	(0) 1
Crewe Alex	(0) 1	Bradford C	(0) 2
Derby Co	(0) 0	Burnley	(0) 1
Exeter C	(0) 0	Everton	(0) 0
Fulham	(2) 2	Luton T	(1) 2
Grimsby T	(1) 3	Stockport Co	(0) 2
Hereford U	(0) 0	Leicester C	(0) 0
Hull C	(1) 1	Chelsea	(2) 6

Norwich C	(0) 1	Coventry C	(0) 3
Preston NE	(1) 2	Oldham Ath	(0) 1
QPR	(1) 1	Torquay U	(0) 1
Reading	(1) 1	Plymouth Arg	(0) 1
Sheffield W	(1) 1	Bristol C	(0) 0
Sunderland	(1) 1	Portsmouth	(0) 0
Tranmere R	(1) 1	West Ham U	(0) 0
Watford	(0) 0	Birmingham C	(0) 1
WBA	(0) 2	Blackburn R	(0) 2
Walsall	(0) 1	Gillingham	(1) 1
Wigan Ath	(0) 0	Wolverhampton W	(0) 1
Wimbledon	(1) 1	Barnsley	(0) 0
Wrexham	(0) 2	Middlesbrough	(1) 1
Chester C	(1) 1	Manchester C	(1) 4
Huddersfield T	(0) 0	Liverpool	(1) 2
Leeds U	(0) 2	Port Vale	(0) 0
Sheffield U	(1) 1	Rushden & D	(1) 1
Tottenham H	(0) 1	Newcastle U	(0) 1
Arsenal	(1) 3	Blackpool	(1) 1
Ipswich T	(0) 0	Southampton	(1) 1
Bolton W	(1) 1	Cardiff C	(0) 0

THIRD ROUND REPLAYS

Everton	(0) 1	Exeter C	(0) 0
Luton T	(0) 0	Fulham	(0) 3
Plymouth Arg	(0) 1	Reading	(0) 0
Rushden & D	(0) 1	Sheffield U	(0) 1
(aet; Sheffield U won 6-5 on penalties.)			
Torquay U	(0) 2	QPR	(0) 3
Blackburn R	(0) 2	WBA	(0) 0
(aet)			
Leicester C	(0) 2	Hereford U	(1) 1
(aet)			
Newcastle U	(3) 6	Tottenham H	(1) 1
Gillingham	(1) 2	Walsall	(1) 1
(aet)			
Oxford U	(0) 1	Nottingham F	(0) 3

FOURTH ROUND

Aston Villa	(1) 1	Southampton	(0) 0
Charlton Ath	(0) 1	QPR	(0) 0
Coventry C	(1) 3	Burnley	(0) 0
Everton	(0) 2	Birmingham C	(0) 0
Fulham	(2) 3	Wimbledon	(0) 0
Grimsby T	(0) 0	Bolton W	(1) 2
Newcastle U	(1) 4	Sheffield U	(1) 1
Plymouth Arg	(0) 0	Preston NE	(1) 3
Sheffield W	(1) 1	Wolverhampton W	(0) 1
Tranmere R	(1) 1	Sunderland	(0) 0
Wrexham	(1) 1	Cambridge U	(1) 2
Arsenal	(0) 0	Leicester C	(0) 0
Manchester C	(2) 2	Leeds U	(3) 5
Liverpool	(0) 0	Blackburn R	(0) 1
Gillingham	(1) 3	Bradford C	(0) 1
Chelsea	(0) 2	Nottingham F	(0) 0

FOURTH ROUND REPLAYS

Wolverhampton W	(0) 0	Sheffield W	(0) 0
(aet; Sheffield W won 4-3 on penalties.)			
Leicester C	(0) 0	Arsenal	(0) 0
(aet; Leicester C won 6-5 on penalties.)			

FIFTH ROUND

Cambridge U	(1) 1	Bolton W	(0) 3
Coventry C	(2) 2	Charlton Ath	(2) 3
Everton	(0) 2	Preston NE	(0) 0
Fulham	(1) 1	Tranmere R	(1) 2
Gillingham	(0) 3	Sheffield W	(1) 1
Aston Villa	(1) 3	Leeds U	(2) 2
Chelsea	(1) 2	Leicester C	(0) 1
Blackburn R	(1) 1	Newcastle U	(1) 2

SIXTH ROUND

Bolton W	(0) 1	Charlton Ath	(0) 0
Chelsea	(1) 5	Gillingham	(0) 0
Everton	(1) 1	Aston Villa	(2) 2
Tranmere R	(1) 2	Newcastle U	(2) 3

SEMI-FINALS (at Wembley)

Bolton W	(0) 0	Aston Villa	(0) 0
(aet; Aston Villa won 4-1 on penalties.)			
Newcastle United	(0) 1	Chelsea	(1) 2

FINAL (at Wembley)

20 MAY

Aston Villa (0) 0
Chelsea (0) 1 *(Di Matteo 72)* 78,217

Aston Villa: James; Delaney, Wright (Hendrie), Southgate, Ehiogu, Barry, Taylor (Stone), Boateng, Dublin, Carbone (Joachim), Merson.
Chelsea: De Goey; Melchiot, Babayaro, Deschamps, Leboeuf, Desailly, Poyet, Di Matteo, Weah (Flo), Zola (Morris), Wise.
Referee: G. Poll (Tring).

PAST FA CUP FINALS

Details of one goalscorer is not available in 1878.

1872	The Wanderers	1	Royal Engineers	0
	Betts			
1873	The Wanderers	2	Oxford University	0
	Kinnaird, Wollaston			
1874	Oxford University	2	Royal Engineers	0
	Mackarness, Patton			
1875	Royal Engineers	1	Old Etonians	1*
	Renny-Tailyour		*Bonsor*	
Replay	Royal Engineers	2	Old Etonians	0
	Renny-Tailyour, Stafford			
1876	The Wanderers	1	Old Etonians	1*
	Edwards		*Bonsor*	
Replay	The Wanderers	3	Old Etonians	0
	Wollaston, Hughes 2			
1877	The Wanderers	2	Oxford University	1*
	Lindsay, Kenrick		*Kinnaird (og)*	
1878	The Wanderers	3	Royal Engineers	1
	Kenrick 2, Kinnaird		*Unknown*	
1879	Old Etonians	1	Clapham Rovers	0
	Clerke			
1880	Clapham Rovers	1	Oxford University	0
	Lloyd-Jones			
1881	Old Carthusians	3	Old Etonians	0
	Wyngard, Parry, Todd			
1882	Old Etonians	1	Blackburn Rovers	0
	Anderson			
1883	Blackburn Olympic	2	Old Etonians	1*
	Costley, Matthews		*Goodhart*	
1884	Blackburn Rovers	2	Queen's Park, Glasgow	1
	Sowerbutts, Forrest		*Christie*	
1885	Blackburn Rovers	2	Queen's Park, Glasgow	0
	Forrest, Brown			
1886	Blackburn Rovers	0	West Bromwich Albion	0
Replay	Blackburn Rovers	2	West Bromwich Albion	0
	Brown, Sowerbutts			
1887	Aston Villa	2	West Bromwich Albion	0
	Hunter, Hodgetts			
1888	West Bromwich Albion	2	Preston NE	1
	Woodhall, Bayliss		*Dewhurst*	
1889	Preston NE	3	Wolverhampton W	0
	Dewhurst, J. Ross, Thompson			
1890	Blackburn Rovers	6	Sheffield W	1
	Walton, John Southworth, Lofthouse, Townley 3		*Bennett*	

Year	Winner		Runner-up	
1891	Blackburn Rovers	3	Notts Co	1
	Dewar, John Southworth, Townley		*Oswald*	
1892	West Browmwich Albion	3	Aston Villa	0
	Geddes, Nicholls, Reynolds			
1893	Wolverhampton W	1	Everton	0
	Allen			
1894	Notts Co	4	Bolton W	1
	Watson, Logan 3		*Cassidy*	
1895	Aston Villa	1	West Bromwich Albion	0
	J. Devey			
1896	Sheffield W	2	Wolverhampton W	1
	Spiksley 2		*Black*	
1897	Aston Villa	3	Everton	2
	Campbell, Wheldon, Crabtree		*Boyle, Bell*	
1898	Nottingham F	3	Derby Co	1
	Cape 2, McPherson		*Bloomer*	
1899	Sheffield U	4	Derby Co	1
	Bennett, Beers, Almond, Priest		*Boag*	
1900	Bury	4	Southampton	0
	McLuckie 2, Wood, Plant			
1901	Tottenham H	2	Sheffield U	2
	Brown 2		*Bennett, Priest*	
Replay	Tottenham H	3	Sheffield U	1
	Cameron, Smith, Brown		*Priest*	
1902	Sheffield U	1	Southampton	1
	Common		*Wood*	
Replay	Sheffield U	2	Southampton	1
	Hedley, Barnes		*Brown*	
1903	Bury	6	Derby Co	0
	Ross, Sagar, Leeming 2, Wood, Plant			
1904	Manchester C	1	Bolton W	0
	Meredith			
1905	Aston Villa	2	Newcastle U	0
	Hampton 2			
1906	Everton	1	Newcastle U	0
	Young			
1907	Sheffield W	2	Everton	1
	Stewart, Simpson		*Sharp*	
1908	Wolverhampton W	3	Newcastle U	1
	Hunt, Hedley, Harrison		*Howey*	
1909	Manchester U	1	Bristol C	0
	A. Turnbull			
1910	Newcastle U	1	Barnsley	1
	Rutherford		*Tufnell*	
Replay	Newcastle U	2	Barnsley	0
	Shepherd 2 (1 pen)			

Year	Winner		Runner-up	
1911	Bradford C	0	Newcastle U	0
Replay	Bradford C	1	Newcastle U	0
	Speirs			
1912	Barnsley	0	West Bromwich Albion	0
Replay	Barnsley	1	West Bromwich Albion	0*
	Tufnell			
1913	Aston Villa	1	Sunderland	0
	Barber			
1914	Burnley	1	Liverpool	0
	Freeman			
1915	Sheffield U	3	Chelsea	0
	Simmons, Masterman, Kitchen			
1920	Aston Villa	1	Huddersfield T	0*
	Kirton			
1921	Tottenham H	1	Wolverhampton W	0
	Dimmock			
1922	Huddersfield T	1	Preston NE	0
	Smith (pen)			
1923	Bolton W	2	West Ham U	0
	Jack, J.R. Smith			
1924	Newcastle U	2	Aston Villa	0
	Harris, Seymour			
1925	Sheffield U	1	Cardiff C	0
	Tunstall			
1926	Bolton W	1	Manchester C	0
	Jack			
1927	Cardiff C	1	Arsenal	0
	Ferguson			
1928	Blackburn Rovers	3	Huddersfield T	1
	Roscamp 2, McLean		*A. Jackson*	
1929	Bolton W	2	Portsmouth	0
	Butler, Blackmore			
1930	Arsenal	2	Huddersfield T	0
	James, Lambert			
1931	West Bromwich Albion	2	Birmingham	1
	W.G. Richardson 2		*Bradford*	
1932	Newcastle U	2	Arsenal	1
	Allen 2		*John*	
1933	Everton	3	Manchester C	0
	Stein, Dean, Dunn			
1934	Manchester C	2	Portsmouth	1
	Tilson 2		*Rutherford*	
1935	Sheffield W	4	West Bromwich Albion	2
	Rimmer 2, Palethorpe, Hooper		*Boyes, Sandford*	
1936	Arsenal	1	Sheffield U	0
	Drake			
1937	Sunderland	3	Preston NE	1
	Gurney, Carter, Burbanks		*F. O'Donnell*	

1938	Preston NE ....1 *Mutch (pen)*	Huddersfield T 0*
1939	Portsmouth ....4 *Parker 2, Barlow, Anderson*	Wolverhampton W ....1 *Dorsett*
1946	Derby Co ....4 *H. Turner (og), Doherty, Stamps 2*	Charlton Ath ....1* *H. Turner*
1947	Charlton Ath ....1 *Duffy*	Burnley 0*
1948	Manchester U ....4 *Rowley 2, Pearson, Anderson*	Blackpool ....2 *Shimwell (pen), Mortensen*
1949	Wolverhampton W ....3 *Pye 2, Smyth,*	Leicester C ....1 *Griffiths*
1950	Arsenal ....2 *Lewis 2*	Liverpool 0
1951	Newcastle U ....2 *Milburn 2*	Blackpool 0
1952	Newcastle U ....1 *G. Robledo*	Arsenal 0
1953	Blackpool ....4 *Mortensen 3, Perry*	Bolton W ....3 *Lofthouse, Moir, Bell*
1954	West Bromwich Albion ....3 *Allen 2 (1 pen), Griffin*	Preston NE ....2 *Morrison, Wayman*
1955	Newcastle U ....3 *Milburn, Mitchell, Hannah*	Manchester C ....1 *Johnstone*
1956	Manchester C ....3 *Hayes, Dyson, Johnstone*	Birmingham C ....1 *Kinsey*
1957	Aston Villa ....2 *McParland 2*	Manchester U ....1 *T. Taylor*
1958	Bolton W ....2 *Lofthouse 2*	Manchester U 0
1959	Nottingham F ....2 *Dwight, Wilson*	Luton T ....1 *Pacey*
1960	Wolverhampton W ....3 *McGrath (og), Deeley 2*	Blackburn Rovers 0
1961	Tottenham H ....2 *Smith, Dyson*	Leicester C 0
1962	Tottenham H ....3 *Greaves, Smith, Blanchflower (pen)*	Burnley ....1 *Robson*
1963	Manchester U ....3 *Herd 2, Law*	Leicester C ....1 *Keyworth*
1964	West Ham U ....3 *Sissons, Hurst, Boyce*	Preston NE ....2 *Holden, Dawson*
1965	Liverpool ....2 *Hunt, St John*	Leeds U ....1* *Bremner*

1966	Everton ......3 *Trebilcock 2, Temple*	Sheffield W ......2 *McCalliog, Ford*
1967	Tottenham H ......2 *Robertson, Saul*	Chelsea ......1 *Tambling*
1968	West Browmwich Albion .....1 *Astle*	Everton 0*
1969	Manchester C ......1 *Young*	Leicester C 0
1970	Chelsea ......2 *Houseman, Hutchinson*	Leeds U ......2* *Charlton, Jones*
Replay	Chelsea ......2 *Osgood, Webb*	Leeds U ......1* *Jones*
1971	Arsenal ......2 *Kelly, George*	Liverpool ......1* *Heighway*
1972	Leeds U ......1 *Clarke*	Arsenal 0
1973	Sunderland ......1 *Porterfield*	Leeds U 0
1974	Liverpool ......3 *Keegan 2, Heighway*	Newcastle 0
1975	West Ham U ......2 *A. Taylor 2*	Fulham 0
1976	Southampton ......1 *Stokes*	Manchester U 0
1977	Manchester U ......2 *Pearson, J. Greenhoff*	Liverpool ......1 *Case*
1978	Ipswich T ......1 *Osborne*	Arsenal 0
1979	Arsenal ......3 *Talbot, Stapleton, Sunderland*	Manchester U ......2 *McQueen, McIlroy*
1980	West Ham U ......1 *Brooking*	Arsenal 0
1981	Tottenham H ......1 *Hutchison (og)*	Manchester C ......1* *Hutchison*
Replay	Totteham H ......3 *Villa 2, Crooks*	Manchester C ......2 *MacKenzie, Reeves (pen)*
1982	Tottenham H ......1 *Hoddle*	QPR ......1* *Fenwick*
Replay	Tottenham H ......1 *Hoddle (pen)*	QPR 0
1983	Manchester U ......2 *Stapleton, Wilkins*	Brighton & HA ......2* *Smith, Stevens*
Replay	Manchester U ......4 *Robson 2, Whiteside, Muhren (pen)*	Brighton & HA 0
1984	Everton ......2 *Sharp, Gray*	Watford 0
1985	Manchester U ......1 *Whiteside*	Everton 0*

1986	Liverpool	3	Everton	1
	Rush 2, Johnston		*Lineker*	
1987	Coventry C	3	Tottenham H	2*
	Bennett, Houchen, Mabbutt (og)		*C. Allen, Kilcline (og)*	
1988	Wimbledon	1	Liverpool	0
	Sanchez			
1989	Liverpool	3	Everton	2*
	Aldridge, Rush 2		*McCall 2*	
1990	Manchester U	3	Crystal Palace	3*
	Robson, Hughes 2		*O'Reilly, Wright 2*	
Replay	Manchester U	1	Crystal Palace	0
	Martin			
1991	Tottenham H	2	Nottingham F	1*
	Stewart, Walker (og)		*Pearce*	
1992	Liverpool	2	Sunderland	0
	Thomas, Rush			
1993	Arsenal	1	Sheffield W	1*
	Wright		*Hirst*	
Replay	Arsenal	2	Sheffield W	1*
	Wright, Linighan		*Waddle*	
1994	Manchester U	4	Chelsea	0
	Cantona 2 (2 pens), Hughes, McClair			
1995	Everton	1	Manchester U	0
	Rideout			
1996	Manchester U	1	Liverpool	0
	Cantona			
1997	Chelsea	2	Middlesbrough	0
	Di Matteo, Newton			
1998	Arsenal	2	Newcastle U	0
	Overmars, Anelka			
1999	Manchester U	2	Newcastle U	0
	Sheringham, Scholes			

**After extra time*

SUMMARY OF FA CUP WINNERS SINCE 1871

Club	Wins
Manchester United	10
Tottenham Hotspur	8
Arsenal	7
Aston Villa	7
Blackburn Rovers	6
Newcastle United	6
Everton	5
Liverpool	5
The Wanderers	5
West Bromwich Albion	5
Bolton Wanderers	4
Manchester City	4
Sheffield United	4
Wolverhampton Wanderers	4
Chelsea	3
Sheffield Wednesday	3
West Ham United	3
Bury	2
Nottingham Forest	2
Old Etonians	2
Preston North End	2
Sunderland	2
Barnsley	1
Blackburn Olympic	1
Blackpool	1
Bradford City	1
Burnley	1
Cardiff City	1
Charlton Athletic	1
Clapham Rovers	1
Coventry City	1
Derby County	1
Huddersfield Town	1
Ipswich Town	1
Leeds United	1
Notts County	1
Old Carthusians	1
Oxford University	1
Portsmouth	1
Royal Engineers	1
Southampton	1
Wimbledon	1

APPEARANCES IN FA CUP FINAL

Club	Appearances
Manchester United	15
Arsenal	13
Newcastle United	13
Everton	12
Liverpool	11
Aston Villa	10
West Bromwich Albion	10
Tottenham Hotspur	9
Blackburn Rovers	8
Manchester City	8
Wolverhampton Wanderers	8
Bolton Wanderers	7
Preston North End	7
Chelsea	6
Old Etonians	6
Sheffield United	6
Sheffield Wednesday	6
Huddersfield Town	5
The Wanderers	5
Derby County	4
Leeds United	4
Leicester City	4
Oxford University	4
Royal Engineers	4
Sunderland	4
West Ham United	4
Blackpool	3
Burnley	3
Nottingham Forest	3
Portsmouth	3
Southampton	3
Barnsley	2
Birmingham City	2
Bury	2
Cardiff City	2
Charlton Athletic	2
Clapham Rovers	2
Notts County	2
Queen's Park (Glasgow)	2
Blackburn Olympic	1
Bradford City	1
Brighton & Hove Albion	1
Bristol City	1
Coventry City	1
Crystal Palace	1
Fulham	1
Ipswich Town	1
Luton Town	1
Middlesbrough	1
Old Carthusians	1
Queen's Park Rangers	1
Watford	1
Wimbledon	1

WORTHINGTON CUP REVIEW 1999–2000

Though their first League Cup final appearance was marred by the 63rd minute dismissal of Clint Hill, goalscoring hero of the first leg semi-final, Tranmere Rovers gave a plucky performance before going down 2-1 to Leicester City at Wembley.

The recent formula of the European Cup committed clubs being given a bye to the third round was continued, but in addition the apparent disinterest of other leading teams saw less than their strongest elevens being wheeled out. Of the seven clubs exempted for this reason, only West Ham managed to reach the fifth round.

Oddly enough Tranmere made an inauspicious start at Blackpool, losing 2-1 at Bloomfield Road, their goal by courtesy of a home defender. And they only edged the return 3-1 after Blackpool had been reduced to ten following a red card.

Top scorers in the first round first leg were Manchester City, 5-0 winners over Burnley. Grimsby Town topped that effort in the second leg taking six goals off Carlisle United.

In the second round, Liverpool began with a 5-1 win at Hull while Tranmere equalled this at the expense of Premiership Coventry City. Once again the losers finished with ten players. There was a slight shock for Watford before they came through on the away goals rule over Wigan Athletic.

Aston Villa after a 6-0 aggregate victory over Chester City, beat an understrength Manchester United 3-0 in the third round. Chelsea, too, had a similar attitude at home to Huddersfield Town and lost by the only goal. Bolton Wanderers won 2-1 at Derby and Leicester emerged as 2-0 winners over Grimsby.

Villa added to their goals tally by hitting Southampton 4-0 but another victim from the top echelon was Tottenham Hotspur, 3-1 losers at Fulham. Bolton made it another uncomfortable night for a Premiership team, this time Sheffield Wednesday going down 1-0 at the Reebok Stadium. Meanwhile Bolton beat Burnley 4-0 in the Lancashire derby.

In the quarter-finals, it was a hat-trick over the Premier League for Bolton, 2-1 winners against Wimbledon. Tranmere accounted for Middlesbrough by the same margin. It was looking good for the Football League representation in the competition. Meanwhile Tranmere beat Barnsley 4-0.

Leicester had a penalty shoot-out success against Leeds and though West Ham United beat Aston Villa via the same method, the match was subsequently scrubbed when it was discovered that Manny Omoyinmi the West Ham player had played in an earlier round on loan to Gillingham. Villa made the most of the reprieve with a 3-1 win at Upton Park. Leicester themselves needed penalty kicks to eliminate Fulham.

Tranmere did well to beat Bolton 1-0 away and emphasised their superiority with a 3-0 second leg win. Leicester held Villa goalless at Villa Park and a Matt Elliott goal was enough in the return leg.

In fact it was a brace from Elliott in the final which accounted for Tranmere in a final watched by 74,313, but the tournament as a whole showed that attendance figures were down on the previous season. At 1,355,548 they were slightly over 200,000 worse than in 1998–99 from the same number of matches.

However in the final Elliott struck first for City in the 29th minute and though Tranmere lost Hill as mentioned previously after 63 minutes, they equalised through David Kelly with 13 minutes remaining. But in the 81st minute it was Elliott who scored again to give Leicester victory.

There was particular satisfaction for Leicester, the beaten finalists of the previous year. They added to their success achieved in 1997 having originally won the League Cup in 1964.

Tranmere's best performance had been reaching the semi-final in 1994 and of course they also enjoyed their best run in the FA Cup in 1999–2000 before being knocked out in the sixth round.

Rovers had in fact completed 14 cup ties in both domestic competitions and added to their League programme had figured in no fewer than 60 top class fixtures, a surprising total for a team outside of the Premier League.

They also managed to have scored at least once in every cup game including a creditable 23 in the League Cup alone.

PAST LEAGUE CUP FINALS

Played as two legs up to 1966

1961	Rotherham U	2	Aston Villa	0
	Webster, Kirkman			
	Aston Villa	3	Rotherham U	0*
	O'Neill, Burrows, McParland			
1962	Rochdale	0	Norwich C	3
			Lythgoe 2, Punton	
	Norwich C	1	Rochdale	0
	Hill			
1963	Birmingham C	3	Aston Villa	1
	Leek 2, Bloomfield		*Thomson*	
	Aston Villa	0	Birmingham C	0
1964	Stoke C	1	Leicester C	1
	Bebbington		*Gibson*	
	Leicester C	3	Stoke C	2
	Stringfellow, Gibson, Riley		*Viollet, Kinnell*	
1965	Chelsea	3	Leicester C	2
	Tambling, Venables (pen), McCreadie		*Appleton, Goodfellow*	
	Leicester C	0	Chelsea	0
1966	West Ham U	2	WBA	1
	Moore, Byrne		*Astle*	
	WBA	4	West Ham U	1
	Kaye, Brown, Clark, Williams		*Peters*	
1967	QPR	3	WBA	2
	Morgan R, Marsh, Lazarus		*Clark C 2*	
1968	Leeds U	1	Arsenal	0
	Cooper			
1969	Swindon T	3	Arsenal	1*
	Smart, Rogers 2		*Gould*	
1970	Manchester C	2	WBA	1*
	Doyle, Pardoe		*Astle*	
1971	Tottenham H	2	Aston Villa	0
	Chivers 2			
1972	Chelsea	1	Stoke C	2
	Osgood		*Conroy, Eastham*	
1973	Tottenham H	1	Norwich C	0
	Coates			
1974	Wolverhampton W	2	Manchester C	1
	Hibbitt, Richards		*Bell*	
1975	Aston Villa	1	Norwich C	0
	Graydon			
1976	Manchester C	2	Newcastle U	1
	Barnes, Tueart		*Gowling*	
1977	Aston Villa	0	Everton	0
Replay	Aston Villa	1	Everton	1*
	Kenyon (og)		*Latchford*	

Replay	Aston Villa 3	Everton 2*
	Little 2, Nicholl	*Latchford, Lyons*
1978	Nottingham F 0	Liverpool 0*
Replay	Nottingham F 1	Liverpool 0
	Robertson (pen)	
1979	Nottingham F 3	Southampton 2
	Birtles 2, Woodcock	*Peach, Holmes*
1980	Wolverhampton W 1	Nottingham F 0
	Gray	
1981	Liverpool 1	West Ham U 1*
	Kennedy A	*Stewart (pen)*
Replay	Liverpool 2	West Ham U 1
	Dalglish, Hansen	*Goddard*
1982	Liverpool 3	Tottenham H 1*
	Whelan 2, Rush	*Archibald*
1983	Liverpool 2	Manchester U 1*
	Kennedy A, Whelan	*Whiteside*
1984	Liverpool 0	Everton 0*
Replay	Liverpool 1	Everton 0
	Souness	
1985	Norwich C 1	Sunderland 0
	Chisholm (og)	
1986	Oxford U 3	QPR 0
	Hebberd, Houghton, Charles	
1987	Arsenal 2	Liverpool 1
	Nicholas 2	*Rush*
1988	Luton T 3	Arsenal 2
	Stein B 2, Wilson	*Hayes, Smith*
1989	Nottingham F 3	Luton T 1
	Clough 2, Webb	*Harford*
1990	Nottingham F 1	Oldham Ath 0
	Jemson	
1991	Sheffield W 1	Manchester U 0
	Sheridan	
1992	Manchester U 1	Nottingham F 0
	McClair	
1993	Arsenal 2	Sheffield W 1
	Merson, Morrow	*Harkes*
1994	Aston Villa 3	Manchester U 1
	Atkinson, Saunders 2 (1 pen)	*Hughes*
1995	Liverpool 2	Bolton W 1
	McManaman 2	*Thompson*
1996	Aston Villa 3	Leeds U 0
	Milosevic, Taylor, Yorke	
1997	Leicester C 1	Middlesbrough 1*
	Heskey	*Ravanelli*
Replay	Leicester C 1	Middlesbrough 0*
	Claridge	
1998	Chelsea 2	Middlesbrough 0*
	Sinclair, Di Matteo	
1999	Tottenham H 1	Leicester C 0
	Nielsen	

**After extra time*

WORTHINGTON CUP 1999–2000

FIRST ROUND, FIRST LEG

Birmingham C	(2) 3	Exeter C	(0) 0
Blackpool	(1) 2	Tranmere R	(1) 1
Bournemouth	(1) 2	Barnet	(0) 0
Bury	(0) 1	Notts Co	(0) 0
Cambridge U	(0) 2	Bristol C	(0) 2
Cardiff C	(0) 1	QPR	(1) 2
Carlisle U	(0) 0	Grimsby T	(0) 0
Chester C	(1) 2	Port Vale	(1) 1
Colchester U	(1) 2	Crystal Palace	(0) 2
Darlington	(1) 1	Bolton W	(0) 1
Halifax T	(0) 0	WBA	(0) 0
Hartlepool U	(1) 3	Crewe Alex	(1) 3
Lincoln C	(1) 2	Barnsley	(3) 4
Luton T	(0) 0	Bristol R	(1) 2
Macclesfield T	(0) 1	Stoke C	(1) 1
Northampton T	(0) 1	Fulham	(0) 2
Norwich C	(2) 2	Cheltenham T	(0) 0
Preston NE	(1) 1	Wrexham	(0) 0
Rochdale	(1) 1	Chesterfield	(0) 2
Rotherham U	(0) 0	Hull C	(1) 1
Scunthorpe U	(0) 0	Huddersfield T	(1) 2
Sheffield U	(0) 3	Shrewsbury T	(0) 0
Southend U	(0) 0	Oxford U	(0) 2
Stockport Co	(0) 2	Oldham Ath	(0) 0
Swindon T	(0) 0	Leyton Orient	(0) 1
Walsall	(1) 4	Plymouth Arg	(1) 1
Wycombe W	(0) 0	Wolverhampton W	(0) 1
York C	(0) 0	Wigan Ath	(0) 1
Brentford	(0) 0	Ipswich T	(0) 2
Brighton & HA	(0) 0	Gillingham	(1) 2
Manchester C	(1) 5	Burnley	(0) 0
Nottingham F	(1) 3	Mansfield T	(0) 0
Reading	(0) 0	Peterborough U	(0) 0
Swansea C	(1) 2	Millwall	(0) 0
Torquay U	(0) 0	Portsmouth	(0) 0

FIRST ROUND, SECOND LEG

Barnet	(2) 3	Bournemouth	(2) 2
Barnsley	(0) 2	Lincoln C	(1) 2
Bolton W	(2) 5	Darlington	(2) 3
Bristol C	(2) 2	Cambridge U	(0) 1
Burnley	(0) 0	Manchester C	(0) 1
Cheltenham T	(0) 2	Norwich C	(0) 1
(aet)			
Chesterfield	(1) 2	Rochdale	(1) 1
Crewe Alex	(0) 1	Hartlepool U	(0) 0
Crystal Palace	(2) 3	Colchester U	(0) 1
Exeter C	(0) 1	Birmingham C	(1) 2
Fulham	(3) 3	Northampton T	(1) 1
Gillingham	(2) 2	Brighton & HA	(0) 0
Grimsby T	(3) 6	Carlisle U	(0) 0
Huddersfield T	(0) 0	Scunthorpe U	(0) 0

Hull C	(1) 2	Rotherham U	(0) 0
Ipswich T	(1) 2	Brentford	(0) 0
Leyton Orient	(0) 1	Swindon T	(0) 1
Mansfield T	(0) 1	Nottingham F	(0) 0
Millwall	(1) 1	Swansea C	(0) 1
Notts Co	(0) 2	Bury	(0) 0
Oldham Ath	(0) 1	Stockport Co	(1) 1
Oxford U	(0) 1	Southend U	(0) 0
Peterborough U	(1) 1	Reading	(1) 2
Plymouth Arg	(1) 1	Walsall	(3) 4
Port Vale	(2) 4	Chester C	(2) 4
Portsmouth	(2) 3	Torquay U	(0) 0
Shrewsbury T	(0) 0	Sheffield U	(2) 3
Tranmere R	(2) 3	Blackpool	(0) 1
WBA	(4) 5	Halifax T	(0) 1
Wigan Ath	(1) 2	York C	(0) 1
Wolverhampton W	(0) 2	Wycombe W	(2) 4
Wrexham	(0) 0	Preston NE	(1) 2
Bristol R	(0) 2	Luton T	(0) 2
QPR	(0) 1	Cardiff C	(1) 2
(aet; Cardiff C won 3-2 on penalties.)			
Stoke C	(0) 3	Macclesfield T	(0) 0

SECOND ROUND, FIRST LEG

Barnsley	(1) 1	Stockport Co	(1) 1
Birmingham C	(0) 2	Bristol R	(0) 0
Bradford C	(1) 1	Reading	(0) 1
Cardiff C	(1) 1	Wimbledon	(0) 1
Charlton Ath	(0) 0	Bournemouth	(0) 0
Chester C	(0) 0	Aston Villa	(0) 1
Chesterfield	(0) 0	Middlesbrough	(0) 0
Crewe Alex	(0) 2	Ipswich T	(1) 1
Crystal Palace	(1) 3	Leicester C	(2) 3
Gillingham	(0) 1	Bolton W	(2) 4
Grimsby T	(2) 4	Leyton Orient	(1) 1
Huddersfield T	(1) 2	Notts Co	(1) 1
Hull C	(0) 1	Liverpool	(2) 5
Norwich C	(0) 0	Fulham	(1) 4
Oxford U	(1) 1	Everton	(1) 1
Portsmouth	(0) 0	Blackburn R	(0) 3
Sheffield U	(2) 2	Preston NE	(0) 0
Stoke C	(0) 0	Sheffield W	(0) 0
Sunderland	(1) 3	Walsall	(2) 2
Swansea C	(0) 0	Derby Co	(0) 0
Tranmere R	(0) 5	Coventry C	(1) 1
WBA	(0) 1	Wycombe W	(0) 1
Watford	(0) 2	Wigan Ath	(0) 0
Manchester C	(0) 0	Southampton	(0) 0
Nottingham F	(1) 2	Bristol C	(1) 1

SECOND ROUND, SECOND LEG

Aston Villa	(2) 5	Chester C	(0) 0
Bolton W	(2) 2	Gillingham	(0) 0
Bournemouth	(0) 0	Charlton Ath	(0) 0
(aet; Bournemouth won 3-1 on penalties.)			
Bristol R	(0) 0	Birmingham C	(0) 1
Fulham	(1) 2	Norwich C	(0) 0

Ipswich T	(1) 1	Crewe Alex	(0) 1
Leyton Orient	(1) 1	Grimsby T	(0) 0
Liverpool	(1) 4	Hull C	(0) 2
Middlesbrough	(1) 2	Chesterfield	(0) 1
Notts Co	(2) 2	Huddersfield T	(2) 2
Preston NE	(1) 3	Sheffield U	(0) 0
Southampton	(2) 4	Manchester C	(1) 3
(aet)			
Stockport Co	(2) 3	Barnsley	(0) 3
(aet; Barnsley won on away goals.)			
Walsall	(0) 0	Sunderland	(2) 5
Wigan Ath	(1) 3	Watford	(0) 1
(aet; Watford won on away goals.)			
Wimbledon	(0) 3	Cardiff C	(1) 1
Wycombe W	(1) 3	WBA	(2) 4
(aet)			
Blackburn R	(0) 3	Portsmouth	(1) 1
Bristol C	(0) 0	Nottingham F	(0) 0
Coventry C	(3) 3	Tranmere R	(1) 1
Derby Co	(1) 3	Swansea C	(0) 1
Everton	(0) 0	Oxford U	(1) 1
Leicester C	(1) 4	Crystal Palace	(0) 2
Reading	(1) 2	Bradford C	(0) 2
(aet; Bradford C won on away goals.)			
Sheffield W	(2) 3	Stoke C	(0) 1

THIRD ROUND

Arsenal	(1) 2	Preston NE	(1) 1
Birmingham C	(1) 2	Newcastle U	(0) 0
Bradford C	(1) 2	Barnsley	(2) 3
Tranmere R	(0) 2	Oxford U	(0) 0
WBA	(1) 1	Fulham	(1) 2
Wimbledon	(0) 3	Sunderland	(0) 2
(aet)			
Aston Villa	(1) 3	Manchester U	(0) 0
Chelsea	(0) 0	Huddersfield T	(0) 1
Derby Co	(1) 1	Bolton W	(1) 2
Leeds U	(0) 1	Blackburn R	(0) 0
Leicester C	(1) 2	Grimsby T	(0) 0
Middlesbrough	(0) 1	Watford	(0) 0
Sheffield W	(1) 4	Nottingham F	(0) 1
Southampton	(0) 2	Liverpool	(0) 1
Tottenham H	(0) 3	Crewe Alex	(0) 1
West Ham U	(0) 2	Bournemouth	(0) 0

FOURTH ROUND

Birmingham C	(0) 2	West Ham U	(1) 3
Bolton W	(0) 1	Sheffield W	(0) 0
Huddersfield T	(1) 1	Wimbledon	(0) 2
(aet)			
Middlesbrough	(1) 2	Arsenal	(1) 2
(aet; Middlesbrough won 3-1 on penalties.)			
Tranmere R	(2) 4	Barnsley	(0) 0
Aston Villa	(1) 4	Southampton	(0) 0
Fulham	(2) 3	Tottenham H	(1) 1
Leicester C	(0) 0	Leeds U	(0) 0
(aet; Leicester C won 4-2 on penalties.)			

FIFTH ROUND

Bolton W	(2) 2	Wimbledon	(1) 1
Tranmere R	(1) 2	Middlesbrough	(0) 1
West Ham U	(0) 2	Aston Villa	(1) 2

(aet; West Ham U won 5-4 on penalties; match ordered to be replayed, West Ham U fielded an ineligible player.)

West Ham U	(0) 1	Aston Villa	(0) 3
Leicester C	(0) 3	Fulham	(0) 3

(aet; Leicester C won 3-0 on penalties.)

SEMI-FINALS, FIRST LEG

Bolton W	(0) 0	Tranmere R	(1) 1
Aston Villa	(0) 0	Leicester C	(0) 0

SEMI-FINALS, SECOND LEG

Tranmere R	(2) 3	Bolton W	(0) 0

(Tranmere R won 4-0 on aggregate.)

Leicester C	(1) 1	Aston Villa	(0) 0

(Leicester C won 1-0 on aggregate.)

FINAL (at Wembley)

27 FEB

Leicester C (1) 2 *(Elliott 29, 81)*
Tranmere R (0) 1 *(Kelly 77)* 74,313

Leicester C: Flowers; Savage, Guppy, Elliott, Taggart, Sinclair, Lennon, Izzet, Cottee (Marshall), Oakes (Impey), Heskey.
Tranmere R: Murphy; Hazell, Roberts, Henry, Hill, Challinor, Mahon, Parkinson (Yates), Jones G, Kelly, Taylor.
Referee: A. Wilkie (Chester-le-Street).
(P. Richards (Preston) (substitute 57 minutes)).

AUTO WINDSCREENS SHIELD 1999–2000

FIRST ROUND

Brighton & HA	(0) 1	Millwall	(0) 0
Gillingham	(0) 0	Torquay U	(0) 3
Hartlepool U	(1) 1	Halifax T	(0) 0
Mansfield T	(1) 2	Bury	(1) 1
(aet; Mansfield T won on sudden death.)			
Northampton T	(0) 1	Cardiff C	(0) 0
Notts Co	(0) 0	Blackpool	(1) 1
Oxford U	(1) 2	Luton T	(0) 0
Preston NE	(3) 4	Wrexham	(1) 1
Rotherham U	(1) 2	Shrewsbury T	(0) 1
Southend U	(0) 0	Cheltenham T	(1) 1
Stoke C	(2) 3	Darlington	(1) 2
(aet; Stoke C won on sudden death.)			
Swansea C	(2) 3	Colchester U	(0) 1
Wigan Ath	(1) 2	Burnley	(1) 1
(aet; Wigan Ath won on sudden death.)			
York C	(0) 0	Hull C	(1) 1
Reading	(1) 1	Leyton Orient	(0) 0
Cambridge U	(1) 1	Barnet	(0) 2
(aet; Barnet won on sudden death.)			

SECOND ROUND

Lincoln C	(0) 1	Scunthorpe U	(1) 2
Preston NE	(0) 1	Hartlepool U	(0) 2
Bournemouth	(0) 1	Brighton & HA	(0) 0
(aet; Bournemouth won on sudden death.)			
Exeter C	(1) 2	Swansea C	(0) 0
Hull C	(1) 2	Chester C	(0) 0
Mansfield T	(0) 0	Blackpool	(1) 1
Northampton T	(0) 0	Bristol R	(0) 0
(aet; Bristol R won 5-3 on penalties.)			
Oldham Ath	(0) 0	Stoke C	(0) 1
(abandoned after 56 mins; floodlight failure.)			
Oldham Ath	(0) 0	Stoke C	(0) 1
(aet; Stoke C won on sudden death.)			
Oxford U	(1) 1	Wycombe W	(1) 1
(aet; Oxford U won 5-3 on penalties.)			
Peterborough U	(0) 0	Brentford	(1) 1
Plymouth Arg	(0) 0	Torquay U	(1) 1
Rochdale	(0) 3	Macclesfield T	(2) 2
(aet; Rochdale won on sudden death.)			
Rotherham U	(0) 1	Chesterfield	(2) 4
Bristol C	(1) 3	Cheltenham T	(0) 1
Barnet	(0) 1	Reading	(1) 2
(aet; Reading won on sudden death.)			
Carlisle U	(2) 2	Wigan Ath	(0) 1

NORTHERN QUARTER-FINALS

Blackpool	(1) 1	Stoke C	(1) 2
Rochdale	(0) 0	Hull C	(0) 0
(aet; Rochdale won 5-4 on penalties.)			

Scunthorpe U	(1) 1	Chesterfield	(1) 2
Carlisle U	(1) 2	Hartlepool U	(0) 1

SOUTHERN QUARTER-FINALS

Bristol R	(0) 1	Reading	(2) 2
Brentford	(0) 2	Oxford U	(0) 0
Bristol C	(1) 1	Bournemouth	(1) 1
(aet; Bristol C won 4-1 on penalties.)			
Exeter C	(1) 1	Torquay U	(0) 0

NORTHERN SEMI-FINALS

Chesterfield	(0) 0	Stoke C	(0) 1
Carlisle U	(0) 0	Rochdale	(0) 1

SOUTHERN SEMI-FINALS

Bristol C	(2) 4	Reading	(0) 0
Exeter C	(2) 3	Brentford	(1) 2

NORTHERN FINAL, FIRST LEG

Rochdale	(0) 1	Stoke C	(3) 3

SOUTHERN FINAL, FIRST LEG

Bristol C	(1) 4	Exeter C	(0) 0

NORTHERN FINAL, SECOND LEG

Stoke C	(0) 1	Rochdale	(0) 0

Stoke C won 4–1 on agg.

SOUTHERN FINAL, SECOND LEG

Exeter C	(1) 1	Bristol C	(0) 1

Bristol C won 5–1 on agg.

FINAL (at Wembley)

16 APR

Bristol C (0) 1 *(Spencer 73)*
Stoke C (1) 2 *(Kavanagh G 31, Thorne 81)* 75,057

Bristol C: Mercer; Carey (Amankwaah), Bell, Jordan, Millen, Holland, Murray, Brown A (Spencer), Beadle, Thorpe, Tinnion.
Stoke C: Ward; Hansson, Clarke, Mohan, Gudjonsson, Gunnlaugsson (Dryden), Gunnarsson, Kavanagh G, Lightbourne (Iwelumo), Thorne, O'Connor.
Referee: K. Lynch (Kirk Hammerton).

FA CHARITY SHIELD WINNERS 1908–99

1908	Manchester U v QPR	4-0 after 1-1 draw
1909	Newcastle U v Northampton T	2-0
1910	Brighton v Aston Villa	1-0
1911	Manchester U v Swindon T	8-4
1912	Blackburn R v QPR	2-1
1913	Professionals v Amateurs	7-2
1920	Tottenham H v Burnley	2-0
1921	Huddersfield T v Liverpool	1-0
1922	Not played	
1923	Professionals v Amateurs	2-0
1924	Professionals v Amateurs	3-1
1925	Amateurs v Professionals	6-1
1926	Amateurs v Professionals	6-3
1927	Cardiff C v Corinthians	2-1
1928	Everton v Blackburn R	2-1
1929	Professionals v Amateurs	3-0
1930	Arsenal v Sheffield W	2-1
1931	Arsenal v WBA	1-0
1932	Everton v Newcastle U	5-3
1933	Arsenal v Everton	3-0
1934	Arsenal v Manchester C	4-0
1935	Sheffield W v Arsenal	1-0
1936	Sunderland v Arsenal	2-1
1937	Manchester C v Sunderland	2-0
1938	Arsenal v Preston NE	2-1
1948	Arsenal v Manchester U	4-3
1949	Portsmouth v Wolverhampton W	1-1*
1950	World Cup Team v Canadian Touring Team	4-2
1951	Tottenham H v Newcastle U	2-1
1952	Manchester U v Newcastle U	4-2
1953	Arsenal v Blackpool	3-1
1954	Wolverhampton W v WBA	4-4*
1955	Chelsea v Newcastle U	3-0
1956	Manchester U v Manchester C	1-0
1957	Manchester U v Aston Villa	4-0
1958	Bolton W v Wolverhampton W	4-1
1959	Wolverhampton W v Nottingham F	3-1
1960	Burnley v Wolverhampton W	2-2*
1961	Tottenham H v FA XI	3-2
1962	Tottenham H v Ipswich T	5-1
1963	Everton v Manchester U	4-0
1964	Liverpool v West Ham U	2-2*
1965	Manchester U v Liverpool	2-2*
1966	Liverpool v Everton	1-0
1967	Manchester U v Tottenham H	3-3*
1968	Manchester C v WBA	6-1
1969	Leeds U v Manchester C	2-1
1970	Everton v Chelsea	2-1
1971	Leicester C v Liverpool	1-0
1972	Manchester C v Aston Villa	1-0
1973	Burnley v Manchester C	1-0
1974	Liverpool† v Leeds U	1-1
1975	Derby Co v West Ham U	2-0
1976	Liverpool v Southampton	1-0
1977	Liverpool v Manchester U	0-0*
1978	Nottingham F v Ipswich T	5-0
1979	Liverpool v Arsenal	3-1
1980	Liverpool v West Ham U	1-0
1981	Aston Villa v Tottenham H	2-2*
1982	Liverpool v Tottenham H	1-0
1983	Manchester U v Liverpool	2-0
1984	Everton v Liverpool	1-0
1985	Everton v Manchester U	2-0
1986	Everton v Liverpool	1-1*
1987	Everton v Coventry C	1-0
1988	Liverpool v Wimbledon	2-1
1989	Liverpool v Arsenal	1-0
1990	Liverpool v Manchester U	1-1*
1991	Arsenal v Tottenham H	0-0*
1992	Leeds U v Liverpool	4-3
1993	Manchester U† v Arsenal	1-1
1994	Manchester U v Blackburn R	2-0
1995	Everton v Blackburn R	1-0
1996	Manchester U v Newcastle U	4-0
1997	Manchester U† v Chelsea	1-1
1998	Arsenal v Manchester U	3-0

*Each club retained shield for six months. †Won on penalties.

AXA FA CHARITY SHIELD 1999

Arsenal (0) 2, Manchester U (1) 1

At Wembley, 1 August 1999, attendance 70,185

Arsenal: Manninger; Dixon, Winterburn, Vieira, Keown, Grimandi, Parlour (Luzhny), Kanu, Petit, Ljungberg, Silvinho (Boa Morte).
Scorers: Kanu 67 (pen), Parlour 77.

Manchester U: Bosnich; Neville P, Irwin, Berg, Scholes, Stam (May), Beckham, Butt (Sheringham), Cole, Yorke, Cruyff (Solskjaer).
Scorer: Yorke 36.

Referee: G. Barber (Tring).

SCOTTISH LEAGUE REVIEW 1999–2000

Rangers won their second successive Scottish Premier League title by the embarrassingly wide margin of 21 points from their eternal rivals Celtic. It might have been worse, had not Rangers suffered only their second defeat of the season at Motherwell on the last day of the season.

Rangers had lost only one other match, 1-0 at home to Dundee, whose manager Jocky Scott had previously stated that Scottish football would be better off without both Rangers and Celtic, because there would at least be level competition.

It was Rangers 48th championship success and Celtic still stand on 36 such wins. Rangers have won 12 of the last 14 titles and finishing second is no consolation for Celtic who parted company with Manager John Barnes shortly after the humiliation of being knocked out of the Scottish Cup on 8 February.

Inverness Caledonian Thistle, relative newcomers to the Scottish League, won 3-1 at Parkhead in a third round tie to produce a shock which rivalled Rangers losing to Berwick Rangers three or more decades earlier. Though Kenny Dalglish was given a more hands on role at the helm, he, too was relieved of his position as Director of Football during the close season, to be replaced by Martin O'Neill the manager of Leicester City.

Scottish football continues to wrestle with its format. After just two seasons of the Premier League there are extensive changes to the pattern for 2000–2001. The top division will be increased to 12 clubs and this situation has forced the Scottish League to add two new clubs in the shape of Elgin City and Peterhead from the Highland League.

Because of these arrangements, it had been decided that while two teams were to be promoted from the Scottish League First Division to the Premier League, a play-off would give a third team the chance to go up with them after meeting the bottom club in the Premier.

For many weeks it seemed likely that Aberdeen would fit this bill admirably. They failed to achieve a point until the eighth game of the season when they drew 2-2 at home to Hibernian. Their next points came in an unexpected and spectacular way when they won 6-5 at Motherwell on 20 October in what was their tenth match.

However, they were spared having to take part in a play-off situation because Falkirk, the third placed team in the First Division, were deemed not to have facilities in keeping with the new requirements of the Premier League.

The reconstruction of Scottish football took a serious turn way back in 1974–75 when the League was rearranged into three divisions. Further changes were made in 1986–87, 1988–89 and 1991–92. Then followed the creation of the breakaway Scottish Premier League.

For 2000–2001, St Mirren and Dunfermline Athletic will be added to the Premier League. Clydebank will become the only relegated team from the First Division, with Clyde, Alloa and Ross County moving into the First Division.

Hamilton Academical, having had 15 points deducted after the players went on strike and refused to play against Stenhousemuir, go down into the Third Division to be replaced by Queen's Park, Berwick Rangers and Forfar Athletic. As previously mentioned, Elgin and Peterhead will restore the Third Division to ten clubs.

However, the 12 clubs in the Scottish Premier League will have a vastly different season with which to contend. After playing each other on a home and away basis, the league will be split into two halves. The top will fight out the championship and other European cup places on offer, while the remainder will be concerned with the fight against relegation.

Such a system has been operated successfully in Switzerland, but the jury is out on whether a similar move will benefit the Scottish clubs. Indeed with financial problems affecting Airdrieonians, Greenock Morton and Clydebank, the entire scene is not a stable one it seems. Clydebank playing home games at Morton had only 29 spectators for one game.

On the Cup front, Rangers managed the double beating Aberdeen 4-0 in the Tennent's Scottish Cup and Celtic made it a miserable season overall for the Dons who beat them 2-0 in the CIS Insurance League Cup. The Challenge Cup was revived and after a 4-4 draw in the final, Alloa won 5-4 on penalties against Inverness.

SCOTTISH LEAGUE TABLES 1999–2000

Premier Division		*Home*			*Goals*		*Away*			*Goals*			
	P	W	D	L	F	A	W	D	L	F	A	Pts	GD
Rangers	36	16	1	1	52	12	12	5	1	44	14	90	70
Celtic	36	12	3	3	58	17	9	3	6	32	21	69	52
Hearts	36	7	6	5	25	18	8	3	7	22	22	54	7
Motherwell	36	8	3	7	27	34	6	7	5	22	29	52	–14
St Johnstone	36	5	7	6	16	18	5	5	7	20	26	42	–8
Hibernian	36	7	6	5	30	27	3	5	10	19	34	41	–12
Dundee	36	4	3	11	20	33	8	2	8	25	31	41	–19
Dundee U	36	6	4	8	16	22	5	2	10	18	35	39	–23
Kilmarnock	36	5	5	8	16	22	3	8	7	22	30	37	–14
Aberdeen	36	6	4	8	28	37	3	2	13	16	46	33	–39

First Division		*Home*			*Goals*		*Away*			*Goals*			
	P	W	D	L	F	A	W	D	L	F	A	Pts	GD
St Mirren	36	12	3	3	42	19	11	4	3	33	20	76	36
Dunfermline Ath	36	10	7	1	34	13	10	4	4	32	20	71	33
Falkirk	36	11	2	5	38	23	9	6	3	29	17	68	27
Livingston	36	9	5	4	29	17	10	2	6	31	28	64	15
Raith R	36	11	3	4	35	21	6	5	7	20	19	59	15
Inverness CT	36	7	6	5	34	25	6	4	8	26	30	49	5
Ayr U	36	6	3	9	25	24	4	5	9	17	28	38	–10
Greenock Morton	36	7	3	8	22	23	3	3	12	23	38	36	–16
Airdrieonians	36	4	5	9	15	26	3	3	12	14	43	29	–40
Clydebank	36	1	3	14	11	40	0	4	14	6	42	10	–65

Second Division		*Home*			*Goals*		*Away*			*Goals*			
	P	W	D	L	F	A	W	D	L	F	A	Pts	GD
Clyde	36	12	5	1	35	7	6	6	6	30	30	65	28
Alloa Ath	36	11	5	2	36	18	6	8	4	22	20	64	20
Ross Co	36	9	5	4	31	20	9	3	6	26	19	62	18
Arbroath	36	6	7	5	28	26	5	7	6	24	29	47	–3
Partick T	36	7	5	6	25	22	5	5	8	17	22	46	–2
Stranraer	36	6	8	4	25	22	3	10	5	22	24	45	1
Stirling Albion	36	7	4	7	34	33	4	3	11	26	39	40	–12
Stenhousemuir	36	6	4	8	24	26	4	4	10	20	33	38	–15
Queen of the S	36	5	6	7	24	32	3	3	12	21	43	33	–30
Hamilton A*	36	5	7	6	18	23	5	7	6	21	21	29	–5

*deducted 15 points for failing to field a team

Third Division		*Home*			*Goals*		*Away*			*Goals*			
	P	W	D	L	F	A	W	D	L	F	A	Pts	GD
Queen's Park	36	11	2	5	28	20	9	7	2	26	17	69	17
Berwick R	36	7	6	5	20	14	12	3	3	33	16	66	23
Forfar Ath	36	10	5	3	39	18	7	5	6	25	22	61	24
East Fife	36	9	6	3	24	16	8	2	8	21	23	59	6
Cowdenbeath	36	6	5	7	30	23	9	4	5	29	20	54	16
Dumbarton	36	7	7	4	26	22	8	1	9	27	29	53	2
East Stirlingshire	36	6	2	10	15	27	5	5	8	13	23	40	–22
Brechin C	36	6	3	9	25	25	4	5	9	17	26	38	–9
Montrose	36	5	2	11	19	31	5	5	8	20	23	37	–15
Albion R	36	2	3	13	13	35	3	4	11	20	40	22	–42

BELL'S SCOTTISH LEAGUE—PREMIER DIVISION RESULTS 1999–2000

	Aberdeen	Celtic	Dundee	Dundee U	Hearts	Hibernian	Kilmarnock	Motherwell	Rangers	St Johnstone
Aberdeen	—	0-5	0-2	1-2	3-1	2-2	2-2	1-1	1-5	0-3
	—	0-6	0-1	3-1	1-2	4-0	5-1	2-1	1-1	2-1
Celtic	7-0	—	6-2	4-1	4-0	4-0	5-1	0-1	1-1	3-0
	5-1	—	2-2	2-0	2-3	1-1	4-2	4-0	0-1	4-1
Dundee	1-3	1-2	—	0-2	1-0	3-4	0-0	0-1	2-3	1-2
	0-2	0-3	—	3-0	0-0	1-0	1-2	4-1	1-7	1-1
Dundee U	3-1	2-1	2-1	—	0-2	3-1	0-0	0-2	0-4	1-0
	1-1	0-1	1-0	—	0-1	0-0	2-2	1-2	0-2	0-1
Hearts	3-0	1-2	4-0	3-0	—	0-3	2-2	1-1	0-4	1-1
	3-0	1-0	2-0	1-2	—	2-1	0-0	0-0	1-2	0-0
Hibernian	2-0	0-2	5-2	3-2	1-1	—	0-3	2-2	0-1	0-1
	1-0	2-1	1-2	1-0	3-1	—	2-2	2-2	2-2	3-3
Kilmarnock	2-0	0-1	0-2	1-1	2-2	0-2	—	0-1	1-1	1-2
	1-0	1-1	2-2	1-0	0-1	1-0	—	0-2	0-2	3-2
Motherwell	5-6	3-2	0-2	2-2	2-1	2-2	0-4	—	1-5	1-0
	1-0	1-1	0-3	1-3	0-2	2-0	2-0	—	2-0	2-1
Rangers	3-0	4-2	1-2	4-1	1-0	2-0	2-1	4-1	—	3-1
	5-0	4-0	3-0	3-0	1-0	5-2	1-0	6-2	—	0-0
St Johnstone	1-1	1-2	0-1	0-1	1-4	1-1	2-0	1-1	0-2	—
	2-1	0-0	2-1	2-0	0-1	1-0	0-0	1-1	1-1	—

BELL'S SCOTTISH LEAGUE—DIVISION ONE RESULTS 1999–2000

	Airdrieonians	Ayr U	Clydebank	Dunfermline Ath	Falkirk	Inverness CT	Livingston	Morton	Raith R	St Mirren
Airdrieonians	—	2-1	1-0	2-2	0-0	1-1	2-3	1-0	1-4	0-2
	—	0-0	0-0	1-2	0-2	1-4	0-2	3-0	0-2	0-1
Ayr U	2-0	—	0-0	0-3	1-1	1-0	1-2	3-0	0-1	0-3
	5-0	—	4-0	0-2	3-3	1-3	0-1	3-2	0-1	1-2
Clydebank	0-2	0-2	—	1-4	0-3	0-3	1-5	1-3	1-1	2-3
	1-1	0-2	—	1-3	0-1	0-1	1-2	0-3	2-1	0-0
Dunfermline Ath	0-0	2-1	2-1	—	1-1	4-0	3-0	2-1	1-1	1-1
	1-0	2-0	6-0	—	2-2	1-0	4-1	1-1	0-2	1-1
Falkirk	2-0	2-1	3-2	1-3	—	0-2	0-2	2-4	2-1	3-1
	8-0	1-0	4-0	1-1	—	2-2	2-3	2-1	1-0	2-0
Inverness CT	2-0	1-1	1-0	1-1	2-3	—	2-0	1-1	0-2	1-1
	1-5	1-1	4-1	1-2	0-3	—	4-1	6-2	1-1	5-0
Livingston	3-0	4-1	2-1	0-1	1-1	2-2	—	2-1	1-1	1-2
	3-2	3-1	3-0	1-0	0-1	1-1	—	1-0	0-0	1-2
Morton	0-2	0-0	0-0	0-3	2-3	5-1	2-2	—	2-0	1-4
	4-0	1-2	1-0	2-0	0-2	0-2	1-0	—	1-0	0-2
Raith R	1-1	5-1	1-0	2-2	2-1	4-2	3-1	3-1	—	0-6
	2-0	2-0	0-0	3-0	0-1	2-0	1-3	3-0	—	1-2
St Mirren	5-0	1-1	2-1	3-1	2-1	3-2	1-1	3-2	3-2	—
	3-1	1-2	8-0	0-2	1-0	2-0	0-2	1-1	3-0	—

BELL'S SCOTTISH LEAGUE—DIVISION TWO RESULTS 1999–2000

	Alloa Ath	Arbroath	Clyde	Hamilton A	Partick Th	Queen of the S	Ross Co	Stenhousemuir	Stirling Alb	Stranraer
Alloa Ath	—	0-0	1-0	1-1	1-0	3-1	2-0	1-4	4-4	1-1
	—	2-1	2-1	2-0	1-1	6-1	1-2	3-1	1-0	4-0
Arbroath	2-2	—	2-1	1-1	0-0	5-2	0-1	0-3	2-1	1-2
	2-0	—	1-1	1-1	3-2	1-2	1-2	2-2	3-2	1-1
Clyde	0-1	0-0	—	2-1	2-0	3-0	3-1	1-0	3-0	0-0
	0-0	4-1	—	1-0	1-0	3-1	0-0	7-0	4-1	1-1
Hamilton A	1-2	2-2	2-3	—	0-0	0-3	1-0	1-1	0-2	2-1
	0-0	2-2	1-1	—	0-1	1-1	0-3	2-1	1-0	2-0
Partick Th	2-2	1-3	0-0	0-1	—	2-0	0-2	0-1	1-0	2-0
	0-1	2-0	1-2	2-2	—	5-4	4-2	1-0	1-1	1-1
Queen of the S	1-1	2-3	1-1	3-2	1-2	—	0-2	0-3	3-3	0-5
	2-1	1-0	3-0	1-1	1-1	—	0-3	3-1	2-3	0-0
Ross Co	1-0	2-0	2-0	2-1	2-1	1-1	—	0-0	1-3	1-1
	3-4	1-1	2-2	0-1	1-3	2-0	—	2-0	5-1	3-1
Stenhousemuir	1-3	1-3	1-3	0-0	0-1	2-1	0-2	—	2-1	1-1
	2-1	3-0	3-4	0-1	2-0	2-0	2-2	—	1-2	1-1
Stirling Alb	0-1	3-4	1-2	2-0	3-1	3-0	2-1	5-1	—	1-1
	1-1	1-1	3-6	1-4	0-2	2-2	3-1	1-0	—	2-5
Stranraer	0-0	2-2	2-2	0-2	1-1	1-0	0-0	2-0	2-1	—
	2-2	0-1	2-1	2-2	3-1	1-2	0-2	2-2	3-1	—

BELL'S SCOTTISH LEAGUE—DIVISION THREE RESULTS 1999–2000

	Albion R	Berwick R	Brechin C	Cowdenbeath	Dumbarton	East Fife	East Stirling	Forfar Ath	Montrose	Queen's P
Albion R	—	0-3	0-0	1-4	1-3	1-3	1-1	0-1	1-3	2-4
	—	0-0	0-2	0-3	3-0	3-1	0-1	0-1	0-2	0-3
Berwick R	1-1	—	2-0	0-2	0-1	0-1	1-0	2-2	0-0	1-2
	2-1	—	3-1	0-0	0-0	0-1	3-0	2-0	2-1	1-1
Brechin C	8-1	0-3	—	2-0	0-2	1-3	1-2	0-2	1-0	1-2
	3-2	1-2	—	1-2	1-2	3-1	1-1	1-0	0-0	0-0
Cowdenbeath	0-0	1-1	6-1	—	0-2	4-0	1-2	0-3	1-1	0-2
	5-0	1-3	1-1	—	1-2	1-0	0-0	4-1	2-1	2-3
Dumbarton	1-1	2-1	1-3	1-1	—	1-1	1-0	3-3	3-4	0-1
	0-0	0-2	2-1	2-0	—	2-1	3-0	0-0	3-2	1-1
East Fife	1-4	1-2	1-0	2-3	1-0	—	1-0	2-0	0-0	0-0
	2-1	3-1	1-1	1-1	2-1	—	3-1	1-1	2-0	0-0
East Stirling	4-3	0-3	0-0	0-1	1-3	0-2	—	0-2	2-0	1-1
	3-1	0-1	0-3	0-4	2-1	1-0	—	0-1	1-0	0-1
Forfar Ath	2-0	1-1	0-0	3-1	5-0	3-2	1-1	—	1-2	2-2
	3-1	2-0	2-0	2-2	4-3	0-1	3-0	—	1-2	4-0
Montrose	2-1	1-2	0-1	0-1	1-4	1-2	1-2	2-0	—	2-1
	1-2	2-3	1-0	1-3	2-1	1-1	0-0	1-5	—	0-2
Queen's P	2-0	1-4	5-3	1-0	3-2	0-1	2-1	1-1	2-1	—
	0-1	0-1	1-0	3-1	2-0	1-0	0-1	3-2	1-1	—

ABERDEEN PREMIER LEAGUE

Ground: Pittodrie Stadium, Aberdeen AB24 5QH (01224) 650400
Ground capacity: 22,199. **Colours:** All red with white trim.
Manager: Ebbe Skovdahl.
League Appearances: Anderson R 34; Belabed R 6(15); Bernard P 24(1); Bett B (1); Buchan J 5(3); Clark C (2); Cobian J 2(1); Dow A 35; Esson R 1; Gillies R 3(7); Guntweit C 20; Hamilton J 3(4); Hart M 2(1); Jess E 25(1); Kiriakov I 6(2); Leighton J 26; Lilley D 14(3); Mackie D 2(2); Mayer A 20(1); McAllister J 29(5); McGuire P (3); Pepper C 4; Perry M 10(8); Preece D 9(1); Rowson D 2(3); Rutkiewicz K 1(9); Smith B 6; Solberg T 26; Stavrum A 22; Whyte D 19(1); Winters R 23(10); Wyness D 1(2); Young Darren 1(2); Young Derek 9(5); Zerouali H 6(8).
Goals – League (44): Stavrum 9 (1 pen), Winters 7, Dow 5, Jess 5, Bernard 4, Solberg 4 (2 pens), Guntweit 3, Zerouali 3, Anderson 1, Belabed 1, Gillies 1, Rowson 1.
Scottish Cup (8): Stavrum 2, Zerouali 2, Bernard 1, Dow 1, Guntweit 1, Jess 1.
CIS Cup (1): Gillies 1.
Honours – Division 1: Champions – 1954-55, **Premier Division:** Champions – 1979-80, 1983-84, 1984-85. **Scottish Cup winners** 1947, 1970, 1982, 1983, 1984, 1986, 1990. **League Cup winners** 1956, 1977, 1986, 1990, 1996. **European Cup-Winners' Cup winners** 1983.

AIRDRIEONIANS DIV. 1

Ground: Shyberry Excelsior Stadium, Airdrie ML6 8QZ (01236) 622000
Ground capacity: 10,000 (all seated). **Colours:** White shirts with red diamond, white shorts.
Manager: Gary Mackay.
League Appearances: Boyce S 6(1); Brady D (4); Conway F 5(5); Dick J 19(3); Easton S 14(3); Evans G 25; Farrell D 14(2); Farrell G 20(1); Forrest E 20(3); Gallacher P 9; Greacen S 2; Holsgrove P 4; Ingram S 7(5); Jack P 29(1); Johnston F 16(3); McCann A 25(4); McClelland J (1); McCormick S 17(4); McGinty B 4; McGuire D 4(14); McKeown S 3(15); Moore A 23(4); Neil A 15(1); Sandison J 25(2); Stewart A 28(1); Struthers W (3); Taylor S 16(6); Thompson N 19(6); Thomson S 22; Wallace R (1); Wilson S 5.
Goals – League (29): Neil 5, Thompson 5, Evans 4, McCormick 4, McKeown 3, McCann 2 (1 pen), Moore 2, Easton 1, Jack 1 (pen), McGuire 1, Taylor 1.
Scottish Cup (1): McCann 1 (pen).
CIS Cup (2): McCormick 2.
Bell's League Cup (3): Moore 2, Johnston 1.
Honours – Division II: Champions – 1902-03, 1954-55, 1973-74. **Scottish Cup winners** 1924. **B&Q Cup winners** 1995.

ALBION ROVERS DIV. 3

Ground: Cliftonhill Stadium, Main Street, Coatbridge ML5 3RB (01236) 606334
Ground capacity: 2496. **Colours:** Yellow shirts with black trim, black shorts.
Manager: John McVeigh.

League Appearances: Best R 1; Bonar S 14(1); Clyde R 4; Coulter J 14(7); Deegan C 7; Diack I 20(12); Dobbins I (1); Duncan G 13; Flannigan C 20(3); Fotheringham G 2(1); Friels G 1; Greenock R 5; Hamilton J 11(2); Harty M 5(9); Hughes M 4(1); Lumsden T 26(1); Lyon M 2; Martin C 7; McArthur S 4(1); McBride K 14(6); McCarroll J 13(3); McCondichie A 2; McGowan N 2; McIntyre J 1(1); McKenzie J 3; McLean M 30; McLees J 27(4); McMillan R 5(5); McMullen S 1(5); McStay J 26(1); Nesovic A 9; Prentice A 9; Rae D 5; Robertson G 6; Russell G 4(2); Silvestro C 23(6); Smith J 23(2); Sutherland D (5); Tait T 30(1); Vennard D 1; Young F 2.
Goals – League (33): Diack 7 (1 pen), McStay 6, Flannigan 4, Duncan 3, Tait 3, McLees 2, Coulter 1, Deegan 1, Hughes 1, Lumsden 1, McCarroll 1, Nesovic 1, Prentice 1, Smith 1.
Scottish Cup (6): Flannigan 3, Duncan 1, McLees 1, McStay 1.
CIS Cup (0).
Bell's League Cup (3): Tait 2, Rae 1.
Honours – Division II: Champions – 1933-34. **Second Division:** Champions 1988-89.

ALLOA ATHLETIC — DIV. 1

Ground: Recreation Park, Alloa FK10 1RR (01259) 722695
Ground capacity: 3142. **Colours:** Gold shirts with black trim, black shorts.
Manager: Terry Christie.
League Appearances: Bannerman S 1(1); Beaton D 34; Boyle J 14(2); Cairns M 20; Cameron M 35; Christie M 20(4); Clark D 31(1); Clark G 18(14); Conway F 13; Cowan M 1(1); Donaghy M 15(11); Farrell G 4(1); Irvine W 36; Little I 29; McAneny P 17(1); McKechnie G 4(5); Menelaus D 6(12); Nelson M 9(2); Nish C 9(4); Sharp R 5(3); Stewart C 16; Valentine C 36; Walker A 4(4); Wilson M 19(2).
Goals – League (58): Cameron 15, Irvine 13, Little 7, Nish 5, Clark G 4, Walker 3, Beaton 2, Clark D 2, Menelaws 2, Boyle 1, Christie 1, Conway 1, McKechnie 1, own goal 1.
Scottish Cup (5): Cameron 2, Beaton 1, Irvine 1, McKechnie 1.
CIS Cup (6): Cameron 2, Irvine 2, McKechnie 2.
Bell's League Cup (14): Cameron 3, Irvine 2 (1 pen), Bannerman 1, Beaton 1, Clark G 1, Donaghy 1, Little 1, McKechnie 1, Nelson 1, Wilson 1, own goal 1.
Honours – Division II: Champions – 1921-22. **Third Division:** Champions – 1997-98. **League Challenge Cup winners** 2000.

ARBROATH — DIV. 2

Ground: Gayfield Park, Arbroath DD11 1QB (01241) 872157
Ground capacity: 6488. **Colours:** Maroon shirts with sky blue trim, white shorts.
Manager: David Baikie.
League Appearances: Arbuckle D 31; Brownlie P 19(5); Bryce T 32(3); Cooper C 6(10); Crawford J 29(2); Desuarte F (2); Devine C 7(14); Florence S 31(3); Gallagher J 14(5); Hinchcliffe C 26; King T 2; McAulay J 35; McGlashan C 34; Mercer J 31; Mols T 3; Peters S 11(5); Raeside J 14; Sellars B 33(2); Steel K 1(4); Thomson J 15; Thomson N 1(3); Tindal K 4(11); Tosh P 3; Webster A 4; Wight C 10.
Goals – League (52): McGlashan 16 (1 pen), Bryce 6 (2 pens), Mercer 6, Brownlie 5, Sellars 4, Arbuckle 3, Gallagher 2, Peters 2, Thomson J 2, Tosh 2, Crawford 1, Devine 1, Raeside 1, Tindal 1.

Scottish Cup (4): Bryce 1, Devine 1, McGlashan 1, Mercer 1.
CIS Cup (0).
Bell's League Cup (4): McGlashan 2, Brownlie 1, Mercer 1.
Honours – Nil.

AYR UNITED DIV. 1

Ground: Somerset Park, Ayr KA8 9NB (01292) 263435
Ground capacity: 10,243 (1549 seated). **Colours:** White shirts with black sleeves, black shorts.
Manager: Gordon Dalziel.
League Appearances: Adams D 4; Armstrong G (2); Bone A 6(3); Bowman G 5(1); Bradford J 5(1); Burns G 1(2); Campbell M 19; Craig D 23; Crilly M 5(8); Davies J 7; Dodds J 2; Duffy C 28; Duncan L (1); Gill T 8; Grant R 9(4); Hansen J 8; Hogg K 2(2); Hurst G 25; Jemson N 9(3); Keane S (2); Kelly R 2(1); Knudsen J 4; Lennon D 3(4); Lindau P 5(11); Lyons A 16(9); McKeown J (1); McMillan A 16(3); McNally M 5(3); Nelson C 18; Nolan J 1; Prenderville B 3(2); Reynolds M 14(13); Robertson J 26(5); Rogers D 13(3); Rõvde M 4; Scally N 15(3); Shepherd P 20(2); Tarrant N 15; Teale G 26(6); Traynor J 1; Wilson M 23(1).
Goals – League (42): Hurst 14 (1 pen), Jemson 5 (3 pens), Tarrant 4, Craig 3, Bone 2, Campbell 2, Grant 2, Hansen 2, Wilson 2, Bradford 1 (pen), Crilly 1, Keane 1, Lennon 1, Rogers 1, Shepherd 1.
Scottish Cup (7): Tarrant 3, Teale 2 (1 pen), Campbell 1, Duffy 1.
CIS Cup (2): Bone 1, Reynolds 1.
Bell's League Cup (0).
Honours – Division II: Champions – 1911-12, 1912-13, 1927-28, 1936-37, 1958-59, 1965-66. **Second Division:** Champions – 1987-88, 1996-97.

BERWICK RANGERS DIV. 2

Ground: Shielfield Park, Berwick-on-Tweed TD15 2EF (01289) 307424
Ground capacity: 4131. **Colours:** Black with two inch gold stripe, black shorts.
Manager: Paul Smith.
League Appearances: Anthony M 32(2); Campbell C 19(3); Carr-Lawton C 4(3); Findlay C 12(14); Forrester P 2(4); Haddow L 31; Harvey J (1); Humphreys M (2); Hunter M 1(4); Laidlaw S 9(3); Leask M 4(7); Magee K 20(9); McNicoll G 26(1); McPherson D (1); Moonie D (1); Neil M 25(1); Neill A 30(3); O'Connor G 29; Oliver N 9; Patterson P 20(7); Porteous A (1); Rafferty K 14(9); Ramsay S 4(2); Ritchie I 29(2); Scrimgour D 7; Smith D 28(7); Watt D 26(2); Wood G 15.
Goals – League (53): Anthony 9, Wood 8 (2 pens), Smith 7, Findlay 5, Haddow 5 (3 pens), Ritchie 5, Laodlaw 3, Watt 3, Patterson 2, Ramsay 2, Leask 1, McNicoll 1, Neill A 1 (pen), Rafferty 1.
Scottish Cup (4): Findlay 2, Haddow 2 (2 pens).
CIS Cup (1): Patterson 1.
Bell's League Cup (5): Patterson 2, Leask 1, Neil M 1, Neill A 1.
Honours – Second Division: Champions – 1978-79.

BRECHIN CITY DIV. 3

Ground: Glebe Park, Brechin DD9 6BJ (01356) 622856
Ground capacity: 3980. **Colours:** Red with white trim.
Manager: Dick Campbell.
League Appearances: Armstrong G 1(2); Bailey L 20(1); Bain K 29; Black R 32(1); Boyle S 4; Brown R 4; Buick G 3(3); Cairney H 31; Campbell S 13(4); Christie G 15(1); Coulston D 12(9); Dailly M 1(2); Dickson J 3(3); Donachie B 23; Durie J 4; Geddes R 36; Harris P (2); Honeyman B 19(3); Hutcheon A 9(9); Kerrigan S 16(14); McKellar J 5(3); Nairn J 9; Price G 4(2); Raynes S 24; Riley P 28; Smith G 25; Sorbie S 24(1); Williamson K 2(3).
Goals – League (42): Honeyman 11, Black 9, Hutcheon 6, Kerrigan 6, Bailey 2, Coulston 2, Sorbie 2, Bain 1, Dickson 1 (pen), own goals 2.
Scottish Cup (6): Black 2, Bailey 1, Christie 1, Nairn 1, Smith 1.
CIS Cup (0).
Bell's League Cup (0).
Honours – Second Division: Champions – 1982-83, 1989-90. **C Division:** Champions – 1953-54.

CELTIC PREMIER LEAGUE

Ground: Celtic Park, Glasgow G40 3RE (0141) 556 2611
Ground capacity: 60,506 (all seated). **Colours:** Green and white hooped shirts, white shorts.
Manager: Martin O'Neill.
League Appearances: Berkovic E 27(1); Blinker R 10(7); Boyd T 10; Brattbakk H (2); Burchill M 12(16); Burley C 6(2); Convery J (1); Crainey S 5(4); De Ornelas F 0(2); Fotheringham M 1(1); Goodwin J 1; Gould J 28(1); Healy C 8(2); Johnson T 7(3); Kennedy J 1(4); Kerr S 4; Kharine D 4; Lambert P 25; Larsson H 8(1); Lynch S 1(1); Mahe S 19; McCann R 1; McColligan B 1; McNamara J 22; Miller L (1); Mjallby J 26(4); Moravcik L 29(1); Petrov S 21(6); Petta B 2(10); Rafael 1(2); Riseth V 28; Shields P (1); Stubbs A 23; Tebily O 19(3); Viduka M 28; Wieghorst M 14(3); Wright I 4(4).
Goals – League (90): Viduka 25 (2 pens), Burchill 11, Berkovic 9, Johnson 9, Moravcik 8, Larsson 7 (1 pen), Blinker 4, Mahe 4, Wieghorst 3, Wright 3, Mjallby 2, Burley 1, Healy 1, Lambert 1, Lynch 1, Petrov 1.
Scottish Cup (1): Burchill 1.
CIS Cup (8): Blinker 1, Johnson 1, Mjallby 1, Moravcik 1, Petta 1, Riseth 1, Viduka 1, Wieghorst 1.
Honours – Division I: Champions – 1892-93, 1893-94, 1895-96, 1897-98, 1904-05, 1905-06, 1906-07, 1907-08, 1908-09, 1909-10, 1913-14, 1914-15, 1915-16, 1916-17, 1918-19, 1921-22, 1925-26, 1935-36, 1937-38, 1953-54, 1965-66, 1966-67, 1967-68, 1968-69, 1969-70, 1970-71, 1971-72, 1972-73, 1973-74. **Premier Division:** Champions – 1976-77, 1978-79, 1980-81, 1981-82, 1985-86, 1987-88, 1997-98. **Scottish Cup winners** 1892, 1899, 1900, 1904, 1907, 1908, 1911, 1912, 1914, 1923, 1925, 1927, 1931, 1933, 1937, 1951, 1954, 1965, 1967, 1969, 1971, 1972, 1974, 1975, 1977, 1980, 1985, 1988, 1989, 1995. **League Cup winners** 1957, 1958, 1966, 1967, 1968, 1969, 1970, 1975, 1983, 1998, 2000. **European Cup winners** 1967.

CLYDE DIV. 1

Ground: Broadwood Stadium, Cumbernauld G68 9NE (01236) 451511
Ground capacity: 8200. **Colours:** White shirts with red and black trim, black shorts.
Manager: Allan Maitland.
League Appearances: Barrett J 9(17); Carrigan B 31(2); Convery S 5(5); Craib S (2); Cranmer C 24(1); Dunn D (3); Farrell T 1(3); Grant A 24(5); Hay P 2(11); Henderson N 6(1); Keogh P 26(4); McClay A 25; McCusker R 27(3); McDonald I 2(3); McGhee G 2(2); McGraw M 4(2); McIntyre G 5; McLauchlan Mart 9(11); McLaughlin Mark 30(1); Mitchell J 15(9); Mols T 1; Murray D 32; Quinn C 1(2); Ross J 29(1); Smith B 35; Spittal I 7; Vickers S (4); Woods T 13(8); Wylie D 31.
Goals – League (65): Carrigan 18 (2 pens), Keogh 11, Grant 7, McLaughlin 6, Cranmer 4, Mitchell 4, McLauchlan 3, Woods 3, Barrett 2, McClay 2, McCusker 2, McGraw 1, Ross 1, Spittal 1.
Scottish Cup (8): Carrigan 5 (3 pens), Grant 1, McLaughlin 1, Woods 1.
CIS Cup (5): Carrigan 2, Farrell 1, Murray 1, Woods 1.
Bell's League Cup (0).
Honours – Division II: Champions – 1904-05, 1951-52, 1956-57, 1961-62, 1972-73. **Second Division:** Champions – 1977-78, 1981-82, 1992-93, 1999-2000. **Scottish Cup winners** 1939, 1955, 1958.

CLYDEBANK DIV. 2

Ground: Cappielow Park, Greenock. (Office) (0141) 9559048. (Match days only) (01475) 723571
Ground capacity: 14,891. **Colours:** Red and white stripes, black shorts.
Player/Manager: Steve Morrison.
League Appearances: Aibache A 1; Beach K 1; Beggs J 2; Brannigan K 19; Cameron I 28(4); Cormack P 19(1); Ewing C 3(7); Gardner L 33(1); Geraghty M 5; Hunter M 8(5); Hutchison S 6; Jackson C 5; McCondichie A 1; McCutcheon G 4; McDonald P (1); McDonald W 3(1); McIntyre P 4(5); McKay J 10(2); McKelvie D 13(16); McKinstrey J 25(6); McLaughlin J 12; McWilliams D 14(6); Miller G 24(11); Morrison S 1(3); Murdoch S 18(4); Murray S 12(1); O'Neil K 9(3); O'Neil M 9(8); O'Sullivan L 5; Oliver N 18; Pheury B 1; Roddie A 4; Scott C 21; Stewart A 3(5); Stewart C 4; Stewart D 8(3); Sutherland C 8; Wishart F 35.
Goals – League (17): Cameron 5, Gardner 4, Cormack 2, Miller 2, McIntyre 1, McKelvie 1, O'Neil 1, own goal 1.
Scottish Cup (2): Gardner 1 (pen), Wishart 1.
CIS Cup (1): Stewart 1.
Bell's League Cup (6): Ewing 3, Cormack 1, McLaughlin 1, McWilliams 1.
Honours – Second Division: Champions – 1975-76.

COWDENBEATH DIV. 3

Ground: Central Park, Cowdenbeath KY4 9EY (01383) 610166
Ground capacity: 5268. **Colours:** Royal blue stripes with red trim, white shorts.
Manager: Craig Levein.
League Appearances: Berry N 3; Bradley M 31(4); Brown G 23(9); Burns J 23(4); Carnie G 4(8); Clark R (1); Cunning J 4(5); Godfrey R 24; Gray D 8(2); Hutchison S 12; Jackson C 5; Johnston D (1); King S 3(2); Lakie J 4; McCulloch K 23(1);

McDonald I 12; McDowell M 27(2); McMillan C 9(7); Mitchell W 1; Neilson R 8; Nicol G 1(1); Porteous A 2(2); Sharp R 5; Simpson P 11; Simpson P 2(6); Snedden S 29(1); Stewart W 10(13); Thomson R 12; Vaugh B (2); White D 34; Wilson W 34(2); Winter C 32; Young C (5).
Goals – League (59): McDowell 13, Brown 12, Bradley 6, Burns 6, Winter 5, Gray 4, Simpson 4, White 2, Carnie 1, McDonald 1, Porteous 1, Sharp 1, Sneddon 1, Wilson 1, own goal 1.
Scottish Cup (2): Brown 2.
CIS Cup (0).
Bell's League Cup (0).
Honours – Division II: Champions – 1913-14, 1914-15, 1938-39.

DUMBARTON DIV. 3

Ground: Cliftonhill Stadium, Main Street, Coatbridge ML5 3RB.
Club Address: 62 Round Riding Road, Dumbarton G82 2JB. (01389) 762569
Ground capacity: 2496. **Colours:** White with yelllow trim, white shorts.
Manager: Jimmy Brown.
League Appearances: Barnes D 24; Bonar S 3; Bradford J 6; Brittain C 35; Brown Alan (3); Brown And 27(7); Bruce J 21; Dickie M 31; Dillon J 17(8); Finnigan P 2; Flannery P 27(2); Gentile C (2); Grace A 26(1); Hringsson H 3(10); Jack S 34; King T 32; McCann K 3; McCormack J 8(10); McHarg S 1(6); Meechan K 12; Melvin M 1(5); Melvin W 8(2); Robertson J 33(3); Smith C 9(11); Stewart D 21; Templeman C 3; Ward H 3(10); Watters W 6(1).
Goals – League (53): Flannery 14, Robertson 7, King 5, Andrew Brown 4, Smith 4, Bradford 3, Hringsson 3, Templeman 3, Grace 2, Melvin W 2, Watters 2, Brittain 1, Dillon 1, Stewart 1, Ward 1.
Scottish Cup (0).
CIS Cup (2): Flannery 2.
Bell's League Cup (1): Dillon 1 (pen).
Honours – Division I: Champions – 1890-91 (Shared), 1891-92. **Division II:** Champions – 1910-11, 1971-72. **Second Division:** Champions – 1991-92. **Scottish Cup winners** 1883.

DUNDEE PREMIER LEAGUE

Ground: Dens Park, Dundee DD3 7JY (01382) 889966
Ground capacity: 12,371 (all seated). **Colours:** Dark blue shirts with red and white trim, white shorts.
Manager: Ivano Bonetti.
League Appearances: Annand E 18(9); Artero J 6(3); Banger N 2(4); Bayne G 3(10); Billio P 16(1); Boyack S 32(4); Coyne T (2); Douglas R 35; Elliott J 0(1); Falconer W 31; Grady J 18(13); Ireland C 14; Langfield J 1; Luna F 5(4); Maddison L 19(1); Matute R 1(4); McSkimming S 20(2); Miller W 10(2); Rae G 35; Raeside R 1; Robertson H 15(9); Sharp L 11(3); Slater M 0(1); Smith B 32; Tweed S 34; Van Eijs F 14(2); Wilkie L 21(3); Yates M 2(3).
Goals – League (45): Falconer 13, Grady 6, Annand 4 (1 pen), Rae 4, Luna 3, McSkimming 2, Robertson 2, Tweed 2, Artero 1, Bayne 1, Billio 1, Boyack 1, Ireland 1, Sharp 1, Yates 1, own goals 2.
Scottish Cup (1): Rae 1.
CIS Cup (7): Falconer 4, Boyack 2, Grady 1
Honours – Division I: Champions – 1961-62. **First Division:** Champions – 1978-79, 1991-92, 1997-98. **Division II:** Champions – 1946-47. **Scottish Cup winners** 1910. **League Cup winners** 1952, 1953, 1974. **B&Q (Centenary) Cup winners** 1991.

DUNDEE UNITED PREMIER LEAGUE

Ground: Tannadice Park, Dundee DD3 7JW (01382) 833166
Ground capacity: 14,209. **Colours:** Tangerine shirts with black trim, black shorts.
Manager: Paul Sturrock.
League Appearances: Bove R (1); Byrne D (1); Combe A 35; Davidson H 17(7); De Vos J 35; Delaunay J 1; Dodds W 15; Easton C 22(10); Ferraz J 15(13); Gallacher P 1; Hamilton J 8(5); Hannah D 33; Jenkins I 1; Jenkinson L 1(3); Jonsson S 14; Malpas M 8(4); Mathie A 10(2); McConalogue S 9(7); McCracken D 2; McCulloch S 10(5); McQuillan J 11; O'Connor S 1; Partridge D 29; Pascual B 30(2); Paterson J 8; Patterson D 6; Preget A 3(1); Skoldmark M 7(3); Smith A 4(3); Telesnikov J 22(3); Thompson S 16(10); Venetis A 12(5); Worrell D 10(3).
Goals – League (34): Dodds 9 (1 pen), Ferraz 6, Hannah 6, Mathie 3, Telesnikov 3, De Vos 2, Easton 1, Hamilton 1, Paterson J 1, Skoldmark 1, Thompson 1.
Scottish Cup (10): Hamilton 3, Hannah 2, Thompson 2, Ferraz 1, Mathie 1, Preget 1.
CIS Cup (8): Thompson 3, Davidson 1, Dodds 1, Easton 1, Ferraz 1, Telesnikov 1.
Honours – Premier Division: Champions – 1982-83. **Division II:** Champions – 1924-25, 1928-29. **Scottish Cup winners** 1994. **League Cup winners** 1980, 1981.

DUNFERMLINE ATHLETIC PREMIER LEAGUE

Ground: East End Park, Dunfermline KY12 7RB (01383) 724295
Ground capacity: 12,500. **Colours:** Black and white striped shirts, black shorts.
Manager: Jim Calderwood.
League Appearances: Bullen L 11(2); Coyle O 23(7); Crawford S 25; Dair J 22(2); Doesburg M 5(1); Dolan J 19; Ferguson I 12; French H 13(8); Graham D (15); Hampshire S 11(8); Huxford R 2; Ireland C 1(2); Mampaey K 14; May E 19(4); McGarty M 1; McGroarty C 13(7); Moss D 18(6); Nish C (2); Petrie S 32; Potter J 17(4); Reid B 21(2); Shields G 3; Skinner J 26(2); Smith A 11(1); Templeman C (1); Thomson S 28(1); Tod A 27(3); Westwater I 22.
Goals – League (66): Crawford 16 (1 pen), Coyle 9, Bullen 7, Moss 6, French 3, Hampshire 3, May 3 (1 pen), Petrie 3, Reid 3, Smith 3, Ferguson 2, Graham 2, Thomson 2, Dair 1, Huxford 1, Potter 1, Tod 1.
Scottish Cup (1): Graham 1.
CIS Cup (4): Coyle 2, Petrie 1, Smith 1.
Bell's League Cup (2): Coyle 2.
Honours – First Division: Champions – 1988-89, 1995-96. **Division II:** Champions – 1925-26. **Second Division:** Champions – 1985-86. **Scottish Cup winners** 1961, 1968.

EAST FIFE DIV. 3

Ground: Bayview Park, Methil, Fife KY8 3RW (01333) 426323
Ground capacity: 2000 (all seated). **Colours:** Amber shirts with black trim, black shorts.
Manager: Rab Shannon.
League Appearances: Agostini D 31(1); Clark P 1(3); Cusick J 23(3); Forrest G 23(3); Gibb R 6(4); Herd W 16; Honeyman B 2(3); Jackson C 11; Kirk S 5(6);

Logan R 21(10); Love G 13(3); Mackay S 26(5); Martin J (1); McAnally D 2; McCloy B 14; McCormick S 11; McCulloch W 36; McGrillen P 3; McManus T 11; Moffat B 28(2); Mooney R (1); Munro K 24(3); O'Hara G 14; Porteous A (1); Ramsay S 6(3); Robertson G 26(7); Shannon R 24(1); Sharpe R 14; Tinley G 1(2); Wright D 4(14).
Goals – League (45): Moffat 11, Robertson 5, Cusick 4, Mackay 4, Logan 3, McCormick 3, McManus 3, Kirk 2, Agostini 1, Forrest 1, Herd 1, Honeyman 1, McGrillen 1, Munro 1, Sharp 1, Wright 1, own goals 2.
Scottish Cup (1): O'Hara 1
CIS Cup (4): Agostini 1, Kirk 1, Logan 1, Robertson 1 (pen).
Bell's League Cup (2): Robertson 1, Wright 1.
Honours – Division II: Champions – 1947-48. **Scottish Cup winners** 1938. **League Cup winners** 1948, 1950, 1954.

EAST STIRLINGSHIRE DIV. 3

Ground: Firs Park, Falkirk FK2 7AY (01324) 623583
Ground capacity: 1880. **Colours:** Black and white stripes, black shorts.
Manager: George Fairley.
League Appearances: Abdulrahman K 1; Allan G 3; Barr A 10(7); Bowsher C 3; Brown M 35(1); Butter J 36; Campbell M 1(1); Crawford G 7(6); Donnelly S 2(3); Elliott A 19(3); Ferguson B 16(7); Gordon K 22(13); Hardie M 21; Hay D 12(3); Higgins G 22(4); Laidlaw S 19; Lynes C 21(5); MacMillan G 2; McCann K 7; McDonald G (2); McNeill W 3(6); McPherson D 1(11); Menmuir S 1; Morrison S 3(3); Muirhead D 36; O'Hara G 2; Ross B 7(1); Russell G 31(1); Scott A 15(1); Storrar A 36; Sutherland M 2(2).
Goals – League (28): Higgins 9, Laidlaw 9, Crawford 2, Storrar 2, Barr 1, Hardie 1, Hay 1, McPherson 1, Muirhead 1, Scott 1.
Scottish Cup (2): Hay 1, Higgins 1.
CIS Cup (2): Higgins 1 (pen), Muirhead 1.
Bell's League Cup (1): Hardie 1.
Honours – Division II: Champions – 1931-32. **C Division:** Champions – 1947-48.

FALKIRK DIV. 1

Ground: Brockville Park, Falkirk FK1 5AX (01324) 624121
Ground capacity: 9706. **Colours:** Navy blue shirts, white shorts.
Manager: Alex Totten.
League Appearances: Christie K 14; Coyne T 6(2); Crabbe S 35; Den Bieman I 15; Hagen D 33(2); Henry J 21; Hogarth M 36; Hutchison G 22(10); Innes C 2; Kerr M 2(5); Lawrie A 33(2); McAllister K 6(3); McDonald C 26(4); McKenzie S 34; McQuilken J 28(3); McStay G 2(4); Morris I 8(7); Moss D 3(1); Nicholls D 32(1); Pearson C (1); Rennie S 10(3); Seaton A 9(10); Sinclair D 19(3); Waddell R (1).
Goals – League (67): Crabbe 14 (3 pens), Nicholls 12, Hagen 6, McDonald 6, Hutchison 5, Lawrie 4, Henry 3, Moss 3, Christie 2, McAllister 2, McStay 2, Morris 2, Coyne 1, Den Bieman 1, Kerr 1, McKenzie 1, McQuilken 1, Sinclair 1.
Scottish Cup (7): Crabbe 2, Hagen 2, Lawrie 1, McQuilken 1, Nicholls 1.
CIS Cup (3): Crabbe 2, own goal 1.
Bell's League Cup (2): Lawrie 1, McDonald 1.
Honours – Division II: Champions – 1935-36, 1969-70, 1974-75. **First Division:** Champions – 1990-91, 1993-94. **Second Division:** Champions – 1979-80. **Scottish Cup winners** 1913, 1957. **League Challenge Cup winners** 1998.

FORFAR ATHLETIC DIV. 2

Ground: Station Park, Forfar, Angus (01307) 463576
Ground capacity: 8732. **Colours:** Sky blue and navy shirts, navy shorts.
Manager: Ian McPhee.
League Appearances: Brand R 17(6); Cargill A 31; Christie S 3(4); Craig D 31; Donaldson E 26(3); Farnan C 19(2); Ferguson G 3; Garden S 36; Horn R 6; Johnston G 13(2); MacDonald I 6(7); McCheyne G 31; McIlravey P 9(11); McKellar J 7(15); McLean B 11(8); McPhee G 22(7); Milne S 35; Morris R 3(5); Nairn J 1(4); Rattray A 31(1); Robson B 25; Taylor A 30(1).
Goals – League (64): Milne 16, Robson 9, Craig 8, Brand 6, McCheyne 4, McIlravey 4, Taylor 4, McKellar 3, Cargill 2, McLean 2, Rattray 2, Donaldson 1, Farnan 1, MacDonald 1, McPhee 1.
Scottish Cup (3): Donaldson 1 (pen), Milne 1, Robson 1.
CIS Cup (1): MacDonald 1.
Bell's League Cup (3): Milne 2, Christie 1.
Honours – Second Division: Champions – 1983-84. **Third Division:** Champions – 1994-95.

GREENOCK MORTON DIV. 1

Ground: Cappielow Park, Greenock (01475) 723571
Ground capacity: 14,891. **Colours:** Royal blue and white shirts, white shorts.
Manager: Allan Evans.
League Appearances: Aitken C 1(1); Aitken S 19(10); Anderson D 28; Anderson J 26(3); Archdeacon O 4; Carlin A 3; Connolly P 5; Curran H 28; Earnshaw R 3; Fenwick P 14; Ferguson I 3(4); Hart M 1(9); Hartley P 3; Hawke N 9(6); Kerr B (4); Matheson R 33(1); Maxwell A 33; McDonald P 16(8); McDonald S 7; McPherson C 14(9); Millen A 28; Morrison G 20(1); Murie D 33(1); Pluck C 3(1); Rice B 1; Robb R (2); Ross M (2); Slavin B 14(6); Stevenson C 1(1); Thomas K 2; Tweedie G 10(8); Walker J 2(5); Whalen S 15(6); Wright K 17(6).
Goals – League (45): Curran 9, Anderson J 5, Connolly 5 (2 pens), Wright 4, McDonald 3, McPherson 3, Earnshaw 2, Matheson 2, Murie 2, Thomas 2, Aitken 1, Anderson D 1, Archdeacon 1, Hartley 1, Hawke 1, Morrison 1, Tweedie 1, Whalen 1.
Scottish Cup (1): Anderson J 1.
CIS Cup (1): Curran 1
Bell's League Cup (2): Hawke 1, Thomas 1.
Honours – First Division: Champions – 1977-78, 1983-84, 1986-87. **Division II:** Champions – 1949-50, 1963-64, 1966-67. **Second Division:** Champions – 1994-95. **Scottish Cup winners** 1922.

HAMILTON ACADEMICAL DIV. 3

Ground: Firhill Stadium, Glasgow G20 7AL. (Match days only): (0141) 5791971(Weekdays): (01698) 286103
Ground capacity: 14,538. **Colours:** Red and white hooped shirts, white shorts.
Manager: Ally Dawson
League Appearances: Bonnar M 30(1); Coubrough J 8; Crossley G 8(9);

Cunnington E 31(1); Davidson W 22(1); Ferguson I 8(2); Gaughan P 22(3); Henderson D 27; Henderson N 19(2); Hillcoat C 5(2); Hunter G 21(1); Kelly R 4(7); Lynn G 4(1); MacFarlane I 12; MacLaren R 30(1); Martin M 15(3); McAulay I 12(3); McCormick S 20(8); McFarlane D 8(5); Miller C 1; Moore M 6(8); Muir D 2; Quitongo J 15; Reid C 24; Renicks S 6(5); Russell A (6); Thomson S 36.
Goals – League (39): Henderson D 6 (1 pen), Henderson N 6 (2 pens), McFarlane D 5, Bonnar 4, Cunnington 4, Ferguson 4, McCormick 3, Coubrough 1, Crossley 1, Gaughan 1, Hunter 1, MacLaren 1, Quitongo 1, Thomson 1.
Scottish Cup (1): Henderson D 1.
CIS Cup (3): Henderson D 3.
Bell's League Cup (3): Henderson N 1 (pen), McCormick 1, Moore 1.
Honours – First Division: Champions – 1985-86, 1987-88. **Divison II:** Champions – 1903-04. **B&Q Cup winners** 1992, 1993.

HEART OF MIDLOTHIAN PREMIER LEAGUE

Ground: Tynecastle Park, Gorgie Road, Edinburgh EH11 2NL (0131) 200 7200
Ground capacity: 18,000. **Colours:** Maroon shirts, white shorts.
Manager: Jim Jefferies.
League Appearances: Adam S 18(7); Cameron C 31(1); Flögel T 28(1); Fulton S 16(10); Graham A (1); Jackson D 31(4); James K 8(2); Juanjo 2(13); Kirk A 1(3); Leclercq F 8(2); Locke G 9(4); Makel L 11(6); McKenzie R 3(2); McKinnon R 3; McSwegan G 23(6); Milne K (1); Murray G 15(6); Naysmith G 34(1); Niemi A 17; Petric G 17(1); Pressley S 36; Quitongo J (1); Ritchie P 14; Rousset G 16; Severin S 18(6); Simpson F 7(4); Tomaschek R 13(1); Wales G 17(7).
Goals – League (47): McSwegan 13, Cameron 8 (2 pens), Jackson 6, Wales 6, Adam 4, Juanjo 3, Severin 2, Flögel 1, Fulton 1, Naysmith 1, Ritchie 1, own goal 1.
Scottish Cup (6): Cameron 2 (2 pens), McSwegan 2, Jackson 1,Wales 1.
CIS Cup (5): Jackson 2, Cameron 1, Holmes 1, Severin 1.
Honours – Division I: Champions – 1894-95, 1896-97, 1957-58, 1959-60. **First Division:** Champions – 1979-80. **Scottish Cup winners** 1891, 1896, 1901, 1906, 1956, 1998. **League Cup winners** 1955, 1959, 1960, 1963.

HIBERNIAN PREMIER LEAGUE

Ground: Easter Road Stadium, Edinburgh EH7 5QG (0131) 661 2159
Ground capacity: 16,032. **Colours:** Green shirts with white sleeves and collar, white shorts.
Manager: Alex McLeish.
League Appearances: Bannerman S (1); Brebner G 27(1); Colgan N 24; Collins D 23(1); Crawford S 1(2); Dempsie M 7(1); Dennis S 23(1); Gottskalksson O 12; Hartley P 14(10); Henry F 6(3); Hughes J 20; Jack M 20(2); Jean E (5); Latapy R 28; Lehmann D 18(12); Lovell S 19(7); Lovering P 9(1); McGinlay P 22(9); McIntosh M 9; McManus T 1(1); Miller K 23(8); Murray I 8(1); Paatelainen M 25(6); Reid A (1); Renwick M 11(2); Sauzee F 24(1); Skinner J 1(1); Smith T 21.
Goals – League (49): Miller 11, Latapy 9 (2 pens), Paatelainen 9, Lehmann 7, Sauzee 5, McGinlay 3, Hartley 1, Jack 1, Lovell 1, own goals 2.
Scottish Cup (12): Latapy 3 (1 pen), Brebner 1, Collins 1, Hartley 1, Lehmann 1, Lovell 1, McGinlay 1, Miller 1, Murray 1, Sauzee 1.
CIS Cup (4): McGinlay 2, Hartley 1, Miller 1.

Honours – Division I: Champions – 1902-03, 1947-48, 1950-51, 1951-52. **First Division:** Champions – 1980-81, 1998-99. **Division II:** Champions – 1893-94, 1894-95, 1932-33. **Scottish Cup winners** 1887, 1902. **League Cup winners** 1973, 1992.

INVERNESS CALEDONIAN THISTLE DIV. 1

Ground: Caledonian Stadium, East Longman, Inverness IV1 1FF (01463) 222880
Ground capacity: 5600. **Colours:** Blue shirts with white trim, blue shorts.
Manager: Steven W.Paterson.
League Appearances: Allan A 4(1); Bavidge M 12(15); Byers K 21(10); Calder J 9; Christie C 22(6); Craig D 6(3); Fridge L 27; Glancy M 6(12); Golabek S 29(2); Hastings R 28; Hind D 2(3); Macdonald N (1); Mann R 27; McCulloch M 35; McLean S 4(7); Munro G 3(1); Robson B 3(1); Shearer D (1); Sheerin P 32; Stewart G (1); Stewart I 3; Teasdale M 23(4); Tokely R 30; Wilson B 30(2); Wyness D 21(5); Xausa D 19.
Goals – League (60): Wilson 13, Sheerin 11 (3 pens), Xausa 10, Wyness 6, Bavidge 5, Glancy 3, Tokely 3, McCulloch 2, McLean 2, Teasdale 2, Byers 1, Christie 1, Golabek 1.
Scottish Cup (4): Mann 1, Sheerin 1 (pen), Wilson 1, own goal 1.
CIS Cup (5): McLean 2, Byers 1, Sheerin 1 (pen), Wilson 1.
Bell's League Cup (11): Sheerin 4, Stewart 2, Glancy 1, McLean 1, Robson 1, Teasdale 1, Wilson 1.
Honours – Third Division: Champions – 1996-97.

KILMARNOCK PREMIER LEAGUE

Ground: Rugby Park, Kilmarnock KA1 2DP (01563) 525184
Ground capacity: 18,128. **Colours:** Blue and white striped shirts, blue shorts.
Manager: Bobby Williamson.
League Appearances: Abou S 5(5); Bagan D 2(1); Baker M 11; Beesley D 1(1); Burke A 3(6); Canero P 6(5); Cocard C 24(1); Davidson S (2); Dindeleux F 28; Durrant I 32; Fowler J 1(4); Hay G 8(2); Henry J 1; Hessey S 7(4); Holt G 35; Innes C 5; Jeffrey M 10(8); Lauchlan J 29; MacPherson A 30; Mahood A 6(12); Marshall G 14; McCoist A 5(4); McCutcheon G (2); McGowne K 9; McKinlay T 14(1); Meldrum C 18; Mitchell A 22(4); Reilly M 28(1); Roberts M 2; Smith A 11(4); Vareille J 13(10); Watt M 4; Wright P 12(4).
Goals – League (38): Cocard 8, Wright 5, Durrant 4, Reilly 3, Vareille 3, Hay 2, Jeffrey 2, Lauchlan 2, Mitchell 2, Dindeleux 1, McCoist 1 (pen), MacPherson 1, Mahood 1, Smith 1, own goals 2.
Scottish Cup (0).
CIS Cup (4): McCoist 2, Jeffrey 1, Vareille 1.
Honours – Division I: Champions – 1964-65. **Division II:** Champions – 1897-98, 1898-99. **Scottish Cup winners** 1920, 1929, 1997.

LIVINGSTON DIV. 1

Ground: Almondvale Stadium, Livingston EH54 7DN (01506) 417 000
Ground capacity: 10,004. **Colours:** Black with yellow trim, black shorts.
Manager: Jim Leishman.

League Appearances: Alexander N 13; Bennett N (1); Bingham D 32; Britton G 13(5); Clark S 2; Coughlan G 26(3); Courts T 2(2); Deas P 33; Feroz C 2(7); Fleming D 17(8); Hart M 3; Keith M 8(1); Kelly P 30(2); King C 20(11); Little I 1(3); McCaldon I 23; McCann G (4); McCormick M 16(12); McDonald W (1); McKinnon R 17(2); McLaren A 5(4); McManus A 28; McPhee B 20(13); Millar J 27(3); Millar M 24; Moffat A (1); Richardson L 6; Robertson J 1(4); Rowson D 6; Smith J 5(1); Sweeney S 15(3); Watson G 1.
Goals – League (60): Bingham 15, McPhee 14, McCormick 6, Britton 5, Keith 4, Deas 2, King 2, McKinnon 2, Millar J 2, Millar M 2, Fleming 1, Robertson 1, Rowson 1, Smith 1, Sweeney 1, own goal 1.
Scottish Cup (8): Keith 3, McKinnon 2, Bingham 1, McPhee 1, own goal 1.
CIS Cup (2): Britton 2.
Bell's League Cup (5): Bingham 2, Britton 1, McPhee 1, Millar M 1.
Honours – Second Division: Champions – 1986-87, 1998-99. **Third Division:** Champions – 1995-96.

MONTROSE DIV. 3

Ground: Links Park, Montrose DD10 8QD (01674) 673200
Ground capacity: 4338. **Colours:** Royal blue with white sleeves, white shorts.
Manager: Kevin Drinkell.
League Appearances: Bennett N 16; Black M 23; Clark S 8; Craib M 33; Craib S 6(3); Craig D 12; Craig M 15(4); Dailly G 2; Dorward R (1); Duffy K 11(11); Farnan C 12; Fitzpatrick F 1; Harrison T 1; Jackson C 1; Mailer C 29; McGlynn G 35; McWilliam R 27(8); Meldrum G 11(9); Mitchell B 6; Niddrie K 13(3); O'Driscoll J 20(4); Ogboke C 3(11); Paterson G 24; Robertson S 13(9); Scott W 25; Shand M 7(11); Stevenson C (2); Taylor S 35; Young J 7.
Goals – League (39): Taylor 12, O'Driscoll 5, Mailer 3, Craib M 2, Craib S 2, Paterson 2, Scott 2, Shand 2, Bennett 1, Craig D 1, Craig M 1, Duffy 1, Farnan 1, McWilliam 1, Meldrum 1, Ogboke 1, own goal 1.
Scottish Cup (1): O'Driscoll 1.
CIS Cup (1): O'Driscoll 1.
Bell's League Cup (1): Taylor 1 (pen).
Honours – Second Division: Champions – 1984-85.

MOTHERWELL PREMIER LEAGUE

Ground: Fir Park, Motherwell ML1 2QN (01698) 333333
Ground capacity: 13,742. **Colours:** Amber shirts with claret trim, white shorts.
Manager: Billy Davies.
League Appearances: Adams D 15(2); Brannan G 33; Corrigan M 18(1); Craigan S 3(2); Curcic S 3(3); Davies J 7(1); Denham G 6; Doesburg M 17(2); Goodman D 25(4); Goram A 22; Halliday S 1(4); Hammell S 3(1); Harvey P 6(7); Kemble B 25; Matthaei R 2(1); McCulloch L 28(1); McGowan J 10(3); McMillan S 31; Nevin P 6(22); Nicholas S 2(19); Ramsay D (2); Spencer J 25(3); Strong G 10; Teale S 16; Thomas A 6; Townsley D 16(9); Twaddle K 18(7); Valakari S 28(2); Woods S 14(1).
Goals – League (49): Spencer 11, McCulloch 9, Goodman 7, Brannan 5, Twaddle 5, McMillan 3, Nevin 2, Teale 2 (1 pen), Adams 1, Corrigan 1, Kemble 1, Nicholas 1, Townsley 1.

Scottish Cup (6): Goodman 3, McCulloch 2, Brannan 1 (pen).
CIS Cup (5): Halliday 1, McCulloch 1, Teale 1, Townsley 1, own goal 1.
Honours – Division I: Champions – 1931-32. **First Division:** Champions – 1981-82, 1984-85. **Division II:** Champions – 1953-54, 1968-69. **Scottish Cup winners** 1952, 1991. **League Cup winners** 1951.

PARTICK THISTLE DIV. 2

Ground: Firhill Park, Glasgow G20 7AL (0141) 579 1971
Ground capacity: 14,538. **Colours:** Red and yellow hooped shirts, black shorts.
Manager: John Lambie.
League Appearances: Archibald A 35; Arthur K 3; Blom J 2; Brannigan K 10; Budinauckas K 33; Callaghan T 3(6); Craig A 28(1); Dallas S 1(1); Docherty S 17(1); Duncan G 12(8); Dunn R 18(9); Elliot D 10(1); English I 7(7); Ferguson D 7; Hardie M 6; Howie W (1); Huggon R 3(1); Jacobs Q 22(5); Kelly R 1(1); Lennon D 19; Lindau P 9; Lyle D 9(13); Martin B 12(4); McAllister T 1; McCann K (1); McGuiness E 1(4); McIntyre P 7(6); McKeown D 31(1); McLean S 7; McVey W (2); McWilliams D 7; Miller S 13(5); Montgomerie R 31(1); Nesovic A 1(1); Newall R (3); Paton E 20(6); Rodden P (1); Rogers D 6; Swan I (2); Walker A 4.
Goals – League (42): Dunn 5, Craig 4, Lindau 4, Lyle 4, Hardie 3, Jacobs 3, McWilliams 3 (1 pen), Miller 3, Elliot 2, Lennon 2, McKeown 2, Blom 1, Docherty 1, English 1, Huggon 1, Kelly 1, McLean 1, Paton 1.
Scottish Cup (6): Lennon 2, Craig 1, Dunn 1, McLean 1, own goal 1.
CIS Cup (0).
Bell's League Cup (0).
Honours – First Division: Champions – 1975-76. **Division II:** Champions – 1896-97, 1899-1900, 1970-71. **Scottish Cup winners** 1921. **League Cup winners** 1972.

QUEEN OF THE SOUTH DIV. 2

Ground: Palmerston Park, Dumfries DG2 9BA (01387) 254853
Ground capacity: 8352. **Colours:** Royal blue shirts, white shorts.
Manager: John Connolly.
League Appearances: Adams C 18(12); Aitken A 33; Bailey L 4(3); Boyle D 17(1); Caldwell B 12(5); Cleeland M 21(1); Davidson S 1(1); Dickson J 23(2); Duncan G 13; Eadie K 5(4); Findlay W 3(4); Gallacher I 1; Gallagher J 3(3); Harvey P 9; Hawke W 17; Hillcoat J 22; Hodge A 26(1); Kerr A 13(8); Leslie S 13(1); Lilley D 2; Mallan S 29(3); Mathieson D 14; McLean S 3; McMillan A 15(1); Paterson G 2; Preston A 6(2); Robison K 14(6); Rowe G 27; Stewart P 19(1); Strain C 1(7); Weir M 10(4).
Goals – League (45): Mallan 13, Adams 4, Eadie 4, Hawke 4, Caldwell 3, Rowe 3, Boyle 2, Harvey 2, Aitken 1, Bailey 1, Dickson 1, Duncan 1, Findlay 1, Hodge 1, Kerr 1, Preston 1, Weir 1, own goal 1.
Scottish Cup (3): Adams 1, Eadie 1, Hawke 1.
CIS Cup (2): Bailey 1, Leslie 1.
Bell's League Cup (1): Adams 1.
Honours – Division II: Champions – 1950-51.

QUEEN'S PARK — DIV. 2

Ground: Hampden Park, Glasgow G42 9BA (0141) 632 1275
Ground capacity: 52,000. **Colours:** Black and white hooped shirts, white shorts.
Coach: John McCormack.
League Appearances: Borland P 19(5); Brown J 28(3); Carmichael D 1; Carroll F 21(6); Caven R 29(1); Connaghan D 30(3); Connell G 30; Edgar S 1(16); Elder G (1); Ferry D 26(4); Finlayson K 8(2); Gallagher M 35; Geoghegan J (1); Inglis N 36; Little T 1(5); MacFarlane N 36; Martin P 27(1); McGoldrick K 13(7); McKee C 2(5); Orr S 5(5); Reid A (1); Scobie R 2(12); Sinclair R 12(3); Travers M 1(2); Tyrrell P (1); Walker P 6(2); Whelan J 27(7).
Goals – League (54): Gallagher 13, Carroll 8, Whelan 8, Brown 7, Caven 6 (4 pens), McGoldrick 3, Connaghan 2, Walker 2, Connell 1, Ferry 1, Finlayson 1, Martin 1, Orr 1.
Scottish Cup (1): Carroll 1.
CIS Cup (2): Brown 1, McGoldrick 1.
Bell's League Cup (4): Gallagher 2, Brown 1, Whelan 1.
Honours – Division II: Champions – 1922-23. **B Division:** Champions – 1955-56. **Second Division:** Champions – 1980-81. **Third Division:** Champions – 1999-2000. **Scottish Cup winners** 1874, 1875, 1876, 1880, 1881, 1882, 1884, 1886, 1890, 1893.

RAITH ROVERS — DIV. 1

Ground: Stark's Park, Pratt Street, Kirkcaldy KY1 1SA (01592) 263514
Ground capacity: 10,104 (all seated). **Colours:** Navy blue shirts, white shorts.
Manager: Peter Hetherston.
League Appearances: Agathe D 30; Agnew P 2(2); Andrews M 29; Begue Y (2); Berthe M 1; Black K 23(2); Browne P 34; Burns A 34; Clark A 3(15); Coyle C 3; Craig S (2); Dargo C 25; Ellis L 4; Fenwick P 2; Gaughan K 6(1); Hamilton S 11(4); Hetherston B 3(11); Javary J 10(1); Kirkwood D 3(1); McCondichie A 1; McCulloch G 13(9); McEwan C 30(4); Nicol K 1; Opinel S 15; Owusu A 8(2); Preget A 2; Roberts M 3; Shields P 1(8); Stein J 32(3); Stewart A (1); Tosh P 10(8); Tosh S 25(6); Van De Kamp G 32.
Goals – League (55): Dargo 12 (1 pen), Agathe 7, Burns 6, Stein 5, Tosh S 5, Browne 4, Tosh P 4, Black 3 (1 pen), Owugu 3, Hetherston 2, Andrews 1, Clark 1, Roberts 1, Shields 1.
Scottish Cup (1): Dargo 1.
CIS Cup (3): Black 1, Burns 1, Dargo 1.
Bell's League Cup (4): Andrews 1, Clark 1, Dargo 1, own goal 1.
Honours – First Division: Champions – 1992-93, 1994-95. **Division II:** Champions – 1907-08, 1909-10 (Shared), 1937-38, 1948-49. **League Cup winners** 1995.

RANGERS — PREMIER LEAGUE

Ground: Ibrox Stadium, Glasgow G51 2XD (0870) 600 1972
Ground capacity: 50,467. **Colours:** Royal blue shirts, red and blue panels, white shorts.
Manager: Dick Advocaat.
League Appearances: Adamczuk D 5(5); Albertz J 30(5); Amato G 4(4); Amoruso L 30; Brown M 1; Charbonnier L 7; Dodds W 16(2); Durie G 1(6); Ferguson B 31;

Ferguson I (2); Gibson J (1); Hendry C 1(1); Hughes S (1); Johansson J 8(8); Kanchelskis A 25(3); Kerimoglu T 9(7); Klos S 24; Malcolm R 1(2); McCann N 12(18); McInnes D (1); Mols M 9; Moore C 22; Myhre T 3; Nicholson B 0(2); Niemi A 1; Numan A 29(1); Penttila T 3; Porrini S 11(1); Reyna C 25(4); Ross M (1); Rozental S 6(5); Van Bronckhorst G 27; Vidmar A 21(6); Wallace R 25(3); Wilson S 9.
Goals – League (96): Albertz 17 (3 pens), Wallace 16, Dodds 10, Mols 9, Johansson 6, Vidmar 6, Reyna 5, Ferguson B 4, Kanchelskis 4, Van Bronckhorst 4, Amato 3, McCann 3, Rozental 3 (1 pen), Amoruso 2, Kerimoglu 1, Moore 1, Numan 1, own goal 1.
Scottish Cup (18): Dodds 5, Numan 2, Rozental 2, Van Bronckhorst 2, Albertz 1, Amoruso 1, Ferguson B 1, Kanchelskis 1, Moore 1, Vidmar 1, Wallace 1.
CIS Cup (0).
Honours – Division I: Champions – 1890-91 (Shared), 1898-99, 1899-1900, 1900-01, 1901-02, 1910-11, 1911-12, 1912-13, 1917-18, 1919-20, 1920-21, 1922-23, 1923-24, 1924-25, 1926-27, 1927-28, 1928-29, 1929-30, 1930-31, 1932-33, 1933-34, 1934-35, 1936-37, 1938-39, 1946-47, 1948-49, 1949-50, 1952-53, 1955-56, 1956-57, 1958-59, 1960-61, 1962-63, 1963-64, 1974-75. **Premier Division:** Champions – 1975-76, 1977-78, 1986-87, 1988-89, 1989-90, 1990-91, 1991-92, 1992-93, 1993-94, 1994-95, 1995-96, 1996-97. **Premier League:** Champions – 1998-99, 1999-2000. **Scottish Cup winners** 1894, 1897, 1898, 1903, 1928, 1930, 1932, 1934, 1935, 1936, 1948, 1949, 1950, 1953, 1960, 1962, 1963, 1964, 1966, 1973, 1976, 1978, 1979, 1981, 1992, 1993, 1996, 1999, 2000. **League Cup winners** 1947, 1949, 1961, 1962, 1964, 1965, 1971, 1976, 1978, 1979, 1982, 1984, 1985, 1987, 1988, 1989, 1991, 1993, 1994, 1997, 1999. **European Cup-Winners' Cup winners** 1972.

ROSS COUNTY DIV. 1

Ground: Victoria Park, Dingwall IV15 9QW (01349) 860860
Ground capacity: 5500 (2700 seated). **Colours:** Dark blue shirts, white shorts.
Manager: Neale Cooper.
League Appearances: Bone A 4(2); Boyle S (3); Campbell C (2); Canning M 5(1); Cormack P 6; Duthie M 24; Escalon F 12(1); Ferguson D 10; Ferguson S 18(1); Feroz C 4; Finlayson K 3(8); Fraser J 16(10); Geraghty M 3(6); Gilbert K 26(1); Hamilton G 1; Hamilton G 7; Hateley M 2; Holmes D 20(5); Irvine B 32; Kinnaird P 22(6); Lennon D 7; Mackay D 13(5); Mackay S (1); Maxwell I 35; McBain R 18(10); McGlashan J 13(3); Mols T 1; Roddie A 1; Ross D 4(7); Shaw G 32(1); Taggart C 9; Thomson P 3; Tully C 12(1); Walker N 25; Wood G 8(4).
Goals – League (57): Shaw 13 (2 pens), Holmes 8, Kinnaird 7, Ferguson 6, Irvine 6, Bone 4, McGlashan 4, Wood 3, Escalon 1, Fraser 1, Gilbert 1, McBain 1, Maxwell 1, Taggart 1.
Scottish Cup (2): Irvine 1, Shaw 1.
CIS Cup (3): Escalon 1, Irvine 1, Shaw 1 (pen).
Bell's League Cup (8): Shaw 3, Irvine 2, Fraser 1, Geraghty 1, Wood 1.
Honours – Third Division: Champions – 1998-99.

ST JOHNSTONE PREMIER LEAGUE

Ground: McDiarmid Park, Crieff Road, Perth PH1 2SJ (01738) 459090
Ground capacity: 10,673. **Colours:** Royal blue shirts with white trim, white shorts.
Manager: Sandy Clark.
League Appearances: Bollan G 34; Connolly P 9(2); Conway C (1); Dasovic N 13;

Dods D 22; Ferguson A 3; Frail S 9; Grant R 1(2); Griffin D 26(3); Jones G 15(4); Kane P 33(1); Lauchlan M (5); Lowndes N 16(9); Main A 21; McAnespie K 14(6); McBride J 18(1); McCluskey S 5(1); McMahon G 9(10); McQuillan J 18; Millar M 3(5); O'Boyle G 4(4); O'Halloran K 31(1); O'Neil J 31(2); Parker K 6(4); Robertson S 12(1); Russell C 1; Simao M 6(11); Thomas K 5(7); Weir J 31.
Goals – League (36): Lowndes 10, Jones 3, O'Neil 3, Bollan 2, Dods 2, Millar 2, Parker 2, Thomas 2, Connolly 1, Griffin 1, Kane 1, McAnespie 1, McBride 1, McQuillan 1, O'Halloran 1, Russell 1, Simao 1, Weir 1.
Scottish Cup (0).
CIS Cup (1): Griffin 1.
Honours – First Division: Champions – 1982-83, 1989-90, 1996-97. **Division II:** Champions – 1923-24, 1959-60, 1962-63.

ST MIRREN — PREMIER LEAGUE

Ground: St Mirren Park, Paisley PA3 2EJ (0141) 889 2558, 840 1337
Ground capacity: 10,866 (all seated). **Colours:** Black and white striped shirts, black shorts.
Manager: Tom Hendrie.
League Appearances: Baltacha S 18(9); Bowman G 10(9); Brown T 19(7); Donnachie S (1); Drew C (6); Gillies R 2(2); Kerr C 3; Lavety B 21(8); McGarry S 22(10); McKnight P 1(3); McLaughlin B 34; McLaughlin J 3; Mendes J 28(5); Murray H 29; Nicolson I 33(1); Paeslack I 1(1); Robinson R (9); Ross I 30(1); Roy L 31; Rudden P 9(7); Scrimgour D 5; Turner T 31; Walker S 33; Yardley M 33(2).
Goals – League (75): Yardley 19, Lavety 16, McGarry 9 (1 pen), Mendes 5, Murray 5, Walker 4, Brown 3, McLaughlin B 3, Ross 3, McKnight 2, Baltacha 1, Bowman 1, McLaughlin J 1, Nicolson 1, Turner 1, own goal 1.
Scottish Cup (1): McGarry 1.
CIS Cup (0).
Bell's League Cup (0).
Honours – First Division: Champions – 1976-77, 1999-2000. **Division II:** Champions – 1967-68. **Scottish Cup winners** 1926, 1959, 1987.

STENHOUSEMUIR — DIV. 2

Ground: Ochilview Park, Stenhousemuir FK5 5QL (01324) 562992
Ground capacity: 3520. **Colours:** Maroon shirts with silver trim, white shorts.
Manager: Brian Fairley.
League Appearances: Armstrong G 23(7); Banks A 18(4); Bradford J 8(5); Connolly J 1(1); Cummings A 1(5); Davidson G 15(1); Fisher J 30; Forrester P 9(3); Fraser G 15(4); Gibson J 14; Graham T 33; Hall M 9; Hamilton L 33; Hamilton R 34(1); Lawrence A 31(3); Lorimer D 9(7); McGurk R 2; McKinnon C 35; McLauchlan M 8(1); Mooney M 17(14); Murphy S 0(1); Roseburgh D (2); Watson G 27; Watters W 4(15); Welsh B 8; Wood D 9(13); Wright K 4(1).
Goals – League (44): Mooney 8, Hamilton R 7, McKinnon 7, Fisher 6, Graham 4, Wood 2, Banks 1, Fraser 1, Lorimer 1, McLauchlan 1, Watson 1, Watters 1, Welsh 1, Wright 1, own goals 2.
Scottish Cup (11): Fisher 3, Graham 2, Hamilton R 2, Mooney 2, Forrester 1, own goal 1.
CIS Cup (1): Mooney 1.
Bell's League Cup (2): Hamilton R 1, Watters 1.
Honours – League Challenge Cup: Winners – 1996.

STIRLING ALBION DIV. 2

Ground: Forthbank Stadium, Springkerse Industrial Estate, Stirling FK7 7UJ (01786) 450399
Ground capacity: 3808. **Colours:** Red and white halves.
Manager: Ray Stewart.
League Appearances: Aitken N 4(10); Bell D (6); Bone A 7(2); Clark P 11(3); Donald G 36; Gardiner J 25; Gardner G 1; Gardner J 29; Gow G 8; Graham A 36; Martin B 11; McAlpine J 3; McCallion K 4(9); McCallum D 12(8); McGrillen P 23(6); McQuade J 34; Mortimer P 19(8); Paterson A 32(1); Philliben J 10(7); Taggart C 27(1); Tortolano J 26(1); Whiteford A 20; Williams A (5); Wood C 18(5).
Goals – League (60): Graham 17, McQuade 15, McGrillen 11, Bone 4, Taggart 3, Aitken 2, Wood 2, Donald 1, Gardner 1, McCallion 1, Mortimer 1, Paterson 1, Whiteford 1.
Scottish Cup (2): Graham 1, Whiteford 1.
CIS Cup (2): Graham 1 (pen), Wood 1.
Bell's League Cup (8): Gardner 2, Graham 2, Aitken 1, McQuade 1, Paterson 1 (pen), Wood 1.
Honours – Division II: Champions – 1952-53, 1957-58, 1960-61, 1964-65. **Second Division:** Champions – 1976-77, 1990-91, 1995-96.

STRANRAER DIV. 2

Ground: Stair Park, Stranraer DG9 8BS (01776) 703271
Ground capacity: 6100. **Colours:** Blue shirts, white shorts.
Manager: Billy McLaren.
League Appearances: Abbott S (2); Bell R 9(5); Black T 16(1); Blaikie A 28(4); Blair P 8(3); Cahoon D 9(4); Duthie M 4; Edgar S 3(6); Feroz C 2; Furphy W 16; George D 22; Harty I 30(2); Jenkins A 17(8); Johnstone D 17(6); Knox K 33; Macdonald W 14; McGeown M 36; McMartin G 14(3); Mitchell A (1); Ramsay D 4; Roddie A 9; Ronald P 17(2); Smith D 3(1); Smith J 30(2); Walker P 8(12); Watson P 19(5); Wright F 19(5); Young J 9(13).
Goals – League (47): Ronald 12, Harty 8 (1 pen), Smith J 7, Roddie 3, Blaikie 2, Johnstone 2, Knox 2, McMartin 2 (2 pens), Blair 1, Cahoon 1, Duthie 1, Edgar 1, George 1, Jenkins 1, MacDonald 1, Wright 1, Young 1.
Scottish Cup (2): Blaikie 1, Ronald 1.
CIS Cup (0).
Bell's League Cup (3): Blaikie 2, Knox 1.
Honours – Second Division: Champions – 1993-94, 1997-98. **League Challenge Cup winners** 1997.

ELGIN CITY DIV. 3

Ground: Borough Briggs, Elgin IV30 1AP (01343) 551114
Ground capacity: 6500 (470 seated). **Colours:** Black and white vertical stripes.
Manager: Alex Caldwell.

PETERHEAD DIV. 3

Ground: Balmoor Stadium, Peterhead AB42 1EU (01779) 478256
Ground capacity: 3250 (1000 seated). **Colours:** Blue and white.
Manager: Ian Wilson.

SCOTTISH LEAGUE HONOURS

*On goal average (ratio)/difference. †Held jointly after indecisive play-off. ‡Won on deciding match. ††Held jointly. ¶Two points deducted for fielding ineligible player. Competition suspended 1940–45 during war; Regional Leagues operating.
‡‡Two points deducted for registration irregularities.

PREMIER LEAGUE

Maximum points: 108

	First	*Pts*	*Second*	*Pts*	*Third*	*Pts*
1998–99	Rangers	77	Celtic	71	St Johnstone	57
1999–00	Rangers	90	Celtic	69	Hearts	54

PREMIER DIVISION

Maximum points: 72

1975–76	Rangers	54	Celtic	48	Hibernian	43
1976–77	Celtic	55	Rangers	46	Aberdeen	43
1977–78	Rangers	55	Aberdeen	53	Dundee U	40
1978–79	Celtic	48	Rangers	45	Dundee U	44
1979–80	Aberdeen	48	Celtic	47	St Mirren	42
1980–81	Celtic	56	Aberdeen	49	Rangers*	44
1981–82	Celtic	55	Aberdeen	53	Rangers	43
1982–83	Dundee U	56	Celtic*	55	Aberdeen	55
1983–84	Aberdeen	57	Celtic	50	Dundee U	47
1984–85	Aberdeen	59	Celtic	52	Dundee U	47
1985–86	Celtic*	50	Hearts	50	Dundee U	47

Maximum points: 88

1986–87	Rangers	69	Celtic	63	Dundee U	60
1987–88	Celtic	72	Hearts	62	Rangers	60

Maximum points: 72

1988–89	Rangers	56	Aberdeen	50	Celtic	46
1989–90	Rangers	51	Aberdeen*	44	Hearts	44
1990–91	Rangers	55	Aberdeen	53	Celtic*	41

Maximum points: 88

1991–92	Rangers	72	Hearts	63	Celtic	62
1992–93	Rangers	73	Aberdeen	64	Celtic	60
1993–94	Rangers	58	Aberdeen	55	Motherwell	54

Maximum points: 108

1994–95	Rangers	69	Motherwell	54	Hibernian	53
1995–96	Rangers	87	Celtic	83	Aberdeen*	55
1996–97	Rangers	80	Celtic	75	Dundee U	60
1997–98	Celtic	74	Rangers	72	Hearts	67

DIVISION 1

Maximum points: 52

1975–76	Partick T	41	Kilmarnock	35	Montrose	30

Maximum points: 78

1976–77	St Mirren	62	Clydebank	58	Dundee	51
1977–78	Morton*	58	Hearts	58	Dundee	57
1978–79	Dundee	55	Kilmarnock*	54	Clydebank	54
1979–80	Hearts	53	Airdrieonians	51	Ayr U*	44
1980–81	Hibernian	57	Dundee	52	St Johnstone	51
1981–82	Motherwell	61	Kilmarnock	51	Hearts	50
1982–83	St Johnstone	55	Hearts	54	Clydebank	50
1983–84	Morton	54	Dumbarton	51	Partick T	46
1984–85	Motherwell	50	Clydebank	48	Falkirk	45
1985–86	Hamilton A	56	Falkirk	45	Kilmarnock	44

Maximum points: 88

1986–87	Morton	57	Dunfermline Ath	56	Dumbarton	53
1987–88	Hamilton A	56	Meadowbank T	52	Clydebank	49

Maximum points: 78

1988–89	Dunfermline Ath	54	Falkirk	52	Clydebank	48
1989–90	St Johnstone	58	Airdrieonians	54	Clydebank	44
1990–91	Falkirk	54	Airdrieonians	53	Dundee	52

Maximum points: 88

1991–92	Dundee	58	Partick T*	57	Hamilton A	57
1992–93	Raith R	65	Kilmarnock	54	Dunfermline Ath	52
1993–94	Falkirk	66	Dunfermline Ath	65	Airdrieonians	54

Maximum points: 108

1994–95	Raith R	69	Dunfermline Ath*	68	Dundee	68
1995–96	Dunfermline Ath	71	Dundee U*	67	Morton	67
1996–97	St Johnstone	80	Airdrieonians	60	Dundee*	58
1997–98	Dundee	70	Falkirk	65	Raith R*	60
1998–99	Hibernian	89	Falkirk	66	Ayr U	62
1999–00	St Mirren	76	Dunfermline Ath	71	Falkirk	68

DIVISION 2

Maximum points: 52

1975–76	Clydebank*	40	Raith R	40	Alloa	35

Maximum points: 78

1976–77	Stirling A	55	Alloa	51	Dunfermline Ath	50
1977–78	Clyde*	53	Raith R	53	Dunfermline Ath	48
1978–79	Berwick R	54	Dunfermline Ath	52	Falkirk	50
1979–80	Falkirk	50	East Stirling	49	Forfar Ath	46
1980–81	Queen's Park	50	Queen of the S	46	Cowdenbeath	45
1981–82	Clyde	59	Alloa*	50	Arbroath	50
1982–83	Brechin C	55	Meadowbank T	54	Arbroath	49
1983–84	Forfar Ath	63	East Fife	47	Berwick R	43
1984–85	Montrose	53	Alloa	50	Dunfermline Ath	49
1985–86	Dunfermline Ath	57	Queen of the S	55	Meadowbank T	49
1986–87	Meadowbank T	55	Raith R*	52	Stirling A*	52
1987–88	Ayr U	61	St Johnstone	59	Queen's Park	51
1988–89	Albion R	50	Alloa	45	Brechin C	43
1989–90	Brechin C	49	Kilmarnock	48	Stirling A	47
1990–91	Stirling A	54	Montrose	46	Cowdenbeath	45
1991–92	Dumbarton	52	Cowdenbeath	51	Alloa	50
1992–93	Clyde	54	Brechin C*	53	Stranraer	53
1993–94	Stranraer	56	Berwick R	48	Stenhousemuir*	47

Maximum points: 108

1994–95	Morton	64	Dumbarton	60	Stirling A	58
1995–96	Stirling A	81	East Fife	67	Berwick R	60
1996–97	Ayr U	77	Hamilton A	74	Livingston	64
1997–98	Stranraer	61	Clydebank	60	Livingston	59
1998–99	Livingston	77	Inverness CT	72	Clyde	53
1999–00	Clyde	65	Alloa	64	Ross County	62

DIVISION 3

Maximum points: 108

1994–95	Forfar Ath	80	Montrose	67	Ross Co	60
1995–96	Livingston	72	Brechin C	63	Caledonian T	57
1996–97	Inverness CT	76	Forfar Ath*	67	Ross Co	67
1997–98	Alloa	76	Arbroath	68	Ross Co*	67
1998–99	Ross Co	77	Stenhousemuir	64	Brechin C	59
1999–00	Queen's Park	69	Berwick R	66	Forfar Ath	61

DIVISION 1 to 1974–75

Maximum points: a 36; *b* 44; *c* 40; *d* 52; *e* 60; *f* 68; *g* 76; *h* 84.

	First	*Pts*	*Second*	*Pts*	*Third*	*Pts*
1890–91*a*	Dumbarton††	29	Rangers††	29	Celtic	21
1891–92*b*	Dumbarton	37	Celtic	35	Hearts	34
1892–93*a*	Celtic	29	Rangers	28	St Mirren	20
1893–94*a*	Celtic	29	Hearts	26	St Bernard's	23
1894–95*a*	Hearts	31	Celtic	26	Rangers	22
1895–96*a*	Celtic	30	Rangers	26	Hibernian	24
1896–97*a*	Hearts	28	Hibernian	26	Rangers	25
1897–98*a*	Celtic	33	Rangers	29	Hibernian	22
1898–99*a*	Rangers	36	Hearts	26	Celtic	24
1899–1900*a*	Rangers	32	Celtic	25	Hibernian	24
1900–01*c*	Rangers	35	Celtic	29	Hibernian	25
1901–02*a*	Rangers	28	Celtic	26	Hearts	22
1902–03*b*	Hibernian	37	Dundee	31	Rangers	29
1903–04*d*	Third Lanark	43	Hearts	39	Celtic*	38
1904–05*d*	Celtic‡	41	Rangers	41	Third Lanark	35
1905–06*e*	Celtic	49	Hearts	43	Airdrieonians	38
1906–07*f*	Celtic	55	Dundee	48	Rangers	45
1907–08*f*	Celtic	55	Falkirk	51	Rangers	50
1908–09*f*	Celtic	51	Dundee	50	Clyde	48
1909–10*f*	Celtic	54	Falkirk	52	Rangers	46
1910–11*f*	Rangers	52	Aberdeen	48	Falkirk	44
1911–12*f*	Rangers	51	Celtic	45	Clyde	42
1912–13*f*	Rangers	53	Celtic	49	Hearts*	41
1913–14*g*	Celtic	65	Rangers	59	Hearts*	54
1914–15*g*	Celtic	65	Hearts	61	Rangers	50
1915–16*g*	Celtic	67	Rangers	56	Morton	51
1916–17*g*	Celtic	64	Morton	54	Rangers	53
1917–18*f*	Rangers	56	Celtic	55	Kilmarnock*	43
1918–19*f*	Celtic	58	Rangers	57	Morton	47
1919–20*h*	Rangers	71	Celtic	68	Motherwell	57
1920–21*h*	Rangers	76	Celtic	66	Hearts	50
1921–22*h*	Celtic	67	Rangers	66	Raith R	51
1922–23*g*	Rangers	55	Airdrieonians	50	Celtic	46
1923–24*g*	Rangers	59	Airdrieonians	50	Celtic	46
1924–25*g*	Rangers	60	Airdrieonians	57	Hibernian	52
1925–26*g*	Celtic	58	Airdrieonians*	50	Hearts	50
1926–27*g*	Rangers	56	Motherwell	51	Celtic	49
1927–28*g*	Rangers	60	Celtic*	55	Motherwell	55
1928–29*g*	Rangers	67	Celtic	51	Motherwell	50
1929–30*g*	Rangers	60	Motherwell	55	Aberdeen	53
1930–31*g*	Rangers	60	Celtic	58	Motherwell	56
1931–32*g*	Motherwell	66	Rangers	61	Celtic	48
1932–33*g*	Rangers	62	Motherwell	59	Hearts	50
1933–34*g*	Rangers	66	Motherwell	62	Celtic	47
1934–35*g*	Rangers	55	Celtic	52	Hearts	50
1935–36*g*	Celtic	66	Rangers*	61	Aberdeen	61
1936–37*g*	Rangers	61	Aberdeen	54	Celtic	52
1937–38*g*	Celtic	61	Hearts	58	Rangers	49
1938–39*g*	Rangers	59	Celtic	48	Aberdeen	46
1946–47*e*	Rangers	46	Hibernian	44	Aberdeen	39
1947–48*e*	Hibernian	48	Rangers	46	Partick T	36

1948–49*e*	Rangers	46	Dundee	45	Hibernian	39
1949–50*e*	Rangers	50	Hibernian	49	Hearts	43
1950–51*e*	Hibernian	48	Rangers*	38	Dundee	38
1951–52*e*	Hibernian	45	Rangers	41	East Fife	37
1952–53*e*	Rangers*	43	Hibernian	43	East Fife	39
1953–54*e*	Celtic	43	Hearts	38	Partick T	35
1954–55*e*	Aberdeen	49	Celtic	46	Rangers	41
1955–56*f*	Rangers	52	Aberdeen	46	Hearts*	45
1956–57*f*	Rangers	55	Hearts	53	Kilmarnock	42
1957–58*f*	Hearts	62	Rangers	49	Celtic	46
1958–59*f*	Rangers	50	Hearts	48	Motherwell	44
1959–60*f*	Hearts	54	Kilmarnock	50	Rangers*	42
1960–61*f*	Rangers	51	Kilmarnock	50	Third Lanark	42
1961–62*f*	Dundee	54	Rangers	51	Celtic	46
1962–63*f*	Rangers	57	Kilmarnock	48	Partick T	46
1963–64*f*	Rangers	55	Kilmarnock	49	Celtic*	47
1964–65*f*	Kilmarnock*	50	Hearts	50	Dunfermline Ath	49
1965–66*f*	Celtic	57	Rangers	55	Kilmarnock	45
1966–67*f*	Celtic	58	Rangers	55	Clyde	46
1967–68*f*	Celtic	63	Rangers	61	Hibernian	45
1968–69*f*	Celtic	54	Rangers	49	DunfermlineAth	45
1969–70*f*	Celtic	57	Rangers	45	Hibernian	44
1970–71*f*	Celtic	56	Aberdeen	54	St Johnstone	44
1971–72*f*	Celtic	60	Aberdeen	50	Rangers	44
1972–73*f*	Celtic	57	Rangers	56	Hibernian	45
1973–74*f*	Celtic	53	Hibernian	49	Rangers	48
1974–75*f*	Rangers	56	Hibernian	49	Celtic	45

DIVISION 2 to 1974–75

Maximum points: a 76; *b* 72; *c* 68; *d* 52; *e* 60; *f* 36; *g* 44.

1893–94*f*	Hibernian	29	Cowlairs	27	Clyde	24
1894–95*f*	Hibernian	30	Motherwell	22	Port Glasgow	20
1895–96*f*	Abercorn	27	Leith Ath	23	Renton	21
1896–97*f*	Partick T	31	Leith Ath	27	Kilmarnock*	21
1897–98*f*	Kilmarnock	29	Port Glasgow	25	Morton	22
1898–99*f*	Kilmarnock	32	Leith Ath	27	Port Glasgow	25
1899–1900*f*	Partick T	29	Morton	28	Port Glasgow	20
1900–01*f*	St Bernard's	25	Airdrieonians	23	Abercorn	21
1901–02*g*	Port Glasgow	32	Partick T	31	Motherwell	26
1902–03*g*	Airdrieonians	35	Motherwell	28	Ayr U*	27
1903–04*g*	Hamilton A	37	Clyde	29	Ayr U	28
1904–05*g*	Clyde	32	Falkirk	28	Hamilton A	27
1905–06*g*	Leith Ath	34	Clyde	31	Albion R	27
1906–07*g*	St Bernard's	32	Vale of Leven*	27	Arthurlie	27
1907–08*g*	Raith R	30	Dumbarton	‡‡27	Ayr U	27
1908–09*g*	Abercorn	31	Raith R*	28	Vale of Leven	28
1909–10*g*	Leith Ath‡	33	Raith R	33	St Bernard's	27
1910–11*g*	Dumbarton	31	Ayr U	27	Albion R	25
1911–12*g*	Ayr U	35	Abercorn	30	Dumbarton	27
1912–13*d*	Ayr U	34	Dunfermline Ath	33	East Stirling	32
1913–14*g*	Cowdenbeath	31	Albion R	27	Dunfermline Ath*	26
1914–15*d*	Cowdenbeath*	37	St Bernard's*	37	Leith Ath	37

1921–22*a*	Alloa	60	Cowdenbeath	47	Armadale	45
1922–23*a*	Queen's Park	57	Clydebank ¶	50	St Johnstone ¶	45
1923–24*a*	St Johnstone	56	Cowdenbeath	55	Bathgate	44
1924–25*a*	Dundee U	50	Clydebank	48	Clyde	47
1925–26*a*	Dunfermline Ath	59	Clyde	53	Ayr U	52
1926–27*a*	Bo'ness	56	Raith R	49	Clydebank	45
1927–28*a*	Ayr U	54	Third Lanark	45	King's Park	44
1928–29*b*	Dundee U	51	Morton	50	Arbroath	47
1929–30*a*	Leith Ath*	57	East Fife	57	Albion R	54
1930–31*a*	Third Lanark	61	Dundee U	50	Dunfermline Ath	47
1931–32*a*	East Stirling*	55	St Johnstone	55	Raith R*	46
1932–33*c*	Hibernian	54	Queen of the S	49	Dunfermline Ath	47
1933–34*c*	Albion R	45	Dunfermline Ath*	44	Arbroath	44
1934–35*c*	Third Lanark	52	Arbroath	50	St Bernard's	47
1935–36*c*	Falkirk	59	St Mirren	52	Morton	48
1936–37*c*	Ayr U	54	Morton	51	St Bernard's	48
1937–38*c*	Raith R	59	Albion R	48	Airdrieonians	47
1938–39*c*	Cowdenbeath	60	Alloa*	48	East Fife	48
1946–47*d*	Dundee	45	Airdrieonians	42	East Fife	31
1947–48*e*	East Fife	53	Albion R	42	Hamilton A	40
1948–49*e*	Raith R*	42	Stirling A	42	Airdrieonians*	41
1949–50*e*	Morton	47	Airdrieonians	44	Dunfermline Ath*	36
1950–51*e*	Queen of the S*	45	Stirling A	45	Ayr U*	36
1951–52*e*	Clyde	44	Falkirk	43	Ayr U	39
1952–53*e*	Stirling A	44	Hamilton A	43	Queen's Park	37
1953–54*e*	Motherwell	45	Kilmarnock	42	Third Lanark*	36
1954–55*e*	Airdrieonians	46	Dunfermline Ath	42	Hamilton A	39
1955–56*b*	Queen's Park	54	Ayr U	51	St Johnstone	49
1956–57*b*	Clyde	64	Third Lanark	51	Cowdenbeath	45
1957–58*b*	Stirling A	55	Dunfermline Ath	53	Arbroath	47
1958–59*b*	Ayr U	60	Arbroath	51	Stenhousemuir	46
1959–60*b*	St Johnstone	53	Dundee U	50	Queen of the S	49
1960–61*b*	Stirling A	55	Falkirk	54	Stenhousemuir	50
1961–62*b*	Clyde	54	Queen of the S	53	Morton	44
1962–63*b*	St Johnstone	55	East Stirling	49	Morton	48
1963–64*b*	Morton	67	Clyde	53	Arbroath	46
1964–65*b*	Stirling A	59	Hamilton A	50	Queen of the S	45
1965–66*b*	Ayr U	53	Airdrieonians	50	Queen of the S	47
1966–67*a*	Morton	69	Raith R	58	Arbroath	57
1967–68*b*	St Mirren	62	Arbroath	53	East Fife	49
1968–69*b*	Motherwell	64	Ayr U	53	East Fife*	48
1969–70*b*	Falkirk	56	Cowdenbeath	55	Queen of the S	50
1970–71*b*	Partick T	56	East Fife	51	Arbroath	46
1971–72*b*	Dumbarton*	52	Arbroath	52	Stirling A	50
1972–73*b*	Clyde	56	Dumfermline Ath	52	Raith R*	47
1973–74*b*	Airdrieonians	60	Kilmarnock	58	Hamilton A	55
1974–75*a*	Falkirk	54	Queen of the S*	53	Montrose	53

Elected to Division 1: 1894 Clyde; 1895 Hibernian; 1896 Abercorn; 1897 Partick T; 1899 Kilmarnock; 1900 Morton and Partick T; 1902 Port Glasgow and Partick T; 1903 Airdrieonians and Motherwell; 1905 Falkirk and Aberdeen; 1906 Clyde and Hamilton A; 1910 Raith R; 1913 Ayr U and Dumbarton.

RELEGATED CLUBS

From Premier League

1998–99 Dunfermline Ath

From Premier Division

1974–75 *No relegation due to League reorganisation*
1975–76 Dundee, St Johnstone
1976–77 Hearts, Kilmarnock
1977–78 Ayr U, Clydebank
1978–79 Hearts, Motherwell
1979–80 Dundee, Hibernian
1980–81 Kilmarnock, Hearts
1981–82 Partick T, Airdrieonians
1982–83 Morton, Kilmarnock
1983–84 St Johnstone, Motherwell
1984–85 Dumbarton, Morton
1985–86 *No relegation due to League reorganization*
1986–87 Clydebank, Hamilton A
1987–88 Falkirk, Dunfermline Ath, Morton
1988–89 Hamilton A
1989–90 Dundee
1990–91 None
1991–92 St Mirren, Dunfermline Ath
1992–93 Falkirk, Airdrieonians
1993–94 *See footnote*
1994–95 Dundee U
1995–96 Partick T, Falkirk
1996–97 Raith R
1997–98 Hibernian

From Division 1

1974–75 *No relegation due to League reorganisation*
1975–76 Dunfermline Ath, Clyde
1976–77 Raith R, Falkirk
1977–78 Alloa Ath, East Fife
1978–79 Montrose, Queen of the S
1979–80 Arbroath, Clyde
1980–81 Stirling A, Berwick R
1981–82 East Stirling, Queen of the S
1982–83 Dunfermline Ath, Queen's Park
1983–84 Raith R, Alloa
1984–85 Meadowbank T, St Johnstone
1985–86 Ayr U, Alloa
1986–87 Brechin C, Montrose
1987–88 East Fife, Dumbarton
1988–89 Kilmarnock, Queen of the S
1989–90 Albion R, Alloa
1990–91 Clyde, Brechin C
1991–92 Montrose, Forfar Ath
1992–93 Meadowbank T, Cowdenbeath
1993–94 *See footnote*
1994–95 Ayr U, Stranraer
1995–96 Hamilton A, Dumbarton
1996–97 Clydebank, East Fife
1997–98 Partick T, Stirling A
1998–99 Hamilton A, Stranraer
1999–00 Clydebank

Relegated from Division 2

1994–95 Meadowbank T, Brechin C
1995–96 Forfar Ath, Montrose
1996–97 Dumbarton, Berwick R
1997–98 Stenhousemuir, Brechin C
1998–99 East Fife, Forfar Ath
1999–00 Hamilton A

Relegated from Division 1 1973–74

1921–22 *Queen's Park, Dumbarton, Clydebank
1922–23 Albion R, Alloa Ath
1923–24 Clyde, Clydebank
1924–25 Third Lanark, Ayr U
1925–26 Raith R, Clydebank
1926–27 Morton, Dundee U
1927–28 Dunfermline Ath, Bo'ness
1928–29 Third Lanark, Raith R
1929–30 St Johnstone, Dundee U
1930–31 Hibernian, East Fife
1931–32 Dundee U, Leith Ath
1932–33 Morton, East Stirling
1933–34 Third Lanark, Cowdenbeath

1934–35 St Mirren, Falkirk
1935–36 Airdrieonians, Ayr U
1936–37 Dunfermline Ath, Albion R
1937–38 Dundee, Morton
1938–39 Queen's Park, Raith R
1946–47 Kilmarnock, Hamilton A
1947–48 Airdrieonians, Queen's Park
1948–49 Morton, Albion R
1949–50 Queen of the S, Stirling A
1950–51 Clyde, Falkirk
1951–52 Morton, Stirling A
1952–53 Motherwell, Third Lanark
1953–54 Airdrieonians, Hamilton A
1954–55 *No clubs relegated*
1955–56 Stirling A, Clyde
1956–57 Dunfermline Ath, Ayr U
1957–58 East Fife, Queen's Park
1958–59 Queen of the S, Falkirk
1959–60 Arbroath, Stirling A
1960–61 Ayr U, Clyde
1961–62 St Johnstone, Stirling A
1962–63 Clyde, Raith R
1963–64 Queen of the S, East Stirling
1964–65 Airdrieonians, Third Lanark
1965–66 Morton, Hamilton A
1966–67 St Mirren, Ayr U
1967–68 Motherwell, Stirling A
1968–69 Falkirk, Arbroath
1969–70 Raith R, Partick T
1970–71 St Mirren, Cowdenbeath
1971–72 Clyde, Dunfermline Ath
1972–73 Kilmarnock, Airdrieonians
1973–74 East Fife, Falkirk

*Season 1921–22 – only 1 club promoted, 3 clubs relegated.

Scottish League championship wins: Rangers 48, Celtic 36, Aberdeen 4, Hearts 4, Hibernian 4, Dumbarton 2, Dundee 1, Dundee U 1, Kilmarnock 1, Motherwell 1, Third Lanark 1.

The Scottish Football League was reconstructed into three divisions at the end of the 1974–75 season, so the usual relegation statistics do not apply. Further reorganization took place at the end of the 1985–86 season. From 1986–87, the Premier and First Division had 12 teams each. The Second Division remained at 14. From 1988–89, the Premier Division reverted to 10 teams, and the First Division to 14 teams but in 1991–92 the Premier and First Division reverted to 12. At the end of the 1997–98 season, the top nine clubs in Premier Division broke away from the Scottish League to form a new competition, the Scottish Premier League, with the club promoted from Division One. At the end of the 1999–2000 season two teams were added to the Scottish League. There was no relegation from the Premier League but two promoted from the First Division and three from each of the Second and Third Divisions. One team was relegated from the First Division and one from the Second Division, leaving 12 teams in each division.

PAST SCOTTISH LEAGUE CUP FINALS

1946–47	Rangers	4	Aberdeen	0
1947–48	East Fife	0 4	Falkirk	0* 1
1948–49	Rangers	2	Raith Rovers	0
1949–50	East Fife	3	Dunfermline	0
1950–51	Motherwell	3	Hibernian	0
1951–52	Dundee	3	Rangers	2
1952–53	Dundee	2	Kilmarnock	0
1953–54	East Fife	3	Partick Thistle	2
1954–55	Hearts	4	Motherwell	2
1955–56	Aberdeen	2	St Mirren	1
1956–57	Celtic	0 3	Partick Thistle	0 0
1957–58	Celtic	7	Rangers	1
1958–59	Hearts	5	Partick Thistle	1
1959–60	Hearts	2	Third Lanark	1
1960–61	Rangers	2	Kilmarnock	0
1961–62	Rangers	1 3	Hearts	1 1
1962–63	Hearts	1	Kilmarnock	0
1963–64	Rangers	5	Morton	0
1964–65	Rangers	2	Celtic	1
1965–66	Celtic	2	Rangers	1
1966–67	Celtic	1	Rangers	0
1967–68	Celtic	5	Dundee	3
1968–69	Celtic	6	Hibernian	2
1969–70	Celtic	1	St Johnstone	0
1970–71	Rangers	1	Celtic	0
1971–72	Partick Thistle	4	Celtic	1
1972–73	Hibernian	2	Celtic	1
1973–74	Dundee	1	Celtic	0
1974–75	Celtic	6	Hibernian	3
1975–76	Rangers	1	Celtic	0
1976–77	Aberdeen	2	Celtic	1
1977–78	Rangers	2	Celtic	1*
1978–79	Rangers	2	Aberdeen	1
1979–80	Aberdeen	0 0	Dundee U	0* 3
1980–81	Dundee	0	Dundee U	3
1981–82	Rangers	2	Dundee U	1
1982–83	Celtic	2	Rangers	1
1983–84	Rangers	3	Celtic	2
1984–85	Rangers	1	Dundee U	0
1985–86	Aberdeen	3	Hibernian	0
1986–87	Rangers	2	Celtic	1
1987–88	Rangers†	3	Aberdeen	3*
1988–89	Aberdeen	2	Rangers	3*
1989–90	Aberdeen	2	Rangers	1
1990–91	Rangers	2	Celtic	1
1991–92	Hibernian	2	Dunfermline Ath	0
1992–93	Rangers	2	Aberdeen	1*
1993–94	Rangers	2	Hibernian	1
1994–95	Raith R†	2	Celtic	2*
1995–96	Aberdeen	2	Dundee	0
1996–97	Rangers	4	Hearts	3
1997–98	Celtic	3	Dundee U	0
1998–99	Rangers	2	St Johnstone	1

*†Won on penalties *After extra time*

CIS SCOTTISH LEAGUE CUP 1999-2000

FIRST ROUND

Albion R	(0) 0	Clyde	(0) 3
(aet)			
Brechin C	(0) 0	Dumbarton	(0) 2
Clydebank	(0) 1	East Stirling	(1) 2
Cowdenbeath	(0) 0	Livingston	(0) 2
East Fife	(0) 2	Stirling Albion	(0) 2
(aet (East Fife won 8-7 on penalties))			
Montrose	(0) 1	Hamilton A	(1) 2
Partick T	(0) 0	Alloa Ath	(0) 2
Queen of the S	(0) 1	Arbroath	(0) 0
(aet)			
Queen's Park	(0) 2	Berwick R	(1) 1
Ross Co	(1) 2	Forfar Ath	(1) 1
(aet)			
Stenhousemuir	(0) 1	Inverness CT	(2) 3
Stranraer	(0) 0	Raith R	(0) 1
(aet)			

SECOND ROUND

Aberdeen	(0) 1	Livingston	(0) 0
Ayr U	(0) 2	Hamilton A	(0) 1
Clyde	(2) 2	Hibernian	(2) 2
(aet (Hibernian won 5-4 on penalties.))			
Dundee	(3) 4	Dumbarton	(0) 0
East Fife	(1) 2	Airdrieonians	(1) 2
(aet (East Fife won 5-4 on penalties))			
Inverness CT	(0) 2	St Mirren	(0) 0
(aet)			
Morton	(1) 1	Alloa Ath	(2) 3
Dundee U	(1) 3	Ross Co	(1) 1
(aet)			
Dunfermline Ath	(3) 4	Queen's Park	(0) 0
East Stirling	(0) 0	Falkirk	(0) 2
(aet)			
Queen of the S	(1) 1	Hearts	(0) 3
Raith R	(0) 2	Motherwell	(1) 2
(aet (Motherwell won 5-4 on penalties))			

THIRD ROUND

Aberdeen	(0) 1	Falkirk	(0) 1
(aet (Aberdeen won 5-3 on penalties))			
Alloa Ath	(1) 1	Dundee	(2) 3
East Fife	(0) 0	Hearts	(1) 2
Inverness CT	(0) 0	Motherwell	(0) 1
Kilmarnock	(2) 3	Hibernian	(1) 2
Rangers	(1) 1	Dunfermline Ath	(0) 0
St Johnstone	(0) 1	Dundee U	(0) 2
Ayr U	(0) 0	Celtic	(0) 4

QUARTER-FINALS

Aberdeen	(0) 1	Rangers	(0) 0
(aet)			
Celtic	(0) 1	Dundee	(0) 0
Dundee U	(2) 3	Motherwell	(0) 2
Kilmarnock	(0) 1	Hearts	(0) 0

SEMI-FINALS

Aberdeen	(0) 1	Dundee U	(0) 0
Celtic	(0) 1	Kilmarnock	(0) 0

FINAL

Celtic	(1) 2	Aberdeen	(0) 0

BELL'S CHALLENGE CUP 1999–2000

FIRST ROUND

Airdrieonians	(1) 2	Dumbarton	(0) 1
Arbroath	(0) 3	East Fife	(1) 2
Ayr U	(0) 0	Raith R	(0) 1
Berwick R	(1) 4	Queen of the S	(0) 1
Brechin C	(0) 0	Queen's Park	(0) 1
Clyde	(0) 0	Ross Co	(2) 4
Cowdenbeath	(0) 0	Alloa Ath	(3) 4
Dunfermline Ath	(0) 2	Morton	(2) 2
(aet (Morton won 5-4 onpenalties)			
East Stirling	(0) 1	Clydebank	(0) 2
(aet)			
Inverness CT	(0) 1	St Mirren	(0) 0
Montrose	(0) 1	Hamilton A	(1) 3
Partick T	(0) 0	Albion R	(1) 2
Stirling Albion	(0) 2	Stenhousemuir	(0) 2
(aet (Stirling Albion won 6-5 on penalties))			
Stranraer	(2) 2	Falkirk	(0) 2
(aet (Stranraer won 5-4 on penalties))			

SECOND ROUND

Airdrieonians	(0) 1	Alloa Ath	(1) 2
Clydebank	(3) 4	Forfar Ath	(2) 3
Hamilton A	(0) 0	Inverness CT	(1) 3
Livingston	(0) 2	Berwick R	(1) 1
(aet)			
Queen's Park	(2) 3	Albion R	(0) 1
Ross Co	(1) 3	Morton	(0) 0
Stirling Albion	(1) 1	Arbroath	(1) 1
(aet (Stirling Albion won 4-3 on penalties))			
Stranraer	(0) 1	Raith R	(1) 2

QUARTER-FINALS

Inverness CT	(1) 2	Clydebank	(0) 0
Livingston	(2) 3	Raith R	(1) 1
Ross Co	(1) 1	Alloa Ath	(0) 2
(aet)			
Stirling Albion	(1) 4	Queen's Park	(0) 0

SEMI-FINALS

Inverness CT	(0) 1	Livingston	(0) 0
Stirling Albion	(1) 1	Alloa Ath	(0) 2

FINAL

Alloa Ath	(2) 4	Inverness CT	(1) 4
(aet (Alloa Ath won 5-4 on penalties))			

SCOTTISH CUP 1999–2000

FIRST ROUND

Hamilton A	(0) 1	Clyde	(1) 2
Huntly	(0) 0	East Stirling	(0) 1
Ross Co	(1) 2	Forfar Ath	(1) 2
Threave R	(0) 1	Stenhousemuir	(4) 7

FIRST ROUND REPLAY

Forfar Ath	(0) 0	Ross Co	(0) 0

(aet (Forfar Ath won 4-2 on penalties))

SECOND ROUND

Albion R	(0) 0	Dalbeattie Star	(0) 0
Arbroath	(0) 0	Fraserburgh	(0) 0
Brechin C	(2) 2	Annan Ath	(0) 2
Cowdenbeath	(0) 2	Clyde	(1) 3
Dumbarton	(0) 0	Stenhousemuir	(1) 2
Montrose	(0) 1	Queen of the S	(1) 3
Partick T	(1) 2	East Stirling	(0) 1
Peterhead	(1) 2	Forfar Ath	(1) 1
Queen's Park	(1) 1	Berwick R	(1) 2
Stirling Albion	(1) 2	East Fife	(1) 1
Stranraer	(0) 1	Clachnacuddin	(0) 0
Whitehill Welfare	(0) 2	Alloa Ath	(1) 2

SECOND ROUND REPLAYS

Annan Ath	(1) 2	Brechin C	(1) 3
(aet)			
Fraserburgh	(0) 1	Arbroath	(1) 3
Dalbeattie Star	(1) 1	Albion R	(1) 5
Alloa Ath	(2) 2	Whitehill Welfare	(0) 0

THIRD ROUND

Albion R	(0) 1	Partick T	(1) 2
Clyde	(0) 3	Raith R	(1) 1
Clydebank	(1) 1	Stirling Albion	(0) 0
Dundee	(0) 0	Ayr U	(0) 0
Falkirk	(2) 3	Peterhead	(1) 1
Hearts	(1) 3	Stenhousemuir	(2) 2
Hibernian	(2) 4	Dunfermline Ath	(1) 1
Queen of the S	(0) 0	Livingston	(1) 7
St Mirren	(0) 1	Aberdeen	(0) 1
Stranraer	(0) 1	Berwick R	(1) 2
Dundee U	(1) 4	Airdrieonians	(0) 1
Morton	(1) 1	Brechin C	(0) 1
St Johnstone	(0) 0	Rangers	(1) 2
Arbroath	(1) 1	Motherwell	(1) 1
Kilmarnock	(0) 0	Alloa Ath	(0) 0
Celtic	(1) 1	Inverness CT	(2) 3

THIRD ROUND REPLAYS

Aberdeen	(0) 2	St Mirren	(0) 0
Brechin C	(0) 0	Morton	(0) 0

(aet (Morton won 4-2 on penalties))

Alloa Ath	(1) 1	Kilmarnock	(0) 0
Ayr U	(0) 1	Dundee	(0) 1
(aet (Ayr U won 7-6 on penalties))			
Motherwell	(1) 2	Arbroath	(0) 0

FOURTH ROUND

Alloa Ath	(2) 2	Dundee U	(0) 2
Berwick R	(0) 0	Falkirk	(0) 0
Clyde	(0) 0	Hearts	(2) 2
Hibernian	(0) 1	Clydebank	(0) 1
Morton	(0) 0	Rangers	(0) 1
Partick T	(1) 2	Livingston	(1) 1
Inverness CT	(0) 1	Aberdeen	(0) 1
Motherwell	(3) 3	Ayr U	(3) 4

FOURTH ROUND REPLAYS

Dundee U	(2) 4	Alloa Ath	(0) 0
Aberdeen	(0) 1	Inverness CT	(0) 0
Clydebank	(0) 0	Hibernian	(1) 3
Falkirk	(1) 3	Berwick R	(0) 0

QUARTER-FINALS

Ayr U	(1) 2	Partick T	(0) 0
Hibernian	(2) 3	Falkirk	(1) 1
Dundee U	(0) 0	Aberdeen	(0) 1
Rangers	(2) 4	Hearts	(1) 1

SEMI-FINALS

Ayr U	(0) 0	Rangers	(3) 7
Hibernian	(0) 1	Aberdeen	(0) 2

FINAL

Aberdeen	(0) 0	Rangers	(1) 4

PAST SCOTTISH CUP FINALS

1874	Queen's Park	2	Clydesdale	0
1875	Queen's Park	3	Renton	0
1876	Queen's Park	1 2	Third Lanark	1 0
1877	Vale of Leven	0 1 3	Rangers	0 1 2
1878	Vale of Leven	1	Third Lanark	0
1879	Vale of Leven	1	Rangers	1
	Vale of Leven awarded cup, Rangers did not appear for replay			
1880	Queen's Park	3	Thornlibank	0
1881	Queen's Park	2 3	Dumbarton	1 1
	Replayed because of protest			
1882	Queen's Park	2 4	Dumbarton	2 1
1883	Dumbarton	2 2	Vale of Leven	2 1
1884	*Queen's Park awarded cup when Vale of Leven did not appear for the final*			
1885	Renton	0 3	Vale of Leven	0 1
1886	Queen's Park	3	Renton	1
1887	Hibernian	2	Dumbarton	1
1888	Renton	6	Cambuslang	1
1889	Third Lanark	3 2	Celtic	0 1
	Replayed because of protest			
1890	Queen's Park	1 2	Vale of Leven	1 1
1891	Hearts	1	Dumbarton	0
1892	Celtic	1 5	Queen's Park	0 1
	Replayed because of protest			
1893	Queen's Park	2	Celtic	1
1894	Rangers	3	Celtic	1
1895	St Bernards	3	Renton	1
1896	Hearts	3	Hibernian	1
1897	Rangers	5	Dumbarton	1
1898	Rangers	2	Kilmarnock	0
1899	Celtic	2	Rangers	0
1900	Celtic	4	Queen's Park	3
1901	Hearts	4	Celtic	3
1902	Hibernian	1	Celtic	0
1903	Rangers	1 0 2	Hearts	1 0 0
1904	Celtic	3	Rangers	2
1905	Third Lanark	0 3	Rangers	0 1
1906	Hearts	1	Third Lanark	0
1907	Celtic	3	Hearts	0
1908	Celtic	5	St Mirren	1
1909	*After two drawn games between Celtic and Rangers, 2.2, 1.1, there was a riot and the cup was withheld*			
1910	Dundee	2 0 2	Clyde	2 0 1
1911	Celtic	0 2	Hamilton Acad	0 0
1912	Celtic	2	Clyde	0
1913	Falkirk	2	Raith R	0
1914	Celtic	0 4	Hibernian	0 1
1920	Kilmarnock	3	Albion R	2
1921	Partick Th	1	Rangers	0
1922	Morton	1	Rangers	0
1923	Celtic	1	Hibernian	0
1924	Airdrieonians	2	Hibernian	0
1925	Celtic	2	Dundee	1
1926	St Mirren	2	Celtic	0
1927	Celtic	3	East Fife	1
1928	Rangers	4	Celtic	0
1929	Kilmarnock	2	Rangers	0
1930	Rangers	0 2	Partick Th	0 1
1931	Celtic	2 4	Motherwell	2 2

1932	Rangers	1 3	Kilmarnock	1 0
1933	Celtic	1	Motherwell	0
1934	Rangers	5	St Mirren	0
1935	Rangers	2	Hamilton Acad	1
1936	Rangers	1	Third Lanark	0
1937	Celtic	2	Aberdeen	1
1938	East Fife	1 4	Kilmarnock	1 2
1939	Clyde	4	Motherwell	0
1947	Aberdeen	2	Hibernian	1
1948	Rangers	1 1	Morton	1 0
1949	Rangers	4	Clyde	1
1950	Rangers	3	East Fife	0
1951	Celtic	1	Motherwell	0
1952	Motherwell	4	Dundee	0
1953	Rangers	1 1	Aberdeen	1 0
1954	Celtic	2	Aberdeen	1
1955	Clyde	1 1	Celtic	1 0
1956	Hearts	3	Celtic	1
1957	Falkirk	1 2	Kilmarnock	1 1
1958	Clyde	1	Hibernian	0
1959	St Mirren	3	Aberdeen	1
1960	Rangers	2	Kilmarnock	0
1961	Dunfermline Ath	0 2	Celtic	0 0
1962	Rangers	2	St Mirren	0
1963	Rangers	1 3	Celtic	1 0
1964	Rangers	3	Dundee	1
1965	Celtic	3	Dunfermline Ath	2
1966	Rangers	0 1	Celtic	0 0
1967	Celtic	2	Aberdeen	0
1968	Dunfermline Ath	3	Hearts	1
1969	Celtic	4	Rangers	0
1970	Aberdeen	3	Celtic	1
1971	Celtic	1 2	Rangers	1 1
1972	Celtic	6	Hibernian	1
1973	Rangers	3	Celtic	2
1974	Celtic	3	Dundee U	0
1975	Celtic	3	Airdrieonians	1
1976	Rangers	3	Hearts	1
1977	Celtic	1	Rangers	0
1978	Rangers	2	Aberdeen	1
1979	Rangers	0 0 3	Hibernian	0 0 2
1980	Celtic	1	Rangers	0
1981	Rangers	0 4	Dundee U	0 1
1982	Aberdeen	4	Rangers	1 (aet)
1983	Aberdeen	1	Rangers	0 (aet)
1984	Aberdeen	2	Celtic	1 (aet)
1985	Celtic	2	Dundee U	1
1986	Aberdeen	3	Hearts	0
1987	St Mirren	1	Dundee U	0 (aet)
1988	Celtic	2	Dundee U	1
1989	Celtic	1	Rangers	0
1990	Aberdeen†	0	Celtic	0
1991	Motherwell	4	Dundee U	3 (aet)
1992	Rangers	2	Airdrieonians	1
1993	Rangers	2	Aberdeen	1
1994	Dundee U	1	Rangers	0
1995	Celtic	1	Airdrieonians	0
1996	Rangers	5	Hearts	1
1997	Kilmarnock	1	Falkirk	0
1998	Hearts	2	Rangers	1
1999	Rangers	1	Celtic	0

†won on penalties

WELSH FOOTBALL 1999–2000

LEAGUE OF WALES

		Home			Goals		Away			Goals			
	P	*W*	*D*	*L*	*F*	*A*	*W*	*D*	*L*	*F*	*A*	*GD*	*Pts*
Total Network Solutions	34	12	2	3	37	14	12	2	3	32	23	+32	76
Barry Town	34	14	3	0	61	17	9	2	6	37	17	+64	74
Cwmbran Town	34	13	1	3	41	17	8	5	4	30	20	+34	69
Carmarthen Town	34	13	1	3	39	21	9	2	6	29	21	+26	69
Llanelli	34	13	1	3	49	24	8	2	7	27	22	+30	66
Aberystwyth Town	34	13	2	2	43	16	6	2	9	27	30	+24	61
Connah's Quay Nomads	34	8	4	5	29	16	9	2	6	28	19	+22	57
Newtown	34	9	2	6	25	13	5	4	8	24	28	+8	48
Bangor City	34	8	3	6	34	27	7	0	10	22	34	−5	48
Afan Lido	34	9	6	2	31	11	3	4	10	13	31	+2	46
Rhyl	34	9	2	6	23	24	4	3	10	17	36	−20	44
Caersws	34	4	3	10	18	28	7	5	5	31	22	−1	41
Flexsys Cefn Druids	34	9	0	8	26	22	4	2	11	18	41	−19	41
Rhayader Town	34	5	3	9	20	23	4	4	9	14	24	−13	34
Haverfordwest County	34	4	5	8	15	31	4	1	12	15	31	−32	30
Inter Cardiff	34	3	8	6	17	34	3	3	11	20	31	−28	28*
Conwy United	34	4	1	12	17	38	2	4	11	16	59	−64	21**
Caernarfon Town	34	1	4	12	12	33	0	4	13	9	48	−60	11

*One point deducted for playing ineligible player.
**Two points deducted for failing to fulfil fixture.

NORTHERN IRISH FOOTBALL 1999–2000

IFL SMIRNOFF

Premiership

	P	*W*	*D*	*L*	*F*	*A*	*GD*	*Pts*
Linfield	36	24	7	5	67	30	+37	79
Coleraine	36	18	7	11	64	42	+22	61
Glenavon	36	17	10	9	55	34	+21	61
Glentoran	36	18	7	11	59	51	+8	61
Portadown	36	15	7	14	64	62	+2	52
Newry Town	36	11	7	18	44	58	−14	40
Crusaders	36	9	13	14	41	55	−14	40
Ballymena United	36	6	16	14	45	62	−17	34
Cliftonville	36	7	13	16	38	59	−21	34
Lisburn Distillery	36	9	5	22	39	63	−24	32

LEAGUE OF WALES—RESULTS 1999–2000

	Aberystwyth Town	Afan Lido	Bangor City	Barry Town	Caernarfon Town	Caersws	Carmarthen Town	Connah's Quay Nomads	Conwy United	Cwmbran Town	Flexys Cefn Druids	Haverfordwest County	Inter Cardiff	Llanelli	Newtown	Rhayader Town	Rhyl	Total Network Solutions
Aberystwyth Town	—	2-0	2-1	3-1	6-0	1-1	2-1	2-1	1-1	1-2	3-0	4-0	1-2	3-1	3-2	3-1	2-1	4-1
Afan Lido	2-1	—	4-0	0-2	4-0	3-0	0-0	1-1	3-0	0-0	2-2	4-3	3-0	0-0	2-1	3-0	0-1	0-0
Bangor City	1-3	4-1	—	3-3	1-0	1-3	0-1	0-2	8-0	1-1	3-3	1-0	3-1	1-3	3-2	1-0	3-2	0-2
Barry Town	3-3	5-0	5-2	—	3-0	1-0	3-1	3-3	4-1	3-1	7-0	3-1	5-1	4-2	4-0	2-0	1-1	5-1
Caernarfon Town	0-0	0-3	1-2	0-3	—	1-3	0-0	0-2	0-2	0-2	2-3	0-4	0-0	0-2	1-1	3-0	2-3	2-3
Caersws	0-3	3-0	2-5	1-2	2-2	—	2-1	0-2	3-3	0-1	3-0	1-0	0-3	0-2	0-1	1-1	0-1	0-1
Carmarthen Town	4-3	3-0	0-1	3-2	3-1	3-2	—	2-0	4-1	3-1	3-0	0-3	0-1	2-1	5-3	1-1	1-0	2-1
Connah's Quay Nomads	0-1	1-1	0-1	2-0	2-1	1-1	0-2	—	10-0	1-2	1-0	2-2	2-1	1-0	2-0	0-0	2-0	2-4
Conwy United	4-2	0-0	0-2	0-4	4-0	0-4	0-2	3-2	—	0-5	1-2	1-0	0-2	0-2	0-1	0-3	0-2	4-5
Cwmbran Town	2-1	3-2	6-0	1-0	4-0	1-1	3-1	0-2	3-1	—	2-1	1-0	3-1	3-1	3-2	1-2	5-0	0-2
Flexys Cefn Druids	2-0	1-0	1-2	0-1	3-0	1-3	0-2	0-2	3-1	3-2	—	2-3	2-1	2-1	2-1	0-2	4-0	0-1
Haverfordwest County	0-5	0-2	2-1	0-6	1-1	0-0	1-6	1-4	1-1	1-1	3-0	—	2-1	1-1	1-1	0-1	2-2	1-1
Inter Cardiff	0-1	1-1	1-0	1-5	1-1	2-7	0-4	2-0	2-0	1-4	0-1	0-0	—	0-3	0-0	1-1	2-1	1-2
Llanelli	5-0	4-2	4-1	2-1	1-1	3-2	7-2	2-0	3-2	1-3	2-1	3-2	3-1	—	0-4	2-0	7-0	0-2
Newtown	2-0	0-0	2-0	1-0	5-0	2-3	0-2	0-1	1-2	2-0	4-1	0-0	2-0	1-2	—	2-1	1-0	0-1
Rhayader Town	0-3	0-1	1-3	0-0	2-1	0-1	1-2	1-2	5-0	1-1	3-1	2-0	1-0	1-3	0-2	—	2-2	0-1
Rhyl	1-0	1-0	1-0	0-5	2-1	2-0	0-1	1-4	1-1	1-2	2-0	3-1	2-0	1-3	2-3	1-0	—	2-4
Total Network Solutions	4-1	3-0	2-1	0-2	4-0	0-0	2-1	1-0	7-0	1-3	0-3	4-1	2-0	2-0	0-0	3-1	2-1	—

EUROPEAN REVIEW 1999–2000

Once upon a time there was a Fairs Cup. This gave way to the UEFA Cup. Meanwhile a European Cup of the Champions was started and subsequently followed by a Cup-Winners' Cup. These three competitions ran pretty successfully with varying degrees of change until the Cup-Winners' Cup was dumped at the end of the 1998–99 season.

Meanwhile another long-standing if lesser known tournament is the Intertoto Cup. Last season there was an English winner in the shape of West Ham United. The reward was a place in the UEFA Cup.

To offset the loss of the Cup-Winners' Cup, it was decided to increase the number of entries in the UEFA Cup. At the same time the expansion of the Champions Cup was such that you no longer had to be a specific country's champions to enter it. Moreover once knocked out of this, you could still find your way into the UEFA Cup! It happened to Arsenal last season as they became the first club in this country to play in two different European cup competitions in the same season - unless you include West Ham as mentioned previously.

The Champions Cup now has a Champions League to start it off and instead of the home and away aggregate scores, there are two series ofgroup matches to be played.

England had two survivors at this knock-outstage – Chelsea and Manchester United, the holders of the cup. Manchester United appeared to have done well enough to hold Real Madrid to a goalless draw in Spain, while Chelsea established a healthy 3-1 first leg lead over Barcelona at Stamford Bridge. Two semi-final teams from England seemed a reasonable choice, but the return legs produced an entirely different outcome.

Chelsea found themselves in all kinds of bother in the return at the Nou Camp and when Barcelona were awarded a penalty kick in the dying minutes the Spaniards merely needed Rivaldo to clinch a 4-1 second leg scoreline from the spot. Alas he missed and it needed extra time before the Spanish team was able to assert its superiority in a 5-1 victory.

A disastrous own goal by Roy Keane gave Real Madrid an early lead at Old Trafford. It was followed early in the second half by the Spaniards scoring twice in as many minutes to roar to a 3-0 lead. Though David Beckham and Paul Scholes from a penalty, reduced the deficit, Real could have afforded the luxury of an equaliser and still qualified for the final.

Thus the semi-finals had three Spanish teams, with Barcelona playing Valencia and Real taking on the Germans from Bayern Munich. It says something for the strength of Spanish club football that Valencia demolished Barcelona in the first leg, winning 4-1, while Real had a respectable 2-0 lead over Bayern. The return matches saw Barcelona only manage to peg back one goal as they won 2-1, while Bayern won by the same scoreline.

Real dominated the final in Paris, winning comfortably 3-0 over Valencia, who had disposed of Barcelona in such convincing fashion.

The quarter-finals of the UEFA Cup also had two English teams in Arsenal and Leeds United. Arsenal who had been eliminated from the Champions League earlier on in the season took a two-goal lead over the Germans Werder Bremen and capped this fine performance with a 4-2 success in the return match. Leeds for their part, took a 3-0 first leg lead over Slavia Prague and won through 4-2 on aggregate.

In the semi-finals, though Dennis Bergkamp gave Arsenal the advantage of a second minute lead over the French club Lens, they were unable to increase the score. Leeds game in Turkey against Galatasaray was in the shadow of the death of two Leeds supporters the previous day in attacks by Turkish supporters. Leeds lost 2-0.

Again Arsenaldid as well away as they had at home and won 2-1 at Lens, but Leeds were unable to improve matters and held to a 2-2 draw were knocked out.

The final in Copenhagen did not enable Arsenal to gain revenge for Leeds against Galatasaray, the match ending as a goalless draw and requiring penalties to resolve it. Once more an English team was found wanting from the resulting spot kicks and Galatsaray won 4-1 from the shoot-out, though two of Arsenal's efforts had managed to hit the woodwork.

EUROPEAN CUP 1999–2000

FIRST QUALIFYING ROUND, FIRST LEG

Barry Town	(0) 0	Valletta	(0) 0
HB Torshavn	(0) 1	Haka	(0) 1
IBV	(1) 1	SK Tirana	(0) 0
Jeunesse Esch	(0) 0	Skonto Riga	(0) 2
Litets	(2) 3	Glentoran	(0) 0
Partizan Belgrade	(3) 6	Flora Tallinn	(0) 0
Sloga	(0) 1	Kapaz	(0) 0
St Patrick's Athletic	(0) 0	Zimbru Chisinau	(3) 5
Zalgiris	(1) 2	Tsement	(0) 0

FIRST QUALIFYING ROUND, SECOND LEG

Flora Tallinn	(0) 1	Partizan Belgrade	(2) 4
Glentoran	(0) 0	Litets	(0) 2
Haka	(2) 6	HB Torshavn	(0) 0
Kapaz	(1) 2	Sloga	(1) 1
Skonto Riga	(2) 8	Jeunesse Esch	(0) 0
SK Tirana	(0) 1	IBV	(2) 2
Tsement	(0) 0	Zalgiris	(2) 3
Valletta	(1) 3	Barry Town	(0) 2
Zimbru Chisinau	(3) 5	St Patrick's Athletic	(0) 0

SECOND QUALIFYING ROUND, FIRST LEG

Anorthosis	(1) 2	Slovan Bratislava	(0) 1
Besiktas	(0) 1	Hapoel Haifa	(0) 1
CSKA Moscow	(1) 2	Molde	(0) 0
Dnepr Mogilev	(0) 0	AIK Stockholm	(0) 1
Dynamo Kiev	(1) 2	Zalgiris	(0) 0
Dynamo Tbilisi	(0) 2	Zimbru Chisinau	(0) 1
Haka	(0) 1	Rangers	(3) 4
IBV	(0) 0	MTK Budapest	(1) 2
Litets	(1) 4	Widzew Lodz	(0) 1
Maribor	(2) 5	Genk	(1) 1
Partizan Belgrade	(2) 3	Rijeka	(0) 1
Rapid Bucharest	(1) 3	Skonto Riga	(2) 3
Rapid Vienna	(0) 3	Valletta	(0) 0
Sloga	(0) 0	Brondby	(1) 1

SECOND QUALIFYING ROUND, SECOND LEG

AIK Stockholm	(0) 2	Dnepr Mogilev	(0) 0
Brondby	(1) 1	Sloga	(0) 0
Genk	(1) 3	Maribor	(0) 0
Hapoel Haifa	(0) 0	Besiktas	(0) 0
Molde	(0) 4	CSKA Moscow	(0) 0
MTK Budapest	(3) 3	IBV	(0) 1
Rangers	(2) 3	Haka	(0) 0
Rijeka	(0) 0	Partizan Belgrade	(2) 3
Skonto Riga	(0) 2	Rapid Bucharest	(1) 1
Slovan Bratislava	(0) 1	Anorthosis	(0) 1
Valletta	(0) 0	Rapid Vienna	(0) 2
Widzew Lodz	(1) 4	Litets	(1) 1
Zalgiris	(0) 0	Dynamo Kiev	(1) 1
Zimbru Chisinau	(1) 2	Dynamo Tbilisi	(0) 0

THIRD QUALIFYING ROUND, FIRST LEG

Aalborg	(0) 1	Dynamo Kiev	(2) 2
AEK Athens	(0) 0	AIK Stockholm	(0) 0

Brondby	(0) 1	Boavista	(1) 2
Chelsea	(0) 3	Skonto Riga	(0) 0
Croatia Zagreb	(0) 0	MTK Budapest	(0) 0
Fiorentina	(1) 3	Widzew Lodz	(0) 1
Hapoel Haifa	(0) 0	Valencia	(0) 2
Hertha Berlin	(1) 2	Anorthosis	(0) 0
Lyon	(0) 0	Maribor	(0) 1
Molde	(0) 0	Mallorca	(0) 0
Rangers	(1) 2	Parma	(0) 0
Rapid Vienna	(0) 0	Galatasaray	(2) 3
Spartak Moscow	(1) 2	Partizan Belgrade	(0) 0
Sturm Graz	(2) 2	Servette	(1) 1
Teplice	(0) 0	Borussia Dortmund	(0) 1
Zimbru Chisinau	(0) 0	PSV Eindhoven	(0) 0

THIRD QUALIFYING ROUND, SECOND LEG

AIK Stockholm	(0) 1	AEK Athens	(0) 0
Anorthosis	(0) 0	Hertha Berlin	(0) 0
Boavista	(1) 4	Brondby	(0) 2
Borussia Dortmund	(0) 1	Teplice	(0) 0
Dynamo Kiev	(0) 2	Aalborg	(1) 2
Galatasaray	(0) 1	Rapid Vienna	(0) 0
Mallorca	(1) 1	Molde	(0) 1
Maribor	(2) 2	Lyon	(0) 0
MTK Budapest	(0) 0	Croatia Zagreb	(0) 2
Parma	(0) 1	Rangers	(0) 0
Partizan Belgrade	(0) 1	Spartak Moscow	(1) 3
PSV Eindhoven	(0) 2	Zimbru Chisinau	(0) 0
Servette	(0) 2	Sturm Graz	(0) 2
Skonto Riga	(0) 0	Chelsea	(0) 0
Valencia	(0) 2	Hapoel Haifa	(0) 0
Widzew Lodz	(0) 0	Fiorentina	(1) 2

CHAMPIONS LEAGUE

GROUP A

Dynamo Kiev	(0) 0	Maribor	(0) 1
Leverkusen	(1) 1	Lazio	(1) 1
Lazio	(0) 2	Dynamo Kiev	(0) 1
Maribor	(0) 0	Leverkusen	(0) 2
Leverkusen	(0) 1	Dynamo Kiev	(0) 1
Lazio	(0) 4	Maribor	(0) 0
Dynamo Kiev	(2) 4	Leverkusen	(1) 2
Maribor	(0) 0	Lazio	(1) 4
Lazio	(1) 1	Leverkusen	(1) 1
Maribor	(0) 1	Dynamo Kiev	(1) 2
Leverkusen	(0) 0	Maribor	(0) 0
Dynamo Kiev	(0) 0	Lazio	(1) 1

Final table	P	W	D	L	F	A	Pts
Lazio	6	4	2	0	13	3	14
Dynamo Kiev	6	2	1	3	8	8	7
Leverkusen	6	1	4	1	7	7	7
Maribor	6	1	1	4	2	12	4

GROUP B

AIK Stockholm	(0) 1	Barcelona	(0) 2
Fiorentina	(0) 0	Arsenal	(0) 0
Arsenal	(1) 3	AIK Stockholm	(0) 1
Barcelona	(2) 4	Fiorentina	(0) 2
AIK Stockholm	(0) 0	Fiorentina	(0) 0

Barcelona	(1) 1	Arsenal	(0) 1
Arsenal	(1) 2	Barcelona	(2) 4
Fiorentina	(2) 3	AIK Stockholm	(0) 0
Arsenal	(0) 0	Fiorentina	(0) 1
Barcelona	(3) 5	AIK Stockholm	(0) 0
AIK Stockholm	(1) 2	Arsenal	(1) 3
Fiorentina	(1) 3	Barcelona	(2) 3

Final table	P	W	D	L	F	A	Pts
Barcelona	6	4	2	0	19	9	14
Fiorentina	6	2	3	1	9	7	9
Arsenal	6	2	2	2	9	9	8
AIK Stockholm	6	0	1	5	4	16	1

GROUP C

Boavista	(0) 0	Rosenborg	(2) 3
Feyenoord	(0) 1	Borussia Dortmund	(0) 1
Borussia Dortmund	(1) 3	Boavista	(1) 1
Rosenborg	(2) 2	Feyenoord	(2) 2
Boavista	(0) 1	Feyenoord	(0) 1
Rosenborg	(1) 2	Borussia Dortmund	(2) 2
Borussia Dortmund	(0) 0	Rosenborg	(1) 3
Feyenoord	(0) 1	Boavista	(0) 1
Borussia Dortmund	(1) 1	Feyenoord	(0) 1
Rosenborg	(0) 2	Boavista	(0) 0
Boavista	(1) 1	Borussia Dortmund	(0) 0
Feyenoord	(0) 1	Rosenborg	(0) 0

Final table	P	W	D	L	F	A	Pts
Rosenborg	6	3	2	1	12	5	11
Feyenoord	6	1	5	0	7	6	8
Borussia Dortmund	6	1	3	2	7	9	6
Boavista	6	1	2	3	4	10	5

GROUP D

Manchester United	(0) 0	Croatia Zagreb	(0) 0
Marseille	(2) 2	Sturm Graz	(0) 0
Croatia Zagreb	(0) 1	Marseille	(1) 2
Sturm Graz	(0) 0	Manchester United	(3) 3
Croatia Zagreb	(2) 3	Sturm Graz	(0) 0
Manchester United	(0) 2	Marseille	(1) 1
Marseille	(0) 1	Manchester United	(0) 0
Sturm Graz	(1) 1	Croatia Zagreb	(0) 0
Croatia Zagreb	(0) 1	Manchester United	(1) 2
Sturm Graz	(1) 3	Marseille	(0) 2
Manchester United	(0) 2	Sturm Graz	(0) 1
Marseille	(0) 2	Croatia Zagreb	(1) 2

Final table	P	W	D	L	F	A	Pts
Manchester United	6	4	1	1	9	4	13
Marseille	6	3	1	2	10	8	10
Sturm Graz	6	2	0	4	5	12	6
Croatia Zagreb	6	1	2	3	7	7	5

GROUP E

Molde	(0) 0	Porto	(0) 1
Olympiakos	(1) 3	Real Madrid	(2) 3
Porto	(1) 2	Olympiakos	(0) 0
Real Madrid	(1) 4	Molde	(0) 1
Olympiakos	(1) 3	Molde	(0) 1
Real Madrid	(2) 3	Porto	(1) 1
Molde	(0) 3	Olympiakos	(2) 2

Porto	(2) 2	Real Madrid	(0) 1
Porto	(2) 3	Molde	(0) 1
Real Madrid	(1) 3	Olympiakos	(0) 0
Molde	(0) 0	Real Madrid	(1) 1
Olympiakos	(0) 1	Porto	(0) 0

Final table	P	W	D	L	F	A	Pts
Real Madrid	6	4	1	1	15	7	13
Porto	6	4	0	2	9	6	12
Olympiakos	6	2	1	3	9	12	7
Molde	6	1	0	5	6	14	3

GROUP F

Bayern Munich	(1) 2	PSV Eindhoven	(0) 1
Valencia	(0) 2	Rangers	(0) 0
PSV Eindhoven	(0) 1	Valencia	(1) 1
Rangers	(1) 1	Bayern Munich	(0) 1
Bayern Munich	(1) 1	Valencia	(0) 1
PSV Eindhoven	(0) 0	Rangers	(0) 1
Rangers	(2) 4	PSV Eindhoven	(1) 1
Valencia	(1) 1	Bayern Munich	(1) 1
PSV Eindhoven	(1) 2	Bayern Munich	(0) 1
Rangers	(0) 1	Valencia	(2) 2
Bayern Munich	(1) 1	Rangers	(0) 0
Valencia	(0) 1	PSV Eindhoven	(0) 0

Final table	P	W	D	L	F	A	Pts
Valencia	6	3	3	0	8	4	12
Bayern Munich	6	2	3	1	7	6	9
Rangers	6	2	1	3	7	7	7
PSV Eindhoven	6	1	1	4	5	10	4

GROUP G

Sparta Prague	(0) 0	Bordeaux	(0) 0
Willem II	(0) 1	Spartak Moscow	(2) 3
Bordeaux	(2) 3	Willem II	(1) 2
Spartak Moscow	(0) 1	Sparta Prague	(1) 1
Bordeaux	(1) 2	Spartak Moscow	(0) 1
Sparta Prague	(3) 4	Willem II	(0) 0
Spartak Moscow	(0) 1	Bordeaux	(1) 2
Willem II	(2) 3	Sparta Prague	(1) 4
Bordeaux	(0) 0	Sparta Prague	(0) 0
Spartak Moscow	(1) 1	Willem II	(0) 1
Sparta Prague	(2) 5	Spartak Moscow	(2) 2
Willem II	(0) 0	Bordeaux	(0) 0

Final table	P	W	D	L	F	A	Pts
Sparta Prague	6	3	3	0	14	6	12
Bordeaux	6	3	3	0	7	4	12
Spartak Moscow	6	1	2	3	9	12	5
Willem II	6	0	2	4	7	15	2

GROUP H

Chelsea	(0) 0	AC Milan	(0) 0
Galatasaray	(1) 2	Hertha Berlin	(2) 2
Hertha Berlin	(1) 2	Chelsea	(0) 1
AC Milan	(2) 2	Galatasaray	(0) 1
Chelsea	(0) 1	Galatasaray	(0) 0
AC Milan	(0) 1	Hertha Berlin	(0) 1
Galatasaray	(0) 0	Chelsea	(1) 5
Hertha Berlin	(1) 1	AC Milan	(0) 0
AC Milan	(0) 1	Chelsea	(0) 1

Hertha Berlin	(1) 1	Galatasaray	(0) 4
Chelsea	(2) 2	Hertha Berlin	(0) 0
Galatasaray	(1) 3	AC Milan	(1) 2

Final table	P	W	D	L	F	A	Pts
Chelsea	6	3	2	1	10	3	11
Hertha Berlin	6	2	2	2	7	10	8
Galatasaray	6	2	1	3	10	13	7
AC Milan	6	1	3	2	6	7	6

SECOND STAGE

GROUP A

Hertha Berlin	(1) 1	Barcelona	(1) 1
Sparta Prague	(0) 0	Porto	(0) 2
Barcelona	(2) 5	Sparta Prague	(0) 0
Porto	(0) 1	Hertha Berlin	(0) 0
Barcelona	(3) 4	Porto	(1) 2
Hertha Berlin	(1) 1	Sparta Prague	(0) 1
Porto	(0) 0	Barcelona	(1) 2
Sparta Prague	(0) 1	Hertha Berlin	(0) 0
Barcelona	(1) 3	Hertha Berlin	(1) 1
Porto	(1) 2	Sparta Prague	(0) 2
Hertha Berlin	(0) 0	Porto	(0) 1
Sparta Prague	(1) 1	Barcelona	(0) 2

Final table	P	W	D	L	F	A	Pts
Barcelona	6	5	1	0	17	5	16
Porto	6	3	1	2	8	8	10
Sparta Prague	6	1	2	3	5	12	5
Hertha Berlin	6	0	2	4	3	8	2

GROUP B

Fiorentina	(1) 2	Manchester United	(0) 0
Valencia	(0) 3	Bordeaux	(0) 0
Bordeaux	(0) 0	Fiorentina	(0) 0
Manchester United	(1) 3	Valencia	(0) 0
Manchester United	(1) 2	Bordeaux	(0) 0
Fiorentina	(1) 1	Valencia	(0) 0
Bordeaux	(1) 1	Manchester United	(1) 2
Valencia	(1) 2	Fiorentina	(0) 0
Bordeaux	(0) 1	Valencia	(1) 4
Manchester United	(2) 3	Fiorentina	(1) 1
Fiorentina	(0) 3	Bordeaux	(1) 3
Valencia	(0) 0	Manchester United	(0) 0

Final table	P	W	D	L	F	A	Pts
Manchester United	6	4	1	1	10	4	13
Valencia	6	3	1	2	9	5	10
Fiorentina	6	2	2	2	7	8	8
Bordeaux	6	0	2	4	5	14	2

GROUP C

Dynamo Kiev	(0) 1	Real Madrid	(1) 2
Rosenborg	(0) 1	Bayern Munich	(1) 1
Bayern Munich	(1) 2	Dynamo Kiev	(0) 1
Real Madrid	(1) 3	Rosenborg	(0) 1
Real Madrid	(1) 2	Bayern Munich	(3) 4
Dynamo Kiev	(2) 2	Rosenborg	(0) 1
Bayern Munich	(2) 4	Real Madrid	(0) 1
Rosenborg	(1) 1	Dynamo Kiev	(1) 2
Bayern Munich	(2) 2	Rosenborg	(0) 1
Real Madrid	(1) 2	Dynamo Kiev	(1) 2

Dynamo Kiev	(1) 2	Bayern Munich	(0) 0
Rosenborg	(0) 0	Real Madrid	(1) 1

Final table	P	W	D	L	F	A	Pts
Bayern Munich	6	4	1	1	13	8	13
Real Madrid	6	3	1	2	11	12	10
Dynamo Kiev	6	3	1	2	10	8	10
Rosenborg	6	0	1	5	5	11	1

GROUP D

Chelsea	(1) 3	Feyenoord	(0) 1
Marseille	(0) 0	Lazio	(0) 2
Feyenoord	(0) 3	Marseille	(0) 0
Lazio	(0) 0	Chelsea	(0) 0
Lazio	(1) 1	Feyenoord	(0) 2
Marseille	(1) 1	Chelsea	(0) 0
Chelsea	(1) 1	Marseille	(0) 0
Feyenoord	(0) 0	Lazio	(0) 0
Feyenoord	(0) 1	Chelsea	(1) 3
Lazio	(3) 5	Marseille	(0) 1
Chelsea	(1) 1	Lazio	(0) 2
Marseille	(0) 0	Feyenoord	(0) 0

Final table	P	W	D	L	F	A	Pts
Lazio	6	3	2	1	10	4	11
Chelsea	6	3	1	2	8	5	10
Feyenoord	6	2	2	2	7	7	8
Marseille	6	1	1	4	2	11	4

QUARTER-FINALS, FIRST LEG

Chelsea	(3) 3	Barcelona	(0) 1
Porto	(0) 1	Bayern Munich	(0) 1
Real Madrid	(0) 0	Manchester United	(0) 0
Valencia	(3) 5	Lazio	(1) 2

QUARTER-FINALS, SECOND LEG

Barcelona	(2) 5	Chelsea	(0) 1
Bayern Munich	(1) 2	Porto	(0) 1
Lazio	(0) 1	Valencia	(0) 0
Manchester United	(0) 2	Real Madrid	(1) 3

SEMI-FINALS, FIRST LEG

Valencia	(3) 4	Barcelona	(1) 1
Real Madrid	(2) 2	Bayern Munich	(0) 0

SEMI-FINALS, SECOND LEG

Barcelona	(0) 2	Valencia	(0) 1
Bayern Munich	(1) 2	Real Madrid	(1) 1

FINAL

Real Madrid (1) 3, Valencia (0) 0

(in Paris, 24 May 2000, 78,759)

Real Madrid: Casillas; Michel Salgado (Hierro 84), Roberto Carlos, Campo, Helguera, Karanka, McManaman, Anelka (Sanchis 80), Raul, Morientes (Savio 72), Redondo.
Scorers: Morientes 39, McManaman 67, Raul 75.
Valencia: Canizares; Angloma, Gerardo, Mendieta, Djukic, Pellegrino, Kili Gonzalez, Farinos, Angulo, Lopez, Gerard (Ilie A 67).
Referee: Braschi (Italy).

UEFA CUP 1999–2000

QUALIFYING ROUND, FIRST LEG

Anderlect	(3) 6	Leiftur	(1) 1
Ankaragucu	(1) 1	B36	(0) 0
Apoel	(0) 0	Levski Sofia	(0) 0
BATE Borisov	(0) 1	Lokomotiv Moscow	(3) 7
Belshina	(1) 1	Omonia	(3) 5
Bodo Glimt	(1) 1	Vaduz	(0) 0
Cwmbran Town	(0) 0	Celtic	(3) 6
Erevan	(0) 0	Hapoel Tel Aviv	(0) 2
Ferencvaros	(2) 3	Constructorul	(0) 1
FK Riga	(0) 0	Helsingborg	(0) 0
Gorica	(0) 2	Inter Cardiff	(0) 0
IFK Gothenburg	(1) 3	Cork City	(0) 0
Grasshoppers	(1) 4	Bray Wanderers	(0) 0
Hajduk Split	(2) 5	Dudelange	(0) 0
HJK Helsinki	(1) 2	Shirak	(0) 0
Inter Bratislava	(2) 3	Bylis	(0) 1
KI	(0) 0	Graz	(3) 5
Krivbas	(2) 3	Shamkir	(0) 0
KR Reykjavik	(0) 1	Kilmarnock	(0) 0
Lantana	(0) 0	Torpedo Kutaisi	(3) 5
Lokomotiv Tbilisi	(1) 1	Linfield	(0) 0
Lyngby	(2) 7	Birkirkara	(0) 0
Maccabi Tel Aviv	(2) 3	Kaunas	(1) 1
Metalurgs	(1) 3	Lech Poznan	(1) 2
Mondercange	(1) 2	Dinamo Bucharest	(2) 6
Neftchi	(1) 2	Red Star Belgrade	(0) 3
Olimpija	(1) 1	Kared	(0) 1
Portadown	(0) 0	CSKA Sofia	(1) 3
Serif	(1) 1	Sigma Olomouc	(1) 1
Shakhtjor Donetsk	(0) 3	Sileks	(0) 1
Sliema Wanderers	(0) 0	Zurich	(1) 3
Steaua	(1) 3	Levadia	(0) 0
Tulevik	(0) 0	FC Brugge	(0) 3
Vardar	(0) 0	Legia Warsaw	(2) 5
Viking	(3) 7	Principat	(0) 0
Vllaznia	(1) 1	Spartak Trnava	(1) 1
Vojvodina	(2) 4	Ujpest	(0) 0
VPS Vaasa	(1) 1	St Johnstone	(0) 1

QUALIFYING ROUND, SECOND LEG

Birkirkara	(0) 0	Lyngby	(0) 0
Bray Wanderers	(0) 0	Grasshoppers	(2) 4
Bylis	(0) 0	Inter Bratislava	(1) 2
B36	(0) 0	Ankaragucu	(0) 1
FC Brugge	(0) 2	Tulevik	(0) 0
Celtic	(1) 4	Cwmbran Town	(0) 0
Constructorul	(1) 1	Ferencvaros	(1) 1
Cork City	(1) 1	IFK Gothenburg	(0) 0
CSKA Sofia	(2) 5	Portadown	(0) 0
Dinamo Bucharest	(4) 7	Mondercange	(0) 0
Dudelange	(0) 1	Hajduk Split	(0) 1
Graz	(0) 4	KI	(0) 0
Hapoel Tel Aviv	(0) 2	Erevan	(0) 1
Helsingborg	(3) 5	FK Riga	(0) 0

Inter Cardiff	(0) 1	Gorica	(0) 0
Kareda	(0) 2	Olimpija	(1) 2
Kaunas	(1) 2	Maccabi Tel Aviv	(0) 1
Kilmarnock	(0) 2	KR Reyjkavik	(0) 0
Lech Poznan	(0) 3	Metalurgs	(0) 1
Legia Warsaw	(2) 4	Vardar	(0) 0
Leiftur	(0) 0	Anderlecht	(2) 3
Levadia	(1) 1	Steaua	(0) 4
Levski Sofia	(0) 2	Apoel	(0) 0
Linfield	(0) 1	Lokomotiv Tbilisi	(0) 1
Lokomotiv Moscow	(3) 5	BATE Borisov	(0) 0
Omonia	(0) 3	Belshina	(0) 0
Principat	(0) 0	Viking	(5) 11
Red Star Belgrade	(0) 1	Neftchi	(0) 0
Shamkir	(0) 0	Krivbas	(1) 2
Shirak	(1) 1	HJK Helsinki	(0) 0
Sigma Olomouc	(0) 0	Serif	(0) 0
Sileks	(1) 2	Shakhtjor Donetsk	(1) 1
Spartak Trnava	(0) 2	Vllaznia	(0) 0
St Johnstone	(0) 2	VPS Vaasa	(0) 0
Torpedo Kutaisi	(3) 4	Lantana	(1) 2
Ujpest	(0) 1	Vojvodina	(0) 1
Vaduz	(1) 1	Bodo Glimt	(1) 2
Zurich	(0) 1	Sliema Wanderers	(0) 0

FIRST ROUND, FIRST LEG

AB Copenhagen	(0) 0	Grasshoppers	(0) 2
Ajax	(2) 6	Bystrica	(1) 1
Amica	(1) 2	Brondby	(0) 0
Anderlecht	(2) 3	Olimpija	(0) 1
Anorthosis	(0) 1	Legia Warsaw	(0) 0
Aris Salonika	(1) 1	Servette	(0) 0
Atletico Madrid	(2) 3	Ankaragucu	(0) 0
Beira Mar	(1) 1	Vitesse	(0) 2
Benfica	(0) 0	Dinamo Bucharest	(1) 1
Bodo Glimt	(0) 0	Werder Bremen	(2) 5
Celtic	(1) 2	Hapoel Tel Aviv	(0) 0
CSKA Sofia	(0) 0	Newcastle United	(0) 2
Gorica	(0) 0	Panathinaikos	(1) 1
Graz	(2) 3	Spartak Trnava	(0) 0
Hajduk Split	(0) 0	Levski Sofia	(0) 0
Hapoel Haifa	(3) 3	FC Brugge	(0) 1
Helsingborg	(0) 1	Karpaty	(1) 1
HJK Helsinki	(0) 0	Lyon	(1) 1
Inter Bratislava	(1) 1	Rapid Vienna	(0) 0
Ionikos	(0) 1	Nantes	(0) 3
Kaiserslautern	(3) 3	Kilmarnock	(0) 0
Lausanne	(2) 3	Celta Vigo	(0) 2
Lech Poznan	(1) 1	IFK Gothenburg	(1) 2
Lokomotiv Tbilisi	(0) 0	PAOK Salonika	(3) 7
Lyngby	(0) 1	Lokomotiv Moscow	(2) 2
Maccabi Tel Aviv	(1) 2	Lens	(1) 2
Monaco	(0) 3	St Johnstone	(0) 0
MTK Budapest	(0) 0	Fenerbahce	(0) 0
Omonia	(0) 2	Juventus	(4) 5
Parma	(2) 3	Krivbas	(1) 2
Partizan Belgrade	(1) 1	Leeds United	(2) 3
Red Star Belgrade	(0) 0	Montpellier	(1) 1

Roda	(2) 2	Shakhtjor Donetsk	(0) 0
Roma	(4) 7	Setubal	(0) 0
Sigma Olomouc	(0) 1	Mallorca	(1) 3
Skonto Riga	(1) 1	Widzew Lodz	(0) 0
Stabaek	(0) 1	La Coruna	(0) 0
Steaua	(0) 2	LASK Linz	(0) 0
Teplice	(1) 3	Ferencvaros	(1) 1
Torpedo Kutaisi	(0) 0	AEK Athens	(0) 1
Tottenham Hotspur	(2) 3	Zimbru Chisinau	(0) 0
Udinese	(1) 1	Aalborg	(0) 0
Viking	(0) 3	Sporting Lisbon	(0) 0
Vojvodina	(0) 0	Slavia Prague	(0) 0
West Ham United	(1) 3	Osijek	(0) 0
Wolfsburg	(0) 2	Debrecen	(0) 0
Zenit	(0) 0	Bologna	(1) 3
Zurich	(1) 1	Lierse	(0) 0

FIRST ROUND, SECOND LEG

Aalborg	(0) 1	Udinese	(0) 2
AEK Athens	(4) 6	Torpedo Kutaisi	(0) 1
Ankaragucu	(0) 1	Atletico Madrid	(0) 0
Bologna	(1) 2	Zenit	(1) 2
Brondby	(1) 4	Amica	(0) 3
FC Brugge	(2) 4	Hapoel Haifa	(1) 2
Bystrica	(1) 1	Ajax	(0) 3
Celta Vigo	(1) 4	Lausanne	(0) 0
Debrecen	(0) 2	Wolfsburg	(0) 1
Dinamo Bucharest	(0) 0	Benfica	(1) 2
Fenerbahce	(0) 0	MTK Budapest	(0) 2
Ferencvaros	(0) 1	Teplice	(0) 1
Grasshoppers	(0) 1	AB Copenhagen	(1) 1
Hapoel Tel Aviv	(0) 0	Celtic	(0) 1
IFK Gothenburg	(0) 0	Lech Poznan	(0) 0
Juventus	(2) 5	Omonia	(0) 0
Karpaty	(0) 1	Helsingborg	(0) 1
Kilmarnock	(0) 0	Kaiserslautern	(2) 2
Krivbas	(0) 0	Parma	(2) 3
La Coruna	(1) 2	Stabaek	(0) 0
LASK Linz	(1) 2	Steaua	(2) 3
Leeds United	(0) 1	Partizan Belgrade	(0) 0
Legia Warsaw	(0) 2	Anorthosis	(0) 0
Lens	(0) 2	Maccabi Tel Aviv	(1) 1
Levski Sofia	(2) 3	Hajduk Split	(0) 0
Lierse	(1) 3	Zurich	(1) 4
Lokomotiv Moscow	(2) 3	Lyngby	(0) 0
Lyon	(3) 5	HJK Helsinki	(1) 1
Mallorca	(0) 0	Sigma Olomouc	(0) 0
Montpellier	(1) 2	Red Star Belgrade	(0) 2
Nantes	(0) 1	Ionikos	(0) 0
Newcastle United	(1) 2	CSKA Sofia	(1) 2
Olimpija	(0) 0	Anderlecht	(0) 3
Osijek	(0) 1	West Ham United	(1) 3
Panathinaikos	(1) 2	Gorica	(0) 0
PAOK Salonika	(0) 2	Lokomotiv Tbilisi	(0) 0
Rapid Vienna	(0) 1	Inter Bratislava	(1) 2
St Johnstone	(2) 3	Monaco	(2) 3
Servette	(1) 1	Aris Salonika	(1) 2
Setubal	(0) 1	Roma	(0) 0

Shakhtjor Donetsk	(1) 1	Roda	(1) 3
Slavia Prague	(1) 3	Vojvodina	(1) 2
Spartak Trnava	(1) 2	Graz	(1) 1
Sporting Lisbon	(0) 1	Viking	(0) 0
Vitesse	(0) 0	Beira Mar	(0) 0
Werder Bremen	(0) 1	Bodo Glimt	(1) 1
Widzew Lodz	(2) 2	Skonto Riga	(0) 0
Zimbru Chisinau	(0) 0	Tottenham Hotspur	(0) 0

SECOND ROUND, FIRST LEG

Anderlecht	(2) 2	Bologna	(0) 1
Aris Salonika	(1) 2	Celta Vigo	(2) 2
Atletico Madrid	(0) 1	Amica	(0) 0
IFK Gothenburg	(0) 0	Roma	(1) 2
Graz	(0) 2	Panathinaikos	(0) 1
Hapoel Haifa	(0) 0	Ajax	(2) 3
Inter Bratislava	(0) 0	Nantes	(2) 3
La Coruna	(1) 3	Montpellier	(1) 1
Leeds United	(2) 4	Lokomotiv Moscow	(0) 1
Lens	(2) 4	Vitesse	(0) 1
Levski Sofia	(0) 1	Juventus	(1) 3
Lyon	(0) 1	Celtic	(0) 0
MTK Budapest	(2) 2	AEK Athens	(0) 1
PAOK Salonika	(0) 1	Benfica	(0) 2
Parma	(1) 1	Helsingborg	(0) 0
Roda	(0) 0	Wolfsburg	(0) 0
Slavia Prague	(2) 3	Grasshoppers	(1) 1
Steaua	(1) 2	West Ham United	(0) 0
Teplice	(0) 1	Mallorc	(2) 2
Tottenham Hotspur	(1) 1	Kaiserslautern	(0) 0
Udinese	(1) 1	Legia Warsaw	(0) 0
Werder Bremen	(0) 0	Viking	(0) 0
Widzew Lodz	(1) 1	Monaco	(1) 1
Zurich	(0) 1	Newcastle United	(0) 2

SECOND ROUND, SECOND LEG

AEK Athens	(0) 1	MTK Budapest	(0) 0
Ajax	(0) 0	Hapoel Haifa	(0) 1
Amica	(1) 1	Atletico Madrid	(3) 4
Benfica	(1) 1	PAOK Salonika	(2) 2
Bologna	(1) 3	Anderlecht	(0) 0
Celta Vigo	(0) 2	Aris Salonika	(0) 0
Celtic	(0) 0	Lyon	(1) 1
Grasshoppers	(0) 1	Slavia Prague	(0) 0
Helsingborg	(0) 1	Parm	(3) 3
Juventus	(0) 1	Levski Sofia	(1) 1
Kaiserslautern	(0) 2	Tottenham Hotspur	(0) 0
Legia Warsaw	(1) 1	Udinese	(1) 1
Lokomotiv Moscow	(0) 0	Leeds United	(3) 3
Mallorca	1) 3	Teplice	(0) 0
Monaco	(0) 2	Widzew Lodz	(0) 0
Montpellier	(0) 0	La Coruna	(1) 2
Nantes	(0) 4	Inter Bratislava	(0) 0
Newcastle United	(1) 3	Zurich	(1) 1
Panathinaikos	(0) 1	Graz	(0) 0
Roma	(0) 1	IFK Gothenburg	(0) 0
Viking	(1) 2	Werder Bremen	(1) 2
Vitesse	(0) 1	Lens	(0) 1

West Ham United	(0) 0	Steaua	(0) 0
Wolfsburg	(0) 1	Roda	(0) 0

THIRD ROUND, FIRST LEG

AEK Athens	(1) 2	Monaco	(1) 2
Ajax	(0) 0	Mallorca	(1) 1
Arsenal	(1) 3	Nantes	(0) 0
Bologna	(0) 1	Galatasaray	(0) 1
Celta Vigo	(4) 7	Benfica	(0) 0
La Coruna	(4) 4	Panathinaikos	(1) 2
Lens	(0) 1	Kaiserslautern	(2) 2
Lyon	(2) 3	Werder Bremen	(0) 0
Olympiakos	(1) 1	Juventus	(1) 3
Parma	(1) 2	Sturm Graz	(1) 1
Rangers	(2) 2	Borussia Dortmund	(0) 0
Roma	(0) 1	Newcastle United	(0) 0
Slavia Prague	(2) 4	Steaua	(0) 1
Spartak Moscow	(1) 2	Leeds United	(1) 1
Udinese	(0) 0	Leverkusen	(0) 1
Wolfsburg	(1) 2	Atletico Madrid	(2) 3

THIRD ROUND, SECOND LEG

Atletico Madrid	(1) 2	Wolfsburg	(0) 1
Benfica	(0) 1	Celta Vigo	(1) 1
Borussia Dortmund	(1) 2	Rangers	(0) 0
Galatasaray	(2) 2	Bologna	(1) 1
Juventus	(1) 1	Olympiakos	(1) 2
Kaiserslautern	(1) 1	Lens	(2) 4
Leeds United	(0) 1	Spartak Moscow	(0) 0
Leverkusen	(1) 1	Udinese	(2) 2
Mallorca	(1) 2	Ajax	(0) 0
Monaco	(1) 1	AEK Athens	(0) 0
Nantes	(1) 3	Arsenal	(3) 3
Newcastle United	(0) 0	Roma	(0) 0
Panathinaikos	(0) 1	La Coruna	(0) 1
Steaua	(0) 1	Slavia Prague	(0) 1
Sturm Graz	(0) 3	Parma	(1) 3
Werder Bremen	(2) 4	Lyon	(0) 0

FOURTH ROUND, FIRST LEG

Atletico Madrid	(1) 2	Lens	(1) 2
Arsenal	(2) 5	La Coruna	(0) 1
Borussia Dortmund	(0) 0	Galatasaray	(2) 2
Juventus	(0) 1	Celta Vigo	(0) 0
Mallorca	(2) 4	Monaco	(1) 1
Parma	(1) 1	Werder Bremen	(0) 0
Roma	(0) 0	Leeds United	(0) 0
Slavia Prague	(0) 1	Udinese	(0) 0

FOURTH ROUND, SECOND LEG

Celta Vigo	(2) 4	Juventus	(0) 0
Galatasaray	(0) 0	Borussia Dortmund	(0) 0
La Coruna	(0) 2	Arsenal	(0) 1
Leeds United	(0) 1	Roma	(0) 0
Lens	(2) 4	Atletico Madrid	(1) 2
Monaco	(1) 1	Mallorca	(0) 0
Udinese	(1) 2	Slavia Prague	(1) 1
Werder Bremen	(2) 3	Parma	(1) 1

QUARTER-FINALS, FIRST LEG

Arsenal	(1) 2	Werder Bremen	(0) 0
Celta Vigo	(0) 0	Lens	(0) 0
Leeds United	(1) 3	Slavia Prague	(0) 0
Mallorca	(0) 1	Galatasaray	(1) 4

QUARTER-FINALS, SECOND LEG

Galatasaray	(1) 2	Mallorca	(0) 1
Lens	(0) 2	Celta Vigo	(0) 1
Slavia Prague	(0) 2	Leeds United	(0) 1
Werder Bremen	(1) 2	Arsenal	(2) 4

SEMI-FINALS, FIRST LEG

Arsenal	(1) 1	Lens	(0) 0
Galatasaray	(2) 2	Leeds United	(0) 0

SEMI-FINALS, SECOND LEG

Leeds United	(1) 2	Galatasaray	(2) 2
Lens	(0) 1	Arsenal	(1) 2

FINAL

Galatasaray (0) 0, Arsenal (0) 0

(in Copenhagen, 17 May 2000, 38,919)

Galatasaray: Taffarel; Capone, Ergun, Umit, Popescu, Bulent, Okan (Hakan Unsal 83), Suat (Ahmet 94), Arif (Hasan 94), Hagi, Hakan Sukur.
Arsenal: Seaman; Dixon, Silvinho, Vieira, Keown, Adams, Parlour, Henry, Petit, Bergkamp (Kanu 74), Overmars (Suker 114).
(aet; Galatasaray won 4-1 on penalties; Ergun (scored) 1-0; Suker (hit post) 1-0; Hakan Sukur (scored) 2-0; Parlour (scored) 2-1; Umit (scored) 3-1; Vieira (hit bar) 3-1; Popescu (scored) 4-1).
Referee: Nieto (Spain).

PAST EUROPEAN CUP FINALS

Year	Winner	Score	Runner-up	Score
1956	Real Madrid	4	Stade de Rheims	3
1957	Real Madrid	2	Fiorentina	0
1958	Real Madrid	3	AC Milan	2*
1959	Real Madrid	2	Stade de Rheims	0
1960	Real Madrid	7	Eintracht Frankfurt	3
1961	Benfica	3	Barcelona	2
1962	Benfica	5	Real Madrid	3
1963	AC Milan	2	Benfica	1
1964	Internazionale	3	Real Madrid	1
1965	Internazionale	1	SL Benfica	0
1966	Real Madrid	2	Partizan Belgrade	1
1967	Celtic	2	Internazionale	1
1968	Manchester U	4	Benfica	1*
1969	AC Milan	4	Ajax	1
1970	Feyenoord	2	Celtic	1*
1971	Ajax	2	Panathinaikos	0
1972	Ajax	2	Internazionale	0
1973	Ajax	1	Juventus	0
1974	Bayern Munich	1 4	Atletico Madrid	1 0
1975	Bayern Munich	2	Leeds U	0
1976	Bayern Munich	1	St Etienne	0
1977	Liverpool	3	Borussia Moenchengladbach	1
1978	Liverpool	1	FC Brugge	0
1979	Nottingham F	1	Malmö	0
1980	Nottingham F	1	Hamburg	0
1981	Liverpool	1	Real Madrid	0
1982	Aston Villa	1	Bayern Munich	0
1983	Hamburg	1	Juventus	0
1984	Liverpool†	1	Roma	1
1985	Juventus	1	Liverpool	0
1986	Steaua Bucharest†	0	Barcelona	0
1987	Porto	2	Bayern Munich	1
1988	PSV Eindhoven†	0	Benfica	0
1989	AC Milan	4	Steaua Bucharest	0
1990	AC Milan	1	Benfica	0
1991	Red Star Belgrade†	0	Marseille	0
1992	Barcelona	1	Sampdoria	0
1993	Marseille	1	AC Milan	0
(*Marseille subsequently stripped of title*)				
1994	AC Milan	4	Barcelona	0
1995	Ajax	1	AC Milan	0
1996	Juventus†	1	Ajax	1
1997	Borussia Dortmund	3	Juventus	1
1998	Real Madrid	1	Juventus	0
1999	Manchester U	2	Bayern Munich	1

PAST EUROPEAN CUP-WINNERS FINALS

Year	Winner	Score	Runner-up	Score
1961	Fiorentina	4	Rangers	1‡
1962	Atletico Madrid	1 3	Fiorentina	1 0
1963	Tottenham H	5	Atletico Madrid	1
1964	Sporting Lisbon	3 1	MTK Budapest	3* 0
1965	West Ham U	2	Munich 1860	0
1966	Borussia Dortmund	2	Liverpool	1*
1967	Bayern Munich	1	Rangers	0*

1968	AC Milan	2	Hamburg	0
1969	Slovan Bratislava	3	Barcelona	2
1970	Manchester C	2	Gornik Zabrze	1
1971	Chelsea	1 2	Real Madrid	1* 1*
1972	Rangers	3	Dynamo Moscow	2
1973	AC Milan	1	Leeds U	0
1974	Magdeburg	2	AC Milan	0
1975	Dynamo Kiev	3	Ferencvaros	0
1976	Anderlecht	4	West Ham U	2
1977	Hamburg	2	Anderlecht	0
1978	Anderlecht	4	Austria Vienna	0
1979	Barcelona	4	Fortuna Dusseldorf	3*
1980	Valencia†	0	Arsenal	0
1981	Dynamo Tbilisi	2	Carl Zeiss Jena	1
1982	Barcelona	2	Standard Liege	1
1983	Aberdeen	2	Real Madrid	1*
1984	Juventus	2	Porto	1
1985	Everton	3	Rapid Vienna	1
1986	Dynamo Kiev	3	Atletico Madrid	0
1987	Ajax	1	Lokomotiv Leipzig	0
1988	Mechelen	1	Ajax	0
1989	Barcelona	2	Sampdoria	0
1990	Sampdoria	2	Anderlecht	0
1991	Manchester U	2	Barcelona	1
1992	Werder Bremen	2	Monaco	0
1993	Parma	3	Antwerp	1
1994	Arsenal	1	Parma	0
1995	Real Zaragoza	2	Arsenal	1*
1996	Paris St Germain	1	Rapid Vienna	0
1997	Barcelona	1	Paris St Germain	0
1998	Chelsea	1	Stuttgart	0
1999	Lazio	2	Mallorca	1

PAST FAIRS CUP FINALS

1958	Barcelona	8	London	2‡
1960	Barcelona	4	Birmingham C	1‡
1961	Roma	4	Birmingham C	2‡
1962	Valencia	7	Barcelona	3‡
1963	Valencia	4	Dynamo Zagreb	1‡
1964	Real Zaragoza	2	Valencia	1
1965	Ferencvaros	1	Juventus	0
1966	Barcelona	4	Real Zaragoza	3‡
1967	Dynamo Zagreb	2	Leeds U	0‡
1968	Leeds U	1	Ferencvaros	0‡
1969	Newcastle U	6	Ujpest Dozsa	2‡
1970	Arsenal	4	Anderlecht	3‡
1971	Leeds U	3**	Juventus	3‡

PAST UEFA CUP FINALS

1972	Tottenham H	2 1	Wolverhampton W	1 1
1973	Liverpool	3 0	Borussia Moenchengladbach	0 2
1974	Feyenoord	2 2	Tottenham H	2 0
1975	Borussia Moenchengladbach	0 5	Twente Enschede	0 1
1976	Liverpool	3 1	FC Brugge	2 1
1977	Juventus**	1 1	Athletic Bilbao	0 2

1978	PSV Eindhoven	0 3	SEC Bastia	0 0
1979	Borussia Moenchengladbach	1 1	Red Star Belgrade	1 0
1980	Borussia Moenchengladbach	3 0	Eintracht Frankfurt**	2 1
1981	Ipswich T	3 2	AZ 67 Alkmaar	0 4
1982	IFK Gothenburg	1 3	SV Hamburg	0 0
1983	Anderlecht	1 1	Benfica	0 1
1984	Tottenham H†	1 1	RSC Anderlecht	1 1
1985	Real Madrid	3 0	Videoton	0 1
1986	Real Madrid	5 0	Cologne	1 2
1987	IFK Gothenburg	1 1	Dundee U	0 1
1988	Bayer Leverkusen†	0 3	Espanol	0 3
1989	Napoli	2 3	Stuttgart	1 3
1990	Juventus	3 0	Fiorentina	1 0
1991	Internazionale	2 0	AS Roma	0 1
1992	Ajax**	0 2	Torino	0 2
1993	Juventus	3 3	Borussia Dortmund	1 0
1994	Internazionale	1 1	Salzburg	0 0
1995	Parma	1 1	Juventus	0 1
1996	Bayern Munich	2 3	Bordeaux	0 1
1997	Schalke*†	1 0	Internazionale	0 1
1998	Internazionale	3	Lazio	0
1999	Parma	3	Marseille	0

** After extra time ** Won on away goals † Won on penalties ‡ Aggregate score*

EURO 2000 REVIEW

If some of the outstanding football during the Euro 2000 finals was featured in the group matches, the drama were unquestionably reserved for the knock-out stages. But on their overall commitment to attack, the French probably deserved to become champions, adding this honour to the World Cup crown they have worn since 1998.

For the first time in a major international competition, the finals were held in two countries, Holland and Belgium. Oddly enough the signal for the standard of play which was to become a speciality of the better matches was given in the inaugural match of the tournament where Belgium edged out Sweden 2-1 in Brussels in Group B. Alas for these two aspirants, neither were able to reproduce the form thus displayed and both failed to reach the quarter-finals.

Italy, though not entirely convincing in this section, won all three matches and it was Turkey who surprisingly elminated Belgium 2-0 in the last of their games to join them in the quarter-finals.

France demonstrated their strength in clinically disposing of Denmark who were to have a wretched time of it, with three defeats and not a single goal to their credit. So the French had started with three goals and three points. Holland joined them on the points level at least by a not over-confident success against an unfortunate Czech Republic team denied a draw by a lucky penalty for the Dutch a minute before the end of normal time converted by Frank de Boer, but a strike which was to haunt his later activities from the same spot.

The group ended with France and Holland not bothered about the result since each team had already qualified. Academically it was the Dutch who beat the French largely reserve team 3-2.

In Group A it had been widely tipped that the Germans had by far the weakest squad they had produced in their lengthy history of international success. They were held 1-1 by Romania. But the shock came in the other game in this section when England carelessly threw away a 2-0 lead inside 20 minutes to lose to a far superior Portuguese team 3-2.

England did manage a 1-0 win over Germany, but could have had no complaints in being knocked-out by a technically sound Romania 3-2 from a late penalty following a sloppy tackle.

Spain again flattered to deceive and were poor in the extreme against Norway, losing 1-0 in Group C. The surprise came from Eastern European sources where ten-man Yugoslavia clawed back to a 3-3 draw after giving Slovenia a three-goal lead. The Yugoslavs managed three goals again against Spain in what has been described as one of the best-ever European Championship encounters of all time, the Spanish scoring twice in injury time, including a penalty, the Slavs again finishing with ten players. The consolation was that both teams progressed as Norway and Slovenia played out a goalless draw.

The quarter-finals began with Portugal enhancing their reputation with a 2-0 win over Turkey. Italy appeared to be getting into their stride with a similar victory against Romania. France had their work cut out against Spain before emerging 2-1, but Holland gave a remarkably confident display of attacking football in destroying Yugoslavia 6-1.

In the semi-finals France needed extra time to dispose of Portugal, who lost their composure and many friends after Abel Xavier handled by the post and Zinedine Zidane, the tournament's outstanding player, converted the goal in sudden death extra time after 117 mintes. for a 2-1 win.

Italy were down to ten men from the 34th minute against Holland, but gave a characteristically cool defensive display apart from conceding two penalties, one from de Boer saved by goalkeeper Toldo, the other from Patrick Kluivert by a post. Extra time produced nothing and it was Italy who won the penalty shoot-out 3-1, the Dutch missing a further three from the spot, de Boer being twice the culprit.

In the final it was tiredness which eventually caused Italy's downfall. Leading by a Marco Delvecchio goal after 53 minutes, they had at least three other reasonable chances to add to their score before in the 94th minute of the match, Sylvain Wiltord equalised for France. Then a wonder volley from David Trezeguet nine minutes later ended it.

EURO 2000 Qualifying Competition

GROUP 1

Minsk, 5 September 1998, 35,000

Belarus (0) 0

Denmark (0) 0

Belarus: Satsunkevich; Yakhimovic, Ostrovski, Shtanyuk, Romashchenko M (Geraschenko 40), Gurenko, Khatskevich, Baranov, Lavrik, Belkevich, Makovski V (Romashchenko MA 89).
Denmark: Schmeichel; Tobiasen, Rieper, Hogh, Heintze, Helveg, Nielsen A, Thomsen, Tomasson (Frederiksen 81), Jorgensen (Andersen 67), Moller (Gravesen 67).
Referee: Dardenne (Germany).

Anfield, 5 September 1998, 23,160

Wales (0) 0

Italy (1) 2 *(Fuser 19, Vieri 76)*

Wales: Jones P; Robinson, Barnard, Symons, Williams, Coleman, Speed, Johnson, Blake (Saunders 66), Hughes M (Savage 80), Giggs.
Italy: Peruzzi; Panucci, Pessotto, Albertini (Di Biagio 68), Cannavaro, Iuliano, Fuser, Dino Baggio, Vieri, Del Piero (Roberto Baggio 74), Di Francesco (Serena 82).
Referee: Hauge (Norway).

Udine, 10 October 1998, 35,247

Italy (1) 2 *(Del Piero 19, 61)*

Switzerland (0) 0

Italy: Buffon; Panucci, Cannavaro, Maldini, Torricelli, Fuser, Dino Baggio, Albertini, Di Francesco (Bachini 63), Inzaghi, Del Piero (Totti 70).
Switzerland: Hilfiker; Wolf (Chassot 68), Vega, Henchoz, Vogel, Wicky (Celestini 86), Sforza, Rothenbuhler, Sesa, Chapuisat, Muller P.
Referee: Sars (France).

Copenhagen, 10 October 1998, 36,009

Denmark (0) 1 *(Frederiksen 57)*

Wales (0) 2 *(Williams 58, Bellamy 86)*

Denmark: Krogh; Tobiasen, Rieper, Hogh, Heintze, Helveg, Frandsen (Gravesen 76), Steen-Nielsen, Jorgensen, Frederiksen, Beck (Sand 65).
Wales: Jones; Savage, Barnard, Williams, Symons, Coleman, Saunders (Robinson 81), Blake (Bellamy 69), Hughes M, Johnson (Pembridge 62), Speed.
Referee: Piller (Hungary).

Cardiff, 14 October 1998, 11,975

Wales (1) 3 *(Robinson 15, Coleman 54, Symons 85)*

Belarus (1) 2 *(Gurenko 21, Belkevich 48)*

Wales: Jones P; Robinson, Barnard, Savage, Symons, Coleman, Saunders, Johnson, Blake, Hughes M, Pembridge.
Belarus: Satsunkevich; Yakhimovic, Ostrovski, Lavrik, Shtanyuk, Baranov (Gerasimets 70), Khatskevich, Geraschenko (Romashchenko MA 88), Gurenko, Belkevich, Makovski V (Katchuro 73).
Referee: Sammut (Malta).

Zurich, 14 October 1998, 12,500

Switzerland (0) 1 (Chapuisat 58)

Denmark (0) 1 *(Tobiasen 90)*

Switzerland: Hilfiker; Jeanneret (Rothenbuhler 76), Sforza, Henchoz, Vogel, Wicky, Sesa (Haas 89), Fournier, Celestini, Chapuisat, Muller P (Di Jorio 78).
Denmark: Krogh; Tobiasen, Rieper, Hogh, Heintze, Helveg, Frandsen (Colding 59), Steen-Nielsen, Tomasson (Beck 78), Fredriksen (Sand 61), Jorgensen.
Referee: Radoman (Yugoslavia).

Minsk, 27 March 1999, 44,000

Belarus (0) 0

Switzerland (0) 1 *(Fournier 72)*

Belarus: Tumilovich; Lavrik, Lukhvich, Yakhimovic, Gurenko, Khatskevich, Belkevich, Geraschenko (Skripchenko 86), Baranov (Chaika 56), Romashchenko MA, Makovski V (Ostrovski 87).
Switzerland: Brunner; Hodel, Henchoz, Vogel, Fournier, Jeanneret, Wicky (Muller P 66), Sforza, Sesa (De Napoli 74), Chapuisat, Comisetti.
Referee: Sarvan (Turkey).

Copenhagen, 27 March 1999, 41,429

Denmark (0) 1 *(Sand 56)*

Italy (1) 2 *(Inzaghi 1, Conte 68)*

Denmark: Schmeichel; Helveg, Henriksen, Hogh, Heintze, Goldbaek (Colding 82), Thomsen, Nielsen A (Tofting 77), Gronkjaer (Molnar 53), Jorgensen, Sand.
Italy: Buffon; Panucci, Nesta, Cannavaro, Maldini, Fuser (Conte 46), Dino Baggio, Di Biagio, Di Francesco, Inzaghi, Chiesa (Totti 63).
Referee: Lopez (Spain).

Ancona, 31 March 1999, 20,735

Italy (1) 1 *(Inzaghi 31 (pen))*

Belarus (1) 1 *(Belkevich 24)*

Italy: Buffon; Panucci, Nesta, Cannavaro, Maldini, Conte, Dino Baggio, Di Biagio (Giannichedda 46), Totti (Di Francesco 46), Inzaghi, Chiesa (Roberto Baggio 64).
Belarus: Tumilovich; Lavrik, Lukhvich, Yakhimovic, Gurenko, Orlovski, Belkevich, Ostrovski, Baranov, Romashchenko MA, Makovski V.
Referee: Piraux (Belgium).

Zurich, 31 March 1999, 13,500

Switzerland (1) 2 *(Chapuisat 4, 70)*

Wales (0) 0

Switzerland: Brunner; Jeanneret, Henchoz, Wolf, Muller P, Vogel, Sforza, Fournier, Wicky, Chapuisat, Comisetti (Buhlmann 67).
Wales: Jones P (Crossley 26); Robinson, Pembridge, Symons, Coleman, Johnson, Saunders, Savage, Blake (Hartson 63), Hughes M (Bellamy 73), Speed.
Referee: Liba (Czech Republic).

Copenhagen, 5 June 1999, 24,876

Denmark (1) 1 *(Heintze 22)*

Belarus (0) 0

Denmark: Schmeichel; Colding, Henriksen, Hogh, Heintze, Goldbaek, Nielsen A, Tofting (Steen-Nielsen 87), Gronkjaer, Jorgensen, Sand (Molnar 78).
Belarus: Tumilovich; Lavrik, Lukhvich, Yakhimovic, Gurenko, Orlovski, Belkevic, Khatskevich (Kulchi 70), Ostrovski (Romashchenko MA 46), Baranov, Makovski V (Ryndyuk 85).
Referee: Baptista (Portugal).

Bologna, 5 June 1999, 12,392

Italy (3) 4 *(Vieri 6, Inzaghi 36, Maldini 39, Chiesa 89)*

Wales (0) 0

Italy: Buffon; Panucci, Maldini, Fuser (Di Livio 68), Negro, Cannavaro, Conte, Albertini, Vieri (Montella 46), Inzaghi (Chiesa 80), Di Francesco.
Wales: Jones P; Robinson (Jenkins 77), Barnard, Page, Melville, Williams, Giggs, Bellamy (Pembridge 79), Saunders (Hartson 46), Hughes M, Speed.
Referee: Steinborn (Germany).

Lausanne, 9 June 1999, 15,800

Switzerland (0) 0

Italy (0) 0

Switzerland: Huber; Wicky (Haas 70), Muller P, Hodel, Jeanneret (Di Jorio 78), Vogel, Sforza, Rothenbuhler, Sesa, Chapuisat, Comisetti (Celestini 57).
Italy: Buffon; Panucci (Pancaro 72), Negro, Cannavaro, Maldini, Fuser (Di Livio 61), Albertini, Conte, Vieri (Chiesa 61), Inzaghi, Di Francesco.
Referee: Poll (England).

Liverpool, 9 June 1999, 10,000

Wales (0) 0

Denmark (0) 2 *(Tomasson 84, Tofting 90 (pen))*

Wales: Jones P; Jenkins, Barnard (Legg 90), Robinson (Pembridge 87), Melville, Coleman, Speed, Saunders, Hartson (Bellamy 89), Hughes M, Giggs.
Denmark: Schmeichel; Colding, Heintze, Gronkjaer, Hogh, Henriksen, Goldbaek, Nielsen A (Tofting 85), Jorgensen (Frandsen 90), Sand, Molnar (Tomasson 72).
Referee: Ancion (Belgium).

Copenhagen, 4 September 1999, 41,667

Denmark (0) 2 *(Nielsen A 53, Tomasson 81)*

Switzerland (0) 1 *(Turkyilmaz 79)*

Denmark: Schmeichel; Helveg, Henriksen, Hogh, Heintze, Goldbaek (Colding 50), Nielsen A (Steen-Nielsen 80), Tofting, Jorgensen, Tomasson (Wieghorst 87), Sand.
Switzerland: Huber; Di Jorio (Turkyilmaz 59), Hodel, Jeanneret, Muller P, Buhlmann, Sforza, Vogel, Wicky (Wyss 88), Chapuisat, Sesa (Muller S 77).
Referee: Wojcik (Poland).

Minsk, 4 September 1999, 25,000

Belarus (1) 1 *(Baranov 30)*

Wales (1) 2 *(Saunders 42, Giggs 86)*

Belarus: Tumilovich; Lavrik, Lukhvich, Ostrovski, Tarlovski, Gurenko, Chaika, Baranov, Kulchi, Orlovski (Romashchenko MA 59), Makovski V.
Wales: Jones P; Robinson J, Barnard, Melville, Page, Coleman, Pembridge (Robinson C 81), Speed, Saunders, Blake, Giggs.
Referee: Ovebro (Norway).

Naples, 8 September 1999, 46,919

Italy (2) 2 *(Fuser 10, Vieiri 34)*

Denmark (1) 3 *(Jorgensen 39 (pen), Wieghorst 57, Tomasson 64)*

Italy: Buffon; Panucci, Nesta, Cannavaro, Pancaro, Fuser, Dino Baggio (Giannichedda 46), Albertini, Di Francesco (Conte 70), Inzaghi, Vieiri (Totti 77).
Denmark: Schmeichel; Colding, Hogh, Henriksen, Heintze, Helveg (Goldbaek 52), Nielsen A, Tofting (Wieghorst 52), Jorgensen, Tomasson (Schjonberg 85), Sand.
Referee: Jol (Holland).

Lausanne, 8 September 1999, 12,000

Switzerland (0) 2 *(Turkyilmaz 68, 87 (pen))*

Belarus (0) 0

Switzerland: Huber; Hodel, Muller P (Wolf 78), Henchoz, Wicky, Vogel, Sforza, Di Jorio, Buhlmann (Sesa 71), Turkyilmaz, Chapuisat (Comisetti 62).
Belarus: Afanasenko; Lukhvich, Lavrik, Yakhimovic, Ostrovski, Gurenko, Kulchi (Katchuro 55), Chaika, Baranov, Tarlovski, Makovski V (Romashchenko MA 69).
Referee: Irvine (Northern Ireland).

Minsk, 9 October 1999, 32,000

Belarus (0) 0

Italy (0) 0

Belarus: Shantalosov; Lukhvich, Yakhimovic, Tarlovski, Orlovski, Gurenko, Romashchenko MA (Makovski V 46), Ostrovski, Chaika, Gerasimets (Kulchi 79), Baranov.
Italy: Buffon; Panucci, Nesta, Cannavaro, Maldini, Moriero, Conte, Di Biagio, Zambrotta, Inzaghi, Vieri (Del Piero 82).
Referee: Colombo (France).

Wrexham, 9 October 1999, 5064

Wales (0) 0

Switzerland (1) 2 *(Rey 17, Buhlmann 59)*

Wales: Jones P; Delaney, Barnard, Savage, Page, Coleman, Robinson J, Blake (Roberts N 78), Saunders (Hartson 67), Oster (Jones M 78), Speed.
Switzerland: Zuberbuhler; Hodel, Henchoz, Jacquet (Wyss 72), Haas, Vogel, Sesa, Di Jorio, Jeanneret, Buhlmann, Rey (Comisetti 67).
Referee: Papadakos (Greece).

Group 1 – Final Table	*P*	*W*	*D*	*L*	*F*	*A*	*Pts*
Italy	8	4	3	1	13	5	15
Denmark	8	4	2	2	11	8	14
Switzerland	8	4	2	2	9	5	14
Wales	8	3	0	5	7	16	9
Belarus	8	0	3	5	4	10	3

GROUP 2

Tbilisi, 5 September 1998, 35,000

Georgia (0) 1 *(Arveladze A 65)*

Albania (0) 0

Georgia: Gvaramadze; Kaladze, Tskitishvili, Silagadze (Kiknadze 42), Tsereteli, Kobiashvili, Nemsadze, Jamarauli, Ketsbaia (Janashia 56), Kinkladze, Iashvili (Arveladze A 60).
Albania: Strakosha; Lala, Shulku, Xhumba, Vata, Pinari, Haxhi, Bushi (Galo 74), Kola, Rrakli, Tare (Peco 67) (Maxhuni 87).
Referee: Tetrucci (Switzerland).

Athens, 6 September 1998, 29,000

Greece (0) 2 *(Mahlas 56 (pen), Frantzeskos 58)*

Slovenia (1) 2 *(Zahovic 19, 73)*

Greece: Atmatsidis; Kalitzakis, Ouzounidis, Dabizas, Borbokis (Liberopoulos 83), Markos, Zagorakis, Tsartas (Frantzeskos 46), Kassapis (Georgatos 78), Mahlas, Nikolaidis.
Slovenia: Simeunovic; Milanic, Galic, Knavs, Novak (Englaro 46), Ceh, Zahovic, Pavlin, Rudonja, Udovic, Osterc (Siljak 68) (Acimovic 72).
Referee: Trentalange (Italy).

Oslo, 6 September 1998, 11,030

Norway (1) 1 *(Solbakken 17)*

Latvia (1) 3 *(Pakhar 11, Shtolcers 53, Zemlinsky 65 (pen))*

Norway: Baardsen; Heggem (Berg 61), Bjornebye, Johnsen, Hoftun, Rekdal, Rudi (Flo H 79), Solbakken, Strandli, Flo T, Solskjaer (Flo J 62).
Latvia: Karavayev; Laizans (Lukashevich 51), Lobanyov, Zemlinsky, Ivanov, Bleidelis, Zakreshevsky, Babichev, Sharando (Boulders 73), Pakhar (Isakov 81), Shtolcers.
Referee: Shmolik (Belarus).

Riga, 10 October 1998, 1900

Latvia (1) 1 *(Shtolcers 2)*

Georgia (0) 0

Latvia: Karavayev; Lukashevich, Zemlinsky, Lobanyov, Sharando, Ivanov, Astafyev (Isakov 75), Bleidelis (Laizans 51), Babichev, Pakhar (Boulders 89), Shtolcers.
Georgia: Gvaramadze; Kaladze, Shekiladze, Kavelashvili, Gakhokidze (Demetradze 60), Kobiashvili, Nemsadze, Jamarauli, Ketsbaia, Kinkladze, Arveladze S.
Referee: Zotta (Romania).

Ljubljana, 10 October 1998, 7000

Slovenia (1) 1 *(Zahovic 24)*

Norway (1) 2 *(Flo T 43, Rekdal 80)*

Slovenia: Simeunovic; Galic, Milanic, Knavs, Rudonja, Novak, Ceh, Zahovic, Pavlin, Osterc (Englaro 46), Udovic (Acimovic 65).
Norway: Grodas; Haaland, Berg, Hoftun, Bjornebye, Heggem (Riseth 86), Strand (Hestad 77), Rekdal, Solbakken, Flo J, Flo T (Rushfeldt 89).
Referee: Schluchter (Switzerland).

Maroussi, 14 October 1998, 15,000

Greece (3) 3 *(Mahlas 13, Liberopoulos 15, Ouzounidis 36)*

Georgia (0) 0

Greece: Atmatsidis; Kalitzakis, Ouzounidis, Dabizas, Zagorakis, Markos, Poursanidis, Frantzeskos (Tsartas 74), Georgatos, Liberopoulos (Yannakopoulos 67), Mahlas (Mavroyenidis 85).
Georgia: Togonidze; Kobiashvili, Kaladze, Shelia, Nemsadze, Shekiladze, Ketsbaia, Jamarauli, Kinkladze, Kavelashvili (Gakhokidze 59), Arveladze S.
Referee: Ouzounov (Bulgaria).

Oslo, 14 October 1998, 17,770

Norway (0) 2 *(Rekdal 80 (pen), Berg 87)*

Albania (1) 2 *(Bushi 38, Tare 53)*

Norway: Grodas; Haaland (Iversen 12), Berg, Hoftun, Bjornebye, Heggem, Strand, Rekdal, Solbakken (Rushfeldt 90), Flo J (Solskjaer 57), Flo T.
Albania: Strakosha; Shulku, Lala, Xhumba, Haxhi, Bushi (Halili 84), Vata, Kola (Dalipi 90), Fakaj, Tare, Rrakli.
Referee: Grabher (Austria).

Maribor, 14 October 1998, 4700

Slovenia (0) 1 *(Udovic 86)*

Latvia (0) 0

Slovenia: Simeunovic; Galic, Milanic, Knavs (Gliha 46), Novak, Istenic (Acimovic 65), Pavlin, Englaro, Zahovic, Udovic (Milinovic 88), Rudonja.
Latvia: Karavayev; Lukashevich, Zemlinsky, Ivanov (Rimkus 87), Lobanyov, Sharando, Bleidelis (Mikholap 51), Astafyev (Boulders 79), Isakov, Pakhar, Shtolcers.
Referee: Nalbandyan (Armenia).

Tirana, 18 November 1998, 14,000

Albania (0) 0

Greece (0) 0

Albania: Strakosha; Dalipi (Halili 52), Haxhi, Vata, Xhumba, Shulku, Fakaj, Kola, Bushi, Rrakli, Tare.
Greece: Atmatsidis; Dabizas (Vokolos 90), Ouzounidis, Kalitzakis, Zagorakis, Poursanidis, Frantzeskos (Liberopoulos 46), Georgatos, Mahlas, Nikolaidis (Konstantinidis K 68), Markos.
Referee: Torres (Spain).

Tbilisi, 27 March 1999, 20,000

Georgia (1) 1 *(Janashia 42)*

Slovenia (0) 1 *(Zahovic 52)*

Georgia: Grishikashvili; Kaladze, Baslashvili, Chkhaidze, Tsereteli, Aleksidze (Kinkladze 46), Nemsadze, Jamarauli (Daraselia 82), Kobiashvili, Janashia, Demetradze (Kavelashvili 74).
Slovenia: Simeunovic; Karic, Milanic, Knavs, Rudonja (Mitrakovic 89), Bulajic, Milinovic, Ceh, Pavlin (Istenic 78), Udovic (Acimovic 60), Zahovic.
Referee: Hamer (Luxembourg).

Athens, 27 March 1999, 42,571

Greece (0) 0

Norway (1) 2 *(Solskjaer 38, 87)*

Greece: Atmatsidis; Dabizas, Ouzounidis, Anatolakis, Zagorakis (Mavroyenidis 46), Yannakopoulos, Poursanidis, Markos (Mahlas 55), Georgatos, Liberopoulos (Frantzeskos 75), Nikolaidis.
Norway: Myhre; Heggem, Berg, Johnsen, Bergdolmo (Halle 65), Iversen, Strand (Bohinen 60), Solbakken, Mykland, Rudi, Solskjaer (Carew 88).
Referee: Irvine (Republic of Ireland).

Riga, 31 March 1999, 3200

Latvia (0) 0

Greece (0) 0

Latvia: Karavayev; Lukashevich, Astafyev, Zemlinsky, Lobanyov, Ivanov (Isakov 27), Sharando (Stepanov 62), Mikholap (Boulders 46), Blagonadezhdin, Pakhar, Shtolcers.
Greece: Atmatsidis; Kassapis, Ouzounidis, Dabizas, Poursanidis, Mavroyenidis, Zagorakis (Yannakopoulos 75), Liberopoulos, Georgatos (Frantzeskos 75), Mahlas (Anastasiou 81), Nikolaidis.
Referee: Fisker (Denmark).

Riga, 28 April 1999, 2700

Latvia (0) 0

Albania (0) 0

Latvia: Karavayev; Stepanov (Sharando 84), Isakov, Lukashevich, Lobanyov, Blagonadezhdin, Ivanov, Boulders, Rubins, Mikholap (Dobretsov 70), Shtolcers (Laizans 60).
Albania: Strakosha; Lala, Shulku, Xhumba, Vata (Jupi 77), Fakaj, Haxhi, Bushi (Halili 87), Kola, Rrakli (Dalipi 82), Tare.
Referee: Romain (Belgium).

Tbilisi, 28 April 1999, 20,000

Georgia (0) 1 *(Janashia 58)*

Norway (4) 4 *(Shekiladze 16 (og), Flo T 26, 38, Solskjaer 35)*

Georgia: Togonidze; Shekiladze (Popkhadze 46), Didava, Tsereteli, Kaladze, Nemsadze, Rekhviashvili (Kiknadze 81), Jamarauli, Kobiashvili, Janashia, Ketsbaia (Demetradze 46).
Norway: Myhre; Haaland, Pedersen, Hoftun, Bergdolmo, Solskjaer (Strand 46), Iversen, Solbakken, Mykland, Rudi (Riseth 82), Flo T (Carew 88).
Referee: Puhl (Hungary).

Oslo, 30 May 1999, 18,236

Norway (1) 1 *(Iversen 4)*

Georgia (0) 0

Norway: Olsen; Heggem, Pedersen, Hoftun, Bergdolmo, Iversen (Dahlum 85), Leonhardsen (Rudi 46), Solbakken, Mykland, Riseth (Rekdal 70), Flo T.
Georgia: Gvaramadze; Guchua (Chichveishvili 62), Kaladze, Didava (Popkhadze 46), Tsereteli, Tskitishvili, Nemsadze, Ketsbaia, Jamarauli, Kavelashvili, Demetradze (Ashvetia 77).
Referee: Huyghe (Belgium).

Tbilisi, 5 June 1999, 15,000

Georgia (0) 1 *(Ketsbaia 55)*

Greece (0) 2 *(Mavroyenidis 88, Mahlas 90)*

Georgia: Gvaramadze; Chichveishvili (Didava 10), Khizaneishvili O, Akhvlediani (Khizaneishvili Z 67), Tsereteli, Tskitishvili (Aleksidze 56), Nemsadze, Ketsbaia, Jamarauli, Ashvetia, Kobiashvili.
Greece: Atmatsidis; Mavroyenidis, Ouzounidis, Anatolakis, Kassapis, Konstantinidis K (Froussas 46), Poursanidis, Zagorakis (Frantzeskos 81), Niniadis, Georgatos (Anastasiou 61), Mahlas.
Referee: Young (Scotland).

Tirana, 5 June 1999, 5000

Albania (1) 1 *(Tare 16)*

Norway (1) 2 *(Iversen 4, Flo T 83)*

Albania: Strakosha; Lala, Shulku, Xhumba, Vata, Haxhi, Bushi, Kola (Duro 69), Fakaj (Bellaj 62), Tare, Rrakli (Bogdani 80).
Norway: Olsen; Haaland, Pedersen (Bragstad 62), Hoftun, Bergdolmo, Iversen, Solbakken (Riseth 89), Rekdal, Mykland, Rudi (Dahlum 78), Flo T.
Referee: Stoica (Romania).

Riga, 5 June 1999, 2500

Latvia (1) 1 *(Pakhar 18)*

Slovenia (2) 2 *(Zahovic 25, 38 (pen))*

Latvia: Kolinko; Lukashevich, Astafyev (Rubins 41), Zemlinsky, Lobanyov (Korablyov 43), Sharando (Bleidelis 69), Laizans, Shtolcers, Pakhar, Babichev, Mikholap.
Slovenia: Simeunovic; Rudonja (Osterc 88), Milinovic, Karic, Galic, Knavs, Novak, Ceh, Udovic (Acimovic 66), Zahovic, Pavlin (Istenic 79).
Referee: Arceo (Spain).

Tirana, 9 June 1999, 8000

Albania (0) 0

Slovenia (1) 1 *(Zahovic 26 (pen))*

Albania: Strakosha; Lala, Shulku, Xhumba, Vata, Duro, Bushi, Bellaj, Bogdani (Dalipi 75), Rrakli (Halili 46), Tare.
Slovenia: Simeunovic; Galic, Knavs, Osterc (Istenic 80), Milinovic, Karic, Novak, Ceh, Udovic (Acimovic 66), Pavlin, Zahovic.
Referee: Stoica (Romania).

Athens, 9 June 1999, 15,000

Greece (1) 1 (Niniadis 38 (pen))

Latvia (1) 2 *(Verpakovskis 24, Zemlinsky 90 (pen))*

Greece: Atmatsidis; Mavroyenidis, Ouzounidis, Anatolakis, Kassapis, Zikos, Zagorakis, Frantzeskos (Anastasiou 60), Niniadis (Froussos 79), Georgatos (Markos 73), Mahlas.
Latvia: Kolinko; Lukashevich, Astafyev (Bleidelis 54), Zemlinsky, Rubins (Sismannovs 64), Pakhar, Babichev, Laizans, Verpakovskis (Mikholap 46), Korablyov, Lobanyov.
Referee: Pucek (Czech Republic).

Ljubljana, 18 August 1999, 8000

Slovenia (0) 2 *(Zahovic 49, Osterc 80)*

Albania (0) 0

Slovenia: Dabanovic; Osterc, Rudonja, Milanic (Milinovic 60), Galic, Knavs, Novak (Istenic 90), Zahovic, Ceh, Udovic (Acimovic 46), Pavlin.
Albania: Strakosha; Pinari, Xhumba, Vata, Shulku, Bellai, Haxhi, Murati (Halili 59), Kola, Rrakli (Bogdani 60), Tare.
Referee: Da Silva (Portugal).

Tirana, 4 September 1999, 3000

Albania (1) 3 *(Bushi 29, 79, Muka 90)*

Latvia (1) 3 *(Astafyev 20, 63, Shtolcers 69)*

Albania: Strakosha; Lala, Shulku, Xhumba, Vata, Fakaj (Bogdani 67), Haxhi, Bellai, Murati (Dalipi 46), Bushi, Tare (Muka 77).
Latvia: Kolinko; Stepanov, Zemlinsky, Lobanov, Lukashevich, Astafyev (Babichev 81), Ivanov (Blagonadezhdin 60), Bleidelis, Rubins, Shtolcers (Boulders 84), Mikholap.
Referee: Hamer (Luxembourg).

Oslo, 4 September 1999, 24,133

Norway (1) 1 *(Leonhardsen 34)*

Greece (0) 0

Norway: Olsen; Heggem, Berg, Hoftun, Bergdolmo, Iversen, Mykland, Skammelsrud, Leonhardsen (Riseth 73), Solskjaer (Rudi 67), Flo T.
Greece: Atmatsidis; Mavrogenidis, Kassapis, Dabizas, Ouzounidis, Poursanidis, Zagorakis (Mahlas 49), Georgatos, Niniadis (Yannakopoulos 46), Nikolaidis, Liberopoulos.
Referee: Merk (Germany).

Ljubljana, 4 September 1999, 8500

Slovenia (0) 2 *(Acimovic 48, Zahovic 80)*

Georgia (0) 1 *(Arveladze S 55)*

Slovenia: Simeunovic; Galic, Milanovic, Knavs, Ceh, Zahovic (Istenic 90), Pavlin, Novak, Osterc (Acimovic 46), Rudonja, Udovic (Karic 75).
Georgia: Gvaramadze; Kaladze, Kobiashvili, Tskitishvili, Didava, Sichinava, Akhvlediani (Shekiladze 46), Potskhveria, Kavelashvili, Arveladze A, Arveladze S.
Referee: Wegereef (Holland).

Tbilisi, 8 September 1999, 15,000

Georgia (1) 2 *(Arveladze S 30, Kavelashvili 52)*

Latvia (0) 2 *(Bleidelis 62, Stepanov 90)*

Georgia: Gvaramadze; Kaladze, Tskitishvili (Sichinava 70), Didava, Tsereteli, Shekiladze, Nemsadze, Jamarauli, Kobiashvili, Kavelashvili (Arveladze A 75), Arveladze S (Demetradze 72).
Latvia: Kolinko; Stepanov, Zemlinsky, Lobanov, Ivanov, Laizans (Boulders 83), Rubins, Bleidelis, Isakov (Babichev 60), Pakhar, Shtolcers (Sharando 74).
Referee: Radoman (Yugoslavia).

Oslo, 8 September 1999, 24,288

Norway (3) 4 *(Istenic 16 (og), Iversen 18, Solskjaer 30, Leonhardsen 68)*

Slovenia (0) 0

Norway: Olsen; Heggem, Berg, Hoftun, Bergdolmo, Iversen, Mykland, Skammelsrud (Sorensen 78), Leonhardsen, Solskjaer (Riseth 78), Flo T (Lund 88).
Slovenia: Simeunovic (Dabanovic 46); Milinovic, Istenic, Knavs, Novak, Ceh, Zahovic, Pavlin, Rudonja, Udovic (Karic 42), Osterc (Acimovic 84).
Referee: Veissiere (France).

Athens, 6 October 1999, 8000

Greece (1) 2 *(Tsartas 1, Georgiadis 87)*

Albania (0) 0

Greece: Atmatsidis; Amanatidis, Ouzounidis, Dabizas, Georgatos (Konstantinidis 66), Poursanidis, Zagorakis (Georgiadis 46), Tsartas (Niniadis 75), Zikos, Mahlas, Nikolaidis.
Albania: Strakosha; Lala, Bellaj (Bogdani 84), Xhumba, Vata, Haxhi, Murazi (Duro 55), Rakli, Bushi, Kola, Tare (Muka 67).
Referee: Ivanov (Bulgaria).

Tirana, 9 October 1999, 3000

Albania (0) 2 *(Rakli 30, Kola 36)*

Georgia (0) 1 *(Arveladze S 52)*

Albania: Beqaj; Lala, Shulku, Xhumba, Vata, Duro, Fakaj, Rakli (Muka 75), Bushi (Murati 54), Kola, Tare (Bogdani 90).
Georgia: Chanturia; Kobiashvili, Didava, Shekiladze, Gakhokidze, Nemsadze, Tskitishvili, Jamarauli, Kaladze, Arveladze S, Arveladze A (Janashia 83).
Referee: Michallef (Malta).

Riga, 9 October 1999, 3000

Latvia (0) 1 *(Pakhar 53)*

Norway (0) 2 *(Solskjaer 52, Flo T 86)*

Latvia: Kolinko; Lukashevich (Laizans 82), Zemlinsky, Lobanyov, Blagonadezhdin, Bleidelis, Ivanov, Astafyev, Rubins, Shtolcers, Pakhar.
Norway: Olsen; Heggem, Bergdolmo, Berg, Hoftun, Leonhardsen, Skammelsrud, Mykland (Solbakken 82), Iversen (Lund 46), Solskjaer (Riseth 87), Flo T.
Referee: Drabek (Austria).

Maribor, 9 October 1999, 2500

Slovenia (0) 0

Greece (2) 3 *(Tsartas 39, Georgiadis 43, Nikolaidis 73)*

Slovenia: Simeunovic; Bajrektarevic, Vugdalic (Englaro 84), Galic, Seslar, Rudonja, Novak, Acimovic, Ceh, Udovic (Karic 46), Simundza (Osterc 60).
Greece: Atmatsidis; Amanatidis, Zikos, Dabizas, Antzas (Zagorakis 71), Georgiadis, Poursanidis, Tsartas (Niniadis 69), Konstantinidis, Limberopoulos, Nikolaidis (Mahlas 75).
Referee: Ghandour (Egypt).

Group 2 – Final Table	*P*	*W*	*D*	*L*	*F*	*A*	*Pts*
Norway	10	8	1	1	21	9	25
Slovenia	10	5	2	3	12	14	17
Greece	10	4	3	3	13	8	15
Latvia	10	3	4	3	13	12	13
Albania	10	1	4	5	8	14	7
Georgia	10	1	2	7	8	18	5

GROUP 3

Helsinki, 5 September 1998, 18,716

Finland (2) 3 *(Kolkka 8, Johansson 44, Paatelainen 62)*

Moldova (2) 2 *(Oprea 10, 11)*

Finland: Niemi; Ylonen, Tuomela, Hyypia, Turpeinen (Reini 46), Wiss, Kautonen, Litmanen, Johansson (Sumiala 80), Paatelainen, Kolkka (Mahlio 73).
Moldova: Coselev; Fistican (Tabanov 76), Rebeja (Pusca 46), Testimitanu, Guzun, Stroenco, Oprea, Gaidamasciuc, Epureanu (Suharev 76), Curtianu, Clescenco.
Referee: Barber (England).

Istanbul, 5 September 1998, 26,500

Turkey (1) 3 *(Oktay 18, 58, Tayfur 49 (pen))*

Northern Ireland (0) 0

Turkey: Rustu; Saffet, Mert, Alpay, Okan (Arif 87), Sergen, Tayfur, Tugay (Oguz 75), Abdullah, Oktay (Hami 79), Hakan Sukur.
Northern Ireland: Fettis; Hughes A, Horlock, Mulryne, Hill, Morrow, Gillespie (Jim Whitley 78), Lennon, Dowie, Rowland (Quinn 46), Hughes M.
Referee: Wojcik (Poland).

Belfast, 10 October 1998, 10,002

Northern Ireland (1) 1 *(Rowland 31)*

Finland (0) 0

Northern Ireland: Fettis; Hughes A, Horlock, Mulryne, Morrow, Patterson, Gillespie (McCarthy 71), Lennon, Dowie (O'Boyle 80), Rowland (Quinn 89), Hughes M.
Finland: Niemi; Ylonen, Ilola, Hyypia, Kautonen, Reini, Riihilahti (Litmanen 75), Valakari, Kolkka, Paatelainen, Johansson.
Referee: Arsic (Yugoslavia).

Bursa, 10 October 1998, 20,000

Turkey (0) 1 *(Hakan Sukur 70)*

Germany (0) 0

Turkey: Rustu; Fatih, Ogun (Unsal 89), Alpay, Tayfun, Tayfur, Tugay (Oktay 61), Abdullah, Mert, Sergen (Saffet 81), Hakan Sukur.
Germany: Kahn; Babbel, Nowotny, Rehmer, Ricken (Bode 81), Ramelow, Beinlich, Jeremies, Heinrich (Neuville 76), Bierhoff, Kirsten.
Referee: Dallas (Scotland).

Chisinau, 14 October 1998, 5000

Moldova (1) 1 *(Guzun 6)*

Germany (3) 3 *(Kirsten 20, 36, Bierhoff 38)*

Moldova: Coselev; Fistican, Stroenco, Testimitanu, Gaidamasciuc, Rebeja, Guzun, Oprea, Curtianu (Suharev 53), Clescenco, Epureanu.
Germany: Kahn; Babbel, Nowotny, Rehmer, Ricken (Neuville 53), Ramelow, Beinlich (Wosz 83), Nerlinger, Tarnat, Kirsten (Jancker 74), Bierhoff.
Referee: Marin (Spain).

Istanbul, 14 October 1998, 25,000

Turkey (0) 1 *(Ogun 73)*

Finland (1) 3 *(Paatelainen 5, Johansson 51, Litmanen 90)*

Turkey: Rustu; Alpay, Ogun, Fatih, Okan (Hami 46), Tugay (Mert 46), Sergen (Hasan Sas 83), Tayfur, Abdullah, Hakan Sukur, Oktay.
Finland: Niemi; Reini, Ylonen (Kolkka 61), Hyypia, Kautonen, Tuomela, Riihilahti (Valakari 76), Litmanen, Ilola, Johansson (Saastamoinen 90), Paatelainen.
Referee: Krondl (Czech Republic).

Belfast, 18 November 1998, 11,137

Northern Ireland (0) 2 *(Dowie 49, Lennon 63)*

Moldova (1) 2 *(Gaidamasciuc 22, Testimitanu 57)*

Northern Ireland: Fettis; Griffin, Kennedy, Lomas, Patterson, Morrow, Gillespie (McCarthy 88), Lennon, Dowie, Rowland (Gray 77), Hughes M.
Moldova: Dinov; Fistican, Guzun (Pusca 71), Stroenco, Rebeja, Curtianu, Stratulat (Suharev 62), Testimitanu (Maievici 86), Epureanu, Gaidamasciuc, Clescenco.
Referee: Hrinak (Slovakia).

Belfast, 27 March 1999, 14,270

Northern Ireland (0) 0

Germany (2) 3 *(Bode 11, 42, Hamann 62)*

Northern Ireland: Taylor; Patterson, Horlock, Lomas, Williams, Morrow, Gillespie (McCarthy 84), Lennon (Sonner 68), Dowie, Rowland (Kennedy 69), Hughes M.
Germany: Kahn; Babbel, Worns, Jeremies, Matthaus (Nowotny 46), Strunz, Heinrich, Hamann, Bierhoff, Neuville (Jancker 69), Bode (Preetz 79).
Referee: Cesari (Italy).

Istanbul, 27 March 1999, 30,000

Turkey (1) 2 *(Hakan Sukur 34, Sergen 90)*

Moldova (0) 0

Turkey: Rustu; Fatih, Ogun, Alpay, Okan, Tugay (Ayhan 85), Sergen, Tayfur, Abdullah, Hakan Sukur, Oktay (Hami 9) (Arif 74).
Moldova: Dinov; Fistican, Rebeja, Tabanov, Guzun, Stroenco, Sischin, Stratulat, Gaidamasciuc, Epureanu, Clescenco (Suharev 81).
Referee: Plautz (Austria).

Nuremberg, 31 March 1999, 40,758

Germany (2) 2 *(Jeremies 31, Neuville 37)*

Finland (0) 0

Germany: Kahn; Babbel, Matthaus, Worns, Strunz, Hamann (Nowotny 72), Jeremies, Heinrich, Neuville (Kirsten 65), Bierhoff, Bode (Jancker 76).
Finland: Niemi; Reini (Lehkosuo 89), Hyypia, Ylonen, Kautonen (Kolkka 72), Kinnunen, Riihilahti, Litmanen, Ilola, Johansson, Paatelainen (Saastamoinen 46).
Referee: Koussainov (Russia).

Chisinau, 31 March 1999, 9237

Moldova (0) 0

Northern Ireland (0) 0

Moldova: Dinov; Fistican, Stroenco, Sosnovschi, Oprea (Stratulat 90), Gaidamasciuc, Epureanu, Rebeja, Guzun, Clescenco, Suharev.
Northern Ireland: Taylor; Patterson (Hughes A 62), Horlock, Lomas, Williams M, Morrow, Gillespie, Lennon, Dowie, Robinson, Hughes M.
Referee: Trivkovic (Croatia).

Leverkusen, 4 June 1999, 21,000

Germany (3) 6 *(Bierhoff 2, 56, 82, Kirsten 27, Bode 38, Scholl 71)*

Moldova (0) 1 *(Stratulat 76)*

Germany: Kahn; Nowotny, Matthaus (Babbel 75), Strunz, Hamann, Jeremies (Scholl 46), Heinrich, Neuville, Bierhoff, Kirsten (Ramelow 54), Bode.
Moldova: Dinov; Fistican, Maievici (Stratulat 55), Stroenco, Rebeja, Gaidamasciuc (Belous 74), Epureanu, Guzun, Curtianu, Oprea, Clescenco (Sischin 81).
Referee: Coroado (Portugal).

Helsinki, 5 June 1999, 36,042

Finland (2) 2 *(Tihinen 10, Paatelainen 14)*

Turkey (2) 4 *(Tayfur 25, 84, Hakan Sukur 34, 87)*

Finland: Niemi; Ylonen, Hyppia, Kuivasto, Tihinen, Riihilahti, Valakari, Litmanen, Kolkka, Paatelainen, Johansson.
Turkey: Rustu; Fatih, Ali Eren, Alpay, Saffet, Sergen (Umit 89), Tayfur, Abdullah (Unsal 90), Tayfun, Hakan Sukur, Ayhan (Tugay 74).
Referee: Jol (Holland).

Chisinau, 9 June 1999, 8000

Moldova (0) 0

Finland (0) 0

Moldova: Dinov; Fistican, Stratulat, Stroenco, Rebeja, Sischin (Belous 75), Guzun, Epureanu, Curtianu, Oprea (Gaidamasciuc 79), Suharev (Chirilov 89).
Finland: Niemi; Ylonen, Reini (Lehkosuo 85), Hyypia, Tininen (Kautonen 46), Riihilahti, Valakari, Paatelainen, Kolkka, Ilola, Johansson (Forssell 60).
Referee: Treossi (Italy).

Helsinki, 4 September 1999, 20,184

Finland (0) 1 *(Salli 63)*

Germany (2) 2 *(Bierhoff 2, 17)*

Finland: Niemi (Laaksonen 46); Saastamoinen, Hyypia, Kuivasto, Ylonen (Kuqi 46), Salli, Wiss, Riihilahti, Tainio, Johansson, Kottila.
Germany: Lehmann; Babbel, Nowotny, Linke, Jeremies, Matthaus, Scholl (Nerlinger 79), Ziege, Neuville (Strunz 85), Bierhoff, Kirsten (Schneider 32).
Referee: Nieto (Spain).

Belfast, 4 September 1999, 7500

Northern Ireland (0) 0

Turkey (0) 3 *(Arif 45, 46, 48)*

Northern Ireland: Taylor; Hughes A, Horlock, Lomas, Williams M, Hunter, McCarthy (Gillespie 62), Lennon, Dowie (Quinn 75), Hughes M, Kennedy.
Turkey: Rustu; Ali Eren, Ogun, Alpay, Tayfun, Tayfur, Tugay, Abdullah (Hakan Unsal 75), Sergen (Umit Karan 90), Arif (Okan 78), Hakan Sukur.
Referee: Sars (France).

Dortmund, 8 September 1999, 41,000

Germany (4) 4 *(Bierhoff 3, Ziege 16, 33, 45)*

Northern Ireland (0) 0

Germany: Lehmann; Linke, Matthaus, Babbel (Strunz 30), Jeremies, Nowotny (Worns 46), Scholl, Ziege, Neuville (Schneider 67), Bierhoff, Bode.
Northern Ireland: Taylor; Nolan, Horlock, Lomas, Williams, Morrow, McCarthy, Lennon (Gillespie 46), Dowie (Quinn 46), Hughes M, Kennedy.
Referee: Bikas (Greece).

Chisinau, 8 September 1999, 6000

Moldova (1) 1 *(Epureanu 3)*

Turkey (0) 1 *(Tayfur 76)*

Moldova: Dinov; Fistican, Stroenco, Boret, Gusin (Siskin 81), Oprea, Epureanu, Osipenco, Rebeja, Clescenco (Chirilov 84), Gaidamasciuc (Stratulat 46).
Turkey: Rustu; Ali Eren, Ogun, Alpay, Okan (Tugay 46), Tayfur, Fatih (Ayhan 46), Hakan Unsal, Sergen (Umit 88), Arif, Hakan Sukur.
Referee: Schluchter (Switzerland).

Helsinki, 9 October 1999, 8217

Finland (1) 4 *(Johansson 9, Hyypia 63, Kolkka 73, 83)*

Northern Ireland (0) 1 *(Jeff Whitley 59)*

Finland: Viander; Lehkosuo, Kuivasto, Hyypia, Tihinen, Wiss (Valakari 87), Litmanen, Riihilahti (Yla-Jussila 87), Kolkka, Paatelainen, Johansson.
Northern Ireland: Taylor; Jenkins (Jim Whitley 79), Nolan, Lennon, Williams, Morrow, McCarthy, Jeff Whitley, Quinn (Coote 68), Kennedy, Hughes M (Johnson 75).
Referee: Ancion (Belgium).

Munich, 9 October 1999, 63,572

Germany (0) 0

Turkey (0) 0

Germany: Kahn; Babbel, Matthaus, Linke, Schneider (Dogan 89), Hamann (Nerlinger 46), Jeremies, Ziege (Bode 76), Neuville, Bierhoff, Scholl.
Turkey: Rustu; Fatih, Ogun, Alpay, Ali Eren, Okan (Arif 72), Tayfun, Sergen, Tayfur (Oktay 85), Abdullah (Ergun 69), Hakan Sukur.
Referee: Collina (Italy).

Group 3 – Final Table	*P*	*W*	*D*	*L*	*F*	*A*	*Pts*
Germany	8	6	1	1	20	4	19
Turkey	8	5	2	1	15	6	17
Finland	8	3	1	4	13	13	10
N. Ireland	8	1	2	5	4	19	5
Moldova	8	0	4	4	7	17	4

GROUP 4

Erevan, 5 September 1998, 2300

Armenia (1) 3 *(Avalyan 40, Yessayan 71, 90)*

Andorra (0) 1 *(Lucendo 86 (pen))*

Armenia: Berezovski; Soukiassian, Krbachian, Hovsepian, Oganessian T (Khodgoyan 83), Vardanian, Sarkissian, Ara Adamian, Art Adamian (Gsepyan 86), Shahgeldian, Avalyan (Yessayan 68).
Andorra: Koldo; Ramirez, Chema, Martin, Lima, Escurza, Garcia, Oscar, Sanchez, Lucendo, Justo.
Referee: O'Hanlon (Republic of Ireland).

Reykjavik, 5 September 1998, 10,500

Iceland (1) 1 *(Dadason 33)*

France (1) 1 *(Dugarry 36)*

Iceland: Kristinsson B; Helgason A, Sigurdsson L, Sverrisson E, Marteinsson, Hreidarsson, Kolvidsson, Gudjonsson T, Kristinsson R, Dadason, Gunnlaugsson A (Thordarson 69).
France: Barthez; Karembeu, Thuram, Leboeuf, Lizarazu, Dugarry (Henry 66), Deschamps, Djorkaeff, Zidane, Pires, Laslandes.
Referee: Blareau (Belgium).

Kiev, 5 September 1998, 18,000

Ukraine (2) 3 *(Popov 14, Skachenko 24, Rebrov 74 (pen))*

Russia (0) 2 *(Varlamov 67, Onopko 87)*

Ukraine: Shovkovskyi; Gusin, Mikitin, Golovko, Vashchuk, Dmitrulin, Skachenko (Kalitvintsev 46), Popov, Kovalov (Kriventsov 87), Shevchenko, Rebrov.
Russia: Kharine; Minko, Chugainov, Kovtun, Yanovski, Semak (Cherchesov 72), Onopko, Alenichev (Mostovoi 64), Kanchelskis (Karpin 71), Kolyvanov, Varlamov.
Referee: Merk (Germany).

Andorra, 10 October 1998, 850

Andorra (0) 0

Ukraine (2) 2 *(Kossovski V 30, Rebrov 43)*

Andorra: Koldo; Ramirez, Chema, Martin, Lima A, Lima I, Pol, Oscar, Emiliano, Sanchez (Jimenez 87), Ruiz.
Ukraine: Shovkovskyi; Luzhny, Golovko, Vashchuk, Mikitin (Kovalov 46), Popov, Maximov (Kriventsov 51), Gusin, Kossovski V, Shevchenko (Mikhailenko 69), Rebrov.
Referee: Guetzov (Bulgaria).

Erevan, 10 October 1998, 6,000

Armenia (0) 0

Iceland (0) 0

Armenia: Berezovski; Soukiassian, Vardanian, Khachatrian V, Hovsepian, Sarkissian, Art Petrossian (Oganessian T 40), Art Adamian, Shahgeldian, Mikaelian, Assadourian (Yessayan 25).
Iceland: Kristinsson B; Jonsson S, Hreidarsson, Adolfsson, Helgason A, Kristinsson R, Kolvidsson, Gunnlaugsson A, Dadason, Gudjonsson T, Sigurdsson L.
Referee: Norman (Sweden).

Moscow, 10 October 1998, 32,500

Russia (1) 2 *(Yanovski 45, Mostovoi 55)*

France (2) 3 *(Anelka 12, Pires 28, Boghossian 81)*

Russia: Ovchinnikov; Kovtun, Onopko, Varlamov, Khlestov, Karpin, Yanovski, Alenichev (Semak 69), Mostovoi, Tikhonov, Bestchastnykh (Gerasimenko 62).
France: Lama; Thuram, Blanc, Desailly, Lizarazu, Deschamps, Petit (Boghossian 46), Pires, Zidane, Djorkaeff (Vieira 54), Anelka (Vairelles 88).
Referee: Ceccarini (Italy).

Paris, 14 October 1998, 75,000

France (0) 2 *(Candela 53, Djorkaeff 61)*

Andorra (0) 0

France: Lama; Candela, Leboeuf, Blanc, Lizarazu, Deschamps, Zidane, Djorkaeff (Boghossian 82), Dugarry (Pires 71), Trezeguet (Anelka 71), Vairelles.
Andorra: Koldo; Ramirez (Sanchez 80), Chema, Martin, Lima A, Lima I, Pol, Oscar, Lucendo (Jimenez 88), Ruiz, Emiliano.
Referee: Koren (Israel).

Reykjavik, 14 October 1998, 3500

Iceland (0) 1 *(Kovtun 88 (og))*

Russia (0) 0

Iceland: Kristinsson B; Jonsson S, Hreidarsson, Adolfsson, Helgason A, Kristinsson R, Kolvidsson (Thordarson 85), Gunnlaugsson A, Dadason, Sigurdsson L, Gudjonsson T (Sigurdsson H 6).
Russia: Cherchesov; Kovtun, Onopko, Smertin, Yanovski, Shalimov, Varlamov (Solomatin 59), Mostovoi, Tikhonov (Igonin 12), Karpin (Khokhlov 59), Titov.
Referee: Temmink (Holland).

Kiev, 14 October 1998, 25,000

Ukraine (1) 2 *(Skachenko 31, Gusin 83)*

Armenia (0) 0

Ukraine: Shovkovskyi; Luzhny, Dmitrulin, Golovko, Vashchuk, Popov (Maximov 75), Skachenko (Kovalov 61), Gusin, Kossovski V, Shevchenko (Kriventsov 80), Rebrov.
Armenia: Berezovski; Soukiassian, Vardanian, Khachatrian V, Hovsepian, Krbachian (Oganessian T 85), Art Petrossian, Ara Adamian, Shahgeldian, Mikaelian (Avalyan 65), Assadourian (Yessayan 73).
Referee: Lica (Romania).

La Vella, 27 March 1999, 1400

Andorra (0) 0

Iceland (0) 2 *(Sverrisson E 58, Adolfsson 67.)*

Andorra: Alvarez; Ramirez (Gonzalez 77), Garcia, Martin, Lima T, Lima I, Pol, Oscar, Jimenez (Sanchez 73), Lucendo, Ruiz (Imbernon 83).
Iceland: Kristinsson B; Jonsson S, Gunnarsson B (Hreidarsson 70), Adolfsson, Helgason A, Kristinsson R, Thordarson, Gunnlaugsson A (Gudmundsson T 81), Sverrisson E (Gretarsson 70), Sigurdsson H, Gudjonsson T.
Referee: Agius (Malta).

Erevan, 27 March 1999, 20,000

Armenia (0) 0

Russia (1) 3 *(Karpin 7, 63 (pen), Bestchastnykh 89)*

Armenia: Berezovski; Mkrchian, Hovsepian, Oganessian S, Karbanian (Harutyunian 65), Vardanian, Art Petrossian, Voskanian (Kakosian 78), Sarkissian, Shahgeldian, Mikalian (Yessayan 81).
Russia: Filimonov; Khlestov, Onopko, Drozdov, Tsymbalar, Karpin, Alenichev (Tikhonov 65), Yanovski, Titov, Yuran (Khokhlov 85), Panov (Bestchastnykh 46).
Referee: Hauge (Norway).

Saint Denis, 27 March 1999, 78,500

France (0) 0

Ukraine (0) 0

France: Barthez; Thuram, Lizarazu, Deschamps, Blanc, Desailly, Pires (Dhorasoo 85), Djorkaeff, Petit (Boghossian 78), Anelka, Dugarry (Wiltord 69).
Ukraine: Shovkovskyi; Luzhny, Vashchuk, Golovko, Mikitin, Gusin (Skrypnyk 85), Popov, Kovalov (Kossovski V 55), Rebrov, Skachenko (Maximov 69), Shevchenko.
Referee: Benko (Austria).

Saint Denis, 31 March 1999, 78,852

France (2) 2 *(Wiltord 3, Dugarry 45)*

Armenia (0) 0

France: Barthez; Thuram (Karembeu 79), Blanc, Desailly, Deschamps, Vieira, Djorkaeff (Pires 69), Boghossian, Anelka, Wiltord, Dugarry (Trezeguet 46).
Armenia: Berezovski; Soukiassian (Khachatrian V 40), Mkrchian, Vardanian, Hovsepian, Oganessian S, Art Petrossian, Voskanian (Hayrapetian 77), Sarkissian, Shahgeldian (Yessayan 53), Mikaelian.
Referee: Bikas (Greece).

Moscow, 31 March 1999, 20,000

Russia (3) 6 *(Titov 8, Bestchastnykh 11, 62, Onopko 42, Tsymbalar 50, Alenichev 90)*

Andorra (0) 1 *(Sanchez 73)*

Russia: Filimonov; Khlestov, Smertin, Tsymbalar, Yevseyev (Tikhonov 46), Alenichev, Onopko, Karpin, Titov, Shirko, Bestchastnykh.
Andorra: Alvarez; Alonso (Gonzalez 57), Garcia, Martin, Lima T, Lima I, Pol, Oscar, Jimenez, Lucendo (Sanchez 65), Ruiz.
Referee: Vuorela (Finland).

Kiev, 31 March 1999, 50,000

Ukraine (0) 1 *(Vashchuk 59)*

Iceland (0) 1 *(Sigurdsson L 66)*

Ukraine: Shovkovskyi; Luzhny, Vashchuk, Golovko, Mikitin, Gusin, Popov (Kalitvintsev 75), Kossovski V, Rebrov, Skachenko (Maximov 46), Shevchenko.
Iceland: Kristinsson B; Jonsson S, Gunnarsson B, Adolfsson, Helgason A, Kristinsson R (Kolvidsson 80), Sigurdsson L, Hreidarsson, Sverrisson E, Sigurdsson H (Sverrisson S 86), Gudjonsson T.
Referee: Dani (Israel).

Saint-Denis, 5 June 1999, 78,000

France (0) 2 *(Petit 48, Wiltord 54)*

Russia (1) 3 *(Panov 40, 75, Karpin 85)*

France: Barthez; Thuram, Blanc, Desailly, Candela (Pires 88), Deschamps, Petit, Djorkaeff (Boghossian 90), Dugarry (Vieira 59), Anelka, Wiltord.
Russia: Filimonov; Khlestov, Onopko, Smertin, Varlamov, Karpin, Semak (Bestchastnykh 60), Mostovoi (Khokhlov 26), Titov, Tikhonov (Tsymbalar 71), Panov.
Referee: Durkin (England).

Reykjavik, 5 June 1999, 5565

Iceland (1) 2 *(Dadason 30, Gunnarsson B 46)*

Armenia (0) 0

Iceland: Kristinsson B; Helgason A (Kolvidsson 72), Hreidarsson, Jonsson S, Marteinsson, Gunnarsson B, Kristinsson R, Sverrisson E, Sigurdsson H (Danielsson 81), Gudjonsson T, Dadason (Helguson 69).
Armenia: Berezovski; Soukiassian (Mkrchian 65), Khachatrian V, Hovsepian, Voskanian (Gregorian 84), Vardanian, Art Petrossian (Hayrapetian 75), Harutyunian, Sarkissian, Shahgeldian, Mikaelian.
Referee: Peltola (Finland).

Kiev, 5 June 1999, 45,000

Ukraine (2) 4 *(Popov 38, Rebrov 41, Dmitrulin 56, Gusin 89)*

Andorra (0) 0

Ukraine: Vorobiov; Luzhny, Mikitin (Mizin 72), Golovko, Vashchuk, Dmitrulin (Maximiuk 78), Tsykhmeistruk, Popov, Gusin, Shevchenko (Skachenko 67), Rebrov.
Andorra: Alvarez; Pol, Martin (Lucendo 53), Garcia, Lima T, Lima I, Gonzalez, Oscar, Ramirez, Sanchez, Ruiz.
Referee: Georgiou (Cyprus).

Barcelona, 9 June 1999, 4000

Andorra (0) 0

France (0) 1 *(Leboeuf 85 (pen))*

Andorra: Alvarez; Pol, Ramirez, Lima T, Lima I, Chema (Jonas 70), Gonzalez, Oscar, Ruiz, Jimenez (Genis 89), Lucendo (Martin 77).
France: Rame; Karembeu, Candela, Boghossian, Leboeuf, Desailly, Wiltord, Dugarry, Anelka, Petit (Vieira 56), Dhorasoo (Pires 60).
Referee: Ross (Northern Ireland).

Erevan, 9 June 1999, 10,000

Armenia (0) 0

Ukraine (0) 0

Armenia: Berezovski; Petrossian T (Gregorian 63), Khachatrian V, Hovsepian, Oganessian S (Harutyunian 46), Vardanian, Art Petrossian, Voskanian, Sarkissian, Shahgeldian, Mikaelian (Mkrchian 46).
Ukraine: Vorobiov; Luzhny, Mikitin, Golovko, Vashchuk, Dmitrulin, Tsykhmeistruk, Popov (Konovalov 34), Gusin, Shevchenko (Cardash 80), Rebrov (Skachenko 70).
Referee: Boggi (Italy).

Moscow, 9 June 1999, 36,000

Russia (1) 1 *(Karpin 44)*

Iceland (0) 0

Russia: Filimonov; Khlestov, Varlamov (Yanovski 56), Onopko, Semak (Bulatov 46), Smertin, Karpin, Khokhlov, Tikhonov, Bestchastnykh (Tsymbalar 71), Panov.
Iceland: Kristinsson B; Helgason A, Hreidarsson (Adolfsson 60), Jonsson S (Kolvidsson 46), Marteinsson, Kristinsson R, Gunnarsson B (Helguson 82), Sverrisson E, Sigurdsson L, Gudjonsson T, Dadason.
Referee: Tokat (Turkey).

Reykjavik, 4 September 1999, 5100

Iceland (2) 3 *(Gudjonsson T 29, Hreidarsson 32, Gudjohnsen E 90)*

Andorra (0) 0

Iceland: Kristinsson B; Helgason A, Hreidarsson, Jonsson S, Sigurdsson L (Vidarsson 26), Gudjonsson B, Gunnarsson, Gudmundsson, Sigurdsson H (Helguson 57), Gudjonsson T, Dadason (Gudjohnsen E 77).
Andorra: Koldo; Martin (Armand Godoy 61), Escura, Ramirez, Garcia J, Sonejee, Pol (Buxo 90), Gonzalez, Jimenez, Sanchez, Alex Godoy (Garcia G 67).
Referee: Liba (Czech Republic).

Moscow, 4 September 1999, 40,000

Russia (1) 2 *(Bestchastnykh 8 (pen), Karpin 70)*

Armenia (0) 0

Russia: Filimonov; Khlestov, Onopko, Smertin, Karpin, Khokhlov, Alenichev, Titov (Semak 80), Panov (Chirko 78), Bestchastnykh, Tikhonov (Yanovski 73).
Armenia: Berezovski; Mkrchian, Khachatrian V, Hovsepian, Oganessian S, Vardanian, Khachatrian R (Art Petrossian 85), Harutyunian (Kakossian 55), Voskanian, Shahgeldian (Devani 78), Mikaelian.
Referee: Agius (Malta).

Kiev, 4 September 1999, 70,000

Ukraine (0) 0

France (0) 0

Ukraine: Shovkovskyi; Luzhny, Golovko, Vashchuk, Dmitrulin (Mitikin 46), Popov, Maximov (Konovalov 70), Gusin (Tsykhmeistruk 84), Kossovski V, Shevchenko, Rebrov.
France: Barthez; Thuram, Blanc, Desailly, Lizarazu, Karembeu, Deschamps, Vieira, Djorkaeff (Pires 69), Zidane, Anelka (Laslandes 52).
Referee: Dallas (Scotland).

La Vella, 8 September 1999, 1000

Andorra (1) 1 *(Ruiz 39 (pen))*

Russia (1) 2 *(Onopko 22, 57)*

Andorra: Koldo; Ramirez, Lima I, Sonejee, Garcia T, Escura, Alex Godoy (Pol 59), Gonzalez, Jimenez, Ruiz, Sanchez (Armand Godoy 89).
Russia: Filimonov; Khlestov, Onopko, Smertin, Karpin, Khokhlov (Bezrodny 55), Alenichev (Yanovski 61), Titov, Bestchastnykh (Panov 46), Chirko, Tikhonov.
Referee: Larsen (Denmark).

Reykjavik, 8 September 1999, 7700

Iceland (0) 0

Ukraine (1) 1 *(Rebrov 43 (pen))*

Iceland: Kristinsson B; Helgason A, Hreidarsson, Jonsson S (Vidarsson 85), Sigurdsson L, Kristinsson R, Gunnarsson, Kolvidsson (Helguson 59), Marteinsson, Gudjonsson T, Dadason (Gudjohnsen E 73).
Ukraine: Shovkovskyi; Luzhny (Mikitin 80), Golovko, Vashchuk, Dmitrulin, Popov, Maximov, Konovalov (Tsykhmeistruk 66), Kossovski V, Shevchenko, Rebrov.
Referee: Pereira (Portugal).

Erevan, 8 September 1999, 20,000

Armenia (1) 2 *(Mikaelian 6, Shakhgeldian 90 (pen))*

France (1) 3 *(Djorkaeff 45 (pen), Zidane 67, Laslandes 74)*

Armenia: Berezovski; Mkrchian, Khachatrian V, Hovsepian, Khachatrian R (Kotcharian 75), Yessayan, Petrossian T, Harutyunian (Gregorian 63), Shakhgeldian, Mikaelian (Devani 67), Sarkissian.
France: Barthez; Thuram, Blanc, Desailly, Lizarazu, Karembeu, Deschamps, Djorkaeff, Zidane (Dehu 72), Wiltord (Robert 63), Laslandes.
Referee: Ouzunov (Bulgaria).

La Vella, 9 October 1999, 700

Andorra (0) 0

Armenia (1) 3 *(Art Petrossian 26, Yessayan 59, Shakhgeldian 65)*

Andorra: Koldo; Ramirez, Escura, Sonejee, Garcia T (Alonso 58), Lima I, Alex Godoy (Pol 46), Gonzalez (Soria 62), Jimenez, Sanchez, Ruiz.
Armenia: Abramian; Soukiassian, Voskanian, Vardanian, Mortigian, Khachatrian, Art Petrossian (Harobian 79), Petrossian T (Krpcharian 82), Sarkissian, Shakhgeldian (Minasian 78), Yessayan.
Referee: Jones (England).

Saint-Denis, 9 October 1999, 80,000

France (2) 3 *(Dadason 17 (og), Djorkaeff 39, Trezeguet 71)*

Iceland (0) 2 *(Sverrisson E 48, Gunnarsson 56)*

France: Lama; Thuram, Blanc, Desailly, Lizarazu, Deschamps, Boghossian (Vieira 90), Zidane, Djorkaeff, Laslandes (Trezeguet 67), Wiltord (Vairelles 84).
Iceland: Kristinsson B; Helgason A, Sigurdsson L, Marteinsson, Hreidarsson, Sverrisson E, Kristinsson R, Gunnarsson, Gudjonsson T (Gudjohnsen E 74), Sigurdsson H (Helguson 72), Dadason.
Referee: Heynemann (Germany).

Moscow, 9 October 1999, 80,000

Russia (0) 1 *(Karpin 72)*

Ukraine (0) 1 *(Shevchenko 87)*

Russia: Filimonov; Khlestov, Onopko, Smertin, Aleinichev, Khokhlov, Drozdov, Titov, Karpin, Panov (Semak 80), Tikhonov (Bestchastnykh 60).
Ukraine: Shovkovskyi; Luzhny, Golovko, Vashchuk, Mizin, Maximov (Moroz 76), Gusin, Dmitrulin (Kovalev 76), Shevchenko, Skachenko (Mikitin 42), Rebrov.
Referee: Elleray (England).

Group 4 – Final Table	*P*	*W*	*D*	*L*	*F*	*A*	*Pts*
France	10	6	3	1	17	10	21
Ukraine	10	5	5	0	14	4	20
Russia	10	6	1	3	22	12	19
Iceland	10	4	3	3	12	7	15
Armenia	10	2	2	6	8	15	8
Andorra	10	0	0	10	3	28	0

GROUP 5

Stockholm, 5 September 1998, 35,394

Sweden (2) 2 *(Andersson A 30, Mjallby 32)*

England (1) 1 *(Shearer 2)*

Sweden: Hedman; Nilsson, Andersson P, Bjorklund, Kamark (Lucic 82), Schwarz, Andersson A (Andersson D 90), Mjallby, Ljungberg, Larsson, Pettersson.
England: Seaman; Anderton (Lee 42), Le Saux, Southgate, Adams, Campbell (Merson 74), Redknapp, Ince, Shearer, Owen, Scholes (Sheringham 85).
Referee: Collina (Italy).

Bourgas, 6 September 1998, 20,000

Bulgaria (0) 0

Poland (2) 3 *(Czereszewski 19, 45, Iwan 47)*

Bulgaria: Zdravkov; Ginchev, Zagorcic (Petkov I 50), Yordanov, Petkov M (Trendafilov 46), Sirakov, Kishishev, Bachev, Borimirov (Gruev 46), Stoichkov, Donev.
Poland: Sidorczuk; Bak, Zielinski, Lapinski, Siadaczka, Hajto (Klos 68), Brzeczek, Czereszewski, Swierczewski (Michalski 76), Iwan, Trzeciak (Juskowiak 83).
Referee: Batta (France).

Wembley, 10 October 1998, 72,974

England (0) 0

Bulgaria (0) 0

England: Seaman; Anderton (Batty 67), Hinchcliffe (Le Saux 34), Neville G, Southgate, Campbell, Lee, Scholes (Sheringham 77), Shearer, Owen, Redknapp.
Bulgaria: Zdravkov; Yordanov, Zagorcic, Kirilov, Kishishev, Iliev (Gruiev 63), Yankov, Petkov M, Naidenov, Stoichkov (Bachev 60), Hristov (Ivanov G 90).
Referee: Vagner (Hungary).

Warsaw, 10 October 1998, 8000

Poland (2) 3 *(Brzeczek 18, Juskowiak 35, Trzeciak 65)*

Luxembourg (0) 0

Poland: Matysek; Zielinski, Lapinski, Ratajczyk (Siadaczka 69), Hajto (Majak 62), Czereszewski (Bak 75), Iwan, Brzeczek, Swierczewski, Juskowiak, Trzeciak.
Luxembourg: Koch; Ferron, Birsens, Funck, Strasser, Holtz (Afrika 69), Theis (Deville F 46), Saibene, Cardoni, Deville L, Christophe (Thill 63).
Referee: Pregia (Albania).

Bourgas, 14 October 1998, 12,000

Bulgaria (0) 0

Sweden (0) 1 *(Larsson 62)*

Bulgaria: Zdravkov; Zagorcic, Yordanov, Kirilov (Parushev 17), Naidenov (Ivanov G 69), Iliev (Bachev 61), Yankov, Petkov M, Petkov I, Stoichkov, Hristov.
Sweden: Hedman; Nilsson, Andersson P, Bjorklund, Lucic (Sundgren 76), Ljungberg, Mild, Mjallby, Schwarz, Larsson (Erlingmark 88), Aslund (Blomqvist 71).
Referee: Heynemann (Germany).

Luxembourg, 14 October 1998, 8000

Luxembourg (0) 0

England (2) 3 *(Owen 19, Shearer 40 (pen), Southgate 90)*

Luxembourg: Koch; Ferron, Deville L, Funck, Deville F, Theis (Holtz 62), Saibene, Strasser, Posing, Cardoni, Christophe.
England: Seaman; Anderton (Lee 64), Neville P, Southgate, Ferdinand, Campbell, Beckham, Batty, Shearer, Owen, Scholes (Wright 76).
Referee: Vorgias (Greece).

Wembley, 27 March 1999, 73,836

England (2) 3 *(Scholes 11, 21, 70)*

Poland (1) 1 *(Brzeczek 29)*

England: Seaman; Neville G, Le Saux, Sherwood, Keown, Campbell, Beckham (Neville P 77), Scholes (Redknapp 83), Shearer, Cole, McManaman (Parlour 69).
Poland: Matysek; Hajto, Zielinski, Lapinski, Ratajczyk, Swierczewski (Klos 46), Bak, Brzeczek, Siadaczka (Kowalczyk 87), Iwan, Trzeciak (Juskowiak 83).
Referee: Pereira (Portugal).

Gothenburg, 27 March 1999, 37,728

Sweden (1) 2 *(Mjallby 34, Larsson 87)*

Luxembourg (0) 0

Sweden: Hedman; Kamark (Lucic 68), Andersson P, Bjorklund, Sundgren, Schwarz, Alexandersson, Mjallby, Ljungberg (Andersson D 79), Larsson, Andersson K.
Luxembourg: Felgen; Ferron, Funck, Birsens, Strasser, Theis (Holtz 70), Vanek, Saibene (Deville F 89), Cardoni, Deville L, Christophe (Zaritski 81).
Referee: Melnitjuk (Ukraine).

Luxembourg, 31 March 1999, 3004

Luxembourg (0) 0

Bulgaria (2) 2 *(Stoichkov 18, Yordanov 38)*

Luxembourg: Felgen; Ferron (Holtz 75), Vanek, Strasser, Deville L, Saibene, Birsens, Theis (Deville F 88), Posing (Zaritski 46), Cardoni, Christophe.
Bulgaria: Zdravkov; Kishishev, Yankov, Stoianov (Petkov I 48), Petkov M, Markov, Yordanov, Petrov, Iliev, Yovov (Ivanov G 79), Stoichkov (Todorov 71).
Referee: Mitrovic (Slovakia).

Chorzow, 31 March 1999, 32,000

Poland (0) 0

Sweden (1) 1 *(Ljungberg 36)*

Poland: Sidorczuk; Waldoch, Lapinski, Zielinski, Siadaczka (Adamczuk 82), Iwan, Michalski (Bak 87), Brzeczek, Majak (Kowalczyk 70), Juskowiak, Trzeciak.
Sweden: Hedman; Kamark, Andersson P, Bjorklund, Lucic, Mild (Alexandersson 72), Schwarz, Mjallby, Ljungberg, Larsson (Pettersson 89), Andersson K.
Referee: Merk (Germany).

Warsaw, 4 June 1999, 8000

Poland (1) 2 *(Hajto 16, Iwan 62)*

Bulgaria (0) 0

Poland: Matysek; Waldoch, Lapinski, Zielinski, Hajto (Majak 80), Nowak (Brzeczek 73), Michalski, Iwan, Siadaczka, Wichniarek (Frankowski 64), Trzeciak.
Bulgaria: Ivankov; Kirilov, Zagorcic, Markov, Kishishev, Petrov, Stoilov, Petkov M, Petkov I (Iliev 80), Stoichkov (Ivanov G 63), Yovov (Bachev 46).
Referee: Braschi (Italy).

Wembley, 5 June 1999, 75,824

England (0) 0

Sweden (0) 0

England: Seaman; Neville P, Le Saux (Gray 46), Batty, Keown (Ferdinand R 35), Campbell, Beckham (Parlour 76), Sherwood, Shearer, Cole, Scholes.
Sweden: Hedman; Nilsson, Kamark, Schwarz, Andersson P, Bjorklund, Mild (Alexandersson 7), Mjallby (Andersson D 82), Andersson K, Larsson (Svensson 70), Ljungberg.
Referee: Aranda (Spain).

Sofia, 9 June 1999, 22,000

Bulgaria (1) 1 *(Markov 18)*

England (1) 1 *(Shearer 15)*

Bulgaria: Ivankov; Kirilov, Stoilov, Kishishev, Zagorcic, Markov, Petrov S, Iliev (Borimirov 61), Petkov M, Stoichkov (Bachev 75), Yovov (Petrov M 46).
England: Seaman; Neville P, Gray, Southgate, Woodgate (Parlour 65), Campbell, Redknapp, Batty, Shearer, Fowler (Heskey 81), Sheringham.
Referee: Van der Ende (Holland).

Luxembourg, 9 June 1999, 2806

Luxembourg (0) 2 *(Birsens 76, Vanek 82)*

Poland (2) 3 *(Siadaczka 22, Wichniarek 45, Iwan 68)*

Luxembourg: Felgen; Vanek, Funck, Birsens, Strasser, Saibene (Alverdi 80), Theis (Schneider 46), Deville F, Cardoni, Christophe, Zaritski (Posing 65).
Poland: Matysek; Waldoch, Lapinski, Klos, Hajto (Brzeczek 65), Nowak, Michalski, Iwan, Siadaczka, Wichniarek (Majak 87), Trzeciak.
Referee: Ivanov (Russia).

Wembley, 4 September 1999, 68,772

England (5) 6 *(Shearer 12 (pen), 28, 34, McManaman 30, 44, Owen 90)*

Luxembourg (0) 0

England: Martyn; Dyer (Neville G 46), Pearce, Batty, Keown, Adams (Neville P 64), Parlour, Beckham (Owen 64), Shearer, Fowler, McManaman.
Luxembourg: Felgen; Ferron, Schauls, Birsens, Funck, Posing (Deville F 83), Vanek, Schneider (Alverdi 46), Saibene, Theis, Christophe (Zaritski 62).
Referee: Shmolik (Belarus).

Stockholm, 4 September 1999, 35,640

Sweden (0) 1 *(Alexandersson 65)*

Bulgaria (0) 0

Sweden: Hedman; Nilsson R, Andersson P, Bjorklund, Kamark, Andersson D, Mild (Svensson 83), Mjallby, Ljungberg (Alexandersson 63), Larsson, Andersson K.
Bulgaria: Ivankov; Stoilov (Gruev 89), Zagorcic (Yankov 26), Petkov I, Markov, Kirilov, Petrov, Petkov M, Todorov, Borimirov, Hristov.
Referee: Koren (Israel).

Luxembourg, 8 September 1999, 4228

Luxembourg (0) 0

Sweden (1) 1 *(Alexandersson 39)*

Luxembourg: Felgen; Funck, Birsens, Schauls, Vanek, Strasser, Saibene (Holtz 87), Schneider (Zaritski 46), Alverdi (Theis 72), Posing, Christophe.
Sweden: Hedman; Nilsson R, Andersson P, Bjorklund, Lucic, Schwarz (Andersson D 81), Mjallby, Alexandersson, Svensson (Zetterberg 46), Larsson, Andersson K.
Referee: Hanacsek (Czech Republic).

Warsaw, 8 September 1999, 17,000

Poland (0) 0

England (0) 0

Poland: Matysek; Klos (Bak 90), Waldoch, Zelinski, Hajto, Iwan, Nowak, Michalski, Siadaczka, Trzeciak (Swierzcewski P 59), Gilewicz (Juskowiak 65).
England: Martyn; Neville G (Neville P 12), Pearce, Batty, Keown, Adams, Beckham, Scholes, Shearer, Fowler (Owen 66), McManaman (Dyer 80).
Referee: Benko (Austria).

Stockholm, 9 October 1999, 35,037

Sweden (0) 2 *(Andersson K 64, Larsson 90)*

Poland (0) 0

Sweden: Hedman; Nilsson R (Sundgren 46), Andersson P, Bjorklund, Kamark, Alexandersson, Mjallby, Schwarz, Ljungberg (Mild 83), Andersson K, Larsson.
Poland: Matysek; Siadaczka, Klos, Zielinski, Waldoch, Hajto, Swierczewski (Wichniarek 89), Michalski, Czereszewski (Nowak 73), Juskowiak (Kryszałowicz 81), Trzeciak.
Referee: Meier (Switzerland).

Sofia, 10 October 1999, 4000

Bulgaria (1) 3 *(Borimirov 40, Petkov I 68, Hristov R 78)*

Luxembourg (0) 0

Bulgaria: Zdravkov; Zagorcic (Ivanov B 84), Stoilov, Petkov I, Yordanov, Borimirov, Markov, Petrov, Bachev (Hristov R 51), Hristov M (Todorov 64), Alexandrov.
Luxembourg: Felgen; Vanek, Schauls, Birsens, Strasser, Alverdi (Theis 71), Saibene, Posing (Deville 59), Cardoni (Holtz 85), Zaritski, Christophe.
Referee: Gadosi (Slovenia).

Group 5 – Final Table	*P*	*W*	*D*	*L*	*F*	*A*	*Pts*
Sweden	8	7	1	0	10	1	22
England	8	3	4	1	14	4	13
Poland	8	4	1	3	12	8	13
Bulgaria	8	2	2	4	6	8	8
Luxembourg	8	0	0	8	2	23	0

GROUP 6

Vienna, 5 September 1998, 20,000

Austria (1) 1 *(Reinmayr 7)*

Israel (0) 1 *(Nimni 68 (pen))*

Austria: Wohlfahrt; Schottel (Hiden 73), Feiersinger, Pfeffer, Cerny (Stoger 74), Kuhbauer, Mahlich, Reinmayr, Amerhauser, Vastic, Haas (Mayrleb 73).
Israel: Cohen; Harazi A, Shelach (Nimni 46), Ben Shimon, Amsalem, Abuksis (Mizrahi A 46), Berkovic, Revivo, Benado, Harazi R (Ghrayib 61), Badir.
Referee: Frisk (Sweden).

Larnaca, 5 September 1998, 3500

Cyprus (1) 3 *(Engomitis 44, Gogic 48, Spoljaric 77)*

Spain (0) 2 *(Raul 72, Morientes 85)*

Cyprus: Panayiotou N; Costa, Ioannou D (Ioakim 84), Charalambous M, Pittas, Melanarkitis, Spoljaric, Christodolou M, Engomitis, Gogic (Agathocleous 61), Malekos (Pounas 55).
Spain: Canizares; Michel Salgado, Nadal (Amor 65), Alkorta, Sergi, Etxeberria J (Ezquerro 59), Hierro, Raul, Luis Enrique, Alfonso (Kiko 39), Morientes.
Referee: Guseinov (Russia).

Larnaca, 10 October 1998, 10,000

Cyprus (0) 0

Austria (0) 3 *(Cerny 53, 61, Reinmayr 74)*

Cyprus: Panayiotou N; Engomitis, Ioannou D, Costa, Charalambous M, Pittas (Georgiou 67), Spoljaric, Melanarkitis (Constandinou M 68), Christodolou M, Agathocleous (Okkas 46), Gogic.
Austria: Wohlfahrt; Hiden, Schottel, Pfeffer, Cerny, Kuhbauer, Mahlich, Reinmayr (Stoger 78), Wetl, Vastic (Glieder 82), Haas (Mayrleb 78).
Referee: Meese (Belgium).

Serravalle, 10 October 1998, 872

San Marino (0) 0

Israel (3) 5 *(Revivo 16, Nimni 19, Mizrahi A 31, 64, Ghrayib 83)*

San Marino: Gasperoni F; Gennari, Guerra, Valentini M, Bacciocchi S (Valentini V 55), Marani, Montagna (Gualtieri 78), Muccioli, Della Valle (Francini 67), Matteoni, Selva A.
Israel: Cohen; Harazi A, Ben Shimon, Telasnikov, Badir, Benado (Shelach 68), Nimni (Banin 59), Ghrayib, Revivo, Berkovic (Shitrit 74), Mizrahi A.
Referee: Khudiev (Azerbaijan).

Tel Aviv, 14 October 1998, 42,000

Israel (0) 1 *(Hazan 63)*

Spain (0) 2 *(Hierro 65, Etxeberria J 77)*

Israel: Cohen; Harazi A, Ben Shimon, Benado, Hazan (Banin 75), Badir, Telasnikov (Mizrahi A 59), Ghrayib, Nimni, Revivo, Berkovic.
Spain: Canizares; Michel Salgado, Hierro, Alkorta, Aranzabal, Luis Enrique, Engonga, Alkiza, De Pedro (Etxeberria J 72), Kiko (Urzaiz 88), Raul (Vales 90).
Referee: Elleray (England).

Serravalle, 14 October 1998, 1000

San Marino (0) 1 *(Selva A 80 (pen))*

Austria (0) 4 *(Vastic 58, Mayrleb 63, Hiden 68, Glieder 76)*

San Marino: Gasperoni F; Gennari, Guerra, Valentini M (Della Valle 80), Bacciocchi S, Marani, Muccioli, Francini (Valentini V 69), Ugolini (Montagna 62), Matteoni, Selva A.
Austria: Wohlfahrt; Hiden, Schottel, Pfeffer, Cerny, Kuhbauer, Heraf, Reinmayr (Mayrleb 46), Wetl, Vastic (Stoger 70), Haas (Glieder 66).
Referee: Onufer (Ukraine).

Serravalle, 18 November 1998, 600

San Marino (0) 0

Cyprus (1) 1 *(Spoljaric 41)*

San Marino: Gasperoni F; Gennari, Valentini M, Guerra, Valentini V, Marani, Gasperoni B, Muccioli (Mularoni 83), Matteoni (Francini 75), Montagna (Bacchiocchi N 67), Ugolini.
Cyprus: Panayiotou N; Pittas, Panayiotou P, Charalambous M, Sophocleous, Engomitis, Melanarkitis, Spoljaric, Agathocleous (Constandinou M 73), Malekos (Ioannou Y 73), Gogic (Okkas 86).
Referee: McDermott (Republic of Ireland).

Nicosia, 10 February 1999, 3000

Cyprus (3) 4 *(Melanarkitis 18, Constantinou M 32, 45, Christodoulou M 88)*

San Marino (0) 0

Cyprus: Panayiotou N; Theodotou, Christodoulou M, Ioakim, Charalambous M, Pittas, Melanarkitis, Spoljaric, Gogic (Ioannou Y 80), Constantinou M (Okkas 80), Malekos (Aristocleous 89).
San Marino: Gasperoni F; Gennari, Marani (Vannucci 84), Gobbi, Valentini V, Guerra, Zonzini, Della Valle (Manzaroli 70), Ugolini (Bacciocchi N 46), Mularoni, Selva A.

Valencia, 27 March 1999, 40,000

Spain (5) 9 *(Raul 5, 17, 47, 74, Urzaiz 30, 44, Hierro 35 (pen), Wetl 76 (og), Fran 84)*

Austria (0) 0

Spain: Canizares; Michel Salgado, Hierro, Marcelino, Sergi, Etxeberria J (Dani 84), Guardiola, Valeron (Mendieta 71), Fran, Raul, Urzaiz (Munitis 61).
Austria: Wohlfahrt; Schottel, Feiersinger (Kogler 54), Pfeffer, Cerny, Mahlich, Neukirchner, Prosenik (Reinmayr 58), Wetl, Herzog, Haas (Mayrleb 69).
Referee: Veissiere (France).

Tel Aviv, 28 March 1999, 30,000

Israel (1) 3 *(Banin 11, Mizrahi A 47, 53)*

Cyprus (0) 0

Israel: Davidovich; Harazi A, Ghrayib, Shelach, Badir (Talker 46), Banin, Benado, Berkovic, Revivo (Tikva 85), Harazi R (Mizrahi A 46), Nimni.
Cyprus: Panayiotou N; Theodotou, Pittas, Ioannou D, Charalambous M, Constandinou M (Okkas 65), Melanarkitis, Spoljaric (Agathocleous 79), Malekos (Nicolaou 46), Sophocleous, Christodolou M.
Referee: Lica (Romania).

Serravalle, 31 March 1999, 1000

San Marino (0) 0

Spain (2) 6 *(Fran 20, Raul 45, 59, 66, Urzaiz 49, Etxeberria J 72)*

San Marino: Gasperoni F; Gennari, Marani, Valentini V, Zonzini, Valentini M, Manzaroli, Gasperoni B (Muccioli 75), Gobbi (Della Balda 51), Selva A, Montagna (Gualtieri 60).
Spain: Canizares; Michel Salgado, Marcelino, Paco, Sergi, Etxeberria J, Guardiola (Engonga 68), Valeron (Helguera 78), Fran, Raul, Urzaiz (Dani 61).
Referee: Maric (Croatia).

Graz, 28 April 1999, 15,000

Austria (3) 7 *(Mayrleb 24, 53, Vastic 42, 44, 84, Amerhauser 71, Herzog 82 (pen))*

San Marino (0) 0

Austria: Wohlfahrt; Winklhofer (Rohseano 80), Feiersinger, Neukirchner, Cerny (Kitzbichler 71), Schopp (Glieder 71), Herzog, Prosenik, Amerhauser, Mayrleb, Vastic.
San Marino: Gasperoni F; Gennari (Bacciocchi S 46), Della Balda, Guerra, Gobbi, Vannucci, Gasperoni B (Manzaroli 15), Zonzini, Muccioli, Selva A, Montagna (Selva R 78).
Referee: Vassaros (Greece).

Villarreal, 5 June 1999, 16,000

Spain (4) 9 *(Hierro 8 (pen), Luis Enrique 22, 67, 71, Etxeberria J 25, 45, Raul 56, Gennari 85 (og), Mendieta 90)*

San Marino (0) 0

Spain: Canizares; Michel Salgado (Munitis 60), Marcelino, Hierro, Aranzabal, Etxeberria J, Guardiola, Guerrero (Mendieta 74), Luis Enrique, Raul (Urzaiz 60), Morientes.
San Marino: Gasperoni F; Gennari (Vannucci 90), Marani, Della Balda, Gobbi, Guerra, Bacciocchi N, Della Valle, Zonzini, Manzaroli (Valentini V 75), Montagna (Ugolini 58).
Referee: Perry (Republic of Ireland).

Tel Aviv, 6 June 1999, 43,000

Israel (2) 5 *(Berkovic 26, 47, Revivo 45, Mizrahi A 54, Ghrayib 75)*

Austria (0) 0

Israel: Davidovich; Shelach, Benado, Harazi A, Ghrayib, Banin, Abuksis (Tal 82), Hazan, Mizrahi A (Tikva 78), Berkovic (Sivilia 77), Revivo.
Austria: Wohlfahrt; Winklhofer, Barisic, Kogler, Cerny, Mahlich, Herzog, Neukirchner, Amerhauser (Prosenik 46), Mayrleb (Haas 67), Vastic (Glieder 57).
Referee: Michel (Slovakia).

Vienna, 4 September 1999, 27,000

Austria (0) 1 *(Hierro 50 (og))*

Spain (1) 3 *(Raul 23, Hierro 54, Luis Enrique 89)*

Austria: Manninger; Streiter, Winklhofer, Hatz, Ibertsberger, Kuhbauer, Vastic, Mahlich (Schopp 60), Kirchler (Weissenberger 67), Cerny, Mayrleb.
Spain: Canizares; Michel Salgado, Hierro, Paco, Sergi, Etxeberria J (Mendieta 81), Valeron (Engonga 72), Guardiola, Luis Enrique, Morientes (Guerrero 88), Raul.
Referee: Piraux (Belgium).

Limassol, 5 September 1999, 16,000

Cyprus (1) 3 *(Engomitis 27, Spoljaric 53, 86 (pen))*

Israel (1) 2 *(Badir 31, Benayoun 82)*

Cyprus: Panayiotou; Engomitis, Pittas, Kostakis, Charalambous, Melanarkitis, Papavassiliou (Christodolou M 64), Kaiafas (Aristocleous 80), Spoljaric, Gogic (Constantinou 72), Okkas.
Israel: Davidovich; Hazan, Harazi A, Benado, Shelach (Civilia 65), Ghrayib, Abuksis (Benayoun 55), Banin, Berkovic (Badir 18), Revivo, Mizrahi A.
Referee: Barber (England).

Tel Aviv, 8 September 1999, 20,000

Israel (3) 8 *(Benayoun 25, 46, 71, Revivo 40, 69, Mizrahi A 38, Sivilia 84, Abuksis 90)*

San Marino (0) 0

Israel: Davidovich; Talkar, Harazi A, Benado (Halfon 66), Amsalem, Telesnikov, Hazan, Tikva (Abuksis 62), Benayoun, Revivo, Mizrahi A (Sivilia 46).
San Marino: Gasperoni F; Gennari, Tomassoni, Bacciocchi S, Della Balda, Pelliccioni, Bacciocchi N (Salva R 59), Gasperoni B, Salva A, Zonzini (Della Valle 75), Montagna (De Luigi 80).
Referee: Kaplan (Turkey).

Badajoz, 8 September 1999, 15,000

Spain (5) 8 *(Urzaiz 19, 25, 37, Guerrero 33, 42, 57, Cesar 82, Hierro 88)*

Cyprus (0) 0

Spain: Canizares (Toni 77); Michel Salgado, Cesar, Hierro, Aranzabal, Etxeberria J (Munitis 46), Guardiola, Guerrero, Luis Enrique (Mendieta 61), Raul, Urzaiz.
Cyprus: Panayiotou; Costa, Nicolaou (Aristocleous 46), Louka, Pittas (Theodotou 46), Melanarkitis, Engomitis, Christodoulou M, Papavassiliou, Gogic (Constandinou 88), Okkas.
Referee: Trentalange (Italy).

Vienna, 10 October 1999, 10,000

Austria (2) 3 *(Glieder 5, Vastic 23, Herzog 81)*

Cyprus (0) 1 *(Costa 64)*

Austria: Manninger; Winklhofer, Neukirchner (Herzog 46), Vastic, Ibertsberger, Cerny (Kauz 75), Kirchler, Kuhbauer, Mayrleb, Glieder, Weissenberger (Wimmer 83).
Cyprus: Panayiotou N; Costa, Christodolou M, Kaiafas, Charalambous M, Engomitis, Spoljaric, Melanarkitis (Demetriou 82), Alexandrou, Gogic (Agathocleous 26), Okkas (Theodotou 46).
Referee: Bazzoli (Italy).

Albacete, 10 October 1999, 12,000

Spain (2) 3 *(Morientes 30, Cesar 37, Raul 51)*

Israel (0) 0

Spain: Toni; Michel Salgado, Hierro (Cesar 22), Paco, Sergi, Etxeberria J, Guardiola, Guerrero (Mendieta 70), Luis Enrique, Morientes (Urzaiz 75), Raul.
Israel: Awat; Gershon, Amsalem, Shelah, Benado (Halfon 49), Hazan (Telesnikov 80), Banin, Tal, Berkovic (Benayoun 67), Revivo, Turgeman.
Referee: Krug (Germany).

Group 6 – Final Table	*P*	*W*	*D*	*L*	*F*	*A*	*Pts*
Spain	8	7	0	1	42	5	21
Israel	8	4	1	3	25	9	13
Austria	8	4	1	3	19	20	13
Cyprus	8	4	0	4	12	21	12
San Marino	8	0	0	8	1	44	0

GROUP 7

Bucharest, 2 September 1998, 6000

Romania (4) 7 *(Gheorge Popescu 18, Munteanu C 30, Ilie A 32, 45, 51, Moldovan 56, Haas 60 (og))*

Liechtenstein (0) 0

Romania: Stelea (Lobont 80); Petrescu, Batranu, Gheorge Popescu, Contra, Petre, Galca, Munteanu C (Sabau 72), Munteanu D, Moldovan, Ilie A (Mihalcea 69).
Liechtenstein: Oehry M; Hefti, Hanselmann, Michael Stocklasa, Telser M (Ender 89), Ritter, Zech, Lingg (Buchel 62), Beck T, Oehri R, Haas (Martin Stocklasa 63).
Referee: Prolic (Bosnia).

Kosice, 5 September 1998, 3243

Slovakia (3) 3 *(Fabus 17, Dubovsky 26 (pen), Moravcik 40)*

Azerbaijan (0) 0

Slovakia: Vencel; Varga, Tomaschek, Tittel, Spilar, Kinder, Sovic, Moravcik, Fabus (Jancula 62), Majoros (Ujlaky 46), Dubovsky (Zvara 62).
Azerbaijan: Kramarenko; Gaisumov, Abusev, Jabarov, Agayev, Lichkin (Rzayev 66), Kasumov (Guseynov 79), Asadov, Sirkhaev, Suleimanov (Kuliyev 46), Kurbanov K.
Referee: Snoddy (Northern Ireland).

Budapest, 6 September 1998, 50,000

Hungary (1) 1 *(Horvath 32)*

Portugal (0) 3 *(Sa Pinto 56, 76, Rui Costa 84)*

Hungary: Kiraly; Feher C (Korsos 78), Lakos, Hrutka, Matyus, Lisztes (Dardai 46), Halmai, Illes, Dombi (Kovacs Z 78), Horvath, Hamar.
Portugal: Vitor Baia; Secretario, Jorge Costa, Paulo Madeira, Dimas, Figo, Paulo Bento, Rui Costa, Paulinho Santos, Joao Pinto, Sa Pinto.
Referee: Meier (Switzerland).

Baku, 10 October 1998, 10,000

Azerbaijan (0) 0

Hungary (0) 4 *(Dardai 58, Illes 85 (pen), Pisont 87, Feher M 90)*

Azerbaijan: Kramarenko (Jidkov 59); Gaisumov, Agayev, Abusev, Kerimov, Asadov (Mamedov I 51), Lichkin, Sirkhaev, Rzayev, Kambarov (Kasumov 46), Kurbanov K.
Hungary: Kiraly; Sebok V (Korsos 65), Feher C, Hrutka, Matyus, Dardai, Pisont, Illes, Lisztes (Dombi 75), Horvath (Feher M 6), Hamar.
Referee: Bre (France).

Vaduz, 10 October 1998, 1900

Liechtenstein (0) 0

Slovakia (3) 4 *(Sovic 3, Dubovsky 13, Tomaschek 36, 61)*

Liechtenstein: Oehry M; Ritter, Hanselmann, Zech, Hefti (Lingg 76), Haas (Martin Stocklasa 33), Oehri R (Ospelt J 46), Hasler, Michael Stocklasa, Frick M, Telser M.
Slovakia: Vencel; Varga (Timko 65), Tittel, Spilar, Sovic, Tomaschek, Moravcik, Dubovsky, Kinder (Kozak 30), Majoros, Fabus (Jancula 61).
Referee: Antonov (Moldova).

Porto, 10 October 1998, 40,000

Portugal (0) 0

Romania (0) 1 *(Munteanu D 90)*

Portugal: Vitor Baia; Abel Xavier (Dani 85), Jorge Costa, Fernando Couto, Dimas, Figo, Paulo Bento (Conceicao 70), Rui Costa, Paulinho Santos, Joao Pinto (Nuno Gomes 79), Sa Pinto.
Romania: Stelea; Petrescu (Contra 83), Filipescu, Gheorge Popescu, Ciobotariu, Petre, Munteanu C (Lupescu 61), Galca, Munteanu D, Rosu, Moldovan (Mihalcea 89).
Referee: Krug (Germany).

Budapest, 14 October 1998, 40,000

Hungary (0) 1 *(Hrutka 82)*

Romania (0) 1 *(Moldovan 51)*

Hungary: Kiraly; Feher C, Sebok V, Hrutka, Matyus, Pisont, Dardai, Illes, Egressy (Lisztes 78), Feher M (Hamori 75), Hamar (Toth 70).
Romania: Stelea; Petrescu, Filipescu, Georghe Popescu, Ciobotariu, Petre (Serban 70), Galca, Lupescu, Munteanu D, Moldovan (Mihalcea 85), Craioveanu (Munteanu C 75).
Referee: Nielsen (Denmark).

Vaduz, 14 October 1998, 1900

Liechtenstein (0) 2 *(Frick M 47 (pen), Telser M 49)*

Azerbaijan (0) 1 *(Kurbanov K 59)*

Liechtenstein: Jehle; Ritter, Zech, Hasler, Martin Stocklasa, Bicker (Ospelt J 67), Lingg, Michael Stocklasa, Beck T (Buchel 74), Frick M, Telser M.
Azerbaijan: Jidkov; Yadullayev, Gaisumov, Agayev, Kerimov, Abusev (Kuliyev 76), KurbanovM (Suleimanov 25), Rzayev, Kambarov (Mamedov I 61), Kurbanov K, Sirkhaev.
Referee: Barr (N Ireland).

Bratislava, 14 October 1998, 22,059

Slovakia (0) 0

Portugal (2) 3 *(Joao Pinto 16, 31, Abel Xavier 72)*

Slovakia: Vencel; Spilar, Kinder (Kozak 46), Tittel, Varga, Sovic (Pinte 82), Tomaschek, Fabus (Nemeth S 57), Moravcik, Majoros, Dubovsky.
Portugal: Vitor Baia; Abel Xavier, Jorge Costa, Fernando Couto, Dimas, Figo (Capucho 89), Paulo Bento, Rui Costa (Da Costa 67), Paulinho Santos, Joao Pinto (Conceicao 46), Sa Pinto.
Referee: Sarvan (Turkey).

Guimaraes, 26 March 1999, 20,000

Portugal (2) 7 *(Sa Pinto 28, Joao Pinto 36, 77, Paulo Madeira 67, Conceicao 75, Pauleta 82, 83)*

Azerbaijan (0) 0

Portugal: Vitor Baia (Espinha 83); Secretario, Paulo Madeira, Fernando Couto, Dimas, Paulo Sousa, Rui Costa (Pedro Barbosa 83), Conceicao, Figo (Pauleta 74), Sa Pinto, Joao Pinto.
Azerbaijan: Kramarenko; Agayev, Asadov, Akhmedov, Stukas, Abusev, Kambarov (Vasiliev 72), Musayev (Rzayev 69), Sirkhaev, Lichkin, Kurbanov K.
Referee: Granat (Poland).

Budapest, 27 March 1999, 9534

Hungary (3) 5 *(Sebok J 17, Sebok V 33, 41, 86, Illes 74)*

Liechtenstein (0) 0

Hungary: Kiraly; Hrutka (Somogyi 79), Sebok V, Korsos, Matyus, Halmai, Sebok J (Dombi 71), Pisont, Illes, Feher M, Toth (Hamar 76).
Liechtenstein: Jehle; Hanselmann (Hefti 46), Martin Stocklasa, Lingg, Ritter, Michael Stocklasa, Wohlwend, Frick M, Hasler, Telser M, Beck M (Ospelt J 78).
Referee: Kapitanis (Cyprus).

Bucharest, 27 March 1999, 15,000

Romania (0) 0

Slovakia (0) 0

Romania: Stelea; Petrescu, Batranu, Gheorge Popescu, Rosu, Petre, Galca, Munteanu C (Lupescu 66), Munteanu D, Moldovan (Craioveanu 64), Ilie A.
Slovakia: Konig; Varga, Zeman, Karhan, Kratochvil, Zatek (Dzurik 75), Tomaschek, Balis, Labant, Dubovsky (Suchancok 78), Majoros (Slicho 62).
Referee: Barber (England).

Baku, 31 March 1999, 25,000

Azerbaijan (0) 0

Romania (0) 1 *(Petre 49)*

Azerbaijan: Magomedov; Kerimov, Poshekhontsev, Asadov, Agayev (Kuliyev 75), Tagizade (Kambarov 69), Kurbanov M (Rzayev 67), Akhmedov, Lichkin, Sirkhaev, Kurbanov K.
Romania: Lobont; Contra, Filipescu, Ciobotariu, Munteanu D, Petre, Galca, Lupescu, Rosu (Florea 75), Moldovan, Craioveanu (Mihalcea 89).
Referee: Luinge (Holland).

Vaduz, 31 March 1999, 3000

Liechtenstein (0) 0

Portugal (1) 5 *(Rui Costa 16 (pen), 79, Figo 49, Paulo Madeira 54, 60)*

Liechtenstein: Jehle; Lingg, Hasler, Hanselmann (Ospelt J 84), Martin Stocklasa, Ritter, Telser M, Frick C, Michael Stocklasa (Beck M 66), Wohlwend (Burgmaier 83), Frick M.
Portugal: Vitor Baia; Secretario, Paulo Madeira, Fernando Couto, Dimas, Conceicao (Capucho 88), Paulo Sousa, Rui Costa, Figo, Sa Pinto (Pauleta 61), Joao Pinto (Nuno Gomes 75).
Referee: Orrason (Iceland).

Bratislava, 31 March 1999, 19,400

Slovakia (0) 0

Hungary (0) 0

Slovakia: Konig; Kratochvil, Zeman (Dzurik 13), Varga, Karhan, Balis, Tomaschek, Dubovsky, Zatek (Hrncar 79), Majoros, Pinte (Slicho 83).
Hungary: Kiraly; Korsos, Sebok V, Hrutka, Matyus, Pisont, Halmai, Illes, Sebok J (Dombi 56), Feher M (Hamar 64), Toth.
Referee: Colombo (France).

Bucharest, 5 June 1999, 23,000

Romania (2) 2 *(Ilie A 2, Munteanu D 15)*

Hungary (0) 0

Romania: Lobont; Petrescu, Filipescu, Gheorge Popescu, Nanu, Petre, Hagi (Lupescu 46), Galca, Munteanu D, Moldovan (Ganea 64), Ilie A (Craioveanu 86).
Hungary: Kiraly; Sebok V, Hrutka, Matyus, Korsos, Dardai, Halmai, Illes (Preisinger 81), Egressy, Sebok J (Herczeg 76), Feher M (Pisont 46).
Referee: Pedersen (Norway).

Baku, 5 June 1999, 8500

Azerbaijan (2) 4 *(Kurbanov K 16, Lichkin 42, Tagizade 60, Isaiev 73)*

Liechtenstein (0) 0

Azerbaijan: Kramarenko; Agayev, Yadullayev, Akhmedov, Kerimov, Kurbanov M, Tagizade (Isaiev 68), Vasiliev (Khankishiev 61), Sirkhaev, Lichkin (Stukas 74), Kurbanov K.
Liechtenstein: Jehle; Lingg, Hasler, Zech, Martin Stocklasa, Ritter, Telser M, Michael Stocklasa (Wohlwend 74), Frick C, Bicker (Beck M 59), Benz (Beck T 46).
Referee: Stadskaar (Denmark).

Lisbon, 5 June 1999, 25,000

Portugal (0) 1 *(Capucho 62)*

Slovakia (0) 0

Portugal: Vitor Baia; Abel Xavier (Conceicao 31), Fernando Couto, Paulo Madeira, Dimas, Paulo Sousa, Paulo Bento, Rui Costa, Figo (Barbosa 89), Joao Pinto (Capucho 61), Sa Pinto.
Slovakia: Konig; Varga, Timko, Karhan, Kratochvil, Zvara (Valachovic 30), Tomaschek, Pinte (Slicho 64), Labant, Dubovsky, Majoros (Kozuch 83).
Referee: Larsen (Denmark).

Gyor, 9 June 1999, 16,500

Hungary (0) 0

Slovakia (0) 1 *(Fabus 53)*

Hungary: Kiraly; Sebok V, Hrutka, Matyus, Korsos, Dardai, Halmai (Pisont 73), Illes, Egressy (Dombi 60), Sebok J, Somogyi (Preisinger 78).
Slovakia: Konig; Varga, Timko, Karhan, Kratochvil, Zvara (Dzurik 81), Valachovic, Pinte, Labant, Nemeth P, Fabus.
Referee: Vega (Spain).

Coimbra, 9 June 1999, 25,000

Portugal (3) 8 *(Sa Pinto 28, 44, Joao Pinto 40, 59, 67, Ritter 52 (og), Rui Costa 80, 90 (pen))*

Liechtenstein (0) 0

Portugal: Vitor Baia; Secretario (Capucho 14), Fernando Couto, Paulo Madeira, Dimas, Paulo Sousa (Barbosa 63), Conceicao, Rui Costa, Figo, Joao Pinto, Sa Pinto.
Liechtenstein: Jehle; Zech, Hasler, Ospelt J, Ritter, Telser D (Lingg 53), Michael Stocklasa (Burgmaier 67), Wohlwend, Telser M (Buchel 73), Bicker, Beck T.
Referee: Drabek (Austria).

Bucharest, 9 June 1999, 8000

Romania (2) 4 *(Ganea 35, Munteanu D 44 (pen), Vladoiu 50, Rosu 90)*

Azerbaijan (0) 0

Romania: Lobont; Petrescu, Filipescu, Gheorge Popescu, Nanu, Petre (Moldovan 68), Galca, Lupescu, Munteanu D, Ganea (Craioveanu 59), Vladoiu (Rosu 79).
Azerbaijan: Kramarenko; Agayev (Getman 71), Jadullayev, Akhmedov, Lichkin (Vasiliev 82), Kerimov, Kurbanov M (Musayev 59), Tagizade, Kurbanov K, Poshekhontsev, Sirkhaev.
Referee: Siric (Croatia).

Baku, 4 September 1999, 8000

Azerbaijan (0) 1 *(Tagizade 51)*

Portugal (0) 1 *(Figo 90)*

Azerbaijan: Kramarenko; Poshekhontsev, Kuliev, Akhmedov, Agayev, Niftaliev, Getman, Tagizade, Musayev (Kurbanov M 58), Vasiliev (Gambarov 54), Lichkin (Stukas 90).
Portugal: Vitor Baia; Secretario, Fernando Couto, Paulo Madeira, Dimas, Paulo Bento (Pauleta 29), Paulo Sousa (Capucho 68), Rui Costa, Figo, Joao Pinto, Sa Pinto (Conceicao 46).
Referee: Gallagher (England).

Vaduz, 4 September 1999, 1700

Liechtenstein (0) 0

Hungary (0) 0

Liechtenstein: Jehle; Zech, Ospelt J, Hasler, Hefti, Gigon, Martin Stocklasa, Telser (Ritter 66), Michael Stocklasa, Frick M (Beck M 90), Beck T (Bicker 83).
Hungary: Kiraly; Korsos, Sebok V, Halmai, Matyus, Dardai, Illes, Feher M (Lendvai 46), Dombi (Sowoumni 60), Horvath (Herczeg 76), Egressy.
Referee: Kaldma (Estonia).

Bratislava, 4 September 1999, 8143

Slovakia (1) 1 *(Labant 22)*

Romania (2) 5 *(Ilie A 6, Hagi 30, Ciobotariu 65, Moldovan 88, 90)*

Slovakia: Konig; Kratochvil (Hrabal 74), Valachovic, Varga, Karhan, Balis (Jancula 68), Nemeth P, Janocko, Labant, Nemeth S, Fabus (Uljaky 81).
Romania: Stelea; Petrescu, Gheorge Popescu, Ciobotariu, Filipescu, Sabau (Stinga 83), Galca, Hagi (Lupescu 75), Munteanu D, Ganea (Moldovan 58), Ilie A.
Referee: Cesari (Italy).

Bucharest, 8 September 1999, 23,000

Romania (1) 1 *(Ilie A 37)*

Portugal (1) 1 *(Figo 45)*

Romania: Stelea; Petrescu (Nanu 46), Gheorge Popescu, Filipescu, Ciobotariu, Sabau, Galca, Hagi, Munteanu D, Moldovan (Lupescu 69), Ilie A (Ganea 85).
Portugal: Vitor Baia; Rui Bento, Fernando Couto, Paulo Madeira, Dimas, Paulo Bento, Paulo Sousa (Conceicao 69), Rui Costa, Figo, Joao Pinto (Pauleta 80), Sa Pinto.
Referee: Strampe (Germany).

Dudnica, 8 September 1999, 3052

Slovakia (1) 2 *(Nemeth S 4, Karhan 56)*

Liechtenstein (0) 0

Slovakia: Susko; Valachovic, Varga, Karhan, Balis, Dzurik, Janocko (Hrabal 41), Ujlaky, Labant, Nemeth S (Kozuch 76), Fabus (Nemeth P 61).
Liechtenstein: Jehle; Ospelt J, Ritter, Martin Stocklasa, Zech, Gigon (Wohlwend 57), Hasler, Telser, Michael Stocklasa (Buchel 12) (Beck M 57), Frick M, Beck T.
Referee: Georgiou (Cyprus).

Budapest, 8 September 1999, 3500

Hungary (1) 3 *(Sebok V 28, Egressy 51, Sowunmi 55)*

Azerbaijan (0) 0

Hungary: Kiraly; Korsos, Sebok V, Hrutka, Matyus, Lendvai, Halmai, Illes, Herczeg (Horvath 74), Sowunmi (Fuzi 89), Egressy.
Azerbaijan: Gassan; Poshekhontsev, Kerimov (Gambarov 61), Getman, Niftialiev, Kuliyev, Asadov, Musayev, Yadullayev, Lichkin (Stukas 68), Vasiliev (Ismailov 90).
Referee: Lazarevski (Macedonia).

Baku, 9 October 1999, 8000

Azerbaijan (0) 0

Slovakia (0) 1 *(Labant 70)*

Azerbaijan: Kramarenko; Agayev (Kerimov 80), Poshekhontsev, Akhmedov, Isayev (Ismailov 56), Getman, Yadullayev, Gambarov (Lichkin 46), Vasiliev, Musayev, Niftalijev.
Slovakia: Susko; Kozak, Sucanchak, Kratochvil, Varga, Labant (Kozuch 84), Timko, Karhan (Zeman 86), Janocko (Pinter 90), Nemeth S, Fabus.
Referee: Vassaras (Greece).

Vaduz, 9 October 1999, 2900

Liechtenstein (0) 0

Romania (1) 3 *(Rosu 26, Ganea 65, 73)*

Liechtenstein: Jehle; Ospelt J, Martin Stocklasa, Hefti, Zech, Ritter, Frick C (Wohlwend 89), Frick M, Telser M (Bicker 69), Beck M, Beck T.
Romania: Stelea; Petrescu, Gheorge Popescu, Ciobotariu, Nanu, Petre, Galca (Lupescu 68), Hagi (Stinga 70), Rosu, Moldovan (Ganea 62), Ilie A.
Referee: Butenko (Russia).

Lisbon, 9 October 1999, 65,000

Portugal (2) 3 *(Rui Costa 15, Joao Pinto 16, Abel Xavier 58)*

Hungary (0) 0

Portugal: Vitor Baia; Secretario (Abel Xavier 46), Paulo Madeira, Jorge Costa, Dimas, Figo, Paulo Sousa, Rui Costa (Paulo Bento 84), Conceicao, Pauleta, Joao Pinto (Sa Pinto 89).
Hungary: Kiraly; Korsos, Dragoner, Lakos, Matyus, Lendvai, Halmai, Pisont (Dardai 24), Sowunmi (Kovacs 83), Egressy, Horvath (Kuttor 75).
Referee: Nielsen (Denmark).

Group 7 – Final Table	*P*	*W*	*D*	*L*	*F*	*A*	*Pts*
Romania	10	7	3	0	25	3	24
Portugal	10	7	2	1	32	4	23
Slovakia	10	5	2	3	12	9	17
Hungary	10	3	3	4	14	10	12
Azerbaijan	10	1	1	8	6	26	4
Liechtenstein	10	1	1	8	2	39	4

GROUP 8

Dublin, 5 September 1998, 34,000

Republic of Ireland (2) 2 *(Irwin 4 (pen), Roy Keane 15)*

Croatia (0) 0

Republic of Ireland: Given; Irwin, Staunton, McAteer, Cunningham, Babb, Kinsella, Roy Keane, O'Neill (Cascarino 9), Robbie Keane (Carsley 62), Duff (Kenna 46).
Croatia: Ladic; Soldo (Tokic 77), Stimac, Simic D, Tudor (Krpan 62), Jurcic, Boban, Asanovic, Jarni, Stanic, Maric (Pamic 46).
Referee: Pereira (Portugal).

Skopje, 6 September 1998, 5000

Macedonia (1) 4 *(Bozinov 20, 48, Sakiri 75, 80)*

Malta (0) 0

Macedonia: Milosevski; Lazarevski, Stojkovski (Gosev 80), Nikolovski (Sainovski 78), Sedloski, Micevski, Stojanoski (Sakiri 70), Trenevski, Zaharievski, Stavrevski, Bozinov.
Malta: Muscat; Said, Overand, Debono, Chetcuti, Turner, Agius (Suda 70), Brincat, Zahra (Carabott 78), Busuttil, Camilleri.
Referee: Wegereef (Holland).

Ta'Qali, 10 October 1998, 8000

Malta (1) 1 *(Suda 28 (pen))*

Croatia (0) 4 *(Simic D 54, Vugrinec 68, 74, Suker 85)*

Malta: Muscat; Buttigieg, Spiteri, Debono, Chetcuti, Suda (Turner 57), Agius (Zammit 11), Brincat, Zahra (Sixsmith 77), Busuttil, Camilleri.
Croatia: Ladic; Simic D (Tokic 81), Soldo, Tudor, Saric, Maric, Boban, Asanovic, Jarni (Cvitanovic 87), Suker, Vucko (Vugrinec 60).
Referee: Benedik (Slovakia).

Zagreb, 14 October 1998, 20,000

Croatia (2) 3 *(Suker 16, Boban 45, 70)*

Macedonia (1) 2 *(Ciric 2, Sainovski 55)*

Croatia: Ladic; Tudor, Stimac, Simic D, Stanic (Jurcic 81), Soldo, Boban, Asanovic (Saric 61), Jarni, Maric, Suker.
Macedonia: Milosevski; Sedloski, Stavrevski, Nikolovski (Stojanoski 77), Sainovski, Zaharievski, Micevski (Gosev 46), Lazarevski (Bozinov 60), Trenevski, Sakiri, Ciric.
Referee: Levnikov (Russia).

Dublin, 14 October 1998, 34,500

Republic of Ireland (2) 5 *(Robbie Keane 16, 18, Roy Keane 54, Quinn 63, Breen 82)*

Malta (0) 0

Republic of Ireland: Given; Kenna, Staunton, McAteer (Carsley 85), Cunningham, Breen, Kinsella, Roy Keane, Quinn (Cascarino 66), Robbie Keane (Kennedy 81), Duff.
Malta: Cini; Debono, Buttigieg, Spiteri, Carabott, Brincat, Zahra (Zammit 70), Sixsmith (Camilleri 66), Chetcuti, Turner, Suda (Agius 65).
Referee: Olsen (Norway).

Valletta, 18 November 1998, 4000

Malta (0) 1 *(Sixsmith 69)*

Macedonia (0) 2 *(Nikolovski 49, Zaharievski 62)*

Malta: Muscat; Sixsmith, Camilleri, Buttigieg, Spiteri, Debono, Busuttil, Saliba (Turner 67), Brincat, Nwoko (Carabott 54), Cutajar (Agius 59).
Macedonia: Milosevski; Veselinovski, Nikolovski, Sedloski, Babunski, Stavrevski, Zaharievski, Micevski, Sainovski, Bozinov (Trenevski 65), Sakiri.
Referee: Smolik (Belarus).

Belgrade, 18 November 1998, 44,000

Yugoslavia (0) 1 *(Mijatovic 65)*

Republic of Ireland (0) 0

Yugoslavia: Kralj; Djukic, Djorovic, Mihajlovic, Jokanovic, Jugovic (Grodzic 77), Stojkovic (Kovacevic 46), Stankovic J, Stankovic D, Mijatovic, Milosevic (Drulovic 77).
Republic of Ireland: Given; Cunningham, Irwin, McLoughlin (Connolly 72), Breen, Staunton, Kinsella, Roy Keane, Quinn (Cascarino 72), McAteer (O'Neill 83), Duff.
Referee: Nilsson (Sweden).

Valletta, 10 February 1999, 7000

Malta (0) 0

Yugoslavia (1) 3 *(Nadj 22, 55, Milosevic 90)*

Malta: Barry; Said, Turner, Spiteri, Camilleri (Sixsmith 73), Buttigieg, Busuttil, Saliba, Carabott, Nwoko (Cutajar 82), Agius (Bencini 59).
Yugoslavia: Kralj; Mirkovic, Djorovic, Jokanovic, Djukic, Mihajlovic, Stankovic D (Grodzic 88), Nadj, Stankovic J (Tomic 75), Mijatovic, Kovacevic (Milosevic 70).
Referee: Garibian (France).

Skopje, 5 June 1999, 14,000

Macedonia (0) 1 *(Hristov 80)*

Croatia (1) 1 *(Suker 19)*

Macedonia: Milosevski; Nikolovski, Stojanovski, Stavrevski, Babunski (Zaharievski 60), Sainovski, Micevski, Trenevski (Bozinov 46), Trajcov (Hristov 80), Sakiri, Ciric.
Croatia: Ladic; Juric, Simic D, Soldo, Saric, Boban, Asanovic, Vugrinec (Vlaovic 19), Jarni, Suker, Boksic (Rapaic 19).
Referee: Dallas (Scotland).

Salonika, 8 June 1999, 2000

Yugoslavia (1) 4 *(Mijatovic 36, Milosevic 49, 90, Kovacevic 75)*

Malta (1) 1 *(Saliba 7)*

Yugoslavia: Kralj; Mirkovic, Djukic, Djorovic, Saveljic, Stojkovic (Drulovic 77), Nadj (Milosevic 46), Jokanovic, Stankovic D (Grozdic 63), Mijatovic, Kovacevic.
Malta: Barry; Buhagiar (Cutajar 80), Said, Debono, Chetcuti, Buttigieg, Saliba, Camilleri (Brincat 64), Carabott, Busuttil, Nwoko (Sultana 83).
Referee: Stahl (Sweden).

Dublin, 9 June 1999, 28,108

Republic of Ireland (0) 1 *(Quinn 67)*

Macedonia (0) 0

Republic of Ireland: Kelly; Carr, Irwin, Duff (Kilbane 63), Cunningham, Breen, Kennedy, Kinsella, Quinn (Connolly 83), Robbie Keane (Cascarino 67), Carsley.
Macedonia: Milosevski; Stavrevski, Babunski, Stojanoski, Trajcev (Memedi 46), Micevski, Trenevski (Hristov 75), Sainovski (Sedloski 70), Nikolovski, Ciric, Sakiri.
Referee: Meier (Switzerland).

Belgrade, 18 August 1999, 52,600

Yugoslavia (0) 0

Croatia (0) 0

Yugoslavia: Kocic; Mirkovic, Djukic, Mihajlovic, Djorovic G (Drulovic 46), Nadj, Jokanovic, Stankovic D, Stankovic J, Mijatovic, Kovacevic (Milosevic 62).
Croatia: Ladic; Kovac, Stimac, Simic D, Jarni, Asanovic, Soldo, Boban (Biscan 75), Jurcic, Stanic, Suker.
Referee: Nielsen (Denmark).

Zagreb, 21 August 1999, 20,000

Croatia (1) 2 *(Stanic 34, Soldo 55)*

Malta (0) 1 *(Carabott 61)*

Croatia: Mrmic; Biscan, Stimac, Simic D, Rapaic, Asanovic, Soldo, Boban (Saric 16), Simic J (Boksic 46), Stanic (Vlaovic 46), Suker.
Malta: Barry; Said, Vella S, Debono, Camilleri, Carabott, Busuttil (Okonkwo 72), Saliba, Nwoko (Mifsud 89), Brincat, Agius (Sultana 83).
Referee: Ouzouniv (Bulgaria).

Dublin, 1 September 1999, 31,400

Republic of Ireland (0) 2 *(Robbie Keane 54, Kennedy 70)*

Yugoslavia (0) 1 *(Stankovic D 61)*

Republic of Ireland: Kelly A; Irwin (Carr 66), Staunton, Breen, Cunningham, Roy Keane (Carsley 69), Kinsella, Robbie Keane, Quinn (Cascarino 80), Kilbane, Kennedy.
Yugoslavia: Kocic; Komljenovic, Djukic, Mihajlovic (Saveljic 68), Bolic, Savicevic (Drulovic 53), Stankovic D, Govedarica, Nadj (Kovacevic 74), Mijatovic, Milosevic.
Referee: Collina (Italy).

Zagreb, 4 September 1999, 25,000

Croatia (0) 1 *(Suker 90)*

Republic of Ireland (0) 0

Croatia: Ladic; Bilic (Rukavina 46), Stimac, Simic D, Stanic (Simic J 84), Kovac, Soldo, Asanovic, Jarni, Suker, Rapaic.
Republic of Ireland: Kelly A; Carr, Kelly G (Harte 72), Breen, Cunningham, Staunton, Carsley, Kinsella, Cascarino (Quinn 82), McLoughlin, Duff (Kilbane 56).
Referee: Vega (Spain).

Belgrade, 5 September 1999, 22,000

Yugoslavia (1) 3 *(Stojkovic 37, 54, Savicevic 77)*

Macedonia (0) 1 *(Ciric 64 (pen))*

Yugoslavia: Kralj; Mirkovic, Krstajic, Jokanovic, Djukic, Saveljic, Stankovic D (Govedarica 75), Mijatovic, Milosevic (Kovacevic 82), Stojkovic (Savicevic 66), Drulovic.
Macedonia: Milosevski; Stavrevski, Jovanovski (Serafimovski 59), Lazarevski, Babunski, Savevski, Veselinovski, Micevski (Gerasimovski 53), Hristov, Ciric (Memedi 77), Sakiri.
Referee: Frisk (Sweden).

Skopje, 8 September 1999, 14,000

Macedonia (0) 2 *(Sakiri 60, Ciric 90)*

Yugoslavia (4) 4 *(Milosevic 1, Babunski 4 (og), Stankovic D 14, Drulovic 38)*

Macedonia: Milosevski; Stavrevski, Jovanovski, Lazarevski, Babunski, Savevski (Gerasimovski 46), Veselinovski (Serafimovski 40), Micevski (Sainovski 40), Hristov, Ciric, Sakiri.
Yugoslavia: Kralj; Mirkovic (Komljenovic 46), Djukic, Mihajlovic, Krstajic, Stankovic D, Stojkovic (Savicevic 46), Jokanovic, Drulovic, Mijatovic, Milosevic (Kovacevic 82).
Referee: Michel (Slovakia).

Valletta, 8 September 1999, 6200

Malta (0) 2 *(Said 62, Carabott 69 (pen))*

Republic of Ireland (2) 3 *(Robbie Keane 13, Breen 21, Staunton 74)*

Malta: Barry; Debono, Buttigieg (Vella S 30), Said, Carabott, Saliba, Camilleri, Agius (Theuma 67), Chetcuti (Buhagiar 24), Busuttil, Nwoko.
Republic of Ireland: Kelly A; Carr, Staunton, Carsley, Cunningham, Breen (Harte 75), Kennedy (McLoughlin 55), Robbie Keane, Quinn, Kilbane (Duff 65), Kinsella.
Referee: Corpodean (Romania).

Zagreb, 9 October 1999, 40,000

Croatia (1) 2 *(Boksic 20, Stanic 47)*

Yugoslavia (2) 2 *(Mijatovic 26, Stankovic D 31)*

Croatia: Ladic; Juric, Kovak (Biscan 61), Tudor (Rapajic 82), Rukavina, Stanic, Soldo, Asanovic, Jarni, Suker, Boksic (Simic J 77).
Yugoslavia: Kralj; Mirkovic, Djukic, Mihajlovic, Djorovic, Jokanovic, Stojkovic (Bolic 54), Nadj (Drulovic 58), Stankovic D, Mijatovic (Savicevic 73), Milosevic.
Referee: Aranda (Spain).

Skopje, 9 October 1999, 4500

Macedonia (0) 1 *(Stavrevski 90)*

Republic of Ireland (1) 1 *(Quinn 19)*

Macedonia: Filevski; Stavrevski, Sedloski, Babunski, Jovanovski (Memedi 78), Gerasimovski, Sainovski, Stanic (Zaharievski 71), Stojanoski (Bekiri 55), Savevski, Hristov.
Republic of Ireland: Kelly A; Irwin, Staunton, McLoughlin, Cunningham, Breen, Kelly G, Kinsella, Robbie Keane (O'Neill 65), Quinn (Cascarino 78), Kennedy (Holland 85).
Referee: Marin (Spain).

Group 8 – Final Table	*P*	*W*	*D*	*L*	*F*	*A*	*Pts*
Yugoslavia	8	5	2	1	18	8	17
Republic of Ireland	8	5	1	2	14	6	16
Croatia	8	4	3	1	13	9	15
Macedonia	8	2	2	4	13	14	8
Malta	8	0	0	8	6	27	0

GROUP 9

Tallinn, 4 June 1998, 3500

Estonia (2) 5 *(Viikmae 13, Reim 43 (pen), Terehhov 76, Oper 87, Kirs 90)*

Faeroes (0) 0

Estonia: Poom; Lemsalu, Kirs, Hohlov-Simson, Meet, Viikmae (O'Konnell-Bronin 80), Terehhov, Oper, Kristal, Reim, Zilinski.
Faeroes: Knudsen; Dam, Hansen J, Thorsteinsson, Hansen O (Jarnskor H 83), Morkore A, Johannesen, Johnsson, Petersen, Muller (Mikkelsen 41), Jonsson (Arge 83).

Sarajevo, 19 August 1998, 20,000

Bosnia (0) 1 *(Baljic 65)*

Faeroes (0) 0

Bosnia: Dedic; Kapetanovic, Barbarez (Mujdza 75), Konjic, Varesanovic, Hibic, Bolic (Mujcin 65), Halilovic, Kodro, Salihamidzic (Sabic 81), Baljic.
Faeroes: Mikkelsen; Hansen H, Hansen JK, Thorsteinsson, Johannesen O, Jarnskor H, Joensen S, Johnsson, Morkore A, Arge (Borg 77), Petersen.
Referee: Mikulski (Poland).

Vilnius, 5 September 1998, 5112

Lithuania (0) 0

Scotland (0) 0

Lithuania: Stauce; Sugzda (Buitkus 61), Semberas, Zutautas R, Zvirgzdauskas, Mikulenas (Slekys 90), Skerla, Baltusnikas, Preiksaitis, Jankauskas, Skarbalius.
Scotland: Leighton; Dailly, Boyd, Elliott, Hendry, Calderwood (Davidson 70), Lambert, Gallacher, McCoist (McCann 82), Jackson (Ferguson B 56), Collins.
Referee: Zotta (Romania).

Sarajevo, 5 September 1998, 21,000

Bosnia (0) 1 *(Barbarez 75 (pen))*

Estonia (1) 1 *(Hibic 28 (og))*

Bosnia: Dedic; Varesanovic, Konjic, Hibic, Kapetanovic, Salihamidzic, Katana (Mujcin 55), Halilovic (Bolic 77), Mujdza (Sabic 65), Barbarez, Baljic.
Estonia: Poom; Rooba U (Meet 81), Kirs, Hohlov-Simson, Reim, Smirnov, Terehov, Kristal, Alonen, Zelinski (Viikmae 81), Oper.
Referee: Agius (Malta).

Toftir, 6 September 1998, 2000

Faeroes (0) 0

Czech Republic (0) 1 *(Smicer 84)*

Faeroes: Mikkelsen; Johannesen O, Hansen JK, Thorsteinsson, Hansen H, Jarnskor H, Arge (Jarnskor M 78), Johnsson, Morkore A, Jonsson T, Petersen.
Czech Republic: Postulka; Rada, Bejbl (Latal 81), Suchoparek, Votava, Cizek (Berger 55), Nemec, Nedved, Lokvenc, Poborsky (Sloncik 81), Smicer.
Referee: Hirviniemi (Finland).

Sarajevo, 10 October 1998, 30,000

Bosnia (0) 1 *(Topic 88)*

Czech Republic (1) 3 *(Baranek 13, Smicer 59, Kuka 90)*

Bosnia: Dedic; Varesanovic, Konjic, Hibic, Kapetanovic, Salihamidzic (Demirovic 66), Katana, Halilovic, Mujcin (Topic 63), Barbarez, Baljic (Besirevic 71).
Czech Republic: Postulka; Baranek (Rada 71), Repka, Suchoparek, Latal, Votava, Nemec, Bejbl, Lokvenc (Kuka 80), Smicer (Sloncik 85), Berger.
Referee: Messina (Italy).

Vilnius, 10 October 1998, 1500

Lithuania (0) 0

Faeroes (0) 0

Lithuania: Stauce; Skerla, Mikalajunas (Zvingilas 74), Zutautas R, Baltusnikas, Zvirgzdauskas, Mikulenas (Buitkus 46), Ivanauskas, Skarbalius, Preiksaitis, Jankauskas.
Faeroes: Mikkelsen; Johannesen O, Hansen JK, Thorsteinsson, Hansen H, Joensen S, Jarnskor H, Johnsson, Arge (Borg 88), Jonsson T, Petersen.
Referee: Schaack (Luxembourg).

Edinburgh, 10 October 1998, 16,930

Scotland (0) 3 *(Dodds 70, 85, Hohlov-Simson 78 (og))*

Estonia (1) 2 *(Hohlov-Simson 35, Smirnov 76)*

Scotland: Leighton; Weir, Davidson, Calderwood (Donnelly 56), Hendry, Boyd, McKinlay W, Durrant, McCoist (Dodds 68), Gallacher (Jackson 17), Johnston.
Estonia: Poom; Kirs, Hohlov-Simson, Reim, Rooba U, Kristal, Smirnov, Alonen, Terehov, Zelinski (Viikmae 86), Oper.
Referee: Marques (Portugal).

Teplice, 14 October 1998, 13,123

Czech Republic (4) 4 *(Nedved 8, Berger 21, 41, Meet 44 (og))*

Estonia (0) 1 *(Arbeiter 90)*

Czech Republic: Postulka; Latal, Suchoparek, Repka, Votava (Rada 53), Nedved, Nemec, Bejbl (Cizek 80), Berger, Lokvenc (Kuka 61), Smicer.
Estonia: Poom; Smirnov (Nommik 46), Meet, Hohlov-Simson, Rooba U, Alonen, Terehov (O'Konnel-Bronin 63), Oper, Viikmae (Arbeiter 46), Reim, Zelinski.
Referee: Olafsson (Iceland).

Vilnius, 14 October 1998, 2000

Lithuania (0) 4 *(Ivanauskas 10, 67, 75, Baltusnikas 90)*

Bosnia (0) 2 *(Konjic 4, Baljic 68)*

Lithuania: Stauce; Skerla, Mikalajunas (Baltusnikas 87), Zutautas R, Gleveckas, Zvirgzdauskas, Semberas, Ivanauskas, Skarbalius (Zvingilas 62), Preiksaitis, Jankauskas (Danilevicius 79).
Bosnia: Dedic; Varesanovic, Konjic, Ramcic, Kapetanovic (Mujdza 80), Salihamidzic, Katana (Topic 75), Halilovic, Mujcin (Besirevic 80), Barbarez, Baljic.
Referee: Schuttengruber (Austria).

Aberdeen, 14 October 1998, 18,517

Scotland (2) 2 *(Burley 22, Dodds 45)*

Faeroes (0) 1 *(Petersen 86 (pen))*

Scotland: Sullivan; Weir, Davidson, Elliott, Hendry, Boyd, McKinlay W (Durrant 46), Donnelly, Dodds, Burley, Johnston (Glass 79).
Faeroes: Mikkelsen; Hansen H, Johannesen O, Hansen JK, Thorsteinsson, Petersen, Joensen S, Johnsson, Jarnskor H (Hansen J 80), Arge (Borg 69), Jonsson T.
Referee: Kapitanis (Cyprus).

Teplice, 27 March 1999, 14,658

Czech Republic (1) 2 *(Hornak 10, Berger 74 (pen))*

Lithuania (0) 0

Czech Republic: Srnicek; Repka, Suchoparek, Hornak, Poborsky (Kuka 63), Hasek, Nemec, Berger, Nedved, Lokvenc (Koller 71), Smicer (Baranek 80).
Lithuania: Stauce; Skerla, Zvirgzdauskas, Zutautas D, Semberas, Vainoras, Preiksaitis, Skarbalius, Mikalajunas (Mikulenas 78), Ivanauskas (Buitkus 83), Jankauskas (Zvingilas 67).
Referee: Juhos (Hungary).

Vilnius, 31 March 1999, 3000

Lithuania (0) 1 *(Fomenka 83)*

Estonia (0) 2 *(Terehov 49, 77)*

Lithuania: Stauce; Skerla, Zutautas R, Zvirgzdauskas, Semberas, Vainoras, Preiksaitis, Maciulevicius, Mikalajunas, Skarbalius (Gleveckas 35) (Buitkus 52), Mikulenas (Fomenka 46).
Estonia: Poom; Lemsalu, Kirs, Hohlov-Simson, Saviauk, Shvets (Kristal 69), Terehov, Oper (Zelinski 67), Viikmae, Smirnov (Alonen 90), Reim.
Referee: Trentalange (Italy).

Glasgow, 31 March 1999, 44,513

Scotland (0) 1 *(Jess 68)*

Czech Republic (2) 2 *(Elliott 27 (og), Smicer 35)*

Scotland: Sullivan; Hopkin, Davidson (Johnston 51), Elliott, Boyd, Weir, Burley, Lambert, McCann, McAllister (Hutchison 62), Jess.
Czech Republic: Srnicek; Hornak, Votava, Suchoparek, Poborsky (Rada 74), Hasek, Nedved, Berger, Nemec, Smicer (Baranek 82), Lokvenc (Kuka 69).
Referee: Nielsen (Denmark).

Sarajevo, 5 June 1999, 5000

Bosnia (1) 2 *(Kodro 26 (pen), Bolic 90)*

Lithuania (0) 0

Bosnia: Dedic; Smajic, Kapetanovic, Varesanovic, Hibic, Repuh (Bolic 87), Besirevic, Sabic, Topic (Turkovic 90), Kodro (Mujcin 79), Salihamidzic.
Lithuania: Leusas; Skerla, Skinderis, Gvildys, Kancelskis, Mikalajunas, Zvirgzdauskas, Semberas (Mikulenas 64), Maciulevicius (Fomenka 46), Ivanauskas, Preiksaitis.
Referee: Ibanez (Spain).

Tallin, 5 June 1999, 3000

Estonia (0) 0

Czech Republic (1) 2 *(Berger 45, Koller 83)*

Estonia: Poom; Lemsalu, Kirs, Hohlov-Simson, Saviauk, Alonen (Smirnov 65) (O'Konnel-Bronin 74), Terehov (Shvets 80), Kristal, Oper, Reim, Viikmae.
Czech Republic: Srnicek; Suchoparek, Repka, Hornak, Poborsky, Hasek, Nedved (Galasek 85), Berger, Nemec, Smicer (Kuka 65), Lokvenc (Koller 70).
Referee: Roca (Spain).

Toftir, 5 June 1999, 4500

Faeroes (0) 1 *(Hansen H)*

Scotland (1) 1 *(Johnston 38)*

Faeroes: Mikkelsen; Johannesen O, Hansen H, Thorsteinsson, Hansen O (Hansen J 87), Johnsson, Joensen J (Borg 73), Joensen S, Jonsson T, Morkore A, Petersen (Arge 82).
Scotland: Sullivan; Weir, Davidson, Elliott, Calderwood, Boyd, Durrant (Cameron 46), Gallacher (Jess 88), Dodds, Lambert, Johnston (Gemmill 85).
Referee: Kalt (France).

Prague, 9 June 1999, 22,000

Czech Republic (0) 3 *(Repka 65, Kuka 75, Koller 87)*

Scotland (1) 2 *(Ritchie 30, Johnston 62)*

Czech Republic: Srnicek; Poborsky (Kuka 68), Berger, Hornak, Suchoparek, Repka, Nedved, Hasek (Baranek 60), Nemec, Lokvenc (Koller 68), Smicer.
Scotland: Sullivan; Johnston, Davidson, Weir, Boyd, Ritchie, Lambert, Calderwood, Gallacher, Dodds, Durrant (Jess 70).
Referee: Krug (Germany).

Tallinn, 9 June 1999, 2500

Estonia (1) 1 *(Oper 10)*

Lithuania (0) 2 *(Ramelis 52, Maciulevicius 56)*

Estonia: Poom; Lemsalu, Kirs, Kaal, Viikmae, Alonen, Terehov (O'Konnel-Bronin 73), Kristal (Shvets 80), Oper, Reim, Zelinski.
Lithuania: Leusas; Skerla, Skinderis, Zutautas D (Maciulevicius 46), Zutautas R, Mikalajunas, Zvirgzdauskas, Ramelis, Razanauskas, Skarbalius, Ivanauskas (Preiksaitis 87).
Referee: Albrecht (Germany).

Toftir, 9 June 1999, 4600

Faeroes (1) 2 *(Arge 38, 48)*

Bosnia (1) 2 *(Bolic 13, 50)*

Faeroes: Mikkelsen; Johannesen O, Joensen S, Thorsteinsson, Hansen O (Jarnskor H 65), Johnsson, Hansen H, Arge (Joensen J 85), Morkore A, Jonsson T, Petersen.
Bosnia: Dedic; Smajic, Besirevic, Varesanovic, Hibic, Repuh (Osmanhodzic 78), Sabic, Topic, Turkovic (Joldic 63), Bolic, Mujcin (Muratovic 85).
Referee: Jones (England).

Sarajevo, 4 September 1999, 26,000

Bosnia (1) 1 *(Bolic 23)*

Scotland (2) 2 *(Hutchison 13, Dodds 45)*

Bosnia: Dedic; Joldic (Repuh 77), Konjic, Hibic, Mujdza (Demirovic 77), Besirevic, Topic, Halilovic (Mujcin 62), Kodro, Barbarez, Bolic.
Scotland: Sullivan; Weir, Burley, Calderwood (Dailly 46), Hendry, Ferguson B (Durrant 69), Hopkin, Collins, Dodds, Hutchison, McCann (Gallacher 75).
Referee: Levnikov (Russia).

Torshavn, 4 September 1999, 2300

Faeroes (0) 0

Estonia (0) 2 *(Reim 88, Piroja 90)*

Faeroes: Mikkelsen; Johannesen O, Hansen JK, Hansen F, Thorsteinsson (Hansen O 75), Johannesen (Jarnskor H 90), Johnsson J, Petersen, Morkore A, Jonsson T, Arge (Borg 90).
Estonia: Poom; Saviauk (Lemsalu 90), Piroja, Hohlov-Simson, Alonen, Terehov, Anniste (O'Konnel Bronin 67), Reim, Kirs, Kristal, Zelinski (Ustritski 75).
Referee: Trivkovic (Croatia).

Vilnius, 4 September 1999, 3000

Lithuania (0) 0

Czech Republic (0) 4 *(Nedved 60, 63, Koller 68, 90)*

Lithuania: Stauce; Semberas (Skerla 55), Zvirgzdauskas, Lencevicius, Zutautas D, Razanauskas, Preiksaitis (Danilevicius 77), Mikalajunas, Tereskinas, Ivanauskas (Ramelis 38), Jankauskas.
Czech Republic: Srnicek; Repka, Rada, Nikl, Poborsky (Sloncik 79), Bejbl, Nedved (Horvath 70), Berger, Nemec (Baranek 78), Kuka, Koller.
Referee: Granat (Poland).

Teplice, 8 September 1999, 10,125

Czech Republic (1) 3 *(Koller 26, Berger 59 (pen), Poborsky 67)*

Bosnia (0) 0

Czech Republic: Srnicek; Niki, Suchoparek, Repka, Nemec, Poborsky, Bejbl, Nedved, Berger (Hasek 83), Kuka (Baranek 79), Koller (Lokvenc 59).
Bosnia: Dedic; Konjic, Barbarez, Hibic, Joldic (Repuh 70), Varesanovic, Ihtijarevic (Bolic 70), Sabic, Besirevic, Kodro, Topic (Demirovic 70).
Referee: Nilsson (Sweden).

Tallinn, 8 September 1999, 4500

Estonia (0) 0

Scotland (0) 0

Estonia: Poom; Kirs, Hohlov-Simson, Piiroja, Saviauk, Kristal, Anniste, Reim, Terehov, O'Konnel-Bronin (Zelinski 46), Oper.
Scotland: Sullivan; Weir, Burley, Davidson, Hendry, Dailly, Durrant (Ferguson B 67), Collins, Dodds, Hutchison, Johnston (McCann 55).
Referee: Stuchlik (Austria).

Torshavn, 8 September 1999, 450

Faeroes (0) 0

Lithuania (0) 1 *(Ramelis 55)*

Faeroes: Mikkelsen; Johannesen O, Hansen JK, Hansen F, Thorsteinsson, Hansen O, Jarnskor H (Lakjuni 84), Johnsson J (Benjaminsen 65), Morkore A, Jonsson T, Arge (Borg 46).
Lithuania: Stauce (Rodimanskas 79); Semberas, Zvrigzdauskas, Vencevicius, Zutautas D, Razanauskas (Skerla 77), Preiksaitis (Danilevicius 88), Mikalajunas, Tereskinas, Ramelis, Skinderis.
Referee: Romain (Belgium).

Ibrox Park, 5 October 1999, 30,574

Scotland (1) 1 *(Collins 26 (pen))*

Bosnia (0) 0

Scotland: Sullivan; Weir, Davidson, Burley, Dailly, Hendry (Calderwood 36), Hopkin, Lambert, Dodds (McSwegan 89), Gallacher (Burchill 79), Collins.
Bosnia: Guso; Hujdorovic, Varesanovic, Barbarez, Kapetanovic, Ihtijarevic (Topic 79), Sabic, Besirevic, Mujcin (Avdic 90), Baljic, Bolic.
Referee: Sundell (Sweden).

Prague, 9 October 1999, 21,326

Czech Republic (1) 2 *(Koller 11, Verbir 84)*

Faeroes (0) 0

Czech Republic: Srnicek; Repka, Suchoparek (Verbir 74), Rada, Poborsky, Baranek (Hornak 58), Nemec, Berger, Bejbl (Horvath 66), Koller, Smicer.
Faeroes: Knudsen; Johannesen O, Hansen JK, Thorsteinsson, Hansen HF, Hansen HJ (Hansen O 88), Johannesen, Johnsson J, Petersen (Jakosen 72), Morkore A, Jonsson T.
Referee: Lica (Romania).

Tallinn, 9 October 1999, 1200

Estonia (1) 1 *(Oper 4)*

Bosnia (1) 4 *(Baljic 42, 57, 67, 87)*

Estonia: Kaalma; Piiroja, Kirs, Hohlov-Simson, Anniste (Saviauk 61), Terehov (O'Konnel-Bronin 74), Alonen, Kristal, Reim, Oper, Zelinski (Viikmae 40).
Bosnia: Guso; Joldic, Kapetanovic, Hujdorovic, Varesanovic, Ihtijarevic, Besirevic, Sabic (Duro 60), Topic, Bolic (Mujcin 80), Baljic (Avdic 89).
Referee: Luinge (Holland).

Hampden Park, 9 October 1999, 22,059

Scotland (0) 3 *(Hutchison 48, McSwegan 50, Cameron 88)*

Lithuania (0) 0

Scotland: Gould; Weir, Davidson, O'Neil, Dailly, Ritchie, Burley (Cameron 46), Lambert, Burchill (Dodds 79), McSwegan (Gallacher 82), Hutchison.
Lithuania: Leus; Zvirgzdauskas, Skinderis, Zutautas D, Skerla, Stumbrys (Vencevicius 54), Razanauskas, Mikalajunas, Tereskinas (Fomenko 65), Dancenko (Maciulevicius 54), Mikulenas.
Referee: Bre (France).

Group 9 – Final Table	*P*	*W*	*D*	*L*	*F*	*A*	*Pts*
Czech Republic	10	10	0	0	26	5	30
Scotland	10	5	3	2	15	10	18
Estonia	10	3	2	5	15	17	11
Bosnia	10	3	2	5	14	17	11
Lithuania	10	3	2	5	8	16	11
Faeroes	10	0	3	7	4	17	3

PLAY-OFFS FIRST LEG

Tel Aviv, 13 November 1999, 45,000

Israel (0) 0

Denmark (2) 5 *(Tomasson 2, 34, Tofting 67, Jorgensen 68, Steen-Nielsen 72)*

Israel: Awat; Harazi A, Amsalem, Benado, Ben Shimon (Tal 38), Hazan, Banin (Telesnikov 79), Berkovic, Revivo, Turjeman, Abuksis (Benayoun 38).
Denmark: Schmeichel; Tofting (Goldbaek 79), Henriksen, Hogh, Heintze, Helveg, Steen-Nielsen, Jorgensen (Schjonberg 86), Gronkjaer, Tomasson (Andersen S 79), Sand.
Referee: Elleray (England).

Dublin, 13 November 1999, 33,610

Republic of Ireland (0) 1 *(Robbie Keane 79)*

Turkey (0) 1 *(Tayfur 83 (pen))*

Republic of Ireland: Kelly A (Kiely 62); Carr, Irwin, Breen, Cunningham, Carsley, Delap (Duff 54), Roy Keane, Robbie Keane, Cascarino (Connolly 76), Kilbane.
Turkey: Rustu; Tayfun, Abdullah, Ali Eren, Alpay, Ogun, Sergen (Korkmaz 86), Umit (Arif 46), Tayfur, Hakan Unsal (Tugay 68), Hakan Sukur.
Referee: Frisk (Sweden).

Hampden Park, 13 November 1999, 50,132

Scotland (0) 0

England (2) 2 *(Scholes 21, 42)*

Scotland: Sullivan; Burley, Ritchie, Weir, Hendry, Dailly, Gallacher (Burchill 83), Ferguson B, Dodds, Hutchison, Collins.
England: Seaman; Campbell, Neville P, Redknapp, Keown, Adams, Beckham, Scholes, Shearer, Owen (Cole 68), Ince.
Referee: Vega (Spain).

Ljubljana, 13 November 1999, 16,000

Slovenia (0) 2 *(Zahovic 53, Asimovic 82)*

Ukraine (1) 1 *(Shevchenko 33)*

Slovenia: Dabanovic; Knavs, Milanic (Osterc 73), Milinovic, Novak, Karic, Ceh, Pavlin, Zahovic, Udovic (Asimovic 46), Rudonja.
Ukraine: Shovkovskyi; Parfionov, Golovko, Vashchuk, Dmitrulin, Popov, Gusin, Kandarov (Kardach 56), Kossovski V, Shevchenko, Rebrov.
Referee: Meier (Switzerland).

PLAY-OFFS SECOND LEG

Copenhagen, 17 November 1999, 41,186

Denmark (2) 3 *(Sand 4, Steen-Nielsen 14, Tomasson 65)*

Israel (0) 0

Denmark: Schmeichel (Sorensen 17); Helveg (Laursen 70), Hogh, Henriksen, Heintze, Tofting, Steen-Nielsen, Gronkjaer (Schjonberg 83), Jorgensen, Sand, Tomasson.
Israel: Elimelech; Talkar, Shelah, Amsalem (Badir 43), Harazi A, Hazan, Banin, Tal (Telesnikov 28), Berkovic (Gershon 72), Benayoun, Turgeman.
Referee: Pereira (Portugal).

Wembley, 17 November 1999, 75,848

England (0) 0

Scotland (1) 1 *(Hutchison 39)*

England: Seaman; Campbell, Neville P, Ince, Southgate, Adams, Beckham, Redknapp, Shearer, Owen (Heskey 64), Scholes (Parlour 90).
Scotland: Sullivan; Burley, Davidson, Weir, Hendry, Dailly, Collins, Ferguson B, Dodds, Hutchison, McCann (Burchill 75).
Referee: Collina (Italy).

Bursa, 17 November 1999, 21,000

Turkey (0) 0

Republic of Ireland (0) 0

Turkey: Rustu (Engin 37); Ali Eren, Ogun, Alpay, Okan, Tayfur, Tayfun (Fatih 46), Abdullah, Arif (Umit 83), Sergen, Hakan Sukur.
Republic of Ireland: Kiely; Carr (Kenna 5) (Cascarino 80), Irwin, Delap, Cunningham, Breen, Kinsella, Roy Keane, Quinn, Connolly (Duff 70), Kilbane.
Referee: Veissiere (France).

Kiev, 17 November 1999, 45,000

Ukraine (0) 1 *(Rebrov 65 (pen))*

Slovenia (0) 1 *(Pavlin 74)*

Ukraine: Shovkovskyi; Luzhny, Golovko, Vashchuk, Dmitrulin, Kandarov (Kovalev 46), Fedorov, Kossovski V (Popov 74), Skachenko (Moroz G 57), Rebrov, Shevchenko.
Slovenia: Dabanovic; Galic, Milanic, Milinovic, Karic (Osterc 74), Novak, Ceh, Pavlin, Zahovic, Udovic (Acimovic 57), Rudonja.
Referee: Heynemann (Germany).

FINAL COMPETITON (played in Holland and Belgium)

GROUP A

Liege, 12 June 2000, 30,000

Germany (1) 1 *(Scholl 29)*

Romania (1) 1 *(Moldovan 5)*

Germany: Kahn; Babbel, Ziege, Linke (Rehmer 46), Matthaus (Deisler 77), Nowotny, Jeremies, Hassler (Hamann 73), Scholl, Bierhoff, Rink.
Romania: Stelea; Petrescu (Contra 69), Chivu, Ciobotariu, Popescu, Filipescu, Munteanu D, Galca, Moldovan (Lupescu 85), Ilie A, Hagi (Mutu 73).
Referee: Nielsen (Denmark).

Eindhoven, 12 June 2000, 33,000

Portugal (2) 3 *(Figo 22, Joao Pinto 38, Nuno Gomes 60)*

England (2) 2 *(Scholes 3, McManaman 18)*

Portugal: Vitor Baia; Xavier, Dimas, Paulo Bento, Fernando Couto, Jorge Costa, Figo, Rui Costa (Beto 84), Nuno Gomes (Capucho 90), Joao Pinto (Conceicao 75), Vidigal.
England: Seaman; Neville G, Neville P, Ince, Campbell, Adams (Keown 81), Beckham, Scholes, Shearer, Owen (Heskey 46), McManaman (Wise 57).
Referee: Frisk (Sweden).

Charleroi, 17 June 2000, 30,000

England (0) 1 *(Shearer 53)*

Germany (0) 0

England: Seaman; Neville G, Neville P, Ince, Keown, Campbell, Beckham, Scholes (Barmby 72), Shearer, Owen (Gerrard 61), Wise.
Germany: Kahn; Babbel, Ziege, Hamann, Matthaus, Nowotny, Deisler (Ballack 72), Scholl, Jancker, Kirsten (Rink 70), Jeremies (Bode 78).
Referee: Collina (Italy).

Arnhem, 17 June 2000, 18,000

Romania (0) 0

Portugal (0) 1 *(Constinha 90)*

Romania: Stelea; Contra, Chivu, Munteanu D, Popescu, Filipescu, Petrescu (Petr 64), Galca, Moldovan (Ganea 69), Ilie A (Rosu 78), Hagi.
Portugal: Vitor Baia; Secretario, Dimas, Vidigal, Fernando Couto, Jorge Costa, Figo, Paulo Bento, Joao Pinto (Conceicao 56), Rui Costa (Constinha 87), Nuno Gomes (Sa Pinto 56).
Referee: Veissiere (France).

Charleroi, 20 June 2000, 30,000

England (2) 2 *(Shearer 40 (pen), Owen 45)*

Romania (1) 3 *(Chivu 22, Munteanu D 48, Ganea 89 (pen))*

England: Martyn; Neville G, Neville P, Ince, Keown, Campbell, Beckham, Scholes (Southgate 81), Shearer, Owen (Heskey 67), Wise (Barmby 75).
Romania: Stelea; Petrescu, Chivu, Contra, Popescu (Belodedici 31), Filipescu, Mutu, Galca (Rosu 68), Moldovan, Ilie A (Ganea 74), Munteanu D.
Referee: Meier (Switzerland).

Rotterdam, 20 June 2000, 44,000

Portugal (1) 3 *(Conceicao 35, 54, 71)*

Germany (0) 0

Portugal: Espinha; Conceicao, Capucho, Beto, Fernando Couto, Jorge Costa, Costinha, Paulo Sousa, Sa Pinto, Pauleta (Nuno Gomez 66), Rui Jorge.
Germany: Kahn; Deisler, Linke, Rehmer, Matthaus, Nowotny, Ballack (Rink 46), Hamann, Jancker, Scholl (Hassler 59), Bode.
Referee: Jol (Holland).

GROUP B

Brussels, 10 June 2000, 50,000

Belgium (1) 2 *(Goor 43, Mpenza E 46)*

Sweden (0) 1 *(Mjallby 53)*

Belgium: De Wilde; Deflandre, Leonard (Van Kerckhoven 72), Verheyen (Peeters 88), Valgaeren, Staelens, Vanderhaeghe, Wilmots, Mpenza E, Strupar (Nilis 69), Goor.
Sweden: Hedman; Nilsson (Lucic 46), Mellberg, Andersson D (Osmanovski 70), Andersson P, Bjorklund, Alexandersson, Mjallby, Andersson K, Pettersson (Larsson 49), Ljungberg.
Referee: Merk (Germany).

Arnhem, 11 June 2000, 25,000

Turkey (0) 1 *(Okan 62)*

Italy (0) 2 *(Conte 52, Inzaghi 70 (pen))*

Turkey: Rustu; Alpay, Fatih, Okan (Ergun 89), Abdullah, Temizkanoglu, Tayfur, Korkut, Hakan Sukur, Sergen (Arif 81), Umit (Tugay 76).
Italy: Toldo; Zambrotta, Pessotto (Iuliano 62), Cannavaro, Nesta, Maldini, Conte, Albertini, Totti (Di Livio 83), Inzaghi, Fiore (Del Piero 74).
Referee: Dallas (Scotland).

Brussels, 14 June 2000, 46,000

Italy (1) 2 *(Totti 6, Fiore 66)*

Belgium (0) 0

Italy: Toldo; Cannavaro, Maldini, Albertini, Nesta, Iuliano, Conte, Zambrotta, Totti (Del Piero 64), Inzaghi (Delvecchio 77), Fiore (Ambrosini 83).
Belgium: De Wilde; Deflandre, Van Kerckhoven (Hendrikx 44), Verheyen (Mpenza M 67), Valgaeren, Staelens, Vanderhaeghe, Wilmots, Mpenza E, Strupar (Nilis 58), Goor.
Referee: Aranda (Spain).

Eindhoven, 15 June 2000, 24,500

Sweden (0) 0

Turkey (0) 0

Sweden: Hedman; Lucic, Sundgren, Mild, Mellberg, Bjorklund, Alexandersson (Andersson A 62), Mjallby, Andersson K (Pettersson 46), Larsson (Svensson 78), Ljungberg.
Turkey: Rustu; Alpay, Unsal, Okan, Fatih, Ogun (Tugay 59), Umit (Tayfun 46), Suat, Hakan Sukur, Izzet (Sergen 58), Arif.
Referee: Jol (Holland).

Eindhoven, 19 June 2000, 25,000

Italy (1) 2 *(Di Biagio 39, Del Piero 88)*

Sweden (0) 1 *(Larsson 77)*

Italy: Toldo; Negro, Pessotto, Ferrara, Iuliano, Maldini (Nesta 42), Di Livio (Fiore 64), Di Biagio, Montella, Del Piero, Ambrosini.
Sweden: Hedman; Svensson (Alexandersson 52), Gustafsson (Andersson K 75), Mellberg, Andersson P, Bjorklund, Mjallby (Andersson D 56), Osmanovski, Mild, Larsson, Ljungberg.
Referee: Pereira (Portugal).

Brussels, 19 June 2000, 48,000

Turkey (1) 2 *(Hakan Sukur 45, 70)*

Belgium (0) 0

Turkey: Rustu; Tayfun, Abdullah, Fatih, Ogun, Alpay, Okan (Ergun 77), Suat, Hakan Sukur, Tugay (Tayfur 37), Arif (Osman 84).
Belgium: De Wilde; Deflandre, Van Kerckhoven, Verheyen (Strupar 64), Staelens, Valgaeren, Vanderhaeghe, Wilmost, Mpenza E, Nilis (De Bilde 77), Goor (Hendrikx 59).
Referee: Nielsen (Denmark) (Benko (Austria) 40).

GROUP C

Rotterdam, 13 June 2000, 45,000

Spain (0) 0

Norway (0) 1 *(Iversen 66)*

Spain: Molina; Michel Salgado, Aranzabal, Guardiola, Paco, Hierro, Etxeberria (Alfonso 71), Valeron (Helguera 80), Raul, Urzaiz, Fran (Mendieta 71).
Norway: Myhre; Heggem, Bergdolmo, Skammelsrud, Berg (Eggen 59), Bragstad, Bakke, Mykland, Flo (Carew 69), Iversen (Riseth 90), Solskjaer.
Referee: Gandour (Egypt).

Charleroi, 13 June 2000, 15,000

Yugoslavia (0) 3 *(Milosevic 67, 73, Drulovic 70)*

Slovenia (2) 3 *(Zahovic 23, 57, Pavlin 52)*

Yugoslavia: Kralj; Jugovic, Nadj, Dudic, Mihajlovic, Djukic, Stankovic D (Stojkovic 36), Jokanovic, Mijatovic (Kezman 82), Kovacevic (Milosevic 52), Drulovic.
Slovenia: Dabanovic; Novak, Karic (Osterc 78), Milinovic, Milanic, Galic, Pavlin (Pavlovic 74), Ceh, Zahovic, Udovic (Acimovic 65), Rudonja.
Referee: Pereira (Portugal).

Liege, 18 June 2000, 24,000

Norway (0) 0

Yugoslavia (1) 1 *(Milosevic 8)*

Norway: Myhre; Heggem (Bjornebye 35), Bergdolmo, Skammelsrud, Eggen, Bragstad, Bakke (Strand 75), Mykland, Flo, Iversen, Solskjaer.
Yugoslavia: Krajl; Saveljic, Djorovic, Jokanovic (Govedarcia 89), Djukic, Komljenovic, Stojkovic (Nadj 83), Jugovic, Milosevic, Mijatovic (Kezman 86), Drulovic.
Referee: Dallas (Scotland).

Amsterdam, 18 June 2000, 45,000

Slovenia (0) 1 *(Zahovic 59)*

Spain (1) 2 *(Raul 5, Etxeberria 60)*

Slovenia: Dabanovic; Novak, Karic, Galic, Milanic (Knavs 67), Milinovic, Pavlin (Acimovic 81), Ceh, Udovic (Osterc 46), Zahovic, Rudonja.
Spain: Canizares; Michel Salgado, Aranzabal, Guardiola (Helguera 81), Hierro, Abelardo, Etxeberria, Valeron (Engonga 89), Raul, Alfonso (Urzaiz 71), Mendieta.
Referee: Merk (Germany).

Arnhem, 21 June 2000, 21,000

Slovenia (0) 0

Norway (0) 0

Slovenia: Dabanovic; Novak, Karic, Milinovic, Galic (Acimovic 83), Knavs, Ceh, Pavlin, Siljak (Osterc 86), Zahovic, Rudonja.
Norway: Myhre; Bergdolmo, Bjornebye, Solbakken, Eggen, Bragstad, Carew (Bakke 61) (Strand 82), Mykland, Flo, Iversen, Solskjaer.
Referee: Poll (England).

Bruges, 21 June 2000, 22,000

Yugoslavia (1) 3 *(Milosevic 31, Govedarica 51, Komljenovic 75)*

Spain (1) 4 *(Alfonso 39, 90, Munitis 53, Mendieta 89 (pen))*

Yugoslavia: Kralj; Komljenovic, Djorovic (Stankovic J 13), Jokanovic, Djukic, Mihaljovic, Stojkovic (Saveljic 69), Jugovic (Govedarica 46), Milosevic, Mijatovic, Drulovic.
Spain: Canizares; Michel Salgado (Munitis 46), Barjuan, Guardiola, Abelardo, Jemez (Urzaiz 64), Helguera, Mendieta, Raul, Alfonso, Gonzalez (Etxeberria 23).
Referee: Veissiere (France).

GROUP D

Bruges, 11 June 2000, 29,000

France (1) 3 *(Blanc 16, Henry 65, Wiltord 90)*

Denmark (0) 0

France: Barthez; Thuram, Lizarazu, Deschamps, Blanc, Desailly, Djorkaeff (Vieira 58), Petit, Henry, Zidane, Anelka (Wiltord 82).
Denmark: Schmeichel; Colding, Heintze, Nielsen A, Schjonberg, Henriksen, Bisgaard (Gravesen 72), Tomasson (Beck 80), Sand, Tofting (Jorgensen 72), Gronkjaer.
Referee: Benko (Austria).

Amsterdam, 11 June 2000, 50,000

Holland (0) 1 *(Frank de Boer 89 (pen))*

Czech Republic (0) 0

Holland: Van der Sar; Reiziger, Van Bronckhorst, Cocu, Frank de Boer, Stam (Konterman 75), Seedorf (Ronald de Boer 57), Davids, Kluivert, Bergkamp, Zenden (Overmars 79).
Czech Republic: Srnicek; Latal (Bejbl 70), Gabriel, Nedved, Rada, Repka, Poborsky, Nemec, Koller, Smicer (Kuka 83), Rosicky.
Referee: Collina (Italy).

Bruges, 16 June 2000, 25,000

Czech Republic (1) 1 *(Poborsky 35 (pen))*

France (1) 2 *(Henry 7, Djorkaeff 60)*

Czech Republic: Srnicek; Poborsky, Nedved, Repka, Rada, Gabriel (Fukal 46), Rosicky (Jankulovski 61), Bejbl, Smicer, Koller, Nemec.
France: Barthez; Thuram, Candela, Vieira, Blanc, Desailly, Deschamps, Petit (Djorkaeff 46), Anelka (Dugarry 64), Zidane, Henry (Wiltord 90).
Referee: Poll (England).

Rotterdam, 16 June 2000, 50,000

Holland (0) 3 *(Kluivert 58, Ronald de Boer 66, Zenden 77)*

Denmark (0) 0

Holland: Van der Sar (Westerveld 88); Reiziger, Van Bronckhorst, Cocu, Konterman, Frank de Boer, Zenden, Davids, Kluivert, Bergkamp (Winter 75), Overmars (Ronald de Boer 61).
Denmark: Schmeichel; Colding, Heintze, Nielsen A, Henriksen, Schjonberg (Helveg 83), Bisgaard, Gravesen, Tomasson, Sand, Gronkjaer.
Referee: Meier (Switzerland).

Liege, 21 June 2000, 25,000

Denmark (0) 0

Czech Republic (0) 2 *(Smicer 64, 67)*

Denmark: Schmeichel; Schjonberg, Helveg, Tofting, Henriksen, Heintze (Colding 68), Goldbaek, Steen-Nielsen, Beck (Molnar 74), Tomasson, Gronkjaer.
Czech Republic: Srnicek; Repka, Nedved, Nemec, Rada, Fukal, Poborsky, Bejbl (Jankulovski 62), Koller (Kuka 74), Smicer (Lokvenc 79), Berger.
Referee: Ghandour (Egypt).

Amsterdam, 21 June 2000, 50,000

France (2) 2 *(Dugarry 8, Trezeguet 32)*

Holland (1) 3 *(Kluivert 14, Frank de Boer 51, Zenden 59)*

France: Lama; Karembeu, Candela, Vieira (Deschamps 90), Leboeuf, Desailly, Pires, Dugarry (Djorkaeff 68), Trezeguet, Wiltord (Anelka 80), Micoud.
Holland: Westerveld; Bosvelt, Numan, Cocu, Frank de Boer, Stam, Zenden, Davids, Kluivert (Makaay 59), Bergkamp (Winter 78), Overmars (Van Vossen 90).
Referee: Frisk (Sweden).

QUARTER-FINALS Brussels, 24 June 2000, 42,500

Italy (2) 2 *(Totte 34, Inzaghi 43)*

Romania (0) 0

Italy: Toldo; Zambrotta, Maldini (Pessotto 46), Cannavaro, Nesta, Iuliano, Conte (Di Biagio 59), Albertini, Inzaghi, Totti (Del Piero 78), Fiore.
Romania: Stelea; Petre, Chivu, Ciobotariu, Belodedici, Filipescu, Mutu, Galca (Lupescu 69), Moldovan (Ganea 54), Munteanu D, Hagi.
Referee: Pereira (Portugal).

Amsterdam, 24 June 2000, 42,000

Portugal (1) 2 *(Nuno Gomes 44, 56)*

Turkey (0) 0

Portugal: Vitor Baia; Conceicao, Dimas, Paulo Bento, Fernando Couto, Jorge Costa, Figo, Costinha (Paulo Sousa 46), Joao Pinto, Nuno Gomes (Sa Pinto 74), Rui Costa (Capucho 87).
Turkey: Rustu; Tayfun, Unsal, Fatih, Ogun (Yalcin 85), Alpay, Tayfur, Okan (Dereli-oglu 62), Ergun, Hakan Sukur, Arif (Kaya 62).
Referee: Jol (Holland).

Bruges, 25 June 2000, 30,000

France (2) 2 *(Zidane 32, Djorkaeff 44)*

Spain (1) 1 *(Mendieta 38 (pen))*

France: Barthez; Thuram, Lizarazu, Vieira, Blanc, Desailly, Deschamps, Dugarry, Henry (Anelka 81), Zidane, Djorkaeff.
Spain: Canizares; Michel Salgado, Aranzabal, Guardiola, Paco, Abelardo, Helguera (Gerard 77), Munitis (Exteberria 73), Alfonso, Raul, Mendieta (Urzaiz 57).
Referee: Collina (Italy).

Rotterdam, 25 June 2000, 50,000

Holland (2) 6 *(Kluivert 23, 38, 54, Overmars 78, 90, Govedarica (og) 51)*

Yugoslavia (0) 1 *(Milosevic 90)*

Holland: Van der Sar (Westerveld 64); Bosvelt, Numan, Cocu, Frank de Boer, Stam, Zenden (Ronald de Boer 79), Davids, Kluivert (Makaay 59), Bergkamp, Overmars.
Yugoslavia: Kralj; Komljenovic, Djukic, Govedarica, Saveljic (Stankovic J 56), Mihajlovic, Stojkovic (Stankovic D 51), Jugovic, Milosevic, Mijatovic, Drulovic (Kovanevic 69).
Referee: Aranda (Spain).

SEMI-FINALS Brussels, 28 June 2000, 50,000

France (0) 2 *(Henry 51, Zidane 117 (pen))*

Portugal (1) 1 *(Nuno Gomes 19)*

France: Barthez; Thuram, Lizarazu, Vieira, Blanc, Desailly, Deschamps, Anelka (Wiltord 71), Henry (Trezeguet 105), Zidane, Petit (Pires 87).
Portugal: Vitor Baia; Xavier, Dimas (Rui Jorge 91), Conceicao, Fernando Couto, Jorge Costa, Costinha, Vidigal (Paulo Bento 60), Figo, Rui Costa (Joao Pinto 76), Nuno Gomes.
France won on sudden death.
Referee: Benko (Austria).

Amsterdam, 29 June 2000, 50,000

Italy (0) 0

Holland (0) 0

Italy: Toldo; Cannavaro, Zambrotta, Nesta, Maldini, Iuliano, Di Biagio, Albertini (Pessotto 78), Inzaghi (Delvecchio 67), Del Piero, Fiore (Totti 82).
Holland: Van der Sar; Bosvelt, Van Bronckhorst, Cocu (Winter 95), Frank de Boer, Stam, Zenden (Van Vossen 77), Davids, Kluivert, Bergkamp (Seedorf 86), Overmars.
aet; Italy won 3-1 on penalties. Di Biagio scored 1-0; Frank de Boer saved 1-0; Pessotto scored 2-0; Stam shot over 2-0; Totti scored 3-0; Kluivert scored 3-1; Maldini saved 3-1; Bosvelt saved 3-1.
Referee: Merk (Germany).

FINAL

Rotterdam, 2 July 2000, 50,000

France (0) 2 *(Wiltord 90, Trezeguet 103)*

Italy (0) 1 *(Delvecchio 55)*

France: Barthez; Thuram, Lizarazu (Pires 85), Vieira, Blanc, Desailly, Deschamps, Dugarry (Wiltord 56), Henry, Zidane, Djorkaeff (Trezeguet 75).
Italy: Toldo; Cannavaro, Maldini, Pessotto, Nesta, Iuliano, Di Biagio (Ambrosini 65), Albertini, Totti, Delvecchio (Montella 85), Fiore (Del Piero 52).
France won on sudden death.
Referee: Frisk (Sweden).

PAST EUROPEAN CHAMPIONSHIP FINALS

Year	*Winners*		*Runners-up*		*Venue*	*Attendance*
1960	USSR	2	Yugoslavia	1	Paris	17,966
1964	Spain	2	USSR	1	Madrid	120,000
1968	Italy	2	Yugoslavia	0	Rome	60,000
	After 1-1 draw					75,000
1972	West Germany	3	USSR	0	Brussels	43,437
1976	Czechoslovakia	2	West Germany	2	Belgrade	45,000
	(Czechoslovakia won on penalties)					
1980	West Germany	2	Belgium	1	Rome	47,864
1984	France	2	Spain	0	Paris	48,000
1988	Holland	2	USSR	0	Munich	72,308
1992	Denmark	2	Germany	0	Gothenburg	37,800
1996	Germany	2	Czech Republic	1	Wembley	73,611
	(Germany won on sudden death)					

PAST WORLD CUP FINALS

Year	**Winners**		**Runners-up**		**Venue**	**Att.**	**Referee**
1930	Uruguay	4	Argentina	2	Montevideo	90,000	Langenus (B)
1934	Italy	2	Czechoslovakia	1	Rome	50,000	Eklind (Se)
	(after extra time)						
1938	Italy	4	Hungary	2	Paris	45,000	Capdeville (F)
1950	Uruguay	2	Brazil	1	Rio de Janeiro	199,854	Reader (E)
1954	West Germany	3	Hungary	2	Berne	60,000	Ling (E)
1958	Brazil	5	Sweden	2	Stockholm	49,737	Guigue (F)
1962	Brazil	3	Czechoslovakia	1	Santiago	68,679	Latychev (USSR)
1966	England	4	West Germany	2	Wembley	93,802	Dienst (Sw)
	(after extra time)						
1970	Brazil	4	Italy	1	Mexico City	107,412	Glockner (EG)
1974	West Germany	2	Holland	1	Munich	77,833	Taylor (E)
1978	Argentina	3	Holland	1	Buenos Aires	77,000	Gonella (I)
	(after extra time)						
1982	Italy	3	West Germany	1	Madrid	90,080	Coelho (Br)
1986	Argentina	3	West Germany	2	Mexico City	114,580	Filho (Br)
1990	West Germany	1	Argentina	0	Rome	73,603	Codesal (Mex)
1994	Brazil	0	Italy	0	Los Angeles	94,194	Puhl (H)
	(Brazil won 3-2 on penalties aet)						
1998	France	3	Brazil	0	St-Denis	75,000	Belqola (Mor)

FIFA WORLD CUP 2002 FIXTURES

EUROPE
(Members 51, Entries 51)

Fourteen or fifteen teams qualify including France as world champions and play-offs between UEFA and Asia.

Group 1
Yugoslavia, Russia, Switzerland, Slovenia, Luxembourg, Faeroes

02.09.00 Luxembourg v Yugoslavia
02.09.00 Faeroes v Slovenia
02.09.00 Switzerland v Russia
07.10.00 Switzerland v Faeroes
07.10.00 Yugoslavia v Russia
07.10.00 Luxembourg v Slovenia
11.10.00 Russia v Luxembourg
11.10.00 Slovenia v Switzerland
11.10.00 Yugoslavia v Faeroes
24.03.01 Russia v Slovenia
24.03.01 Luxembourg v Faeroes
24.03.01 Yugoslavia v Switzerland
28.03.01 Slovenia v Yugoslavia
28.03.01 Russia v Faeroes
28.03.01 Switzerland v Luxembourg
02.06.01 Slovenia v Luxembourg
02.06.01 Faeroes v Switzerland
02.06.01 Russia v Yugoslavia
06.06.01 Switzerland v Slovenia
06.06.01 Faeroes v Yugoslavia
06.06.01 Luxembourg v Russia
01.09.01 Faeroes v Luxembourg
01.09.01 Switzerland v Yugoslavia
01.09.01 Slovenia v Russia
05.09.01 Yugoslavia v Slovenia
05.09.01 Faeroes v Russia
05.09.01 Luxembourg v Switzerland
06.10.01 Russia v Switzerland
06.10.01 Slovenia v Faeroes
06.10.01 Yugoslavia v Luxembourg

Group 2
Holland, Portugal, Republic of Ireland, Cyprus, Andorra, Estonia

16.08.00 Estonia v Andorra
02.09.00 Andorra v Cyprus
02.09.00 Holland v Republic of Ireland
03.09.00 Estonia v Portugal
07.10.00 Cyprus v Holland
07.10.00 Portugal v Republic of Ireland
07.10.00 Andorra v Estonia
11.10.00 Holland v Portugal
11.10.00 Republic of Ireland v Estonia
15.11.00 Cyprus v Andorra
14.02.01 Portugal v Andorra
24.03.01 Andorra v Holland
24.03.01 Cyprus v Republic of Ireland
28.03.01 Cyprus v Estonia
28.03.01 Andorra v Republic of Ireland
28.03.01 Portugal v Holland
24.04.01 Holland v Cyprus
25.04.01 Republic of Ireland v Andorra
02.06.01 Estonia v Holland
02.06.01 Republic of Ireland v Portugal
06.06.01 Portugal v Cyprus
06.06.01 Estonia v Republic of Ireland
15.08.01 Estonia v Cyprus
01.09.01 Republic of Ireland v Holland
01.09.01 Andorra v Portugal
05.09.01 Holland v Estonia
05.09.01 Cyprus v Portugal
06.10.01 Republic of Ireland v Cyprus
06.10.01 Holland v Andorra
06.10.01 Portugal v Estonia

Group 3
Czech Republic, Denmark, Bulgaria, Iceland, Northern Ireland, Malta

02.09.00 Iceland v Denmark
02.09.00 Northern Ireland v Malta
02.09.00 Bulgaria v Czech Republic
07.10.00 Czech Republic v Iceland
07.10.00 Northern Ireland v Denmark
07.10.00 Bulgaria v Malta
11.10.00 Iceland v Northern Ireland
11.10.00 Malta v Czech Republic
11.10.00 Denmark v Bulgaria
25.03.01 Malta v Denmark
25.03.01 Bulgaria v Iceland
25.03.01 Northern Ireland v Czech Republic
28.03.01 Czech Republic v Denmark
28.03.01 Bulgaria v Northern Ireland
25.04.01 Malta v Iceland
02.06.01 Iceland v Malta
02.06.01 Denmark v Czech Republic
02.06.01 Northern Ireland v Bulgaria
06.06.01 Denmark v Malta
06.06.01 Iceland v Bulgaria
06.06.01 Czech Republic v Northern Ireland
01.09.01 Denmark v Northern Ireland
01.09.01 Malta v Bulgaria
01.09.01 Iceland v Czech Republic
05.09.01 Northern Ireland v Iceland
05.09.01 Czech Republic v Malta
05.09.01 Bulgaria v Denmark
06.10.01 Czech Republic v Bulgaria
06.10.01 Malta v Northern Ireland
06.10.01 Denmark v Iceland

Group 4
Sweden, Turkey, Slovakia, Macedonia, Azerbaijan, Moldova

02.09.00 Slovakia v Macedonia
02.09.00 Azerbaijan v Sweden
02.09.00 Turkey v Moldova
07.10.00 Moldova v Slovakia
07.10.00 Macedonia v Azerbaijan
07.10.00 Sweden v Turkey
11.10.00 Azerbaijan v Turkey
11.10.00 Moldova v Macedonia
11.10.00 Slovakia v Sweden
24.03.01 Turkey v Slovakia
24.03.01 Azerbaijan v Moldova
24.03.01 Sweden v Macedonia
28.03.01 Moldova v Sweden
28.03.01 Slovakia v Azerbaijan
28.03.01 Macedonia v Turkey
02.06.01 Macedonia v Moldova
02.06.01 Sweden v Slovakia
02.06.01 Turkey v Azerbaijan

06.06.01 Azerbaijan v Slovakia
06.06.01 Turkey v Macedonia
06.06.01 Sweden v Moldova
01.09.01 Moldova v Azerbaijan
01.09.01 Slovakia v Turkey
01.09.01 Macedonia v Sweden
05.09.01 Turkey v Sweden
05.09.01 Azerbaijan v Macedonia
05.09.01 Slovakia v Moldova
07.10.01 Sweden v Azerbaijan
07.10.01 Moldova v Turkey
07.10.01 Macedonia v Slovakia

Group 5
Norway, Ukraine, Poland, Wales, Armenia, Belarus
02.09.00 Ukraine v Poland
02.09.00 Norway v Armenia
02.09.00 Belarus v Wales
07.10.00 Poland v Belarus
07.10.00 Armenia v Ukraine
07.10.00 Wales v Norway
10.10.00 Poland v Wales
10.10.00 Norway v Ukraine
10.10.00 Belarus v Armenia
24.03.01 Ukraine v Belarus
24.03.01 Norway v Poland
24.03.01 Armenia v Wales
27.03.01 Poland v Armenia
27.03.01 Wales v Ukraine
27.03.01 Belarus v Norway
02.06.01 Ukraine v Norway
02.06.01 Armenia v Belarus
02.06.01 Wales v Poland
05.06.01 Armenia v Poland
05.06.01 Ukraine v Wales
05.06.01 Norway v Belarus
01.09.01 Wales v Armenia
01.09.01 Belarus v Ukraine
01.09.01 Poland v Norway
04.09.01 Norway v Wales
04.09.01 Belarus v Poland
04.09.01 Ukraine v Armenia
06.10.01 Armenia v Norway
06.10.01 Poland v Ukraine
06.10.01 Wales v Belarus

Group 6
Belgium, Scotland, Croatia, Latvia, San Marino
02.09.00 Latvia v Scotland
02.09.00 Belgium v Croatia
07.10.00 Latvia v Belgium
07.10.00 San Marino v Scotland
11.10.00 Croatia v Scotland
15.11.00 San Marino v Latvia
14.02.01 Belgium v San Marino
24.03.01 Scotland v Belgium
24.03.01 Croatia v Latvia
28.03.01 Scotland v San Marino
25.04.01 Latvia v San Marino
02.06.01 Croatia v San Marino
02.06.01 Belgium v Latvia
06.06.01 San Marino v Belgium
06.06.01 Latvia v Croatia
01.09.01 Scotland v Croatia
05.09.01 Belgium v Scotland
05.09.01 San Marino v Croatia
06.10.01 Scotland v Latvia
06.10.01 Croatia v Belgium

Group 7
Spain, Austria, Israel, Bosnia, Liechtenstein
02.09.00 Bosnia v Spain
03.09.00 Israel v Liechtenstein
07.10.00 Liechtenstein v Austria
07.10.00 Spain v Israel
11.10.00 Israel v Bosnia
11.10.00 Austria v Spain
24.03.01 Bosnia v Austria
24.03.01 Spain v Liechtenstein
28.03.01 Austria v Israel
28.03.01 Liechtenstein v Bosnia
02.06.01 Spain v Bosnia
02.06.01 Liechtenstein v Israel
06.06.01 Austria v Liechtenstein
06.06.01 Israel v Spain
01.09.01 Spain v Austria
01.09.01 Bosnia v Israel
05.09.01 Liechtenstein v Spain
05.09.01 Austria v Bosnia
07.10.01 Bosnia v Liechtenstein
07.10.01 Israel v Austria

Group 8
Romania, Italy, Lithuania, Hungary, Georgia
02.09.00 Romania v Lithuania
02.09.00 Hungary v Italy
07.10.00 Italy v Romania
07.10.00 Lithuania v Georgia
11.10.00 Lithuania v Hungary
11.10.00 Italy v Georgia
24.03.01 Hungary v Lithuania
24.03.01 Romania v Italy
28.03.01 Georgia v Romania
28.03.01 Italy v Lithuania
02.06.01 Romania v Hungary
02.06.01 Georgia v Italy
06.06.01 Lithuania v Romania
06.06.01 Hungary v Georgia
01.09.01 Lithuania v Italy
01.09.01 Georgia v Hungary
05.09.01 Georgia v Lithuania
05.09.01 Hungary v Romania
06.10.01 Romania v Georgia
06.10.01 Italy v Hungary

Group 9
Germany, England, Greece, Finland, Albania
02.09.00 Finland v Albania
02.09.00 Germany v Greece
07.10.00 Greece v Finland
07.10.00 England v Germany
11.10.00 Finland v England
11.10.00 Albania v Greece
24.03.01 Germany v Albania
24.03.01 England v Finland
28.03.01 Albania v England
28.03.01 Greece v Germany
02.06.01 Finland v Germany
02.06.01 Greece v Albania
06.06.01 Greece v England
06.06.01 Albania v Germany
01.09.01 Albania v Finland
01.09.01 Germany v England
05.09.01 Finland v Greece
05.09.01 England v Albania
06.10.01 Germany v Finland
06.10.01 England v Greece

WORLD CLUB CHAMPIONSHIP

Played annually up to 1974 and intermittently since then between the winners of the European Cup and the winners of the South American Champions Cup — known as the Copa Libertadores. In 1980 the winners were decided by one match arranged in Tokyo in February 1981 and the venue has been the same since. AC Milan replaced Marseille who had been stripped of their European Cup title in 1993.

1960 Real Madrid beat Penarol 0-0, 5-1
1961 Penarol beat Benfica 0-1, 5-0, 2-1
1962 Santos beat Benfica 3-2, 5-2
1963 Santos beat AC Milan 2-4, 4-2, 1-0
1964 Inter-Milan beat Independiente 0-1, 2-0, 1-0
1965 Inter-Milan beat Independiente 3-0, 0-0
1966 Penarol beat Real Madrid 2-0, 2-0
1967 Racing Club beat Celtic 0-1, 2-1, 1-0
1968 Estudiantes beat Manchester United 1-0, 1-1
1969 AC Milan beat Estudiantes 3-0, 1-2
1970 Feyenoord beat Estudiantes 2-2, 1-0
1971 Nacional beat Panathinaikos* 1-1, 2-1
1972 Ajax beat Independiente 1-1, 3-0
1973 Independiente beat Juventus* 1-0
1974 Atlético Madrid* beat Independiente 0-1, 2-0
1975 Independiente and Bayern Munich could not agree dates; no matches.
1976 Bayern Munich beat Cruzeiro 2-0, 0-0
1977 Boca Juniors beat Borussia Moenchengladbach* 2-2, 3-0
1978 Not contested
1979 Olimpia beat Malmö* 1-0, 2-1
1980 Nacional beat Nottingham Forest 1-0
1981 Flamengo beat Liverpool 3-0
1982 Penarol beat Aston Villa 2-0
1983 Gremio Porto Alegre beat SV Hamburg 2-1
1984 Independiente beat Liverpool 1-0
1985 Juventus beat Argentinos Juniors 4-2 on penalties after a 2-2 draw
1986 River Plate beat Steaua Bucharest 1-0
1987 FC Porto beat Penarol 2-1 after extra time
1988 Nacional (Uru) beat PSV Eindhoven 7-6 on penalties after 1-1 draw
1989 AC Milan beat Atletico Nacional (Col) 1-0 after extra time
1990 AC Milan beat Olimpia 3-0
1991 Red Star Belgrade beat Colo Colo 3-0
1992 Sao Paulo beat Barcelona 2-1
1993 Sao Paulo beat AC Milan 3-2
1994 Velez Sarsfield beat AC Milan 2-0
1995 Ajax beat Gremio Porto Alegre 4-3 on penalties after 0-0 draw
1996 Juventus beat River Plate 1-0
1997 Borussia Dortmund beat Cruzeiro 2-0
1998 Real Madrid beat Vasco da Gama 2-1
*European Cup runners-up; winners declined to take part.

1999

30 November in Tokyo

Manchester U (1) 1

Palmeiras (0) 0 53,372

Manchester U: Bosnich; Neville G, Irwin, Silvestre, Keane, Stam, Beckham, Butt, Solskjaer (York 46), Scholes (Sheringham 74), Giggs.
Scorer: Keane 35.
Palmeiras: Marcos; Arce, Roque Junior, Cesar Sampaio, Junior Baiano, Junior, Galeano (Evair 54), Alex, Asprilla (Oseas 56), Nunes (Euller 77), Zinho.
Referee: Krug (Germany).

EUROPEAN SUPER CUP

Played annually between the winners of the European Champions' Cup and the European Cup-Winners' Cup. AC Milan replaced Marseille in 1993–94.

Previous Matches
1972 Ajax beat Rangers 3-1, 3-2
1973 Ajax beat AC Milan 0-1, 6-0
1974 Not contested
1975 Dynamo Kiev beat Bayern Munich 1-0, 2-0
1976 Anderlecht beat Bayern Munich 4-1, 1-2
1977 Liverpool beat Hamburg 1-1, 6-0
1978 Anderlecht beat Liverpool 3-1, 1-2
1979 Nottingham F beat Barcelona 1-0, 1-1
1980 Valencia beat Nottingham F 1-0, 1-2
1981 Not contested
1982 Aston Villa beat Barcelona 0-1, 3-0
1983 Aberdeen beat Hamburg 0-0, 2-0
1984 Juventus beat Liverpool 2-0
1985 Juventus v Everton not contested due to UEFA ban on English clubs
1986 Steaua Bucharest beat Dynamo Kiev 1-0
1987 FC Porto beat Ajax 1-0, 1-0
1988 KV Mechelen beat PSV Eindhoven 3-0, 0-1
1989 AC Milan beat Barcelona 1-1, 1-0
1990 AC Milan beat Sampdoria 1-1, 2-0
1991 Manchester U beat Red Star Belgrade 1-0
1992 Barcelona beat Werder Bremen 1-1, 2-1
1993 Parma beat AC Milan 0-1, 2-0
1994 AC Milan beat Arsenal 0-0, 2-0
1995 Ajax beat Zaragoza 1-1, 4-0
1996 Juventus beat Paris St Germain 6-1, 3-1
1997 Barcelona beat Borussia Dortmund 2-0, 1-1
1998 Chelsea beat Real Madrid 1-0

1999

27 August 1999, Monaco

Lazio (1) 1 *(Salas 35)*

Manchester U (0) 0 14,461

Lazio: Marchegiani; Negro, Pancaro, Nedved (Simeone 65), Nesta, Mihajlovic, Stankovic, Veron, Inzaghi (Salas 23), Mancini (Lombardo 83), Almeyda.
Manchester U: Van der Gouw; Neville G, Neville P, Berg, Keane, Stam (Curtis 56), Beckham (Cruyff 57), Scholes, Cole (Greening 77), Sheringham, Solskjaer.
Referee: Wojcik (Poland).

FIFA CLUB WORLD CHAMPIONSHIP

GROUP A

Corinthians (0) 2 *(Luizao 50, Fabio Luciano 65)*
Raja (0) 0

Real Madrid (1) 3 *(Anelka 21, Raul 62, Savio 71 (pen))*
Al Nassr (1) 1 *(Al-Husseini 45 (pen))*

GROUP B

Manchester United (0) 1 *(Yorke 82)*
Necaxa (1) 1 *(Montecinos 15)*

Vasco da Gama (0) 2 *(Felipe 53, Edmundo 86)*
South Melbourne (0) 0

GROUP A

Al Nassr (1) 4 *(Fuad Amin 3, Ahmed Bahja 48, Al-Husseini 50, Moussa Saib 85)*
Raja (1) 3 *(Al-Husseini 24 (og), El-Moubarki 67, El-Karkouri 73)*

Corinthians (1) 2 *(Edilson 28, 63)*
Real Madrid (1) 2 *(Anelka 19, 70)*

GROUP B

Necaxa (2) 3 *(Montecinos 18, Delgado 28, Cabrera 78)*
South Melbourne (0) 1 *(Anastasiadis 48)*

Vasco da Gama (3) 3 *(Romario 24, 26, Edmundo 43)*
Manchester United (0) 1 *(Butt 81)*

GROUP A

Al Nassr (0) 0
Corinthians (1) 2 *(Ricardinho 24, Rincon 81)*

Real Madrid (0) 3 *(Hierro 38, Morientes 52, Geremi 88)*
Raja (1) 2 *(Achami 28, Moustaoudia 59)*

GROUP B

Manchester United (2) 2 *(Fortune 8, 20)*
South Melbourne (0) 0

Vasco da Gama (1) 2 *(Odvan 14, Romario 69)*
Necaxa (1) 1 *(Aguinaga 5)*

THIRD PLACE PLAY-OFF

Real Madrid (1) 1 *(Raul 15)*
Necaxa (0) 1 *(Delgado 58)*

FINAL

Corinthians (0) 0
Vasco da Gama (0) 0

Corinthians: Dida; Indio, Adilson, Vampeta (Gilmar 91), Kieber, Marcelinho, Rincon, Fabio Luciano, Edilson (Fernando Baiano 113), Ricardinho (Edu 46), Luizao.
Vasco da Gama: Helton; Odvan, Amaral, Paulo Miranda, Mauro Galvao, Felipe (Alex de Oliveira 102), Juninho (Viola 96), Gilberto, Ramon (Donizete 111), Romario, Edmundo.
aet; Corinthians won 4-3 on penalties.
Referee: Jol (Holland).

SOUTH AMERICAN CHAMPIONSHIP

(Copa America)

1916	Uruguay	1937	Argentina	1959	Uruguay
1917	Uruguay	1939	Peru	1963	Bolivia
1919	Brazil	1941	Argentina	1967	Uruguay
1920	Uruguay	1942	Uruguay	1975	Peru
1921	Argentina	1945	Argentina	1979	Paraguay
1922	Brazil	1946	Argentina	1983	Uruguay
1923	Uruguay	1947	Argentina	1987	Uruguay
1924	Uruguay	1949	Brazil	1989	Brazil
1925	Argentina	1953	Paraguay	1991	Argentina
1926	Uruguay	1955	Argentina	1993	Argentina
1927	Argentina	1956	Uruguay	1995	Uruguay
1929	Argentina	1957	Argentina	1997	Brazil
1935	Uruguay	1959	Argentina	1999	Brazil

SOUTH AMERICAN CUP

(Copa Libertadores)

1960	Penarol (Uruguay)	1981	Flamengo (Brazil)
1961	Penarol	1982	Penarol
1962	Santos (Brazil)	1983	Gremio Porto Alegre (Brazil)
1963	Santos	1984	Independiente
1964	Independiente (Argentina)	1985	Argentinos Juniors (Argentina)
1965	Independiente	1986	River Plate (Argentina)
1966	Penarol	1987	Penarol
1967	Racing Club (Argentina)	1988	Nacional (Uruguay)
1968	Estudiantes (Argentina)	1989	Nacional (Colombia)
1969	Estudiantes	1990	Olimpia
1970	Estudiantes	1991	Colo Colo (Chile)
1971	Nacional (Uruguay)	1992	São Paulo (Brazil)
1972	Independiente	1993	São Paulo
1973	Independiente	1994	Velez Sarsfield (Argentina)
1974	Independiente	1995	Gremio Porto Alegre
1975	Independiente	1996	River Plate
1976	Cruzeiro (Brazil)	1997	Cruzeiro
1977	Boca Juniors (Argentina)	1998	Vasco da Gama
1978	Boca Juniors	1999	Palmeiras
1979	Olimpia (Paraguay)	2000	Boca Juniors
1980	Nacional		

OTHER BRITISH AND IRISH INTERNATIONAL MATCHES 1999–2000

Sunderland, 10 October 1999, 40,897

England (1) 2 *(Shearer 6, Redknapp 66)*

Belgium (1) 1 *(Strupar 14)*

England: Seaman (Martyn 46); Dyer (Neville P 57), Guppy, Keown, Adams, Southgate, Lampard (Wise 75), Redknapp, Shearer (Heskey 85), Phillips (Owen 57), Ince.
Belgium: De Vlieger (Gaspercic 46); Deflandre, Peeters, Van Meir, Oyen, Tanghe (Walem 46), Vanderhaeghe, Wilmots, Van Kerckhoven, De Bilde, Strupar (Brogno 72).
Referee: Frisk (Sweden).

Wembley, 23 February 2000, 74,008

England (0) 0

Argentina (0) 0

England: Seaman; Dyer (Neville P 59), Wilcox, Southgate, Keown (Ferdinand R 46), Campbell, Beckham (Parlour 73), Scholes, Shearer (Phillips 78), Heskey (Cole 79), Wise.
Argentina: Cavallero; Zanetti, Arruabarrena (Vivas 67), Ayala, Sensini (Pochettino 34), Chamot, Simeone, Veron, Batistuta (Crespo 57), Ortega (Lopez 90), Gonzalez.
Referee: Merk (Germany).

Wembley, 27 May 2000, 73,956

England (1) 1 *(Owen 38)*

Brazil (1) 1 *(Franca 45)*

England: Seaman; Neville G, Neville P, Ince (Parlour 60 (Barmby 90)), Keown, Campbell, Beckham, Scholes, Shearer (Fowler 84), Owen (Phillips 84), Wise.
Brazil: Dida; Carlos (Carvalho 81), Aldair, Cafu, Cesar Sampaio, Emerson, Silvinho (Roberto Carlos 60), Ze Roberto, Franca, Rivaldo, Amoroso (Denilson 68).
Referee: Wojcik (Poland).

Wembley, 31 May 2000, 55,975

England (1) 2 *(Fowler 44, Adams 68)*

Ukraine (0) 0

England: Martyn; Gerrard (Dyer 81), Neville P (Barry 73), Southgate, Adams, Campbell, Beckham, Scholes (Barmby 73), Shearer, Fowler (Heskey 46), McManaman.
Ukraine: Kernozenko (Virt 84); Luzhny, Dmitrulin, Golovko, Popov, Vashchuk, Kandaurov (Moroz 46), Tymoschuk, Shevchenko, Rebrov, Gusin.
Referee: Michel (Slovakia).

Valletta, 3 June 2000, 10,023

Malta (1) 1 *(Wright 29 (og))*

England (1) 2 *(Keown 23, Heskey 75)*

Malta: Barry (Muscat 90); Debono (Camilleri 33), Buttigieg (Chetcuti 54), Said (Okonkwo 77), Carabott (Ciantar 90), Brincat (Holland 82), Vella (Theuma 41), Turner (Veselji 86), Spiteri (Dimech 77), Busuttil (Nwoko 46), Agius (Mallia 59).

England: Wright; Neville G, Neville P, Wise (Ince 68), Keown (Southgate 58), Campbell, Beckham (Barry 79), Barmby, Shearer (Heskey 50), Phillips (Fowler 58), Scholes (McManaman 68).
Referee: Braschi (Italy).

Hampden Park, 29 March 2000, 48,157

Scotland (0) 0

France (0) 2 *(Wiltord 54, Henry 89)*

Scotland: Sullivan; Telfer (Johnston 68), Davidson, Dailly, Hendry, Ritchie (Pressley 46), Cameron (McCann 46), Ferguson B, Dodds, Gallacher (Burchill 79), Hutchison.
France: Rame; Thuram, Lizarazu, Deschamps (Vieira 59), Blanc, Desailly, Giuly (Wiltord 46), Dugarry (Pires 72), Henry, Djorkaeff (Micoud 46), Petit.
Referee: Pedersen (Norway).

Arnhem, 26 April 2000, 24,500

Holland (0) 0

Scotland (0) 0

Holland: Van der Sar; Ooijer, Numan, Bosvelt, Konterman, Frank de Boer, Makaay (Talan 60), Hasselbaink (Van Hooijdonk 66), Bergkamp (Kluivert 46), Davids, Overmars (Zenden 46).
Scotland: Sullivan; McNamara (Burchill 66), Ritchie, Dailly (O'Neil 84), Elliott, Weir, Burley (Durrant 46), Lambert, Dodds, Hutchison, McCann.
Referee: Strampe (Germany).

Dublin, 30 May 2000, 30,213

Republic of Ireland (1) 1 *(Kennedy 2)*

Scotland (2) 2 *(Hutchison 15, Ferguson B 27)*

Republic of Ireland: Kelly A; Carr, Kilbane, McAteer, Breen (Dunne 75), Babb, Finnan, Kennedy (Duff 64), McPhail (Phelan 63), Quinn (Foley 75), Robbie Keane.
Scotland: Sullivan; Burley, Naysmith (Holt 89), O'Neil, Elliott, Dailly, Ferguson B (Cameron 84), Lambert (Johnston 75), Dodds (Gallacher 46), Hutchison, McCann (Pressley 90).
Referee: Pereira (Portugal).

Doha, 23 February 2000, 2000

Qatar (0) 0

Wales (1) 1 *(Robinson J 10)*

Qatar: Khalil (Hussain 81); Z Al Kuwari (Saad 65), Al Tamimi, Fatah, Al Nobbi, Kuwari, Jassim (Obaildy 71), Nadmi (Hasan 90), Hassan (Mohd 78), F Al Kuwari, Salim Al Enizi (Mubarek 63).
Wales: Jones P; Delaney, Barnard (Simons 90), Page, Coleman, Melville, Robinson J, Jones M, Blake, Pembridge, Speed.
Referee: Aziz (Bahrain).

Millennium Stadium, Cardiff, 29 March 2000, 66,500

Wales (0) 1 *(Giggs 60)*

Finland (2) 2 *(Litmanen 21, Blake 42 (og))*

Wales: Crossley; Savage (Johnson 79), Barnard (Roberts G 70), Page, Coleman, Melville, Robinson J, Pembridge (Roberts I 85), Blake (Saunders 79), Speed, Giggs.

Finland: Enckelman (Moilanen 46); Reini, Tihinen, Hyypia, Saastamoinen (Tuomela 46), Kolkka, Valakari (Wiss 65), Litmanen (Lehkuoso 70), Forssell (Paatelainen 46), Riihilahti, Nurmela.
Referee: Ross (Northern Ireland).

Millennium Stadium, Cardiff, 23 May 2000, 72,500

Wales (0) 0

Brazil (0) 3 *(Elber 62, Cafu 70, Rivaldo 72)*

Wales: Freestone; Delaney, Roberts G, Page, Melville, Savage (Bellamy 75), Robinson J, Jones M (Johnson 75), Saunders (Barnard 84), Roberts I, Speed.
Brazil: Dida; Carlos (Assuncao 83), Silvinho, Cafu, Aldair (Denilson 71), Cesar Sampaio (Carvalho 83), Ze Roberto, Emerson, Rivaldo (Evanilson 83), Elber, Franca.
Referee: Pereira (Portugal).

Chaves, 2 June 2000, 11,000

Portugal (2) 3 *(Figo 21, Sa Pinto 44, Capucho 66)*

Wales (0) 0

Portugal: Vitor Baia; Secretario (Costinha 59), Dimas (Rui Jorge 69), Fernando Couto, Jorge Costa, Vidigal (Conceicao 46), Paulo Bento, Figo (Capucho 59), Rui Costa, Joao Pinto (Pauleta 78), Sa Pinto (Nuno Gomes 62).
Wales: Ward; Delaney, Roberts G (Weston 83), Page, Melville, Barnard (Robinson C 66), Robinson J, Jones M, Roberts I, Bellamy, Speed (Johnson 31).
Referee: Bleeckere (Belgium).

Windsor Park, Belfast, 18 August 2000, 11,804

Northern Ireland (0) 0

France (0) 1 *(Laslandes 67)*

Northern Ireland: Taylor (Wright 46); Hughes A, Horlock, Lomas, Williams M, Hunter, McCarthy, Lennon, Dowie (Quinn 55), Hughes M, Kennedy (Gillespie 74).
France: Barthez; Thuram, Lizarazu (Candela 55), Vieira (Dehu 83), Blanc, Desailly (Leboeuf 65), Pires, Boghossian, Laslandes (Vairelles 75), Micoud, Wiltord (Robert 55).
Referee: Young (Scotland).

Luxembourg, 23 February 2000, 1818

Luxembourg (1) 1 *(Cardoni 41)*

Northern Ireland (1) 3 *(Healy 21, 48, Quinn 87)*

Luxembourg: Besic; Vanek, Schaack, Birsens (Alverdi 5), Strasser, Saibene, Deville F, Holtz (Huss 75), Braun (Zaritski 61), Cardoni, Schneider (Christophe 46).
Northern Ireland: Carroll (Taylor 75); Nolan, Hughes A, Griffin (McGibbon 87), Williams M (Murdock 65), Lomas, Magilton (Sonner 75), Johnson (Hughes M 77), Quinn (Coote 87), Healy, Gillespie (Robinson 87).
Referee: Schutiengruber (Austria).

Valletta, 28 March 2000, 956

Malta (0) 0

Northern Ireland (3) 3 *(Hughes M 13 (pen), Quinn 15, Healy 41)*

Malta: Barry (Muscat 46); Said, Debono, Buttigieg (Turner 46), Chetcuti, Carabott (Ifeanyi 46), Busuttil (Veselji 63), Vella (Azzopardi 56), Ciantar, Nwoko (Mallia 78), Agius (Miscud 46).

Northern Ireland: Carroll (Taylor 86); Nolan, Griffin, Lomas, Williams M, Murdock (Sonner 46), Gillespie (Johnson 63), Quinn (Coote 70), Healy, Hughes M (Horlock 77).
Referee: De Santis (Italy).

Windsor Park, Belfast, 26 April 2000, 9140

Northern Ireland (0) 0

Hungary (0) 1 *(Horvath 61)*
Northern Ireland: Taylor; Griffin (Johnson 72), Nolan, Lennon, Hughes A, Taggart (Williams M 58), Gillespie (Murdock 73), Sonner, Kirk (Coote 58), Healy, Hughes M.
Hungary: Kiraly; Hrutka, Sebok V, Matyus, Feher C, Lendvai, Dardai (Halmai 46), Illes, Peto (Korsos 56), Preisinger (Herczeg 77), Horvath (Hamar 88).
Referee: Richards (Wales).

Dublin, 23 February 2000, 30,543

Republic of Ireland (2) 3 *(Rada 16 (og), Harte 43, Robbie Keane 87)*

Czech Republic (2) 2 *(Koller 4, 35)*
Republic of Ireland: Kelly A; Kelly G, Harte, Kilbane (Staunton 83), Cunningham, Butler (Babb 46), Kennedy (McAteer 46), Kinsella, Quinn, Robbie Keane (Connolly 90), Roy Keane.
Czech Republic: Maier; Repka (Suchoparek 46), Rada, Gabriel, Poborsky, Bejbl, Nedved (Rosicky 83), Nemec (Latal 63), Smicer (Wagner 66), Koller (Kuka 69), Berger (Horvath 73).
Referee: Coue (France).

NIKE CUP

Chicago, 4 June 2000

Republic of Ireland (0) 2 *(Dunne 59, Foley 71)*

Mexico (1) 2 *(Osorno 37, Sanchez 53)*
Republic of Ireland: Kiely; Carr, Phelan, Breen, Dunne (Babb 81), Holland, McAteer, Quinn B (Kilbane 41), Quinn N, Robbie Keane (Foley 46), Kennedy.
Mexico: Bernal; Beltran, Ramirez (Giminez 69), Alpizar, Lopez, Torrado, Perez, Sancho, Sanchez (Galinda 81), Gonzalez, Osorno.
Referee: Stott (USA).

Boston, 6 June 2000

Republic of Ireland (1) 1 *(Foley 31)*

USA (0) 1 *(Razov 68)*
Republic of Ireland: Kelly; Carr, Phelan, Breen, Babb, Holland, Farrelly (Kennedy 72), McPhail (McAteer 37), Doherty (Quinn N 72), Foley (Quinn B 88), Kilbane.
USA: Friedel; Hejduk, Berhalter, Brown, Vanney, O'Brien (Reyna 58), Kirovski, Olsen (Zanneh 75), Ralston (Stewart 46), Kreis (Jones 65), Razov (McBride 88).
Referee: Archondia (Mexico).

New Jersey, 11 June, 2000

Republic of Ireland (1) 2 *(McPhail 43, Quinn N 69)*

South Africa (1) 1 *(Bartlett 17)*
Republic of Ireland: Given; Carr, Phelan, Breen, Babb, Holland, McAteer (Kennedy 44), McPhail (Quinn B 85), Quinn N (Doherty 76), Foley (Robbie Keane 46), Mahon (Kilbane 42).
South Africa: Arendse; Lekgetho, Rabuta, Mokoena, Nzama, Buckley, Fortune (Swane 76), Ngobe (Mayo 46), Mhkalele (Mngomeni 76), McCartay (Sheppard 46), Bartlett.
Referee: Badilla (Mexico).

ENGLAND UNDER-21 TEAMS 1999–2000

3 Sept

England (2) 5 *(Gerrard 12, Jeffers 31, Hendrie 60, Cort 69, Lampard 79)*

Luxembourg (0) 0 18,094

England: Weaver; Mills, Ball, Gerrard, Carragher, Upson (King 69), Lampard (Thompson 82), Chadwick, Heskey (Cort 49), Jeffers, Hendrie.

7 Sept

Poland (0) 3 *(Kubik 46, Dawidowski 57, Sobczak 61)*

England (0) 1 *(Mills 48)* 1500

England: Weaver; Curtis (Woodhouse 65), Robinson, Carragher, Mills, Upson, Greening (Thompson 80), Gerrard, Beattie, Cort (Vassell 46), Morris.

8 Oct

England (2) 4 *(Smith 19, Bowyer 30, Cort 83, Thompson 90)*

Denmark (0) 1 *(Magleby 72)* 15,220

England: Robinson; Mills, Johnson (Ball 83), Carragher (Young 75), Gerrard, Upson, Chadwick, Bowyer (Thompson 65), Smith, Hendrie, Bridges (Cort 75).

22 Feb

England (0) 1 *(Hendrie 68)*

Argentina (0) 0 15,748

England: Weaver; Mills (Young 46), Naylor (Johnson 69), Carragher, Lampard, Woodgate, Chadwick, Bowyer (Cole 46), Cort, Hendrie, Jeffers (Smith 8 (Harley 80)).

29 Mar

England (1) 3 *(Campbell 24, Lampard 49 (pen), Hendrie 64)*

Yugoslavia (0) 0 1000

England: Wright; Dyer, Johnson, Carragher, Ferdinand, Barry, Lampard, Gerrard, Heskey (Davies 77), Hendrie (Mills 87), Campbell (Cadamarteri 86).

27 May

Italy (2) 2 *(Comandini 24, Pirlo 45 (pen))*

England (0) 0

England: Weaver; Mills, Carragher, King, Thompson (Chadwick 74), Lampard, Murphy, Johnson, Hendrie (Dunn 46), Cort (Jansen 66), Jeffers.

29 May

England (2) 6 *(Lampard 28, Jeffers 45, Cort 66, King 73, Mills 77, Campbell 90)*

Turkey (0) 0 250

England: Weaver; Young, Carragher, King, Mills, Murphy (Thompson 79), Lampard, Dunn, Johnson (Harley 79), Cort, Jeffers (Campbell 75).

1 June

England (0) 0

Slovakia (0) 2 *(Babnic 67, Nemeth 74)* 9113

England: Weaver; Young, Carragher, King, Mills, Murphy, Lampard, Dunn (Campell 46), Harley (Hendrie 46), Cort, Jeffers (Chadwick 78).

POST-WAR INTERNATIONAL APPEARANCES

As at July 2000 *(Season of first cap given)*

ENGLAND

A'Court, A. (5) 1957/8 Liverpool
Adams, T. A. (64) 1986/7 Arsenal
Allen, C. (5) 1983/4 QPR, Tottenham H
Allen, R. (5) 1951/2 WBA
Allen, T. (3) 1959/60 Stoke C
Anderson, S. (2) 1961/2 Sunderland
Anderson, V. (30) 1978/9 Nottingham F, Arsenal, Manchester U
Anderton, D. R. (27) 1993/4 Tottenham H
Angus, J. (1) 1960/1 Burnley
Armfield, J. (43) 1958/9 Blackpool
Armstrong, D. (3) 1979/80 Middlesbrough, Southampton
Armstrong, K. (1) 1954/5 Chelsea
Astall, G. (2) 1955/6 Birmingham C
Astle, J. (5) 1968/9 WBA
Aston, J. (17) 1948/9 Manchester U
Atyeo, J. (6) 1955/6 Bristol C

Bailey, G. R. (2) 1984/5 Manchester U
Bailey, M. (2) 1963/4 Charlton
Baily, E. (9) 1949/50 Tottenham H
Baker, J. (8) 1959/60 Hibernian, Arsenal
Ball, A. (72) 1964/5 Blackpool, Everton, Arsenal
Banks, G. (73) 1962/3 Leicester C, Stoke C
Banks, T. (6) 1957/8 Bolton W
Bardsley, D. (2) 1992/3 QPR
Barham, M. (2) 1982/3 Norwich C
Barlow, R. (1) 1954/5 WBA
Barmby, N. J. (15) 1994/5 Tottenham H, Middlesbrough, Everton
Barnes, J. (79) 1982/3 Watford, Liverpool
Barnes, P. (22) 1977/8 Manchester C, WBA, Leeds U
Barrass, M. (3) 1951/2 Bolton W
Barrett, E. D. (3) 1990/1 Oldham Ath, Aston Villa
Barry, G. (2) 1999/00 Aston Villa
Barton, W. D. (3) 1994/5 Wimbledon, Blackburn R
Batty, D. (42) 1990/1 Leeds U, Blackburn R, Newcastle U, Leeds U
Baynham, R. (3) 1955/6 Luton T
Beardsley, P. A. (59) 1985/6 Newcastle U, Liverpool, Newcastle U
Beasant, D. J. (2) 1989/90 Chelsea
Beattie, T. K. (9) 1974/5 Ipswich T
Beckham, D. R. J. (34) 1996/7 Manchester U
Bell, C. (48) 1967/8 Manchester C
Bentley, R. (12) 1948/9 Chelsea
Berry, J. (4) 1952/3 Manchester U
Birtles, G. (3) 1979/80 Nottingham F, Manchester U
Blissett, L. (14) 1982/3 Watford, AC Milan
Blockley, J. (1) 1972/3 Arsenal
Blunstone, F. (5) 1954/5 Chelsea
Bonetti, P. (7) 1965/6 Chelsea
Bould, S. A. (2) 1993/4 Arsenal
Bowles, S. (5) 1973/4 QPR
Boyer, P. (1) 1975/6 Norwich C
Brabrook, P. (3) 1957/8 Chelsea
Bracewell, P. W. (3) 1984/5 Everton
Bradford, G. (1) 1955/6 Bristol R
Bradley, W. (3) 1958/9 Manchester U
Bridges, B. (4) 1964/5 Chelsea
Broadbent, P. (7) 1957/8 Wolverhampton W
Broadis, I. (14) 1951/2 Manchester C, Newcastle U
Brooking, T. (47) 1973/4 West Ham U
Brooks, J. (3) 1956/7 Tottenham H
Brown, A. (1) 1970/1 WBA
Brown, K. (1) 1959/60 West Ham U
Brown, W. M. (1) 1998/9 Manchester U
Bull, S. G. (13) 1988/9 Wolverhampton W
Butcher, T. (77) 1979/80 Ipswich T, Rangers
Butt, N. (8) 1996/7 Manchester U
Byrne, G. (2) 1962/3 Liverpool
Byrne, J. (11) 1961/2 Crystal P, West Ham U
Byrne, R. (33) 1953/4 Manchester U

Callaghan, I. (4) 1965/6 Liverpool
Campbell, S. (36) 1995/6 Tottenham H
Carragher, J. L. (1) 1998/9 Liverpool
Carter, H. (7) 1946/7 Derby C
Chamberlain, M. (8) 1982/3 Stoke C
Channon, M. (46) 1972/3 Southampton, Manchester C
Charles, G. A. (2) 1990/1 Nottingham F
Charlton, J. (35) 1964/5 Leeds U
Charlton, R. (106) 1957/8 Manchester U
Charnley, R. (1) 1961/2 Blackpool
Cherry, T. (27) 1975/6 Leeds U
Chilton, A. (2) 1950/1 Manchester U
Chivers, M. (24) 1970/1 Tottenham H
Clamp, E. (4) 1957/8 Wolverhampton W
Clapton, D. (1) 1958/9 Arsenal
Clarke, A. (19) 1969/70 Leeds U
Clarke, H. (1) 1953/4 Tottenham H
Clayton, R. (35) 1955/6 Blackburn R
Clemence, R (61) 1972/3 Liverpool, Tottenham H

Clement, D. (5) 1975/6 QPR
Clough, B. (2) 1959/60 Middlesbrough
Clough, N. H. (14) 1988/9 Nottingham F
Coates, R. (4) 1969/70 Burnley, Tottenham H
Cockburn, H. (13) 1946/7 Manchester U
Cohen, G. (37) 1963/4 Fulham
Cole, A. (7) 1994/5 Manchester U
Collymore, S. V. (3) 1994/5 Nottingham F
Compton, L. (2) 1950/1 Arsenal
Connelly J. (20) 1959/60 Burnley, Manchester U
Cooper, C. T. (2) 1994/5 Nottingham F
Cooper, T. (20) 1968/9 Leeds U
Coppell, S. (42) 1977/8 Manchester U
Corrigan J. (9) 1975/6 Manchester C
Cottee, A. R. (7) 1986/7 West Ham U, Everton
Cowans, G. (10) 1982/3 Aston Villa, Bari, Aston Villa
Crawford, R. (2) 1961/2 Ipswich T
Crowe, C. (1) 1962/3 Wolverhampton W
Cunningham, L. (6) 1978/9 WBA, Real Madrid
Curle, K. (3) 1991/2 Manchester C
Currie, A. (17) 1971/2 Sheffield U, Leeds U

Daley, A. M. (7) 1991/2 Aston Villa
Davenport, P. (1) 1984/5 Nottingham F
Deane, B. C. (3) 1990/1 Sheffield U
Deeley, N. (2) 1958/9 Wolverhampton W
Devonshire, A. (8) 1979/80 West Ham U
Dickinson, J. (48) 1948/9 Portsmouth
Ditchburn, E. (6) 1948/9 Tottenham H
Dixon, K. M. (8) 1984/5 Chelsea
Dixon, L. M. (22) 1989/90 Arsenal
Dobson, M. (5) 1973/4 Burnley, Everton
Dorigo, A. R. (15) 1989/90 Chelsea, Leeds U
Douglas, B. (36) 1957/8 Blackburn R
Doyle, M. (5) 1975/6 Manchester C
Dublin, D. (4) 1997/8 Coventry C, Aston Villa
Duxbury, M. (10) 1983/4 Manchester U
Dyer, K. C. (5) 1999/00 Newcastle U

Eastham, G. (19) 1962/3 Arsenal
Eckersley, W. (17) 1949/50 Blackburn R
Edwards, D. (18) 1954/5 Manchester U
Ehiogu, U. (1) 1995/6 Aston Villa
Ellerington, W. (2) 1948/9 Southampton
Elliott, W. H. (5) 1951/2 Burnley

Fantham, J. (1) 1961/2 Sheffield W
Fashanu, J. (2) 1988/9 Wimbledon
Fenwick, T. (20) 1983/4 QPR, Tottenham H
Ferdinand, L. (17) 1992/3 QPR, Newcastle U, Tottenham H
Ferdinand, R. G. (9) 1997/8 West Ham U
Finney, T. (76) 1946/7 Preston NE
Flowers, R. (49) 1954/5 Wolverhampton W
Flowers, T. (11) 1992/3 Southampton, Blackburn R
Foster, S. (3) 1981/2 Brighton
Foulkes, W. (1) 1954/5 Manchester U
Fowler, R. B. (14) 1995/6 Liverpool
Francis, G. (12) 1974/5 QPR
Francis, T. (52) 1976/7 Birmingham C, Nottingham F, Manchester C, Sampdoria
Franklin, N. (27) 1946/7 Stoke C
Froggatt, J. (13) 1949/50 Portsmouth
Froggatt, R. (4) 1952/3 Sheffield W

Garrett, T. (3) 1951/2 Blackpool
Gascoigne, P. J. (57) 1988/9 Tottenham H, Lazio, Rangers, Middlesbrough
Gates, E. (2) 1980/1 Ipswich T
George, F. C. (1) 1976/7 Derby C
Gerrard, S. G. (2) 1999/00 Liverpool
Gidman, J. (1) 1976/7 Aston Villa
Gillard, I. (3) 1974/5 QPR
Goddard, P. (1) 1981/2 West Ham U
Grainger, C. (7) 1955/6 Sheffield U, Sunderland
Gray, A. A. (1) 1991/2 Crystal P
Gray, M. (3) 1998/9 Sunderland
Greaves, J. (57) 1958/9 Chelsea, Tottenham H
Greenhoff, B. (18) 1975/6 Manchester U
Gregory, J. (6) 1982/3 QPR
Guppy, S. (1) 1999/00 Leicester C

Hagan, J. (1) 1948/9 Sheffield U
Haines, J. (1) 1948/9 WBA
Hall, J. (17) 1955/6 Birmingham C
Hancocks, J. (3) 1948/9 Wolverhampton W
Hardwick, G. (13) 1946/7 Middlesbrough
Harford, M. G. (2) 1987/8 Luton T
Harris, G. (1) 1965/6 Burnley
Harris, P. (2) 1949/50 Portsmouth
Harvey, C. (1) 1970/1 Everton
Hassall, H. (5) 1950/1 Huddersfield T, Bolton W
Hateley, M. (32) 1983/4 Portsmouth, AC Milan, Monaco, Rangers
Haynes, J. (56) 1954/5 Fulham
Hector, K. (2) 1973/4 Derby C
Hellawell, M. (2) 1962/3 Birmingham C
Hendrie, L. A. (1) 1998/9 Aston Villa
Henry, R. (1) 1962/3 Tottenham H
Heskey, E. W. (9) 1998/9 Leicester C, Liverpool
Hill, F. (2) 1962/3 Bolton W
Hill, G. (6) 1975/6 Manchester U
Hill, R. (3) 1982/3 Luton T

Hinchcliffe, A. G. (7) 1996/7 Everton, Sheffield W
Hinton A. (3) 1962/3 Wolverhampton W, Nottingham F
Hirst, D. E. (3) 1990/1 Sheffield W
Hitchens, G. (7) 1960/1 Aston Villa, Internazionale
Hoddle, G. (53) 1979/80 Tottenham H, Monaco
Hodge, S. B. (24) 1985/6 Aston Villa, Tottenham H, Nottingham F
Hodgkinson, A. (5) 1956/7 Sheffield U
Holden, D. (5) 1958/9 Bolton W
Holliday, E. (3) 1959/60 Middlesbrough
Hollins, J. (1) 1966/7 Chelsea
Hopkinson, E. (14) 1957/8 Bolton W
Howe, D. (23) 1957/8 WBA
Howe, J. (3) 1947/8 Derby C
Howey, S. N. (4) 1994/5 Newcastle U
Hudson, A. (2) 1974/5 Stoke C
Hughes, E. (62) 1969/70 Liverpool, Wolverhampton W
Hughes, L. (3) 1949/50 Liverpool
Hunt, R. (34) 1961/2 Liverpool
Hunt, S. (2) 1983/4 WBA
Hunter, N. (28) 1965/6 Leeds U
Hurst, G. (49) 1965/6 West Ham U

Ince, P. (53) 1992/3 Manchester U, Internazionale, Liverpool, Middlesbrough

James, D. B. (1) 1996/7 Liverpool
Jezzard, B. (2) 1953/4 Fulham
Johnson, D. (8) 1974/5 Ipswich T, Liverpool
Johnston, H. (10) 1946/7 Blackpool
Jones, M. (3) 1964/5 Sheffield U, Leeds U
Jones, R. (8) 1991/2 Liverpool
Jones, W. H. (2) 1949/50 Liverpool

Kay, A. (1) 1962/3 Everton
Keegan, K. (63) 1972/3 Liverpool, SV Hamburg, Southampton
Kennedy, A. (2) 1983/4 Liverpool
Kennedy, R. (17) 1975/6 Liverpool
Keown, M. R. (33) 1991/2 Everton, Arsenal
Kevan, D. (14) 1956/7 WBA
Kidd, B. (2) 1969/70 Manchester U
Knowles, C. (4) 1967/8 Tottenham H

Labone, B. (26) 1962/3 Everton
Lampard, F. J. (1) 1999/00 West Ham U
Lampard, F. (2) 1972/3 West Ham U
Langley, J. (3) 1957/8 Fulham
Langton, R. (11) 1946/7 Blackburn R, Preston NE, Bolton W
Latchford, R. (12) 1977/8 Everton
Lawler, C. (4) 1970/1 Liverpool
Lawton, T. (15) 1946/7 Chelsea, Notts C
Lee, F. (27) 1968/9 Manchester C
Lee, J. (1) 1950/1 Derby C
Lee, R. M. (21) 1994/5 Newcastle U
Lee, S. (14) 1982/3 Liverpool
Le Saux, G. P. (35) 1993/4 Blackburn R, Chelsea
Le Tissier, M. P. (8) 1993/4 Southampton
Lindsay, A. (4) 1973/4 Liverpool
Lineker, G. (80) 1983/4 Leicester C, Everton, Barcelona, Tottenham H
Little, B. (1) 1974/5 Aston Villa
Lloyd, L. (4) 1970/1 Liverpool, Nottingham F
Lofthouse, N. (33) 1950/1 Bolton W
Lowe, E. (3) 1946/7 Aston Villa

Mabbutt, G. (16) 1982/3 Tottenham H
Macdonald, M. (14) 1971/2 Newcastle U, Arsenal
Madeley, P. (24) 1970/1 Leeds U
Mannion, W. (26) 1946/7 Middlesbrough
Mariner, P. (35) 1976/7 Ipswich T, Arsenal
Marsh, R. (9) 1971/2 QPR, Manchester C
Martin, A. (17) 1980/1 West Ham U
Martyn, A. N. (14) 1991/2 Crystal P, Leeds U
Marwood, B. (1) 1988/9 Arsenal
Matthews, R. (5) 1955/6 Coventry C
Matthews, S. (37) 1946/7 Stoke C, Blackpool
McDermott, T. (25) 1977/8 Liverpool
McDonald, C. (8) 1957/8 Burnley
McFarland, R. (28) 1970/1 Derby C
McGarry, W. (4) 1953/4 Huddersfield T
McGuinness, W. (2) 1958/9 Manchester U
McMahon, S. (17) 1987/8 Liverpool
McManaman, S. (29) 1994/5 Liverpool, Real Madrid
McNab, R. (4) 1968/9 Arsenal
McNeil, M. (9) 1960/1 Middlesbrough
Meadows, J. (1) 1954/5 Manchester C
Medley, L. 1950/1 Tottenham H
Melia, J. (2) 1962/3 Liverpool
Merrick, G. (23) 1951/2 Birmingham C
Merson, P. C. (21) 1991/2 Arsenal, Middlesbrough, Aston Villa
Metcalfe, V. (2) 1950/1 Huddersfield T
Milburn, J. (13) 1948/9 Newcastle U
Miller, B. (1) 1960/1 Burnley
Mills, M. (42) 1972/3 Ipswich T
Milne, G. (14) 1962/3 Liverpool
Milton, C. A. (1) 1951/2 Arsenal
Moore, R. (108) 1961/2 West Ham U
Morley, A. (6) 1981/2 Aston Villa
Morris, J. (3) 1948/9 Derby C
Mortensen, S. (25) 1946/7 Blackpool
Mozley, B. (3) 1949/50 Derby C

Mullen, J. (12) 1946/7 Wolverhampton W
Mullery, A. (35) 1964/5 Tottenham H

Neal, P. (50) 1975/6 Liverpool
Neville, G. A. (39) 1994/5 Manchester U
Neville, P. J. (29) 1995/6 Manchester U
Newton, K. (27) 1965/6 Blackburn R, Everton
Nicholls, J. (2) 1953/4 WBA
Nicholson, W. (1) 1950/1 Tottenham H
Nish, D. (5) 1972/3 Derby C
Norman, M. (23) 1961/2 Tottenham H

O'Grady, M. (2) 1962/3 Huddersfield T, Leeds U
Osgood, P. (4) 1969/70 Chelsea
Osman, R. (11) 1979/80 Ipswich T
Owen, M. J. (22) 1997/8 Liverpool
Owen, S. (3) 1953/4 Luton T

Paine, T. (19) 1962/3 Southampton
Pallister, G. (22) 1987/8 Middlesbrough, Manchester U
Palmer, C. L. (18) 1991/2 Sheffield W
Parker, P. A. (19) 1988/9 QPR, Manchester U
Parkes, P. (1) 1973/4 QPR
Parlour, R. (7) 1998/9 Arsenal
Parry, R. (2) 1959/60 Bolton W
Peacock, A. (6) 1961/2 Middlesbrough, Leeds U
Pearce, S. (78) 1986/7 Nottingham F, West Ham U
Pearson, Stan (8) 1947/8 Manchester U
Pearson, Stuart (15) 1975/6 Manchester U
Pegg, D. (1) 1956/7 Manchester U
Pejic, M. (4) 1973/4 Stoke C
Perry, W. (3) 1955/6 Blackpool
Perryman, S. (1) 1981/2 Tottenham H
Peters, M. (67) 1965/6 West Ham U, Tottenham H
Phelan, M. C. (1) 1989/90 Manchester U
Phillips, K. (5) 1998/9 Sunderland
Phillips, L. (3) 1951/2 Portsmouth
Pickering, F. (3) 1963/4 Everton
Pickering, N. (1) 1982/3 Sunderland
Pilkington, B. (1) 1954/5 Burnley
Platt, D. (62) 1989/90 Aston Villa, Bari, Juventus, Sampdoria, Arsenal
Pointer, R. (3) 1961/2 Burnley
Pye, J. (1) 1949/50 Wolverhampton W

Quixall, A. (5) 1953/4 Sheffield W

Radford, J. (2) 1968/9 Arsenal
Ramsey, A. (32) 1948/9 Southampton, Tottenham H
Reaney, P. (3) 1968/9 Leeds U
Redknapp, J. F. (17) 1995/6 Liverpool
Reeves, K. (2) 1979/80 Norwich C
Regis, C. (5) 1981/2 WBA, Coventry C
Reid, P. (13) 1984/5 Everton
Revie, D. (6) 1954/5 Manchester C
Richards, J. (1) 1972/3 Wolverhampton W
Richardson, K. (1) 1993/4 Aston Villa
Rickaby, S. (1) 1953/4 WBA
Rimmer, J. (1) 1975/6 Arsenal
Ripley, S. E. (2) 1993/4 Blackburn R
Rix, G. (17) 1980/1 Arsenal
Robb, G. (1) 1953/4 Tottenham H
Roberts, G. (6) 1982/3 Tottenham H
Robson, B. (90) 1979/80 WBA, Manchester U
Robson, R. (20) 1957/8 WBA
Rocastle, D. (14) 1988/9 Arsenal
Rowley, J. (6) 1948/9 Manchester U
Royle, J. (6) 1970/1 Everton, Manchester C
Ruddock, N. (1) 1994/5 Liverpool

Sadler, D. (4) 1967/8 Manchester U
Salako, J. A. (5) 1990/1 Crystal P
Sansom, K. (86) 1978/9 Crystal P, Arsenal
Scales, J. R. (3) 1994/5 Liverpool
Scholes, P. (27) 1996/7 Manchester U
Scott, L. (17) 1946/7 Arsenal
Seaman, D. A. (59) 1988/9 QPR, Arsenal
Sewell, J. (6) 1951/2 Sheffield W
Shackleton, L. (5) 1948/9 Sunderland
Sharpe, L. S. (8) 1990/1 Manchester U
Shaw, G. (5) 1958/9 Sheffield U
Shearer, A. (63) 1991/2 Southampton, Blackburn R, Newcastle U
Shellito, K. (1) 1962/3 Chelsea
Sheringham, E. (38) 1992/3 Tottenham H, Manchester U
Sherwood, T. A. (3) 1998/9 Tottenham H
Shilton, P. (125) 1970/1 Leicester C, Stoke C, Nottingham F, Southampton, Derby C
Shimwell, E. (1) 1948/9 Blackpool
Sillett, P. (3) 1954/5 Chelsea
Sinton, A. (12) 1991/2 QPR, Sheffield W
Slater, W. (12) 1954/5 Wolverhampton W
Smith, A. M. (13) 1988/9 Arsenal
Smith, L. (6) 1950/1 Arsenal
Smith, R. (15) 1960/1 Tottenham H
Smith, Tom (1) 1970/1 Liverpool
Smith, Trevor (2) 1959/60 Birmingham C
Southgate, G. (37) 1995/6 Aston Villa
Spink, N. (1) 1982/3 Aston Villa
Springett, R. (33) 1959/60 Sheffield W
Staniforth, R. (8) 1953/4 Huddersfield T
Statham, D. (3) 1982/3 WBA
Stein, B. (1) 1983/4 Luton T
Stepney, A. (1) 1967/8 Manchester U
Sterland, M. (1) 1988/9 Sheffield W

Steven, T. M. (36) 1984/5 Everton, Rangers, Marseille
Stevens, G. A. (7) 1984/5 Tottenham H
Stevens, M. G. (46) 1984/5 Everton, Rangers
Stewart, P. A. (3) 1991/2 Tottenham H
Stiles, N. (28) 1964/5 Manchester U
Stone, S. B. (9) 1995/6 Nottingham F
Storey-Moore, I. (1) 1969/70 Nottingham F
Storey, P. (19) 1970/1 Arsenal
Streten, B. (1) 1949/50 Luton T
Summerbee, M. (8) 1967/8 Manchester C
Sunderland, A. (1) 1979/80 Arsenal
Sutton, C. R. (1) 1997/8 Blackburn R
Swan, P. (19) 1959/60 Sheffield W
Swift, F. (19) 1946/7 Manchester C

Talbot, B. (6) 1976/7 Ipswich T
Tambling, R. (3) 1962/3 Chelsea
Taylor, E. (1) 1953/4 Blackpool
Taylor, J. (2) 1950/1 Fulham
Taylor, P. H. (3) 1947/8 Liverpool
Taylor, P. J. (4) 1975/6 Crystal P
Taylor, T. (19) 1952/3 Manchester U
Temple, D. (1) 1964/5 Everton
Thomas, Danny (2) 1982/3 Coventry C
Thomas, Dave (8) 1974/5 QPR
Thomas, G. R. (9) 1990/1 Crystal P
Thomas, M. L. (2) 1988/9 Arsenal
Thompson, P. (16) 1963/4 Liverpool
Thompson, P. B. (42) 1975/6 Liverpool
Thompson, T. (2) 1951/2 Aston Villa, Preston NE
Thomson, R. (8) 1963/4 Wolverhampton W
Todd, C. (27) 1971/2 Derby C
Towers, T. (3) 1975/6 Sunderland
Tueart, D. (6) 1974/5 Manchester C

Ufton, D. (1) 1953/4 Charlton Ath
Unsworth, D. G. (1) 1994/5 Everton

Venables, T. (2) 1964/5 Chelsea
Venison, B. (2) 1994/5 Newcastle U
Viljoen, C. (2) 1974/5 Ipswich T
Viollet, D. (2) 1959/60 Manchester U

Waddle, C. R. (62) 1984/5 Newcastle U, Tottenham H, Marseille
Waiters, A. (5) 1963/4 Blackpool
Walker, D. S. (59) 1988/9 Nottingham F, Sampdoria, Sheffield W
Walker, I. M. (3) 1995/6 Tottenham H
Wallace, D. L. (1) 1985/6 Southampton
Walsh, P. (5) 1982/3 Luton T
Walters, K. M. (1) 1990/1 Rangers
Ward, P. (1) 1979/80 Brighton
Ward, T. (2) 1947/8 Derby C
Watson, D. (12) 1983/4 Norwich C, Everton
Watson D. V. (65) 1973/4 Sunderland, Manchester C, Southampton, Werder Bremen, Southampton, Stoke C
Watson, W. (4) 1949/50 Sunderland
Webb, N. (26) 1987/8 Nottingham F, Manchester U
Weller, K. (4) 1973/4 Leicester C
West, G. (3) 1968/9 Everton
Wheeler, J. (1) 1954/5 Bolton W
White, D. (1) 1992/3 Manchester C
Whitworth, S. (7) 1974/5 Leicester C
Whymark, T. (1) 1977/8 Ipswich T
Wignall, F. (2) 1964/5 Nottingham F
Wilcox, J. M. (3) 1995/6 Blackburn R, Leeds U
Wilkins, R. (84) 1975/6 Chelsea, Manchester U, AC Milan
Williams, B. (24) 1948/9 Wolverhampton W
Williams, S. (6) 1982/3 Southampton
Willis, A. (1) 1951/2 Tottenham H
Wilshaw, D. (12) 1953/4 Wolverhampton W
Wilson, R. (63) 1959/60 Huddersfield T, Everton
Winterburn, N. (2) 1989/90 Arsenal
Wise, D. F. (19) 1990/1 Chelsea
Withe, P. (11) 1980/1 Aston Villa
Wood, R. (3) 1954/5 Manchester U
Woodcock, A. (42) 1977/8 Nottingham F, FC Cologne, Arsenal
Woodgate, J. S. (1) 1998/9 Leeds U
Woods, C. C. E. (43) 1984/5 Norwich C, Rangers, Sheffield W
Worthington, F. (8) 1973/4 Leicester C
Wright, I. E. (33) 1990/1 Crystal P, Arsenal, West Ham U
Wright M. (45) 1983/4 Southampton, Derby C, Liverpool
Wright R. I. (1) 1999/00 Ipswich T
Wright, T. (11) 1967/8 Everton
Wright, W. (105) 1946/7 Wolverhampton W

Young, G. (1) 1964/5 Sheffield W

NORTHERN IRELAND

Aherne, T. (4) 1946/7 Belfast Celtic, Luton T
Anderson, T. (22) 1972/3 Manchester U, Swindon T, Peterborough U
Armstrong, G. (63) 1976/7 Tottenham H, Watford, Real Mallorca, WBA, Chesterfield

Barr, H. (3) 1961/2 Linfield, Coventry C
Best, G. (37) 1963/4 Manchester U, Fulham
Bingham, W. (56) 1950/1 Sunderland, Luton T, Everton, Port Vale
Black, K. (30) 1987/8 Luton T, Nottingham F
Blair, R. (5) 1974/5 Oldham Ath
Blanchflower, D. (54) 1949/50 Barnsley, Aston Villa, Tottenham H
Blanchflower, J. (12) 1953/4 Manchester U
Bowler, G. (3) 1949/50 Hull C
Braithwaite, R. (10) 1961/2 Linfield, Middlesbrough
Brennan, R. (5) 1948/9 Luton T, Birmingham C, Fulham
Briggs, R. (2) 1961/2 Manchester U, Swansea
Brotherston, N. (27) 1979/80 Blackburn R
Bruce, W. (2) 1960/1 Glentoran

Campbell, A. (2) 1962/3 Crusaders
Campbell, D. A. (10) 1985/6 Nottingham F, Charlton Ath
Campbell, J. (2) 1950/1 Fulham
Campbell, R. M. (2) 1981/2 Bradford C
Campbell, W. (6) 1967/8 Dundee
Carey, J. (7) 1946/7 Manchester U
Carroll, R. E. (4) 1996/7 Wigan Ath
Casey, T. (12) 1954/5 Newcastle U, Portsmouth
Caskey, A. (7) 1978/9 Derby C, Tulsa Roughnecks
Cassidy, T. (24) 1970/1 Newcastle U, Burnley
Caughey, M. (2) 1985/6 Linfield
Clarke, C. J. (38) 1985/6 Bournemouth, Southampton, Portsmouth
Cleary, J. (5) 1981/2 Glentoran
Clements, D. (48) 1964/5 Coventry C, Sheffield W, Everton, New York Cosmos
Cochrane, D. (10) 1946/7 Leeds U
Cochrane, T. (26) 1975/6 Coleraine, Burnley, Middlesbrough, Gillingham
Coote, A. (6) 1998/9 Norwich C
Cowan, J. (1) 1969/70 Newcastle U
Coyle, F. (4) 1955/6 Coleraine, Nottingham F
Coyle, L. (1) 1988/9 Derry C
Coyle, R. (5) 1972/3 Sheffield W
Craig, D. (25) 1966/7 Newcastle U
Crossan, E. (3) 1949/50 Blackburn R
Crossan, J. (23) 1959/60 Sparta Rotterdam, Sunderland, Manchester C, Middlesbrough
Cunningham, W. (30) 1950/1 St Mirren, Leicester C, Dunfermline Ath
Cush, W. (26) 1950/1 Glentoran, Leeds U, Portadown

D'Arcy, S. (5) 1951/2 Chelsea, Brentford
Davison, A. J. (3) 1995/6 Bolton W, Bradford C, Grimsby T
Dennison, R. (18) 1987/8 Wolverhampton W
Devine, J. (1) 1989/90 Glentoran
Dickson, D. (4) 1969/70 Coleraine
Dickson, T. (1) 1956/7 Linfield
Dickson, W. (12) 1950/1 Chelsea, Arsenal
Doherty, L. (2) 1984/5 Linfield
Doherty, P. (6) 1946/7 Derby C, Huddersfield T, Doncaster R
Donaghy, M. (91) 1979/80 Luton T, Manchester U, Chelsea
Dougan, D. (43) 1957/8 Portsmouth, Blackburn R, Aston Villa, Leicester C, Wolverhampton W
Douglas, J. P. (1) 1946/7 Belfast Celtic
Dowd, H. (3) 1972/3 Glentoran, Sheffield W
Dowie, I. (59) 1989/90 Luton T, Southampton, Crystal P, West Ham, QPR
Dunlop, G. (4) 1984/5 Linfield

Eglington, T. (6) 1946/7 Everton
Elder, A. (40) 1959/60 Burnley, Stoke C

Farrell, P. (7) 1946/7 Everton
Feeney, J. (2) 1946/7 Linfield, Swansea C
Feeney, W. (1) 1975/6 Glentoran
Ferguson, G. (1) 1998/9 Linfield
Ferguson, W. (2) 1965/6 Linfield
Ferris, R. (3) 1949/50 Birmingham C
Fettis, A. (25) 1991/2 Hull C, Nottingham F, Blackburn R
Finney, T. (14) 1974/5 Sunderland, Cambridge U
Fleming, J. G. (31) 1986/7 Nottingham F, Manchester C, Barnsley
Forde, T. (4) 1958/9 Ards

Gallogly, C. (2) 1950/1 Huddersfield T
Garton, R. (1) 1968/9 Oxford U

Gillespie, K. R. (32) 1994/5 Manchester U, Newcastle U, Blackburn R
Gorman, W. (4) 1946/7 Brentford
Graham, W. (14) 1950/1 Doncaster R
Gray, P. (21) 1992/3 Luton T, Sunderland, Nancy, Luton T
Gregg, H. (25) 1953/4 Doncaster R, Manchester U
Griffin, D. J. (12) 1995/6 St Johnstone

Hamill, R. (1) 1998/9 Glentoran
Hamilton, B. (50) 1968/9 Linfield, Ipswich T, Everton, Millwall, Swindon T
Hamilton, W. (41) 1977/8 QPR, Burnley, Oxford U
Harkin, T. (5) 1967/8 Southport, Shrewsbury T
Harvey, M. (34) 1960/1 Sunderland
Hatton, S. (2) 1962/3 Linfield
Healy, D. J. (3) 1999/00 Manchester U
Healy, P. J. (4) 1981/2 Coleraine, Glentoran
Hegan, D. (7) 1969/70 WBA, Wolverhampton W
Hill, C. F. (27) 1989/90 Sheffield U, Leicester C, Trelleborg, Northampton T
Hill, J. (7) 1958/9 Norwich C, Everton
Hinton, E. (7) 1946/7 Fulham, Millwall
Horlock, K. (21) 1994/5 Swindon T, Manchester C
Hughes, A. W. (12) 1997/8 Newcastle U
Hughes, M. E. (54) 1991/2 Manchester C, Strasbourg, West Ham U, Wimbledon
Hughes, P. (3) 1986/7 Bury
Hughes, W. (1) 1950/1 Bolton W
Humphries, W. (14) 1961/2 Ards, Coventry C, Swansea T
Hunter, A. (53) 1969/70 Blackburn R, Ipswich T
Hunter, B. V. (15) 1994/5 Wrexham, Reading

Irvine, R. (8) 1961/2 Linfield, Stoke C
Irvine, W. (23) 1962/3 Burnley, Preston NE, Brighton & HA

Jackson, T. (35) 1968/9 Everton, Nottingham F, Manchester U
Jamison, A. (1) 1975/6 Glentoran
Jenkins, I. (6) 1996/7 Chester C, Dundee U
Jennings, P. (119) 1963/4 Watford, Tottenham H, Arsenal, Tottenham H, Everton, Tottenham H
Johnson, D. M. (5) 1998/9 Blackburn R
Johnston, W. (1) 1961/2 Glentoran, Oldham Ath
Jones, J. (3) 1955/6 Glenavon

Keane, T. (1) 1948/9 Swansea T
Kee, P. V. (9) 1989/90 Oxford U, Ards
Keith, R. (23) 1957/8 Newcastle U
Kelly, H. (4) 1949/50 Fulham, Southampton
Kelly, P. (1) 1949/50 Barnsley
Kennedy, P. H. (6) 1998/9 Watford
Kirk, A. (1) 1999/00 Heart of Midlothian

Lawther, I. (4) 1959/60 Sunderland, Blackburn R
Lennon, N. F. (33) 1993/4 Crewe Alexandra, Leicester C
Lockhart, N. (8) 1946/7 Linfield, Coventry C, Aston Villa
Lomas, S. M. (35) 1993/4 Manchester C, West Ham U
Lutton, B. (6) 1969/70 Wolverhampton W, West Ham U

Magill, E. (26) 1961/2 Arsenal, Brighton & HA
Magilton, J. (40) 1990/1 Oxford U, Southampton, Sheffield W, Ipswich T
Martin, C. (6) 1946/7 Glentoran, Leeds U, Aston Villa
McAdams, W. (15) 1953/4 Manchester C, Bolton W, Leeds U
McAlinden, J. (2) 1946/7 Portsmouth, Southend U
McBride, S. (4) 1990/1 Glenavon
McCabe, J. (6) 1948/9 Leeds U
McCarthy, J. D. (16) 1995/6 Port Vale, Birmingham C
McCavana, T. (3) 1954/5 Coleraine
McCleary, J. W. (1) 1954/5 Cliftonville
McClelland, J. (6) 1960/1 Arsenal, Fulham
McClelland, J. (53) 1979/80 Mansfield T, Rangers, Watford, Leeds U
McCourt, F. (6) 1951/2 Manchester C
McCoy, R. (1) 1986/7 Coleraine
McCreery, D. (67) 1975/6 Manchester U, QPR, Tulsa Roughnecks, Newcastle U, Heart of Midlothian
McCrory, S. (1) 1957/8 Southend U
McCullough, W. (10) 1960/1 Arsenal, Millwall
McCurdy, C. (1) 1979/80 Linfield
McDonald, A. (52) 1985/6 QPR
McElhinney, G. (6) 1983/4 Bolton W
McFaul, I. (6) 1966/7 Linfield, Newcastle U
McGarry, J. K. (3) 1950/1 Cliftonville
McGaughey, M. (1) 1984/5 Linfield
McGibbon, P. C. G. (7) 1994/5 Manchester U, Wigan Ath
McGrath, R. (21) 1973/4 Tottenham H, Manchester U

McIlroy, J. (55) 1951/2 Burnley, Stoke C
McIlroy, S. B. (88) 1971/2 Manchester U, Stoke C, Manchester C
McKeag, W. (2) 1967/8 Glentoran
McKenna, J. (7) 1949/50 Huddersfield T
McKenzie, R. (1) 1966/7 Airdrieonians
McKinney, W. (1) 1965/6 Falkirk
McKnight, A. (10) 1987/8 Celtic, West Ham U
McLaughlin, J. (12) 1961/2 Shrewsbury T, Swansea C
McMahon, G. J. (17) 1994/5 Tottenham H, Stoke C
McMichael, A. (39) 1949/50 Newcastle U
McMillan, S. (2) 1962/3 Manchester U
McMordie, E. (21) 1968/9 Middlesbrough
McMorran, E. (15) 1946/7 Belfast Celtic, Barnsley, Doncaster R
McNally, B. A. (5) 1985/6 Shrewsbury T
McParland, P. (34) 1953/4 Aston Villa, Wolverhampton W
McVeigh, P. (1) 1998/9 Tottenham H
Montgomery, F. J. (1) 1954/5 Coleraine
Moore, C. (1) 1948/9 Glentoran
Moreland, V. (6) 1978/9 Derby C
Morgan, S. (18) 1971/2 Port Vale, Aston Villa, Brighton & HA, Sparta Rotterdam
Morrow, S. J. (39) 1989/90 Arsenal, QPR
Mullan, G. (4) 1982/3 Glentoran
Mulryne, P. P. (8) 1996/7 Manchester U, Norwich C
Murdock, C. J. (3) 1999/00 Preston NE

Napier, R. (1) 1965/6 Bolton W
Neill, T. (59) 1960/1 Arsenal, Hull C
Nelson, S. (51) 1969/70 Arsenal, Brighton & HA
Nicholl, C. (51) 1974/5 Aston Villa, Southampton, Grimsby T
Nicholl, J. M. (73) 1975/6 Manchester U, Toronto Blizzard, Sunderland, Rangers, WBA
Nicholson, J. (41) 1960/1 Manchester U, Huddersfield T
Nolan, I. R. (12) 1996/7 Sheffield W

O'Boyle, G. (13) 1993/4 Dunfermline Ath, St Johnstone
O'Doherty, A. (2) 1969/70 Coleraine
O'Driscoll, J. (3) 1948/9 Swansea C
O'Kane, L. (20) 1969/70 Nottingham F
O'Neill, C. (3) 1988/9 Motherwell
O'Neill, H. M. (64) 1971/2 Distillery, Nottingham F, Norwich C, Manchester C, Norwich C, Notts C
O'Neill, J. (1) 1961/2 Sunderland
O'Neill, J. (39) 1979/80 Leicester C
O'Neill, M. A. (31) 1987/8 Newcastle U, Dundee U, Hibernian, Coventry C

Parke, J. (13) 1963/4 Linfield, Hibernian, Sunderland
Patterson, D. J. (17) 1993/4 Crystal P, Luton T, Dundee U
Peacock, R. (31) 1951/2 Celtic, Coleraine
Penney, S. (17) 1984/5 Brighton & HA
Platt, J. A. (23) 1975/6 Middlesbrough, Ballymena U, Coleraine

Quinn, J. M. (46) 1984/5 Blackburn R, Leicester, Bradford C, West Ham U, Bournemouth, Reading
Quinn, S. J. (21) 1995/6 Blackpool, WBA

Rafferty, P. (1) 1979/80 Linfield
Ramsey, P. (14) 1983/4 Leicester C
Rice, P. (49) 1968/9 Arsenal
Robinson, S. (5) 1996/7 Bournemouth
Rogan, A. (18) 1987/8 Celtic, Sunderland, Millwall
Ross, E. (1) 1968/9 Newcastle U
Rowland, K. (19) 1994/5 West Ham U
Russell, A. (1) 1946/7 Linfield
Ryan, R. (1) 1949/50 WBA

Sanchez, L. P. (3) 1986/7 Wimbledon
Scott, J. (2) 1957/8 Grimsby T
Scott, P. (10) 1974/5 Everton, York C, Aldershot
Sharkey, P. (1) 1975/6 Ipswich T
Shields, J. (1) 1956/7 Southampton
Simpson, W. (12) 1950/1 Rangers
Sloan, D. (2) 1968/9 Oxford
Sloan, T. (3) 1978/9 Manchester U
Sloan, W. (1) 1946/7 Arsenal
Smyth, S. (9) 1947/8 Wolverhampton W, Stoke C
Smyth, W. (4) 1948/9 Distillery
Sonner, D. J. (6) 1997/8 Ipswich T, Sheffield W
Spence, D. (29) 1974/5 Bury, Blackpool, Southend U
Stevenson, A. (3) 1946/7 Everton
Stewart, A. (7) 1966/7 Glentoran, Derby
Stewart, D. (1) 1977/8 Hull C
Stewart, I. (31) 1981/2 QPR, Newcastle U
Stewart, T. (1) 1960/1 Linfield

Taggart, G. P. (46) 1989/90 Barnsley, Bolton W, Leicester C
Taylor, M. S. (11) 1998/9 Fulham
Todd, S. (11) 1965/6 Burnley, Sheffield W
Trainor, D. (1) 1966/7 Crusaders
Tully, C. (10) 1948/9 Celtic

Uprichard, N. (18) 1951/2 Swindon T, Portsmouth

Vernon, J. (17) 1946/7 Belfast Celtic, WBA

Walker, J. (1) 1954/5 Doncaster R
Walsh, D. (9) 1946/7 WBA
Walsh, W. (5) 1947/8 Manchester C
Watson, P. (1) 1970/1 Distillery
Welsh, S. (4) 1965/6 Carlisle U
Whiteside, N. (38) 1981/2 Manchester U, Everton
Whitley, Jeff (4) 1996/7 Manchester C
Whitley, Jim (3) 1997/8 Manchester C
Williams, M. S. (11) 1998/9 Chesterfield, Watford
Williams, P. (1) 1990/1 WBA
Wilson, D. J. (24) 1986/7 Brighton & HA, Luton, Sheffield W
Wilson, K. J. (42) 1986/7 Ipswich T, Chelsea, Notts C, Walsall
Wilson, S. (12) 1961/2 Glenavon, Falkirk, Dundee
Wood, T. J. (1) 1995/6 Walsall
Worthington, N. (66) 1983/4 Sheffield W, Leeds U, Stoke C
Wright, T. J. (31) 1988/9 Newcastle U, Nottingham F, Manchester C

SCOTLAND

Aird, J. (4) 1953/4 Burnley
Aitken, G. G. (8) 1948/9 East Fife, Sunderland
Aitken, R. (57) 1979/80 Celtic, Newcastle U, St Mirren
Albiston, A. (14) 1981/2 Manchester U
Allan, T. (2) 1973/4 Dundee
Anderson, J. (1) 1953/4 Leicester C
Archibald, S. (27) 1979/80 Aberdeen, Tottenham H, Barcelona
Auld, B. (3) 1958/9 Celtic

Baird, H. (1) 1955/6 Airdrieonians
Baird, S. (7) 1956/7 Rangers
Bannon, E. (11) 1979/80 Dundee U
Bauld, W. (3) 1949/50 Heart of Midlothian
Baxter, J. (34) 1960/1 Rangers, Sunderland
Bell, W. (2) 1965/6 Leeds U
Bernard, P. R. (2) 1994/5 Oldham Ath
Bett, J. (25) 1981/2 Rangers, Lokeren, Aberdeen
Black, E. (2) 1987/8 Metz
Black, I. (1) 1947/8 Southampton
Blacklaw, A. (3) 1962/3 Burnley
Blackley, J. (7) 1973/4 Hibernian
Blair, J. (1) 1946/7 Blackpool
Blyth, J. (2) 1977/8 Coventry C
Bone, J. (2) 1971/2 Norwich C
Booth, S. (17) 1992/3 Aberdeen, Borussia Dortmund
Bowman, D. (6) 1991/2 Dundee U
Boyd, T. (65) 1990/1 Motherwell, Chelsea, Celtic
Brand, R. (8) 1960/1 Rangers
Brazil, A. (13) 1979/80 Ipswich T, Tottenham H
Bremner, D. (1) 1975/6 Hibernian
Bremner, W. (54) 1964/5 Leeds U
Brennan, F. (7) 1946/7 Newcastle U
Brogan, J. (4) 1970/1 Celtic
Brown, A. (14) 1949/50 East Fife, Blackpool
Brown, H. (3) 1946/7 Partick Thistle
Brown, J. (1) 1974/5 Sheffield U
Brown, R. (3) 1946/7 Rangers
Brown, W. (28) 1957/8 Dundee, Tottenham H
Brownlie, J. (7) 1970/1 Hibernian
Buchan, M. (34) 1971/2 Aberdeen, Manchester U
Buckley, P. (3) 1953/4 Aberdeen
Burchill, M. J. (6) 1999/00 Celtic
Burley, C. W. (38) 1994/5 Chelsea, Celtic, Derby Co
Burley, G. (11) 1978/9 Ipswich T
Burns, F. (1) 1969/70 Manchester U
Burns, K. (20) 1973/4 Birmingham C, Nottingham F
Burns, T. (8) 1980/1 Celtic

Calderwood, C. (36) 1994/5 Tottenham H, Aston Villa
Caldow, E. (40) 1956/7 Rangers
Callaghan, W. (2) 1969/70 Dunfermline
Cameron, C. (5) 1998/9 Heart of Midlothian
Campbell, R. (5) 1946/7 Falkirk, Chelsea
Campbell, W. (5) 1946/7 Morton
Carr, W. (6) 1969/70 Coventry C
Chalmers, S. (5) 1964/5 Celtic
Clark, J. (4) 1965/6 Celtic
Clark, R. (17) 1967/8 Aberdeen
Clarke, S. (6) 1987/8 Chelsea
Collins, J. (58) 1987/8 Hibernian, Celtic, Monaco, Everton
Collins, R. (31) 1950/1 Celtic, Everton, Leeds U
Colquhoun, E. (9) 1971/2 Sheffield U
Colquhoun, J. (1) 1987/8 Heart of Midlothian
Combe, R. (3) 1947/8 Hibernian

Conn, A. (1) 1955/6 Heart of Midlothian
Conn, A. (2) 1974/5 Tottenham H
Connachan, E. (2) 1961/2 Dunfermline Ath
Connelly, G. (2) 1973/4 Celtic
Connolly, J. (1) 1972/3 Everton
Connor, R. (4) 1985/6 Dundee, Aberdeen
Cooke, C. (16) 1965/6 Dundee, Chelsea
Cooper, D. (22) 1979/80 Rangers, Motherwell
Cormack, P. (9) 1965/6 Hibernian, Nottingham F
Cowan, J. (25) 1947/8 Morton, Motherwell
Cowie, D. (20) 1952/3 Dundee
Cox, C. (1) 1947/8 Heart of Midlothian
Cox, S. (24) 1947/8 Rangers
Craig, J. (1) 1976/7 Celtic
Craig, J. P. (1) 1967/8 Celtic
Craig, T. (1) 1975/6 Newcastle U
Crawford, S. (1) 1994/5 Raith R
Crerand, P. (16) 1960/1 Celtic, Manchester U
Cropley, A. (2) 1971/2 Hibernian
Cruickshank, J. (6) 1963/4 Heart of Midlothian
Cullen, M. (1) 1955/6 Luton T
Cumming, J. (9) 1954/5 Heart of Midlothian
Cunningham, W. (8) 1953/4 Preston NE
Curran, H. (5) 1969/70 Wolverhampton W

Dailly, C. (23) 1996/7 Derby C, Blackburn R
Dalglish, K. (102) 1971/2 Celtic, Liverpool
Davidson, C. I. (12) 1998/9 Blackburn R
Davidson, J. (8) 1953/4 Partick Thistle
Dawson, A. (5) 1979/80 Rangers
Deans, D. (2) 1974/5 Celtic
Delaney, J. (4) 1946/7 Manchester U
Dick, J. (1) 1958/9 West Ham U
Dickson, W. (5) 1969/70 Kilmarnock
Docherty, T. (25) 1951/2 Preston NE, Arsenal
Dodds, D. (2) 1983/4 Dundee U
Dodds, W. (18) 1996/7 Aberdeen, Dundee U, Rangers
Donachie, W. (35) 1971/2 Manchester C
Donnelly, S. (10) 1996/7 Celtic
Dougall, C. (1) 1946/7 Birmingham C
Dougan, R. (1) 1949/50 Heart of Midlothian
Doyle, J. (1) 1975/6 Ayr U
Duncan, A. (6) 1974/5 Hibernian
Duncan, D. (3) 1947/8 East Fife
Duncanson, J. (1) 1946/7 Rangers
Durie, G. S. (43) 1987/8 Chelsea, Tottenham H, Rangers
Durrant, I. (19) 1987/8 Rangers, Kilmarnock

Elliott, M. S. (9) 1997/8 Leicester C
Evans, A. (4) 1981/2 Aston Villa
Evans, R. (48) 1948/9 Celtic, Chelsea
Ewing, T. (2) 1957/8 Partick Thistle

Farm, G. (10) 1952/3 Blackpool
Ferguson, B. (7) 1998/9 Rangers
Ferguson, Derek (2) 1987/8 Rangers
Ferguson, Duncan (7) 1991/2 Dundee U, Everton
Ferguson, I. (9) 1988/9 Rangers
Ferguson, R. (7) 1965/6 Kilmarnock
Fernie, W. (12) 1953/4 Celtic
Flavell, R. (2) 1946/7 Airdrieonians
Fleck, R. (4) 1989/90 Norwich C
Fleming, C. (1) 1953/4 East Fife
Forbes, A. (14) 1946/7 Sheffield U, Arsenal
Ford, D. (3) 1973/4 Heart of Midlothian
Forrest, J. (1) 1957/8 Motherwell
Forrest, J. (5) 1965/6 Rangers, Aberdeen
Forsyth, A. (10) 1971/2 Partick Thistle, Manchester U
Forsyth, C. (4) 1963/4 Kilmarnock
Forsyth, T. (22) 1970/1 Motherwell, Rangers
Fraser, D. (2) 1967/8 WBA
Fraser, W. (2) 1954/5 Sunderland

Gabriel, J. (2) 1960/1 Everton
Gallacher, K. W. (49) 1987/8 Dundee U, Coventry C, Blackburn R, Newcastle U
Galloway, M. (1) 1991/2 Celtic
Gardiner, W. (1) 1957/8 Motherwell
Gemmell, T. (2) 1954/5 St Mirren
Gemmell, T. (18) 1965/6 Celtic
Gemmill, A. (43) 1970/1 Derby C, Nottingham F, Birmingham C
Gemmill, S. (15) 1994/5 Nottingham F, Everton
Gibson, D. (7) 1962/3 Leicester C
Gillespie, G. T. (13) 1987/8 Liverpool, Celtic
Gilzean, A. (22) 1963/4 Dundee, Tottenham H
Glass, S. (1) 1998/9 Newcastle U
Glavin, R. (1) 1976/7 Celtic
Glen, A. (2) 1955/6 Aberdeen
Goram, A. L. (43) 1985/6 Oldham Ath, Hibernian, Rangers
Gough, C. R. (61) 1982/3 Dundee U, Tottenham H, Rangers
Gould, J. (1) 1999/00 Celtic
Govan, J. (6) 1947/8 Hibernian
Graham, A. (10) 1977/8 Leeds U
Graham, G. (12) 1971/2 Arsenal, Manchester U
Grant, J. (2) 1958/9 Hibernian
Grant, P. (2) 1988/9 Celtic

Gray, A. (20) 1975/6 Aston Villa, Wolverhampton W, Everton
Gray, E. (12) 1968/9 Leeds U
Gray F. (32) 1975/6 Leeds U, Nottingham F, Leeds U
Green, A. (6) 1970/1 Blackpool, Newcastle U
Greig, J. (44) 1963/4 Rangers
Gunn, B. (6) 1989/90 Norwich C

Haddock, H. (6) 1954/5 Clyde
Haffey, F. (2) 1959/60 Celtic
Hamilton, A. (24) 1961/2 Dundee
Hamilton, G. (5) 1946/7 Aberdeen
Hamilton, W. (1) 1964/5 Hibernian
Hansen, A. (26) 1978/9 Liverpool
Hansen J. (2) 1971/2 Partick Thistle
Harper, J. (4) 1972/3 Aberdeen
Hartford, A. (50) 1971/2 WBA, Manchester C, Everton, Manchester C
Harvey, D. (16) 1972/3 Leeds U
Haughney, M. (1) 1953/4 Celtic
Hay, D. (27) 1969/70 Celtic
Hegarty, P. (8) 1978/9 Dundee U
Henderson, J. (7) 1952/3 Portsmouth, Arsenal
Henderson, W. (29) 1962/3 Rangers
Hendry, E. C. J. (45) 1992/3 Blackburn R, Rangers, Coventry C
Herd, D. (5) 1958/9 Arsenal
Herd, G. (5) 1957/8 Clyde
Herriot, J. (8) 1968/9 Birmingham C
Hewie, J. (19) 1955/6 Charlton Ath
Holt, D. D. (5) 1962/3 Heart of Midlothian
Holt, G. J. (1) 1999/00 Kilmarnock
Holton, J. (15) 1972/3 Manchester U
Hope, R. (2) 1967/8 WBA
Hopkin, D. (7) 1996/7 Crystal P, Leeds U
Houliston, W. (3) 1948/9 Queen of the South
Houston, S. (1) 1975/6 Manchester U
Howie, H. (1) 1948/9 Hibernian
Hughes, J. (8) 1964/5 Celtic
Hughes, W. (1) 1974/5 Sunderland
Humphries, W. (1) 1951/2 Motherwell
Hunter, A. (4) 1971/2 Kilmarnock, Celtic
Hunter, W. (3) 1959/60 Motherwell
Husband, J. (1) 1946/7 Partick Thistle
Hutchison, D. (10) 1998/9 Everton
Hutchison, T. (17) 1973/4 Coventry C

Imlach, S. (4) 1957/8 Nottingham F
Irvine, B. (9) 1990/1 Aberdeen

Jackson, C. (8) 1974/5 Rangers
Jackson, D. (28) 1994/5 Hibernian, Celtic
Jardine, A. (38) 1970/1 Rangers
Jarvie, A. (3) 1970/1 Airdrieonians
Jess, E. (18) 1992/3 Aberdeen, Coventry C, Aberdeen
Johnson, A. (9) 1998/9 Sunderland
Johnston, M. (38) 1983/4 Watford, Celtic, Nantes, Rangers
Johnston, W. (22) 1965/6 Rangers, WBA
Johnstone, D. (14) 1972/3 Rangers
Johnstone, J. (23) 1964/5 Celtic
Johnstone, L. (2) 1947/8 Clyde
Johnstone, R. (17) 1950/1 Hibernian, Manchester C
Jordan, J. (52) 1972/3 Leeds U, Manchester U, AC Milan

Kelly, H. (1) 1951/2 Blackpool
Kelly, J. (2) 1948/9 Barnsley
Kennedy, J. (6) 1963/4 Celtic
Kennedy, S. (8) 1977/8 Aberdeen
Kennedy, S. (5) 1974/5 Rangers
Kerr, A. (2) 1954/5 Partick Thistle

Lambert, P. (24) 1994/5 Motherwell, Borussia Dortmund, Celtic
Law, D. (55) 1958/9 Huddersfield T, Manchester C, Torino, Manchester U, Manchester C
Lawrence, T. (3) 1962/3 Liverpool
Leggat, G. (18) 1955/6 Aberdeen, Fulham
Leighton, J. (91) 1982/3 Aberdeen, Manchester U, Hibernian, Aberdeen
Lennox, R. (10) 1966/7 Celtic
Leslie, L. (5) 1960/1 Airdrieonians
Levein, C. (16) 1989/90 Heart of Midlothian
Liddell, W. (28) 1946/7 Liverpool
Linwood, A. (1) 1949/50 Clyde
Little, A. (1) 1952/3 Rangers
Logie, J. (1) 1952/3 Arsenal
Long, H. (1) 1946/7 Clyde
Lorimer, P. (21) 1969/70 Leeds U

Macari, L. (24) 1971/2 Celtic, Manchester U
Macaulay, A. (7) 1946/7 Brentford, Arsenal
MacDougall, E. (7) 1974/5 Norwich C
Mackay, D. (22) 1956/7 Heart of Midlothian, Tottenham H
Mackay, G. (4) 1987/8 Heart of Midlothian
Malpas, M. (55) 1983/4 Dundee U
Marshall, G. (1) 1991/2 Celtic
Martin, B. (2) 1994/5 Motherwell
Martin, F. (6) 1953/4 Aberdeen
Martin, N. (3) 1964/5 Hibernian, Sunderland
Martis, J. (1) 1960/1 Motherwell
Mason, J. (7) 1948/9 Third Lanark
Masson, D. (17) 1975/6 QPR, Derby C
Mathers, D. (1) 1953/4 Partick Thistle
McAllister, B. (3) 1996/7 Wimbledon

McAllister, G. (57) 1989/90 Leicester C, Leeds U, Coventry C
McAvennie, F. (5) 1985/6 West Ham U, Celtic
McBride, J. (2) 1966/7 Celtic
McCall, S. M. (40) 1989/90 Everton, Rangers
McCalliog, J. (5) 1966/7 Sheffield W, Wolverhampton W
McCann, N. D. (8) 1998/9 Heart of Midlothian, Rangers
McCann, R. (5) 1958/9 Motherwell
McClair, B. (30) 1986/7 Celtic, Manchester U
McCloy, P. (4) 1972/3 Rangers
McCoist, A. (61) 1985/6 Rangers, Kilmarnock
McColl, I. (14) 1949/50 Rangers
McCreadie, E. (23) 1964/5 Chelsea
MacDonald, A. (1) 1975/6 Rangers
MacDonald, J. (2) 1955/6 Sunderland
McFarlane, W. (1) 1946/7 Heart of Midlothian
McGarr, E. (2) 1969/70 Aberdeen
McGarvey, F. (7) 1978/9 Liverpool, Celtic
McGhee, M. (4) 1982/3 Aberdeen
McGinlay, J. (13) 1993/4 Bolton W
McGrain, D. (62) 1972/3 Celtic
McGrory, J. (3) 1964/5 Kilmarnock
McInally, A. (8) 1988/9 Aston Villa, Bayern Munich
McInally, J. (10) 1986/7 Dundee U
McKay, D. (14) 1958/9 Celtic
McKean, R. (1) 1975/6 Rangers
McKenzie, J. (9) 1953/4 Partick Thistle
McKimmie, S. (40) 1988/9 Aberdeen
McKinlay, T. (22) 1995/6 Celtic
McKinlay, W. (29) 1993/4 Dundee U, Blackburn R
McKinnon, R. (28) 1965/6 Rangers
McKinnon, R. (3) 1993/4 Motherwell
McLaren, A. (4) 1946/7 Preston NE
McLaren, A. (24) 1991/2 Heart of Midlothian, Rangers
McLean, G. (1) 1967/8 Dundee
McLean, T. (6) 1968/9 Kilmarnock
McLeish, A. (77) 1979/80 Aberdeen
McLeod, J. (4) 1960/1 Hibernian
MacLeod, M. (20) 1984/5 Celtic, Borussia Dortmund, Hibernian
McLintock, F. (9) 1962/3 Leicester C, Arsenal
McMillan, I. (6) 1951/2 Airdrieonians, Rangers
McNamara, J. (10) 1996/7 Celtic
McNaught, W. (5) 1950/1 Raith R
McNeill, W. (29) 1960/1 Celtic
McPhail, J. (5) 1949/50 Celtic
McPherson, D. (27) 1988/9 Heart of Midlothian, Rangers
McQueen, G. (30) 1973/4 Leeds U, Manchester U
McStay, P. (76) 1983/4 Celtic
McSwegan, G. (2) 1999/00 Heart of Midlothian
Millar, J. (2) 1962/3 Rangers
Miller, W. (6) 1946/7 Celtic
Miller, W. (65) 1974/5 Aberdeen
Mitchell, R. (2) 1950/1 Newcastle U
Mochan, N. (3) 1953/4 Celtic
Moir, W. (1) 1949/50 Bolton W
Moncur, R. (16) 1967/8 Newcastle U
Morgan, W. (21) 1967/8 Burnley, Manchester U
Morris, H. (1) 1949/50 East Fife
Mudie, J. (17) 1956/7 Blackpool
Mulhall, G. (3) 1959/60 Aberdeen, Sunderland
Munro, F. (9) 1970/1 Wolverhampton W
Munro, I. (7) 1978/9 St Mirren
Murdoch, R. (12) 1965/6 Celtic
Murray, J. (5) 1957/8 Heart of Midlothian
Murray, S. (1) 1971/2 Aberdeen

Narey, D. (35) 1976/7 Dundee U
Naysmith, G. A. (1) 1999/00 Heart of Midlothian
Nevin, P. K. F. (28) 1985/6 Chelsea, Everton, Tranmere R
Nicholas, C. (20) 1982/3 Celtic, Arsenal, Aberdeen
Nicol, S. (27) 1984/5 Liverpool

O'Donnell, P. (1) 1993/4 Motherwell
O'Hare, J. (13) 1969/70 Derby C
O'Neil, B. (5) 1995/6 Celtic, Wolfsburg
Ormond, W. (6) 1953/4 Hibernian
Orr, T. (2) 1951/2 Morton

Parker, A. (15) 1954/5 Falkirk
Parlane, D. (12) 1972/3 Rangers
Paton, A. (2) 1951/2 Motherwell
Pearson, T. (2) 1946/7 Newcastle U
Penman, A. (1) 1965/6 Dundee
Pettigrew, W. (5) 1975/6 Motherwell
Plenderleith, J. (1) 1960/1 Manchester C
Pressley, S. J. (2) 1999/00 Heart of Midlothian
Provan, D. (5) 1963/4 Rangers
Provan, D. (10) 1979/80 Celtic

Quinn, P. (4) 1960/1 Motherwell

Redpath, W. (9) 1948/9 Motherwell
Reilly, L. (38) 1948/9 Hibernian
Ring, T. (12) 1952/3 Clydebank
Rioch, B. (24) 1974/5 Derby C, Everton, Derby C

Ritchie, P. S. (6) 1998/9 Heart of Midlothian, Bolton W
Robb, D. (5) 1970/1 Aberdeen
Robertson, A. (5) 1954/5 Clyde
Robertson, D. (3) 1991/2 Rangers
Robertson, H. (1) 1961/2 Dundee
Robertson, J. (16) 1990/1 Heart of Midlothian
Robertson, J. G. (1) 1964/5 Tottenham H
Robertson, J. N. (28) 1977/8 Nottingham F, Derby C
Robinson, B. (4) 1973/4 Dundee
Rough, A. (53) 1975/6 Partick Thistle, Hibernian
Rougvie, D. (1) 1983/4 Aberdeen
Rutherford, E. (1) 1947/8 Rangers

St John, I. (21) 1958/9 Motherwell, Liverpool
Schaedler, E. (1) 1973/4 Hibernian
Scott, A. (16) 1956/7 Rangers, Everton
Scott, J. (1) 1965/6 Hibernian
Scott, J. (2) 1970/1 Dundee
Scoular, J. (9) 1950/1 Portsmouth
Sharp, G. M. (12) 1984/5 Everton
Shaw, D. (8) 1946/7 Hibernian
Shaw, J. (4) 1946/7 Rangers
Shearer, D. (7) 1993/4 Aberdeen
Shearer, R. (4) 1960/1 Rangers
Simpson, N. (4) 1982/3 Aberdeen
Simpson, R. (5) 1966/7 Celtic
Sinclair, J. (1) 1965/6 Leicester C
Smith, D. (2) 1965/6 Aberdeen, Rangers
Smith, E. (2) 1958/9 Celtic
Smith, G. (18) 1946/7 Hibernian
Smith, H. G. (3) 1987/8 Heart of Midlothian
Smith, J. (4) 1967/8 Aberdeen, Newcastle U
Souness, G. (54) 1974/5 Middlesbrough, Liverpool, Sampdoria
Speedie, D. R. (10) 1984/5 Chelsea, Coventry C
Spencer, J. (14) 1994/5 Chelsea, QPR
Stanton, P. (16) 1965/6 Hibernian
Steel, W. (30) 1946/7 Morton, Derby C, Dundee
Stein, C. (21) 1968/9 Rangers, Coventry C
Stephen, J. (2) 1946/7 Bradford C
Stewart, D. (1) 1977/8 Leeds U
Stewart, J. (2) 1976/7 Kilmarnock, Middlesbrough
Stewart, R. (10) 1980/1 West Ham U
Strachan, G. (50) 1979/80 Aberdeen, Manchester U, Leeds U
Sturrock, P. (20) 1980/1 Dundee U
Sullivan, N. (16) 1996/7 Wimbledon

Telfer, P. N. (1) 1999/00 Coventry C
Telfer, W. (1) 1953/4 St Mirren
Thomson, W. (7) 1979/80 St Mirren
Thornton, W. (7) 1946/7 Rangers
Toner, W. (2) 1958/9 Kilmarnock
Turnhull, E. (8) 1947/8 Hibernian

Ure, I. (11) 1961/2 Dundee, Arsenal

Waddell, W. (17) 1946/7 Rangers
Walker, A. (3) 1987/8 Celtic
Walker, J. N. (2) 1992/3 Heart of Midlothian, Partick Thistle
Wallace, L. A. (3) 1977/8 Coventry C
Wallace, W. S. B. (7) 1964/5 Heart of Midlothian, Celtic
Wardhaugh, J. (2) 1954/5 Heart of Midlothian
Wark, J. (29) 1978/9 Ipswich T, Liverpool
Watson, J. (2) 1947/8 Motherwell, Huddersfield T
Watson, R. (1) 1970/1 Motherwell
Weir, A. (6) 1958/9 Motherwell
Weir, D. G. (20) 1996/7 Heart of Midlothian, Everton
Weir, P. (6) 1979/80 St Mirren, Aberdeen
White, J. (22) 1958/9 Falkirk, Tottenham H
Whyte, D. (12) 1987/8 Celtic, Middlesbrough, Aberdeen
Wilson, A. (1) 1953/4 Portsmouth
Wilson, D. (22) 1960/1 Rangers
Wilson, I. A. (5) 1986/7 Leicester C, Everton
Wilson, P. (1) 1974/5 Celtic
Wilson, R. (2) 1971/2 Arsenal
Winters, R. (1) 1998/9 Aberdeen
Wood, G. (4) 1978/9 Everton, Arsenal
Woodburn, W. (24) 1946/7 Rangers
Wright, K. (1) 1991/2 Hibernian
Wright, S. (2) 1992/3 Aberdeen
Wright, T. (3) 1952/3 Sunderland

Yeats, R. (2) 1964/5 Liverpool
Yorston, H. (1) 1954/5 Aberdeen
Young, A. (9) 1959/60 Heart of Midlothian, Everton
Young, G. (53) 1946/7 Rangers
Younger, T. (24) 1954/5 Hibernian, Liverpool

WALES

Aizlewood, M. (39) 1985/6 Charlton Ath, Leeds U, Bradford C, Bristol C, Cardiff C
Allchurch, I. (68) 1950/1 Swansea T, Newcastle U, Cardiff C, Swansea T
Allchurch, L. (11) 1954/5 Swansea T, Sheffield U
Allen, B. (2) 1950/1 Coventry C
Allen, M. (14) 1985/6 Watford, Norwich C, Millwall, Newcastle U

Baker, C. (7) 1957/8 Cardiff C
Baker, W. (1) 1947/8 Cardiff C
Barnard, D. S. (12) 1997/8 Barnsley
Barnes, W. (22) 1947/8 Arsenal
Bellamy, C. D. (9) 1997/8 Norwich C
Berry, G. (5) 1978/9 Wolverhampton W, Stoke C
Blackmore, C. G. (39) 1984/5 Manchester U, Middlesbrough
Blake, N. (15) 1993/4 Sheffield U, Bolton W, Blackburn R
Bodin, P. J. (23) 1989/90 Swindon T, Crystal P, Swindon T
Bowen, D. (19) 1954/5 Arsenal
Bowen, J. P. (2) 1993/4 Swansea C, Birmingham C
Bowen, M. R. (41) 1985/6 Tottenham H, Norwich C, West Ham U
Boyle, T. (2) 1980/1 Crystal P
Browning, M. T. (5) 1995/6 Bristol R, Huddersfield T
Burgess, R. (32) 1946/7 Tottenham H
Burton, O. (9) 1962/3 Norwich C, Newcastle U

Cartwright, L. (7) 1973/4 Coventry C, Wrexham
Charles, J. (38) 1949/50 Leeds U, Juventus, Leeds U, Cardiff C
Charles, J. M. (19) 1980/1 Swansea T, QPR, Oxford U
Charles, M. (31) 1954/5 Swansea T, Arsenal, Cardiff C
Clarke, R. (22) 1948/9 Manchester C
Coleman, C. (28) 1991/2 Crystal P, Blackburn R, Fulham
Cornforth, J. M. (2) 1994/5 Swansea C
Coyne, D. (1) 1995/6 Tranmere R
Crossley, M. G. (3) 1996/7 Nottingham F
Crowe, V. (16) 1958/9 Aston Villa
Curtis, A. (35) 1975/6 Swansea C, Southampton, Cardiff C

Daniel, R. (21) 1950/1 Arsenal, Sunderland
Davies, A. (13) 1982/3 Manchester U, Newcastle U, Swansea C, Bradford C
Davies, D. (52) 1974/5 Everton, Wrexham, Swansea C
Davies, G. (16) 1979/80 Fulham, Chelsea, Manchester C
Davies, R. Wyn (34) 1963/4 Bolton W, Newcastle U, Manchester C, Manchester U, Blackpool
Davies, Reg (6) 1952/3 Newcastle U
Davies, Ron (29) 1963/4 Norwich C, Southampton, Portsmouth
Davies, S. I. (1) 1995/6 Manchester U
Davis, C. (1) 1971/2 Charlton Ath
Davis, G. (4) 1977/8 Wrexham
Deacy, N. (11) 1976/7 PSV Eindhoven, Beringen
Delaney, M. A. (4) 1999/00 Aston Villa
Derrett, S. (4) 1968/9 Cardiff C
Dibble, A. (3) 1985/6 Luton T, Manchester C
Durban, A. (27) 1965/6 Derby C
Dwyer, P. (10) 1977/8 Cardiff C

Edwards. C. N. H. (1) 1995/6 Swansea C
Edwards, G. (12) 1946/7 Birmingham C, Cardiff C
Edwards, I. (4) 1977/8 Chester
Edwards, R. W. (4) 1997/8 Bristol C
Edwards, T. (2) 1956/7 Charlton Ath
Emanuel, J. (2) 1972/3 Bristol C
England, M. (44) 1961/2 Blackburn R, Tottenham H
Evans, B. (7) 1971/2 Swansea C, Hereford U
Evans, I. (13) 1975/6 Crystal P
Evans, R. (1) 1963/4 Swansea T

Felgate, D. (1) 1983/4 Lincoln C
Flynn, B. (66) 1974/5 Burnley, Leeds U, Burnley
Ford, T. (38) 1946/7 Swansea C, Aston Villa, Sunderland, Cardiff C
Foulkes, W. (11) 1951/2 Newcastle U
Freestone, R. (1) 1999/00 Swansea C

Giggs, R. J. (26) 1991/2 Manchester U
Giles, D. (12) 1979/80 Swansea C, Crystal P
Godfrey, B. (3) 1963/4 Preston NE
Goss, J. (9) 1990/1 Norwich C
Green, C. (15) 1964/5 Birmingham C
Green, R. M. (2) 1997/8 Wolverhampton W
Griffiths, A. (17) 1970/1 Wrexham
Griffiths, H. (1) 1952/3 Swansea T
Griffiths, M. (11) 1946/7 Leicester C

Hall, G. D. (9) 1987/8 Chelsea

Harrington, A. (11) 1955/6 Cardiff C
Harris, C. (24) 1975/6 Leeds U
Harris, W. (6) 1953/4 Middlesbrough
Hartson, J. (18) 1994/5 Arsenal, West Ham U, Wimbledon
Haworth, S. O. (5) 1996/7 Cardiff C, Coventry C
Hennessey, T. (39) 1961/2 Birmingham C, Nottingham F, Derby C
Hewitt, R. (5) 1957/8 Cardiff C
Hill, M. (2) 1971/2 Ipswich T
Hockey, T. (9) 1971/2 Sheffield U, Norwich C, Aston Villa
Hodges, G. (18) 1983/4 Wimbledon, Newcastle U, Watford, Sheffield U
Holden, A. (1) 1983/4 Chester C
Hole, B. (30) 1962/3 Cardiff C, Blackburn R, Aston Villa, Swansea T
Hollins, D. (11) 1961/2 Newcastle U
Hopkins, J. (16) 1982/3 Fulham, Crystal P
Hopkins, M. (34) 1955/6 Tottenham H
Horne, B. (59) 1987/8 Portsmouth, Southampton, Everton, Birmingham C
Howells, R. (2) 1953/4 Cardiff C
Hughes, C. M. (8) 1991/2 Luton T, Wimbledon
Hughes, I. (4) 1950/1 Luton T
Hughes, L. M. (72) 1983/4 Manchester U, Barcelona, Manchester U, Chelsea, Southampton
Hughes, W. (3) 1946/7 Birmingham C
Hughes, W. A. (5) 1948/9 Blackburn R
Humphreys, J. (1) 1946/7 Everton

Jackett, K. (31) 1982/3 Watford
James, G. (9) 1965/6 Blackpool
James, L. (54) 1971/2 Burnley, Derby C, QPR, Burnley, Swansea C, Sunderland
James, R. M. (47) 1978/9 Swansea C, Stoke C, QPR, Leicester C, Swansea C
Jarvis, A. (3) 1966/7 Hull C
Jenkins, S. R. (12) 1995/6 Swansea C, Huddersfield T
Johnson, A. J. (7) 1998/9 Nottingham F
Johnson, M. (1) 1963/4 Swansea C
Jones, A. (6) 1986/7 Port Vale, Charlton Ath
Jones, Barrie (15) 1962/3 Swansea T, Plymouth Argyle, Cardiff C
Jones, Bryn (4) 1946/7 Arsenal
Jones, C. (59) 1953/4 Swansea T, Tottenham H, Fulham
Jones, D. (8) 1975/6 Norwich C
Jones, E. (4) 1947/8 Swansea T, Tottenham H
Jones, J. (72) 1975/6 Liverpool, Wrexham, Chelsea, Huddersfield T
Jones, K. (1) 1949/50 Aston Villa
Jones, M. G. (4) 1999/00 Leeds U
Jones, P. L. (2) 1996/7 Liverpool, Tranmere R
Jones, P. S. (14) 1996/7 Stockport C, Southampton
Jones, R. (1) 1993/4 Sheffield W
Jones, T. G. (13) 1946/7 Everton
Jones, V. P. (9) 1994/5 Wimbledon
Jones, W. (1) 1970/1 Bristol C

Kelsey, J. (41) 1953/4 Arsenal
King, J. (1) 1954/5 Swansea T
Kinsey, N. (7) 1950/1 Norwich C, Birmingham C
Knill, A. R. (1) 1988/9 Swansea C
Krzywicki, R. 1969/70 WBA, Huddersfield T

Lambert, R. (5) 1946/7 Liverpool
Law, B. J. (1) 1989/90 QPR
Lea, C. (2) 1964/5 Ipswich T
Leek, K. (13) 1960/1 Leicester C, Newcastle U, Birmingham C
Legg, A. (5) 1995/6 Birmingham C, Cardiff C
Lever, A. (1) 1952/3 Leicester C
Lewis, D. (1) 1982/3 Swansea C
Llewellyn, C. M. (2) 1997/8 Norwich C
Lloyd, B. (3) 1975/6 Wrexham
Lovell, S. (6) 1981/2 Crystal P, Millwall
Lowndes, S. (10) 1982/3 Newport C, Millwall, Barnsley
Lowrie, G. (4) 1947/8 Coventry C, Newcastle U
Lucas, M. (4) 1961/2 Leyton Orient
Lucas, W. (7) 1948/9 Swansea T

Maguire, G. T. (7) 1989/90 Portsmouth
Mahoney, J. (51) 1967/8 Stoke C, Middlesbrough, Swansea C
Mardon, P. J. (1) 1995/6 WBA
Marriott, A. (5) 1995/6 Wrexham
Marustik, C. (6) 1981/2 Swansea C
Medwin, T. (30) 1952/3 Swansea T, Tottenham H
Melville, A. K. (39) 1989/90 Swansea C, Oxford U, Sunderland, Fulham
Mielczarek, R. (1) 1970/1 Rotherham U
Millington, A. (21) 1962/3 WBA, Crystal P, Peterborough U, Swansea C
Moore, G. (21) 1959/60 Cardiff C, Chelsea, Manchester U, Northampton T, Charlton Ath
Morris, W. (5) 1946/7 Burnley

Nardiello, D. (2) 1977/8 Coventry C
Neilson, A. B. (5) 1991/2 Newcastle U, Southampton

Nicholas, P. (73) 1978/9 Crystal P, Arsenal, Crystal P, Luton T, Aberdeen, Chelsea, Watford
Niedzwiecki, E. A. (2) 1984/5 Chelsea
Nogan, L. M. (2) 1991/2 Watford, Reading
Nurse, E. A. (2) 1984/5 Chelsea
Norman, A. J. (5) 1985/6 Hull C
Nurse, M. (12) 1959/60 Swansea T, Middlesbrough

O'Sullivan, P. (3) 1972/3 Brighton & HA
Oster, J. M. (3) 1997/8 Everton, Sunderland

Page, M. (28) 1970/1 Birmingham C
Page, R. J. (13) 1996/7 Watford
Palmer, D. (3) 1956/7 Swansea T
Parry, J. (1) 1950/1 Swansea T
Pascoe, C. (10) 1983/4 Swansea C, Sunderland
Paul, R. (33) 1948/9 Swansea T, Manchester C
Pembridge, M. A. (36) 1991/2 Luton T, Derby C, Sheffield W, Benfica, Everton
Perry, J. (1) 1993/4 Cardiff C
Phillips, D. (62) 1983/4 Plymouth Argyle, Manchester C, Coventry C, Norwich C, Nottingham F
Phillips, J. (4) 1972/3 Chelsea
Phillips, L. (58) 1970/1 Cardff C, Aston Villa, Swansea C, Charlton Ath
Pontin, K. (2) 1979/80 Cardiff C
Powell, A. (8) 1946/7 Leeds U, Everton, Birmingham C
Powell, D. (11) 1967/8 Wrexham, Sheffield U
Powell, I. (8) 1946/7 QPR, Aston Villa
Price, P. (25) 1979/80 Luton T, Tottenham H
Pring, K. (3) 1965/6 Rotherham U
Pritchard, H. K. (1) 1984/5 Bristol C

Rankmore, F. (l) 1965/6 Peterborough U
Ratcliffe, K. (59) 1980/1 Everton, Cardiff C
Ready, K. (5) 1996/7 QPR
Reece, G. (29) 1965/6 Sheffield U, Cardiff C
Reed, W. (2) 1954/5 Ipswich T
Rees, A. (1) 1983/4 Birmingham C
Rees, J. M. (1) 1991/2 Luton T
Rees, R. (39) 1964/5 Coventry C, WBA, Nottingham F
Rees, W. (4) 1948/9 Cardiff C, Tottenham H
Richards, S. (1) 1946/7 Cardiff C
Roberts, A. M. (2) 1992/3 QPR
Roberts, D. (17) 1972/3 Oxford U, Hull C
Roberts, G. W. (3) 1999/00 Tranmere R
Roberts, I. W. (10) 1989/90 Watford, Huddersfield T, Leicester C, Norwich C
Roberts, J. G. (22) 1970/1 Arsenal, Birmingham C
Roberts, J. H. (1) 1948/9 Bolton W
Roberts, N. W. (1) 1999/00 Wrexham
Roberts, P. (4) 1973/4 Portsmouth
Robinson, C. P. (2) 1999/00 Wolverhampton W
Robinson, J. R. C. (22) 1995/6 Charlton Ath
Rodrigues, P. (40) 1964/5 Cardiff C, Leicester C, Sheffield W
Rouse, V. (1) 1958/9 Crystal P
Rowley, T. (1) 1958/9 Tranmere R
Rush, I. (73) 1979/80 Liverpool, Juventus, Liverpool

Saunders, D. (73) 1985/6 Brighton & HA, Oxford U, Derby C, Liverpool, Aston Villa, Galatasaray, Nottingham F, Sheffield U, Benfica, Bradford C
Savage, R. W. (16) 1995/6 Crewe Alexandra, Leicester C
Sayer, P. (7) 1976/7 Cardiff C
Scrine, F. (2) 1949/50 Swansea T
Sear, C. (1) 1962/3 Manchester C
Sherwood, A. (41) 1946/7 Cardiff C, Newport C
Shortt, W. (12) 1946/7 Plymouth Argyle
Showers, D. (2) 1974/5 Cardiff C
Sidlow, C. (7) 1946/7 Liverpool
Slatter, N. (22) 1982/3 Bristol R, Oxford U
Smallman, D. (7) 1973/4 Wrexham, Everton
Southall, N. (92) 1981/2 Everton
Speed, G. A. (58) 1989/90 Leeds U, Everton, Newcastle U
Sprake, G. (37) 1963/4 Leeds U, Birmingham C
Stansfield, F. (1) 1948/9 Cardiff C
Stevenson, B. (15) 1977/8 Leeds U, Birmingham C
Stevenson, N. (4) 1981/2 Swansea C
Stitfall, R. (2) 1952/3 Cardiff C
Sullivan, D. (17) 1952/3 Cardiff C
Symons, C. J. (32) 1991/2 Portsmouth, Manchester C, Fulham

Tapscott, D. (14) 1953/4 Arsenal, Cardiff C
Taylor, G. K. (8) 1995/6 Crystal P, Sheffield U
Thomas, D. (2) 1956/7 Swansea T
Thomas, M. (51) 1976/7 Wrexham, Manchester U, Everton, Brighton & HA, Stoke C, Chelsea, WBA
Thomas, M. R. (1) 1986/7 Newcastle U
Thomas, R. (50) 1966/7 Swindon T, Derby C, Cardiff C
Thomas, S. (4) 1947/8 Fulham
Toshack, J. (40) 1968/9 Cardiff C, Liverpool, Swansea C
Trollope, P. J. (5) 1996/7 Derby C, Fulham

Van Den Hauwe, P. W. R. (13) 1984/5 Everton
Vaughan, N. (10) 1982/3 Newport C, Cardiff C
Vearncombe, G. (2) 1957/8 Cardiff C
Vernon, R. (32) 1956/7 Blackburn R, Everton, Stoke C
Villars, A. (3) 1973/4 Cardiff C

Walley, T. (1) 1970/1 Watford
Walsh, I. (18) 1979/80 Crystal P, Swansea C
Ward, D. (2) 1958/9 Bristol R, Cardiff C
Ward, D. (1) 1999/00 Notts C
Webster, C. (4) 1956/7 Manchester U
Weston, R. D. (1) 1999/00 Arsenal
Williams, A. (12) 1993/4 Reading, Wolverhampton W
Williams, A. P. (2) 1997/8 Southampton
Williams, D. G. 1987/8 13, Derby C, Ipswich T
Williams, D. M. (5) 1985/6 Norwich C
Williams, G. (1) 1950/1 Cardiff C
Williams, G. E. (26) 1959/60 WBA
Williams, G. G. (5) 1960/1 Swansea T
Williams, H. (4) 1948/9 Newport C, Leeds U
Williams, Herbert (3) 1964/5 Swansea T
Williams, S. (43) 1953/4 WBA, Southampton
Witcomb, D. (3) 1946/7 WBA, Sheffield W
Woosnam, P. (17) 1958/9 Leyton Orient, West Ham U, Aston Villa

Yorath, T. (59) 1969/70 Leeds U, Coventry C, Tottenham H, Vancouver Whitecaps
Young, E. (21) 1989/90 Wimbledon, Crystal P, Wolverhampton W

EIRE

Aherne, T. (16) 1945/6 Belfast Celtic, Luton T
Aldridge, J. W. (69) 1985/6 Oxford U, Liverpool, Real Sociedad, Tranmere R
Ambrose, P. (5) 1954/5 Shamrock R
Anderson, J. (16) 1979/80 Preston NE, Newcastle U

Babb, P. (34) 1993/4 Coventry C, Liverpool
Bailham, E. (1) 1963/4 Shamrock R
Barber, E. (2) 1965/6 Shelbourne, Birmingham C
Beglin, J. (15) 1983/4 Liverpool
Bonner, P. (80) 1980/1 Celtic
Braddish, S. (1) 1977/8 Dundalk
Brady, T. R. (6) 1963/4 QPR
Brady, W. L. (72) 1974/5 Arsenal, Juventus, Sampdoria, Internazionale, Ascoli, West Ham U
Branagan, K. G. (1) 1996/7 Bolton W
Breen, G. (31) 1995/6 Birmingham C, Coventry C
Breen, T. (3) 1946/7 Shamrock R
Brennan, F. (1) 1964/5 Drumcondra
Brennan, S. A. (19) 1964/5 Manchester U, Waterford
Browne, W. (3) 1963/4 Bohemians
Buckley, L. (2) 1983/4 Shamrock R, Waregem
Burke, F. (1) 1951/2 Cork Ath
Butler, P. J. (1) 1999/00 Sunderland
Byrne, A. B. (14) 1969/70 Southampton
Byrne, J. (23) 1984/5 QPR, Le Havre, Brighton & HA, Sunderland, Millwall
Byrne, P. (8) 1983/4 Shamrock R

Campbell, A. (3) 1984/5 Santander
Campbell, N. (11) 1970/1 St Patrick's Ath, Fortuna Cologne
Cantwell, N. (36) 1953/4 West Ham U, Manchester U
Carey, B. P. (3) 1991/2 Manchester U, Leicester C
Carey, J. J. (21) 1945/6 Manchester U
Carolan, J. (2) 1959/60 Manchester U
Carr, S. (12) 1998/9 Tottenham H
Carroll, B. (2) 1948/9 Shelbourne
Carroll, T. R. (17) 1967/8 Ipswich T, Birmingham C
Carsley, L. K. (15) 1997/8 Derby C, Blackburn R
Cascarino, A. G. (88) 1985/6 Gillingham, Millwall, Aston Villa, Celtic, Chelsea, Marseille, Nancy
Chandler, J. (2) 1979/80 Leeds U
Clarke, J. (1) 1977/8 Drogheda U
Clarke, K. (2) 1947/8 Drumcondra
Clarke, M. (1) 1949/50 Shamrock R
Clinton, T. J. (3) 1950/1 Everton
Coad, P. (11) 1946/7 Shamrock R
Coffey, T. (1) 1949/50 Drumcondra
Colfer, M. D. (2) 1949/50 Shelbourne
Conmy, O. M. (5) 1964/5 Peterborough U
Connolly, D. J. (22) 1995/6 Watford, Feyenoord, Wolverhampton W, Excelsior
Conroy, G. A. (27) 1969/70 Stoke C
Conway, J. P. (20) 1966/7 Fulham, Manchester C
Corr, P. J. (4) 1948/9 Everton
Courtney, E. (1) 1945/6 Cork U
Coyle, O. (1) 1993/4 Bolton W

Coyne, T. (22) 1991/2 Celtic, Tranmere R, Motherwell
Cummins, G. P. (19) 1953/4 Luton T
Cuneen, T. (1) 1950/1 Limerick
Cunningham, K. (31) 1995/6 Wimbledon
Curtis, D. P. (17) 1956/7 Shelbourne, Bristol C, Ipswich T, Exeter C
Cusack, S. (1) 1952/3 Limerick

Daish, L. S. (5) 1991/2 Cambridge U, Coventry C
Daly, G. A. (48) 1972/3 Manchester U, Derby C, Coventry C, Birmingham C, Shrewsbury T
Daly, M. (2) 1977/8 Wolverhampton W
Daly, P. (1) 1949/50 Shamrock R
Delap, R. J. (6) 1997/8 Derby C
De Mange, K. J. P. P. (2) 1986/7 Liverpool, Hull C
Deacy, E. (4) 1981/2 Aston Villa
Dempsey, J. T. (19) 1966/7 Fulham, Chelsea
Dennehy, J. (11) 1971/2 Cork Hibernian, Nottingham F, Walsall
Desmond, P. (4) 1949/50 Middlesbrough
Devine, J. (12) 1979/80 Arsenal, Norwich C
Doherty, G. M. T. (3) 1999/00 Luton T, Tottenham H
Donovan, D. C. (5) 1954/5 Everton
Donovan, T. (1) 1979/80 Aston Villa
Doyle, C. (1) 1958/9 Shelbourne
Duff, D. A. (14) 1997/8 Blackburn R
Duffy, B. (1) 1949/50 Shamrock R
Dunne, A. P. (33) 1961/2 Manchester U, Bolton W
Dunne, J. C. (1) 1970/1 Fulham
Dunne, P. A. J. (5) 1964/5 Manchester U
Dunne, R. P. (3) 1999/00 Everton
Dunne, S. (15) 1952/3 Luton T
Dunne, T. (3) 1955/6 St Patrick's Ath
Dunning, P. (2) 1970/1 Shelbourne
Dunphy, E. M. (23) 1965/6 York C, Millwall
Dwyer, N. M. (14) 1959/60 West Ham U, Swansea T

Eccles, P. (1) 1985/6 Shamrock R
Eglington, T. J. (24) 1945/6 Shamrock R, Everton
Evans, M. J. (1) 1997/8 Southampton

Fagan, E. (1) 1972/3 Shamrock R
Fagan, F. (8) 1954/5 Manchester C, Derby C
Fairclough, M. (2) 1981/2 Dundalk
Fallon, S. (8) 1950/1 Celtic
Farrell, P. D. (28) 1945/6 Shamrock R, Everton
Farrelly, G. (6) 1995/6 Aston Villa, Everton, Bolton W
Finnan, S. (2) 1999/00 Fulham
Finucane, A. (11) 1966/7 Limerick
Fitzgerald, F. J. (2) 1954/5 Waterford
Fitzgerald, P. J. (5) 1960/1 Leeds U, Chester
Fitzpatrick, K. (1) 1969/70 Limerick
Fitzsimons, A. G. (26) 1949/50 Middlesbrough, Lincoln C
Fleming, C. (10) 1995/6 Middlesbrough
Fogarty, A. (11) 1959/60 Sunderland, Hartlepool U
Foley, D. J. (4) 1999/00 Watford
Foley, T. C. (9) 1963/4 Northampton T
Fullam, J. 1960/1 Preston NE, Shamrock R

Gallagher, C. (2) 1966/7 Celtic
Gallagher, M. (1) 1953/4 Hibernian
Galvin, A. (29) 1982/3 Tottenham H, Sheffield W
Gannon, E. (14) 1948/9 Notts C, Sheffield W, Shelbourne K
Gannon, M. (1) 1971/2 Shelbourne
Gavin, J. T. (7) 1949/50 Norwich C, Tottenham H, Norwich C
Gibbons, A. (4) 1951/2 St Patrick's Ath
Gilbert, R. (1) 1965/6 Shamrock R
Giles, C. (1) 1950/1 Doncaster R
Giles, M. J. (59) 1959/60 Manchester U, Leeds U, WBA, Shamrock R
Given, S. J. J. (25) 1995/6 Blackburn R, Newcastle U
Givens, D. J. (56) 1968/9 Manchester U, Luton T, QPR, Birmingham C, Neuchatel Xamax
Glynn, D. (2) 1951/2 Drumcondra
Godwin, T. F. (13) 1948/9 Shamrock R, Leicester C, Bournemouth
Goodman, J. (4) 1996/7 Wimbledon
Gorman, W. C. (2) 1946/7 Brentford
Grealish, A. (44) 1975/6 Orient, Luton T, Brighton & HA, WBA
Gregg, E. (8) 1977/8 Bohemians
Grimes, A. A. (17) 1977/8 Manchester U, Coventry C, Luton T

Hale, A. (13) 1961/2 Aston Villa, Doncaster R, Waterford
Hamilton, T. (2) 1958/9 Shamrock R
Hand, E. K. (20) 1968/9 Portsmouth
Harte, I. P. (22) 1995/6 Leeds U
Hartnett, J. B. (2) 1948/9 Middlesbrough
Haverty, J. (32) 1955/6 Arsenal, Blackburn R, Millwall, Celtic, Bristol R, Shelbourne
Hayes, A. W. P. (1) 1978/9 Southampton
Hayes, W. E. (2) 1946/7 Huddersfield T
Hayes, W. J. (1) 1948/9 Limerick
Healey, R. (2) 1976/7 Cardiff C
Heighway, S . D. (34) 1970/1 Liverpool, Minnesota Kicks
Henderson, B. (2) 1947/8 Drumcondra

Hennessy, J. (5) 1955/6 Shelbourne, St Patrick's Ath
Herrick, J. (3) 1971/2 Cork Hibernians, Shamrock R
Higgins, J. (1) 1950/1 Birmingham C
Holland, M. R. (4) 1999/00 Ipswich T
Holmes, J. 1970/1 Coventry C, Tottenham H, Vancouver Whitecaps
Houghton, R. J. (73) 1985/6 Oxford U, Liverpool, Aston Villa, Crystal P, Reading
Howlett, G. (1) 1983/4 Brighton & HA
Hughton, C. (53) 1979/80 Tottenham H, West Ham U
Hurley, C. J. (40) 1956/7 Millwall, Sunderland, Bolton W

Irwin, D. J. (56) 1990/1 Manchester U

Kavanagh, G. A. (3) 1997/8 Stoke C
Keane, R. D. (18) 1997/8 Wolverhampton W, Coventry C
Keane, R. M. (46) 1990/1 Nottingham F, Manchester U
Keane, T. R. (4) 1948/9 Swansea T
Kearin, M. (1) 1971/2 Shamrock R
Kearns, F. T. (1) 1953/4 West Ham U
Kearns, M. (18) 1969/70 Oxford U, Walsall, Wolverhampton W
Kelly, A. T. (30) 1992/3 Sheffield U, Blackburn R
Kelly, D. T. (26) 1987/8 Walsall, West Ham U, Leicester C, Newcastle U, Wolverhampton W, Sunderland, Tranmere R
Kelly, G. (31) 1993/4 Leeds U
Kelly J. A. (48) 1956/7 Drumcondra, Preston NE
Kelly, J. P. V. (5) 1960/1 Wolverhampton W
Kelly, M. J. (4) 1987/8 Portsmouth
Kelly, N. (1) 1953/4 Nottingham F
Kenna, J. J. (27) 1994/5 Blackburn R
Kennedy, M. (30) 1995/6 Liverpool, Wimbledon, Manchester C
Kennedy, M. F. (2) 1985/6 Portsmouth
Keogh, J. (1) 1965/6 Shamrock R
Keogh, S. (1) 1958/9 Shamrock R
Kernaghan, A. N. (22) 1992/3 Middlesbrough, Manchester C
Kiely, D. L. (4) 1999/00 Charlton Ath
Kiernan, F. W. (5) 1950/1 Shamrock R, Southampton
Kilbane, K. D. (16) 1997/8 WBA, Sunderland
Kinnear, J. P. (26) 1966/7 Tottenham H, Brighton & HA
Kinsella, M. A. (16) 1997/8 Charlton Ath

Langan, D. (25) 1977/8 Derby C, Birmingham C, Oxford U
Lawler, J. F. (8) 1952/3 Fulham
Lawlor, J. C. (3) 1948/9 Drumcondra, Doncaster R
Lawlor, M. (5) 1970/1 Shamrock R
Lawrenson, M. (39) 1976/7 Preston NE, Brighton & HA, Liverpool
Leech, M. (8) 1968/9 Shamrock R
Lowry, D. (1) 1961/2 St Patrick's Ath

McAlinden, J. (2) 1945/6 Portsmouth
McAteer, J. W. (35) 1993/4 Bolton W, Liverpool, Blackburn R
McCann, J. (1) 1956/7 Shamrock R
McCarthy, M. (57) 1983/4 Manchester C, Celtic, Lyon, Millwall
McConville, T. (6) 1971/2 Dundalk, Waterford
McDonagh, J. (24) 1980/1 Everton, Bolton W, Notts C
McDonagh, Joe (3) 1983/4 Shamrock R
McEvoy, M. A. (17) 1960/1 Blackburn R
McGee, P. (15) 1977/8 QPR, Preston NE
McGoldrick, E. J. (15) 1991/2 Crystal P, Arsenal
McGowan, D. (3) 1948/9 West Ham U
McGowan, J. (1) 1946/7 Cork U
McGrath, M. (22) 1957/8 Blackburn R, Bradford Park Avenue
McGrath, P. (83) 1984/5 Manchester U, Aston Villa, Derby C
Macken, A. (1) 1976/7 Derby C
Mackey, G. (3) 1956/7 Shamrock R
McLoughlin, A. F. (42) 1989/90 Swindon T, Southampton, Portsmouth
McMillan, W. (2) 1945/6 Belfast Celtic
McNally, J. B. (3) 1958/9 Luton T
McPhail, S. (3) 1999/00 Leeds U
Mahon, A. J. (2) 1999/00 Tranmere R
Malone, G. (1) 1948/9 Shelbourne
Mancini, T. J. (5) 1973/4 QPR, Arsenal
Martin, C. J. (30) 1945/6 Glentoran, Leeds U, Aston Villa
Martin, M. P. (51) 1971/2 Bohemians, Manchester U, WBA, Newcastle U
Maybury, A. (2) 1997/8 Leeds U
Meagan, M. K. (17) 1960/1 Everton, Huddersfield T, Drogheda
Milligan, M. J. (1) 1991/2 Oldham Ath
Mooney, J. (2) 1964/5 Shamrock R
Moore, A. (8) 1995/6 Middlesbrough
Moran, K. (70) 1979/80 Manchester U, Sporting Gijon, Blackburn R
Moroney, T. (12) 1947/8 West Ham U
Morris, C. B. (35) 1987/8 Celtic, Middlesbrough
Moulson, G. B. (3) 1947/8 Lincoln C
Mucklan, C. (1) 1977/8 Drogheda

Mulligan, P. M. (50) 1968/9 Shamrock R, Chelsea, Crystal P, WBA, Shamrock R
Munroe, L. (1) 1953/4 Shamrock R
Murphy, A. (1) 1955/6 Clyde
Murphy, B. (1) 1985/6 Bohemians
Murphy, J. (1) 1979/80 Crystal P
Murray, T. (1) 1949/50 Dundalk

Newman, W. (1) 1968/9 Shelbourne
Nolan, R. (10) 1956/7 Shamrock R

O'Brien, F. (4) 1979/80 Philadelphia Fury
O'Brien, L. (16) 1985/6 Shamrock R, Manchester U, Newcastle U, Tranmere R
O'Brien, R. (4) 1975/6 Notts C
O'Byrne, L. B. (1) 1948/9 Shamrock R
O'Callaghan, B. R. (6) 1978/9 Stoke C
O'Callaghan, K. (20) 1980/1 Ipswich T, Portsmouth
O'Connnell, A. (2) 1966/7 Dundalk, Bohemians
O'Connor, T. (4) 1949/50 Shamrock R
O'Connor, T. (7) 1967/8 Fulham, Dundalk, Bohemians
O'Driscoll, J. F. (3) 1948/9 Swansea T
O'Driscoll, S. (3) 1981/2 Fulham
O'Farrell, F. (9) 1951/2 West Ham U, Preston NE
O'Flanagan, K. P. (3) 1946/7 Arsenal
O'Flanagan, M. (1) 1946/7 Bohemians
O'Hanlon, K. G. (1) 1987/8 Rotherham U
O'Keefe, E. (5) 1980/1 Everton, Port Vale
O'Leary, D. (68) 1976/7 Arsenal
O'Leary, P. (7) 1979/80 Shamrock R
O'Neill, F. S. (20) 1961/2 Shamrock R
O'Neill, J. (17) 1951/2 Everton
O'Neill, J. (1) 1960/1 Preston NE
O'Neill, K. P. (13) 1995/6 Norwich C, Middlesbrough
O'Regan, K. (4) 1983/4 Brighton & HA
O'Reilly, J. (2) 1945/6 Cork U

Peyton, G. (33) 1976/7 Fulham, Bournemouth, Everton
Peyton, N. (6) 1956/7 Shamrock R, Leeds U
Phelan, T. (42) 1991/2 Wimbledon, Manchester C, Chelsea, Everton, Fulham

Quinn, B. S. (4) 1999/00 Coventry C
Quinn, N. J. (79) 1985/6 Arsenal, Manchester C, Sunderland

Richardson, D. J. (3) 1971/2 Shamrock R, Gillingham
Ringstead, A. (20) 1950/1 Sheffield U
Robinson, M. (23) 1980/1 Brighton & HA, Liverpool, QPR
Roche, P. J. (8) 1971/2 Shelbourne, Manchester U
Rogers, E. (19) 1967/8 Blackburn R, Charlton Ath
Ryan, G. (16) 1977/8 Derby C, Brighton & HA
Ryan, R. A. (16) 1949/50 WBA, Derby C

Savage, D. P. T. (5) 1995/6 Millwall
Saward, P. (18) 1953/4 Millwall, Aston Villa, Huddersfield T
Scannell, T. (1) 1953/4 Southend U
Scully, P. J. (1) 1988/9 Arsenal
Sheedy, K. (45) 1983/4 Everton, Newcastle U
Sheridan, J. J. (34) 1987/8 Leeds U, Sheffield W
Slaven, B. (7) 1989/90 Middlesbrough
Sloan, J. W. (2) 1945/6 Arsenal
Smyth, M. (1) 1968/9 Shamrock R
Stapleton, F. (70) 1976/7 Arsenal, Manchester U, Ajax, Derby C, Le Havre, Blackburn R
Staunton, S. (84) 1988/9 Liverpool, Aston Villa, Liverpool
Stevenson, A. E. (6) 1946/7 Everton
Strahan, F. (5) 1963/4 Shelbourne
Swan, M. M. G. (1) 1959/60 Drumcondra
Synott, N. (3) 1977/8 Shamrock R

Thomas, P. (2) 1973/4 Waterford
Tsend, A. D. (70) 1988/9 Norwich C, Chelsea, Aston Villa, Middlesbrough
Traynor, T. J. (8) 1953/4 Southampton
Treacy, R. C. P. (42) 1965/6 WBA, Charlton Ath, Swindon T, Preston NE, WBA, Shamrock R
Tuohy, L. (8) 1955/6 Shamrock R, Newcastle U, Shamrock R
Turner, P. (2) 1962/3 Celtic

Vernon, J. (2) 1945/6 Belfast Celtic

Waddock, G. (20) 1979/80 QPR, Millwall
Walsh, D. J. (20) 1945/6 WBA, Aston Villa
Walsh, J. (1) 1981/2 Limerick
Walsh, M. (21) 1975/6 Blackpool, Everton, QPR, Porto
Walsh, M. (4) 1981/2 Everton, Norwich C
Walsh, W. (9) 1946/7 Manchester C
Waters, J. (2) 1976/7 Grimsby T
Whelan, R. (2) 1963/4 St Patrick's Ath
Whelan, R. (53) 1980/1 Liverpool, Southend U
Whelan, W. (4) 1955/6 Manchester U
Whittaker, R. (1) 1958/9 Chelsea

BRITISH ISLES INTERNATIONAL GOALSCORERS SINCE 1946

ENGLAND

A'Court, A.	1
Adams, T.A.	5
Allen, R.	2
Anderson, V.	2
Anderton, D.R.	7
Astall, G.	1
Atyeo, P.J.W.	5
Baily, E.F.	5
Baker, J.H.	3
Ball, A.J.	8
Barnes, J.	11
Barnes, P.S.	4
Barmby, N.J.	3
Beardsley, P.A.	9
Beattie, J.K.	1
Beckham, D.R.J.	1
Bell, C.	9
Bentley, R.T.F.	9
Blissett, L.	3
Bowles, S.	1
Bradford, G.R.W.	1
Bradley, W.	2
Bridges, B.J.	1
Broadbent, P.F.	2
Broadis, I.A.	8
Brooking, T.D.	5
Brooks, J.	2
Bull, S.G.	4
Butcher, T.	3
Byrne, J.J.	8
Carter, H.S.	5
Chamberlain, M.	1
Channon, M.R.	21
Charlton, J.	6
Charlton, R.	49
Chivers, M.	13
Clarke, A.J.	10
Connelly, J.M.	7
Coppell, S.J.	7
Cowans, G.	2
Crawford, R.	1
Currie, A.W.	3
Dixon, L.M.	1
Dixon, K.M.	4
Douglas, B.	11
Eastham, G.	2
Edwards, D.	5
Elliott, W.H.	3
Ferdinand, L.	5
Finney, T.	30
Flowers, R.	10
Fowler, R.B.	3
Francis, G.C.J.	3
Francis, T.	12
Froggatt, J.	2
Froggatt, R.	2
Gascoigne, P.J.	10
Goddard, P.	1
Grainger, C.	3
Greaves, J.	44
Haines, J.T.W.	2
Hancocks, J.	2
Hassall, H.W.	4
Hateley, M.	9
Haynes, J.N.	18
Heskey, E.W.	1
Hirst, D.E.	1
Hitchens, G.A.	5
Hoddle, G.	8
Hughes, E.W.	1
Hunt, R.	18
Hunter, N.	2
Hurst, G.C.	24
Johnson, D.E.	6
Kay, A.H.	1
Keegan, J.K.	21
Kennedy, R.	3
Keown, M.R.	2
Kevan, D.T.	8
Kidd, B.	1
Langton, R.	1
Latchford, R.D.	5
Lawler, C.	1
Lawton, T.	16
Lee, F.	10
Lee, J.	1
Lee, R.M.	2
Lee, S.	2
Le Saux, G.P.	1
Lineker, G.	48
Lofthouse, N.	30
Mabbutt, G.	1
McDermott, T.	3
Macdonald, M.	6
McManaman, S.	3
Mannion, W.J.	11
Mariner, P.	13
Marsh, R.W.	1
Matthews, S.	3
Medley, L.D.	1
Melia, J.	1
Merson, P.C.	3
Milburn, J.E.T.	10
Moore, R.F.	2
Morris, J.	3
Mortensen, S.H.	23
Mullen, J.	6
Mullery, A.P.	1
Neal, P.G.	5
Nicholls, J.	1
Nicholson, W.E.	1
O'Grady, M.	3
Owen, M.J.	7
Own goals	23
Paine, T.L.	7
Palmer, C.L.	1
Parry, R.A.	1
Peacock, A.	3
Pearce, S.	5
Pearson, J.S.	5
Pearson, S.C.	5
Perry, W.	2
Peters, M.	20
Pickering, F.	5
Platt, D.	27
Pointer, R.	2
Ramsay, A.E.	3
Redknapp, J.F.	1
Revie, D.G.	4
Robson, B.	26
Robson, R.	4
Rowley, J.F.	6
Royle, J.	2

Sansom, K.	1
Scholes, P.	10
Sewell, J.	3
Shackleton, L.F.	1
Shearer, A.	30
Sheringham, E.P.	9
Smith, A.M.	2
Smith, R.	13
Southgate, G.	1
Steven, T.M.	4
Stiles, N.P.	1
Stone, S.B.	2
Summerbee, M.G.	1
Tambling, R.V.	1
Taylor, P.J.	2
Taylor, T.	16
Thompson, P.B.	1
Tueart, D.	2
Viollet, D.S.	1
Waddle, C.R.	6
Wallace, D.L.	1
Walsh, P.	1
Watson, D.V.	4
Webb, N.	4
Weller, K.	1
Wignall, F.	2
Wilkins, R.G.	3
Wilshaw, D.J.	10
Wise, D.F.	1
Withe, P.	1
Woodcock, T.	16
Worthington, F.S.	2
Wright, I.E.	9
Wright, M.	1
Wright, W.A.	3

SCOTLAND

Aitken, R.	1
Archibald, S.	4
Baird, S.	2
Bannon, E.	1
Bauld, W.	2
Baxter, J.C.	3
Bett, J.	1
Bone, J.	1
Booth, S.	5
Boyd, T.	1
Brand, R.	8
Brazil, A.	1
Bremner, W.J.	3
Brown, A.D.	6
Buckley, P.	1
Burley, C.W.	3
Burns, K.	1
Calderwood, C.	1
Caldow, E.	4
Cameron, C.	1
Campbell, R.	1
Chalmers, S.	3
Collins, J.	12
Collins, R.V.	10
Combe, J.R.	1
Conn, A.	1
Cooper, D.	6
Craig, J.	1
Crawford, S.	1
Curran, H.P.	1
Dailly, C.	1
Dalglish, K.	30
Davidson, J.A.	1
Docherty, T.H.	1
Dodds, D.	1
Dodds, W.	4
Duncan, D.M.	1
Durie, G.S.	7
Ferguson, B.	1
Fernie, W.	1
Flavell, R.	2
Fleming, C.	2
Gallacher, K.W.	8
Gemmell, T.K *(St Mirren)*	1
Gemmell, T.K *(Celtic)*	1
Gemmill, A.	8
Gibson, D.W.	3
Gilzean, A.J.	12
Gough, C.R.	6
Graham, A.	2
Graham, G.	3
Gray, A.	5
Gray, E.	3
Gray, F.	1
Greig, J.	3
Hamilton, G.	4
Harper, J.M.	2
Hartford, R.A.	4
Henderson, J.G.	1
Henderson, W.	5
Hendry, E.C.J.	1
Herd, D.G.	3
Herd, G.	1
Hewie, J.D.	2
Holton, J.A.	2
Hopkin, D.	2
Houliston, W.	2
Howie, H.	1
Hughes, J.	1
Hunter, W.	1
Hutchison, D.	5
Hutchison, T.	1
Jackson, C.	1
Jackson, D.	4
Jardine, A.	1
Jess, E.	2
Johnston, A.	2
Johnston, L.H.	1
Johnston, M.	14
Johnstone, D.	2
Johnstone, J.	4
Johnstone, R.	9
Jordan, J.	11
Law, D.	30
Leggat, G.	8
Lennox, R.	3
Liddell, W.	6
Linwood, A.B.	1
Lorimer, P.	4
Macari, L.	5
McAllister, G.	5
MacDougall, E.J.	3
MacKay, D.C.	4
Mackay, G.	1
MacKenzie, J.A.	1
MacLeod, M.	1
McAvennie, F.	1
McCall, S.M.	1
McCalliog, J.	1
McClair, B.	2
McCoist, A.	19
McGhee, M.	2
McGinlay, J.	3
McInally, A.	3
McKimmie, S.I.	1
McKinlay, W.	4
McKinnon, R.	1
McLaren, A.	4

McLean, T.	1
McLintock, F.	1
McMillan, I.L.	2
McNeill, W.	3
McPhail, J.	3
McQueen, G.	5
McStay, P.	9
McSwegan, G.J.	1
Mason, J.	4
Masson, D.S.	5
Miller, W.	1
Mitchell, R.C.	1
Morgan, W.	1
Morris, H.	3
Mudie, J.K.	9
Mulhall, G.	1
Murdoch, R.	5
Murray, J.	1
Narey, D.	1
Nevin, P.K.F.	5
Nicholas, C.	5
O'Hare, J.	5
Ormond, W.E.	1
Orr, T.	1
Own goals	9
Parlane, D.	1
Pettigrew, W.	2
Provan, D.	1
Quinn, J.	7
Quinn, P.	1
Reilly, L.	22
Ring, T.	2
Rioch, B.D.	6
Ritchie, P.S.	1
Robertson, A.	2
Robertson, J.	2
Robertson, J.N.	9
St John, I.	9
Scott, A.S.	5
Sharp, G.	1
Shearer, D.	2
Smith, G.	4
Souness, G.J.	4
Steel, W.	12
Stein, C.	10
Stewart, R.	1
Strachan, G.	5
Sturrock, P.	3
Thornton, W.	1
Waddell, W.	6
Wallace, I.A.	1
Wark, J.	7
Weir, A.	1
White, J.A.	3
Wilson, D.	9
Young, A.	2

WALES

Allchurch, I.J.	23
Allen, M.	3
Barnes, W.	1
Bellamy, C.D.	2
Blackmore, C.G.	1
Blake, N.A.	2
Bodin, P.J.	3
Bowen, D.I.	3
Bowen, M.	2
Boyle, T.	1
Burgess, W.A.R.	1
Charles, J.	1
Charles, M.	6
Charles, W.J.	15
Clarke, R.J.	5
Coleman, C.	4
Curtis, A.	6
Davies, G.	2
Davies, R.T.	9
Davies, R.W.	6
Deacy, N.	4
Durban, A.	2
Dwyer, P.	2
Edwards, G.	2
Edwards, R.I.	4
England, H.M.	4
Evans, I.	1
Flynn, B.	7
Ford, T.	23
Foulkes, W.J.	1
Giggs, R.J.	7
Giles, D.	2
Godfrey, B.C.	2
Griffiths, A.T.	6
Griffiths, M.W.	2
Harris, C.S.	1
Hartson, J.	2
Hewitt, R.	1
Hockey, T.	1
Hodges, G.	2
Horne, B.	2
Hughes, L.M.	16
James, L.	10
James, R.	7
Jones, A.	1
Jones, B.S.	2
Jones, Cliff	16
Jones, D.E.	1
Jones, J.P.	1
Kryzwicki, R.I.	1
Leek, K.	5
Lovell, S.	1
Lowrie, G.	2
Mahoney, J.F.	1
Medwin, T.C.	6
Melville, A.K.	3
Moore, G.	1
Nicholas, P.	2
O'Sullivan, P.A.	1
Own goals	5
Palmer, D.	1
Paul, R.	1
Pembridge, M.A.	5
Phillips, D.	2
Powell, A.	1
Powell, D.	1
Price, P.	1
Reece, G.I.	2
Rees, R.R.	3
Roberts, P.S.	1
Robinson, J.R.C.	3
Rush, I.	28
Saunders, D.	22
Savage R.W.	1
Slatter, N.	2
Smallman, D.P.	1
Speed, G.A.	3
Symons, C.J.	2

Tapscott, D.R.	4
Thomas, M.	4
Toshack, J.B.	12
Vernon, T.R.	8
Walsh, I.	7
Williams, A.	1
Williams, G.E.	1
Williams, G.G.	1
Woosnam, A.P.	3
Yorath, T.C.	2
Young, E.	1

NORTHERN IRELAND

Anderson, T.	4
Armstrong, G.	12
Barr, H.H.	1
Best, G.	9
Bingham, W.L.	10
Black, K.	1
Blanchflower, D.	2
Blanchflower, J.	1
Brennan, R.A.	1
Brotherston, N.	3
Campbell, W.G.	1
Casey, T.	2
Caskey, W.	1
Cassidy, T.	1
Clarke, C.J.	13
Clements, D.	2
Cochrane, T.	1
Crossan, E.	1
Crossan, J.A.	10
Cush, W.W.	5
D'Arcy, S.D.	1
Doherty, I.	1
Doherty, P.D.	2
Dougan, A.D.	8
Dowie, I.	12
Elder, A.R.	1
Ferguson, W.	1
Ferris, R.O.	1
Finney, T.	2
Gillespie, K.R.	1
Gray, P.	5
Griffin, D.J.	1
Hamilton, B.	4
Hamilton, W.	5
Harkin, J.T.	2
Harvey, M.	3
Healy, D.J.	3
Hill, C.F.	1
Humphries, W.	1
Hughes, M.E.	4
Hunter, A.	1
Hunter, B.V.	1
Irvine, W.J.	8
Johnston, W.C.	1
Jones, J.	1
Lennon, N.F.	2
Lockhart, N.	3
Lomas, S.M.	2
Magilton, J.	5
McAdams, W.J.	7
McClelland, J.	1
McCrory, S.	1
McCurdy, C.	1
McDonald, A.	3
McGarry, J.K.	1
McGrath, R.C.	4
McIlroy, J.	10
McIlroy, S.B.	5
McLaughlin, J.C.	6
McMahon, G.J.	2
McMordie, A.S.	3
McMorran, E.J.	4
McParland, P.J.	10
Moreland, V.	1
Morgan, S.	3
Morrow, S.J.	1
Mulryne, P.P.	1
Neill, W.J.T.	2
Nelson, S.	1
Nicholl, C.J.	3
Nicholl, J.M.	1
Nicholson, J.J.	6
O'Boyle, G.	1
O'Kane, W.J.	1
O'Neill, J.	2
O'Neill, M.A.	4
O'Neill, M.H.	8
Own goals	5
Patterson, D.J.	1
Peacock, R.	2
Penney, S.	2
Quinn, J.M.	12
Quinn, S.J.	3
Rowland, K.	1
Simpson, W.J.	5
Smyth, S.	5
Spence, D.W.	3
Stewart, I.	2
Taggart, G.P.	7
Tully, C.P.	3
Walker, J.	1
Walsh, D.J.	5
Welsh, E.	1
Whiteside, N.	9
Whitley, Jeff	1
Wilson, D.J.	1
Wilson, K.J.	6
Wilson, S.J.	7

EIRE

Aldridge, J.	19
Ambrose, P.	1
Anderson, J.	1
Brady, L.	9
Breen, G.	4
Byrne, J. *(QPR)*	4
Cantwell, J.	14
Carey, J.	3
Carroll, T.	1
Cascarino, A.	19
Coad, P.	3
Connolly, D.J.	7
Conroy, T.	2
Conway, J.	3
Coyne, T.	6
Cummings, G.	5
Curtis, D.	8
Daly, G.	13
Dempsey, J.	1

Dennehy, M. 2
Duffy, B. 1
Dunne, R.P. 1

Eglinton, T. 2

Fagan, F. 5
Fallon, S. 2
Farrell, P. 3
Fitzgerald, J. 1
Fitzgerald, P. 2
Fitzsimons, A. 7
Fogarty, A. 3
Foley, D. 2
Fullam, J. 1

Galvin, A. 1
Gavin, J. 2
Giles, J. 5
Givens, D. 19
Glynn, D. 1
Grealish, T. 8
Grimes, A.A. 1

Hale, A. 2
Hand, E. 2
Harte, I.P. 3
Haverty, J. 3
Holmes, J. 1
Houghton, R. 6
Hughton, C. 1
Hurley, C. 2

Irwin, D. 4

Kavanagh, G.A. 1
Keane, R.D. 2
Keane, R.M. 5
Kelly, D. 9
Kelly, G. 1
Kennedy, M. 3
Kernaghan, A. 1

Lawrenson, M. 5
Leech, M. 2

McAteer, J.W. 1
McCann, J. 1
McCarthy, M. 2
McEvoy, A. 6
McGee, P. 4
McGrath, P. 8
McLoughlin, A. 2
McPhail; S. 1
Mancini, T. 1
Martin, C. 6
Martin, M. 4
Mooney, J. 1
Moran, K. 6
Moroney, T. 1
Mulligan, P. 1

O'Callaghan, K. 1
O'Connor, T. 2
O'Farrell, F. 2
O'Keefe, E. 1
O'Leary, D.A. 1
O'Neill, F. 1
O'Neill, K.P. 4
O'Reilly, J. 1
Own goals 8

Quinn, N. 20

Ringstead, A. 7
Robinson, M. 4
Rogers, E. 5
Ryan, G. 1
Ryan, R. 3

Sheedy, K. 9
Sheridan, J. 5
Slaven, B. 1
Sloan, W. 1
Stapleton, F. 20
Staunton, S. 7
Strahan, F. 1

Townsend, A.D. 7
Treacy, R. 5
Tuohy, L. 4

Waddock, G. 3
Walsh, D. 5
Walsh, M. 3
Waters, J. 1
Whelan, R. 3

UEFA UNDER-21 CHAMPIONSHIP 1998–2000

GROUP 1
Belarus 0, Denmark 2
Wales 1, Italy 2
Denmark 2, Wales 2
Italy 1, Switzerland 0
Switzerland 2, Denmark 0
Wales 0, Belarus 0
Denmark 1, Italy 2
Switzerland 1, Wales 0
Italy 4, Belarus 1
Denmark 2, Belarus 0
Italy 6, Wales 2
Wales 1, Denmark 2
Switzerland 0, Italy 0
Belarus 1, Switzerland 0
Belarus 1, Wales 0
Denmark 1, Switzerland 3
Switzerland 2, Belarus 1
Italy 3, Denmark 1
Wales 0, Switzerland 0
Belarus 1, Italy 2

GROUP 2
Latvia 1, Georgia 2
Georgia 0, Albania 1
Slovenia 1, Norway 3
Norway 4, Albania 1
Greece 3, Georgia 2
Slovenia 0, Latvia 1
Norway 2, Latvia 0
Greece 2, Slovenia 2
Albania 0, Greece 5
Greece 2, Norway 1
Georgia 0, Slovenia 0
Latvia 0, Greece 2
Georgia 0, Norway 3
Latvia 0, Albania 0
Norway 0, Georgia 0
Albania 1, Norway 2
Georgia 1, Greece 1
Latvia 1, Slovenia 1
Albania 1, Slovenia 4
Greece 6, Latvia 0
Norway 2, Greece 1
Georgia 4, Latvia 2
Norway 3, Slovenia 0
Greece 5, Albania 2
Slovenia 0, Greece 5
Latvia 2, Norway 1
Albania 0, Georgia 0
Albania 1, Latvia 1
Slovenia 2, Georgia 2
Slovenia 0, Albania 1

GROUP 3
Turkey 2, N Ireland 0
N Ireland 1, Finland 1
Turkey 2, Germany 0
Moldova 0, Germany 2
Turkey 1, Finland 1
Finland 1, Moldova 0
N Ireland 1, Moldova 1
N Ireland 1, Germany 0
Turkey 2, Moldova 0
Moldova 0, N Ireland 0
Germany 2, Finland 0
Germany 2, Moldova 0
Finland 0, Turkey 0
Moldova 1, Finland 1
Finland 3, Germany 1
N Ireland 1, Turkey 2
Germany 1, N Ireland 0
Moldova 1, Turkey 1
Finland 2, N Ireland 1
Germany 1, Turkey 1

GROUP 4
Ukraine 1, Russia 0
Armenia 3, Iceland 1
Russia 2, France 1
Ukraine 8, Armenia 0
Iceland 1, Russia 2
Iceland 0, France 2
France 4, Ukraine 0
Armenia 0, Russia 2
Ukraine 5, Iceland 1
France 3, Armenia 1
Iceland 2, Armenia 0
France 2, Russia 0
Armenia 1, Ukraine 1
Russia 3, Iceland 0
Ukraine 0, France 0
Armenia 1, France 4
Russia 6, Armenia 0
Iceland 4, Ukraine 1
France 2, Iceland 0
Russia 2, Ukraine 0

GROUP 5
Sweden 0, England 2
England 1, Bulgaria 0
Poland 5, Luxembourg 0
Bulgaria 2, Sweden 1
Luxembourg 0, England 5
Bulgaria 2, Poland 2
Sweden 3, Luxembourg 0
England 5, Poland 0
Poland 2, Sweden 0
Luxembourg 0, Bulgaria 3
England 3, Sweden 0
Poland 3, Bulgaria 3
Bulgaria 0, England 1
Luxembourg 0, Poland 4
England 5, Luxembourg 0
Poland 3, England 1
Luxembourg 0, Sweden 1
Sweden 1, Poland 2
Bulgaria 3, Luxembourg 0
Sweden 1, Bulgaria 4

GROUP 6
Austria 0, Israel 1
Cyprus 1, Spain 3
Cyprus 2, Austria 1
Holland 3, Israel 0
Israel 0, Spain 4
Holland 3, Austria 2
Cyprus 0, Holland 3
Spain 4, Austria 0
Israel 1, Cyprus 1
Holland 0, Spain 1
Austria 0, Holland 1
Spain 4, Holland 1
Israel 2, Austria 1
Holland 5, Cyprus 1
Austria 1, Spain 2
Israel 0, Holland 1
Spain 1, Cyprus 1
Spain 2, Israel 1
Austria 3, Cyprus 0
Cyprus 1, Israel 1

GROUP 7
Portugal 1, Romania 1
Azerbaijan 2, Hungary 1
Slovakia 1, Portugal 0
Hungary 1, Romania 2
Hungary 0, Portugal 3
Slovakia 2, Azerbaijan 1
Portugal 5, Azerbaijan 0
Romania 0, Slovakia 1
Azerbaijan 0, Romania 2
Slovakia 4, Hungary 1
Romania 2, Hungary 1
Portugal 1, Slovakia 1
Romania 1, Azerbaijan 1
Hungary 3, Slovakia 0
Romania 2, Portugal 3
Azerbaijan 0, Slovakia 3
Portugal 2, Hungary 1
Azerbaijan 0, Portugal 2
Slovakia 0, Romania 0
Hungary 4, Azerbaijan 1

GROUP 8
Republic of Ireland 2, Croatia 2
Malta 0, Croatia 3

Republic of Ireland 2, Malta 1
Croatia 4, Macedonia 0
Macedonia 1, Malta 0
Yugoslavia 1, Republic of Ireland 1
Malta 5, Macedonia 1
Malta 1, Yugoslavia 5
Macedonia 0, Croatia 2
Republic of Ireland 0, Macedonia 0
UEFA awarded Republic of Ireland a 3-0 win; Macedonia fielded a suspended player.
Yugoslavia 7, Malta 0
Republic of Ireland 0, Yugoslavia 2
Croatia 5, Republic of Ireland 1
Malta 1, Republic of Ireland 3
Macedonia 0, Y ugoslavia 8
Macedonia 0, Republic of Ireland 1
Croatia 2, Yugoslavia 2
Yugoslavia 2, Macedonia 0
Croatia 1, Malta 0
Yugoslavia 2, Croatia 6

GROUP 9
Lithuania 0, Scotland 0
Scotland 2, Estonia 0
Bosnia 0, Czech Republic 0
Lithuania 0, Belgium 1
Lithuania 4, Bosnia 0
Czech Republic 3, Estonia 0
Belgium 2, Scotland 0
Belgium 0, Czech Republic 2
Bosnia 3, Estonia 2
Scotland 2, Belgium 2
Czech Republic 1, Lithuania 0
Lithuania 4, Estonia 1
Scotland 0, Czech Republic 1
Belgium 4, Bosnia 0
Bosnia 1, Lithuania 2
Estonia 0, Czech Republic 3
Czech Republic 3, Scotland 2
Estonia 0, Lithuania 2
Belgium 5, Estonia 0
Lithuania 0, Czech Republic 2
Estonia 0, Scotland 4
Czech Republic 1, Bosnia 0
Belgium 3, Lithuania 0
Scotland 2, Bosnia 0
Scotland 1, Lithuania 2
Czech Republic 1, Belgium 3
Estonia 0, Bosnia 2
Bosnia 2, Scotland 5
Estonia 1, Belgium 7
Bosnia 3, Belgium 4

PLAY-OFFS

FIRST LEG
Czech Republic 3, Greece 0
Holland 2, Belgium 2
Norway 1, Spain 3
Portugal 2, Croatia 0
Russia 0, Slovakia 1
France 1, Italy 1

PLAY-OFFS

SECOND LEG
Belgium 0, Holland 2
Croatia 3, Portugal 0
Greece 1, Czech Republic 0
Slovakia 3, Russia 1
Italy 2, France 1

1 game:
England 3, Yugoslavia 0

FINALS (in Slovakia)

GROUP A
Croatia 1, Holland 2
Spain 1, Czech Republic 1
Czech Republic 3, Holland 1
Spain 0, Croatia 0
Holland 0, Spain 1
Czech Republic 4, Croatia 3

GROUP B
Italy 2, England 0
Slovakia 2, Turkey 1
England 6, Turkey 0
Italy 1, Slovakia 1
England 0, Slovakia 2
Turkey 1, Italy 3

THIRD PLACE PLAY-OFF
Spain 1, Slovakia 0

FINAL
Czech Republic 1, Italy 2

REPUBLIC OF IRELAND LEAGUE

	P	W	D	L	F	A	Pts
Shelbourne	33	19	12	2	49	20	69
Cork City	33	16	10	7	53	32	58
Bohemians	33	16	9	8	40	22	57
UCD	33	13	12	8	40	29	51
Shamrock Rovers	33	13	11	9	49	36	50
St Patrick's Ath	33	13	11	9	40	31	50
Derry City	33	12	10	11	32	38	46
Finn Harps	33	8	10	15	39	41	34
Galway United	33	8	10	15	32	49	34
Waterford United	33	7	12	14	24	38	33
Sligo Rovers	33	5	10	18	31	60	25
Drogheda United	33	4	11	18	20	53	23

HIGHLAND LEAGUE

		Home			Away			Goals			
	P	W	D	L	W	D	L	F	A	Pts	GD
Keith	30	11	1	3	10	2	3	76	38	66	38
Fraserburgh	30	8	6	1	9	4	2	75	32	61	43
Buckie Thistle	30	8	4	2	10	3	3	58	31	61	27
Peterhead	30	9	4	2	9	0	6	66	39	58	27
Huntly	30	9	3	3	6	4	5	69	46	52	23
Forres Mechanics	30	8	3	4	7	4	4	60	42	52	18
Clachnacuddin	30	6	1	8	8	5	2	55	37	48	18
Cove Rangers	30	7	2	6	5	4	6	81	54	42	27
Elgin City	30	8	3	4	4	3	8	45	44	42	1
Lossiemouth	30	6	3	6	6	3	6	51	54	42	−3
Deveronvale	30	7	1	7	4	4	7	51	63	38	−12
Brora Rangers	30	2	5	8	7	1	7	53	61	33	−8
Rothes	30	3	2	10	5	3	7	41	52	29	−11
Wick Academy	30	5	2	8	1	3	11	36	84	23	−48
Nairn County	30	3	3	9	0	5	10	24	91	17	−67
Fort William	30	0	5	11	1	0	13	34	107	8	−73

NATIONWIDE CONFERENCE 1999–2000

		Home			*Goals*		*Away*			*Goals*		
	P	*W*	*D*	*L*	*F*	*A*	*W*	*D*	*L*	*F*	*A*	*Pts*
Kidderminster Harriers	42	16	3	2	47	16	10	4	7	28	24	85
Rushden & Diamonds	42	11	8	2	37	18	10	5	6	34	24	76
Morecambe	42	10	7	4	46	29	8	9	4	24	19	70
Scarborough	42	10	6	5	36	14	9	6	6	24	21	69
Kingstonian	42	9	4	8	30	24	11	3	7	28	20	67
Dover Athletic	42	10	7	4	43	26	8	5	8	22	30	66
Yeovil Town	42	11	4	6	37	28	7	6	8	23	35	64
Hereford United	42	9	6	6	43	31	6	8	7	18	21	59
Southport	42	10	5	6	31	21	5	8	8	24	35	58
Stevenage Borough	42	8	5	8	26	20	8	4	9	34	34	57
Hayes	42	7	3	11	24	28	9	5	7	33	30	56
Doncaster Rovers	42	7	5	9	19	21	8	4	9	27	27	54
Kettering Town	42	8	10	3	25	19	4	6	11	19	31	52
Woking	42	5	6	10	17	27	8	7	6	28	26	52
Nuneaton Borough	42	7	6	8	28	25	5	9	7	21	28	51
Telford United	42	12	4	5	34	21	2	5	14	22	45	51
Hednesford Town	42	10	3	8	27	23	5	3	13	18	45	51
Northwich Victoria	42	10	8	3	33	25	3	4	14	20	53	51
Forest Green Rovers	42	11	2	8	35	23	2	6	13	19	40	47
Welling United	42	6	5	10	27	32	7	3	11	27	34	47
Altrincham	42	6	8	7	31	26	3	11	7	20	34	46
Sutton United	42	4	8	9	23	32	4	2	15	16	43	34

Leading Goalscorers 1999–2000

Conf.			*FAC*	*ECT*	*UT*
29	Justin Jackson (Morecambe)	+	1	—	1
24	Carl Alford (Stevenage Borough)	+	—	1	1
18	Neil Davis (Hereford United)	+	1	—	2
17	Ian Foster (Kidderminster Harriers)	+	—	—	—
15	Joff Vansittart (Dover Athletic)	+	—	—	4
14	Ian Arnold (Southport)	+	1	—	3
	Kevin Ellison (Altrincham)	+	1	—	—
13	Steve Brodie (Scarborough)	+	—	1	2
	Lee Charles (Hayes)	+	5	—	—
	Robin Elmes (Hereford United)	+	1	—	1
	Paul Fewings (Hereford United)	+	2	—	—
	Warren Patmore (Yeovil Town)	+	—	2	2
12	Nassim Akrour (Woking)	+	—	2	3
	Stewart Hadley (Kidderminster Harriers)	+	—	—	—
	Ritchie Hanlon (Welling United)	+	—	1	1
	Richard Landon (Altrincham)	+	1	—	1
	David Leworthy (Kingstonian)	+	2	1	2
	Marc McGregor (Forest Green Rovers)	+	1	—	1
	Val Owen (Northwich Victoria)	+	1	—	—
11	Darren Collins (Rushden & Diamonds)	+	2	—	2
	Phil Eastwood (Morecambe)	+	—	—	2
	Lee Elam (Southport)	+	—	—	1
	Mike McElhatton (Rushden & Diamonds)	+	2	—	—
	Zeke Rowe (Welling United)	+	—	—	—
	Dave Stevens (Hayes)	+	—	—	—
	Mark Watson (Sutton United)	+	—	—	1

AC: FA Cup; ECT: Endsleigh Challenge Trophy; UT Umbro Trophy.

NATIONWIDE CONFERENCE RESULTS 1999–2000

	Altrincham	Doncaster Rovers	Dover Athletic	Forest Green Rovers	Hayes	Hednesford Town	Hereford United	Kettering Town	Kidderminster Harriers	Kingstonian	Morecambe	Northwich Victoria	Nuneaton Borough	Rushden & Diamonds	Scarborough	Southport	Stevenage Borough	Sutton United	Telford United	Welling United	Woking	Yeovil Town
Altrincham	—	1-2	3-0	1-1	1-2	0-1	2-1	1-1	0-0	1-3	2-2	2-0	2-2	1-2	2-1	3-0	0-1	3-0	3-3	0-1	1-1	2-2
Doncaster Rovers	0-1	—	0-1	3-2	0-0	2-1	2-2	2-1	1-2	1-0	0-1	2-0	0-1	0-1	0-1	1-1	1-2	1-0	2-0	1-1	0-0	0-3
Dover Athletic	2-2	1-3	—	4-0	2-2	4-1	2-0	1-1	0-1	0-1	3-1	4-1	3-1	0-4	1-1	1-1	4-2	1-1	3-0	2-1	2-2	3-0
Forest Green Rovers	1-1	1-0	3-1	—	0-1	3-0	0-1	2-0	3-2	0-3	1-2	5-1	1-2	1-0	0-1	1-0	3-2	1-2	5-2	1-2	0-0	3-0
Hayes	1-1	3-4	1-2	3-0	—	2-1	0-0	0-1	2-0	1-2	0-1	2-1	3-0	0-5	0-1	0-2	1-2	1-0	1-2	1-0	0-0	2-3
Hednesford Town	5-0	2-1	1-0	1-0	2-1	—	0-1	1-1	0-2	2-3	1-3	1-0	0-0	1-2	0-3	1-2	2-2	1-0	2-1	0-1	3-0	1-0
Hereford United	2-2	5-3	2-0	1-0	0-2	3-0	—	4-2	1-1	0-2	1-1	3-0	1-1	4-0	4-4	2-1	1-2	4-1	2-2	1-2	2-4	0-1
Kettering Town	0-0	2-2	1-2	1-0	1-1	4-2	2-0	—	3-1	2-1	1-1	1-1	1-1	1-1	0-0	0-3	1-0	1-0	0-0	2-1	0-0	1-2
Kidderminster Harriers	1-1	1-0	1-2	3-3	2-1	3-0	1-1	1-0	—	2-0	2-1	3-1	1-2	2-0	2-0	5-0	3-1	1-0	2-0	4-1	3-2	4-0
Kingstonian	2-2	0-1	4-1	0-1	1-3	0-2	0-0	2-0	0-1	—	0-0	3-3	2-0	0-1	2-0	4-2	1-0	4-2	4-2	1-0	0-2	0-1
Morecambe	3-3	1-1	2-0	1-1	1-4	4-0	3-2	2-1	0-1	1-2	—	5-0	1-1	0-0	0-1	3-3	3-3	6-2	5-2	2-1	1-0	1-1
Northwich Victoria	1-1	2-1	1-1	0-0	0-0	3-2	0-0	2-6	1-1	0-3	0-0	—	3-1	2-1	2-0	0-1	3-3	2-0	2-1	3-2	3-1	3-0
Nuneaton Borough	3-1	0-0	0-2	2-3	2-1	3-0	0-1	0-1	2-3	2-0	1-1	3-1	—	1-1	1-1	0-2	0-1	2-0	1-1	4-3	0-1	1-1
Rushden & Diamonds	1-0	0-0	1-1	3-2	1-0	1-1	0-0	2-0	5-3	1-0	0-2	6-0	1-1	—	0-0	4-2	2-1	4-0	1-1	2-0	1-3	1-1
Scarborough	1-0	0-0	1-2	5-0	4-1	1-1	3-0	0-0	0-0	0-1	0-2	3-0	1-1	0-1	—	3-0	1-3	3-0	2-0	0-0	3-2	5-0
Southport	2-0	1-0	1-2	2-1	4-1	2-0	0-1	0-1	0-1	0-0	1-1	0-1	2-0	2-1	2-2	—	2-1	1-1	1-3	3-2	4-1	1-1
Stevenage Borough	1-1	3-0	3-1	1-1	3-0	0-1	0-3	3-0	0-2	0-1	1-2	3-1	2-1	2-2	0-1	1-1	—	1-0	2-0	0-1	0-1	0-0
Sutton United	3-0	1-0	0-1	3-2	2-2	0-0	1-1	1-1	0-3	2-2	0-1	2-2	1-2	0-4	1-2	1-1	0-2	—	2-1	2-3	1-1	0-1
Telford United	0-1	0-2	1-1	2-0	1-2	6-2	1-1	3-1	3-2	1-0	3-2	0-1	1-0	1-1	1-0	0-0	2-1	2-0	—	2-1	1-2	3-1
Welling United	2-2	0-1	1-1	1-1	1-2	1-2	3-1	1-0	1-2	0-1	0-0	1-3	0-0	0-3	2-1	4-1	2-1	2-3	2-0	—	1-2	2-5
Woking	0-1	1-3	2-0	2-1	0-3	0-1	0-2	1-1	1-0	1-1	0-0	1-1	1-1	1-3	0-2	0-0	0-2	1-2	1-0	2-3	—	2-0
Yeovil Town	3-0	1-3	1-1	1-0	2-4	3-0	1-0	2-0	1-0	3-2	2-0	3-2	1-3	5-1	1-2	1-1	2-2	1-2	2-1	1-1	0-3	—

DR MARTENS LEAGUE 1999–2000

Premier Division

	P	*W*	*D*	*L*	*F*	*A*	*Pts*	*GD*
Boston United	42	27	11	4	102	39	92	63
Burton Albion	42	23	9	10	73	43	78	30
Margate	42	23	8	11	64	43	77	21
Bath City	42	19	15	8	70	49	72	21
King's Lynn	42	19	14	9	59	43	71	16
Tamworth	42	20	10	12	80	51	70	29
Newport County	42	16	18	8	67	50	66	17
Clevedon Town	42	18	9	15	52	52	63	0
Ilkeston Town	42	16	12	14	77	69	60	8
Weymouth	42	14	16	12	60	51	58	9
Halesowen Town	42	14	14	14	52	54	56	−2
Crawley Town	42	15	8	19	68	82	53	−14
Havant & Waterlooville	42	13	13	16	63	68	52	−5
Cambridge City	42	14	10	18	52	66	52	−14
Worcester City	42	13	11	18	60	66	50	−6
Salisbury City	42	14	8	20	70	84	50	−14
Merthyr Tydfil	42	13	9	20	51	63	48	−12
Dorchester Town	42	10	17	15	56	65	47	−9
Grantham Town	42	14	5	23	63	76	47	−13
Gloucester City	42	8	14	20	40	82	38	−42
Rothwell Town	42	5	14	23	48	85	29	−37
Atherstone United	42	5	13	24	30	76	28	−46

Leading Goalscorers 1999–2000
(League and Cup)

Premier Division

Mark Hallam (Tamworth)	35
James Taylor (Havant & Waterlooville)	32
Christian Moore (Burton Albion)	29
Paul Sales (Salisbury City)	27
Philip Collins (Margate)	25
Mark Owen (Worcester City)	24
Martin Paul (Bath City)	20
Mark Rawle (Boston United)	20
James Smith (Salisbury City)	20
Carl Dale (Newport County)	19
Daniel O'Hagan (Dorchester Town)	19
Warren Haughton (Tamworth)	18
David Laws (Weymouth)	18
Ian Cambridge (Cambridge City)	14

DR MARTENS PREMIER LEAGUE RESULTS 1999–2000

	Atherstone United	Bath City	Boston United	Burton Albion	Cambridge City	Clevedon Town	Crawley Town	Dorchester Town	Gloucester City	Grantham Town	Halesowen Town	Havant & Waterlooville	Ilkeston Town	King's Lynn	Margate	Merthyr Tydfil	Newport County	Rothwell Town	Salisbury City	Tamworth	Weymouth	Worcester City
Atherstone United	—	0-0	1-1	0-2	0-1	1-3	0-1	1-1	1-0	0-2	4-5	0-1	3-2	0-2	0-1	0-3	0-1	3-1	0-3	0-5	1-1	2-1
Bath City	2-0	—	2-0	2-1	2-2	2-1	7-0	1-1	5-1	2-1	0-1	1-1	0-0	1-1	1-1	0-1	1-1	1-0	4-4	4-1	2-0	1-1
Boston United	3-0	1-1	—	3-1	5-0	5-1	1-0	3-0	6-1	3-1	4-1	4-2	3-2	1-2	3-0	4-1	1-1	2-0	6-0	1-0	3-0	2-1
Burton Albion	5-1	3-0	1-1	—	3-0	1-0	3-0	5-0	3-0	1-0	2-4	3-0	3-1	1-0	0-1	2-0	1-1	2-1	4-1	1-1	1-0	2-3
Cambridge City	3-2	0-2	0-2	0-1	—	1-1	3-2	0-1	2-1	0-2	1-1	4-1	3-2	2-3	0-0	0-0	0-0	1-0	1-3	1-2	2-3	4-2
Clevedon Town	1-0	3-0	0-0	0-0	1-0	—	1-1	2-1	3-0	2-2	0-0	0-0	2-0	4-2	1-0	1-2	1-0	1-1	1-2	1-0	1-1	1-0
Crawley Town	0-0	4-1	1-6	1-4	1-2	1-3	—	3-1	2-1	3-2	2-2	2-3	1-1	1-2	5-3	2-0	2-2	4-1	4-1	3-0	1-0	2-2
Dorchester Town	2-2	0-0	3-4	0-1	1-2	2-1	0-2	—	1-2	0-1	2-2	4-1	1-1	3-4	1-0	0-0	1-2	0-0	4-4	2-1	0-1	3-0
Gloucester City	1-1	1-1	2-2	2-1	1-0	1-5	2-2	0-0	—	2-0	2-2	1-1	1-0	0-1	0-4	1-0	1-1	3-1	3-3	0-0	1-1	2-1
Grantham Town	6-0	1-3	0-3	0-1	2-0	2-0	4-2	0-2	1-1	—	1-0	2-0	1-0	1-3	1-2	1-1	0-1	1-0	5-1	0-3	3-3	0-2
Halesowen Town	0-1	0-3	1-1	2-1	1-2	3-0	1-0	0-1	4-2	2-1	—	1-0	3-0	0-0	0-3	0-1	2-0	3-3	3-1	0-3	0-0	2-1
Havant & Waterlooville	1-1	1-2	3-3	6-0	3-1	1-2	1-0	1-2	1-1	1-0	2-1	—	2-3	2-2	3-3	1-2	2-2	5-2	0-1	0-2	1-2	1-0
Ilkeston Town	1-0	2-2	1-0	4-1	2-2	4-1	2-0	3-1	1-0	5-4	0-0	2-1	—	2-1	1-2	2-1	2-1	3-3	6-0	4-4	2-2	2-2
King's Lynn	1-1	4-1	0-0	0-1	0-0	1-0	1-0	4-1	2-0	3-3	1-0	0-1	1-1	—	0-0	4-2	2-2	0-0	2-0	1-0	1-0	0-1
Margate	2-0	1-1	2-1	1-0	1-2	2-1	1-0	1-1	3-0	1-2	3-1	0-0	3-2	1-0	—	0-0	2-1	4-1	2-0	1-2	2-0	0-1
Merthyr Tydfil	2-0	0-2	0-2	1-1	1-0	2-0	2-3	0-0	5-0	5-2	1-0	0-2	1-3	0-0	3-4	—	2-5	3-1	1-1	1-1	1-2	0-3
Newport County	1-1	0-1	2-2	1-1	2-2	5-0	0-1	1-1	2-1	2-1	0-0	3-3	2-1	1-2	3-1	2-0	—	1-1	0-0	2-0	2-1	1-0
Rothwell Town	3-3	2-3	0-2	1-1	1-4	0-2	3-3	1-4	2-0	2-0	2-2	1-1	2-2	2-1	0-2	2-0	0-3	—	3-2	1-1	1-2	0-1
Salisbury City	1-0	1-3	1-2	0-3	4-0	1-2	4-1	1-1	2-0	5-0	2-0	1-2	1-2	2-3	2-0	2-3	1-2	4-2	—	1-1	1-1	1-3
Tamworth	4-0	3-2	1-2	1-1	1-2	4-1	3-0	1-1	1-1	3-4	1-2	5-0	2-1	3-0	2-0	3-1	2-2	2-1	1-2	—	3-1	4-2
Weymouth	0-0	3-0	2-2	1-2	0-0	0-1	4-0	2-2	4-1	3-2	0-0	2-2	4-1	1-1	0-1	2-1	4-2	3-0	1-0	1-2	—	1-1
Worcester City	0-0	0-1	1-2	2-2	3-2	1-0	2-5	4-4	4-0	3-1	0-0	0-3	2-1	1-1	1-3	2-1	3-4	0-0	2-3	0-1	1-1	—

UNIBOND LEAGUE 1999–2000

Premier Division		*Home*			*Goals*		*Away*			*Goals*		
	P	W	D	L	F	A	W	D	L	F	A	Pts
Leigh RMI	44	15	3	4	42	17	13	5	4	49	28	92
Hyde United	44	14	5	3	47	20	10	8	4	30	24	85
Gateshead	44	12	6	4	41	17	11	7	4	38	24	82
Marine	44	10	9	3	40	25	11	7	4	38	21	79
Emley	44	9	7	6	25	18	11	5	6	29	23	72
Lancaster City	44	14	4	4	40	18	6	7	9	25	37	71
Stalybridge Celtic	44	13	5	4	42	27	5	7	10	22	27	66
Bishop Auckland	44	9	8	5	33	23	9	3	10	30	38	65
Runcorn	44	11	4	7	36	25	7	6	9	28	30	64
Worksop Town	44	10	3	9	44	29	9	3	10	34	36	63
Gainsborough Trinity	44	12	6	4	40	22	4	9	9	19	27	63
Whitby Town	44	11	7	4	38	24	4	6	12	28	42	58
Barrow	44	6	7	9	35	40	8	8	6	30	19	57
Blyth Spartans	44	10	2	10	39	34	5	7	10	23	33	54
Droylsden	44	9	4	9	26	26	5	8	9	27	34	54
Frickley Athletic	44	8	8	6	39	40	7	1	14	25	45	54
Bamber Bridge	44	7	7	8	38	32	7	4	11	32	35	53
Hucknall Town	44	11	5	6	33	22	3	6	13	22	39	53
Leek Town	44	8	5	9	30	34	6	5	11	28	45	52
Colwyn Bay	44	5	7	10	20	35	7	5	10	26	50	48
Spennymoor United**	44	6	10	6	23	24	4	3	15	18	47	42
Guiseley	44	3	8	11	23	36	5	9	8	29	36	41
Winsford United	44	2	3	17	24	58	1	4	17	16	58	16

*** –1 point deducted for breach of rule*

Leading Goalscorers

(In order of League Goals)

Premier Division

Lge	*Cup*	*Tot*	
23	14	37	Simon Yeo (Hyde United)
21	9	30	Simon Parke (Guiseley)
21	6	27	Andy Whittaker (Bamber Bridge)
20	13	33	Paul Kiely (Leek Town, now Stafford Rangers)
19	15	34	Andy Hayward (Frickley Athletic)
19	8	27	Nicky Peverill (Barrow)

UNIBOND LEAGUE—PREMIER DIVISION RESULTS 1999–2000

	Bamber Bridge	Barrow	Bishop Auckland	Blyth Spartans	Colwyn Bay	Droylsden	Emley	Frickley Athletic	Gainsborough Trinity	Gateshead	Guiseley	Hucknall Town	Hyde United	Lancaster City	Leek Town	Leigh RMI	Marine	Runcorn	Spennymoor United	Stalybridge Celtic	Whitby Town	Winsford United	Worksop Town
Bamber Bridge	—	2-3	4-0	1-1	1-2	1-3	0-1	2-1	0-0	0-3	2-2	1-1	0-0	6-1	5-0	2-2	0-2	2-0	2-0	1-4	2-2	2-1	2-3
Barrow	4-0	—	1-3	3-2	4-0	0-3	0-2	2-0	1-1	3-5	1-1	4-2	1-2	2-2	1-4	2-2	2-2	0-2	1-0	1-1	0-3	0-0	2-3
Bishop Auckland	0-1	1-3	—	1-1	4-0	1-0	1-1	3-2	0-0	1-1	1-0	3-1	2-2	1-1	1-1	1-1	0-2	2-0	0-3	1-0	4-0	4-1	1-2
Blyth Spartans	1-2	1-1	0-2	—	4-1	3-0	3-2	4-1	1-1	0-1	1-2	1-0	3-4	0-2	2-3	0-1	3-1	4-2	2-3	1-4	2-0	1-0	2-1
Colwyn Bay	0-7	0-0	0-1	0-0	—	1-2	0-1	1-0	0-0	1-3	0-2	2-0	2-3	1-1	1-1	3-5	0-5	1-1	0-2	0-0	2-0	2-0	3-1
Droylsden	2-0	0-3	1-0	1-0	1-2	—	1-1	1-1	1-0	2-2	3-0	0-0	1-3	3-4	1-2	0-2	0-1	1-0	0-1	1-0	3-2	3-0	0-2
Emley	3-0	0-0	2-0	2-0	1-2	1-0	—	1-3	0-0	1-1	1-1	1-1	0-1	0-0	0-0	3-1	0-2	1-0	2-0	0-1	2-1	3-2	1-2
Frickley Athletic	2-0	2-5	4-2	1-1	4-1	0-4	0-0	—	0-0	1-4	2-2	3-2	3-1	3-2	1-1	2-4	2-2	1-2	1-1	1-1	2-1	3-1	1-3
Gainsborough Trinity	1-0	1-3	4-1	0-1	2-0	2-1	2-1	1-2	—	1-2	0-0	5-2	1-1	1-0	3-2	4-3	0-0	1-1	4-0	1-1	1-1	3-0	2-0
Gateshead	2-1	0-0	0-0	3-0	6-0	1-1	0-1	2-0	0-1	—	3-1	0-0	2-3	4-0	2-1	1-1	2-0	0-3	6-2	2-0	0-0	2-0	3-2
Guiseley	2-4	0-0	0-3	2-1	2-2	2-0	1-1	0-1	1-3	1-1	—	1-2	0-1	0-1	1-1	0-3	1-3	2-2	3-1	2-2	0-1	2-2	0-1
Hucknall Town	2-1	0-3	1-0	0-1	2-2	3-3	2-0	2-1	1-0	1-0	1-1	—	0-1	1-3	2-0	1-2	2-0	1-1	0-0	4-0	3-2	4-0	0-1
Hyde United	3-1	1-0	1-1	5-2	3-0	2-0	2-3	2-3	4-0	1-1	2-0	4-3	—	4-1	2-0	1-2	1-1	0-0	2-1	1-0	4-1	2-0	0-0
Lancaster City	1-1	1-0	0-1	3-0	3-0	4-0	2-1	2-0	2-0	1-1	2-0	1-0	1-0	—	1-3	1-3	1-1	3-2	3-0	3-2	1-2	4-1	0-0
Leek Town	0-0	2-1	1-4	1-4	0-2	0-0	1-3	1-2	3-2	1-2	2-2	2-2	2-0	3-1	—	2-0	2-4	0-1	1-0	0-0	2-1	1-2	3-1
Leigh RMI	3-0	1-0	4-1	2-0	1-2	1-2	1-0	5-0	1-1	3-1	0-1	1-0	0-0	2-1	0-2	—	2-1	2-0	4-0	2-0	2-1	3-2	2-2
Marine	0-3	1-0	3-1	0-0	1-1	3-2	3-1	1-0	2-2	1-1	2-2	3-0	0-0	0-0	6-1	1-1	—	0-1	3-0	1-3	3-3	3-1	3-2
Runcorn	2-0	2-2	2-0	3-0	1-2	1-1	1-3	2-1	3-2	2-0	2-2	0-1	0-3	0-1	5-0	0-2	1-2	—	3-2	0-0	3-1	1-0	2-0
Spennymoor United	3-1	0-0	0-1	0-0	1-1	1-1	2-3	3-2	0-2	0-2	1-4	1-1	0-0	0-0	3-1	1-3	0-0	3-0	—	1-0	1-1	0-0	2-1
Stalybridge Celtic	2-2	3-1	5-0	2-0	3-1	0-0	0-0	2-3	2-0	1-0	2-1	2-1	3-1	1-1	3-2	1-3	0-3	1-1	1-0	—	0-3	4-1	4-3
Whitby Town	1-1	1-1	2-2	1-2	1-1	5-2	0-1	3-0	2-1	0-2	3-1	2-1	1-1	1-0	3-1	2-0	0-3	4-0	1-1	1-0	—	2-2	2-1
Winsford United	1-5	0-2	2-5	0-5	1-2	1-1	1-2	1-2	1-2	1-3	4-2	1-2	1-2	0-2	0-2	0-5	2-2	1-6	3-0	1-2	1-1	—	1-3
Worksop Town	0-2	0-2	1-2	2-2	4-2	1-1	0-1	4-0	2-1	1-2	1-2	1-0	1-1	4-1	2-0	0-3	0-1	0-3	5-1	2-1	4-1	9-0	—

RYMAN FOOTBALL LEAGUE 1999–2000

Premier Division

		Home					*Away*					
	P	W	D	L	F	A	W	D	L	F	A	Pts
Dagenham & Redbridge	42	20	1	0	58	13	12	4	5	39	22	101
Aldershot Town	42	13	2	6	39	23	11	3	7	32	28	77
Chesham United	42	11	6	4	33	21	9	4	8	31	29	70
Purfleet	42	10	8	3	39	22	8	7	6	31	26	69
Canvey Island	42	13	2	6	37	18	8	4	9	33	35	69
St Albans City	42	8	6	7	37	26	11	4	6	38	29	67
Billericay Town	42	10	6	5	36	28	8	6	7	26	34	66
Hendon	42	11	4	6	38	31	7	4	10	23	33	62
Slough Town	42	10	3	8	37	30	7	6	8	24	29	60
Dulwich Hamlet	42	10	2	9	32	31	7	3	11	30	37	56
Gravesend & Northfleet	42	9	6	6	36	25	6	4	11	30	42	55
Farnborough Town	42	8	5	8	25	19	6	6	9	27	36	53
Hampton & Richmond	42	8	4	9	26	28	5	9	7	23	29	52
Enfield	42	9	6	6	42	34	4	5	12	22	34	50
Heybridge Swifts	42	7	5	9	34	33	6	6	9	23	32	50
Hitchin Town	42	10	4	7	36	29	3	7	11	23	43	50
Carshalton Athletic	42	6	9	6	30	30	6	3	12	25	35	48
Basingstoke Town	42	10	6	5	31	24	3	3	15	25	47	48
Harrow Borough	42	7	4	10	31	26	7	2	12	23	44	48
Aylesbury United	42	9	4	8	38	33	4	5	12	26	48	48
Boreham Wood	42	3	6	12	21	40	8	4	9	23	31	43
Walton & Hersham	42	4	4	13	19	38	7	4	10	25	32	41

Leading Goalscorers

Premier Division		*Lge*	*RLC*	*PC*
29	Gary Abbott (Aldershot Town)	29		
27	George Georgiou (Purfleet)	20		7
25	Steve Darlington (Farnborough Town)	19	5	1
23	Paul Coombs (Purfleet)	15	1	7
22	Terry Bowes (Chesham United)	18	3	1
21	Wayne Andrews (Aldershot Town)	17	2	2
	(includes while at St Albans City)	11	2	2
21	Simon Parker (Heybridge Swifts)	16	5	

RYMAN FOOTBALL LEAGUE—PREMIER DIVISION RESULTS 1999–2000

	Aldershot Town	Aylesbury United	Basingstoke Town	Billericay Town	Boreham Wood	Canvey Island	Carshalton Athletic	Chesham United	Dagenham & Redbridge	Dulwich Hamlet	Enfield	Farnborough Town	Gravesend & Northfleet	Hampton & Richmond	Harrow Borough	Hendon	Heybridge Swifts	Hitchin Town	Purfleet	Slough Town	St Albans City	Walton & Hersham
Aldershot Town	—	1-1	5-2	0-1	1-0	3-1	4-0	4-1	1-0	3-2	0-4	1-0	2-1	1-1	1-2	2-1	0-1	5-1	0-2	2-0	0-2	3-0
Aylesbury United	3-0	—	3-0	0-1	0-1	3-3	3-2	3-2	0-2	2-3	1-0	1-2	4-1	2-2	3-1	2-3	2-2	3-1	0-3	2-2	0-2	1-0
Basingstoke Town	2-1	4-2	—	2-0	1-1	0-1	2-0	0-1	0-4	2-0	2-1	2-2	2-0	2-0	2-0	1-1	2-2	1-1	2-2	1-0	0-2	1-3
Billericay Town	3-2	5-0	1-0	—	1-0	0-0	2-0	2-1	0-4	3-5	0-0	0-3	3-3	1-0	5-0	1-1	1-2	1-1	1-1	3-1	3-1	0-3
Boreham Wood	2-5	2-2	3-4	0-2	—	3-2	0-2	1-3	0-1	0-0	1-0	1-1	3-4	0-4	0-1	0-2	0-0	0-0	1-1	1-3	2-3	1-0
Canvey Island	2-1	2-3	3-1	3-0	0-1	—	1-0	2-1	3-1	0-1	1-0	2-0	4-1	1-2	2-0	0-0	6-1	0-3	2-0	2-0	0-1	1-1
Carshalton Athletic	3-0	2-1	3-3	3-3	3-0	3-1	—	0-3	1-1	0-5	2-2	1-1	1-2	1-1	3-1	0-1	1-1	2-0	0-0	1-1	0-1	0-2
Chesham United	2-0	1-1	1-1	1-1	5-0	2-1	0-0	—	0-3	1-2	1-0	2-1	1-1	1-0	1-2	2-1	1-1	2-1	1-0	3-0	3-4	2-1
Dagenham & Redbridge	3-1	4-1	1-0	2-1	2-0	2-0	3-1	1-1	—	3-0	4-0	3-2	2-1	5-0	4-1	4-0	2-0	4-1	3-1	2-1	2-1	2-0
Dulwich Hamlet	1-2	3-0	3-2	1-2	1-2	2-0	1-3	1-2	0-0	—	0-0	1-3	1-5	2-0	2-0	1-0	2-1	1-2	3-2	2-3	3-2	1-0
Enfield	1-4	3-1	2-0	1-1	1-1	1-1	3-2	2-2	1-1	3-2	—	3-0	0-1	2-3	0-3	5-3	3-2	1-1	1-2	1-3	4-0	4-1
Farnborough Town	0-0	3-1	3-0	2-0	0-2	1-2	4-1	0-1	2-1	2-0	1-1	—	3-2	0-1	0-0	0-1	0-1	1-1	1-1	0-1	1-0	1-2
Gravesend & Northfleet	1-1	5-0	1-0	2-2	3-0	0-1	0-5	3-2	1-2	3-1	1-2	5-1	—	0-0	4-1	1-0	1-1	1-1	1-2	1-0	1-2	1-1
Hampton & Richmond	0-1	2-1	2-1	1-2	1-1	0-2	0-1	0-1	2-3	3-0	2-1	1-0	1-0	—	3-1	1-2	1-4	2-1	1-1	1-1	2-2	0-2
Harrow Borough	0-1	4-1	1-1	1-1	1-3	1-3	0-0	0-2	1-1	1-0	1-2	1-3	6-0	3-0	—	2-1	2-0	4-0	2-3	0-1	0-2	0-1
Hendon	1-2	1-0	4-3	3-2	2-1	3-2	2-0	4-2	0-1	1-2	2-2	5-3	2-0	1-0	0-1	—	2-0	1-1	1-3	1-1	0-3	2-2
Heybridge Swifts	1-3	0-0	2-0	1-2	0-1	3-0	0-2	2-1	5-4	1-1	2-1	1-2	2-4	2-2	1-2	1-2	—	2-3	0-0	1-1	2-1	5-1
Hitchin Town	1-2	4-3	2-0	4-0	1-3	3-3	3-2	0-2	0-2	2-0	2-1	1-1	1-0	2-2	4-0	1-0	1-2	—	1-0	1-2	2-2	0-2
Purfleet	2-4	0-2	1-2	2-2	3-2	2-0	1-1	0-0	2-0	1-1	4-2	4-0	0-0	0-0	1-1	4-1	1-0	3-0	—	2-0	3-3	3-1
Slough Town	0-0	1-2	1-4	4-0	2-3	1-2	2-1	2-0	2-3	2-1	2-1	1-2	2-1	1-1	2-3	1-1	2-1	3-0	3-0	—	0-3	3-1
St Albans City	0-1	1-1	4-1	1-2	0-0	2-5	4-0	1-1	1-3	4-1	5-0	0-0	0-1	1-1	3-2	3-0	2-0	2-1	2-4	0-1	—	1-1
Walton & Hersham	0-1	0-3	1-0	0-1	3-1	0-3	0-2	1-2	0-2	0-3	0-2	0-0	2-2	1-3	3-1	1-2	0-1	4-3	0-3	2-2	1-1	—

PONTIN'S LEAGUE

Premier Division

	P	W	D	L	F	A	Pts
Manchester C	22	13	5	4	42	24	44
Huddersfield T	22	12	4	6	35	22	40
Birmingham C	22	9	8	5	31	22	35
Port Vale	22	8	8	6	32	26	32
Tranmere R	22	9	3	10	28	31	30
Wolverhampton W	22	9	3	10	27	30	30
Oldham Ath	22	7	8	7	35	34	29
Preston NE	22	7	8	7	35	36	29
WBA	22	8	5	9	23	24	29
Burnley	22	6	9	7	29	34	27
Stoke C	22	3	8	11	21	37	17
Grimsby T	22	2	9	11	23	41	15

Division One

	P	W	D	L	F	A	Pts
Rotherham U	22	11	6	5	30	18	39
Stockport Co	22	11	5	6	39	26	38
Wrexham	22	10	6	6	36	27	36
Blackpool	22	9	6	7	27	22	33
Scunthorpe U	22	9	5	8	29	27	32
Lincoln C	22	8	7	7	25	27	31
Sheffield U	22	8	6	8	30	26	30
York C	22	9	3	10	23	33	30
Shrewsbury T	22	6	9	7	19	23	27
Walsall	22	6	6	10	34	33	24
Notts Co	22	6	6	10	32	37	24
Scarborough	22	3	7	12	17	42	16

Division Two

	P	W	D	L	F	A	Pts
Wigan Ath	20	12	5	3	39	21	41
Darlington	20	13	1	6	48	25	40
Bury	20	13	1	6	44	26	40
Hull C	20	9	4	7	32	26	31
Chesterfield	20	7	7	6	30	28	28
Macclesfield T	20	7	4	9	27	29	25
Hartlepool U	20	7	4	9	27	32	25
Mansfield T	20	7	3	10	27	36	24
Halifax T	20	5	4	11	20	34	19
Rochdale	20	4	6	10	23	38	18
Chester C	20	5	3	12	29	51	18

AVON INSURANCE COMBINATION

Division One

	P	*W*	*D*	*L*	*F*	*A*	*GD*	*Pts*
Millwall	21	14	8	1	40	14	+26	48
QPR	21	14	3	4	53	21	+32	45
Ipswich T	21	13	4	4	49	27	+22	43
Fulham	21	12	5	4	42	21	+21	41
Bristol C	21	12	5	4	37	25	+12	41
Swindon T	21	12	4	5	38	26	+12	40
Bournemouth	21	10	4	7	35	33	+2	34
Peterborough U	21	9	5	7	39	27	+12	32
Cambridge U	21	9	4	8	39	33	+6	31
Bristol R	21	8	6	7	28	27	+1	30
Brighton & HA	21	8	5	8	34	30	+4	29
Norwich C	21	7	6	8	30	24	+6	27
Leyton Orient	21	7	5	9	30	40	−10	26
Colchester U	21	6	7	8	29	39	−10	25
Portsmouth	21	7	4	10	29	40	−11	25
Gillingham	21	6	5	10	23	39	−16	23
Northampton T	21	6	4	11	27	36	−9	22
Barnet	21	5	6	10	26	33	−7	21
Southend U	21	5	2	14	25	48	−23	17
Luton T	21	3	7	11	19	33	−14	16
Oxford U	21	4	4	13	27	45	−18	16
Wycombe W	21	2	3	16	19	57	−38	9

Division Two

	P	*W*	*D*	*L*	*F*	*A*	*GD*	*Pts*
Plymouth Arg	8	6	1	1	11	8	+3	19
Cardiff C	8	3	3	2	16	10	+6	12
Exeter C	8	4	0	4	11	9	+2	12
Swansea C	8	3	1	4	11	10	+1	10
Torquay U	8	1	1	6	8	20	−12	4

Avon Insurance Combination – League Cup Winners
Division One – Bournemouth
Division Two – Cardiff C

FA ACADEMY UNDER-19 LEAGUE

GROUP A	P	W	D	L	F	A	GD	Pts
Sunderland	22	15	5	2	62	24	+38	50
Barnsley	22	12	4	6	52	38	+14	40
Sheffield W	22	10	1	11	39	49	−10	31
Middlesbrough	22	9	2	11	32	40	−8	29
Leeds U	22	7	4	11	32	48	−16	25
Newcastle U	22	7	3	12	37	53	−16	24
Huddersfield T	22	4	1	17	34	68	−34	13

GROUP B	P	W	D	L	F	A	GD	Pts
Blackburn R	22	15	5	2	55	18	+37	50
Everton	22	14	3	5	38	22	+16	45
Manchester U	22	11	5	6	47	22	+25	38
Manchester C	22	12	2	8	45	32	+13	38
Liverpool	22	11	3	8	45	37	+8	36
Crewe Alex	22	7	8	7	29	34	−5	29
Bolton W	22	3	3	16	18	55	−37	12

GROUP C	P	W	D	L	F	A	GD	Pts
Nottingham F	22	15	2	5	63	29	+34	47
Leicester C	22	11	5	6	32	29	+3	38
Coventry C	22	11	4	7	38	33	+5	37
Aston Villa	22	8	6	8	34	31	+3	30
Derby Co	22	6	5	11	26	33	−7	23
Peterborough U	22	5	6	11	29	41	−12	21
Birmingham C	22	6	3	13	23	36	−13	21
Stoke C	22	3	5	14	17	47	−30	14

GROUP D	P	W	D	L	F	A	GD	Pts
Arsenal	22	14	4	4	50	25	+25	46
Fulham	22	11	7	4	43	25	+18	40
Bristol C	22	9	5	8	35	24	+11	32
Crystal Palace	22	9	5	8	37	31	+6	32
Millwall	22	9	1	12	25	34	−9	28
Chelsea	22	7	6	9	26	28	−2	27
Southampton	22	6	4	12	28	46	−18	22
Reading	22	6	3	13	27	40	−13	21

GROUP E	P	W	D	L	F	A	GD	Pts
West Ham U	22	13	5	4	46	20	+26	44
Wimbledon	22	12	5	5	30	22	+8	41
QPR	22	9	9	4	39	29	+10	36
Charlton Ath	22	8	6	8	35	39	−4	30
Tottenham H	22	7	7	8	36	31	+5	28
Watford	22	6	4	12	34	49	−15	22
Ipswich T	22	6	3	13	26	41	−15	21
Norwich C	22	4	1	17	19	60	−41	13

UNDER-19 PLAY-OFFS

First Round
Southampton 1 Ipswich T 3
Peterborough U 2 Norwich C 0
Watford 1 Reading 1*
Chelsea 3 Stoke C 0
Newcastle U 4 Bolton W 1
Birmingham C 0 Huddersfield T 2

Second Round
Blackburn R 3 Ipswich T 1
Middlesbrough 2 Aston Villa 2*
Manchester U 6 Leeds U 1
West Ham U 3 Peterborough U 0
Barnsley 0 Crewe Alex 2
Wimbledon 3 Liverpool 4 *(aet)*
Coventry C 2 Charlton Ath 1
Sunderland 4 Reading 0
Nottingham F 3* Chelsea 3
Bristol C 1 Manchester C 1*
Fulham 2 Derby Co 0
Leicester C 1 Newcastle U 4
Everton 1 Tottenham H 0
Sheffield W 2 Crystal Palace 1
QPR 0 Millwall 1
Arsenal 2 Huddersfield T 1

Third Round
Blackburn R 4 Aston Villa 1
West Ham U 5 Manchester U 0
Crewe Alex 2 Liverpool 1
Sunderland 0 Coventry C 1
Nottingham F 3 Manchester C 2
Newcastle U 1 Fulham 2
Everton 2 Sheffield W 0
Arsenal 2 Millwall 0

Fourth Round
Blackburn R 1 West Ham U 2
Coventry C 0 Crewe Alex 1
Nottingham F 1 Fulham 2
Arsenal 2 Everton 0

Semi-finals
Crewe Alex 0 West Ham U 1
Arsenal 4 Fulham 1

Final (2 legs)
West Ham U 5 Arsenal 5
Arsenal 1 West Ham U 1*
(6-6 on aggregate. West Ham U won 4-2 on penalties)
* = won on penalties

FA ACADEMY UNDER-17 LEAGUE

GROUP A	P	W	D	L	F	A	GD	Pts
Newcastle U	22	11	5	6	37	30	+7	38
Sunderland	22	11	4	7	29	23	+6	37
Middlesbrough	22	9	9	4	44	25	+19	36
Sheffield W	22	9	6	7	41	33	+8	33
Leeds U	22	9	0	13	46	52	−6	27
Barnsley	22	4	2	16	22	76	−54	14

GROUP B	P	W	D	L	F	A	GD	Pts
Crewe Alex	22	13	3	6	74	35	+39	42
Manchester U	22	13	2	7	59	29	+30	41
Blackburn R	22	11	5	6	43	34	+9	38
Liverpool	22	12	2	8	41	32	+9	38
Manchester C	22	11	2	9	42	25	+17	35
Bolton W	22	3	1	18	19	61	−42	10

GROUP C	P	W	D	L	F	A	GD	Pts
Aston Villa	22	14	6	2	57	29	+28	48
Leicester C	22	9	6	7	29	25	+4	33
Coventry C	22	8	7	7	40	33	+7	31
Nottingham F	22	9	3	10	31	45	−14	30
Birmingham C	22	3	6	13	27	60	−33	15

GROUP D	P	W	D	L	F	A	GD	Pts
Arsenal	22	17	4	1	65	13	+52	55
Bristol C	22	9	6	7	28	28	+0	33
Millwall	22	9	4	9	41	36	+5	31
Reading	22	8	7	7	33	31	+2	31
Southampton	22	3	7	12	34	52	−18	16
Crystal Palace	22	4	4	14	24	52	−28	16
Fulham	22	3	5	14	22	59	−37	14

GROUP E	P	W	D	L	F	A	GD	Pts
West Ham U	22	14	3	5	48	21	+27	45
Watford	22	11	4	7	37	35	+2	37
QPR	22	10	6	6	40	32	+8	36
Wimbledon	22	8	5	9	31	30	+1	29
Charlton Ath	22	5	4	13	25	49	−24	19
Tottenham H	22	2	8	12	17	41	−24	14

UNDER-17 PLAY-OFFS

First Round
Blackburn R 1 Sheffield W 3
Sunderland 2 Birmingham C 1
Aston Villa 6 Bolton W 2
Manchester U 3 Leeds U 1
Coventry C 5 Liverpool 1
Middlesbrough 2 Manchester C 3
Crewe Alex 7 Barnsley 2
QPR 2 Reading 1
Leicester C 4 Southampton 2
Bristol C 2 Tottenham H 1
Watford 3 Crystal Palace 2
Millwall 3 Charlton Ath 2
Wimbledon 1 Nottingham F 0
West Ham U 2* Fulham 2

Second Round
Newcastle U 3 Sheffield W 0
Aston Villa 2 Sunderland 0
Manchester U 2 Coventry C 3
Crewe Alex 1 Manchester C 0
Arsenal 3 QPR 0
Bristol C 2 Leicester C 3
Watford 1 Millwall 1*
West Ham U 3 Wimbledon 1

Third Round
Newcastle U 1 Aston Villa 3
Crewe Alex 4 Coventry C 1
Arsenal 2 Leicester C 0
West Ham U 1 Millwall 0

Semi-finals
Crewe Alex 1 Aston Villa 0
West Ham U 2 Arsenal 3

Final (2 legs)
Crewe Alex 1 Arsenal 0
Arsenal 4 Crewe 2
(Arsenal won 4-3 on aggregate)
* = won on penalties

FA PREMIER RESERVE LEAGUES

NORTH

		Home			Goals		Away			Goals			
	P	W	D	L	F	A	W	D	L	F	A	GD	Pts
Liverpool	24	7	5	0	28	9	9	2	1	27	9	+37	55
Sunderland	24	8	4	0	21	4	4	1	7	14	23	+8	41
Blackburn R	24	7	1	4	22	13	4	5	3	15	13	+11	39
Bradford C	24	7	2	3	24	16	5	1	6	20	29	−1	39
Newcastle U	24	8	0	4	21	12	3	4	5	16	23	+2	37
Manchester U	24	7	2	3	29	14	4	1	7	17	18	+14	36
Leeds U	24	6	3	3	30	19	4	3	5	18	19	+10	36
Middlesbrough	24	6	2	4	18	18	4	4	4	16	15	+1	36
Everton	24	4	5	3	21	17	3	5	4	23	23	+4	31
Aston Villa	24	3	3	6	18	24	5	2	5	19	18	−5	29
Bolton W	24	4	2	6	13	25	2	2	8	9	34	−37	22
Sheffield W	24	5	1	6	23	21	0	3	9	12	31	−17	19
Barnsley	24	2	4	6	14	22	1	1	10	8	26	−27	14

SOUTH

		Home			Goals		Away			Goals			
	P	W	D	L	F	A	W	D	L	F	A	GD	Pts
Derby Co	24	9	3	0	22	9	5	3	4	23	19	+17	48
Charlton Ath	24	8	1	3	34	19	7	1	4	23	17	+21	47
Tottenham H	24	6	4	2	19	16	6	2	4	23	19	+7	42
Southampton	24	7	3	2	28	13	5	2	5	15	14	+16	41
Coventry C	24	5	3	4	18	17	6	3	3	20	13	+8	39
Arsenal	24	6	3	3	28	15	4	4	4	21	17	+17	37
Chelsea	24	4	6	2	14	13	4	3	5	17	17	+1	33
Wimbledon	24	5	3	4	21	17	3	4	5	17	18	+3	31
Nottingham F	24	6	3	3	19	13	1	4	7	15	25	−4	28
Leicester C	24	3	4	5	17	20	4	3	5	19	24	−8	28
West Ham U	24	4	0	8	17	25	3	3	6	10	18	−16	24
Watford	24	3	2	7	15	20	2	2	8	12	30	−23	19
Crystal Palace	24	2	2	8	8	24	1	3	8	6	29	−39	14

FA UMBRO TROPHY 1999–2000

FINAL (at Wembley)

13 MAY

Kettering Town (0) 2 *(Vowden 55, Norman 64 (pen))*

Kingstonian (1) 3 *(Akuamoah 40, 69, Simba 75)* 20,034

Kettering Town: Solitt; Shutt, Setchell (Hopkins 80), Perkins, Vowden, Norman (Diuk 73), Brown, Fisher, McNamara, Watkins (Hudson 46), Adams.
Kingstonian: Farrelly; Mustafa, Luckett, Stewart (Saunders 75), Crossley, Harris, Pitcher, Kadi (Leworthy 82), Akuamoah, Simba, Green (Basford 85).
Referee: S. Dunn (Gloucester).

FA CARLSBERG VASE 1999–2000

FINAL (at Wembley)

6 MAY

Chippenham Town (0) 0

Deal Town (0) 1 *(Graham 87)* 20,083

Chippenham Town: Jones; James (Tiley 89), Andrews, Woods, Murphy, Burns, Collier, Charity, Godley (Cutler 69), Tweddle, Brown (Godwin 90).
Deal Town: Tucker; Ribbens, Monteith (Roberts 10), Ash (Warden 73), Martin, Best, Kempster, Seager, Lovell (Turner 58), Marshall, Graham.
Referee: D. Laws (Whitley Bay).

THE TIMES FA YOUTH CUP 1999–2000

FINAL First Leg

4 MAY

Coventry City (0) 1 *(McSheffrey 85)*

Arsenal (0) 3 *(Thomas 48, Barratt 65, Sidwell 68)* 10,280

Coventry City: Montgomery; Spong, Hall D, Davenport, Cudworth, Betts, Pead (Grant 75), Strachan C, Parkinson (Ashby 67), McSheffrey, Fowler.
Arsenal: Stack; Da Silva, Chilvers, Noble, Halls, Galli, Sidwell, Ricketts, Barratt, Bothroyd, Thomas (Osei-Kuffour 79).
Referee: S. Bennett (Orpington).

FINAL Second Leg

12 MAY

Arsenal (1) 2 *(Bothroyd 38, Sidwell 72)*

Coventry City (0) 0 14,706

Arsenal: Stack; Volz, Chilvers, Noble, Halls, Galli, Pennant, Ricketts, Barratt, Bothroyd, Sidwell.
Coventry City: Montgomery; Spong, Hall D, Betts, Cudworth, Davenport, Strachan C (Shanahan 85), Fowler, Pead, McSheffrey (Parkinson 57), Ashby (Magennis 73).
Referee: S. Bennett (Orpington).

NATIONAL LIST OF REFEREES FOR SEASON 2000–2001

Alcock, P.E. (Halstead, Kent)
*Armstrong, P. (Thatcham, Berkshire)
Baines, S.J. (Chesterfield)
Barber, G.P. (Tring, Hertfordshire)
Barry, N.S. (Roxby, N. Lincolnshire)
Bates, A. (Stoke-on-Trent)
Beeby, R.J. (Northampton)
Bennett, S.G. (Orpington, Kent)
Brandwood, M.J. (Lichfield, Staffordshire)
Burns, W.C. (Scarborough)
Butler, A.N. (Sutton-in-Ashfield, Notts)
Cable, L.E. (Woking)
Cain, G. (Seaforth, Merseyside)
*Clattenburg, M. (Chester-le-Street)
*Cooper, M.A. (Walsall)
Cowburn, M.G. (Blackpool)
Crick, D.R. (Worcester Park, Surrey)
*Curson, B. (Hinckley, Leicestershire)
Danson, P.S. (Leicester)
¶Dean, M.L. (Heswall, Wirral)
Dowd, P. (Stoke-on-Trent)
Dunn, S.W. (Bristol)
Durkin, P.A. (Portland, Dorset)
D'Urso, A.P. (Billericay, Essex)
Elleray, D.R. (Harrow-on-the-Hill)
Fletcher, M. (Wolverley, Worcestershire)
Foy, C.J. (St Helens, Merseyside)
Frankland, G.B. (Middlesbrough)
Furnandiz, R.D. (Doncaster)
Gallagher, D.J. (Banbury, Oxfordshire)
Hall, A.R. (Birmingham)
Halsey, M.R. (Welwyn Garden City)
Harris, R.J. (Oxford)
Hill, K.D. (Royston, Hertfordshire)
Jones, M.J. (Chester)
Jones, P. (Loughborough)
Jones, T. (Dalton-in-Furness, Cumbria)
Jordan, W.M. (Tring, Hertfordshire)
Joslin, P.J. (Newark, Nottinghamshire)
Kaye, A. (Wakefield)
Knight, B. (Orpington, Kent)
Laws, D. (Whitley Bay)
Laws, G. (Whitley Bay)
Leake, A.R. (Darwen, Lancashire)
Lodge, S.J. (Barnsley)
Lomas, E. (Manchester)
Mathieson, S.W. (Stockport)
Messias, M.D. (York)
*North, M.J. (Poole, Dorset)
Olivier, R.J. (Sutton Coldfield)
Parkes, T.A. (Birmingham)
Pearson, R. (Peterlee, Durham)
Pike, M.S. (Barrow-in-Furness)
Poll, G. (Tring, Hertfordshire)
*Prosser, P.J. (Abbeymead, Glos)
Pugh, D. (Bebington, Merseyside)
Rejer, P. (Droitwich Spa, Worcestershire)
Rennie, U.D. (Sheffield)
Richards, P.R. (Darwen, Lancashire)
Riley, M.A. (Leeds)
Robinson, J.P. (Hull)
Ryan, M. (Preston)
Stretton, F.G. (Nottingham)
¶Styles, R. (Waterlooville, Hampshire)
¶Taylor, P. (Cheshunt, Hertfordshire)
Tomlin, S.G. (Lewes, East Sussex)
Walton, P. (Long Buckby, Northants)
Warren, M.R. (Walsall)
*Webb, H.M. (Rotherham)
*Webster, C.H. (Shotley Bridge, Durham)
Wiley, A.G. (Burntwood, Staffordshire)
Wilkes, C.R. (Gloucester)
Winter, J.T. (Stockton-on-Tees)
Wolstenholme, E.K. (Blackburn)

* New for season 2000–2001 ¶ New to Premier League 2000–2001

USEFUL ADDRESSES

The Football Association: The Secretary, 16 Lancaster Gate, London W2 3LW *020 7262 4542*
Scotland: The Secretary, 6 Park Gardens, Glasgow G3 7YE. *0141-332 6372*
Northern Ireland (Irish FA): D. I. Bowen, 20 Windsor Avenue, Belfast BT9 6EG. *01232-669458*
Wales: A. Evans, 3 Westgate Street, Cardiff, South Glamorgan CF1 1JF. *01222-372325*
Republic of Ireland (FA of Ireland): B. O'Byrne, 80 Merrion Square South, Dublin 2. *00353-16766864*
International Federation (FIFA): M. Zen-Ruffinen, P. O. Box 85 8030 Zurich, Switzerland. *00 411 384 9595. Fax: 00 411 384 9696*
Union of European Football Associations: G. Aigner, Route de Geneve 46, Case Postal, CH-1260 Nyon, Switzerland. *0041 22 994 4444. Fax: 0041 22 994 4488*
The Premier League: The Secretary, 11 Connaught Place, London W2 2ET. *020 7298 1600*
The Football League: J. D. Dent, F.C.I.S., The Football League, Unit 5, Edward VII Quay, Navigation Way, Preston, Lancashire PR2 2YF. *01772 325800. Fax 01772 325801*
Scottish Premier League: R. Mitchell, Hampden Park, Somerville Drive, Glasgow G42 9BA. *0141 646 6962*
The Scottish League: P. Donald, 188 West Regent Street, Glasgow G2 4RY. *0141-248 3844*
The Irish League: H. Wallace, 87 University Street, Belfast BT7 1HP. *01232-242888*
Football League of Ireland: E. Morris, 80 Merrion Square South, Dublin 2. *003531 765120*
The Nationwide Football Conference: J. A. Moules, Riverside House, 14b High Street, Crayford DA1 4HG. *01322 411021*
Northern Premier: R. D. Bayley, 22 Woburn Drive, Hale, Altrincham, Cheshire, WA15 8LZ. *0161-980 7007*
Isthmian League: N. Robinson, 226 Rye Lane, Peckham, SE15 4NL. *020 8409 1978. Fax 020 7639 5726*
English Schools FA: M. R. Berry, 1/2 Eastgate Street, Stafford ST16 2NN. *01785-51142*
Southern League: D. J. Strudwick, PO Box 90, Worcester WR3 8RX. *01905-757509.*
National Federation of Football Supporters' Clubs: Chairman: Ian D. Todd MBE, 8 Wyke Close, Wyke Gardens, Isleworth, Middlesex TW7 5PE. *020 8847 2905 (and fax). Mobile: 0961-558908.* National Secretary: Mark Agate, "The Stadium", 14 Coombe Close, Lordswood, Chatham, Kent ME5 8NU. *01634 319461 (and fax)*
Professional Footballers' Association: G. Taylor, 2 Oxford Court, Bishopsgate, Off Lower Mosley Street, Manchester M2 3WQ. *0161-236 0575*
Referees' Association: A. Smith, 1 Westhill Road, Coundon, Coventry CV6 2AD. *01203 601701*
Women's Football Alliance: Miss K. Simmons, 9 Wyllyotts Place, Potters Bar, Herts EN6 2JD. *01707 651840*
The Association of Football Statisticians: R. J. Spiller, PO Box 5828, Basildon, Essex SS15 5GQ. *01268 416020 (and fax 01268 543559)*
The Football Programme Directory: David Stacey, 'The Beeches', 66 Southend Road, Wickford, Essex SS11 8EN. *01268 732041 (and fax)*
England Football Supporters Association: Publicity Officer, David Stacey, 66 Southend Road, Wickford, Essex SS11 8EN. *01268 732041 (and fax)*
World Cup (1966) Association: as above.
The Football Trust: Second Floor, Walkden House, 10 Melton Street, London NW1 2EJ. *020 7388 4504*

ENGLISH LEAGUE FIXTURES 2000–2001

Saturday, 12 August 2000
Nationwide Football League Division 1
Barnsley v Norwich C
Blackburn R v Crystal Palace
Bolton W v Burnley
Fulham v Crewe Alex
Gillingham v Stockport Co
Grimsby T v Preston NE
Huddersfield T v Watford
Nottingham F v WBA
QPR v Birmingham C
Sheffield U v Portsmouth
Wimbledon v Tranmere R

Nationwide League Division 2
Bristol R v AFC Bournemouth
Cambridge U v Bury
Luton T v Notts Co
Millwall v Reading
Northampton T v Brentford
Oldham Ath v Port Vale
Oxford U v Peterborough U
Rotherham U v Walsall
Stoke C v Wycombe W
Swansea C v Wigan Ath
Swindon T v Colchester U
Wrexham v Bristol C

Nationwide League Division 3
Barnet v Shrewsbury T
Blackpool v Hull C
Carlisle U v Halifax T
Cheltenham T v Mansfield T
Chesterfield v York C
Exeter C v Cardiff C
Kidderminster H v Torquay U
Lincoln C v Hartlepool U
Macclesfield T v Scunthorpe U
Plymouth Arg v Leyton Orient
Rochdale v Darlington
Southend U v Brighton & HA

Sunday, 13 August 2000
Nationwide Football League Division 1
Wolverhampton W v Sheffield W (12.30)

Friday, 18 August 2000
Birmingham C v Fulham (7.45)

Saturday, 19 August 2000
FA Carling Premiership
Charlton Ath v Manchester C
Chelsea v West Ham U
Coventry C v Middlesbrough
Derby Co v Southampton
Leeds U v Everton
Leicester C v Aston Villa
Liverpool v Bradford C
Sunderland v Arsenal
Tottenham H v Ipswich T

Nationwide Football League Division 1
Burnley v Wimbledon
Crewe Alex v Blackburn R
Norwich C v Nottingham F
Portsmouth v Grimsby T
Preston NE v Sheffield U
Sheffield W v Huddersfield T
Stockport Co v Wolverhampton W
Tranmere R v Gillingham
Watford v Barnsley
WBA v Bolton W

Nationwide League Division 2
AFC Bournemouth v Cambridge U
Brentford v Swansea C
Bristol C v Stoke C
Bury v Wrexham
Colchester U v Rotherham U
Notts Co v Millwall
Peterborough U v Bristol R
Port Vale v Oxford U
Reading v Swindon T
Walsall v Oldham Ath
Wigan Ath v Luton T
Wycombe W v Northampton T

Nationwide League Division 3
Brighton & HA v Rochdale
Cardiff C v Blackpool
Darlington v Exeter C
Halifax T v Lincoln C
Hartlepool U v Chesterfield
Hull C v Plymouth Arg
Leyton Orient v Carlisle U
Mansfield T v Barnet
Scunthorpe U v Kidderminster H
Shrewsbury T v Macclesfield T
Torquay U v Southend U
York C v Cheltenham T

Sunday, 20 August 2000
FA Carling Premiership
Manchester U v Newcastle U (4.00)

Nationwide Football League Division 1
Crystal Palace v QPR (1.00)

Monday, 21 August 2000
FA Carling Premiership
Arsenal v Liverpool (8.00)

Tuesday, 22 August 2000
FA Carling Premiership
Bradford C v Chelsea
Ipswich T v Manchester U
Middlesbrough v Tottenham H

Wednesday, 23 August 2000
FA Carling Premiership
Aston Villa v Leeds U
Everton v Charlton Ath (8.00)
Manchester C v Sunderland
Newcastle U v Derby Co
Southampton v Coventry C
West Ham U v Leicester C

Friday, 25 August 2000
Nationwide Football League Division 1
Gillingham v Portsmouth (7.45)

Saturday, 26 August 2000

FA Carling Premiership
Arsenal v Charlton Ath
Bradford C v Leicester C
Everton v Derby Co
Ipswich T v Sunderland
Manchester C v Coventry C
Middlesbrough v Leeds U
Newcastle U v Tottenham H
Southampton v Liverpool
West Ham U v Manchester U

Nationwide Football League Division 1
Barnsley v WBA
Blackburn R v Norwich C
Bolton W v Preston NE
Fulham v Stockport Co
Grimsby T v Sheffield W
Huddersfield T v Crystal Palace
Nottingham F v Birmingham C
QPR v Crewe Alex
Sheffield U v Tranmere R
Wimbledon v Watford
Wolverhampton W v Burnley

Nationwide League Division 2
Bristol R v Port Vale
Cambridge U v Bristol C
Luton T v AFC Bournemouth
Millwall v Wycombe W
Northampton T v Reading
Oldham Ath v Peterborough U
Oxford U v Brentford
Rotherham U v Bury
Stoke C v Notts Co
Swansea C v Colchester U
Swindon T v Walsall
Wrexham v Wigan Ath

Nationwide League Division 3
Barnet v Cardiff C
Blackpool v Leyton Orient
Carlisle U v York C
Cheltenham T v Torquay U
Chesterfield v Shrewsbury T
Exeter C v Hartlepool U
Kidderminster H v Halifax T
Lincoln C v Brighton & HA
Macclesfield T v Hull C
Plymouth Arg v Mansfield T
Rochdale v Scunthorpe U
Southend U v Darlington

Sunday, 27 August 2000

FA Carling Premiership
Aston Villa v Chelsea (4.00)

Monday, 28 August 2000

Nationwide Football League Division 1
Birmingham C v Barnsley
Burnley v Gillingham
Crewe Alex v Grimsby T
Crystal Palace v Nottingham F
Norwich C v Fulham
Portsmouth v Wolverhampton W
Preston NE v Wimbledon
Sheffield W v Blackburn R (8.00)
Stockport Co v Huddersfield T
Tranmere R v Bolton W
Watford v Sheffield U
WBA v QPR

Nationwide League Division 2
AFC Bournemouth v Wrexham
Brentford v Bristol R
Bristol C v Rotherham U
Bury v Northampton T
Colchester U v Oldham Ath
Notts Co v Cambridge U
Peterborough U v Swansea C
Port Vale v Swindon T
Reading v Stoke C
Walsall v Oxford U
Wigan Ath v Millwall
Wycombe W v Luton T

Nationwide League Division 3
Brighton & HA v Kidderminster H
Cardiff C v Southend U
Darlington v Plymouth Arg
Halifax T v Rochdale
Hartlepool U v Cheltenham T
Hull C v Lincoln C
Leyton Orient v Exeter C
Mansfield T v Macclesfield T
Scunthorpe U v Chesterfield
Shrewsbury T v Carlisle U
Torquay U v Blackpool
York C v Barnet

Friday, 1 September 2000

Nationwide Football League Division 1
Tranmere R v Stockport Co (7.45)

Saturday, 2 September 2000

Nationwide Football League Division 1
Barnsley v Blackburn R
Bolton W v QPR
Burnley v Crewe Alex
Gillingham v Wolverhampton W
Norwich C v Birmingham C
Preston NE v Portsmouth
Sheffield U v Fulham
Watford v Sheffield W
WBA v Crystal Palace
Wimbledon v Grimsby T

Nationwide League Division 2
Brentford v Wycombe W
Bristol R v Millwall
Colchester U v AFC Bournemouth
Northampton T v Stoke C
Oldham Ath v Notts Co
Oxford U v Cambridge U
Peterborough U v Bury
Port Vale v Reading
Rotherham U v Luton T
Swansea C v Bristol C
Swindon T v Wrexham
Walsall v Wigan Ath

Nationwide League Division 3
Brighton & HA v Torquay U
Chesterfield v Barnet
Darlington v York C
Exeter C v Mansfield T
Halifax T v Leyton Orient
Hartlepool U v Shrewsbury T
Hull C v Cheltenham T
Kidderminster H v Carlisle U
Lincoln C v Southend U
Plymouth Arg v Macclesfield T
Rochdale v Cardiff C
Scunthorpe U v Blackpool

Sunday, 3 September 2000

Nationwide League Division 1
Nottingham F v Huddersfield T (1.00)

Tuesday, 5 September 2000

FA Carling Premiership
Charlton Ath v Southampton
Leeds U v Manchester C
Sunderland v West Ham U
Tottenham H v Everton

Wednesday, 6 September 2000

FA Carling Premiership
Chelsea v Arsenal (8.00)
Coventry C v Newcastle U
Derby Co v Middlesbrough
Leicester C v Ipswich T
Liverpool v Aston Villa
Manchester U v Bradford C

Friday, 8 September 2000

Nationwide League Division 2
Wycombe W v Oxford U (7.45)

Saturday, 9 September 2000

FA Carling Premiership
Bradford C v Arsenal
Coventry C v Leeds U
Ipswich T v Aston Villa
Leicester C v Southampton
Liverpool v Manchester C
Manchester U v Sunderland
Middlesbrough v Everton
Newcastle U v Chelsea

Nationwide Football League Division 1
Birmingham C v Sheffield U
Blackburn R v Nottingham F
Crewe Alex v Norwich C
Crystal Palace v Burnley
Grimsby T v Gillingham
Huddersfield T v Bolton W
Portsmouth v Watford
QPR v Preston NE
Sheffield W v Wimbledon
Stockport Co v WBA
Wolverhampton W v Tranmere R

Nationwide League Division 2
AFC Bournemouth v Port Vale
Bristol C v Swindon T
Bury v Walsall
Cambridge U v Rotherham U
Luton T v Northampton T
Millwall v Swansea C
Notts Co v Bristol R
Reading v Brentford
Stoke C v Peterborough U
Wigan Ath v Colchester U
Wrexham v Oldham Ath

Nationwide League Division 3
Barnet v Kidderminster H
Blackpool v Hartlepool U
Cardiff C v Brighton & HA
Carlisle U v Rochdale
Cheltenham T v Chesterfield
Leyton Orient v Hull C
Macclesfield T v Exeter C
Mansfield T v Halifax T
Shrewsbury T v Darlington
Southend U v Plymouth Arg
Torquay U v Lincoln C
York C v Scunthorpe U

Sunday, 10 September 2000

FA Carling Premiership
Derby Co v Charlton Ath (4.00)

Nationwide Football League Division 1
Fulham v Barnsley (1.00)

Monday, 11 September 2000

FA Carling Premiership
Tottenham H v West Ham U (8.00)

Tuesday, 12 September 2000

Nationwide Football League Division 1
Birmingham C v Preston NE
Crewe Alex v WBA
Crystal Palace v Barnsley
Fulham v Burnley
Grimsby T v Bolton W
Huddersfield T v Wimbledon (8.00)
Portsmouth v Tranmere R
Stockport Co v Norwich C
Wolverhampton W v Sheffield U

Nationwide League Division 2
AFC Bournemouth v Swindon T
Bristol C v Brentford
Bury v Colchester U
Cambridge U v Port Vale
Luton T v Walsall
Millwall v Northampton T
Notts Co v Swansea C
Reading v Oldham Ath
Wigan Ath v Peterborough U
Wrexham v Rotherham U
Wycombe W v Bristol R

Nationwide League Division 3
Barnet v Exeter C
Blackpool v Brighton & HA
Cardiff C v Halifax T
Carlisle U v Chesterfield
Cheltenham T v Darlington
Leyton Orient v Scunthorpe U
Macclesfield T v Lincoln C
Mansfield T v Hull C
Shrewsbury T v Plymouth Arg
Southend U v Kidderminster H
Torquay U v Hartlepool U
York C v Rochdale

Wednesday, 13 September 2000

Nationwide Football League Division 1
Blackburn R v Watford
QPR v Gillingham
Sheffield W v Nottingham F

Nationwide League Division 2
Stoke C v Oxford U

Friday, 15 September 2000

Nationwide Football League Division 1
Sheffield U v Blackburn R (7.45)

Saturday, 16 September 2000

FA Carling Premiership
Arsenal v Coventry C

Aston Villa v Bradford C
Charlton Ath v Tottenham H
Chelsea v Leicester C
Everton v Manchester U
Leeds U v Ipswich T
Southampton v Newcastle U
Sunderland v Derby Co
West Ham U v Liverpool

Nationwide Football League Division 1
Barnsley v QPR
Bolton W v Portsmouth
Burnley v Grimsby T
Gillingham v Huddersfield T
Norwich C v Crystal Palace
Nottingham F v Fulham
Preston NE v Stockport Co
Tranmere R v Sheffield W
Watford v Crewe Alex
WBA v Birmingham C
Wimbledon v Wolverhampton W

Nationwide League Division 2
Brentford v Millwall
Bristol R v Wigan Ath
Colchester U v Wrexham
Northampton T v Notts Co
Oldham Ath v Bristol C
Oxford U v Bury
Peterborough U v Reading
Rotherham U v Wycombe W
Swansea C v Luton T
Swindon T v Cambridge U
Walsall v AFC Bournemouth

Nationwide League Division 3
Brighton & HA v Cheltenham T
Chesterfield v Mansfield T
Darlington v Barnet
Exeter C v York C
Halifax T v Southend U
Hartlepool U v Macclesfield T
Hull C v Shrewsbury T
Kidderminster H v Leyton Orient
Lincoln C v Blackpool
Plymouth Arg v Carlisle U
Rochdale v Torquay U
Scunthorpe U v Cardiff C

Sunday, 17 September 2000

FA Carling Premiership
Manchester C v Middlesbrough (4.00)

Nationwide League Division 2
Port Vale v Stoke C (1.00)

Friday, 22 September 2000

Nationwide Football League Division 3
Macclesfield T v Darlington (7.45)

Saturday, 23 September 2000

FA Carling Premiership
Bradford C v Southampton
Coventry C v West Ham U
Derby Co v Leeds U
Ipswich T v Arsenal
Liverpool v Sunderland
Manchester U v Chelsea (11.30)
Middlesbrough v Aston Villa
Newcastle U v Charlton Ath
Tottenham H v Manchester C

Nationwide Football League Division 1
Birmingham C v Tranmere R
Blackburn R v Bolton W
Crewe Alex v Barnsley
Crystal Palace v Sheffield U
Fulham v Gillingham
Grimsby T v Nottingham F
Huddersfield T v Burnley
Portsmouth v WBA
QPR v Wimbledon
Sheffield W v Preston NE
Stockport Co v Watford

Nationwide League Division 2
AFC Bournemouth v Oldham Ath
Bristol C v Colchester U
Bury v Port Vale
Cambridge U v Bristol R
Luton T v Swindon T
Millwall v Oxford U
Notts Co v Brentford
Reading v Swansea C
Stoke C v Rotherham U
Wigan Ath v Northampton T
Wrexham v Walsall
Wycombe W v Peterborough U

Nationwide League Division 3
Barnet v Hull C
Blackpool v Chesterfield
Cardiff C v Kidderminster H
Carlisle U v Exeter C
Cheltenham T v Plymouth Arg
Leyton Orient v Lincoln C
Mansfield T v Hartlepool U
Shrewsbury T v Rochdale
Southend U v Scunthorpe U
Torquay U v Halifax T
York C v Brighton & HA

Sunday, 24 September 2000

FA Carling Premiership
Leicester C v Everton (4.00)

Nationwide League Division 1
Wolverhampton W v Norwich C (1.00)

Friday, 29 September 2000

Nationwide League Division 3
Kidderminster H v Blackpool (7.45)

Saturday, 30 September 2000

FA Carling Premiership
Aston Villa v Derby Co
Charlton Ath v Coventry C
Chelsea v Liverpool
Everton v Ipswich T
Leeds U v Tottenham H
Manchester C v Newcastle U
Southampton v Middlesbrough
Sunderland v Leicester C
West Ham U v Bradford C

Nationwide Football League Division 1
Barnsley v Grimsby T
Bolton W v Fulham
Burnley v Portsmouth
Gillingham v Sheffield W
Norwich C v Huddersfield T
Nottingham F v Wolverhampton W
Preston NE v Crystal Palace

Sheffield U v QPR
Tranmere R v Crewe Alex
WBA v Blackburn R
Wimbledon v Stockport Co

Nationwide League Division 2
Brentford v AFC Bournemouth
Bristol R v Luton T
Colchester U v Stoke C
Northampton T v Wrexham
Oldham Ath v Cambridge U
Oxford U v Bristol C
Peterborough U v Millwall
Port Vale v Wycombe W
Rotherham U v Reading
Swansea C v Bury
Swindon T v Wigan Ath
Walsall v Notts Co

Nationwide League Division 3
Brighton & HA v Leyton Orient
Chesterfield v Macclesfield T
Darlington v Carlisle U
Exeter C v Cheltenham T
Halifax T v Shrewsbury T
Hartlepool U v York C
Hull C v Cardiff C
Lincoln C v Mansfield T
Plymouth Arg v Barnet
Rochdale v Southend U
Scunthorpe U v Torquay U

Sunday, 1 October 2000

FA Carling Premiership
Arsenal v Manchester U (4.00)

Nationwide Football League Division 1
Watford v Birmingham C (1.00)

Friday, 6 October 2000

Nationwide Football League Division 1
Blackburn R v Preston NE (7.45)

Saturday, 7 October 2000

Nationwide Football League Division 1
Crewe Alex v Birmingham C
Crystal Palace v Wimbledon
Gillingham v Bolton W
Huddersfield T v Barnsley
Norwich C v Watford
Nottingham F v Sheffield U
Sheffield W v WBA
Stockport Co v Portsmouth
Tranmere R v Burnley
Wolverhampton W v Grimsby T

Nationwide League Division 2
Bristol C v AFC Bournemouth
Bury v Bristol R
Colchester U v Walsall
Luton T v Millwall
Northampton T v Swansea C
Peterborough U v Port Vale
Rotherham U v Oldham Ath
Stoke C v Brentford
Swindon T v Oxford U
Wigan Ath v Reading
Wrexham v Cambridge U
Wycombe W v Notts Co

Nationwide League Division 3
Barnet v Macclesfield T
Blackpool v Southend U
Cardiff C v Lincoln C
Cheltenham T v Carlisle U
Chesterfield v Plymouth Arg
Hartlepool U v Darlington
Hull C v Brighton & HA
Kidderminster H v Rochdale
Scunthorpe U v Halifax T
Shrewsbury T v Exeter C
Torquay U v Leyton Orient
York C v Mansfield T

Sunday, 8 October 2000

Nationwide Football League Division 1
QPR v Fulham (1.00)

Saturday, 14 October 2000

FA Carling Premiership
Arsenal v Aston Villa
Coventry C v Tottenham H
Everton v Southampton
Ipswich T v West Ham U
Leeds U v Charlton Ath
Leicester C v Manchester U
Manchester C v Bradford C
Sunderland v Chelsea

Nationwide Football League Division 1
Barnsley v Nottingham F
Birmingham C v Crystal Palace
Bolton W v Wolverhampton W
Burnley v Stockport Co
Grimsby T v Huddersfield T
Portsmouth v Sheffield W
Preston NE v Tranmere R
Sheffield U v Crewe Alex
Watford v QPR
WBA v Norwich C
Wimbledon v Gillingham

Nationwide League Division 2
AFC Bournemouth v Rotherham U
Brentford v Peterborough U
Bristol R v Northampton T
Cambridge U v Luton T
Millwall v Bury
Notts Co v Wigan Ath
Oldham Ath v Swindon T
Oxford U v Wrexham
Port Vale v Colchester U
Reading v Wycombe W
Swansea C v Stoke C
Walsall v Bristol C

Nationwide League Division 3
Brighton & HA v Scunthorpe U
Carlisle U v Barnet
Darlington v Torquay U
Exeter C v Chesterfield
Halifax T v Hull C
Leyton Orient v Cardiff C
Lincoln C v Kidderminster H
Macclesfield T v Cheltenham T
Mansfield T v Shrewsbury T
Plymouth Arg v Blackpool
Rochdale v Hartlepool U
Southend U v York C

Sunday, 15 October 2000

FA Carling Premiership
Derby Co v Liverpool (4.00)

Nationwide Football League Division 1
Fulham v Blackburn R (1.00)

Monday, 16 October 2000

FA Carling Premiership
Middlesbrough v Newcastle U (8.00)

Tuesday, 17 October 2000

Nationwide Football League Division 1
Barnsley v Tranmere R
Birmingham C v Stockport Co
Bolton W v Nottingham F
Burnley v Sheffield W
Fulham v Crystal Palace
Grimsby T v QPR
Portsmouth v Crewe Alex
Preston NE v Norwich C
Sheffield U v Huddersfield T
Watford v Gillingham
WBA v Wolverhampton W (8.00)
Wimbledon v Blackburn R

Nationwide League Division 2
AFC Bournemouth v Wigan Ath
Brentford v Colchester U
Bristol R v Rotherham U
Cambridge U v Stoke C
Millwall v Bristol C
Notts Co v Bury
Oldham Ath v Wycombe W
Oxford U v Luton T
Port Vale v Northampton T
Reading v Wrexham
Swansea C v Swindon T
Walsall v Peterborough U

Nationwide League Division 3
Brighton & HA v Hartlepool U
Carlisle U v Cardiff C
Darlington v Kidderminster H
Exeter C v Hull C
Halifax T v Cheltenham T
Leyton Orient v Shrewsbury T
Lincoln C v York C
Macclesfield T v Torquay U
Mansfield T v Blackpool
Plymouth Arg v Scunthorpe U
Rochdale v Chesterfield
Southend U v Barnet

Saturday, 21 October 2000

FA Carling Premiership
Bradford C v Ipswich T
Charlton Ath v Middlesbrough
Chelsea v Coventry C
Liverpool v Leicester C
Manchester U v Leeds U (11.30)
Newcastle U v Everton
Tottenham H v Derby Co
West Ham U v Arsenal

Nationwide Football League Division 1
Blackburn R v Grimsby T
Crewe Alex v Wimbledon
Crystal Palace v Portsmouth
Gillingham v Barnsley
Huddersfield T v Preston NE
Norwich C v Sheffield U
Nottingham F v Watford
QPR v Burnley
Stockport Co v Bolton W
Tranmere R v WBA
Wolverhampton W v Fulham

Nationwide League Division 2
Bristol C v Reading
Bury v AFC Bournemouth
Colchester U v Cambridge U
Luton T v Brentford
Northampton T v Oldham Ath
Peterborough U v Notts Co
Rotherham U v Oxford U
Stoke C v Millwall
Swindon T v Bristol R
Wigan Ath v Port Vale
Wrexham v Swansea C
Wycombe W v Walsall

Nationwide League Division 3
Barnet v Halifax T
Blackpool v Macclesfield T
Cardiff C v Mansfield T
Cheltenham T v Rochdale
Chesterfield v Brighton & HA
Hartlepool U v Plymouth Arg
Hull C v Southend U
Kidderminster H v Exeter C
Scunthorpe U v Darlington
Shrewsbury T v Lincoln C
Torquay U v Carlisle U
York C v Leyton Orient

Sunday, 22 October 2000

FA Carling Premiership
Aston Villa v Sunderland (4.00)

Nationwide Football League Division 1
Sheffield W v Birmingham C (1.00)

Monday, 23 October 2000

FA Carling Premiership
Southampton v Manchester C (8.00)

Tuesday, 24 October 2000

Nationwide Football League Division 1
Barnsley v Wolverhampton W
Birmingham C v Gillingham
Crewe Alex v Huddersfield T
Crystal Palace v Grimsby T
Fulham v Preston NE
Norwich C v Portsmouth
Sheffield U v Stockport Co
Watford v Bolton W (8.00)
WBA v Wimbledon

Nationwide League Division 2
AFC Bournemouth v Notts Co
Bristol C v Peterborough U
Bury v Reading
Cambridge U v Northampton T
Colchester U v Bristol R
Oldham Ath v Luton T
Oxford U v Wigan Ath
Port Vale v Brentford
Rotherham U v Swansea C
Swindon T v Millwall
Walsall v Stoke C
Wrexham v Wycombe W

Nationwide League Division 3
Blackpool v Carlisle U
Brighton & HA v Plymouth Arg
Cardiff C v Darlington
Halifax T v York C
Hull C v Hartlepool U
Kidderminster H v Chesterfield
Leyton Orient v Barnet
Lincoln C v Cheltenham T
Rochdale v Macclesfield T
Scunthorpe U v Shrewsbury T
Southend U v Exeter C
Torquay U v Mansfield T

Wednesday, 25 October 2000

Nationwide Football League Division 1
Blackburn R v Tranmere R
Nottingham F v Burnley
QPR v Sheffield W

Friday, 27 October 2000

Nationwide Football League Division 1
Preston NE v Barnsley (7.45)

Saturday, 28 October 2000

FA Carling Premiership
Arsenal v Manchester C
Aston Villa v Charlton Ath
Chelsea v Tottenham H
Ipswich T v Middlesbrough
Leicester C v Derby Co
Liverpool v Everton
Manchester U v Southampton
Sunderland v Coventry C
West Ham U v Newcastle U

Nationwide Football League Division 1
Bolton W v Crystal Palace
Burnley v Norwich C
Gillingham v Crewe Alex
Huddersfield T v Blackburn R
Portsmouth v Birmingham C
Sheffield W v Fulham
Stockport Co v Nottingham F
Tranmere R v QPR
Wimbledon v Sheffield U
Wolverhampton W v Watford

Nationwide League Division 2
Brentford v Walsall
Bristol R v Oldham Ath
Luton T v Wrexham
Millwall v Cambridge U
Northampton T v Rotherham U
Notts Co v Swindon T
Peterborough U v Colchester U
Reading v Oxford U
Stoke C v AFC Bournemouth
Swansea C v Port Vale
Wigan Ath v Bury
Wycombe W v Bristol C

Nationwide League Division 3
Barnet v Lincoln C
Carlisle U v Scunthorpe U
Cheltenham T v Blackpool
Chesterfield v Cardiff C
Darlington v Brighton & HA
Exeter C v Rochdale
Hartlepool U v Leyton Orient
Macclesfield T v Halifax T
Mansfield T v Southend U
Plymouth Arg v Kidderminster H
Shrewsbury T v Torquay U
York C v Hull C

Sunday, 29 October 2000

FA Carling Premiership
Bradford C v Leeds U (4.00)

Nationwide Football League Division 1
Grimsby T v WBA (1.00)

Saturday, 4 November 2000

FA Carling Premiership
Charlton Ath v Bradford C
Coventry C v Manchester U
Leeds U v Liverpool (11.30)
Manchester C v Leicester C
Middlesbrough v Arsenal
Newcastle U v Ipswich T
Southampton v Chelsea
Tottenham H v Sunderland

Nationwide Football League Division 1
Birmingham C v Bolton W
Blackburn R v Stockport Co
Crewe Alex v Wolverhampton W
Crystal Palace v Sheffield W
Fulham v Huddersfield T
Norwich C v Tranmere R
Nottingham F v Preston NE
QPR v Portsmouth
Sheffield U v Gillingham
Watford v Grimsby T
WBA v Burnley

Nationwide League Division 2
AFC Bournemouth v Peterborough U
Bristol C v Notts Co
Bury v Luton T
Cambridge U v Brentford
Colchester U v Northampton T
Oldham Ath v Swansea C
Oxford U v Bristol R
Port Vale v Millwall
Rotherham U v Wigan Ath
Swindon T v Wycombe W
Walsall v Reading
Wrexham v Stoke C

Nationwide League Division 3
Blackpool v Shrewsbury T
Brighton & HA v Carlisle U
Cardiff C v York C
Halifax T v Exeter C
Hull C v Darlington
Kidderminster H v Cheltenham T
Leyton Orient v Mansfield T
Lincoln C v Chesterfield
Rochdale v Barnet
Scunthorpe U v Hartlepool U
Southend U v Macclesfield T
Torquay U v Plymouth Arg

Sunday, 5 November 2000

FA Carling Premiership
Everton v Aston Villa (4.00)

Nationwide Football League Division 1
Barnsley v Wimbledon (1.00)

Monday, 6 November 2000

FA Carling Premiership
Derby Co v West Ham U (8.00)

Friday, 10 November 2000

Nationwide Football League Division 1
Preston NE v Crewe Alex (7.45)

Saturday, 11 November 2000

FA Carling Premiership
Arsenal v Derby Co
Aston Villa v Tottenham H
Bradford C v Everton
Ipswich T v Charlton Ath
Leicester C v Newcastle U
Liverpool v Coventry C
Manchester U v Middlesbrough
Sunderland v Southampton
West Ham U v Manchester C

Nationwide Football League Division 1
Bolton W v Barnsley
Burnley v Sheffield U
Grimsby T v Birmingham C
Huddersfield T v WBA
Portsmouth v Blackburn R
Sheffield W v Norwich C
Stockport Co v QPR
Tranmere R v Watford
Wimbledon v Fulham
Wolverhampton W v Crystal Palace

Nationwide League Division 2
Brentford v Rotherham U
Bristol R v Walsall
Luton T v Bristol C
Millwall v Wrexham
Northampton T v AFC Bournemouth
Notts Co v Port Vale
Peterborough U v Swindon T
Reading v Colchester U
Stoke C v Oldham Ath
Swansea C v Oxford U
Wigan Ath v Cambridge U
Wycombe W v Bury

Nationwide League Division 3
Barnet v Blackpool
Carlisle U v Southend U
Cheltenham T v Leyton Orient
Chesterfield v Hull C
Darlington v Halifax T
Exeter C v Scunthorpe U
Hartlepool U v Kidderminster H
Macclesfield T v Brighton & HA
Mansfield T v Rochdale
Plymouth Arg v Lincoln C
Shrewsbury T v Cardiff C
York C v Torquay U

Sunday, 12 November 2000

FA Carling Premiership
Chelsea v Leeds U (4.00)

Nationwide Football League Division 1
Gillingham v Nottingham F (1.00)

Saturday, 18 November 2000

FA Carling Premiership
Charlton Ath v Chelsea
Derby Co v Bradford C
Everton v Arsenal
Leeds U v West Ham U
Manchester C v Manchester U (11.30)
Middlesbrough v Leicester C
Newcastle U v Sunderland
Southampton v Aston Villa

Nationwide Football League Division 1
Barnsley v Sheffield W
Birmingham C v Burnley
Blackburn R v Wolverhampton W
Crewe Alex v Stockport Co
Crystal Palace v Tranmere R
Fulham v Portsmouth
Norwich C v Bolton W
Nottingham F v Wimbledon
QPR v Huddersfield T
Sheffield U v Grimsby T
Watford v Preston NE
WBA v Gillingham

Sunday, 19 November 2000

FA Carling Premiership
Tottenham H v Liverpool (4.00)

Monday, 20 November 2000

FA Carling Premiership
Coventry C v Ipswich T (8.00)

Saturday, 25 November 2000

FA Carling Premiership
Charlton Ath v Sunderland
Coventry C v Aston Villa
Derby Co v Manchester U
Everton v Chelsea
Manchester C v Ipswich T
Middlesbrough v Bradford C
Newcastle U v Liverpool
Southampton v West Ham U
Tottenham H v Leicester C

Nationwide Football League Division 1
Barnsley v Portsmouth
Birmingham C v Huddersfield T
Blackburn R v Gillingham
Crewe Alex v Sheffield W
Crystal Palace v Stockport Co
Fulham v Grimsby T
Norwich C v Wimbledon
Nottingham F v Tranmere R
QPR v Wolverhampton W
Sheffield U v Bolton W
Watford v Burnley
WBA v Preston NE

Nationwide League Division 2
AFC Bournemouth v Reading
Bristol C v Wigan Ath
Bury v Brentford
Cambridge U v Swansea C
Colchester U v Wycombe W
Oldham Ath v Millwall
Oxford U v Notts Co
Port Vale v Luton T
Rotherham U v Peterborough U
Swindon T v Stoke C
Walsall v Northampton T
Wrexham v Bristol R

Nationwide League Division 3
Blackpool v Darlington
Brighton & HA v Shrewsbury T
Cardiff C v Hartlepool U
Halifax T v Chesterfield
Hull C v Carlisle U
Kidderminster H v York C
Leyton Orient v Macclesfield T
Lincoln C v Exeter C
Rochdale v Plymouth Arg
Scunthorpe U v Mansfield T
Southend U v Cheltenham T
Torquay U v Barnet

Sunday, 26 November 2000
Leeds U v Arsenal (4.00)

Saturday, 2 December 2000
FA Carling Premiership
Arsenal v Southampton
Aston Villa v Newcastle U
Bradford C v Coventry C
Ipswich T v Derby Co
Leicester C v Leeds U
Liverpool v Charlton Ath
Manchester U v Tottenham H
West Ham U v Middlesbrough

Nationwide Football League Division 1
Bolton W v Watford
Burnley v Nottingham F
Gillingham v Birmingham C
Grimsby T v Crystal Palace
Huddersfield T v Crewe Alex
Portsmouth v Norwich C
Preston NE v Fulham
Sheffield W v QPR
Stockport Co v Sheffield U
Tranmere R v Blackburn R
Wimbledon v WBA
Wolverhampton W v Barnsley

Nationwide League Division 2
Brentford v Wigan Ath
Bristol C v Bury
Colchester U v Notts Co
Northampton T v Swindon T
Oldham Ath v Oxford U
Peterborough U v Wrexham
Reading v Cambridge U
Rotherham U v Millwall
Stoke C v Luton T
Swansea C v Bristol R
Walsall v Port Vale
Wycombe W v AFC Bournemouth

Nationwide League Division 3
Brighton & HA v Halifax T
Carlisle U v Lincoln C
Cheltenham T v Barnet
Chesterfield v Leyton Orient
Darlington v Mansfield T
Exeter C v Plymouth Arg
Hartlepool U v Southend U
Kidderminster H v Macclesfield T
Rochdale v Blackpool
Scunthorpe U v Hull C
Torquay U v Cardiff C
York C v Shrewsbury T

Sunday, 3 December 2000
FA Carling Premiership
Chelsea v Manchester C (4.00)

Monday, 4 December 2000
FA Carling Premiership
Sunderland v Everton (8.00)

Saturday, 9 December 2000
FA Carling Premiership
Arsenal v Newcastle U
Bradford C v Tottenham H
Charlton Ath v Manchester U
Chelsea v Derby Co
Liverpool v Ipswich T
Manchester C v Everton
Southampton v Leeds U
Sunderland v Middlesbrough
West Ham U v Aston Villa

Nationwide Football League Division 1
Barnsley v Sheffield U
Birmingham C v Wimbledon
Blackburn R v QPR
Bolton W v Crewe Alex
Crystal Palace v Watford
Huddersfield T v Wolverhampton W
Norwich C v Gillingham
Nottingham F v Portsmouth
Preston NE v Burnley
Sheffield W v Stockport Co
Tranmere R v Grimsby T
WBA v Fulham

Sunday, 10 December 2000
FA Carling Premiership
Coventry C v Leicester C (4.00)

Saturday, 16 December 2000
FA Carling Premiership
Aston Villa v Manchester C
Derby Co v Coventry C
Everton v West Ham U
Ipswich T v Southampton
Leeds U v Sunderland
Leicester C v Charlton Ath
Middlesbrough v Chelsea
Newcastle U v Bradford C

Nationwide Football League Division 1
Crewe Alex v Crystal Palace
Fulham v Tranmere R
Gillingham v Preston NE
Grimsby T v Norwich C
Portsmouth v Huddersfield T
QPR v Nottingham F
Sheffield U v Sheffield W (11.30)
Stockport Co v Barnsley
Watford v WBA
Wimbledon v Bolton W
Wolverhampton W v Birmingham C

Nationwide League Division 2
AFC Bournemouth v Swansea C
Bristol R v Stoke C
Bury v Oldham Ath
Cambridge U v Peterborough U
Luton T v Colchester U
Millwall v Walsall
Notts Co v Reading

Oxford U v Northampton T
Port Vale v Bristol C
Swindon T v Rotherham U
Wigan Ath v Wycombe W
Wrexham v Brentford

Nationwide League Division 3
Barnet v Scunthorpe U
Blackpool v Exeter C
Cardiff C v Cheltenham T
Halifax T v Hartlepool U
Hull C v Torquay U
Leyton Orient v Darlington
Lincoln C v Rochdale
Macclesfield T v Carlisle U
Mansfield T v Brighton & HA
Plymouth Arg v York C
Shrewsbury T v Kidderminster H
Southend U v Chesterfield

Sunday, 17 December 2000

FA Carling Premiership
Manchester U v Liverpool (12.00)

Nationwide Football League Division 1
Burnley v Blackburn R (4.00)

Monday, 18 December 2000

FA Carling Premiership
Tottenham H v Arsenal (8.00)

Friday, 22 December 2000

Nationwide Football League Division 1
Bristol C v Bristol R (7.45)

Saturday, 23 December 2000

FA Carling Premiership
Charlton Ath v Everton
Chelsea v Bradford C
Coventry C v Southampton
Derby Co v Newcastle U
Leeds U v Aston Villa
Leicester C v West Ham U
Liverpool v Arsenal (11.30)
Manchester U v Ipswich T
Sunderland v Manchester C
Tottenham H v Middlesbrough

Nationwide Football League Division 1
Birmingham C v QPR
Burnley v Bolton W
Crewe Alex v Fulham
Crystal Palace v Blackburn R
Norwich C v Barnsley
Portsmouth v Sheffield U
Preston NE v Grimsby T
Sheffield W v Wolverhampton W
Stockport Co v Gillingham
Tranmere R v Wimbledon
Watford v Huddersfield T
WBA v Nottingham F

Nationwide League Division 2
AFC Bournemouth v Millwall
Brentford v Oldham Ath
Bury v Swindon T
Colchester U v Oxford U
Notts Co v Wrexham
Peterborough U v Northampton T
Port Vale v Rotherham U
Reading v Luton T
Walsall v Cambridge U

Wigan Ath v Stoke C
Wycombe W v Swansea C

Nationwide League Division 3
Brighton & HA v Exeter C
Cardiff C v Macclesfield T
Darlington v Lincoln C
Halifax T v Plymouth Arg
Hartlepool U v Barnet
Hull C v Kidderminster H
Leyton Orient v Rochdale
Mansfield T v Carlisle U
Scunthorpe U v Cheltenham T
Shrewsbury T v Southend U
Torquay U v Chesterfield
York C v Blackpool

Tuesday, 26 December 2000

FA Carling Premiership
Arsenal v Leicester C
Aston Villa v Manchester U (1.00)
Bradford C v Sunderland
Everton v Coventry C
Ipswich T v Chelsea
Manchester C v Derby Co
Middlesbrough v Liverpool
Newcastle U v Leeds U
West Ham U v Charlton Ath

Nationwide Football League Division 1
Barnsley v Burnley
Blackburn R v Birmingham C
Bolton W v Sheffield W
Fulham v Watford
Gillingham v Crystal Palace
Grimsby T v Stockport Co
Huddersfield T v Tranmere R
Nottingham F v Crewe Alex
QPR v Norwich C
Sheffield U v WBA
Wimbledon v Portsmouth
Wolverhampton W v Preston NE

Nationwide League Division 2
Bristol R v Reading
Cambridge U v Wycombe W
Luton T v Peterborough U
Millwall v Colchester U
Northampton T v Bristol C
Oldham Ath v Wigan Ath
Oxford U v AFC Bournemouth
Rotherham U v Notts Co
Stoke C v Bury
Swansea C v Walsall
Swindon T v Brentford
Wrexham v Port Vale

Nationwide League Division 3
Barnet v Brighton & HA
Blackpool v Halifax T
Carlisle U v Hartlepool U
Cheltenham T v Shrewsbury T
Chesterfield v Darlington
Exeter C v Torquay U
Kidderminster H v Mansfield T
Lincoln C v Scunthorpe U
Macclesfield T v York C
Plymouth Arg v Cardiff C
Rochdale v Hull C
Southend U v Leyton Orient

Wednesday, 27 December 2000

FA Carling Premiership
Southampton v Tottenham H (8.00)

Saturday, 30 December 2000

FA Carling Premiership
Arsenal v Sunderland
Aston Villa v Leicester C
Bradford C v Liverpool
Everton v Leeds U
Ipswich T v Tottenham H
Manchester C v Charlton Ath
Middlesbrough v Coventry C
Newcastle U v Manchester U
Southampton v Derby Co
West Ham U v Chelsea

Nationwide Football League Division 1
Barnsley v Watford
Blackburn R v Crewe Alex
Bolton W v WBA
Fulham v Birmingham C
Gillingham v Tranmere R
Grimsby T v Portsmouth
Huddersfield T v Sheffield W
Nottingham F v Norwich C
QPR v Crystal Palace
Sheffield U v Preston NE
Wimbledon v Burnley
Wolverhampton W v Stockport Co

Nationwide League Division 2
Bristol R v Peterborough U
Cambridge U v AFC Bournemouth
Luton T v Wigan Ath
Millwall v Notts Co
Northampton T v Wycombe W
Oldham Ath v Walsall
Oxford U v Port Vale
Rotherham U v Colchester U
Stoke C v Bristol C
Swansea C v Brentford
Swindon T v Reading
Wrexham v Bury

Nationwide League Division 3
Barnet v Mansfield T
Blackpool v Cardiff C
Carlisle U v Leyton Orient
Cheltenham T v York C
Chesterfield v Hartlepool U
Exeter C v Darlington
Kidderminster H v Scunthorpe U
Lincoln C v Halifax T
Macclesfield T v Shrewsbury T
Plymouth Arg v Hull C
Rochdale v Brighton & HA
Southend U v Torquay U

Monday, 1 January 2001

FA Carling Premiership
Charlton Ath v Arsenal
Chelsea v Aston Villa
Coventry C v Manchester C
Derby Co v Everton
Leeds U v Middlesbrough
Leicester C v Bradford C
Liverpool v Southampton
Manchester U v West Ham U
Sunderland v Ipswich T
Tottenham H v Newcastle U

Nationwide Football League Division 1
Birmingham C v Nottingham F
Burnley v Wolverhampton W
Crewe Alex v QPR
Crystal Palace v Huddersfield T
Norwich C v Blackburn R
Portsmouth v Gillingham
Preston NE v Bolton W
Sheffield W v Grimsby T
Stockport Co v Fulham
Tranmere R v Sheffield U
Watford v Wimbledon
WBA v Barnsley

Nationwide League Division 2
AFC Bournemouth v Luton T
Brentford v Oxford U
Bristol C v Cambridge U
Bury v Rotherham U
Colchester U v Swansea C
Notts Co v Stoke C
Peterborough U v Oldham Ath
Port Vale v Bristol R
Reading v Northampton T
Walsall v Swindon T
Wigan Ath v Wrexham
Wycombe W v Millwall

Nationwide League Division 3
Brighton & HA v Southend U
Cardiff C v Exeter C
Darlington v Rochdale
Halifax T v Carlisle U
Hartlepool U v Lincoln C
Hull C v Blackpool
Leyton Orient v Plymouth Arg
Mansfield T v Cheltenham T
Scunthorpe U v Macclesfield T
Shrewsbury T v Barnet
Torquay U v Kidderminster H
York C v Chesterfield

Saturday, 6 January 2001

Nationwide Football League Division 2
AFC Bournemouth v Bristol R
Brentford v Northampton T
Bristol C v Wrexham
Bury v Cambridge U
Colchester U v Swindon T
Notts Co v Luton T
Peterborough U v Oxford U
Port Vale v Oldham Ath
Reading v Millwall
Walsall v Rotherham U
Wigan Ath v Swansea C
Wycombe W v Stoke C

Nationwide League Division 3
Brighton & HA v Lincoln C
Cardiff C v Barnet
Darlington v Southend U
Halifax T v Kidderminster H
Hartlepool U v Exeter C
Hull C v Macclesfield T
Leyton Orient v Blackpool
Mansfield T v Plymouth Arg

Scunthorpe U v Rochdale
Shrewsbury T v Chesterfield
Torquay U v Cheltenham T
York C v Carlisle U

Saturday, 13 January 2001

FA Carling Premiership
Arsenal v Chelsea
Aston Villa v Liverpool
Bradford C v Manchester U
Everton v Tottenham H
Ipswich T v Leicester C
Manchester C v Leeds U
Middlesbrough v Derby Co
Newcastle U v Coventry C
Southampton v Charlton Ath
West Ham U v Sunderland

Nationwide Football League Division 1
Barnsley v Birmingham C
Blackburn R v Sheffield W
Bolton W v Tranmere R
Fulham v Norwich C
Gillingham v Burnley
Grimsby T v Crewe Alex
Huddersfield T v Stockport Co
Nottingham F v Crystal Palace
QPR v WBA
Sheffield U v Watford
Wimbledon v Preston NE
Wolverhampton W v Portsmouth

Nationwide League Division 2
Bristol R v Brentford
Cambridge U v Notts Co
Luton T v Wycombe W
Millwall v Wigan Ath
Northampton T v Bury
Oldham Ath v Colchester U
Oxford U v Walsall
Rotherham U v Bristol C
Stoke C v Reading
Swansea C v Peterborough U
Swindon T v Port Vale
Wrexham v AFC Bournemouth

Nationwide League Division 3
Barnet v York C
Blackpool v Torquay U
Carlisle U v Shrewsbury T
Cheltenham T v Hartlepool U
Chesterfield v Scunthorpe U
Exeter C v Leyton Orient
Kidderminster H v Brighton & HA
Lincoln C v Hull C
Macclesfield T v Mansfield T
Plymouth Arg v Darlington
Rochdale v Halifax T
Southend U v Cardiff C

Saturday, 20 January 2001

FA Carling Premiership
Charlton Ath v West Ham U
Chelsea v Ipswich T
Coventry C v Everton
Derby Co v Manchester C
Leeds U v Newcastle U
Leicester C v Arsenal
Liverpool v Middlesbrough
Manchester U v Aston Villa
Sunderland v Bradford C
Tottenham H v Southampton

Nationwide Football League Division 1
Birmingham C v Blackburn R
Burnley v Barnsley
Crewe Alex v Nottingham F
Crystal Palace v Gillingham
Norwich C v QPR
Portsmouth v Wimbledon
Preston NE v Wolverhampton W
Sheffield W v Bolton W
Stockport Co v Grimsby T
Tranmere R v Huddersfield T
Watford v Fulham
WBA v Sheffield U

Nationwide League Division 2
AFC Bournemouth v Oxford U
Brentford v Swindon T
Bristol C v Northampton T
Bury v Stoke C
Colchester U v Millwall
Notts Co v Rotherham U
Peterborough U v Luton T
Port Vale v Wrexham
Reading v Bristol R
Walsall v Swansea C
Wigan Ath v Oldham Ath
Wycombe W v Cambridge U

Nationwide League Division 3
Brighton & HA v Barnet
Cardiff C v Plymouth Arg
Darlington v Chesterfield
Halifax T v Blackpool
Hartlepool U v Carlisle U
Hull C v Rochdale
Leyton Orient v Southend U
Mansfield T v Kidderminster H
Scunthorpe U v Lincoln C
Shrewsbury T v Cheltenham T
Torquay U v Exeter C
York C v Macclesfield T

Saturday, 27 January 2001

Nationwide Football League Division 2
Bristol R v Bristol C
Cambridge U v Walsall
Luton T v Reading
Millwall v AFC Bournemouth
Northampton T v Peterborough U
Oldham Ath v Brentford
Oxford U v Colchester U
Rotherham U v Port Vale
Stoke C v Wigan Ath
Swansea C v Wycombe W
Swindon T v Bury
Wrexham v Notts Co

Nationwide League Division 3
Barnet v Hartlepool U
Blackpool v York C
Carlisle U v Mansfield T
Cheltenham T v Scunthorpe U
Chesterfield v Torquay U
Exeter C v Brighton & HA
Kidderminster H v Hull C
Lincoln C v Darlington
Macclesfield T v Cardiff C

Plymouth Arg v Halifax T
Rochdale v Leyton Orient
Southend U v Shrewsbury T

Tuesday, 30 January 2001

FA Carling Premiership
Arsenal v Bradford C
Charlton Ath v Derby Co
Leeds U v Coventry C
Sunderland v Manchester U

Wednesday, 31 January 2001

FA Carling Premiership
Aston Villa v Ipswich T
Chelsea v Newcastle U
Everton v Middlesbrough
Manchester C v Liverpool
Southampton v Leicester C
West Ham U v Tottenham H

Saturday, 3 February 2001

FA Carling Premiership
Bradford C v Aston Villa
Coventry C v Arsenal
Derby Co v Sunderland
Ipswich T v Leeds U
Leicester C v Chelsea
Liverpool v West Ham U
Manchester U v Everton
Middlesbrough v Manchester C
Newcastle U v Southampton
Tottenham H v Charlton Ath

Nationwide Football League Division 1
Birmingham C v Norwich C
Blackburn R v Barnsley
Crewe Alex v Burnley
Crystal Palace v WBA
Fulham v Sheffield U
Grimsby T v Wimbledon
Huddersfield T v Nottingham F
Portsmouth v Preston NE
QPR v Bolton W
Sheffield W v Watford
Stockport Co v Tranmere R
Wolverhampton W v Gillingham

Nationwide League Division 2
AFC Bournemouth v Colchester U
Bristol C v Swansea C
Bury v Peterborough U
Cambridge U v Oxford U
Luton T v Rotherham U
Millwall v Bristol R
Notts Co v Oldham Ath
Reading v Port Vale
Stoke C v Northampton T
Wigan Ath v Walsall
Wrexham v Swindon T
Wycombe W v Brentford

Nationwide League Division 3
Barnet v Chesterfield
Blackpool v Scunthorpe U
Cardiff C v Rochdale
Carlisle U v Kidderminster H
Cheltenham T v Hull C
Leyton Orient v Halifax T
Macclesfield T v Plymouth Arg
Mansfield T v Exeter C
Shrewsbury T v Hartlepool U
Southend U v Lincoln C
Torquay U v Brighton & HA
York C v Darlington

Saturday, 10 February 2001

FA Carling Premiership
Arsenal v Ipswich T
Aston Villa v Middlesbrough
Charlton Ath v Newcastle U
Chelsea v Manchester U
Everton v Leicester C
Leeds U v Derby Co
Manchester C v Tottenham H
Southampton v Bradford C
Sunderland v Liverpool
West Ham U v Coventry C

Nationwide Football League Division 1
Barnsley v Fulham
Bolton W v Huddersfield T
Burnley v Crystal Palace
Gillingham v Grimsby T
Norwich C v Crewe Alex
Nottingham F v Blackburn R
Preston NE v QPR
Sheffield U v Birmingham C
Tranmere R v Wolverhampton W
Watford v Portsmouth
WBA v Stockport Co
Wimbledon v Sheffield W

Nationwide League Division 2
Brentford v Reading
Bristol R v Notts Co
Colchester U v Wigan Ath
Northampton T v Luton T
Oldham Ath v Wrexham
Oxford U v Wycombe W
Peterborough U v Stoke C
Port Vale v AFC Bournemouth
Rotherham U v Cambridge U
Swansea C v Millwall
Swindon T v Bristol C
Walsall v Bury

Nationwide League Division 3
Brighton & HA v Cardiff C
Chesterfield v Cheltenham T
Darlington v Shrewsbury T
Exeter C v Macclesfield T
Halifax T v Mansfield T
Hartlepool U v Blackpool
Hull C v Leyton Orient
Kidderminster H v Barnet
Lincoln C v Torquay U
Plymouth Arg v Southend U
Rochdale v Carlisle U
Scunthorpe U v York C

Saturday, 17 February 2001

Nationwide Football League Division 1
Birmingham C v WBA
Blackburn R v Sheffield U
Crewe Alex v Watford
Crystal Palace v Norwich C
Fulham v Nottingham F
Grimsby T v Burnley
Huddersfield T v Gillingham
Portsmouth v Bolton W

QPR v Barnsley
Sheffield W v Tranmere R
Stockport Co v Preston NE
Wolverhampton W v Wimbledon

Nationwide League Division 2
AFC Bournemouth v Walsall
Bristol C v Oldham Ath
Bury v Oxford U
Cambridge U v Swindon T
Luton T v Swansea C
Millwall v Brentford
Notts Co v Northampton T
Reading v Peterborough U
Stoke C v Port Vale
Wigan Ath v Bristol R
Wrexham v Colchester U
Wycombe W v Rotherham U

Nationwide League Division 3
Barnet v Darlington
Blackpool v Lincoln C
Cardiff C v Scunthorpe U
Carlisle U v Plymouth Arg
Cheltenham T v Brighton & HA
Leyton Orient v Kidderminster H
Macclesfield T v Hartlepool U
Mansfield T v Chesterfield
Shrewsbury T v Hull C
Southend U v Halifax T
Torquay U v Rochdale
York C v Exeter C

Tuesday, 20 February 2001
Nationwide Football League Division 1
Barnsley v Crystal Palace
Bolton W v Grimsby T
Burnley v Fulham
Gillingham v QPR
Norwich C v Stockport Co
Preston NE v Birmingham C
Sheffield U v Wolverhampton W
Tranmere R v Portsmouth
Watford v Blackburn R
WBA v Crewe Alex
Wimbledon v Huddersfield T

Nationwide League Division 2
Brentford v Bristol C
Bristol R v Wycombe W
Colchester U v Bury
Northampton T v Millwall
Oldham Ath v Reading
Oxford U v Stoke C
Peterborough U v Wigan Ath
Port Vale v Cambridge U
Rotherham U v Wrexham
Swansea C v Notts Co
Swindon T v AFC Bournemouth
Walsall v Luton T

Nationwide League Division 3
Brighton & HA v Blackpool
Chesterfield v Carlisle U
Darlington v Cheltenham T
Exeter C v Barnet
Halifax T v Cardiff C
Hartlepool U v Torquay U
Hull C v Mansfield T
Kidderminster H v Southend U
Lincoln C v Macclesfield T
Plymouth Arg v Shrewsbury T
Rochdale v York C
Scunthorpe U v Leyton Orient

Wednesday, 21 February 2001
Nationwide Football League Division 1
Nottingham F v Sheffield W

Saturday, 24 February 2001
FA Carling Premiership
Bradford C v West Ham U
Coventry C v Charlton Ath
Derby Co v Aston Villa
Ipswich T v Everton
Leicester C v Sunderland
Liverpool v Chelsea
Manchester U v Arsenal
Middlesbrough v Southampton
Newcastle U v Manchester C
Tottenham H v Leeds U

Nationwide Football League Division 1
Barnsley v Crewe Alex
Bolton W v Blackburn R
Burnley v Huddersfield T
Gillingham v Fulham
Norwich C v Wolverhampton W
Nottingham F v Grimsby T
Preston NE v Sheffield W
Sheffield U v Crystal Palace
Tranmere R v Birmingham C
Watford v Stockport Co
WBA v Portsmouth
Wimbledon v QPR

Nationwide League Division 2
Brentford v Notts Co
Bristol R v Cambridge U
Colchester U v Bristol C
Northampton T v Wigan Ath
Oldham Ath v AFC Bournemouth
Oxford U v Millwall
Peterborough U v Wycombe W
Port Vale v Bury
Rotherham U v Stoke C
Swansea C v Reading
Swindon T v Luton T
Walsall v Wrexham

Nationwide League Division 3
Brighton & HA v York C
Chesterfield v Blackpool
Darlington v Macclesfield T
Exeter C v Carlisle U
Halifax T v Torquay U
Hartlepool U v Mansfield T
Hull C v Barnet
Kidderminster H v Cardiff C
Lincoln C v Leyton Orient
Plymouth Arg v Cheltenham T
Rochdale v Shrewsbury T
Scunthorpe U v Southend U

Saturday, 3 March 2001
FA Carling Premiership
Arsenal v West Ham U
Coventry C v Chelsea
Derby Co v Tottenham H
Everton v Newcastle U

Ipswich T v Bradford C
Leeds U v Manchester U
Leicester C v Liverpool
Manchester C v Southampton
Middlesbrough v Charlton Ath
Sunderland v Aston Villa

Nationwide Football League Division 1
Birmingham C v Watford
Blackburn R v WBA
Crewe Alex v Tranmere R
Crystal Palace v Preston NE
Fulham v Bolton W
Grimsby T v Barnsley
Huddersfield T v Norwich C
Portsmouth v Burnley
QPR v Sheffield U
Sheffield W v Gillingham
Stockport Co v Wimbledon
Wolverhampton W v Nottingham F

Nationwide League Division 2
AFC Bournemouth v Brentford
Bristol C v Oxford U
Bury v Swansea C
Cambridge U v Oldham Ath
Luton T v Bristol R
Millwall v Peterborough U
Notts Co v Walsall
Reading v Rotherham U
Stoke C v Colchester U
Wigan Ath v Swindon T
Wrexham v Northampton T
Wycombe W v Port Vale

Nationwide League Division 3
Barnet v Plymouth Arg
Blackpool v Kidderminster H
Cardiff C v Hull C
Carlisle U v Darlington
Cheltenham T v Exeter C
Leyton Orient v Brighton & HA
Macclesfield T v Chesterfield
Mansfield T v Lincoln C
Shrewsbury T v Halifax T
Southend U v Rochdale
Torquay U v Scunthorpe U
York C v Hartlepool U

Tuesday, 6 March 2001

Nationwide Football League Division 1
Crewe Alex v Sheffield U
Crystal Palace v Birmingham C
Gillingham v Wimbledon
Huddersfield T v Grimsby T
Norwich C v WBA
Stockport Co v Burnley
Tranmere R v Preston NE
Wolverhampton W v Bolton W

Nationwide League Division 2
Bristol C v Walsall
Bury v Millwall
Colchester U v Port Vale
Luton T v Cambridge U
Northampton T v Bristol R
Peterborough U v Brentford
Rotherham U v AFC Bournemouth
Swindon T v Oldham Ath
Wigan Ath v Notts Co
Wrexham v Oxford U
Wycombe W v Reading

Nationwide League Division 3
Barnet v Carlisle U
Blackpool v Plymouth Arg
Cardiff C v Leyton Orient
Cheltenham T v Macclesfield T
Chesterfield v Exeter C
Hartlepool U v Rochdale
Hull C v Halifax T
Kidderminster H v Lincoln C
Scunthorpe U v Brighton & HA
Shrewsbury T v Mansfield T
Torquay U v Darlington
York C v Southend U

Wednesday, 7 March 2001

Nationwide Football League Division 1
Blackburn R v Fulham
Nottingham F v Barnsley
QPR v Watford
Sheffield W v Portsmouth

Nationwide League Division 2
Stoke C v Swansea C

Saturday, 10 March 2001

Nationwide Football League Division 1
Barnsley v Huddersfield T
Birmingham C v Crewe Alex
Bolton W v Gillingham
Burnley v Tranmere R
Fulham v QPR
Grimsby T v Wolverhampton W
Portsmouth v Stockport Co
Preston NE v Blackburn R
Sheffield U v Nottingham F
Watford v Norwich C
WBA v Sheffield W
Wimbledon v Crystal Palace

Nationwide League Division 2
AFC Bournemouth v Bristol C
Brentford v Stoke C
Bristol R v Bury
Cambridge U v Wrexham
Millwall v Luton T
Notts Co v Wycombe W
Oldham Ath v Rotherham U
Oxford U v Swindon T
Port Vale v Peterborough U
Reading v Wigan Ath
Swansea C v Northampton T
Walsall v Colchester U

Nationwide League Division 3
Brighton & HA v Hull C
Carlisle U v Cheltenham T
Darlington v Hartlepool U
Exeter C v Shrewsbury T
Halifax T v Scunthorpe U
Leyton Orient v Torquay U
Lincoln C v Cardiff C
Macclesfield T v Barnet
Mansfield T v York C
Plymouth Arg v Chesterfield
Rochdale v Kidderminster H
Southend U v Blackpool

Saturday, 17 March 2001

FA Carling Premiership

Aston Villa v Arsenal
Bradford C v Manchester C
Charlton Ath v Leeds U
Chelsea v Sunderland
Liverpool v Derby Co
Manchester U v Leicester C
Newcastle U v Middlesbrough
Southampton v Everton
Tottenham H v Coventry C
West Ham U v Ipswich T

Nationwide Football League Division 1

Blackburn R v Wimbledon
Crewe Alex v Portsmouth
Crystal Palace v Fulham
Gillingham v Watford
Huddersfield T v Sheffield U
Norwich C v Preston NE
Nottingham F v Bolton W
QPR v Grimsby T
Sheffield W v Burnley
Stockport Co v Birmingham C
Tranmere R v Barnsley
Wolverhampton W v WBA

Nationwide League Division 2

Bristol C v Millwall
Bury v Notts Co
Colchester U v Brentford
Luton T v Oxford U
Northampton T v Port Vale
Peterborough U v Walsall
Rotherham U v Bristol R
Stoke C v Cambridge U
Swindon T v Swansea C
Wigan Ath v AFC Bournemouth
Wrexham v Reading
Wycombe W v Oldham Ath

Nationwide League Division 3

Barnet v Southend U
Blackpool v Mansfield T
Cardiff C v Carlisle U
Cheltenham T v Halifax T
Chesterfield v Rochdale
Hartlepool U v Brighton & HA
Hull C v Exeter C
Kidderminster H v Darlington
Scunthorpe U v Plymouth Arg
Shrewsbury T v Leyton Orient
Torquay U v Macclesfield T
York C v Lincoln C

Saturday, 24 March 2001

Nationwide Football League Division 1

Barnsley v Gillingham
Birmingham C v Sheffield W
Bolton W v Stockport Co
Burnley v QPR
Fulham v Wolverhampton W
Grimsby T v Blackburn R
Portsmouth v Crystal Palace
Preston NE v Huddersfield T
Sheffield U v Norwich C
Watford v Nottingham F
WBA v Tranmere R
Wimbledon v Crewe Alex

Nationwide League Division 2

AFC Bournemouth v Bury
Brentford v Luton T
Bristol R v Swindon T
Cambridge U v Colchester U
Millwall v Stoke C
Notts Co v Peterborough U
Oldham Ath v Northampton T
Oxford U v Rotherham U
Port Vale v Wigan Ath
Reading v Bristol C
Swansea C v Wrexham
Walsall v Wycombe W

Nationwide League Division 3

Brighton & HA v Chesterfield
Carlisle U v Torquay U
Darlington v Scunthorpe U
Exeter C v Kidderminster H
Halifax T v Barnet
Leyton Orient v York C
Lincoln C v Shrewsbury T
Macclesfield T v Blackpool
Mansfield T v Cardiff C
Plymouth Arg v Hartlepool U
Rochdale v Cheltenham T
Southend U v Hull C

Saturday, 31 March 2001

FA Carling Premiership

Arsenal v Tottenham H
Bradford C v Newcastle U
Charlton Ath v Leicester C
Chelsea v Middlesbrough
Coventry C v Derby Co
Liverpool v Manchester U
Manchester C v Aston Villa
Southampton v Ipswich T
Sunderland v Leeds U
West Ham U v Everton

Nationwide Football League Division 1

Barnsley v Stockport Co
Birmingham C v Wolverhampton W
Blackburn R v Burnley
Bolton W v Wimbledon
Crystal Palace v Crewe Alex
Huddersfield T v Portsmouth
Norwich C v Grimsby T
Nottingham F v QPR
Preston NE v Gillingham
Sheffield W v Sheffield U
Tranmere R v Fulham
WBA v Watford

Nationwide League Division 2

Brentford v Wrexham
Bristol C v Port Vale
Colchester U v Luton T
Northampton T v Oxford U
Oldham Ath v Bury
Peterborough U v Cambridge U
Reading v Notts Co
Rotherham U v Swindon T
Stoke C v Bristol R
Swansea C v AFC Bournemouth
Walsall v Millwall
Wycombe W v Wigan Ath

Nationwide League Division 3
Brighton & HA v Mansfield T
Carlisle U v Macclesfield T
Cheltenham T v Cardiff C
Chesterfield v Southend U
Darlington v Leyton Orient
Exeter C v Blackpool
Hartlepool U v Halifax T
Kidderminster H v Shrewsbury T
Rochdale v Lincoln C
Scunthorpe U v Barnet
Torquay U v Hull C
York C v Plymouth Arg

Saturday, 7 April 2001

FA Carling Premiership
Aston Villa v West Ham U
Derby Co v Chelsea
Everton v Manchester C
Ipswich T v Liverpool
Leeds U v Southampton
Leicester C v Coventry C
Manchester U v Charlton Ath
Middlesbrough v Sunderland
Newcastle U v Arsenal
Tottenham H v Bradford C

Nationwide Football League Division 1
Burnley v Preston NE
Crewe Alex v Bolton W
Fulham v WBA
Gillingham v Norwich C
Grimsby T v Tranmere R
Portsmouth v Nottingham F
QPR v Blackburn R
Sheffield U v Barnsley
Stockport Co v Sheffield W
Watford v Crystal Palace
Wimbledon v Birmingham C
Wolverhampton W v Huddersfield T

Nationwide League Division 2
AFC Bournemouth v Wycombe W
Bristol R v Swansea C
Bury v Bristol C
Cambridge U v Reading
Luton T v Stoke C
Millwall v Rotherham U
Notts Co v Colchester U
Oxford U v Oldham Ath
Port Vale v Walsall
Swindon T v Northampton T
Wigan Ath v Brentford
Wrexham v Peterborough U

Nationwide League Division 3
Barnet v Cheltenham T
Blackpool v Rochdale
Cardiff C v Torquay U
Halifax T v Brighton & HA
Hull C v Scunthorpe U
Leyton Orient v Chesterfield
Lincoln C v Carlisle U
Macclesfield T v Kidderminster H
Mansfield T v Darlington
Plymouth Arg v Exeter C
Shrewsbury T v York C
Southend U v Hartlepool U

Saturday, 14 April 2001

FA Carling Premiership
Arsenal v Middlesbrough
Aston Villa v Everton
Bradford C v Charlton Ath
Chelsea v Southampton
Ipswich T v Newcastle U
Leicester C v Manchester C
Liverpool v Leeds U
Manchester U v Coventry C
Sunderland v Tottenham H
West Ham U v Derby Co

Nationwide Football League Division 1
Bolton W v Birmingham C
Burnley v WBA
Gillingham v Sheffield U
Grimsby T v Watford
Huddersfield T v Fulham
Portsmouth v QPR
Preston NE v Nottingham F
Sheffield W v Crystal Palace
Stockport Co v Blackburn R
Tranmere R v Norwich C
Wimbledon v Barnsley
Wolverhampton W v Crewe Alex

Nationwide League Division 2
Brentford v Port Vale
Bristol R v Colchester U
Luton T v Oldham Ath
Millwall v Swindon T
Northampton T v Cambridge U
Notts Co v AFC Bournemouth
Peterborough U v Bristol C
Reading v Bury
Stoke C v Walsall
Swansea C v Rotherham U
Wigan Ath v Oxford U
Wycombe W v Wrexham

Nationwide League Division 3
Barnet v Leyton Orient
Carlisle U v Blackpool
Cheltenham T v Lincoln C
Chesterfield v Kidderminster H
Darlington v Cardiff C
Exeter C v Southend U
Hartlepool U v Hull C
Macclesfield T v Rochdale
Mansfield T v Torquay U
Plymouth Arg v Brighton & HA
Shrewsbury T v Scunthorpe U
York C v Halifax T

Monday, 16 April 2001

FA Carling Premiership
Charlton Ath v Aston Villa
Coventry C v Sunderland
Derby Co v Leicester C
Everton v Liverpool
Leeds U v Bradford C
Manchester C v Arsenal
Middlesbrough v Ipswich T
Newcastle U v West Ham U
Southampton v Manchester U
Tottenham H v Chelsea

Nationwide Football League Division 1
Barnsley v Preston NE

Birmingham C v Portsmouth
Blackburn R v Huddersfield T
Crewe Alex v Gillingham
Crystal Palace v Bolton W
Fulham v Sheffield W
Norwich C v Burnley
Nottingham F v Stockport Co
QPR v Tranmere R
Sheffield U v Wimbledon
Watford v Wolverhampton W
WBA v Grimsby T

Nationwide League Division 2
AFC Bournemouth v Stoke C
Bristol C v Wycombe W
Bury v Wigan Ath
Cambridge U v Millwall
Colchester U v Peterborough U
Oldham Ath v Bristol R
Oxford U v Reading
Port Vale v Swansea C
Rotherham U v Northampton T
Swindon T v Notts Co
Walsall v Brentford
Wrexham v Luton T

Nationwide League Division 3
Blackpool v Cheltenham T
Brighton & HA v Darlington
Cardiff C v Chesterfield
Halifax T v Macclesfield T
Hull C v York C
Kidderminster H v Plymouth Arg
Leyton Orient v Hartlepool U
Lincoln C v Barnet
Rochdale v Exeter C
Scunthorpe U v Carlisle U
Southend U v Mansfield T
Torquay U v Shrewsbury T

Saturday, 21 April 2001

FA Carling Premiership
Arsenal v Everton
Aston Villa v Southampton
Bradford C v Derby Co
Chelsea v Charlton Ath
Ipswich T v Coventry C
Leicester C v Middlesbrough
Liverpool v Tottenham H
Manchester U v Manchester C
Sunderland v Newcastle U
West Ham U v Leeds U

Nationwide Football League Division 1
Bolton W v Norwich C
Burnley v Birmingham C
Gillingham v WBA
Grimsby T v Sheffield U
Huddersfield T v QPR
Portsmouth v Fulham
Preston NE v Watford
Sheffield W v Barnsley
Stockport Co v Crewe Alex
Tranmere R v Crystal Palace
Wimbledon v Nottingham F
Wolverhampton W v Blackburn R

Nationwide League Division 2
Brentford v Cambridge U
Bristol R v Oxford U
Luton T v Bury
Millwall v Port Vale
Northampton T v Colchester U
Notts Co v Bristol C
Peterborough U v AFC Bournemouth
Reading v Walsall
Stoke C v Wrexham
Swansea C v Oldham Ath
Wigan Ath v Rotherham U
Wycombe W v Swindon T

Nationwide League Division 3
Barnet v Rochdale
Carlisle U v Brighton & HA
Cheltenham T v Kidderminster H
Chesterfield v Lincoln C
Darlington v Hull C
Exeter C v Halifax T
Hartlepool U v Scunthorpe U
Macclesfield T v Southend U
Mansfield T v Leyton Orient
Plymouth Arg v Torquay U
Shrewsbury T v Blackpool
York C v Cardiff C

Saturday, 28 April 2001

FA Carling Premiership
Charlton Ath v Ipswich T
Coventry C v Liverpool
Derby Co v Arsenal
Everton v Bradford C
Leeds U v Chelsea
Manchester C v West Ham U
Middlesbrough v Manchester U
Newcastle U v Leicester C
Southampton v Sunderland
Tottenham H v Aston Villa

Nationwide Football League Division 1
Barnsley v Bolton W
Birmingham C v Grimsby T
Blackburn R v Portsmouth
Crewe Alex v Preston NE
Crystal Palace v Wolverhampton W
Fulham v Wimbledon
Norwich C v Sheffield W
Nottingham F v Gillingham
QPR v Stockport Co
Sheffield U v Burnley
Watford v Tranmere R
WBA v Huddersfield T

Nationwide League Division 2
AFC Bournemouth v Northampton T
Bristol C v Luton T
Bury v Wycombe W
Cambridge U v Wigan Ath
Colchester U v Reading
Oldham Ath v Stoke C
Oxford U v Swansea C
Port Vale v Notts Co
Rotherham U v Brentford
Swindon T v Peterborough U
Walsall v Bristol R
Wrexham v Millwall

Nationwide League Division 3
Blackpool v Barnet
Brighton & HA v Macclesfield T
Cardiff C v Shrewsbury T
Halifax T v Darlington
Hull C v Chesterfield

Kidderminster H v Hartlepool U
Leyton Orient v Cheltenham T
Lincoln C v Plymouth Arg
Rochdale v Mansfield T
Scunthorpe U v Exeter C
Southend U v Carlisle U
Torquay U v York C

Saturday, 5 May 2001

FA Carling Premiership
Arsenal v Leeds U
Aston Villa v Coventry C
Bradford C v Middlesbrough
Chelsea v Everton
Ipswich T v Manchester C
Leicester C v Tottenham H
Liverpool v Newcastle U
Manchester U v Derby Co
Sunderland v Charlton Ath
West Ham U v Southampton

Nationwide Football League Division 2
Brentford v Bury
Bristol R v Wrexham
Luton T v Port Vale
Millwall v Oldham Ath
Northampton T v Walsall
Notts Co v Oxford U
Peterborough U v Rotherham U
Reading v AFC Bournemouth
Stoke C v Swindon T
Swansea C v Cambridge U
Wigan Ath v Bristol C
Wycombe W v Colchester U

Nationwide League Division 3
Barnet v Torquay U
Carlisle U v Hull C
Cheltenham T v Southend U
Chesterfield v Halifax T
Darlington v Blackpool
Exeter C v Lincoln C
Hartlepool U v Cardiff C
Macclesfield T v Leyton Orient
Mansfield T v Scunthorpe U
Plymouth Arg v Rochdale
Shrewsbury T v Brighton & HA
York C v Kidderminster H

Sunday, 6 May 2001

Nationwide Football League Division 1
Bolton W v Sheffield U
Burnley v Watford
Gillingham v Blackburn R
Grimsby T v Fulham
Huddersfield T v Birmingham C
Portsmouth v Barnsley
Preston NE v WBA
Sheffield W v Crewe Alex
Stockport Co v Crystal Palace
Tranmere R v Nottingham F
Wimbledon v Norwich C
Wolverhampton W v QPR

Saturday, 19 May 2001

FA Carling Premiership
Charlton Ath v Liverpool
Coventry C v Bradford C
Derby Co v Ipswich T
Everton v Sunderland
Leeds U v Leicester C
Manchester C v Chelsea
Middlesbrough v West Ham U
Newcastle U v Aston Villa
Southampton v Arsenal
Tottenham H v Manchester U

SCOTTISH LEAGUE FIXTURES 2000–2001

Saturday, 29 July 2000

Scottish Premier League
Dunfermline Ath v Aberdeen
Hearts v Hibernian
Motherwell v Dundee
Rangers v St Johnstone
St Mirren v Kilmarnock

Sunday, 30 July 2000

Scottish Premier League
Dundee U v Celtic

Saturday, 5 August 2000

Scottish Premier League
Aberdeen v St Mirren
Celtic v Motherwell
Dundee v Dunfermline Ath
Hibernian v Dundee U
Kilmarnock v Rangers

Scottish League Division 1
Ayr U v Ross Co
Clyde v Falkirk
Inverness CT v Airdrieonians
Greenock Morton v Livingston
Raith R v Alloa Ath

Scottish League Division 2
Arbroath v Partick T
Queen's Park v Berwick R
Stenhousemuir v Queen of the S
Stirling A v Clydebank
Stranraer v Forfar Ath

Scottish League Division 3
Albion R v East Fife
Brechin C v Elgin
East Stirlingshire v Cowdenbeath
Hamilton A v Dumbarton
Peterhead v Montrose

Sunday, 6 August 2000

Scottish Premier League
St Johnstone v Hearts

Saturday, 12 August 2000

Scottish Premier League
Dundee U v Motherwell
Dunfermline Ath v St Johnstone
Hibernian v Dundee

Scottish League Division 1
Airdrieonians v Raith R
Alloa Ath v Ayr U
Falkirk v Greenock Morton
Livingston v Inverness CT
Ross Co v Clyde

Scottish League Division 2
Berwick R v Arbroath
Clydebank v Stenhousemuir
Forfar Ath v Queen's Park
Partick T v Stranraer
Queen of the S v Stirling A

Scottish League Division 3
Cowdenbeath v Albion R
Dumbarton v Brechin C
East Fife v Peterhead

Elgin v Hamilton A
Montrose v East Stirlingshire

Sunday, 13 August 2000

Scottish Premier League
Aberdeen v Hearts
Celtic v Kilmarnock
St Mirren v Rangers

Tuesday, 15 August 2000

Scottish Premier League
Dundee v Dundee U

Wednesday, 16 August 2000

Scottish Premier League
Hearts v St Mirren
Kilmarnock v Hibernian
Motherwell v Dunfermline Ath
Rangers v Aberdeen
St Johnstone v Celtic

Saturday, 19 August 2000

Scottish Premier League
Aberdeen v Hibernian
Dundee U v St Johnstone
Hearts v Celtic
Kilmarnock v Motherwell
Rangers v Dunfermline Ath
St Mirren v Dundee

Scottish League Division 1
Ayr U v Airdrieonians
Clyde v Livingston
Inverness CT v Falkirk
Greenock Morton v Alloa Ath
Raith R v Ross Co

Scottish League Division 2
Arbroath v Clydebank
Queen's Park v Queen of the S
Stenhousemuir v Partick T
Stirling A v Forfar Ath
Stranraer v Berwick R

Scottish League Division 3
Albion R v Elgin
Brechin C v Cowdenbeath
East Stirlingshire v East Fife
Hamilton A v Montrose
Peterhead v Dumbarton

Saturday, 26 August 2000

Scottish Premier League
Dunfermline Ath v Dundee U
Hibernian v St Mirren
St Johnstone v Kilmarnock

Scottish League Division 1
Alloa Ath v Livingston
Ayr U v Falkirk
Clyde v Greenock Morton
Raith R v Inverness CT
Ross Co v Airdrieonians

Scottish League Division 2
Clydebank v Queen of the S
Forfar Ath v Stenhousemuir
Partick T v Berwick R
Stirling A v Queen's Park
Stranraer v Arbroath

Scottish League Division 3
Albion R v Dumbarton
Cowdenbeath v Elgin
East Stirlingshire v Hamilton A
Montrose v East Fife
Peterhead v Brechin C

Sunday, 27 August 2000

Scottish Premier League
Celtic v Rangers
Dundee v Hearts
Motherwell v Aberdeen

Saturday, 9 September 2000

Scottish Premier League
Aberdeen v St Johnstone
Celtic v Hibernian
Dundee v Rangers
Hearts v Dunfermline Ath
Kilmarnock v Dundee U
St Mirren v Motherwell

Scottish League Division 1
Airdrieonians v Alloa Ath
Falkirk v Raith R
Inverness CT v Clyde
Livingston v Ayr U
Greenock Morton v Ross Co

Scottish League Division 2
Arbroath v Forfar Ath
Berwick R v Clydebank
Queen of the S v Stranraer
Queen's Park v Partick T
Stenhousemuir v Stirling A

Scottish League Division 3
Brechin C v Montrose
Dumbarton v East Stirlingshire
East Fife v Cowdenbeath
Elgin v Peterhead
Hamilton A v Albion R

Saturday, 16 September 2000

Scottish Premier League
Dundee U v St Mirren
Hibernian v Motherwell
Kilmarnock v Aberdeen
Rangers v Hearts
St Johnstone v Dundee

Scottish League Division 1
Clyde v Airdrieonians
Falkirk v Alloa Ath
Inverness CT v Ross Co
Livingston v Raith R
Greenock Morton v Ayr U

Scottish League Division 2
Arbroath v Stenhousemuir
Berwick R v Queen of the S
Forfar Ath v Clydebank
Partick T v Stirling A
Stranraer v Queen's Park

Scottish League Division 3
Albion R v Brechin C
Cowdenbeath v Hamilton A
East Fife v Elgin
Montrose v Dumbarton
Peterhead v East Stirlingshire

Monday, 18 September 2000

Scottish Premier League
Dunfermline Ath v Celtic

Saturday, 23 September 2000

Scottish Premier League
Celtic v Dundee
Dundee U v Aberdeen
Dunfermline Ath v Hibernian
Motherwell v Rangers
St Mirren v St Johnstone

Scottish League Division 1
Airdrieonians v Livingston
Alloa Ath v Inverness CT
Ayr U v Clyde
Raith R v Greenock Morton
Ross Co v Falkirk

Scottish League Division 2
Clydebank v Partick T
Queen of the S v Forfar Ath
Queen's Park v Arbroath
Stenhousemuir v Berwick R
Stirling A v Stranraer

Scottish League Division 3
Brechin C v East Fife
Dumbarton v Cowdenbeath
East Stirlingshire v Albion R
Elgin v Montrose
Hamilton A v Peterhead

Sunday, 24 September 2000

Scottish Premier League
Hearts v Kilmarnock

Saturday, 30 September 2000

Scottish Premier League
Aberdeen v Celtic
Dundee v Kilmarnock
Hearts v Motherwell
St Johnstone v Hibernian
St Mirren v Dunfermline Ath

Scottish League Division 1
Ayr U v Inverness CT
Clyde v Raith R
Falkirk v Livingston
Greenock Morton v Airdrieonians
Ross Co v Alloa Ath

Scottish League Division 2
Arbroath v Queen of the S
Berwick R v Stirling A
Partick T v Forfar Ath
Queen's Park v Stenhousemuir
Stranraer v Clydebank

Scottish League Division 3
Albion R v Peterhead
Brechin C v East Stirlingshire
Cowdenbeath v Montrose
East Fife v Hamilton A
Elgin v Dumbarton

Sunday, 1 October 2000

Scottish Premier League
Rangers v Dundee U

Saturday, 7 October 2000

Scottish League Division 1
Airdrieonians v Falkirk
Alloa Ath v Clyde
Inverness CT v Greenock Morton
Livingston v Ross Co
Raith R v Ayr U

Scottish League Division 2
Clydebank v Queen's Park
Forfar Ath v Berwick R
Queen of the S v Partick T
Stenhousemuir v Stranraer
Stirling A v Arbroath

Scottish League Division 3
Dumbarton v East Fife
East Stirlingshire v Elgin
Hamilton A v Brechin C
Montrose v Albion R
Peterhead v Cowdenbeath

Saturday, 14 October 2000

Scottish Premier League
Aberdeen v Dundee
Celtic v St Mirren
Dundee U v Hearts
Hibernian v Rangers
Kilmarnock v Dunfermline Ath
Motherwell v St Johnstone

Scottish League Division 1
Airdrieonians v Inverness CT
Alloa Ath v Raith R
Falkirk v Clyde
Livingston v Greenock Morton
Ross Co v Ayr U

Scottish League Division 2
Berwick R v Queen's Park
Clydebank v Stirling A
Forfar Ath v Stranraer
Partick T v Arbroath
Queen of the S v Stenhousemuir

Scottish League Division 3
Cowdenbeath v East Stirlingshire
Dumbarton v Hamilton A
East Fife v Albion R
Elgin v Brechin C
Montrose v Peterhead

Saturday, 21 October 2000

Scottish Premier League
Aberdeen v Dunfermline Ath
Celtic v Dundee U
Dundee v Motherwell
Kilmarnock v St Mirren
St Johnstone v Rangers

Scottish League Division 1
Ayr U v Alloa Ath
Clyde v Ross Co
Inverness CT v Livingston
Greenock Morton v Falkirk
Raith R v Airdrieonians

Scottish League Division 2
Arbroath v Berwick R
Queen's Park v Forfar Ath
Stenhousemuir v Clydebank
Stirling A v Queen of the S
Stranraer v Partick T

Scottish League Division 3
Albion R v Cowdenbeath
Brechin C v Dumbarton
East Stirlingshire v Montrose
Hamilton A v Elgin
Peterhead v East Fife

Sunday, 22 October 2000

Scottish Premier League
Hibernian v Hearts

Saturday, 28 October 2000

Scottish Premier League
Dundee U v Hibernian
Dunfermline Ath v Dundee
Hearts v St Johnstone
Rangers v Kilmarnock
St Mirren v Aberdeen

Scottish League Division 1
Airdrieonians v Ross Co
Falkirk v Ayr U
Inverness CT v Raith R
Livingston v Alloa Ath
Greenock Morton v Clyde

Scottish League Division 2
Arbroath v Stranraer
Berwick R v Partick T
Queen of the S v Clydebank
Queen's Park v Stirling A
Stenhousemuir v Forfar Ath

Scottish League Division 3
Brechin C v Peterhead
Dumbarton v Albion R
East Fife v Montrose
Elgin v Cowdenbeath
Hamilton A v East Stirlingshire

Sunday, 29 October 2000

Scottish Premier League
Motherwell v Celtic

Saturday, 4 November 2000

Scottish Premier League
Hearts v Aberdeen
Kilmarnock v Celtic
Motherwell v Dundee U
Rangers v St Mirren
St Johnstone v Dunfermline Ath

Scottish League Division 1
Alloa Ath v Airdrieonians
Ayr U v Livingston
Clyde v Inverness CT
Raith R v Falkirk
Ross Co v Greenock Morton

Scottish League Division 2
Clydebank v Berwick R
Forfar Ath v Arbroath
Partick T v Queen's Park
Stirling A v Stenhousemuir
Stranraer v Queen of the S

Scottish League Division 3
Albion R v Hamilton A
Cowdenbeath v East Fife
East Stirlingshire v Dumbarton
Montrose v Brechin C
Peterhead v Elgin

Sunday, 5 November 2000

Scottish Premier League
Dundee v Hibernian

Saturday, 11 November 2000

Scottish Premier League
Celtic v St Johnstone
Dundee U v Dundee
Dunfermline Ath v Motherwell
Hibernian v Kilmarnock
St Mirren v Hearts

Scottish League Division 1
Clyde v Ayr U
Falkirk v Ross Co
Inverness CT v Alloa Ath
Livingston v Airdrieonians
Greenock Morton v Raith R

Scottish League Division 2
Arbroath v Queen's Park
Berwick R v Stenhousemuir
Forfar Ath v Queen of the S
Partick T v Clydebank
Stranraer v Stirling A

Scottish League Division 3
Albion R v East Stirlingshire
Cowdenbeath v Dumbarton
East Fife v Brechin C
Montrose v Elgin
Peterhead v Hamilton A

Sunday, 12 November 2000

Scottish Premier League
Aberdeen v Rangers

Saturday, 18 November 2000

Scottish Premier League
Celtic v Hearts
Dundee v St Mirren
Dunfermline Ath v Rangers
Hibernian v Aberdeen
Motherwell v Kilmarnock
St Johnstone v Dundee U

Scottish League Division 1
Airdrieonians v Clyde
Alloa Ath v Falkirk
Ayr U v Greenock Morton
Raith R v Livingston
Ross Co v Inverness CT

Scottish League Division 2
Clydebank v Forfar Ath
Queen of the S v Berwick R
Queen's Park v Stranraer
Stenhousemuir v Arbroath
Stirling A v Partick T

Scottish League Division 3
Brechin C v Albion R
Dumbarton v Montrose
East Stirlingshire v Peterhead
Elgin v East Fife
Hamilton A v Cowdenbeath

Saturday, 25 November 2000
Scottish Premier League
Aberdeen v Motherwell
Dundee U v Dunfermline Ath
Hearts v Dundee
Kilmarnock v St Johnstone
St Mirren v Hibernian

Scottish League Division 1
Ayr U v Raith R
Clyde v Alloa Ath
Falkirk v Airdrieonians
Greenock Morton v Inverness CT
Ross Co v Livingston

Scottish League Division 2
Arbroath v Stirling A
Berwick R v Forfar Ath
Partick T v Queen of the S
Queen's Park v Clydebank
Stranraer v Stenhousemuir

Scottish League Division 3
Albion R v Montrose
Brechin C v Hamilton A
Cowdenbeath v Peterhead
East Fife v Dumbarton
Elgin v East Stirlingshire

Sunday, 26 November 2000
Scottish Premier League
Rangers v Celtic

Wednesday, 29 November 2000
Scottish Premier League
Dundee U v Kilmarnock
Dunfermline Ath v Hearts
Hibernian v Celtic
Motherwell v St Mirren
Rangers v Dundee
St Johnstone v Aberdeen

Saturday, 2 December 2000
Scottish Premier League
Aberdeen v Kilmarnock
Celtic v Dunfermline Ath
Dundee v St Johnstone
Hearts v Rangers
Motherwell v Hibernian
St Mirren v Dundee U

Scottish League Division 1
Airdrieonians v Greenock Morton
Alloa Ath v Ross Co
Inverness CT v Ayr U
Livingston v Falkirk
Raith R v Clyde

Scottish League Division 2
Clydebank v Stranraer
Forfar Ath v Partick T
Queen of the S v Arbroath
Stenhousemuir v Queen's Park
Stirling A v Berwick R

Scottish League Division 3
Dumbarton v Elgin
East Stirlingshire v Brechin C
Hamilton A v East Fife
Montrose v Cowdenbeath
Peterhead v Albion R

Saturday, 9 December 2000
Scottish Premier League
Aberdeen v Dundee U
Dundee v Celtic
Hibernian v Dunfermline Ath
Kilmarnock v Hearts
Rangers v Motherwell
St Johnstone v St Mirren

Scottish League Division 1
Airdrieonians v Ayr U
Alloa Ath v Greenock Morton
Falkirk v Inverness CT
Livingston v Clyde
Ross Co v Raith R

Saturday, 16 December 2000
Scottish Premier League
Celtic v Aberdeen
Dundee U v Rangers
Dunfermline Ath v St Mirren
Hibernian v St Johnstone
Kilmarnock v Dundee
Motherwell v Hearts

Scottish League Division 1
Ayr U v Ross Co
Clyde v Falkirk
Inverness CT v Airdrieonians
Greenock Morton v Livingston
Raith R v Alloa Ath

Scottish League Division 2
Arbroath v Partick T
Queen's Park v Berwick R
Stenhousemuir v Queen of the S
Stirling A v Clydebank
Stranraer v Forfar Ath

Scottish League Division 3
Albion R v East Fife
Brechin C v Elgin
East Stirlingshire v Cowdenbeath
Hamilton A v Dumbarton
Peterhead v Montrose

Saturday, 23 December 2000
Scottish Premier League
Dundee v Aberdeen
Dunfermline Ath v Kilmarnock
Hearts v Dundee U
Rangers v Hibernian
St Johnstone v Motherwell
St Mirren v Celtic

Tuesday, 26 December 2000
Scottish Premier League
Dundee U v Celtic
Dunfermline Ath v Aberdeen
Hearts v Hibernian
Motherwell v Dundee
Rangers v St Johnstone
St Mirren v Kilmarnock

Scottish League Division 1
Airdrieonians v Alloa Ath
Falkirk v Raith R
Inverness CT v Clyde
Livingston v Ayr U
Greenock Morton v Ross Co

Scottish League Division 2
Berwick R v Stranraer
Clydebank v Arbroath
Forfar Ath v Stirling A
Partick T v Stenhousemuir
Queen of the S v Queen's Park

Scottish League Division 3
Cowdenbeath v Brechin C
Dumbarton v Peterhead
East Fife v East Stirlingshire
Elgin v Albion R
Montrose v Hamilton A

Saturday, 30 December 2000
Scottish Premier League
Aberdeen v St Mirren
Celtic v Motherwell
Dundee v Dunfermline Ath
Hibernian v Dundee U
Kilmarnock v Rangers
St Johnstone v Hearts

Scottish League Division 1
Alloa Ath v Livingston
Ayr U v Falkirk
Clyde v Greenock Morton
Raith R v Inverness CT
Ross Co v Airdrieonians

Scottish League Division 2
Clydebank v Queen of the S
Forfar Ath v Stenhousemuir
Partick T v Berwick R
Stirling A v Queen's Park
Stranraer v Arbroath

Scottish League Division 3
Albion R v Dumbarton
Cowdenbeath v Elgin
East Stirlingshire v Hamilton A
Montrose v East Fife
Peterhead v Brechin C

Tuesday, 2 January 2001
Scottish Premier League
Aberdeen v Hearts
Celtic v Kilmarnock
Dundee U v Motherwell
Dunfermline Ath v St Johnstone
Hibernian v Dundee
St Mirren v Rangers

Scottish League Division 1
Clyde v Airdrieonians
Falkirk v Alloa Ath
Inverness CT v Ross Co
Livingston v Raith R
Greenock Morton v Ayr U

Scottish League Division 2
Arbroath v Forfar Ath
Berwick R v Clydebank
Queen of the S v Stranraer
Queen's Park v Partick T
Stenhousemuir v Stirling A

Scottish League Division 3
Brechin C v Montrose
Dumbarton v East Stirlingshire
East Fife v Cowdenbeath
Elgin v Peterhead
Hamilton A v Albion R

Saturday, 6 January 2001

Scottish League Division 1
Airdrieonians v Livingston
Alloa Ath v Inverness CT
Ayr U v Clyde
Raith R v Greenock Morton
Ross Co v Falkirk

Saturday, 13 January 2001

Scottish League Division 1
Ayr U v Inverness CT
Clyde v Raith R
Falkirk v Livingston
Greenock Morton v Airdrieonians
Ross Co v Alloa Ath

Scottish League Division 2
Arbroath v Stenhousemuir
Berwick R v Queen of the S
Forfar Ath v Clydebank
Partick T v Stirling A
Stranraer v Queen's Park

Scottish League Division 3
Albion R v Brechin C
Cowdenbeath v Hamilton A
East Fife v Elgin
Montrose v Dumbarton
Peterhead v East Stirlingshire

Saturday, 20 January 2001

Scottish League Division 1
Airdrieonians v Falkirk
Alloa Ath v Clyde
Inverness CT v Greenock Morton
Livingston v Ross Co
Raith R v Ayr U

Scottish League Division 2
Clydebank v Partick T
Queen of the S v Forfar Ath
Queen's Park v Arbroath
Stenhousemuir v Berwick R
Stirling A v Stranraer

Scottish League Division 3
Brechin C v East Fife
Dumbarton v Cowdenbeath
East Stirlingshire v Albion R
Elgin v Montrose
Hamilton A v Peterhead

Wednesday, 31 January 2001

Scottish Premier League
Dundee v Dundee U
Hearts v St Mirren
Kilmarnock v Hibernian
Motherwell v Dunfermline Ath
Rangers v Aberdeen
St Johnstone v Celtic

Saturday, 3 February 2001

Scottish Premier League
Aberdeen v Hibernian
Dundee U v St Johnstone
Hearts v Celtic
Kilmarnock v Motherwell
Rangers v Dunfermline Ath
St Mirren v Dundee

Scottish League Division 1
Ayr U v Airdrieonians
Clyde v Livingston
Inverness CT v Falkirk
Greenock Morton v Alloa Ath
Raith R v Ross Co

Scottish League Division 2
Clydebank v Queen's Park
Forfar Ath v Berwick R
Queen of the S v Partick T
Stenhousemuir v Stranraer
Stirling A v Arbroath

Scottish League Division 3
Dumbarton v East Fife
East Stirlingshire v Elgin
Hamilton A v Brechin C
Montrose v Albion R
Peterhead v Cowdenbeath

Saturday, 10 February 2001

Scottish Premier League
Celtic v Rangers
Dundee v Hearts
Dunfermline Ath v Dundee U
Hibernian v St Mirren
Motherwell v Aberdeen
St Johnstone v Kilmarnock

Scottish League Division 1
Airdrieonians v Raith R
Alloa Ath v Ayr U
Falkirk v Greenock Morton
Livingston v Inverness CT
Ross Co v Clyde

Scottish League Division 2
Arbroath v Queen of the S
Berwick R v Stirling A
Partick T v Forfar Ath
Queen's Park v Stenhousemuir
Stranraer v Clydebank

Scottish League Division 3
Albion R v Peterhead
Brechin C v East Stirlingshire
Cowdenbeath v Montrose
East Fife v Hamilton A
Elgin v Dumbarton

Saturday, 17 February 2001

Scottish League Division 2
Arbroath v Clydebank
Queen's Park v Queen of the S
Stenhousemuir v Partick T
Stirling A v Forfar Ath
Stranraer v Berwick R

Scottish League Division 3
Albion R v Elgin
Brechin C v Cowdenbeath
East Stirlingshire v East Fife
Hamilton A v Montrose
Peterhead v Dumbarton

Saturday, 24 February 2001

Scottish Premier League
Aberdeen v St Johnstone
Celtic v Hibernian
Dundee v Rangers
Hearts v Dunfermline Ath
Kilmarnock v Dundee U
St Mirren v Motherwell

Scottish League Division 1
Airdrieonians v Ross Co
Falkirk v Ayr U
Inverness CT v Raith R
Livingston v Alloa Ath
Greenock Morton v Clyde

Scottish League Division 2
Berwick R v Arbroath
Clydebank v Stenhousemuir
Forfar Ath v Queen's Park
Partick T v Stranraer
Queen of the S v Stirling A

Scottish League Division 3
Cowdenbeath v Albion R
Dumbarton v Brechin C
East Fife v Peterhead
Elgin v Hamilton A
Montrose v East Stirlingshire

Saturday, 3 March 2001

Scottish Premier League
Dundee U v St Mirren
Dunfermline Ath v Celtic
Hibernian v Motherwell
Kilmarnock v Aberdeen
Rangers v Hearts
St Johnstone v Dundee

Scottish League Division 1
Alloa Ath v Airdrieonians
Ayr U v Livingston
Clyde v Inverness CT
Raith R v Falkirk
Ross Co v Greenock Morton

Scottish League Division 2
Clydebank v Berwick R
Forfar Ath v Arbroath
Partick T v Queen's Park

Stirling A v Stenhousemuir
Stranraer v Queen of the S

Scottish League Division 3
Albion R v Hamilton A
Cowdenbeath v East Fife
East Stirlingshire v Dumbarton
Montrose v Brechin C
Peterhead v Elgin

Saturday, 10 March 2001
Scottish League Division 2
Arbroath v Stranraer
Berwick R v Partick T
Queen of the S v Clydebank
Queen's Park v Stirling A
Stenhousemuir v Forfar Ath

Scottish League Division 3
Brechin C v Peterhead
Dumbarton v Albion R
East Fife v Montrose
Elgin v Cowdenbeath
Hamilton A v
East Stirlingshire

Saturday, 17 March 2001
Scottish Premier League
Celtic v Dundee
Dundee U v Aberdeen
Dunfermline Ath v Hibernian
Hearts v Kilmarnock
Motherwell v Rangers
St Mirren v St Johnstone

Scottish League Division 1
Clyde v Ayr U
Falkirk v Ross Co
Inverness CT v Alloa Ath
Livingston v Airdrieonians
Greenock Morton v Raith R

Scottish League Division 2
Arbroath v Queen's Park
Berwick R v Stenhousemuir
Forfar Ath v Queen of the S
Partick T v Clydebank
Stranraer v Stirling A

Scottish League Division 3
Albion R v East Stirlingshire
Cowdenbeath v Dumbarton
East Fife v Brechin C
Montrose v Elgin
Peterhead v Hamilton A

Saturday, 31 March 2001
Scottish Premier League
Aberdeen v Celtic
Dundee v Kilmarnock
Hearts v Motherwell
Rangers v Dundee U
St Johnstone v Hibernian
St Mirren v Dunfermline Ath

Scottish League Division 1
Airdrieonians v Clyde
Alloa Ath v Falkirk
Ayr U v Greenock Morton
Raith R v Livingston
Ross Co v Inverness CT

Scottish League Division 2
Clydebank v Forfar Ath
Queen of the S v Berwick R
Queen's Park v Stranraer
Stenhousemuir v Arbroath
Stirling A v Partick T

Scottish League Division 3
Brechin C v Albion R
Dumbarton v Montrose
East Stirlingshire v Peterhead
Elgin v East Fife
Hamilton A v Cowdenbeath

Saturday, 7 April 2001
Scottish Premier League
Aberdeen v Dundee
Celtic v St Mirren
Dundee U v Hearts
Hibernian v Rangers
Kilmarnock v
Dunfermline Ath
Motherwell v St Johnstone

Scottish League Division 1
Ayr U v Raith R
Clyde v Alloa Ath
Falkirk v Airdrieonians
Greenock Morton v
Inverness CT
Ross Co v Livingston

Scottish League Division 2
Arbroath v Stirling A
Berwick R v Forfar Ath
Partick T v Queen of the S
Queen's Park v Clydebank
Stranraer v Stenhousemuir

Scottish League Division 3
Albion R v Montrose
Brechin C v Hamilton A
Cowdenbeath v Peterhead
East Fife v Dumbarton
Elgin v East Stirlingshire

Saturday, 14 April 2001
Scottish League Division 1
Airdrieonians v
Greenock Morton
Alloa Ath v Ross Co
Inverness CT v Ayr U
Livingston v Falkirk
Raith R v Clyde

Scottish League Division 2
Clydebank v Stranraer
Forfar Ath v Partick T
Queen of the S v Arbroath
Stenhousemuir v Queen's Park
Stirling A v Berwick R

Scottish League Division 3
Dumbarton v Elgin
East Stirlingshire v Brechin C
Hamilton A v East Fife
Montrose v Cowdenbeath
Peterhead v Albion R

Saturday, 21 April 2001
Scottish League Division 1
Airdrieonians v Inverness CT
Alloa Ath v Raith R
Falkirk v Clyde
Livingston v Greenock Morton
Ross Co v Ayr U

Scottish League Division 2
Berwick R v Queen's Park
Clydebank v Stirling A
Forfar Ath v Stranraer
Partick T v Arbroath
Queen of the S v
Stenhousemuir

Scottish League Division 3
Cowdenbeath v
East Stirlingshire
Dumbarton v Hamilton A
East Fife v Albion R
Elgin v Brechin C
Montrose v Peterhead

Saturday, 28 April 2001
Scottish League Division 1
Ayr U v Alloa Ath
Clyde v Ross Co
Inverness CT v Livingston
Greenock Morton v Falkirk
Raith R v Airdrieonians

Scottish League Division 2
Arbroath v Berwick R
Queen's Park v Forfar Ath
Stenhousemuir v Clydebank
Stirling A v Queen of the S
Stranraer v Partick T

Scottish League Division 3
Albion R v Cowdenbeath
Brechin C v Dumbarton
East Stirlingshire v Montrose
Hamilton A v Elgin
Peterhead v East Fife

Saturday, 5 May 2001
Scottish League Division 1
Airdrieonians v Ayr U
Alloa Ath v Greenock Morton
Falkirk v Inverness CT
Livingston v Clyde
Ross Co v Raith R

Scottish League Division 2
Berwick R v Stranraer
Clydebank v Arbroath
Forfar Ath v Stirling A
Partick T v Stenhousemuir
Queen of the S v Queen's Park

Scottish League Division 3
Cowdenbeath v Brechin C
Dumbarton v Peterhead
East Fife v East Stirlingshire
Elgin v Albion R
Montrose v Hamilton A

OTHER FIXTURES – SEASON 2000–2001

July 2000

1 Sat UEFA Intertoto Cup 2 (1)
2 Sun Euro 2000 Final
8 Sat UEFA Intertoto Cup 2 (2)
11 Tue U16 Nationwide Tournament – England v Thailand *at York City FC – 7.15pm*
12 Wed UEFA Champions League 1Q (1)
15 Sat UEFA Intertoto Cup 3 (1)
16 Sun U16 Nationwide Tournament – England v Brazil *at Sunderland AFC – 2.30pm*
19 Wed UEFA Champions League 1Q (2)
22 Sat UEFA Intertoto Cup 3 (2)
26 Wed UEFA Champions League 2Q (1)
UEFA Intertoto Cup SF (1)

August 2000

2 Wed UEFA Champions League 2Q (2)
UEFA Intertoto Cup SF (2)
5 Sat
8/9 Tue/Wed UEFA Champions League 3Q (1)
9 Wed UEFA Intertoto Cup Final (1)
10 Thu UEFA Cup Qualifying Round (1)
12 Sat Start of Football League
13 Sun One2One Charity Shield
16 Wed International – Friendly
19 Sat Start of F.A. Premier League
22/23 Tue/Wed UEFA Champions Leagues 3Q (2)
23 Wed UEFA Intertoto Cup Final (2)
Worthington Cup 1 (1)
24 Thu UEFA Cup Qualifying Round (2)
25 Fri UEFA Super Cup
26 Sat F.A. Cup sponsored by AXA Extra Preliminary Round
28 Mon Bank Holiday

September 2000

2 Sat France v England – Friendly International
F.A. Cup sponsored by AXA Preliminary Round
AXA F.A. Youth Cup 1Q*
6 Wed Worthington Cup 1 (2)
9 Sat F.A. Carlsberg Vase 1Q
10 Sun AXA F.A. Women's Cup Extra Preliminary Round
AXA F.A. Premier League Cup Preliminary Round
12/13 Tue/Wed UEFA Champions League – Group 1 – Match Day 1
14 Thu UEFA Cup 1 (1)
16 Sat F.A. Cup sponsored by AXA 1Q
19/20 Tue/Wed UEFA Champions League – Group 1 – Match Day 2
20 Wed Worthington Cup 2 (1)
23 Sat F.A. Carlsberg Vase 2Q
AXA F.A. Youth Cup 2Q*
24 Sun AXA F.A. Women's Cup Preliminary Round
AXA F.A. Women's Premier League Cup 1
26/27 Tue/Wed UEFA Champions League – Group 1 – Match Day 3
27 Wed Worthington Cup 2 (2)
28 Thu UEFA Cup 1 (2)
30 Sat F.A. Cup sponsored by AXA 2Q

October 2000

1 Sun F.A. Umbro Sunday Cup 1
7 Sat England v Germany – FIFA World Cup Qualifier
AXA F.A. Youth Cup 3Q*
F.A. County Youth Cup 1*
11 Wed Finland v England – FIFA World Cup Qualifier
14 Sat F.A. Cup sponsored by AXA 3Q
17/18 Tue/Wed UEFA Champions League – Group 1 – Match Day 4
20 Fri U15 Victory Shield – Northern Ireland v England – venue tbc
21 Sat F.A. Carlsberg Vase 1P
24/25 Tue/Wed UEFA Champions League – Group 1 – Match Day 5
26 Thu UEFA Cup 2 (1)
28 Sat F.A. Cup sponsored by AXA 4Q
AXA F.A. Youth Cup 1P*
29 Sun AXA F.A. Women's Cup 1
AXA F.A. Women's Premier League Cup 2

November 2000

1 Wed Worthington Cup 3
3 Fri U15 Victory Shield – Wales v England – venue tbc
4 Sat F.A. Umbro Trophy 1
5 Sun F.A. Umbro Sunday Cup 2
7/8 Tue/Wed UEFA Champions League – Group 1 – Match Day 6
9 Thu UEFA Cup 2 (2)
11 Sat F.A. Carslberg Vase 2P
AXA F.A. Youth Cup 2P*
F.A. County Youth Cup 2*
12 Sun AXA F.A. Women's Premier League 3
15 Wed International – Friendly
18 Sat F.A. Cup sponsored by AXA 1P
19 Sun AXA F.A. Women's Cup 2
20 Mon F.A. XI v Northern Premier League
21 Tue F.A. XI v Southern League
21/22 Tue/Wed UEFA Champions League – Group 2 – Match Day 1
22 Wed F.A. XI v Isthmian League
23 Thu UEFA Cup 3 (1)
25 Sat
28 Tue Inter-Continental Cup
29 Wed F.A. Cup sponsored by AXA 1P replays
Worthington Cup 4

December 2000

1 Fri U15 Victory Shield – England v Scotland – venue tbc
2 Sat F.A. Umbro Trophy 2
3 Sun F.A. Umbro Sunday Cup 3
5/6 Tue/Wed UEFA Champions League – Group 2 – Match Day 2
7 Thu UEFA Cup 3 (2)
9 Sat F.A. Cup sponsored by AXA 2P
F.A. Carlsberg Vase 3P
AXA F.A. Youth Cup 3P*
10 Sun AXA F.A. Women's Cup 3
13 Wed Worthington Cup 5

16 Sat F.A. County Youth Cup 3
17 Sun AXA F.A. Women's Premier League Cup SF
20 Wed F.A. Cup sponsored by AXA 2P replays
25 Mon Christmas Day
26 Tue Boxing Day
30 Sat

January 2001
1 Mon New Year's Day
6 Sat F.A. Cup sponsored by AXA 3P
7 Sun AXA F.A. Women's Cup 4
8 Mon F.A. XI v British Universities
10 Wed Worthington Cup SF1
13 Sat F.A. Umbro Trophy 3
14 Sun F.A. Umbro Sunday Cup 4
17 Wed F.A. Cup sponsored by AXA 3P replays
20 Sat F.A. Carlsberg Vase 4P
AXA F.A. Youth Cup 4P*
24 Wed Worthington Cup SF2
27 Sat F.A. Cup sponsored by AXA 4P
F.A. County Youth Cup 4*
28 Sun AXA F.A. Women's Cup 5
30 Mon F.A. XI v Combined Services

February 2001
3 Sat F.A. Umbro Trophy 4
4 Sun F.A. Umbro Sunday Cup 5
7 Wed F.A. Cup sponsored by AXA 4P replays
10 Sat F.A. Carslberg Vase 5P
AXA F.A. Youth Cup 5P*
13 Tue England Semi-Professional International
13/14 Tue/Wed UEFA Champions League – Group 2 – Match Day 3
14 Wed International – Friendly
15 Thu UEFA Cup 4 (1)
17 Sat F.A. Cup sponsored by AXA 5P
18 Sun AXA F.A. Women's Cup 6
20/21 Tue/Wed UEFA Champions League – Group 2 – Match Day 4
22 Thu UEFA Cup 4 (2)
24 Sat F.A. Umbro Trophy 5
25 Sun F.A. Umbro Sunday Cup SF
28 Wed F.A. Cup sponsored by AXA 5P replays
International Friendly

March 2001
3 Sat F.A. Carlsberg Vase 6P
AXA F.A. Youth Cup 6P*
4 Sun Worthington Cup Final
6/7 Tue/Wed UEFA Champions League – Group 2 – Match Day 5
8 Thu UEFA Cup QF (1)
10 Sat F.A. Cup sponsored by AXA 6P
F.A. Umbro Trophy 6
F.A. County Youth Cup SF*
11 Sun AXA F.A. Women's Premier League Cup Final
13/14 Tue/Wed UEFA Champions League – Group 2 – Match Day 6
15 Thu UEFA Cup QF (2)
17 Sat F.A. Carlsberg Vase SF1
AXA F.A. Youth Cup SF1*
20 Tue England Semi-Professional International
21 Wed F.A. Cup sponsored by AXA 6P replays
24 Sat England v Finland – FIFA World Cup Qualifier
F.A. Carlsberg Vase SF2
25 Sun AXA F.A. Women's Cup SF
28 Wed Albania v England – FIFA World Cup Qualifier
31 Sat F.A. Umbro Trophy SF1

April 2001
3/4 Tue/Wed UEFA Champions League QF (1)
5 Thu UEFA Cup SF (1)
7 Sat F.A. Umbro Trophy SF2
AXA F.A. Youth Cup SF2*
8 Sun F.A. Cup sponsored by AXA SF
13 Fri Good Friday
14 Sat
15 Sun Easter Sunday
16 Mon Easter Monday
17/18 Tue/Wed UEFA Champions League QF (2)
19 Thu UEFA Cup SF (2)
25 Wed International – Friendly
28 Sat F.A. County Youth Cup Final (fixed date)

May 2001
1/2 Tue/Wed UEFA Champions League SF (1)
5 Sat Football League ends
7 Mon AXA F.A. Women's Cup Final
Bank Holiday
9 Wed UEFA Champions League SF (2)
11 Fri AXA F.A. Youth Cup Final (1)
12 Sat F.A. Cup sponsored by AXA Final
13 Sun Football League Play-Off SF (1)
16 Wed UEFA Cup Final
Football League Play-Off SF (2)
18 Fri AXA F.A. Youth Cup Final (2)
19 Sat Premier League ends
23 Wed UEFA Champions League Final
26 Sat Football League Division 3 Play-Off Final
27 Sun Football League Division 2 Play-Off Final
28 Mon Football League Division 1 Play-Off Final

June 2001
2 Sat International (World Cup Qualifier) – no England fixture
6 Wed Greece v England – FIFA World Cup Qualifier

September 2001
1 Sat Germany v England – FIFA World Cup Qualifier

.* = closing date of Round
to be decided:
F.A. Carlsberg Vase Final
F.A. Umbro Trophy Final
F.A. Umbro Sunday Cup Final